The Dynamics of Inequality

Race, Class, Gender, and Sexuality in the United States

Edited by

Patricia Gagné
Richard Tewksbury

both of The University of Louisville

Prentice
Hall

Upper Saddle River, New Jersey 07458

Library of Congress Cataloging-in-Publication Data

The dynamics of inequality : race, class, gender, and sexuality in the United States /
edited by Patricia Gagné, Richard Tewksbury.
      p. cm.
   ISBN 0-13-097637-7
   1. Equality—United States. 2. Discrimination—United States. 3. Prejudices—United
States. 4. Minorities—United States. 5. Marginality, Social—United States. I. Gagné,
Patrica. II. Tewksbury, Richard A.
   HN90.S6 D96 2002
   305—dc21

                                                              2002019513

AVP, Publisher: Nancy Roberts
Editorial Assistant: Lee Peterson
Project Manager: Merrill Peterson
Cover Director: Jayne Conte
Cover Designer: Joseph Sengotta
Cover Credit: Lisa Henderling/Stock Illustration Source, Inc.
Prepress and Manufacturing Buyer: Mary Ann Gloriande
Senior Marketing Manager: Amy Speckman
Marketing Assistant: Anne Marie Fritzky

This book was set in 10/11 New Baskerville by TSI Graphics
and was printed and bound by Hamilton Printing Company.
The cover was printed by Phoenix Color Corp.

© 2003 by Pearson Education, Inc.
Upper Saddle River, New Jersey 07458

Printed in the United States of America

10 9 8 7 6 5 4 3 2 1

ISBN 0-13-097637-7

Pearson Education LTD., London
Pearson Education Australia PTY, Limited, Sydney
Pearson Education Singapore, Pte. Ltd
Pearson Education North Asia Ltd, Hong Kong
Pearson Education Canada, Ltd., Toronto
Pearson Educación de Mexico, S.A. de C.V.
Pearson Education—Japan, Tokyo
Pearson Education Malaysia, Pte. Ltd
Pearson Education, Upper Saddle River, New Jersey

Contents

CHAPTER 4

Barriers to Equality   143

CHAPTER 6

Theoretical Perspectives on Race, Class, Gender, and Sexualities   393

CHAPTER 7

Social Movements and Resistance   447

Preface

What is it about the United States that makes it so unique? It may be the freedoms U.S. citizens enjoy, yet in many democracies of the world, people enjoy similar liberties. Some say the United States offers an unparalleled standard of living, but luxury is common in many nations of the world. What makes the United States different from any other nation in the world is its cultural diversity. The United States is the only nation on earth founded by immigrants and based on the premise that all who enter U.S. borders can expect to find opportunities and freedoms that, as newcomers, they would fail to find anywhere else in the world. There are differences in the amount of wealth Americans enjoy; still, each person is constitutionally entitled to the same protections as any other citizen, regardless of race, ethnicity, national origin, religion, social class, sex, gender, or sexual orientation. And with very few exceptions, each person is legally entitled to the same opportunities as everyone else. Indeed, these are laudable ideals. But has the United States lived up to them?

This book suggests that U.S. society has a long way to go before equal protection under the law and equality of opportunity are realities. The articles here give voice to the Americans that freedom and opportunity have neglected. In the first section, authors talk about their personal experiences with prejudice and discrimination, demonstrating just some of the ways that inequality is perpetuated in U.S. society today. The second section offers insights into the nation's long history of inequality based on race, ethnicity, class, gender, and sexuality. The authors discuss racial inequality and violence, lack of political liberties for women, distrust of new immigrants, and discrimination in official government policy against gay men and lesbians. The articles in the third section examine the impact of today's dominant culture in perpetuating inequality. The authors examine belief systems, stereotypes, and prejudices and discuss some of the ways that racist, sexist, classist, and homophobic biases are perpetuated by the media and certain social groups.

The fourth section provides articles that explain some of the ways that inequalities have been built into the very structure of U.S. society. That section is divided into four subsections, which discuss how key social institutions—the economy, education, medicine, and legal system—perpetuate prejudice, discrimination, and inequality. In the fifth section, authors discuss some of the ways that violence against women, people of color, gay men, lesbians, and others is used to intimidate individuals and perpetuate the dominance of those who perpetrate violence against them. As these articles make clear, violence affects not only individual victims, but also all those who are intimidated from exercising their rights and freedoms for fear of attack.

Since the United States was founded on principles of equality of opportunity and equal protection under the law, how is it that inequalities continue? In the sixth section, authors offer explanations for inequality based on race, class, gender, and sexuality, as well as the myriad ways in which these individual characteristics and social statuses intersect with one another. Such explanations are crucial to efforts to challenge, resist, and overthrow the barriers to equality that continue to exist in U.S. society.

A number of social movements of the twentieth century focused on resisting and challenging systems of domination. These and continuing efforts are the focus of the seventh section of this book. The civil rights movement made unprecedented gains in challenging the system of social, political, and economic apartheid that was part of the fabric of U.S. society. And people of color of all races benefitted from that movement's efforts. Similarly, the women's movement challenged the oppression of women, and the gay and lesbian movement resisted prejudice and worked to change institutionalized discrimination. Yet one of the most daunting challenges of the twenty-first century will be for activists to find ways to address prejudice, discrimination, and oppression that occur at the intersections of race, ethnicity, social class, gender, and sexuality.

Specifically, the civil rights movement succeeded at improving the rights and liberties of African Americans, while the feminist movement increased the rights of women. Yet women of color find that they continue to be targets of prejudice and discrimination in ways neither movement has understood or anticipated. Furthermore, identity-based politics, through which people work together to improve their status—as people of color, as women, as gay men, as lesbians, as transgenders, as poor people, or as members of the working class—makes it increasingly difficult for individuals to reach beyond group boundaries. Even as these groups struggle for full and equal participation in society, each has a tendency to isolate itself from others who are different.

The only way that inequality will be successfully challenged in the twenty-first century is for these groups and others to reach beyond the boundaries that have allowed each to work for its own members' rights. People of color, women, sexual minorities, the poor, and members of the working class must work together in coalition, focusing on the intersections of race, ethnicity, class, gender, and sexualities. It is only by working for unity while celebrating diversity that all people will come to enjoy the freedoms, civil liberties, and equality of opportunity that are the foundation upon which the United States claims to be founded. With this book, we hope to show some of the challenges that people in the United States have faced and continue to encounter as they strive to overcome the barriers to equality and enjoy full participation in society.

We wish to thank Nancy Roberts, Merrill Peterson, Cynthia McCloud, Deanna McGaughey, and Mark Richard for their editorial and administrative assistance in the production of this book. We could not have produced it without their valuable help. We also wish to thank the following reviewers: Susan E. Chase, University of Tulsa; Trudie Coker, Florida Atlantic University; William P. Nye, Hollins University; and Magalene Harris Taylor, University of Arkansas.

Chapter 1

The Personal Experience of Inequality

When we look around today, evidence of inequality is everywhere. Some people own $100,000 cars, for example, while others lack a decent home or adequate food and clothing. However, people disagree about whether inequality is a problem. Some think that inequality of result—such as differences in income, wealth, or property— should be minimized and that it is up to the government to help equalize differences among us. Others think that inequality of result is inevitable and even desirable because the chance to own a big house, a luxury car, or a great deal of money motivates people to work hard. But even those who hold the latter view believe that everyone deserves a fair chance to get ahead. They believe in equality of opportunity and think the government should make sure that everyone who wants a fair chance to get a good education and to compete for jobs has those opportunities.

To make the competition for opportunities more fair, the U.S. government implemented a number of programs to help people get a good education and to make sure that they get a fair chance to compete for good jobs. Partly because of those programs, racial and ethnic minorities, women, and gay men and lesbians have been given opportunities to advance that were previously unavailable to them. As a result, today many people, particularly those who do not directly experience the sting of unfair treatment, think that inequality is no longer a problem. Many people, for example, believe that racism and sexism—prejudice and discrimination on the basis of race and sex—are relics of the past. They may also believe that class-based inequality results from differences in individual ability and motivation and that any judgment of an individual's worth based on sexuality is based on moral principles and concrete ideas of right and wrong. In other words, some people today believe that others are not discriminated against, and that those who face prejudice and unfair treatment probably deserve what they get.

Nonetheless, research consistently shows us that racism, sexism, class-based inequality, and heterosexism—prejudice and discrimination based upon the belief that heterosexuality is the only appropriate expression of sexuality—continue to exist, albeit sometimes in forms that are more subtle and difficult to detect. The articles in this section provide insights into how these forms of inequality directly and indirectly impact the lives of individuals who have one or more "different" social statuses. Differences may be based upon race, ethnicity, sex, gender, social class, sexuality, or any combination of these statuses. Being different is not the problem; it is the basis upon which the prejudice and discrimination that limit equal opportunity are exercised. That is the problem.

Individuals view the world through the lens of their own personal experiences. For most, experiences constitute the information people use to understand how the world works and why society operates the way it does. If an individual does not personally experience prejudice or discrimination, she or he is likely to view society as fair and just. For this reason, it is important to start with a basic understanding of how individuals of all statuses directly experience discrimination and prejudice, sometimes based upon one social status but more often based upon a combination of differences.

The authors of the readings in this chapter discuss the personal experience of inequality. Some draw upon their own lives; others discuss research they have conducted. No matter what the articles are based upon, these readings all provide insights into how inequalities impact the everyday lives of real people in the United States.

In the first article in this chapter, White draws upon his own experience as a young African-American man who, along with three other African-American men, directly and forcefully felt the effects of racism. Specifically, these four men were arrested solely because they were racial minorities in a building where the police had received a report of Hispanic men with guns. They did not come close to the physical descriptions of the suspects, but they were detained nonetheless. This article exemplifies the practice of racial profiling, which is police action that relies on the race, ethnicity, or national origin of an individual, rather than on that person's behavior or on information that may lead the police to believe the individual has engaged in illegal behavior (Ramirez, McDevitt, and Farrell 2000). Racial profiling is a practice with which African-Americans, and particularly black men, must contend on a daily basis.

Although some inequality is the result of face-to-face interactions, such as with the police, some is an outcome of institutional or structural changes in society. In the second article in this section, Freedman presents the story of one family who was deeply affected by changes in technology and the economy. Although no one specifically singled out the Perillo family for discrimination, technological and economic changes caused the closing of the factory in which two previous generations had worked. As a result, the lifestyle and opportunities available to the family were radically changed in a negative way. Jason Perillo, the main character of the story, had always assumed that he would get a job where his father and grandfather had worked. Jason is representative of millions of high school graduates who do not hold college degrees and are vulnerable to low-wage jobs and job insecurity simply because opportunities that were available to previous generations no longer exist for them.

In the third article, Baker and Joseph present a different focus, looking at how an individual's sexuality can have far-reaching consequences for his or her life. The focus in this reading is on an eighteen-year-old gay man. The authors discuss the difficulties gay and lesbian youth encounter in their day-to-day lives. Moreover, they examine social improvements that help nonheterosexual young people cope with their sexual differences and the negative social reactions they frequently encounter.

In the fourth article, Asanti builds upon the ideas of Baker and Joseph but goes a step farther by looking at differences within the gay and lesbian community. As a lesbian, Asanti expected to find unity, based upon sexuality, within the gay and lesbian community. Instead she was surprised to find that even when people share one important social status, such as sexuality, they also are likely to focus upon a number of differences. Even within a minority community, these differences may outweigh the commonalities, leading to prejudice and discrimination among community members.

Asanti argues that it is necessary to look beyond individual statuses, including master statuses such as gender or sexuality. She says that instead of focusing on differences, gay men, lesbians—indeed, all people—should work toward unity and harmony.

One population that has had to fight for inclusion in the gay and lesbian group are transsexuals—individuals whose experience and gender identity differ from their biological sex. (Transsexuals include people who live, or want to live, as the other sex and who sometimes undergo medical treatment, including sex reassignment surgery, in order to do so.) Transsexuals are one of the most commonly maligned and misunderstood minority groups in the United States today. In the final article in this chapter, Rees, who was born female and now lives as a man, gives a first-person account of his early experiences with gender and his transformation from female to male.

Sociologist C. Wright Mills argued that in order to change society, people must understand the ways in which social forces impact their own lives. Taken as a group, these six articles provide us with an opening glimpse into the ways in which social forces have an effect on the day-to-day lives of individuals in a number of minority groups. Prejudice and discrimination may occur on an individual, face-to-face level, or they may occur at an institutional level, resulting in a negative impact on one group even when there is nothing personal about the results. Either way, the fact remains that inequalities lead to suffering for some groups more than others. If we are ever to alleviate that suffering, it is imperative that we recognize the myriad ways in which inequality manifests itself in the lives of individuals.

REFERENCE

RAMIREZ, DEBORAH, JACK MCDEVITT, and AMY FARRELL. 2000. *A Resource Guide on Racial Profiling Data Collection Systems*. Washington, DC: United States Department of Justice.

Reading 1

Ragtime, My Time

Alton Fitzgerald White

In this article, White discusses his personal experiences with racism at the hands of the police.

As the youngest of five girls and two boys growing up in Cincinnati, Ohio, I was raised to believe that if I worked hard, was a good person and always told the truth, the world would be my oyster. I was taught to be courteous and polite. I was raised a gentleman and learned that these fine qualities would bring me one very important, hard-earned human quality: Respect!

Source: Reprinted with permission from *The Nation* (October 11, 1999): 11–12.

While respect is indeed something one has to earn, consideration is something owed to every human being, even total strangers. On Friday, June 16, 1999, when I was wrongfully arrested while trying to leave my building in Harlem, my perception of everything I had learned as a young man was forever changed—not only because of the fact that I wasn't given even a second to use any of the wonderful manners and skills my parents had taught me as a child, but mostly because the police, who I'd always naively thought were supposed to serve and protect me, were actually hunting me.

I had planned the day to be a pleasant one. The night before was not only payday but also I received a rousing standing ovation after portraying the starring role of Coalhouse Walker Jr. in *Ragtime* on Broadway. It is a role I've worked very hard for professionally, and emotionally as well. A role that requires not only talent but also an honest emotional investment, including the morals and lessons I learned as a child.

Coalhouse Walker Jr. is a victim (an often misused word but in this case the true definition) of overt racism. His story is every black man's nightmare. He is hard-working, successful, talented, charismatic, friendly and polite. Perfect prey for someone with authority and not even a fraction of those qualities. The fictional character I portrayed on Thursday night became a part of my reality on Friday afternoon. Nothing in the world could have prepared me for it. Nothing I had seen on television. Not even stories told to me by other black men who had suffered similar injustices.

Most Fridays for me mean a trip to the bank, errands, the gym, dinner and then to the theater. On this particular day, I decided to break my usual pattern of getting up and running right out of the house. Instead, I took my time, slowed down my pace and splurged by making myself some homemade strawberry pancakes. It was a way of spoiling myself in preparation for my demanding, upcoming four-show weekend. Before I knew

it, it was 2:45, and my bank closes at 3:30, leaving me less than forty-five minutes to get to midtown on the train. I was pressed for time but in a relaxed, blessed state of mind. When I walked through the lobby of my building, I noticed two light-skinned Hispanic men I'd never seen before. Not thinking much of it, I continued on to the vestibule, which is separated from the lobby by a locked door.

As I approached the exit, I saw people in uniforms rushing toward the door. I sped up to open it for them, especially after noticing that the first of them was a woman. My first thought was that they were paramedics, seeing as many of the building's occupants are retired and/or elderly. It wasn't until I had opened the door and greeted the woman that I recognized that they were the police. Within seconds I was told to "hold it" because they had received a call about young Hispanics with guns. I was told to get against the wall. I was searched, stripped of my backpack (which was searched repeatedly), put on my knees, handcuffed and told to be quiet when I tried to ask any questions.

With me were three other innocent black men. They had been on their way to their U-Haul, parked on the side of the building. They were moving into the apartment beneath me and were still glowing from the tour I'd given them of the beautiful historic landmark building. I had just bragged to them about how safe it was and how proud I was to have been living there for over five years. And now here the four of us were being told to get on our knees, handcuffed and not allowed to say a word in our defense. As a matter of fact, it was one of these gentlemen who got off his knees, still handcuffed, and unlocked the door for the policemen to get into the lobby where the two strangers were. Instead of being thanked or even acknowledged, we were led out the door past our neighbors, who were all but begging the police in our defense.

We were put into cars with the two strangers and taken to the 33rd Precinct at 165th and

Amsterdam. The police automatically linked us to them with no questions and no regard for our character or our lives. No consideration was given to where we were going or what we were in need of doing before they came into our building. Suppose I had an ailing relative upstairs in my apartment waiting for me to return with her emergency remedy? Or young children who were told Daddy is running to the corner store for milk and will be right back? These three gentlemen weren't even allowed to lock their apartment or check on the U-Haul full of their personal belongings.

After we were lined up in the station, the younger of the two Hispanic men was immediately identified as an experienced criminal, and drug residue was found in a pocket of the other. I now realize how naive I was to think the police would then uncuff me, apologize for their terrible mistake and let me go. Instead, they continued to search my backpack repeatedly, questioned me and put me in jail with the criminals.

The rest of the nearly five-hour ordeal was like a horrible dream, putting me in a surreal state of shock. Everything from being handcuffed, strip-searched, taken in and out for questioning, to being told that they knew exactly who I was and my responsibility to the show and that in fact they knew they already had whom they wanted, left me in absolute disbelief.

When I asked how they could keep me there, or have brought me there in the first place with nothing found and a clean record, I was told it was standard procedure. As if the average law-abiding citizen knows what that is and can dispute it. From what I now know, "standard procedure" is something that every citizen, black and white, needs to learn, and fast. Even though they knew I was innocent, they made me feel completely powerless. All for one reason. Why do you think? Here I was, young, pleasant and successful, in good physical shape, dressed in clean athletic attire. I was carrying a backpack, containing a substantial pay-

check and deposit slip, on my way to the bank and to enjoy a well-deserved great day. Yet after hours and hours I was sitting at a desk with two officers who not only couldn't tell me why I was there but seemed determined to find something on me, to the point of making me miss my performance.

It was because I am a black man!

I sat in that cell crying silent tears of disappointment and injustice with the realization of how many innocent black men are convicted for no reason. When I was handcuffed, my first instinct had been to pull away out of pure insult and violation as a human being. Thank God I was calm enough to do what they said. When I was thrown in jail with the criminals and strip-searched, I somehow knew to put my pride aside, be quiet and do exactly what I was told, hating it but coming to terms with the fact that in this situation I was powerless. I was a victim. They had guns!

Before I was finally let go, exhausted, humiliated, embarrassed and still in shock, I was led to a room and given a pseudo-apology. I was told that I was at the wrong place at the wrong time. My reply? "I was where I live."

As a result, what I learned growing up in Cincinnati has been shattered. Life will never be the same.

CRITICAL THINKING QUESTIONS

1. Why did the police focus on White and his friends? Is there a problem with this practice? Explain.

2. As long as they are eventually released and not charged with a crime, does any actual harm come to individuals who are wrongly arrested because they meet the physical description of actual criminals? Explain.

3. Does any harm come to society when individuals are singled out for closer scrutiny or are detained for questioning based solely upon their physical appearance? Explain.

Reading 2

The End of the Line

Samuel G. Freedman

> *This article discusses the experiences of one working-class family and their struggles to cope in a changing economy.*

For a working-class kid like Jason Perillo, the future holds fear and confusion. The factory jobs that lifted his father and grandfather into the middle class have vanished. School hasn't prepared him for a high-tech economy. Life inside a blue-collar family at the end of the line.

Late one afternoon in 1972, when Dave Perillo was 15 years old and America was the industrial titan of the world, he took his first steps inside the General Motors plant where his father worked. The factory was no place for kids, not with welders spewing fire and forklifts rumbling down the aisles and presses as tall as the ceiling smashing their jaws shut. Four thousand men and women made a million square feet throb with production, and when the shifts changed, the traffic jams in the parking lot were of epic dimension. So until that moment, Dave had come no closer than sitting across the street with his mother in the family Oldsmobile, trying to pick out the wiry figure of his old man.

On this day, though, this one day every year, the factory threw open its gate to welcome the husbands, wives and children of its workers and show them prosperity's reward. The latest GM models, donated by local dealers, stood behind bunting like contestants in a beauty pageant. Brand-new washers, dryers and refrigerators, all made by GM's subsidiary Frigidaire, gleamed in coronas of light. Guides handed out key rings, balloons and money clips to the visitors, then led them

through the departments that built door handles, rearview mirrors and seat adjusters. All these parts and others, manufactured here in the Trenton suburb of Ewing, N.J., would be shipped to GM assembly plants across the country to be incorporated into finished automobiles.

Dave had been pestering his father about the open house for weeks. And Michael Perillo, for his part, was not going to let his son just tag along on the standard tour. No, he would escort Dave himself. Michael was the best buffer in the place, the one who could burnish even the most angular pieces of chrome, and he had finished his daily quota two hours early to meet his boy. They moved down the aisles, the father in sweaty khaki and the son in a suit usually reserved for Mass at St. Ann's. Michael pointed out the various departments—here, anodizing; there, extruding; around the corner, molding—but mostly he showed Dave off to his buddies who had teenagers of their own. It was for the kids' futures that they worked.

Leaving the factory in the twilight of early evening, Dave implicitly understood. "I saw our family living well," he would recall. "I looked at what my father did for us. And I thought, 'If I do the same as my dad did, I'll be satisfied.'"

On another afternoon, 21 years after that first visit to the plant, Dave Perillo welcomed his own son to another open house. This time, the new models sat on the lawn near the main entrance. A few workers displayed the antique cars they had restored as hobbies. There were free hot dogs and soda, and a rock station was

Source: Reprinted with permission from *Rolling Stone,* 754 (February 20, 1997): 54–61.

broadcasting live. The festive air relieved Dave, because it would help hide the truth from his son.

Inside the plant, where guests were not permitted, the 4,000 jobs of 1972 had by 1993 dwindled to just 1,900. Of the 30 buffing machines in Michael Perillo's old department, only a handful remained. The entire second floor of the factory, once bustling with the paint shop and assembly lines for vent windows and door supports, now sprawled, nearly deserted, the sunlight falling—uninterrupted by man or machine—from massive windows onto the plank floor.

Jason Perillo, a boy of 14, smiled and shook hands as his father introduced him to co-workers. There had been a time, not many years earlier, when Jason had all but assumed he would follow family tradition into GM. His parents and his grandparents, even a few great-aunts and -uncles, had worked here, and Jason had grown up amid middle-class households built and sustained by GM paychecks.

More recently, though, that security had begun to dissolve in ways that defied Dave's attempts to shield his son. Jason's mother, Joyce, had taken early retirement after 15 years in the plant, fearful of reports that it would imminently close. Now she was waitressing at the same greasy spoon where Jason bused tables. The stress of constant layoffs and the fear of a shutdown of the factory had given Dave gout, insomnia, high blood pressure, a breathing disorder called sleep apnea and, most apparent to Jason, a wicked temper for unkempt rooms and unfinished chores. At the dinner table, the Perillos talked about moving to West Virginia or Tennessee, or anywhere the auto plants were hiring. GM in Ewing hadn't added a permanent full-time job in eight years. . . .

On yet another afternoon, this one in the autumn of 1996, Jason Perillo, now 17, pulls a standard-issue green and orange smock over his school clothes and begins his shift at 7-Eleven. He stations himself at the cash register—cigarette racks to his left, lottery machine to the right, safe at his knees, where the customers can't see it—and sets about earning $5.85 an hour.

Jason has held the job for two years, more than long enough for it to bore him. He knows that the customers arrive in waves just after every hour, as shifts change or workdays end, and they lay on the counter their Big Gulps and TastyKakes, their Slurpees and Super Pretzels. Hot dogs rotate beneath heat lamps. The hum from the cooler blots out other noise. It's all too familiar. Every so often, somebody calls up to solicit advice on lucky numbers. . . .

. . . Today in particular, behind the opaque obedience he shows to customers, he feels "all messed up." He is thinking about the future. He just got his best report card in several years, 4 B's and a C, and had a conversation with his guidance counselor about applying to Mercer County Community College, near Trenton. Instead of clarifying his direction, the good news only added to the muddle of confusion and self-doubt.

Jason can see himself becoming a cop, but he's not even sure the community college offers criminal-justice courses. He's heard his father preach about the importance of higher education, and Jason got a glimpse of it this fall when a girlfriend from high school started her freshman year at Rutgers University. He liked what he heard about the Thursday night parties on Frat Row. . . . But the idea of handing in a paper every Monday, as his girlfriend must, intimidates him. The other day, Jason's history teacher told the class that during his first semester of college he wrote 200 pages of term papers. "Oh, my God," Jason found himself thinking, "what college did you go to?"

This sense of inadequacy strikes him often. Jason languishes in the middle tracks of a high school struggling against mediocrity, and he aspires only with trepidation. For a while, he had imagined a career in architecture. He enjoyed his mechanical-drawing class, craved the challenge of building models from paper and tape. Yet when the architect of the new aquarium in Camden, N.J. spoke at Ewing High School, Jason withered upon realizing how demanding the profession truly is.

"I thought it was just about drawing," he says of architecture. "I'm not a high-class student.

I'm not on top of things. I try my best. . . ." His hands form a pyramid as his voice trails off in resignation.

This past semester, at the behest of his guidance counselor, Jason took an auto-mechanics class at a local vocational school, the Arthur Sypek Center. A starting job as a mechanic for a dealership might bring $7 or $8 an hour—the same pay his mother and father were making as 19-year-olds at GM some 20 years ago. A recruiter from an automotive trade school in Philadelphia recently tried to persuade Jason to enroll there after graduation. But after the recruiter had made his pitch around the Perillos' kitchen table, spreading out his charts and brochures in their full-color resplendence, Jason was left with two facts: Tuition would cost $16,000, exactly the amount he could expect to earn in his first year on the job.

"I never, ever want to have to borrow money from my family," Jason says. "I don't want to be a burden on them. Like this week—I need $20 for the yearbook, and my dad tells me he'll pay for it. But I feel guilty. Last year I didn't even get one because I felt so guilty."

Then there was the $100 due for the senior trip to Busch Gardens in Virginia. Jason covered it with one of his twice-monthly paychecks from 7-Eleven. That left him short on the insurance for his 13-year-old car. But, again, he refused to ask for help from his father. Jason is accustomed to providing for himself. His earnings as a busboy and clerk have purchased many of his clothes. And while his classmates spend extravagantly on brand names . . . Jason wears unadorned jeans and rugby shirts. He saved for years, literally—from the time he was a preteen with a paper route—for his Pro-Flex mountain bike and a 150-watt Denon stereo.

That stereo occupies most of the single closet in the 10-by-12 bedroom that Jason shares with his 6-year-old brother, David Jr. They sleep in bunk beds and divide the wall space between Jason's poster of a prowling panther and David Jr.'s of the Little Rascals. Atop a bureau, Jason keeps several dozen CDs,

ranging from Pearl Jam to Crosby, Stills and Nash, a group he learned about from his father. It was Jason's parents, in fact, who took him to his first concert (the Moody Blues) and who rescued him just the other week when his car died while he was on the way to Philadelphia to see a show by his current favorite, the Dave Matthews Band. . . .

Even the teachers and counselors who grieve over Jason's grades admire his character. Honest, responsible, unafraid of physical labor, willing to defer gratification, he would have thrived in the foundries, steel mills and auto plants that once defined the American economy. These days, Jason's attributes have gotten him as far as the 7-Eleven. And there is no assurance that they will get him any further.

From his post at the counter, Jason serves people who work jobs that are little better than his own. They arrive with dusk, middle-aged men in the uniforms of landscapers or security guards or carpet installers, making dinner of a $1.09 burrito. It would not surprise Jason if some of them used to work at GM. His mother, after all, waits tables for $2.35 an hour plus tips.

For Jason, there is no hope of working at GM. The Ewing plant has shrunk to 840 workers. One of Dave's most recent assignments on the job was to clean the area where yet another assembly line had been phased out. Around him, the shop floor looks like a city ruined by bombing, with uninhabited stretches and activity visible only in scattered clusters. In order to obtain contracts from the parent corporation, the Ewing plant and its United Auto Workers local must not only bid against brethren in other GM-parts factories—a process known as whipsawing—but also against nonunion shops. And under the latest contract between GM and the UAW, the corporation will be permitted to close certain unprofitable plants. The last Dave heard, Ewing was losing several million dollars a year.

Given such a backdrop, Jason is glad to be working this 7-Eleven shift with his classmate

Jackson, who plays cutup to Jason's loner. Jackson wears a Ralph Lauren headband with his 7-Eleven shirt. He jokes about a late-shift employee nicknamed Stink because his clothes always reek of gasoline from his day job at a service station. Taking a bag of garbage to a dumpster in the parking lot, Jackson pauses outside the front window to get Jason's attention, then heaves the load onto the roof of the store. Finally, with an audience of customers and commuters, he climbs up to fetch it.

A little later, Jackson pulls a couple of Ewing High sweat shirts from his backpack. He and the other players on the hockey team are selling them for $10 apiece to raise money.

"It's nice," Jason says wanly. "Too bad I'm broke."

"Hey," Jackson persists, "I told you it's nine bucks for you."

Jason laughs, then opens the register and removes a $10 bill. Like all employees, he may borrow money from the till for meals on the job and have the amount deducted from his next paycheck. He notes the withdrawal on the appropriate form. But instead of immediately giving Jackson the bill, he crams it into a pocket.

There it remains for the next two hours. Then, abruptly, Jason returns the $10 to the register.

"I don't care about school spirit," he tells Jackson.

"Yes, you do."

"I do," Jason acknowledges. "But not that much."

"They sell that at the store for $40," Jackson says, brandishing a sweat shirt one last time.

Jason's voice turns hard and impatient.

"I can't afford 10."

The events of these three afternoons distill the experience of three generations. And the experience of three generations traces the trajectory of much of the American working class during the past half-century. Michael Perillo rose from penury to comfort on the wages of GM. David and Joyce Perillo, welcomed into that comfort while still teenagers, approach

middle age desperately, precariously clinging to its vestiges. And Jason Perillo, nearing adulthood, stands little chance of living as well as his forebears.

In his plight, Jason represents the nearly 30 million Americans in their 20s who do not hold college degrees and so remain most vulnerable to low wages and job insecurity in the increasingly global and technological economy of the 1990s. Despite the perception of the United States as a country of higher education on a mass scale, the vast majority of young adults—three-quarters of those age 28, according to one study—have not graduated from college. Ignored by the media, they occupy the distant shore in the growing divide between the skilled and unskilled, white collar and blue, more educated and less. Call them Generation Expendable.

"It doesn't get the tears on *60 Minutes* that a plant closing or downsizing would," says Gary Burtless, a labor economist at the Brookings Institution, "but you've got the situation of a 22-year-old or a 27-year-old who's living in a trailer or still living with parents. That person's prospects haven't declined, because they started out so low. When they enter the work force, their starting wage is so much lower than their parents', and their improvement is so much slower."

Generation Expendable is the product of a quiet catastrophe that has struck the American labor market during the past 25 years. On the surface, the economy as expressed by the gross domestic product has grown during that time by an average of about 2.7 percent annually. But unlike the growth of the 1950s and 1960s, which raised the living standard of most workers, this one has excluded the middle and lower echelons. Even as high technology has boomed, driving up salaries for the intellectual elite, a male without a college diploma has lost one-fifth of his real income since the early 1970s. . . .

As a result, the level of income inequality in the Untied States has soared to its highest point in 70 years. Labor economists find the consequences in the tendency of young adults to postpone marrying or having children, or simply living independently, because they cannot afford to do so. More profoundly, the growing gap between winners and losers has tested the beliefs of families like the Perillos that America is, if not exactly a classless nation, at least an overwhelmingly middle-class one.

"The economic trends are forcing the society apart," says Arnold Packer, a senior fellow at the Institute for Policy Studies, in Baltimore. "The schools are not closing the gap. It'll widen. It's hard to run a democracy in which that's the prevalent expectation. You get anger and bitterness, and the wealthy distancing themselves—gated communities, private schools, private security forces. You have a Latin American country."

Several factors have rendered Jason Perillo and his peers the campesinos of the service economy. The industrial sector has shriveled, particularly in the urban Northeast and Midwest. New York and Philadelphia, the big cities that bracket Ewing, a suburb of 35,000, collectively lost 680,000 manufacturing jobs from 1967 to 1987, the renowned sociologist William Julius Wilson reports in his book *When Work Disappears: The World of the New Urban Poor.* Put another way, Philadelphia lost 64 percent and New York 58 percent of their industrial jobs. In the immediate vicinity of Ewing, GM employs about one-seventh of its plant's 5,700-person capacity; the Fairless Hills steel mill has slashed its work force from 9,000 to 700; and the Hill Refrigeration, American Steel and Lenox China plants have closed entirely. A bridge across the Delaware River still bears a decades-old sign, Trenton makes—the world takes, but the slogan is a chilling anachronism.

Into the vacuum have poured service jobs, both high paid and low. Just 10 miles from the Perillo home flourishes one of America's hotbeds of computer activity—a collection of consultants, software developers, Web-page designers and research labs known loosely as Video Valley. During the next decade, New Jersey expects a greater growth in systems analysts than in any other occupation. But it is just such an occupation that requires a demanding education. The other jobs in which New Jersey expects to abound are those of janitor, waitress and orderly, to cite a few examples from a Rutgers University study. In the smugger precincts of Video Valley, these people, people like the Perillos, are dismissed as the information superhighway's "road kill."

As industry has atrophied, so has organized labor. Upward of one in three American workers belonged to a union in the early 1950s; now barely one in 10 does. Thus labor no longer exerts the pressure it once did on management to raise wages and benefits—a pressure so effective that even nonunion shops felt it was necessary to offer competitive packages. At the same time, the minimum wage has lost much of its actual value, which peaked in 1969 at today's equivalent of more than $6 an hour. So for blue-collar workers, both the ceiling and the floor have dropped simultaneously.

"We're seeing the consequences," says the Brookings Institution's Bill Dickens, who served as a senior economist on President Bill Clinton's Council of Economic Advisers, in 1993 and 1994. "A lot of people are thinking their kids won't have as good a life as they had. And the people who want to live the life their parents led can't do it."

The life that Jason Perillo will not be able to lead had its genesis in the depths of the Great Depression. In 1937, with the economy sinking again despite the New Deal, General Motors broke ground amid the apple orchards and rural crossroads of Ewing for an 86-acre plant capable of producing 2,500 sets of autobody hardware and fittings every day. So grateful were local residents for the factory that its opening merited a 600-person banquet at the Stacy-Trent Hotel and a commemorative issue of Trenton magazine.

"Employees . . . will have the privilege of working under ideal conditions in the finest plant of its kind in the world," the magazine declared. "Furthermore, the benefits from this new payroll will reach every Trenton citizen either directly or indirectly. Merchants, professional men, landlords, taxpayers—all of them will reap some gain."

One of those who joined the payroll in 1942 was Michael Perillo, Jason's grandfather. The seventh of nine children of an immigrant house painter, Michael had dropped out of school in ninth grade to help support the family. The Perillos were so poor at some points that the children would taunt railroad guards into running them off by throwing chunks of coal that had fallen from the freight trains. The coal fed the household furnace.

Ultimately, three brothers from the Perillo family worked in the Ewing plant. When the factory converted to military production during World War II, Michael riveted wings onto Avenger aircraft, the planes that bombed Iwo Jima and Tokyo. Harry Truman visited in 1943 to pay his personal thanks to the workers, many of whom were women and blacks gaining their first berths in the industrial economy. In the decade after the war ended, the Ewing plant swelled to a record peacetime employment of 5,700. "If you die on the job," went a joke, "just don't fall onto the [assembly] line." That way, someone else could step in without production stopping for a second.

With GM's wages, Michael bought his first car, a Chevy, in 1947, and his first home, for $9,000, three years later. A brand-new two-bedroom Cape Cod with a finished basement, it nestled among identical houses owned by an insurance agent, a lawyer and an engineer. GM had put Michael in the middle class alongside men far better educated than he.

Dave Perillo, the second of three children, seemed destined for college, if not as a scholar then as an athlete. He was a big, talented lineman and punter on an unbeaten high school team. His football career ended, however, with a severe car accident after his freshman

year at Trenton State College. In August 1976 he took up his father's offer to get him on the line at GM, taking classes all day and then reporting for the second shift.

There, to his amazement, Dave worked beside a man with a degree in psychology from Michigan State who had discovered that GM paid better than teaching did. Dave was making $7.25 an hour—the equivalent of more than $19 in late 1996. Within 90 days of starting, he was earning just 20 cents an hour less than his father, a man with 34 years of seniority. "I used to be embarrassed by the money I was making," Dave recalls. Not too embarrassed, however, to drop out of college in favor of GM and its paychecks.

Joyce Henry, the woman whom Dave would ultimately marry, shared the experience. A job at GM had rescued her mother from the depleted coal fields of eastern Pennsylvania, and a job at GM gave Joyce more money than a friend of hers was earning after seven years as a dental hygienist. Joyce paid off a new Camaro in one year, spent weekends at the Jersey Shore, and went to see Peter Frampton and Yes in concert at the Philadelphia Spectrum. "Look at this," she remembers thinking. "Look at what I have."

In their late teens and early 20s, Joyce and Dave could afford to move out of their parents' houses, get married and start families. . . .

For a time, the Perillo home seemed the portrait of stability. Joyce and Dave were each making $35,000 or more a year with full benefits. They owned a new three-bedroom home—a handsome gray and maroon colonial in a subdivision with curving streets named for flowers and brooks—that was on its way to doubling in value from its $70,000 purchase price; they kept two cars, bought an above-ground pool for the kids and treated themselves to Eagles season tickets. Dave helped Jason and Jamie with homework on school nights; he quizzed them orally on the eve of a test. And together, as Halloween approached each year, the Perillos would transform their driveway and front lawn into a spectacle that was the talk of the neighborhood—skeletons downing beers at a bar, a coffin with a mechanical lid that creaked open, skeins of Spanish moss dangling from the drainpipes to the lawn.

Then, on Dec. 3, 1992, everything changed.

When Jason came home from school that afternoon, he heard muffled, worried talk. He followed the sound into the kitchen, where his mother, grandmother and a family friend, all of them current or former workers at the Ewing plant, were gathered around a small television. Silent but curious, Jason fixed his eyes, too, on CNN. A map of the United States filled the screen, a map with pinpoints of light marking places like Kalamazoo, Mich.; Syracuse, N.Y.; Sioux City, Iowa—and Ewing. Every spot indicated a factory that GM had just announced would close within three and a half years, eradicating a total of 18,000 jobs. . . .

The previous few years had made Jason an excellent eavesdropper, a scavenger of the bad news his parents tried to keep secret by whispering. In just the last few days at school, he had heard the rumors of a shutdown. He never let on what he knew; it seemed to his parents that he was the same Jason as always, busy riding his bike or running his remote-control car. Only now, with the worst speculation confirmed, did he speak.

"What's going on?" he asked his mother. "What does this mean?"

"We don't know what's going on with the plant," Joyce said, even though she knew all too well. She caught herself and added, "Don't worry about it." A few hours later, Dave arrived home shellshocked.

Joyce tried her best to buoy the whole family. "This is a blessing in disguise," she said. "We need to get away from this place anyway. We'll do better in another state."

Because the UAW contract with GM guaranteed that the employees of a closed plant be given priority for jobs elsewhere in the corporation, other GM facilities set up recruiting tables and began accepting applications in Ewing. As Dave walked to the personnel department during lunch one day, he noticed that the guys headed in the same direction were moving faster and faster—nobody wanting to actually run, but nobody daring to fall behind. Dave ultimately applied for jobs in the Saturn plant in Tennessee and GM-parts warehouses in Pennsylvania and West Virginia. Then he and Joyce set about persuading their children that forced upheaval was actually some sort of adventure.

One night that December, Joyce laid pamphlets about several other plants across the kitchen table, banished the anguish from her face and asked, "Wouldn't it be interesting to live somewhere else?"

"No," Jason and Jamie answered.

They had lived virtually their entire lives in one town with one school district, enmeshed in an extended family. Jamie, so social that she says "the phone is my life," could not imagine leaving her friends. Jason, the introvert, could not imagine making new ones in a strange place.

"Well, we might have to," Joyce said, the veneer of enthusiasm sliding off her features. "It's a job or no job."

It was no job. Even with 16 years of seniority, Dave did not make the cut at the other GM sites. And every time the UAW or the local politicians suggested that the Ewing plant could be saved with yet another round of union concessions, management warned against false hope.

"It's time to buckle down and get the job done," plant manager Terry Marquis wrote to the employees in February 1993. "The job is to shut the plant down. Let me leave no doubt—the plant is closing. Many people take the absence of visible movement of jobs, tools and equipment as a sign something is up. Not so!"

Many nights, as his parents wrestled anew with their future and his own, Jason withdrew up the stairs and into his bedroom. Sometimes he lost himself in the idealized family of Full House on TV. Sometimes, with his growing interest in things mechanical, he built cars from the plastic pieces called K'Nex and then piled his dumbbells and encyclopedia volumes on top. He wanted to see just how much pressure a seemingly fragile structure could bear.

The same test was being made of his family. There was talk that GM would sell the Ewing plant to an investor—provided that wages were capped at $12 an hour, a loss of about $15,000 annually for Dave. When the deal collapsed, he considered moving the family to Pennsylvania's coal country, from which Joyce's parents had fled decades earlier. A job he had been offered there, in a medical-equipment factory, meant taking a pay cut of $10,000.

Jason could see a transformation in his father. Dave used to bring home chocolate doughnuts for the children or have shaving-cream fights with Jason. Now, Dave's joints ached from gout, his neck burned from high blood pressure, and he lurched through his shifts, exhausted from sleepless nights. When he returned from work one afternoon to discover that Jason had left an empty carton of milk on the kitchen counter, he hurled it at the boy's bed. "You didn't throw it away," Dave explained sarcastically, "so I thought you were saving it for something."

"Damn, why's he like that?" Jason remembers thinking. "Man, what's wrong with him?"

Report cards, in particular, set Dave off. In every C or D, he saw tragedy etched. Every C or D meant his children not getting into college, not finding a way out of GM's meltdown. Instead of playing the patient tutor, as he had in the past, he turned dictatorial. He banned Jason and Jamie from using the phone, going on dates, leaving the house except for their classes and jobs. Even Joyce grew to dread the end of the school marking period, knowing the tirades that were bound to follow.

And Jason was now practically failing. What had happened to the boy who had been nominated seven times in junior high school for Student of the Month? Dave grew obsessed with the question. Was it uncool to get good grades? One afternoon, he dragged a bunch of the neighbor kids into his living room to ask them. Another time, to his exasperation, he chanced upon a letter Jason was writing to his girlfriend at Rutgers: "You're studying tonight? You loser." Or, Dave sometimes wondered, was he pushing his children too hard? Making them rebel by failing?

"Stop tearing their heads off," Joyce pleaded with Dave one night. Next thing, he was yelling at her for contradicting him. Then Jamie was crying at the top of the stairs. And then Jason was heading into his bedroom, the sanctuary of Full House and K'Nex.

In the summer of 1994, the Ewing plant won a reprieve from GM, which allowed it to survive for another three-year contract, based on more givebacks from the UAW local. But as Dave gained a semblance of security, Joyce was losing hers. Nearly all of the $40,000 that she had cleared after taxes by taking early retirement was gone within two years. She tried to compensate by providing day care in her home, which also allowed her to stay with her toddler. No more than five children ever enrolled, though, and when the number dropped to two last summer and her weekly income to $135, Joyce gave up and turned to waitressing.

It has been a battle ever since to get the best schedule: the closing shift that can bring $60 in tips in just a few hours. Too often, she has ended a 30-hour week with $200 rather than the $350 she had anticipated. When she has searched for better jobs, she has found none.

"Where are all these jobs people at the White House are talking about?" she asks. "Where are they? Who has them? I was telling Dave, 'This is really scary. There's nothing left.' If you don't have an education, there's nothing but minimum wage. It seems like nothing's gonna work out down the line. That's why we talk to Jason and Jamie: 'You gotta get serious. You gotta look down the line.' You look at the big picture, and it's actually pretty scary."

The outward appearance of the good life appears intact—two cars in the garage, television sets upstairs and down, nothing in visible neglect. But this equilibrium is precarious. The major appliances are now all 13 years old, and after Dave paid $100 to repair the dishwasher, he couldn't afford the $165 necessary to fix the dryer. (Ultimately, a GM buddy did the job in exchange for Dave's help around his house.) One local bank refused to refinance the Perillo's mortgage because the plant's shaky future made them a poor credit risk (another bank did make the loan). The money for the last big-ticket items the family added—a 35-inch Mitsubishi TV in the living room and central air conditioning for the house—came from Joyce's buyout, which was more than five years ago.

Most often, Jason and Jamie see the little pictures, miniatures of life on the brink. Sometimes Jason catches sight of his father bent over a stack of bills, audibly groaning. Or Jamie watches her mother trudge through the door wordlessly, strands of hair askew, and knows the closing shift didn't come through. After just such a day recently, Jamie bought her a small ceramic teddy bear with a card saying, a bear hug for my mother.

But then came the dinner when Jason was chiding Joyce about her unpredictable schedule: "You don't do nothin' in your job, Mom. You're just here all day." He was kidding with her, in fact, trying to deflate the tension of a miserable day, but Dave heard it as ridicule. That very day, Joyce had called him at the plant in tears because her shift had been canceled. And now his son was mocking her.

Even more hulking now than in his football days, Dave shoved back his chair and stood nose to nose with Jason.

"You will never, ever raise your voice to your mother like that," he screamed. "You will regret it. You will regret every word that came out of your mouth. Or your life will be a living hell, and I will make sure." He drew breath, then hissed, "I want you out of my sight."

Jason retreated to his bedroom. Hours passed. Eventually, Dave came in and told Jason about the phone call from Joyce that afternoon, about all the fears and disappointments.

Without quite apologizing, he had made reconciliation possible. A few days later, when Jason noticed Dave alone in the master bedroom, the most private place in the house, he asked, "Dad, how come you're like this? So nasty."

"You can't imagine the pressure your mother and I are under," Dave said. "I even hide things from your mother. When I come home, I don't want to relive everything that went wrong. And I don't want to put it on your shoulders." Then, as if to ask forgiveness, he added, "Say to yourself, 'Something must've been tough on Dad today.'"

Crouching in oil-streaked jeans, squinting behind safety glasses, Jason ponders the right rear wheel of his 1983 Eldorado. The car rests on a hydraulic lift three feet off the floor in the Arthur Sypek Center, the county-wide vocational school where Jason starts his day. Four classmates, each as confounded as Jason, cluster around a work light dangling from the car's undercarriage. None of them has ever done a wheel alignment, a basic procedure for any mechanic, and this wheel is being aligned in a 21st-century way.

An electronic sensor grips the wheel and registers its position on the screen of a nearby computer. With every tweak of tool against metal, every shove of shoulder against tire, the digits report imperfection: "+0.18 . . . -0.07 . . . +0.11." The other boys step outside for cigarettes at the midperiod break. Jason remains fixated on the task, inured to the sound of Jimi Hendrix on a blaster, muttering to himself, "I'm gonna end up driving home sideways."

Like Jason, the other 20 boys in the class are the children of a destabilized working class—telephone installers and truck drivers, roofers and exterminators, secretaries and millwrights. Like him, they will struggle just to stay even with parents who are themselves struggling to stay afloat. Jason's teacher Keith Fennimore calculates that a graduate of the Sypek Center needs to earn $30,000 a year to support himself in this part of the country. Yet even as a mechanic's duties have grown far more sophisticated—today's Cadillacs use a half-dozen on-board computers; auto emissions are measured with 486 processors—Fennimore has seen wages stall during the seven years he has taught at Sypek. A starting mechanic at a local dealership will earn perhaps $16,000 annually.

Fennimore does more to prepare his students for the real world than simply teach them repairs and tuneups. He requires them to bring in help-wanted ads from the newspapers to get a sense of the job market. He encourages them to understand the economic currents swirling around them. Back in 1992, he noticed that many of the students rooted for Ross Perot, who was predicting that the enactment of the North American Free Trade Agreement would cause a "giant sucking sound" of jobs leaving the United States for low-wage, nonunion sites in Mexico. This year, though, only one student in Jason's class could even identify NAFTA. Few followed the presidential election. "They don't know the news," Fennimore says with a sigh, "unless it's on MTV."

Until recently, Ewing High School seemed equally oblivious. Erected during the industrial glory days of 1950, it depended on plants like GM to employ the students who never attended college or dropped out of high school. For a long time, the unstated compact held. A majority of Ewing's adults have no education beyond high school, the 1990 census found, yet only a tiny percentage were jobless or on welfare.

But at the same time that manufacturing jobs were hemorrhaging, at the same time that education was becoming more closely tied to earning power, at the same time that Jason Perillo was making his way through the elementary and middle grades, Ewing High School was convulsing. Prior to the 1994–95 academic year, the school had gone through eight principals in nine years. It did not have a computer lab and had only three advanced-placement classes. Ewing's voters, at least the minority who bothered to turn out, defeated the proposed school-district budget almost annually. . . .

The so-called digital divide among Information Age schools gaped between Ewing High and West Windsor-Plainsboro, a nearby public school that educated the children of the Video Valley. In the 1993–94 school year, as Jason Perillo entered Ewing High, fewer than two-thirds of its juniors passed all three sections of the state's basic-skills tests, and its seniors scored an average of 953 (using the newly re-centered formula) on the Scholastic Aptitude Test, placing Ewing in the 40th percentile nationally. West Windsor-Plainsboro, meanwhile, registered SATs of an average of 1,145 and a 91 percent pass rate on the basic-skills test. More than 300 students were enrolled in advanced-placement classes.

A new principal, Edward Barry, assumed control of Ewing High in September 1994, at the start of Jason's sophomore year. During Barry's tenure, the school has raised its scores steadily on the SATs and the basic-skills tests. It has installed a computer lab and more than doubled the number of advanced-placement courses. Half of last June's graduates went on to four-year colleges, including Brandeis, New York University, and William and Mary.

Still, the improvements have reached Jason only slightly, if at all. He has spent his high school years in the middle academic tracks—not quite remedial but far from college prep. And although Barry has reduced the number of tracks from six to three to soften the academic caste system, seniors like Jason are graduating under the old system. A visitor to Ewing High can sense how thoroughly the students in the bottom tiers have accepted their station as their destiny.

"Kids don't actually go up to you and say, 'Why are you doin' well?'" Jason says. "But in the classroom, the learning environment is not there. People start talking to you, you start answering—even if you didn't want to. And braggin' about how they didn't study for the test. They fail and laugh at it. It's not like, 'Oh, my God.'"

"I've had a lot of kids ask me, 'What track am I in? What level am I in?'" says Dena Lavery, an English teacher who is a favorite of Jamie Perillo's. "If they find out it's college prep, they're more motivated from that alone." If not, "they feel, because they're in this [lower] level, they're not required to do as much."

To follow Jason and Jamie through several days of class is to encounter genuinely gifted teachers, particularly the younger faculty recruited by Barry, amid an overall climate of limited expectations. Many of the classes consist largely of a teacher reviewing the previous night's homework, whether that homework happens to be vocabulary or equations, verb conjugations or chemical valences. The state basic-skills tests loom over such drills, for any public school in New Jersey ignores them at its peril. They are second only to SAT scores as the journalistic shorthand for evaluating districts and are the favored sales tool of real-estate brokers.

For his part, the same Jason who toils through his break at the Sypek Center merely tolerates his academic classes. He does his homework, yes, and he behaves respectfully. Yet never does he appear intellectually engaged. The last time that school excited him, he says, was back in seventh grade, when a social-studies teacher had the class act out such events as the assassination of Abraham Lincoln. So, one semester shy of graduation, he has a C average and a combined SAT score of 850 to show for his own efforts and the school's. "If you come to class and do what you're supposed to do," he says, "you pass."

Hillary Freundlich, Jason's guidance counselor, has observed in many students that same acquiescence, that same ennui. It does not puzzle her, though. A child who grows up being abused, she says by way of metaphor, comes to believe that abuse is normal. The same holds true for a child reared in the De-Industrial Revolution. "When we describe what it was like for us—that we knew we'd have better jobs than our parents—for these kids that is as much of a fairy tale, a vapor, as what our parents told us about the Great Depression," she says. "They don't know the world is skewed."

On the day after the Presidential election, a torpor hangs over the Perillo home. Joyce wonders if she should take the two-hour dinner shift she's been offered; it means $20 at most. Dave frets over a *Wall Street Journal* article that made the rounds at work today, about

how GM may sell the division that includes its Ewing plant. Knowing her parents are captives of their worries, Jamie minds Dave Jr. while Jason, recovering from an emergency appendectomy over the weekend, sleeps off a painkiller.

In this house, the election brings neither joy nor relief. . . .

"A bunch of "b.s." Joyce says of . . . claims of economic recovery.

"Yeah, thanks for creating all those $5.25-an-hour jobs," Dave adds. "You don't hear about all the $20-an-hour jobs that left the country."

Even Halloween, usually such a diversion for the family, failed to dispel the gloom. They felt too dispirited to take a hayride together at the orchard like they usually do, and the $100 it would have cost seemed better spent elsewhere. Only Dave Jr. got a new costume. It felt like drudgery stuffing the dummies and stringing the lights for the annual extravaganza out front.

Now, with the holiday over, the whole display has to be packed away. Dave and Joyce have crammed much of it behind the garage door, out of sight of the neighbors at least. But a twine cobweb still hangs between two trees along the driveway. Spanish moss sags from the eaves. And in the center of the lawn, just below Jason Perillo's bedroom window, lies a coffin.

CRITICAL THINKING QUESTIONS

1. What factors lead to the economic problems of the Perillo family?

2. Some people would say the Perillo family is to blame for their own problems. Support or refute this statement.

3. Capitalist societies, such as that in the United States, cannot survive and grow unless businesses are free to hire and fire workers as they need them. When families such as the Perillos suffer, who in society benefits?

Reading 3

Coming Out Now

J. Baker and N. Joseph

In this article, the authors focus on the difficulties gay youth encounter in their everyday lives.

For gay teens, life is better—and worse. They see more role models but AIDS is unrelenting.

Here's how Daniel Paul Layer Jr., 18, of Castro Valley, Calif., sees himself in 20 years: "I'll have my own business and have made enough money to do what I want . . . I'll have a house in the country . . . I'll have been settled down with somebody for a long time, and have three children: a boy to carry on my family name, a girl to spoil and an 'It'—whatever the third child happens to be. The first two will be mine, but the third could be adopted."

An ordinary enough dream for a teenager—but Daniel Layer is gay. Ten years ago not many gay adolescents would have considered such a dream obtainable. Traditionally, growing up gay has meant years of self-loathing and a sense of isolation from classmates and family. Hesitant to combat the social sentiments that gay is not good, many gay teenagers still repress their homosexuality until adulthood, spending their adolescence pretending to be straight. Meanwhile, other impulses are at work: in an era when teens feel peer pressure to experiment with sex earlier, many are often forced to face the question, "Am I gay or not?" long before they're ready. For those who are gay, the strain often leads to depression. Paul Gibson, a San Francisco social worker who did a study of teen suicide for the U.S. Department of Health and Human Services, believes gays nationwide account for 30 percent of all teen attempts. "The root of the problem," says Gibson, "is a society that stigmatizes homosex-

uals while failing to recognize that a substantial number of its youth are gay."

On top of that, young gay men must now confront the specter of an early death from AIDS. But ironically the AIDS crisis has also made it easier for some homosexual teenagers: over the last decade Gay America has become more visible, often in a positive light as it took care of its own sick and dying. Gay characters now show up on television and in movies, such as the recent *Longtime Companion,* the first feature film about AIDS in the gay community. News reports proliferate about the gay-rights movement, the phenomena of gay surrogate parenting and adoption, and about prominent figures who are homosexual—all of them, from congressmen to local AIDS volunteers, providing high-profile role models and raising the expectations of gay youth. Daniel Layer believes AIDS has made many Americans recognize that a gay subculture exists. "AIDS has gotten the straight world involved in the gay world," he says.

The future looks bright to Daniel, thanks to good counseling and an understanding mother. But getting this far was a struggle. His parents divorced when their only child was 3, and Daniel lived with his mother in Auburn, Wash., where she was studying to be a draftsman. On some weekends he visited Daniel Sr., a diesel mechanic, and after his father remarried, Daniel was joined by a stepbrother and a baby sister. Though Daniel liked having a family, he says his father, once a paratrooper in Vietnam, could be intense. His stepmother was a fundamentalist Christian, and Daniel says that she and his father were strict disciplinarians who didn't hesitate to punish him severely. "When he'd come back it'd take two weeks to put him back together," says Heather, 37, Daniel's mother. In 1981, to get a fresh start, Heather took her son to live in Tulsa, Okla., her hometown.

In sixth grade, Daniel got an early taste of homophobia. He and Heather had just moved back west to Tracy, Calif. "A redneck town," says Daniel. "The kids were all Chicanos and cowboys, very rough." On his first day Daniel wore a brightly colored jacket with a big collar that he thought was hip and would help him fit in. He miscalculated—drastically—and heard himself called "fag" for the first time. "The word meant absolutely nothing to me," he said. "I just knew I'd gone from being a popular kid [in Tulsa] to one of the biggest nerds in school."

Daniel says junior high was a nightmare. Because he didn't conform to the local macho standards of dress and behavior, he was challenged to fistfights daily. Once in biology lab classmates threw frogs that they had been dissecting at him. Another time, after a water-polo game, a student held him underwater so long that he almost drowned. Daniel grew depressed, got erratic grades and became rebellious. His weight shot up—"I oinked out," he says—and he quarreled constantly with Heather.

At the same time, Daniel says he recognized that the name-calling wasn't entirely off the mark. "Their words hurt a lot worse because I knew they were true," he says. He was beginning to realize he was sexually attracted to boys, and went to the library to find books and magazine articles on homosexuality. He also started seeing a family counselor to make peace at home, and a school counselor with whom he discussed his feelings of homosexuality. The school counselor's response was orthodox; she told him youngsters often go through a homosexual phase and that he could still grow up straight, marry and have a family. Hoping the counselor was right, he dated girls, but says he soon realized he was deceiving himself. Daniel kept his homosexuality from his mother and the family counselor, but his sexual confusion and years of taunting had taken their toll. "The family counselor told me to take him out of there and move to the Bay Area," says Heather, "or I would wind up with a dead son." Daniel never considered suicide, but he believes he might have if he had stayed in Tracy.

During his four high-school years in the suburban Bay Area, Daniel continued the painstaking process of accepting his homosexuality. Students at Castro Valley High School are tolerant of differences—one popular clique, with spiky, tie-dyed hair, would look at home in New York's East Village. Though he never came out publicly at school, he was discreetly involved with another gay student for two years.

What helped most was his improved relationship with his mother. Heather says she always worried about the absence of a male role model; she suspected he might be gay, but says, "He had me fooled with all that talk about wanting children." When, at 15, he finally told her he was homosexual, he says she didn't berate him, but instead tracked down a counseling group for gay teenagers in Berkeley. "She thought I would make friends," says Daniel.

Daniel's development took a critical turn in the summer of 1988. Working as a salesclerk at a shopping mall, he fell in with a suburban network of young gay men who copied the fast-track behavior of San Francisco: a steady round of dance clubs, stylish clothes—and casual sex. Daniel followed the pack, but says he has since pulled away. He wants someone steady in his life, and doesn't think he can find him there. "They see someone for a month and say they have a boyfriend," he says.

In this period, Daniel also learned firsthand about fear of AIDS. He insists that he and his generation practice safe sex as a matter of course. "We grew up with AIDS," Daniel says. "You just use condoms without thinking about it." But as his sexual experience grew, Daniel began to worry that he may have somehow been exposed to the virus. In October 1989 he took the HIV antibody test—and was negative.

Daniel appears to have adjusted to his homosexuality at an age when many teenagers are just beginning the struggle. "My friends are starting to call me the gay poster child," he says. But he still attends a group-therapy session in San Francisco where gay teens complain of being harassed for their sexuality. "When I say, 'Mom, Dad, I can't solve this math equation'," says Peter, a member of Daniel's group, "they answer, 'Well, if you weren't gay . . .'" The group shares its thoughts of suicide, fear of AIDS and anger at being ostracized by classmates. "You miss out on dating," says another group member. "You feel socially retarded."

Adolescence is never easy, but growing up gay has always been trying. For Daniel Layer, the path to self-esteem and sexual maturity dovetails with a quest for stability in his home life. Recently he walked around San Francisco's predominantly gay Castro district where bar-hopping young men bustle past neighbors on canes, their unearthly pale faces the hallmark of AIDS. But which of all the images of gay life in the Castro struck Daniel most? A couple in their 70s, helping each other down the street, both of them men.

CRITICAL THINKING QUESTIONS

1. In what ways are the lives of gay youth different from heterosexual youth?
2. Why are support groups and a sense of community important for gay youth?
3. Discuss the ways in which gay or lesbian young people's equality of opportunity may be limited when their sexuality is known to others.

Reading 4

Race, Skin Color and Body Parts

Ta'Shia Asanti

Asanti addresses the ways that gay men and lesbian women contend with their multiple forms of minority status and how such differences can impede the development of a sense of community.

At the beginning of my career as a political and cultural worker, I unrealistically expected and took for granted that there was unity and cohesiveness in the struggle for equality among people of color, women and people from diverse sexual communities. I also be-

Source: Updated version; originally published in *Lesbian News* 21, no. 6 (January 1996) with permission from the author.

Ta'Shia Asanti is a human rights activist, award-winning journalist, poet, fiction writer and filmmaker. She was nominated for the Courage in Journalism award in 2002, given by the International Women's Media Foundation.

lieved that there was an invisible bond that existed, based purely on the color of people's skin. My political immaturity placed me in a position of vulnerability on many levels, as soon I would face attacks not just from the people who I felt oppressed me, but the very people I was fighting for. These experiences were so painful, that in an effort to understand this division, I posted my thoughts on the subject on a popular site for lesbians of color. One member wrote back to me explaining how I shouldn't have any romanticized expectations of my Black sisters or brothers based on skin color. These sentiments hurt me even deeper. However, it was true. The majority of people of color lack the ability to work with each other in any large numbers and will trust someone who is not a person of color before they can trust or bond with someone from their own ethnic background. In evaluating the effects of the historic Willie Lynch Letter,[1] one can easily understand why this is so. But in exploring the technical definitions for words such as ethnicity and culture, we are able to understand how cultural upbringing and socialization impacts one's ability to connect with others who "look" like them.

Webster's Dictionary defines ethnicity with words like "native, race, religion and culture." It defines culture as "enlightenment, enrichment and knowledge." Many people of color, particularly people of African descent, have not been socialized to affirm, celebrate and have "enlightenment" about their culture. In understanding the political and social ramifications of the skin color in America, or the "presence of melanin" issue, it is important to understand race and skin color in the context of history. The teaching by European slave owners that "the darker the person was the more inferior the person was" is at the core of self-hate and division among poc [people of color] communities, and misperception and fear in non-poc communities. Prohibiting African slaves to practice or emulate anything that related to traditional African culture and socializing American Blacks to imitate White culture has rendered most Blacks completely ignorant to the knowledge of their own cultural heritage. This is a subject I could go on and on about but I'll move on to body parts. . . .

The issue of body parts relates to gender differences, perceived and actual. The issue of sexism and gender oppression has existed throughout history. Sexism is so ingrained in

our global culture that there is not a country in the world that doesn't face issues in this arena. Even in the queer community, lesbians discriminate against gay men often preferring lesbians only at social events. Male children are often barred from attending lesbian only events that allow children. Male-to-female transsexuals are barred from lesbian and women's events. They are resented for enjoying what some women would call the "fruits of womanhood without the trials of womanhood" as I heard one lesbian call it. But I ponder the trials that transsexuals must face in order to assume life as a woman and wonder why such a sacrifice is not deemed enough by my lesbian sisters. In addition, shouldn't any one who would subject themselves to the pain of the sex change, the ostracism of such a life decision and the work of learning to live in a new body, be respected for who and how they identify? Do body parts determine who we are? If that's the case, all women should be with men, right? And regarding the issue of sexism, I've observed women who label themselves or are labeled as "butch" who act and play out sexist roles in their relationships and in society. They act as if they truly believe feminine looking women should be subservient and weak. Gay men often describe themselves as drama queens, a term used to describe women who are overly emotional. There goes the myth that men don't have any feelings. The famous singer and recording artist, "Prince" once asked the question to his fans, "Am I Black or White, am I straight or gay?" That song became one of his top sellers. In truth, due to the mixing of the races during the middle passage, most of us are not pure anything. And almost everyone can attest to feeling curiosity about what same-gender-love would be like at least one time in his or her life, although they'd never admit it.

Even in the lesbian-gay-bisexual-transgender (lgbt) community, where I thought surely there would be unity based on mutual struggles, there exist walls of division based on sexual orientation, socio-economic status and ethnicity. As I interact in Black communities which "appear" primarily heterosexual, I face

---

1. The Willie Lynch Letter is a historical document written by a slave owner to slave owners around the world. The Willie Lynch Letter outlined a master plan to keep Blacks enslaved through maintaining division among their communities by programming them to divide themselves based on skin color, age, where they worked on the plantation, gender, hair texture and facial features.

discrimination again, regardless of my achievements in and dedication to fighting for ideals
that could better the entire race. I have
learned through this journey to see each and
every person as an individual, to focus on their
humanness instead of human made titles. I
have learned to analyze myself for stereotypes
and personal prejudices against any one
group. And more importantly, I have learned
to believe in the work that I am doing, regardless of the opinions of others. The results have
truly been freeing.

CRITICAL THINKING QUESTIONS

1. Asanti says that she thought she would find
unity in the gay/lesbian community. Why?

2. What are the bases upon which there are
divisions in the gay/lesbian community?

3. Explain why other social statuses appear to
be more important than sexuality for some
members of the gay/lesbian community. How
might differences in this community be overcome?

Reading 5

Becoming a Man:
The Personal Account of a
Female-to-Male Transsexual

Mark Rees

In this article Rees discusses his experiences and struggles as a female-to-male transsexual.

BACKGROUND

My parents were married in 1938. Mother
was a secretary in a City of London firm and
my father was in the Merchant Navy. For a
couple of years they lived in London but in
1940 my mother's firm was evacuated to
Rusthall, a village near Tunbridge Wells in
Kent. My mother moved with her widowed
mother whilst my father sailed to places unknown—wartime security meant that his
whereabouts could not be revealed, even to
his family.

I was born in December 1942, the survivor
of two-month premature non-identical twins.

Source: Richard Ekins & Dave King (Eds). 1996. *Blending
Genders: Social Aspects of Cross-dressing and Sex-changing.*
NY: Routledge.

My sister, Carol, died five days after birth due
to "prematurity." I was a weakly child and succumbed easily to illness, which meant much
missed schooling. A younger sister, Rosemary,
was born in 1946. She was much more robust
than I had been and sailed through her
schooling, passing the eleven-plus scholarship examination, which I did not. Rosemary
went to the local grammar school, a privilege
denied me, but ultimately my academic
achievements were greater, if considerably be-
lated. Although the move to Rusthall had not
been my parents' original plan, both of them
spent the rest of their lives there and became
greatly liked members of the local community. At the time of writing my sister lives in
Tunbridge Wells, a couple of miles distant,
whilst I remain in Rusthall, which has been
my home all my life.

BECOMING AWARE—CHILDHOOD, ADOLESCENCE AND ADULTHOOD, BEFORE MY ROLE CHANGE

My childhood was better than people imagine. Life for the potential female-to-male transsexual is undoubtedly easier than for the male-to-female. Tomboys, even in the 1940s and 1950s when I was a child, were acccept-able and treated with good-humored toler-ance, whilst feminine boys known by the more derogatory name of sissies were—and re-main—subject to derision.

My younger sister and I played with both boys' and girls' toys but once I had my own pocket money and was able to buy my own playthings, masculine toys predominated. In spite of playing with toy soldiers and trains my sister did not become a transsexual, whilst I, in spite of the dolls, did not become a normal woman. Our friends were of both sexes. My best pals were a boy (whose electric train I shamelessly coveted) and an assertive and confident girl. I never cultivated the friend-ship of 'frilly' girls.

For most of my school career I was at all-girl schools and lived with my sister, mother and grandmother—even the cat was female! My fa-ther was in the Merchant Navy for most of the time, so female influence was strong and male influence correspondingly weak. My condi-tion could not therefore be ascribed to a lack of female environment. My mother was the closer parent and remained so for the rest of her life, but it was my father who was my role model—I adored Mum, whilst wanting to be like Dad.

It did not occur to me that my female peers didn't want to be boys, nor did I consider that I was destined for womanhood myself. This was totally outside my childish scheme of life, wholly detached from my thinking, as incon-ceivable as the notion of becoming a giraffe. I was therefore, until puberty, happily unaware of the problems to come.

Yet others, even if they did not verbalise it at the time, sensed that all was not as ex-pected. When I was a small child my mother consulted a doctor, because she was con-cerned that my clitoris was larger than nor-mal, but was reassured. Much later, both she and a close family friend were to make inde-pendent statutory declarations to the effect that I had been masculine from a very early age, both in looks and in behaviour. The friend added that I looked like a boy even when wearing the dresses mother put on me. Few friends and neighbours were surprised when I eventually changed roles.

The realisation of puberty was one of the most terrible traumas of my whole life, before or since. My peers were all more advanced than me so for a while my hopes were raised. Perhaps it wouldn't happen to me and I would change into a boy? But at fourteen I started having periods. I was consumed with anger, despair and anguish. My body was repugnant, something alien, almost a deformity, although as far as breast development was concerned, that was never very great—but sufficient to cause me abhorrence.

It was paradoxical that whilst supposingly passing into womanhood I was apparently be-coming more ambiguous, judging by the number of mistakes made about my sex, not to mention the deliberate jeers. Even when I was wearing ostensibly female attire people thought me male. The caretaker at my new college tried to allocate me a locker in the boys' cloakroom, irrespective of the fact that I was dressed in a skirt and nylons at the time— a somewhat embarrassing encounter since it took place in front of several other students. Such mistakes were bad enough, reinforcing my sense of being an oddity, but less forgive-able were the thoughtless remarks from peo-ple who should have known better. 'He, she or it?' sneered a friend of my parents in my presence.

Little sympathy was forthcoming from my family over such incidents. Wasn't I inviting such remarks by my behaviour? Didn't I make matters worse by walking like a boy? I was ac-cused of being abnormal, especially because I refused to wear a bra. I was seen as awkward. No one seemed to understand that I hadn't set out to be awkward but was just behaving in a way which seemed natural.

Had it not been for the feeling of shame and guilt over my problem I might have sought professional help sooner than I did. It took the combined efforts of my 'assertive and confident' childhood friend and a sympathetic college tutor to get me to see a doctor. I expected to be told to pull myself together—hadn't others said as much?—but Dr. G. took me seriously and was very sympathetic. She referred me to a psychiatrist.

The psychiatrist offered to admit me into hospital. By now almost unable to cope with all the taunts, I accepted and became the hospital's youngest patient. I was seventeen. It was a refuge but little else. I certainly wasn't 'cured'. When I was discharged the lady psychiatrist said: 'Good-bye my dear, enjoy being a woman'.

I was now blighted with a psychiatric history. It prevented me from succeeding in my efforts to enter either the police or the Women's Royal Air Force (WRAF). The WRAF rejected my application on the grounds of 'temperamental instability'. Eventually I was given a chance by the Women's Royal Naval Service (WRNS) which accepted me after writing to Dr. G.

By now, convinced that my conflict of mind and body and the accompanying isolation from normal society could never be resolved, I decided to cope by acting out the female role as far as dress was concerned—no further would I have gone. I donned a dress and court shoes and ventured forth, hating every moment.

'My God', exclaimed one of my WRNS friends, 'You look like a bloke in drag!' That's exactly how I felt. Nor were my superiors fooled by my role-playing: 'Tell me, Wren Rees,' asked my divisional officer, 'Why are you so mannish?'

As if that was not enough, I fell in love with a fellow Wren, although I didn't want a relationship with her as a woman myself. I thought I must be homosexual—there seemed to be no other label to give to my undiagnosed and apparently unique condition, but I was very uneasy with it. When later I met lesbians my uneasiness was confirmed. I wasn't one of them but very much heterosexual, although afflicted with the wrong genitalia.

There followed a very stressful period after my fellow Wren discovered my feelings for her and threatened to report me to the Commanding Officer. Not long afterwards I was given a medical discharge with the diagnosis of 'homosexual tendencies'. I knew this was wrong, but what was I?

By now life was barely tolerable. I avoided social gatherings and tried to bury myself in study. Contact with doctors and clergy proved unhelpful. The doctors told me I would grow out of it (at 25?) and would have to learn to live with it. A clergyman told me that one could live a fulfilling life as a non-practising homosexual!

In 1969, four years after my WRNS' discharge, I chanced to see an article in *The Times* of London which described the condition of transsexualism. It was a moment of enlightenment; at last it all fitted into place. I was transsexual. It was a year or more before I managed to find a specialist and heard the words I never believed possible: 'I can help you live as a man'.

Having gained some 'A' levels since leaving the WRNS I was about to embark upon a degree course in dental surgery at the University of Birmingham. In theory it seemed wise to complete the course before changing roles, but in reality life was intolerable for me in the female role. I was acting out a part which was alien to me, suppressing my sexual feelings and suffering a perpetual onslaught of comments and mistakes about my sex. I decided to change roles as soon as possible.

My consultant agreed and prescribed methyl testosterone. I knew that the process would be long and arduous, but once I'd taken the hormone the depression which had hung over me since puberty lifted. I felt a new person, both mentally and physically. At the age of 28 I was about to start living.

BECOMING A MAN—PHYSICALLY

Practically and emotionally, becoming a man, physically, was the least difficult part of my role reassignment. It was, however, the most frustrating because it was only a compromise. I knew that, however good the treatment, I'd never be fully male, functionally, anatomically or chromosomally; but to be accepted socially as such was a tremendous release, a miracle.

The action of the hormones was almost immediate. A couple of weeks later I had my last period and within a month or so people began to notice a change in my voice. (Since I was still living as a woman, I told enquirers that I had a heavy cold!) Although the growth of my facial hair took much longer, I was surprised by the rapidity of the changes generally. How much the lifting of my underlying depression was due to the hormone intake, and how much to the relief of knowing that at long last I was being enabled to change roles, I do not know.

My superficial veins especially in the forearms, became more obvious as the subcutaneous fat decreased. This decrease was most obvious around the breasts, hips and thighs. There was an increase in muscle development with a corresponding weight increase, redistribution and increase in body hair and clitoral enlargement. After six months I was able to live successfully as a man.

In retrospect, whilst very grateful at the time, I realise that my treatment was somewhat arbitrary. The 'gender identity clinic' I attended seemed to consist solely of one psychiatrist. I had no physical examination or biochemical tests. It was the psychiatrist, not an endocrinologist, who prescribed the hormone preparation which was later found to put the liver at risk of cancer. Once this was known I was submitted to a liver scan, but otherwise did not receive any form of physical monitoring. All hormone treatment was stopped for six months during this period. Then, when I expressed concern about this—chiefly because I had lost all my chest hairs—another oral preparation was prescribed. It is now understood that these oral preparations and long periods without any hormone replacement therapy (HRT) render one prone to osteoporosis, a condition which has been diagnosed in some female-to-male transsexuals.

My recent—and first—density scan showed a below average reading but 'acceptable' unless a continuous loss is observed.

It was not until just before surgery, in 1974, that I received any form of physical examination, and it was eight years after my first hormone tablets, when I had transferred myself to another gender clinic, that I was examined by an endocrinologist and biochemical tests carried out. An appropriate dosage was prescribed and later intra-muscular injections replaced the more risky—and less effective—oral preparations. My 'defection' meant that I have been monitored ever since, not only for osteoporosis but also signs of cardio-vascular disease. I see an endocrinologist annually and the practice nurses who administer the injections keep a check on my blood pressure and cholesterol levels.

I recently opted to reduce my hormone intake from monthly injections to about three or four annually, but began to feel less than fully fit, slightly depressed and lethargic, and experienced a return of a certain amount of subcutaneous fat. To avoid these eunuchoid symptoms I returned to a monthly regime, so far with no adverse effects.

Surgery is often depicted, especially by the more ignorant members of the media, as the sum total of a 'sex-change'. A man goes into hospital and comes out a woman, or vice versa. I find this utter nonsense. It is but part of a process which can take months, probably years. Alone it would achieve little. For myself the most wonderful thing was being enabled to live in the male role. This was achieved by the hormones, not by the scalpel. I had been living as a man for nearly three years before undergoing a bilateral mastectomy. This was straightforward and relatively painless. Prior to the surgery I had imagined that once relieved of what seemed like unnatural appendages I would go into paroxysms of delight, but this was not so. To discover myself with a flat, barely scarred chest seemed so absolutely normal; my previous form seemed a bad dream, something from another life.

The hysterectomy and oophorectomy (removal of the ovaries) a year later was less easy;

I developed a massive haematoma which necessitated blood transfusions. I felt unwell and wondered if I'd been right to voluntarily undergo surgery on an otherwise healthy body, although medical friends had advised it, fearing the risk of cancer in the unused organs. None the less I felt guilty because of the bother caused to the medical and nursing staff and, not least, the anxiety undergone by my mother and friends. These qualms were finally laid to rest by a visiting friend who firmly told me that the treatment had been justified. As my friend put it: 'You were only half a person before, now you are whole.'

As time went on adhesions developed in my chest and rather unsightly concavities appeared. The surgeon who had carried out the mastectomy advised rubbing the affected parts with cold cream. This proved a totally useless exercise. By now I had 'defected' to the new clinic and its plastic surgeon performed corrective surgery in February 1985. To date there have been no problems since. None the less I remain somewhat apprehensive about being seen without a shirt. The possibility of liposuction was discussed with the team, since large hips are as much a bane to the female-to-male transsexual as the presence of breasts, but I decided that I would be foolish to undergo the risk of surgery unless it were absolutely necessary. Besides, surgery could not alter the underlying bone structure. Bearing in mind that in my former role my sex had been questioned almost daily, whereas since my role-change it had been questioned only twice in some thirteen years, I felt such a procedure was not absolutely necessary.

A phalloplasty (the construction of a penis) is probably what most female-to-male transsexuals yearn for more than anything else, yet it is a most difficult, risky and unsatisfactory procedure. Had I been offered a phalloplasty when first changing roles it is possible that I may have accepted, but now, many years later and with considerably more knowledge, it is an operation I would not wish to undergo. Some techniques appear better than others but all involve considerable pain and scarring. Other areas of the body have to be mutilated in order to acquire tissue for the construction. The involvement of the urethra increases the risk of infection and the ability to [urinate] in a male fashion cannot be guaranteed. Indeed some patients are unable, after surgery, to pass water in either a male or female way. I met one who has to carry a jug everywhere he goes. Erection by natural means is, of course, impossible and no amount of surgery will render the female-to-male transsexual capable of fathering children. An added risk is the fact that the procedure often leaves the constructed phallus totally insensitive. Far from the phalloplasty being the philosophers' stone, it has instead made life worse, not better, for many of those desperate enough to undergo it.

Rather than enter the fraught area of phalloplasties, a number of female-to-male transsexuals have equipped themselves with very realistic looking prostheses, which can enable them to urinate in a male fashion if desired. I would not use one myself—they are expensive and add bother to life, both in the fixing and the cleaning. I suppose I feel, too, that their use is a little dishonest, which is illogical because a man with a false leg would not be so regarded.

Of course I despise my female body and the practical and psychological problems it causes. If some wonderful technique could be perfected whereby the hated vagina could be excised and a fully functional and aesthetically acceptable phallus constructed without the need for mutilation elsewhere, then I'd be as keen as any female-to-male transsexual to have it done. But, unlike some of my colleagues, I realise that maleness is not bestowed by genitalia alone. I have not needed a penis to be accepted as male. As Professor Milton Diamond says: "The most powerful sex organ is between the ears, not the legs."

BECOMING A MAN—SEXUALLY

It was during my teens that I discovered that women sexually aroused me, but it has been only recently that I came to the view that this experience was physically dissimilar from that of a normal woman, although our equipment was identical. Women, of my acquaintance, speak of an arousal which seems to be diffuse, whereas I had what I later recognised as a clitoral erection and this was over ten years before my hormone therapy.

I consider it impossible to become a man sexually as far as sexual intercourse is concerned. However good a phalloplasty, which they seldom are, no constructed organ will have a natural erection or impregnate a female.

Many female-to-male transsexuals do, however, have lasting relationships with normal, non-lesbian women, which include a sexual element. I believe that their partners do not see their lovers as women, but as men, albeit without penises and that many experience orgasms for the first time with these lovers. I am less certain of the satisfaction obtained by the female-to-male transsexual. One is in the unhappy situation of being stimulated by the same signals which would arouse a heterosexual genetic male, but having female genitalia which react in a way appropriate to a woman. Some may be able to cope with these unwelcome reminders of one's condition, but I find it difficult.

BECOMING A MAN— ADMINISTRATIVELY AND SOCIALLY

Faced with all the documentation to be changed I decided that if there were any doubts about changing roles, this would be the point at which they would surface. I had none.

A change of name brings about an appreciation of just how many documents bear it. The initial deed poll on change of name was straightforward. 'Brenda' became 'Brendan' and 'Margaret' became 'Mark'. (Although not my intention at the time, a few years later I dropped 'Brendan' making 'Mark' [by which I'd been known socially] my first name.) My original change had been made in a way to ease life of those around me who found it difficult to use my new name—'Bren' covered

everything. Once established, I wanted to use a name which had no ties with the past. This undoubtedly had psychological benefits for me.

The university authorities were very discreet and helpful but there still remained much that I had to do. Names had to be changed on bank accounts, insurance policies, passport, driving license, club membership, and on Department of Social Security, Department of Employment, Inland Revenue and medical records. The list seemed interminable. Some time later, when applying for another course, I discovered one omission— my examination certificates, so that required some explanatory letters to various examining authorities. All the official bodies with which I dealt endeavoured to be discreet and helpful. Bureaucracy had got a human face.

There was also the change of wardrobe, although having worn unisex clothes for some time this was less of a total change than an amendment. The few clothes I bought new were supplemented by gleaning from charity shops—I didn't want everything to look new! I took my feminine clothes back to the charity shops.

My father was dead by the time I changed roles, so it is useless to speculate as to how he would have reacted. Understandably, my mother found it hard, saying that she'd never realised my feelings. However, since all the neighbours had guessed, I suspect that it was a case of not seeing what was obvious because it was too painful. It was a very difficult period for all of us, but, as my sister predicted, once my mother realised how much happier I had become as a result, she was more able to accept it. We must not, however, underestimate the trauma families and close friends may undergo. There is a tendency, I believe, for transsexuals to be so wrapped up in their own problems that they do not see the anguish which those around them are also experiencing.

I found dealing with friends and acquaintances almost as fraught as coping with the family. Those who were close knew of my situation and were very supportive. I was in for some surprises from the others. My 'pious' and older friends, who I thought would be narrow-minded and condemnatory, turned out to be very helpful and accepting; whilst my acquaintances in the WRNS, sure, I thought, to be broad-minded and understanding, were, with one or two exceptions, the least so.

Some people were surprised that I chose to remain in my home instead of 'vanishing', which seems to be a common transsexual practice. I saw no reason to do so. It was, admittedly, a little daunting to face the local community as 'Mark' after having been known as the rather ambiguous 'Brenda' for years. Of course, there was gossip, but it died down and now I am re-assimilated into the community, even singing bass in the choir where I once sang soprano! Twenty years on I can confidently say that my condition is not a barrier to social acceptance. In my experience, if one lives a normal life and makes a contribution to the well-being of the community in which one lives, then transsexualism is hardly worth a thought. This is borne out by the fact that recently I was invited to stand as a local candidate for the council elections and was duly elected.

BECOMING A MAN— PSYCHOLOGICALLY

For the transsexual, a change of role does not mean a change of personality, although that seems to be a popular notion. One relative suggested to me that I should take up pipe-smoking! I replied that I had no need of a nipple-substitute! The treatment may have changed the body and hence the world's perception of one, but the person is the same. It seems absurd to undergo all that a role-change involves in order to become a male (or female) stereotype. That would be as much of a prison as being trapped in the wrong body. Treatment has rendered my body as congruent as possible with my gender identity—my sense of myself as male.

There were changes, however. One of the most immediate was to be rid of my premenstrual depression. My change of roles en-abled me to behave in a way which came naturally and no longer did I feel as if I were acting a role. As a consequence I became less self-conscious, more relaxed, sociable and, so I am told, a more pleasant person. Psychologically, I did not 'become a man'. I became myself.

BECOMING A MAN—LEGALLY

The problems which would beset me as a result of the United Kingdom law were not uppermost in my mind when I initially changed roles. I knew that I could not change my name and sex on my birth certificate, the document being considered a record of fact at the time of registration. I knew, too, that the birth certificate was not technically an identity document, even though it might be used as such. What I did not bargain for, however, was how I would feel on the occasions when it was necessary for me to produce it. I deeply resented having to disclose my medical condition to people to whom it was not directly relevant and who may or may not have been sympathetic. I felt my privacy was being invaded.

I gradually realised that the legal situation had more far-reaching implications than I had originally thought. It was not just the birth certificate but the non-recognition of one's current status which placed considerable burdens upon the transsexual.

At that time, although a change of name was permitted on the passport, no gender prefix was allowed, a concession later granted. Whenever sex was legally relevant I was designated as a female and would be to the grave, since that is what should be recorded on my death certificate. I was barred from marriage with a woman, although not with a man!

I felt that my inability to marry a woman meant that it was unlikely that I would be able to adopt a child. Were a partner to have a child by artificial insemination I could not be recorded as its legal father. It was clear that not only transsexuals, but those closely associated with them were also adversely affected by the legal situation.

After years of solitary campaigning I took my case to the European Commission of Human Rights, spurred on not just by the bar to marriage but also because possible career prospects had been ruined. At that time, in 1979, I was just completing a degree course in religious studies and English literature at an Anglican College of Higher Education and was intending to be ordained as a priest. The Church deemed otherwise because I was legally a woman.

We sought to have my . . . identity as a man recognised for all legal purposes. . . . We alleged that by its non-activity the United Kingdom government was in breach of Articles 8 (right to private life) and 12 (right to marriage) of the European Convention of Human Rights. The European Commission of Human Rights declared my application admissable and, following the refusal of the United Kingdom government to reach a friendly settlement, presented the case before the Court. Judgment was handed down on 17 October 1986. By twelve votes to three the Court ruled that there had been no violation of Article 8 and was unanimous in holding that Article 12 had not been violated. . . . I was angry and shocked.

Now with support from many members of the public and the media, I battled on, but to little avail. A motion from the Committee on Petitions of the European Parliament calling, *inter alia*, for 'legal recognition; change of first name; change of sex on birth certificates and identity documents', was adopted by the European Parliament on 12 September 1989. The United Kingdom government has ignored it. The matter is under review! More recently, I founded the pressure group Press for Change . . . which is seeking full legal recognition for United Kingdom transsexuals in their reassigned sex.[1]

At the time of writing progress towards reform seems slow. We need also to educate in order to gain support. With an increasing amount of backing from Members of Parliament, leading lawyers, medical experts, church people and the public at large, we are confident that change will come. For the present, our struggle will continue. One day I shall legally become a man.

CONCLUSIONS

'Becoming a man', physically, was apparently the most major and drastic part of my transition experience, but it was the process which brought peace of mind because at last society saw the outward manifestation of what I was within. After years of conflict between what I was inside and what I appeared outside, medical science had brought them into harmony. I was enabled to be true to myself. The discomfort of surgery and the risks associated with hormone replacement therapy were but a small price to pay for the reconciliation of my physical and psychological selves.

I feel I have always been a heterosexual male, psychologically. I did not 'become' one. The 'becoming' was the freedom to form relationships with non-lesbian, heterosexual women. Sadly, my experience in this area has been very limited, but enough to realise that women see me as a man in spite of my lack of male genitalia. My anxiety over this matter is not shared by women of my acquaintance. It is a far greater obstacle to me than to the women, especially now that my contemporaries are women who have finished child-rearing.

'Becoming a man', administratively, was tedious but not insurmountable, except for the wretched government's stance on legal recognition. Social acceptance was perhaps the easiest 'becoming' to achieve. That began immediately I changed roles, if not earlier. Paradoxically, this almost effortless 'becoming' was also the most important. By the same token, the 'becoming' which I have not yet attained and which would affect my daily life very little—legal recognition—is the one which has demanded the greatest effort, so far with apparently fruitless results.

For me, it is most important to become male socially. Without acceptance in my male

1. The position of transsexual rights world-wide is outlined in McMullan and Whittle (1994: 104–17).

role, life would be intolerable. Full legal recognition and miraculous surgery to construct almost perfect male genitalia would, without this acceptance, be worse than useless. People see a male or female person. They do not usually demand presentation of a legal document or medical examination of one's genitalia before deciding that someone is a man or woman.

Of course there are practical and psychological problems caused by my physical and legal situation, but they occupy a relatively minute part of everyday life. I have been indisputably accepted as a man socially. The world now sees me as I see myself. In its eyes I have become a man; in my own eyes I have become myself.

CRITICAL THINKING QUESTIONS

1. Explain why an individual would choose to change his or her sex.

2. How might equality of opportunity increase or decrease for an individual who changes sex? Explain.

3. What is society's reaction to transsexuals? Why do people react in this way?

Getting Involved

1. Identify a student organization on your campus whose mission it is to support a particular minority group. Talk to the leaders of that group, attend a meeting or group function, and ask members how the organization helps them.

2. Research the personnel policies of your university or a local business as it pertains to issues of diversity. Specifically, how does the policy affect individuals on the basis of race, ethnicity, sex, gender (including transsexuals), and sexuality.

3. Interview someone who is different from you in two or more of the following social statuses: race, sex, social class, sexuality. Ask that person to explain how he or she arrived at today's position and how the statuses that are different from yours have impacted his or her life. Write an essay comparing how the social statuses of each of you have helped or hindered your ability to achieve what you want in life.

Site-Seeing

1. For more information on the practice of racial profiling, visit the American Civil Liberties Union web site at **http://www.aclu.org/profiling/**.

2. For information on the demise of well-paid factory jobs and the growth of poorly-paid service sector jobs, visit **http://www.tradewatch.org/nafta/naftapg.html**.

3. To learn more about National Coming Out Day, visit **http://www.youth resource.com**.

4. For more information about transsexualism, visit **http://www.pridenet.com/ trans.html**.

Chapter 2

Linking the Past with the Present

To understand inequality today, we need to examine the historical roots of contemporary arrangements. History is more than the story of how things were at one time. Indeed, as historians have long recognized, anyone who ignores history is destined to repeat its mistakes. Why? Because contemporary social arrangements are largely dependent upon the way societies were organized in the past, as well as on historical events that have perpetuated or altered social patterns. If we hope to avoid repeating past mistakes, any understanding of society and social inequality today must include an examination of the historical roots of oppression and emancipation.

Looking at history can help us understand the way things were, how they developed to their current state, and how the social world operates today. Historical patterns and arrangements influence the way individuals and social groups perceive themselves and others, just as they affect people's expectations about how others will view and interact with them. These ideas about what groups of people are like often come from deep-seated values and long-standing patterns of behavior that continue to influence society today. History, then, is an important factor that helps us shape a sense of personal and group identity, as well as our expectations of how society should be organized. Specifically, when history defines a particular group as weaker, less intelligent, or less valued, those beliefs carry over and influence contemporary ideologies, even when such ideas are repeatedly challenged by social movements and individual resistance. Thus, for example, even today African-Americans must overcome stereotypes that they are more dangerous than whites, poor people must prove that they are not lazy, women must strive to prove their intelligence, and gay men, lesbians, and transsexuals are challenged by long-standing assumptions of mental illness. Many people today would argue that these are mistaken assumptions, but others continue to believe these myths.

In the first article in this chapter, Davis reviews the history of African-American professionals' struggles to get jobs, initially by encouraging individual companies to hire one black employee and later through legislation. Although African-Americans have made important strides in gaining economic and workplace equality, Davis points out that there continues to be significant resistance to the full and equal inclusion of African-Americans in all aspects of society. This article touches upon the ongoing interaction between groups seeking social change and those seeking to preserve these long-standing arrangements.

The ways that historical values and practices continue to influence contemporary values and practices are at the center of the Anderson, Dyson, and Brooks article. Through their examination of the "new" correctional sanction of chain gangs, the authors demonstrate how historical practices can be reinvigorated, often packaged as a new idea. The authors argue that chain gangs revert to old southern institutionalized forms of racism. Moreover, they emphasize the negative consequences that the contemporary use of chain gangs can have on race relations. This article demonstrates that even when society breaks from its old racist practices, it is easy to revert to such arrangements if the values and beliefs upon which they were based are not altered.

Just as the United States has demonstrated a long history of racism, its historical and contemporary culture is imbued with a distrust of immigrants and ethnic differences. Even among women, who might be expected to be unified on the basis of gender, historical differences on the basis of ethnicity and social class have been evident. At the beginning of the twentieth century, during a massive wave of immigration, upper middle-class women played a major role in efforts to "Americanize" these newcomers. In the third article in this chapter, McClymer argues that the Americanization of women was meant to teach them to be good homemakers and mothers in the "American" tradition and to train them away from participation in civic life. Ironically, those who trained immigrant women in this so-called American way engaged in careers and public lives themselves.

Although immigrants were subjected to efforts to strip them of their cultural heritage, perhaps the most egregious of these efforts were aimed at Native Americans. In the fourth article, Almeida discusses the history of European American efforts to educate Native American children by sending them to boarding schools. In this way, children were separated from their families and tribes and from their traditional systems of education and socialization. The effect was to strip nearly half of all Native Americans of their cultural heritage, which has led to a number of social problems among this population. Ultimately, however, Almeida documents the role of women in preserving the history and culture, resisting European American domination, and reestablishing a system of education that respects and teaches Native American culture.

As evidenced by Americans' assumption that certain immigrants and all Native Americans needed to be Americanized, U.S. citizens at the turn of the twentieth century were fearful of difference, whether based on ethnicity, social class, or other statuses. In the fifth article in this chapter, Turner discusses legislation enacted by Congress in 1917 that denied immigration for a number of medical conditions, including homosexuality. This standard held legally until the passage of the 1990 Immigration Act, even though homosexuality was declassified as a mental illness in 1973. Despite these changes, however, U.S. society continues to exhibit a strong distrust of sexual minorities. Although gay men, lesbians, and other sexual minorities are now free to immigrate to the United States, they continue to face discrimination in many social institutions, not least of which is the government itself. For example, in the last article, Lewis discusses the post–World War II history of U.S. government policy toward federal gay and lesbian employees. The central point of the article is that although the government has prohibited discrimination against gays and lesbians, legal protections remain weak and gay men, lesbians, and other sexual minorities continue to face prejudice and discrimination. Here, again, the point is raised that without changes in values and beliefs, social institutions, as well as individual behaviors, are unlikely to change significantly, even when the government takes an official stance against discrimination.

As these articles show, the United States has a long history of official and unofficial prejudice and discrimination against people considered different. In the wake of minority group struggles to achieve social equality, significant progress has been made. Nonetheless, remnants of past inequalities continue to exist, with some bygone practices being recycled. In this way, inequality is perpetuated, even as it continues to be challenged. Change occurs, but it takes place slowly and in small steps, in large part because many people continue to believe that the old ways are the best.

Reading 1

The Struggle for Equal Employment Opportunity in Corporate America

George Davis

In this article, Davis looks at the historical and present barriers to equal employment experienced by African-Americans, as well as some of the strategies they have used to increase their opportunities.

Before the days of Affirmative Action, African Americans were a rare sight among corporate workers. Once Upon a Time When We Were "Negroes"

It was different back in the 1940s and early '50s when some of the grandparents of the present generation came into Corporate America. Only a few of them came. Everything was segregated.

The reputation of most big White businesses was known in the Black community. If a particular company was willing to hire a Negro (as we called ourselves back then), the word would spread. If another company did not make it a practice of hiring Negroes, then none would apply.

Employment agencies also knew which companies to avoid in sending Negro applicants. In

places like New York, employment agencies like Richard Clark Associates made a successful business out of directing Negro applicants toward the few open doors in American industry.

Some companies advertised in Negro magazines. All during this time, prominent Negroes were pressuring "good White people" to pressure business executives to hire a Negro. A few companies hired Negroes in clerical positions in records keeping and personnel, out of the main line of the company's business.

Because of shortages of technically trained workers, the color line in many large companies was first broken by Negro scientists and engineers back in the 1940s and early '50s.

Back then there were laws in several states that outlawed discrimination in employment. Organizations like the Urban League and the National Association for the Advancement of Colored People sent qualified Negroes into a variety of businesses as "test cases."

When they got turned down for employment, the organization could threaten or ac-

Source: Reprinted from *Black Collegian* 26, no. 3 (April 1996): 47–50 with permission from the author. George Davis is author of *Black Life in Corporate America.*

tually institute lawsuits. But battles had to be fought case-by-case, so the going was somewhat like trench warfare.

As far back as 1941, federal contracts had standard clauses in them banning any type of discrimination because of race, religion, or national origin. But for the most part, little pressure was brought to bear on contractors to comply with these clauses.

Various organizations worked with willing businesses by running placement services to help find qualified Negroes. There were many other volunteer organizations in every city in the nation that focused on bringing Negroes into major companies and bringing these companies into compliance with the law.

One of the most effective, The American Friends Service Committee, launched its Job Opportunities Program (JOP) in Philadelphia in 1945 and expanded its activities into more than a dozen cities during the 1950s.

JOP methods ranged from moral persuasion to economic pressure. For example, an article in the *Indianapolis Recorder,* a Negro weekly, reported that "all of the large downtown department stores except one have embraced the JOP Program and employed some Negroes above the usual menial categories. If Negroes would give their patronage to these stores, this might cause the holdout to see the error of its ways."

During this time, all attempts by the federal government to set up a Federal Fair Employment Practices Commission were repeatedly blocked in Congress until, in 1953, President Eisenhower went around Congress and set up the Committee on Government Contracts (CGC) headed by Vice President Nixon.

The CGC did not have enforcement authority, but it did become a clearinghouse for complaints. These complaints were forwarded to the NAACP, which was mounting very intense legal battles in local and federal courts and making passionate legal and moral arguments before various commissions.

Complaints were also forwarded to contracting agencies. Some put pressure on contractors; some didn't. In 1961, the Kennedy Administration set up the President's Committee on Equal Employment Opportunities

under Vice President Lyndon Johnson and gave it more power than the Eisenhower Committee to crack down on those who discriminated against Negroes.

In one of the directives, government contractors were told that they must take "affirmative action to ensure" that there is no discrimination in connection with work under federal contract. This was not the first time that the term Affirmative Action was used. It was used without much effect by the Eisenhower Committee back in the 1950s.

But somehow these weren't the "bad old days." They were days of joy and challenge, on the one hand, and hope and eagerness, on the other. The joy and challenge came to those who, as tokens, broke into the mainstream. It was like being "chosen," culled from among the others and honored with a job "downtown," as the White business sections of American cities were called. This was before corporations started to move out to the corporate parks in the suburbs.

Hope and eagerness arose in those who had the skill and inclination to make the leap into the mainstream, but who had not yet been chosen. In the "Speaking of People" columns in *Ebony* magazine, each month the hopeful would see the pictures of the chosen. The columns would feature six of the hundreds of "breakthroughs" being made at that time. Most of those pictured had found jobs in city, state, or federal agencies, but of the six there was usually one who had broken into Corporate America.

In these columns and in a feature article in *Ebony* in 1961, the hopeful read, "Campbell Soups Corporation has hired a Negro; Burke Pierce, a Cornell graduate and incidentally son-in-law of Ralph Bunche, has been hired by General Foods Corporation. RCA has hired one in personnel, and so has the Metropolitan Life Insurance Co., as an assistant to the personnel director."

To the educated middle class, this was like hearing that Jackie Robinson had achieved another home run or had stolen three bases in a single game, or that Sugar Ray Robinson had scored another knockout.

The *Ebony* article continued: "Levi Jackson, former Yale football captain, is with Ford Motor Co., and Macy's in New York has Fred Wilkerson. This accumulation," *Ebony* concluded, "is a mere spit in the ocean compared to employment potential."

Because of the terrain and the objectives, the battle in Corporate America was nowhere near as intense as it was in schools, colleges, hotels, swimming pools, hospitals, or even some labor unions. In the early 1960s more than 200 companies, including General Electric, Honeywell, and Xerox, had joined a voluntary association pledged to work actively to hire more Negroes. A survey by P.F.P. revealed that only about 12 in every 1000 white-collar workers in a 1000-company survey were Negroes, and most were confined to low-level clerical positions.

"Until now business has been left pretty much alone, and for the most part management has followed a do-nothing policy," said the *Harvard Business Review* of March 1963. The magazine warned, however, that "forces are gathering which may well develop into active conflict."

Examples of these forces were the picket lines in front of General Motors facilities in 23 cities in 1964, and the picket lines in front of Bank of America branches later that year.

Despite the battles, there was still a mood of optimism in the Negro community, so much so that in March 1964 *Ebony* published an editorial entitled "It's Great to Be a Negro." The article declared: "Opportunity for young trained Negroes is not just knocking, it's pounding on the door . . . White businesses are seeking more Negro white collar workers than ever before."

The optimism was echoed in an article in *Time* of June 1964, which quoted a college placement director as saying, "If a white and a Negro graduate were competing for the same job and were equal in every respect save skin color, the job would go to the Negro."

This is one of the areas that perhaps fuels the argument that anti-discrimination measures amounted to "preferential treatment," and "reverse discrimination." There was never a time when it was not generally an advantage to be a White male, but there were specific instances when this advantage was nullified by extraordinary steps taken to advance racial fairness.

The *Time* article continued: "Some defense contractors feel it is good business to display Negroes conspicuously at drafting tables and in labs. Consumer-oriented companies are inclined to woo Negro trainees to avoid the unpleasantness of picket lines and sit-ins."

AFFIRMATIVE ACTION, NEGATIVE BACKLASH

The big victory resulting from all of the optimism and agitation was the passage of the 1964 Civil Rights Bill. It was also this bill that started the avalanche of complaints by employers that the government had put on too much pressure.

The federal government did not back off, because the numbers confirmed that Blacks (as we came to be called during this period) were not being hired fast enough. In 1966, under Executive Order 11246, the Department of Labor began keeping personnel records by race and using them to evaluate hiring practices.

Out of this action grew the request for targets and timetables, which the popular press began classifying as "quotas." In 1968 the Office of Federal Contract Compliance went even further by declaring that employers must submit a written Affirmative Action Plan with "an evaluation of opportunities for the utilization of minority group personnel."

Enemies of Affirmative Action began calling this an attempt by the government to tell companies whom they can and cannot hire. Political conservatives warned that seeking a group approach to equality of opportunity would hurt psychologically, even if not materially, thousands of White males. Liberals argued that conservatives created the kind of resistances and dodges that made group solutions necessary.

Resentment grew, but corporations were expanding rapidly, so they created add-on positions to meet the requirement to hire more women and minorities. The battle raged, but liberals seemed to be winning it.

Corporate employment opportunities opened up remarkably for the Black middle class during the late 1960s and early 1970s. In 1973 the Department of Labor won a monumental suit against AT&T, the nation's largest employer, for back wages for 13,000 women and 2,000 minority men.

Other large court victories followed. However, a turning point came in 1978 with the famous *Bakke* Case in which a White male successfully sued the University of California, charging that by reserving 16 slots in the freshman class of its medical school for minorities, the University was denying access to competition for these slots to White people like himself.

In *Meanness Mania,* his 1976 book, Gerald Gill described what he called "a mania increasingly adamant against governmental and societal efforts to help Blacks, other minorities and the poor." Gill continued, "It is not too much to suggest that behind this mania is a growing feeling of meanness. While 'meanness' is a strong categorization, it is an apt one to explain the current mood of selfishness, stinginess and malice among much of the American populace."

Meanwhile, corporations themselves had joined the battle against what was being called "reverse discrimination," or "minority preferences." In 1972 the Business Roundtable was formed as a probusiness organization composed of the CEOs of major American companies. In 1972 there were 89 Political Action Committees (PACs) spending $8 million on political campaigns. By 1980 there were 1251 PACs spending $39 million. Many of the PACs were financed by big business. Ronald Reagan came to the Presidency on the promise that he was going to get the government off the backs of the middle class.

One of the things that this meant was that he was intent on crippling governmental efforts to enforce Equal Opportunity laws. With the help of men like Edwin Meese and William Bedford Reynolds at the Justice Department and Clarence Thomas at the Equal Employment Opportunities Commission, he was able to do just that. Enforcement was slowed.

However, middle class workers still took a drubbing as governmental policies began to favor the rich to the extent that even conservative writer Kevin Phillips wrote in *The Politics of Rich and Poor* that the 1980s witnessed the biggest transfer in history of money from the hands of the middle class into the hands of the very wealthy.

After having benefitted from the atmosphere created by Affirmative Action, Clarence Thomas, as head of the EEOC, said he was "unalterably opposed to programs that forced or even cajoled people to hire a certain percentage of minorities."

In 1981 and 1983 the budgets for the EEOC and Office of Federal Contract Compliance were slashed. In 1988 in *Watson v. Fort Worth Bank and Trust,* federal courts held that the "ultimate burden of proving that discrimination against a protected group has been caused by a specific employment practice rest" with the person bringing the suit, at all times.

Democrats, still in power in Congress, passed another Civil Rights Bill. President Bush vetoed it, saying that it "employs a maze of highly legalistic language to introduce the destructive force of quotas into our nation's employment system."

But due largely to the political backlash from the Anita Hill–Clarence Thomas hearings when Thomas was being elevated to the Supreme Court, Bush signed a Civil Rights Bill in 1991 in which the burden of proof shifts back to the employer.

Setting the tone for more inclusion of minorities and women into all aspects of national life, President Clinton's initial cabinet was composed of three women, four African Americans, and two Hispanics. But in 1994 the anti-Affirmative Action forces energized the American electorate and ended Democratic rule in the Congress for the first time in 40 years. The House under Speaker Newt Gingrich and the

Senate under Majority Leader Robert Dole have declared war on Affirmative Action. By 5–4 votes the Supreme Court has in recent decisions also expressed its opposition to much of the spirit of Affirmative Action.

CRITICAL THINKING QUESTIONS

1. How has government policy encouraged the inclusion of African-Americans in corporate jobs? What are the advantages and disadvantages of these policies for both African-Americans and corporations?

2. What are the arguments made by those who oppose affirmative action? Do you agree or disagree with them? Why?

3. Propose an alternative policy to ensure equality of opportunity in corporate jobs. Who is likely to support your proposal? Why? Who is likely to oppose your proposal? Why?

Reading 2

Alabama Prison Chain Gangs: Reverting to Archaic Punishment to Reduce Crime and Discipline Offenders

James F. Anderson, Laronistine Dyson, and Willie Brooks, Jr.

> *In this reading, the authors argue that the historical and contemporary use of prison chain gangs is a racist criminal justice practice.*

INTRODUCTION

In the 1940s, chain gangs were outlawed as an appropriate correctional practice. Chain gangs became unpopular and started to decline because prisoners who were sentenced to them suffered disturbing abuses by those who operated prison systems, and from others who provided direct supervision over inmates assigned to work details. However, because of its increasing crime problem, Alabama has resurged chain gangs as a viable correctional policy (Donziger, 1996). Alabama prison officials argue that the purposes of chain gangs are fourfold: (1) To re-

duce the number of crimes committed; (2) to reduce repeat offenders; (3) to address disciplinary problems; and (4) to shame offenders into a life of conformity (*The Mobile Press Register,* 1996, 4B).

Chain gangs are work details that permit prison inmates to leave a traditional prison setting for a specified period of time to be shackled with other inmates in leg irons to perform manual labor. The work details in which participants engage include: Removing trash from interstate roads; cleaning parks; painting shelters and benches; and repairing roads and fences (Donziger, 1996; *The Mobile Press Register,* 1996, 4B).

Chain gangs have ignited controversy in Alabama and have captured national attention. For example, though some residents of

Source: Western Journal of Black Studies Vol. 24, No. 1, Washington State University.

Alabama concede that chain gangs are punitive, they still favor using them as "a necessary evil." They contend that humiliation and hard work should deter criminals and potential law violators from engaging in crime. Yet, others oppose chain gangs and argue that this form of punishment conjures up memories of slavery and extreme brutality that blacks endured in the antebellum south. Moreover, the Alabama Department of Corrections (ADC) and other southern states have poor histories of affording fairness to black inmates. Therefore, implementing this type of punishment to an inmate population that is disproportionately African-American spotlights the brutality that has historically been given to blacks in southern states. Furthermore, the national audience has voiced its opposition to chain gangs by labeling them as discriminatory, repressive, brutal, unconstitutional, and shameful. However, despite the mixed feelings surrounding chain gangs lodged by Alabamians and national commentators, chain gangs are still used in Alabama and neighboring states. Despite criticisms, some officials of ADC contend that chain gangs will remain a part of the Alabama correctional arsenal (*The Mobile Press Register*, 1996, 4B).

This paper is divided into four parts. Part one addresses the historical use of chain gangs. Part two describes Alabama chain gangs. Part three discusses the unsafe aspects of chain gangs and the legal liabilities that could ensue from their use. Part four focuses on whether Alabama chain gangs are aimed at rehabilitating or punishing offenders. In the final analysis, we contend that chain gangs are a form of cruel and unusual punishment designed to dehumanize offenders.

PART I: THE HISTORICAL USE OF CHAIN GANGS IN THE UNITED STATES

In 1878, as an attempt to reform the penal system, William Penn created the Philadelphia Society for Alleviating the Miseries of Public Prisons to reduce the high levels of corporal and capital punishment to which prisoners were subjected (McKelvey, 1972; Sellin, 1967; Duffee, 1989). With this new penal code, insufferable conditions such as floggings, mutilations, and executions of inmates were replaced by imprisonment with hard labor (McKelvey, 1972; Sellin, 1967). One immediate result of this reformative effort was that inmates were quickly placed on chain gangs to work on city streets. The inmates assigned to work details were made to wear highly visible uniforms and engage in hard labor while chained to other inmates.

Historical commentators note that during the 18th century to the mid–19th century, it was commonly assumed that subjecting inmates to hard work was necessary to assist them in atoning for their misdeeds (Duffee, 1989). During this period, however, states recognized the economic potential of having a vast number of prisoners and began exploiting inmates as a viable labor pool (Duffee, 1989; Walker, 1988). The use of inmate labor would ultimately develop into a lease system (Walker, 1988). Under the lease system, many states benefitted from this penal practice because corporations and profiteers leased inmates for a cheap rate. This provided contractors the opportunity to maximize profits by investing in cheap labor since they paid states a flat fee and avoided hiring free citizens to work countless hours (Walker, 1988). Under this system, contractors promised to be responsible for the care of inmates; however, this rarely occurred. Walker (1988) argues that for many contractors, being responsible for inmates had little to do with providing the inmates' physical and psychological needs. Instead, contractors focused on providing supervision and control so that inmates would work hard enough to turn a profit and not escape. For example, Walker (1988:126) explains:

Despite the provisions in the 1883 rules and regulations that sought to provide better care for prisoners in the outside camps, life outside the prisons remained almost unendurable. Sergeants and guards in the camps, although employed and paid by the state, succumbed frequently to the economic blandishment of contractors who promised generous pay incentives to the state personnel in return for increased production. Generally, great production could be accomplished only by working prisoners beyond reasonable limits.

Walker (1988) indicates that a substantial number of inmates either died as a result of brutal working conditions or were killed by guards who watched over them. Before the lease system was abolished in 1934, nearly every state had some type of lease system in place. Despite the Congressional Act of 1934 that prohibited leasing inmates, chaining inmates together was not completely abandoned. For example, while the Act prohibited inmates from being leased to private individuals and corporations, it did not apply to state and local government. As a result, chained inmates and prison labor flourished for both security and economic reasons. Because of the Congressional Act of 1934, inmate labor could no longer be exploited by private individuals for personal consumption, but rather, inmates were now used for road construction and repair, and for providing farm labor. The government contended that inmates should be responsible for sustaining the institutions that confined them. As a result, many of the resources generated from prison labor were used to purchase inmates' food, clothing, shelter, and to operate the correctional facility (Walker, 1988). Consequently, the government, rather than corporations, was now the new recipient of inmate labor. Despite this shift, abuses were prevalent and the conditions of confinement for inmates in road camps were still shocking to the human conscience (Walker, 1988).

During post World War II, chain gangs had been nearly abolished in the northern states. However, many southern states held to this correctional practice. Robin (1987) reports that many states felt compelled to abolish chain gangs because they were tied to slavery. Some commentators (see Walker, 1988) contend that those states which continued to employ chain gangs used them as a cost control tool. For example, by using chain gangs, prisons could work more inmates with fewer guards to watch them. Moreover, along with an increase in inmates came an increase in profits made from inmate labor. For southerners, chain gangs reduced the amount of money needed to manage an inmate population. It also allowed them the occasion to control their black populations with the threat of and/or use of corporal punishment since the majority of the inmates in southern states were African-Americans. According to Sellin (1967), the contract, or lease system, flourished in southern states after slavery (Civil War) and was used as a way to punish former slaves and their descendants.

In the 1960s, chain gangs still existed in some southern states. However, because the levels of brutality were so intense, it was inevitable that they would soon be abolished. For instance, in 1964, an investigation into an Arkansas work farm (the Tucker farm) showed signs of corruption, brutality, and mistreatment of chain gang offenders that ultimately led to the crumbling of this correctional practice in Arkansas. Moreover, in 1967, Georgia used labor camps as part of its correctional practice until it was revealed that the camps were operating in horrific fashions. Commentators report that young male offenders, chained together, were given the daily task of breaking rocks. The working conditions became so insufferable that the inmates began breaking their own legs to prevent from having to work. This incident captured national attention and ultimately contributed to the abolition of Georgia's work camps (Robin, 1987).

The 1990s bear witness to increases in the prison population and a decline in the number of economic resources allocated to prison facilities. At the same time, public outcry to take a strong stance against crime has never been greater (Eskridge, 1996). Therefore, faced with exuberant levels of crime, increased prison populations, and a demanding constituency, many legislators have begun advocating crime control and harsh punishment to better control inmates and potential law violators. As a result, in 1995, states such as Alabama, Arizona, and Florida reinstituted archaic forms of punishment (chain gangs and hitching posts) to deter criminal offenders. Alabama, however, was the first state to return to this old-fashioned method of punishment.

PART II: ALABAMA CHAIN GANGS

Chain gangs are not a recent phenomenon in Alabama, but rather, they date back to the mid-nineteenth century. They came into being shortly after the abolition of slavery. For this reason, some critics charge that they were created to control blacks (see Sellin, 1967). As early as 1866, Alabama operated chain gangs. Archival data from Alabama indicate that, at their inception, chain gangs were created to prevent prisoners from escaping a sentence to hard labor (see The Penal Code of Alabama 1866). The courts intended prisoners to remain sentenced to labor camps until their sentence was completely served. The courts created elaborate plans drawing the conditions of which contractors could hire and work prisoners. It also required that money earned from inmate services be used to benefit the helpless who resided in poor houses or houses of corrections, but not the inmate laborers themselves. According to The Alabama Penal Code of 1866, persons sentenced to hard labor could be confined, chained, or shackled if a sentence was imposed by the court or county commissioners. The Code made it legal to shackle offenders if: (1) They were given a sentence of two or more months for having committed a crime; (2) prisoners either ran away or tried to escape; or (3) offenders failed or refused to work.

Alabama chain gangs in the 1990s, like their predecessors, are relegated to inmates laboring on public roads, public bridges, and other public works. Similarly, chain gangs today, like those in the past, are being used in Alabama as an attempt to reduce prison overcrowding. This is the best justification given by ADC for resurging this archaic form of punishment. Recent crime statistics from the Alabama Criminal Justice Information Center (1996) support this contention. Alabama crime estimates demonstrate that violent crime increased from 1990 to 1994. Therefore, the contention of using chain gangs to reduce the level of crime appears to be legitimate. However, the Southern Poverty Law Center has filed a class action suit (*Michael Austin et al. v. Fob James Jr., Governor of Alabama and Ron Jones, Commissioner of ADC,* Case No. 95-T-637-N) challenging the constitutionality of chain gangs calling them dehumanizing, cruel and unusual, and reminiscent of slavery because of its practices and its almost entirely African-American work crews.

Currently, there are 700 inmates who participate in the Alabama chain gangs. These offenders are easily identified by their white uniforms with the label "chain gang" affixed to them. Chain gangs are located at Limestone, Staton, Easterling, Fountain, and Draper Correctional Facilities. The facilities that hold these offenders are often former warehouses that are too small to accommodate the number of prisoners placed in them. For example, the Limestone Correctional Facility was designed to hold 315 inmates, yet it houses more than 400 prisoners. Inmates at Limestone sleep in double or triple bunk beds (see *Michael Austin et al. v. Fob James Jr., Governor of Alabama and Ron Jones, Commissioner of ADC,* Case No. 95-T-637-N).

A sentence to chain gangs is given at the discretion of Alabama judges. However, offenders are typically given the sentence to chain gangs if they violate conditions of parole or fail to adhere to prison rules. Inmates who receive this sentence must serve a minimum of six months. Therefore, repeat chain gang offenders could spend a year or more on these work crews. Those who are sentenced to chain gangs for disciplinary reasons spend between fifteen and forty-five days. Alabama requires that inmates not have any visitation privileges while serving this sentence. Moreover, while on chain gangs, inmates are chained together with leg irons in groups of four or five. They work as many as ten hours each day equipped with blades, sledgehammers, axes, and other tools to engage in highway maintenance, splitting rocks, building demolitions, and farm work. Despite their many work details, they are disproportionately assigned to work along city interstates. Observers warn that these work details are potentially dangerous.

PART III: UNSAFE ASPECTS AND THE LEGAL LIABILITIES OF CHAIN GANGS

Critics of the Alabama chain gangs contend that they are unsafe and could have the unintended effect of causing death and injury to prisoners. For example, a substantial number of arguments and fights have occurred among shackled inmates that have resulted in them using rocks, tools, and even leg irons as weapons against each other (*The Mobile Press Register,* 1996 4B). The Southern Poverty Law Center has responded to these incidences by filing suit citing violations of prisoners' First, Eighth, and Fourteenth Amendment rights. The Center claims that the use of chain gangs creates a substantial and constant risk of violence among chain gang members and poses a serious and constant threat to their health and safety (*The Mobile Press Register,* 1996 4B). More specifically, the suit alleges that chain gangs deprive prisoners of their associational rights, innate human dignity, and subject them to brutal working conditions. Therefore, they constitute cruel and unusual punishment (see *Michael Austin et al. v. Fob James Jr., Governor of Alabama and Ron Jones, Commissioner of ADC,* Case No. 95-T-637-N).

The Southern Poverty Law Center contends that chain gangs subject inmates to inhumane conditions that could cause severe physical and psychological damage. For example, the Center contends that inmates working on chain gangs are dehumanized when they are forced to defecate in the presence of other chain gang prisoners and passersby travelling on the highways. Furthermore, if prisoners refuse, they are handcuffed to hitching posts until they comply

with orders. As a punishment, when inmates can no longer work because of exhaustion or physical illness, they are handcuffed and made to stand at hitching posts for hours without food and water. Moreover, while assigned to clean roads, prisoners are constantly mocked and are subjected to racial epithets from passersby. There has even been one instance when a passerby shot above the heads of a work crew. Further, prisoners suffer physical pain since they must wear leg irons. They often complain that leg irons are too tight causing their ankles to swell. Inmates report that this form of punishment subjects them to sun strokes, poison ivy, and chigger bites (see *Michael Austin et al. v. Fob James Jr., Governor of Alabama and Ron Jones, Commissioner of ADC,* Case No. 95-T-637-N).

The Center has also reported that a number of traffic accidents and deaths have occurred in Alabama chain gangs. Those involved in these tragedies were motorists traveling the highways, inmates, and correctional guards. For example, the presence of inmates on the side of roads presents a health risk because chain gangs distract motorists. Motorists are sometimes diverted from what they are doing to focus on chain gang activities. For example, in November 1995, a motorist lost control of his vehicle and injured many chain gang participants. Critics argued that if the inmates were not wearing leg irons, perhaps they could have run from the swerving car (see *Michael Austin et al. v. Fob James Jr., Governor of Alabama and Ron Jones, Commissioner of ADC,* Case No. 95-T-637-N).

Violence occurs regularly on chain gang work details. When prison inmates are placed together to work ten hours each day, they are placed in great jeopardy. Sometimes inmates are frustrated by unending hard work and the reality of being chained with other inmates for long periods of time. They sometimes become agitated by trivial matters and lash out at those in close proximity. Critics ask why would prison officials arm inmates who have criminal histories of engaging in violent crime with potential weapons? They (inmates) are a disaster waiting to happen. Chain gang prisoners are armed with axes, shovels, blades, sledge-hammers, and rocks. Because they are chained together, the potential for deadly violence is sometimes unavoidable especially for innocent members who are not involved in disputes. The leg irons do not allow escape, and since there is only one guard for every forty inmates, the chance of protection is almost non-existent (see *Michael Austin et al. v. Fob James Jr., Governor of Alabama and Ron Jones, Commissioner of ADC,* Case No. 95-T-637-N). Ironically, when a guard intervenes, he points his weapon at the entire chained group.

A tragedy that occurred on May 15, 1996 highlights this point. *The Mobile Press Register,* (1996, 4B) reported that an inmate was shot and killed by a corrections guard on Interstate 65 south of Montgomery after ignoring a warning to stop fighting another inmate. The prison spokesperson stated that the inmate was shot because he continued to attack another inmate with an ax when he was warned to stop fighting. Officials of ADC have downplayed the shooting. However, those at the Southern Poverty Law Center contend that since the ADC continues to subject offenders to constant risk of serious body and psychological damage, via chain gangs, hitching posts, and the indignity of forcing prisoners to defecate in public, they have shown deliberate indifference to the welfare of offenders in their custody. Therefore, this constitutes cruel and unusual punishment protected by the Eighth and Fourteenth Amendments. The class action suit that is being filed by the Southern Poverty Law Center is seeking that ADC desist from subjecting prisoners to this barbaric practice (see *Michael Austin et al. v. Fob James Jr., Governor of Alabama and Ron Jones, Commissioner of ADC,* Case No. 95-T-637-N). While the current lawsuit does not seek compensation for offenders injured from this archaic practice, the potential exists for such litigation to occur in the future. For example, damages could be sought in federal and state courts claiming civil rights violations under Section 1983 or a wrongful death action (see Collins, 1990). O'Leary (1989) contends that the likelihood for such litigation exists be-cause after inmates are taken into custody and can no longer provide for themselves, custodians must provide inmates' health and safety needs.

PART IV: CHAIN GANGS: PUNISHMENT OR REHABILITATION

Alabama chain gangs, without question, are designed to punish offenders for the crimes that they have committed. Moreover, officials of ADC have stated that they want to make the punishment for committing crime so punitive that it would have a specific and general deterrent effect on criminals and potential law violators (*The Mobile Press Register,* 1996, 4B). While this "get tough" approach to crime might appeal to some citizens who are fearful of increasing crime rates, this same approach could have the unintended effect of making the crime problem worse and costing Alabamians more to confine its prison populations. Chain gangs are very punitive and prisoners have stated that they wish they were not on them, but this does not mean they will not reoffend after release. While a sentence to a chain gang is more punitive than getting a traditional sentence, it comes at the expense of sacrificing rehabilitation and treatment programs. Such programs could help some offenders to become law abiding, thereby reducing already scarce resources needed to operate state correctional budgets.

Though rehabilitation is certainly not guaranteed to all offenders after treatment is given to them, a substantial number of offenders receiving treatment programs indicate they have a better chance of not reoffending after release (see Anderson and Dyson, 1996; Anderson, Dyson, and Carson, 1995). In contrast, chain gang prisoners work constantly. Prison officials fail to provide them any type of self-help programs. They sometimes work as long as ten hours a day until their assignment is completed and then they move to the next job until their sentence has been completely served.

After chain gangs, prisoners return to their former communities to face the same dismal future they faced before going to prison. They must now avoid the same criminogenic factors that they were unable to avoid before being sentenced to a chain gang. Without rehabilitation and treatment programs aimed at giving offenders a better prospect on life, one has to wonder if Alabama correctional officials realistically believe that these parolees can survive without reoffending in communities that are saturated with unemployment, despair, gangs, guns, random violence, drugs, teenage pregnancies, and social disorganization (see Anderson and Dyson, 1996). In essence, while Alabama chain gangs make good on the promise to shame and punish offenders, they could undermine their own efforts to reduce crime since chain gang offenders are not given the proper skills needed to better themselves after returning to their respective communities. Braithwaite (1992) argues that reintegrative shaming (that removes the stigma of crime and punishment and provides ceremonies that embrace the offender back into the community) could deter future criminal behavior. However, he cautions that shaming simply for the sake of punishment (without ceremonies recognizing the behavior as bad, but the offender as good) could have detrimental consequences that cause similarly labeled offenders to unite and engage in future crime.

Chain gangs punish; they do not attempt to rehabilitate or teach offenders marketable job skills. They do not prepare offenders for a competitive labor force, nor teach offenders how to diffuse their aggressive behavior. Instead, chain gang guards are there to watch and punish offenders and make them hate the chain gang experience in hopes that this alone will serve as a panacea or be so compelling that offenders will not want to recidivate. The irony of the Alabama chain gang experience is that correctional officials truly desire to reduce the crime problem, yet they do nothing to prevent the continuation of crime. Perhaps Alabama prison officials should invest in the future of its citizens instead of its prisons.

Unfortunately, if chain gangs fail to reduce crime and the number of repeat offenders increase, Alabama will have to spend more money to house the same offenders.

CONCLUSION

Since the resurgence of Alabama chain gangs in 1995, no one has examined the recidivism of chain gang prisoners. Though it usually takes three years to determine if correctional practices have had a deterrent effect on recidivism, the future looks grim for Alabama chain gang prisoners since they are not provided treatment and rehabilitation opportunities to better themselves after release. While many crime control policies advocate harsher punishment, the history of correctional practices indicate that programs devoid of rehabilitation and treatment efforts have failed to discourage future criminal behavior. Therefore, the authors reject chain gangs as a viable approach to reducing crime and recidivism, and contend they are cruel and unusual forms of punishment that could increase the Alabama prison population and litigation in the future.

REFERENCES

Alabama Criminal Justice Information Center (1996). *1994: Crime in Alabama.* Statistical Analysis Center.

ANDERSON, J. F., AND DYSON, L. (1996). Community strategies to neutralize gang proliferation. *Journal of Gang Research* 3(2)17–26.

ANDERSON, J. F., AND DYSON, L. (1996). A tracking investigation to determine boot camp success and offender risk assessment for CRIPP participants. *Journal of Crime and Justice* 19(1)179–190.

ANDERSON, J. F., DYSON, L., AND CARSON, G. (1995). Drug use history and shock incarceration outcome. *Journal of Contemporary Criminal Justice* 11(3)196–200.

BRAITHWAITE, J. (1992). *Crime, shame and reintegration.* Cambridge: Cambridge University Press.

COLLINS, W.C. (1990). *Correctional law for the correctional officer.* Washington, D.C.: St. Mary's Press.

DONZIGER, S.R. (1996). *The real war on crime: The report of the national criminal justice commission.* New York: Harper Perennial Publishers.

DUFFEE, D.E. (1989). *Corrections: Practice and policy.* New York: Random House.

ESKRIDGE, C.W. (1996). *Criminal justice: Concepts and issues.* Los Angeles: Roxbury Publishing Company.

MCKELVEY, B. (1972). *American prisons: A study of American social history prior to 1915.* Montclair, New Jersey: Patterson Smith Publishers.

O'LEARY, W.D. (1989). Custodial suicides: Evolving liability considerations. *Psychiatric Quarterly* 31:34–36.

ROBIN, G.D. (1987). *Introduction to the criminal justice system.* New York: Harper & Row Publishers.

SELLIN, T. (1967). A look at prison history. *Federal Probation* 31(3):18–23.

The Mobile Press Register, Lawyer: Shooting shows chain gang problem. May 17, 1996, 4B.

The Mobile Press Register, State chain gangs fate 1st anniversary. May 3, 1996, 4B.

The Penal Code of Alabama (1866). Montgomery, Reid & Screws State Printers.

WALKER, D.R. (1988). *Penology for profit: A history of the Texas prison system 1867–1912.* College Station: Texas A & M University Press.

CASE

Michael Austin et al. v. Fob James Jr., Governor of the State of Alabama and Ron Jones, Commissioner of the Alabama Department of Corrections, Case No. 95-T-637-N.

CRITICAL THINKING QUESTIONS

1. How are prison chain gangs today similar and different from those of the nineteenth century?

2. Explain why critics believe prison chain gangs are racist. Do you agree or disagree? Why?

3. What are the costs and benefits of using chain gangs—to society in general and to correctional officials specifically?

Reading 3

Gender and the "American Way of Life": Women in the Americanization Movement

John F. McClymer

> *In this article, the author focuses on the role of women in the "Americanization" movement and the ways that women contributed to the perpetuation of stereotypes about gender, race, ethnicity, and social class.*

"Only an agile and determined immigrant, possessed of over-mastering devotion to the land of his birth," wrote the *Chicago Tribune* in its 14 April 1919 edition, "can hope to escape Americanization by at least one of the many processes now being prepared for his special benefit, in addition to those which have sur- rounded him in the past."[1] The immediate postwar years, in fact, did mark the apogee of the Americanization movement. By then it had grown into one of the largest social and political movements in American history. So large was it that a United States Bureau of Education "list of lists" of public and private agencies actively engaged in some sort of Americanization work contained 108 entries. They ranged from "Secretaries of Americanization Committees of Chambers of Commerce" to "Sons of Italy

Source: Reprinted from *Journal of American Ethnic History* 10, no. 3 (Spring, 1991): 3–20.

Local Branches in New York State," from "Four Minute Men—State Chairman" to "General Federation of Women's Clubs—State Chairmen of Civics." And the Bureau's list was far from exhaustive.[2]

There were Americanization classes in the public schools, and programs run by the Young Men's and the Young Women's Christian Associations. There were employer-sponsored and union-sponsored campaigns. The Daughters and the Sons of the American Revolution were active in programs to promote greater loyalty among the foreign born and their children. And there were numerous organizations founded especially to advance one or another version of Americanization. Attempts to determine the full extent of the movement, both at the time and subsequently, have fallen short of complete accuracy. Still, even the most conservative estimates calculate that thousands of Americanization programs existed and, if the *Chicago Tribune*'s claim that only the most agile immigrant could avoid participation in one or another of them overstated the case, it exaggerated only somewhat.[3]

Despite its size and the furor it occasioned in the decade following the outbreak of war in Europe, Americanization remains one of the least studied movements in United States history.[4] It has been largely over-shadowed by two competing solutions to the immigrant "problem," namely, the "Great Red Scare" and restriction based upon national quotas. A cartoon in the *Toledo (Ohio) Blade* of 24 October 1919 aptly captured the spirit of the Scare. It portrayed "the alien in America" standing at a fork in the road. To the left lay a path labelled "To Americanization" while to the right lay one marked "To Deportation." The caption read: "There Should Be but Two Roads for Him." The Palmer Raids and subsequent deportations demonstrated the Wilson administration's willingness to push aliens down the path to the right.[5]

Even as the deportation mania faded in the early 1920s, restriction triumphed. Once it did, Americanization lost its urgency. As the *New York Times* argued in a 15 August 1927 editorial on "The Year's Newcomers," "Whatever danger existed from excessive numbers of aliens in this country is . . . almost certain to disappear in time, so long as the principle of restriction remains in force." This was because "most of the valid arguments" against immigration held "that the foreign-born form such large groups that they are indigestible" so "mere numerical restriction" should prove "satisfactory."[6]

With the passage of a permanent restriction law in 1924, the Americanization movement virtually died. But its effects, especially on the emerging public understanding of "true" Americanism were profound and long lasting. One of the most important of these was the way the movement politicized domestic stereotypes of women—transforming images of women as homemakers, wives, and mothers into key components of the "American Way of Life." To understand this dimension of the movement's impact upon American public culture we must first appreciate the roles of women within, and without, its vast network of organizations and activities. Women were key players in the Americanization crusade both as policy makers in public and private agencies and as teachers and administrators in states and local communities. As a result, there is considerable irony in the movement's idealization of traditional images of women.

Women came to play such important roles in the movement in part because of the way gender influenced the public life of the Progressive Era and in part because of the timing of the national concern over Americanization. This was the generation of women who developed that William L. O'Neill called "social feminism," an orientation towards increasing women's "sphere" which used traditional stereotypes about domesticity and maternal instincts to argue that women were peculiarly well suited for a whole range of public tasks. These tasks included fields such as nursing and teaching, which an earlier generation of women had claimed as their own, and such new areas of professional activity as social and settlement house work, factory safety inspection, and consumer protection. By 1914 this generation of women had assumed important positions of leadership in all of these fields, and this fact means that they were thereby well placed to claim leadership of the Americanization crusade when the outbreak of war suddenly catapulted it into prominence.[7]

Prior to World War I few native-born Americans had thought of the immigration "problem" in cultural terms. Most instead had worried about the "new" immigrant's allegedly inferior racial characteristics or they had fretted that the newcomer's supposed willingness to work for low wages would drive down the American standard of living. Old fears, about the immigrants' proclivity for radical politics or blind adherence to papist superstitions, persisted as well. There were some, however, who did see the immigration problem as one of acculturation. Settlement house workers tended to this view as did educators, perhaps because such a definition of the problem maximized the relevance of their own expertise. Some business leaders, looking to apply modern management techniques to their labor forces, also saw formal Americanization work as part of the solution to an immigration "problem" they defined in terms of labor unrest, high turnover rates, and poor workmanship.[8]

So, although the cultural viewpoint was a minority one, it did have a strong institutional base in settlements and other service agencies, such as the YMCA and YWCA, in the schools, and in the employer groups like the North American Civic League for Immigrants. Further, in each of these agencies women held important leadership positions.[9]

The most important case in point was Frances A. Kellor. An attorney, a former settlement worker, and an industrial safety expert Kellor was, in 1916, the vice-chair—and effective head—of the National Americanization Committee and of its parent organization, the Committee for Immigrants. Both organizations were outgrowths of the New York–New Jersey branch of the North American Civic League. She was also the assistant to the chair, and day-to-day executive officer, of the Committee on Immigration of the United States Chamber of Commerce. Later, after the United States entered the war, she headed up the Americaniza-

tion work of the federal Bureau of Education as well. After the war, she was instrumental in organizing the Inter-Racial Council, a business association which sought to exercise editorial control over the foreign-language press.[10] . . .

Women were key players in state and local school programs as well, an important fact given the highly decentralized nature of the movement. Marguerite H. Burnett directed the state program in Delaware; Laura Selden Peck headed up the public school programs in Sioux Falls, South Dakota; S. Alice Smith was director of adult education, which included Americanization classes, in Utica, New York. There were many others because, by the World War I period, women had begun to hold a number of supervisory posts in public schools. Once public officials, such as Raymond Crist of the federal Bureau of Naturalization, employers, union leaders, and their counterparts in an array of other organizations began to define the Americanization issue in educational terms, that is, by 1915, women educators necessarily had significant voices in saying what the content of the resulting courses would be.[11]

Equally important, women had long since dominated the ranks of grammar school teachers, and it was from their ranks that the large majority of Americanization teachers would come. Women teachers, as a result, would implement in the classroom Americanization curricula which women supervisors, principals, and department heads would do much to design.[12]

Other women made important contributions to the movement as well. They include settlement house leaders, like Mary Kingsbury Simkhovitch of New York's United Neighborhood Houses, other social service professionals, such as Edith Terry Bremer who headed the International Institutes program of the Young Women's Christian Association, and Grace Abbott who directed the Chicago-based Immigrant Protective Association, and club women like Maine's Margaret B. DeGarme. Historians of Americanization, myself included, have noted the important role played by individual women. But, our biographical approach, recounting the career of Frances Kellor and then that of Josephine Roche and so on, although it does have the merit of giving those individuals their due, can never explain the collective importance of women in the movement.[13]

Biography also cannot easily address the sexual politics of a movement, articulated in terms of a male-centered and dominated political culture, and aimed largely at men, but substantially directed—and overwhelmingly carried out—by women. To get at these dimensions of the Americanization movement it is necessary to place it in the context of the ongoing debate about what being an American would entail, on the one hand, and in the context of the efforts by social feminists to use certain aspects of traditional stereotypes to advance their own positions and their reform agendas, on the other.

Getting at these issues poses several complex methodological problems. One derives from the fact that the manifest content of Americanization materials concerning gender, which was that public life in the United States is a male preserve, was at odds with the latent message carried by the highly visible activities of women Americanizers.[14] The historian must somehow give both their proper weight.

Another methodological challenge springs from the contrast between the indifference and hostility with which many immigrants, both male and female, reacted to official efforts to Americanize them and the powerful attraction these same immigrants felt to most things American.

Ethnic critics of the movement were numerous, despite the risk they ran of being accused of disloyalty to their new homeland. One Polish-language newspaper in Chicago struck a common note when it called for the "Americanization of Poles by the Poles." A second decried "American chauvinists" who understood by Americanization "only one language, unity of thought and opinion, one sympathy and antipathy." Still a third charged that the movement had "in it not the smallest particle of the true American spirit, the spirit of freedom, the brightest virtue of which is the broadest possible tolerance." Among Italians the term "Americanate" became a bitter insult. Equally revealing is the way in which immigrants, especially women resisted formal Americanization work. One Cleveland head worker ruefully confessed that the settlement's "house-to-house canvass" to recruit students for an "English class for foreign women" was a "failure." The women regarded "the sudden invitation to learn English . . . with suspicion as part of a plan of the American government to 'make soldiers of their husbands.'"[15]

Americanizers sought to dictate the pace and the content of cultural assimilation. Often they acted as though their programs were the only elements in the lives of immigrants which could offset the pull of Old World customs and values. Or they worried that their programs were all that might keep the newcomers from yielding to the siren songs of anarchists or Bolsheviki. Almost never did they acknowledge that most immigrant families were being "Americanized," as settlement leader Robert A. Woods phrased it in pre-War days, "not by a tradition or other educational process than that of having the typical American experience in . . . the heart of the country."[16]

Cultural assimilation would go forward whether there was an Americanization movement or not. Since Americanizers grossly overstated the dangers of ethnic disloyalty and severely understated the attractive force of American culture (because in this sense there was so much less at stake than they thought) it is easy to underestimate the full import of their movement. It is clear in retrospect that Americanization was not so much a way of transforming immigrants and their children into real Americans as a campaign to fix the public meaning of Americanism. Americanizers would have much of lasting influence to say on that score, and they would say it in terms of traditional gender roles.

This point was clearest in the public meaning of Americanization as put forward in public school courses and other curricula. Such courses varied widely, given the local control of education in the United States. Some schools contented themselves with elementary school primers. Others designed materials intended to meet the special needs of the adult learner. Most classes were conducted entirely in English, but a few programs sought to reach immigrants in their native languages.[17]

For all of their differences, however, Americanization curricula were invariant in their portrayal of the public domain of American life as an all-male preserve. Indeed Americanization itself seemed, at first blush, to have been for men only. Certainly the *Chicago Tribune*'s agile immigrant was male. And a large majority of the formal citizenship classes were designed for adult males. The reasons are clear. Women, even after the suffrage amendment passed, were not fully citizens in their own right in the way that men were. Women shared the citizenship status of their fathers, if they were minors, and then of their husbands, if they married, whatever their nativity or age. This situation held for all women. If a native-born woman married an alien, she automatically forfeited her United States citizenship. Similarly, if a foreign-born woman's husband was, or became, an American citizen, then she became one as well. So, to the extent that the Americanization movement focused upon citizenship and had naturalization as its goal, the crusade necessarily directed most of its energies at men.

The Americanization crusade quickly moved beyond simple citizenship and naturalization to more all-encompassing definitions of loyalty and "100% Americanism." This broadened notion of what it meant to be a good American would, in due course, convince Americanizers that they had to turn their energies to the immigrant woman as well as the immigrant man. At the outset, however, it tended to have the opposite effect as those determined to eliminate the threat of alien disloyalty attended first to allegations of sabotage and espionage and then to the ticklish question of whether aliens should be exempt from military service.[18] All were presumed to be matters involving men alone.

So were matters involving strikes and other forms of union militancy. Right from the beginning of the movement employer groups sought to wrap their own programs of company unionism and "welfare capitalism" in the banner of "real" Americanism and to stigmatize the activities of their class enemies as "unAmerican." For example, the business-sponsored Americanization Day Committee offered as its first definition of "What The Americanization Of The Foreign Born Means To America" that "it means industrial peace." This was to be a peace based upon the immigrants' repudiation of "radical agitators addressing them in their own language." That these employer groups were preoccupied with the immigrant workingman can be seen in the most famous visual image of the whole movement, the graduation ceremony at Henry Ford's River Rouge factory Americanization school. The ceremony consisted of Ford workers, all men, marching across a stage while dressed in ethnic costumes. They climbed up a ladder and into a huge pot, fittingly labeled the "melting pot," and then re-emerged to climb down on the other side dressed in "American" clothes.[19]

Public school classes continued this practice of defining the unit to be Americanized as the foreign-born working-class adult male. A 1916 article on Rochester's public school program was entitled "An Americanization Factory" and began by noting that in the class of "fifty or more" there was only one woman. In like fashion Pittsburgh's citizenship courses were explicitly designed for men, and were keyed to the stages of the naturalization process. Its "Beginning Course is primarily for men who have a very limited knowledge of English and have taken the first step in naturalization," who had, that is, applied for their first papers.[20]

Nonetheless women Americanizers had long insisted on the importance of reaching the foreign-born woman. Indeed settlement programs for immigrant wives and daughters were usually larger and better funded than were comparable programs for men. In fact this attention to women drew the fire of one of the Carnegie Corporation's students of the Americanization movement. According to John Daniels, "the man, not the woman, is the determining factor in immigrant groups." Not only had he "been the lord and master" in the old country "from time immemorial," but "the great adventure of establishing a new home in America gives him even more responsibility and authority." The man was "the explorer," "the pioneer." "He is the breadwinner and the guardian, on whom the mother and her brood depend for livelihood and protection. Consequently his is the deciding voice."

Women Americanizers who challenged this male supremacist view did so in terms of traditional gender roles. According to Edith Terry Bremer of the YWCA's International Institutes program, "to men it may appear that America's great concern is over the immigrants who could be citizens and soldiers." But, "to America the 'Immigration problem' is a great 'problem' of homes." The "real question," said Bremer, was "what kind of homes" do the newcomers make. "When it comes to homes, women and not men become the important factors." To direct Americanization "as if it aimed at men only," she concluded, "is both un-American and dangerous."[21]

Bremer's social feminist position prevailed throughout much of the movement. According to the federal Bureau of Naturalization, the answer to Daniels' arguments about male dominance was also that "America is no better than its homes." Of course it was the mother, its pamphlet offering Suggestions For Americanization Work Among Foreign-Born Women maintained, who "determines the kind of home and the health and happiness of the family." Further, these same mothers "have much of the responsibility of determining what kind of citizens their children shall become." Left to their own devices, these women would fail. The Bureau of Naturalization argued that "the schooling of the mother is the only effective way to enable her to take her full responsibility in the home and in the community."[22]

Other Americanizers agreed. The federal Bureau of Education detailed the dangers posed by the unAmericanized mother. "From babyhood to adolescence the child suffers through the mother's ignorance of the language. Juvenile delinquency is reported widely where children are blunderingly acquiring American ways apart from the parents' direction." In addition to delinquency, such mothers were supposedly responsible in large measure for high rates of infant mortality and disease. "Later on, when the child reaches the age limit of compulsory school attendance, the non-English speaking mother, failing to realize the advantages of a longer period of schooling, frequently allows the boy or girl to leave school and go to work, although an economic necessity may not exist." Worse still, some of those daughters would wind up in unspecified but improper surroundings because "the immigrant mother, as a rule, remains ignorant of the nature of the work . . . and of the people with whom she associates."[23]

All of these were serious problems, but why were they Americanization issues? John J. Mahoney, Massachusetts state supervisor of Americanization, made the connection this way. "The immigrant is becoming either Americanized or anarchized by every experience which he undergoes, every condition to which he is subjected." This meant Americanization was not only a matter of promoting loyalty to the United States. It was "also a matter of prevention of exploitation, of good housing, of clean milk for babies, of adequate wages, of satisfactory industrial conditions, of the spirit of neighborliness between Americans, old and new." Americanization, that is, dealt with the whole of life. "Everything that touches the immigrant's life is an instrumentality for his Americanization or the reverse."[24]

Josephine Roche's Division of Work with the Foreign-Born in the wartime Committee on Public Information took an equally sweeping approach. The Division held that "influence must be brought to bear upon the individual who is to be Americanized in every thing that concerns his mind and his heart" and even argued that "whoever is homesick for another country is lost for America."[25]

Prior to World War I loyalty had meant political allegiance and had been measured by the newcomer's willingness to become a law-abiding citizen of the new land. War-inspired fears of a Balkanized United States helpless to defend its national interests changed all that.

Woodrow Wilson dramatically signaled the change when he excoriated his German and Irish-American critics in his 1915 State of the Union message as "infinitely malignant." They had "poured the poison of disloyalty into the very arteries of our national life" and sought "to debase our politics to the uses of foreign intrigue."[26]

As the distinction between criticism and sedition evaporated, loyalty came to mean conformity. One Polish-language newspaper in Chicago caught the import of this development perfectly when it warned its readers that "the average American does not well understand" the Poles' distaste for the Austro-Hungarian and German empires and so suspects them simply because they speak or dress differently. Poles needed "not only to obey all laws and avoid doing anything which may even cast the slightest suspicion upon us of aiding the Germans and their allies but also to observe carefully everything about us."[27]

Once loyalty became a matter of "100% Americanism," once Americanism became a matter of cultural conformity, Americanizers set themselves the task of entirely remaking the immigrant in their own image. This shift, in turn, meant that stereotypical notions of the woman's proper sphere would become articles of patriotic faith. And it indicated that old ideas of the cultural significance of that sphere, e.g., the centrality of the home in the raising of good citizens, would gain a renewed lease on life.

One measure of the sweep of the resulting notion of domestic Americanism is the campaign against "foreign" vegetables, especially cabbage. Americanism truly extended to every detail of life, and each detail became highly significant once it officially became part of the "American Way." The General Federation of Women's Clubs made eliminating cabbage a major objective of its Americanization work and club women were not alone in crusading against the vegetable. The Carnegie Corporation's Americanization Study commended an "enlightened" company which discovered that the "dampness in Polish houses and the tendency of paper to come off the walls were due

to the continual flow of steam from the kitchen stove" where the workers' wives were wont to cook "cabbage soup." Happily, the company quickly launched a program to teach those women to cook "American" foods. Similarly, club women resolved to "carry the English language and American ways of caring for babies, ventilating the house, preparing American vegetables, instead of the inevitable cabbage, right into the new homes."[28]

What was at stake, thought the club women, was nothing less than the sanctity of the American way of life. Margaret B. DeGarme, chair of the Maine Federation's Americanization Committee, asked "What are these aliens doing to us?" The answer, she said, spelled "disaster. They deride our Bible and our Public Schools, and for our stars and stripes, flaunt the red flag of anarchy, anarchy that they actually preach in English." The national Federation agreed and, in 1921, allied itself with the National Security League, the American Legion, and more than a dozen other organizations to form a National Committee for the Co-ordination of Patriotic and Civic Work in order to help "eradicate, root and branch, the loathsome growth of radicalism." Not all women Americanizers jumped on this right-wing bandwagon of course, although Frances Kellor, easily the most influential woman in the movement, certainly did. But, all did join in attributing life-and-death significance to matters of domestic routine.[29]

School programs offer cases in point. The federal Bureau of Naturalization's "Suggestive Lesson Topics" for work with foreign-born women began with "the home" went on to "child welfare" and then to "the mother and the neighborhood," "the mother and the school," and "the mother and the community" before concluding with a catchall "general topics" category. Americanization work, the bureau held, entailed teaching immigrant women about "keeping out mosquitoes and flies" while still "opening windows for ventilation." It involved informing them about "suitable play clothes for children" and instructing them in "good taste in home furnishing." There were lessons on weaning children and on "harmful and wholesome comic pictures." There was a lesson on "measuring cloth in a dry-goods store." Listed last, and presumably least, was citizenship.[30] Missing altogether were the standard lessons on the form and structure of local, state, and national government, on the judicial system, or on voting which were standard and important parts of Americanization curricula designed for men.

The Carnegie Corporation's Americanization study took the same tack. It called "the problem of the immigrant woman in the home" the "most difficult one confronting Americanization forces to-day." To meet it local school boards should hire "home teachers," i.e., women who could conduct classes for immigrant mothers in their own homes—a necessity since few of the newcomers were willing or able to attend public school classes and since the latter were aimed at men in any event. The home teacher could "demonstrate the benign intent of the state in offering helpful services to all strangers who have come among us" even if "she does not teach the mother English." What were the "helpful services" in question? They were "explaining to immigrant mothers the laws and customs of American life, the school attendance requirements for children, the existence and location of public baths, libraries, dispensaries" and the like.[31]

The program in Akron, Ohio appears to have been typical. At first the city organized "mother's classes in the schools and club houses and social centers," but soon "it was found necessary to take the Americanization class to the home of the foreign-born mother." The city's Americanization director described the work of the home class teacher this way: "Up and down the unimproved streets, into the alleys, and the rear apartments, the home class teacher has gone." She has had the "tremendous task" of teaching these women "a new language, and in so doing to teach American standards and cleanliness, health for children, and civic pride."[32]

Suffrage did not change this virtually exclusive preoccupation with maternal and domestic responsibilities. Consider the federal Bureau of Education's response to the "fact that in a number of States, women whose husbands are American citizens automatically receive the right to vote, whether or not they speak or understand English." Their ignorance, the bureau warned, "injects an element of danger into this new electoral power." The bureau did urge that public school teachers use the occasions of home visits and mothers' meetings to teach civics, but it laid far more stress on the need to assist the immigrant mother to find American dietary substitutes "to the diet upon which she has been dependent" and to "introduce the mothers . . . to American institutions, such as art museums . . . and other places of interest which will help them to understand and feel acquainted with the new country." This advice stands in sharp contrast to the bureau's detailed instructions to these same teachers about the fathers of their pupils. They should "find out in what families the father has not taken out his first naturalization papers; and find out why." They should attempt to interest him in taking this "first step." They should locate the nearest night school and "offer to direct him there and give him a note of introduction to the teacher in charge."[33]

If suffrage did not prompt Americanizers to do more than pay lip service to the idea of civics programs for women, it did provide many with a reason for urging that women's citizenship status be separated from that of their husbands. Their object was not that women have full equality under the law although their reform would in fact be a step in that direction. Rather their goal was to decrease the number of women voters. As the National Committee for Constructive Immigration Legislation put it, the "separation of the citizenship of a wife from that of her husband . . . will prevent large numbers of uneducated and wholly unqualified foreign-born women from voting merely because their husbands may have become naturalized citizens."[34]

John Palmer Gavit, writing on behalf of the Carnegie Corporation's Americanization study, agreed that "the real problem of the foreign-born woman, so far as her equipment as a voter is concerned, has reference almost entirely to the vast number of women who are carried into citizenship and potential voting power by the naturalization of their husbands. This is a serious matter."[35] Gavit's operating assumption, one shared by other Americanizers both male and female, was that the immigrant woman was, and ought to remain, an entirely house-bound and tradition-bound creature. As a result, he and his colleagues were able to contemplate calmly with respect to women a prospect which, where the immigrant man was concerned, they regarded with horror. A great mass of unnaturalized women threatened no Balkanization of the United States, no "poisoning" of public life.

Immigrant women mattered to Americanizers as mothers and homemakers. Yet, despite all the emphasis upon traditional roles in the content of Americanization programs, the highly visible, if anomalous, activities of female Americanization workers carried a very different message. The worker indoctrinated immigrant men in the proper exercise of civic responsibilities which she did not share. Meanwhile, as the teacher, she asserted a direct authority over those same men even as she taught them that public life in the United States was for men only. She also explained the proper way to run a home to immigrant women even as she actively pursued a career outside the home herself. She emphasized the primacy of motherhood and maternal duties even as her presence away from her own home demonstrated that some women could assume other responsibilities.

A case in point is the career of the otherwise unidentified Miss W., the moving spirit behind Americanization work in Hughson, California. She had first become active in the movement while teaching at the Glendale High School in Los Angeles. When she moved to Hughson to become cashier at the local bank, "she felt as never before the crying need for education of the many Portuguese and Mexicans with whom she came in contact from day to day." She began visiting their homes, "teaching the men to write their signatures, advising them in business and legal matters, and incidentally becoming acquainted with their children and wives." Next she organized night classes for the men and a Saturday afternoon school for their wives and sisters. Within a year Miss W. was a full-time director of Americanization as a member of the Hughson high school faculty. In addition to her evening and Saturday classes she used "the beautiful home she purchased in Hughson" as a social center. She "constantly entertained" groups of foreigners at dinners and luncheons with her women pupils delightedly helping her in the dining room and kitchen." Often she invited prominent Americans, such as the chaplain at San Quentin penitentiary and his wife, to meet her immigrant pupils thereby "bringing them into contact with the best in American life and letting them absorb it in their own way."[36]

Americanization workers like Miss W. could be models for immigrant women seeking to adjust to a culture where, compared to their native countries, more women were active in the wage labor market, where single women had less supervision and more freedom of choice about whom they could keep company with, and where—in short—the range of acceptable female behavior, however confined it seems in retrospect, seemed vast in prospect. Miss W., with her independent ways, her careers as banker and educator, her home, her important friends, her ability to organize an elaborate series of social programs, embodied much of the promise of a freer life many immigrant women associated with America.

The social activism of women Americanizers broadcast a message deeply subversive of the traditional notions of women's "proper sphere" that they urged upon their clients. This counter-message may well have been just as salient as the domestic orthodoxy found in Americanization curricula. Historians have long appreciated the irony of women activists preaching social conservatism, often criticizing them for not fully liberating themselves from the sexist notions of their age.[37] We have been less appreciative of the fact that the social feminists among the Americanizers, like their sisters in other Progressive Era reform movements, did hew out a place for women in public policy formation and implementation. This was no small accomplishment. It meant that even as the Americanization movement turned conventional wisdom about a woman's proper role in public life into part of the "American Way" women like Frances Kellor and Miss W. were pioneering new roles for women.

NOTES

1. *Chicago Daily Tribune,* 14 April 1919, clipping in Department of Labor, Immigration and Naturalization Service, Americanization Section, "Sundry Press Clippings Relative To Education Work of Bureau of Education," File No. 27671/2680, in Record Group 85, National Archives [hereinafter cited as RG 85].

2. "List Of Lists Found In the Office," 6/24/18, in U.S., Department of Interior, Bureau of Education, Record Group 12, Box 106, Americanization—War Work [hereinafter cited as RG 12]. During World War I Four Minute Men gave patriotic speeches between features at movie theaters using material provided by the federal Committee on Public Information.

3. The best contemporary analyses were those undertaken as part of the Carnegie Corporation's Americanization Studies series of which Allen T. Burns was general editor. These include: W. I. Thomas [credited to Robert E. Park and Herbert A. Miller], *Old Worm Traits Transplanted* (New York, 1921); John Palmer Gavit, *Americans By Choice* (New York, 1922); and William M. Leiserson, *Adjusting Immigrant and Industry* (New York, 1924). One of the Carnegie volumes, Frank V. Thompson, *Schooling of the Immigrant* (New York, 1920) contained a sharply worded critique of federally-sponsored Americanization programs, especially those connected with the Bureau of Naturalization (Chapter X, "Schooling in Citizenship," prepared by Raymond Moley). One criticism, that the Bureau grossly overstated the reach of its program, led Naturalization to undertake its own "Survey of Immigrant Education in the United States (Development and Status of State programs of Immigrant Education)," RG 85, File No. E16075-1. The Survey was later published. Margaret D. Moore, *Citizenship Training of Adult Immigrants in the United States: Its Status in Relation to the Census of 1920* (Washington, D.C., 1925). An effort to estimate the numbers of adult immigrants who actually enrolled in, and did or did not complete, a formal Americanization program is John F. McClymer, "The Americanization Movement and the Education of the Foreign-Born Adult, 1914–1925," in *American Education and the European Immigrant, 1840–1940,* ed. Bernard J. Weiss (Urbana, Ill., 1982), especially pp. 102–105. For an account of federal Americanization efforts see McClymer, "The Fed-

eral Government and the Americanization Movement, 1915–1924," *Prologue,* 10 (Spring, 1978): 22–41.

4. Edward G. Hartmann, *The Movement To Americanize The Immigrant* (New York, 1948) is a largely acritical study of the largest employer-based Americanization organization. John Higham's masterful synthesis, *Strangers In The Land: Patterns of American Nativism, 1860–1925* (1955; reprinted, New York, 1970) pp. 234–263, contains a much more insightful account of the movement. Gerd Korman, *Industrialization, Immigrants, And Americanizers: The View from Milwaukee* (Madison, Wis., 1967) is a good case study. So is Frederick C. Luebke, *Bonds Of Loyalty: German Americans and World War I* (DeKalb, Ill., 1974). Also useful is Stephen Meyer, "Adapting The Immigrant To The Line: Americanization in the Ford Factory, 1914–1921," *Journal of Social History,* 14 (Fall, 1980): 67–82.

5. *Toledo (Ohio) Blade,* 24 October 1919, clipping in RG 85, File E 6298. See William Preston, *Aliens and Dissenters* (New York, 1963) and Horace C. Peterson and Gilbert C. Fite, *Opponents of War, 1917–1918* (Seattle, 1957).

6. *New York Times,* 15 August 1927, clipping in American Council of Nationality Services Papers, Shipment 2, Box 5, Immigration History Research Center, University of Minnesota, Twin Cities [hereinafter cited as ACNS Papers].

7. See William L. O'Neill, *Everyone Was Brave: A History of Feminism in America* (Chicago, 1971) and John F. McClymer, *War and Welfare: Social Engineering in America, 1890–1925* (Westport, Conn., 1980), pp. 14–24.

8. A compendium of prewar concerns over immigration is *Reports of the Immigration Commission,* 41 vols. (Washington, D.C., 1911). The classic critique of the Commission's work is Oscar Handlin, "Old Immigrants and New," in his *Race and Nationality in American Life* (Boston, 1957). A full statement of the standard of living argument is Jeremiah W. Jenks and W. Jett Lauck, *The Immigration Problem: A Study of American Immigration Conditions and Needs* (New York, 1917). Edward A. Ross, *The Old World in the New* (New York, 1914) was an influential version of the racial argument.

9. McClymer, *War and Welfare,* pp. 82–104, 110–114.

10. See McClymer, "The Federal Government and the Americanization Movement."

11. No complete listing of local and state school Americanization officials exists so it is not possible to calculate the exact share of these positions held by women. One straw in the wind is a list, compiled in the Bureau of Naturalization in 1923, of school officials in charge of Americanization programs which published their own periodicals for their students. Women were exactly 50 percent of those officials. "Periodicals Issued by Americanization Classes with Public School Officials in Charge," Federal Council of Citizenship Training, RG 85, Box 3.

12. The Federal Bureau of Education's training manual for Americanization teachers, *Training Teachers For Americanization: A Course of Study for Normal Schools and Teachers' Institutes,* Bureau of Education Bulletin No. 12 (Washington, D.C., 1920) was written by John J. Mahoney, State Supervisor of Americanization of Massachusetts "with the assistance of Frances K. Wetmore, of the

public schools of Chicago, and Helen Winkler and Elsa Alsberg, of the Council of Jewish Women." The manual simply assumed the Americanization teacher would be a woman. So did the federal Bureau of Naturalization's *Teacher's Manual* (preliminary edition) to accompany its *Federal Citizenship Textbook* (Washington, D.C., 1922). The textbook was used in hundreds of public school programs across the country. The Manual relied heavily on Rose M. O'Toole, *Practical English for New Americans, Teacher's Manual* (Boston, ca. 1920–1923). Several model lessons in the *Naturalization's Teacher's Manual* were furnished by Marguerite T. Hickey, a field agent with the Americanization Department of the Connecticut State Board of Education.

13. In addition to the works cited in notes 3, 4, and 11, see Raymond A. Mohl, "The International Institutes and Immigrant Education, 1910–40," and Nicholas V. Montalto, "The Intercultural Education Movement, 1924–1941: The Growth of Tolerance as a Form of Intolerance," both in *American Education and the European Immigrant.*

14. Dziennik Zjednoczenia, vol. 36, no. 112 (13 May 1922); Narod Polski, vol. 23, no. 6 (5 February 1919); Dziennik Zwiazkowy, (7 August 1918), all in Chicago Foreign Language Press Survey, Reel 55. Enrico C. Sartorio, "Americanization," from his *Social and Religious Life of Italians in America* (Boston, 1918) as reprinted in Francesco Cordasco and Eugene Bucchioni, eds., *The Italians: Social Backgrounds Of An American Group* (Clifton, N.J., 1974), p. 199. The Cleveland headworker's account is reprinted in John Daniels, *America Via The Neighborhood* (New York, 1920), p. 232.

15. Robert A. Woods, "Pittsburgh: An Interpretation of Its Growth," *Charities and The Commons,* 21 (2 January 1909): 528. Ethnic fiction often pivots upon the many and subtle attractions American popular culture held for immigrant women and their daughters. See, for example, Anzia Yezierska, *Hungry Hearts* (Boston, 1920). See also Robert Anthony Orsi, *The Madonna of 115th Street: Faith and Community in Italian Harlem, 1880–1950* (New Haven, 1985).

16. See Herbert Adolphus Miller, *The School and the Immigrant* (Cleveland, 1916) and Frank V. Thompson, *Schooling of the Immigrant* (New York, 1920) for insightful contemporary analyses.

17. See Higham, *Strangers In The Land.* What made the issue of military service so controversial was the problematic status of unnaturalized immigrants from the German, Austro-Hungarian, or Ottoman Empires who might serve in the United States military. Since they were still, under the terms of international law, subjects of those empires, they were not entitled to the protections created for prisoners of war. They were liable to summary trial as traitors and could be executed. The Wilson administration exempted enemy aliens from the draft and provided expeditious naturalization for those who volunteered. There is no published study of military programs of citizenship training. Gavit, *Americans By Choice* provides a brief narrative.

18. Mimeographed circular, "Some Facts For Speakers at Americanization Day Celebrations," n.d. [1915], in Americanization Section, Sundry Correspondence . . .

Americanization Day Committee, RG 85, File No. 27671/30. The Americanization Day Committee was a creation of the National Americanization Committee. See McClymer, War and Welfare, pp. 110–112. See also Meyer, "Adapting The Immigrant To The Line."

19. Gregory Mason, "An Americanization Factory," *The Outlook,* 112 (23 February 1916): pp. 430–448; *Evening Schools and Extension Work: Course of Study Manual, Pittsburgh Public Schools* (Pittsburgh, 1915). The quotation is on p. 29. 24. Daniels, *America Via The Neighborhood,* p. 193.

20. Edith Terry Bremer, "Foreign Community And Immigration Work Of The National Young Women's Christian Association," reprinted from *Immigrants In America Review,* January 1916, Bulletin No. 3, Committee For Foreign Community and Immigration Work, National Board, Y.W.C.A. in American Council of Nationality Services Papers, Shipment 3, Box 1, Immigration History Research Center.

21. *Suggestions For Americanization Work Among Foreign-Born Women* (Washington, 1921), p. 2.

22. The Kindergarten And Americanization, Kindergarten Circular No. 3 (November 1918) (Washington, D.C., 1918), pp. 1–2.

23. Mahoney, *Training Teachers for Americanization,* p. 14.

24. "In Literature and Song: How can Americanization be furthered by the Stage?" *German Democracy Bulletin,* 2, no. 3 (1919): 2 in Committee on Public Information Papers, microfilm reel 31, Immigration History Research Center.

25. Woodrow Wilson, Public Papers, 3:423–424.

26. Dziennik Zwiazkowy, 18 April 1917, in Chicago Foreign Language Press Survey, Reel 51, Immigration History Research Center.

27. William M. Leiserson, *Adjusting Immigrant and Industry* (New York, 1924), pp. 66–70; Helen Varick Boswell, "Promoting Americanization," *Annals of the American Academy of Political and Social Science,* 64 (March 1916): 205, 206.

28. Margaret B. DeGarme et al., to "the President of and to the other members of the State Federation interested in Americanization work," 7 April 1924, in American Council of Nationality Services Papers, Shipment 2, Box 1; National Security League and Allied Organizations (1921) and "Americanization Program of the General Federation of Women's Clubs," both in American Council of Nationality Services Papers. In sharp contrast are the programs of the Y.W.C.A.'s International Institutes. See Edith Terry Bremer, The International Institutes in Foreign Community Work: Their Program and Philosophy, undated [1923] Y.W.C.A. pamphlet in Ibid., Shipment 3, Box 3. For Kellor's role in wartime and postwar anti-radical campaigns, see War and Welfare, pp. 112–13, 116–22.

29. *Suggestions For Americanization Work Among Foreign-Born Women,* pp. 6–8. Three of 151 lesson topics dealt with the woman as a citizen in her own right. All 148 of the others dealt with domestic and maternal duties.

30. Thompson, *Schooling Of The Immigrant,* pp. 109, 111.

31. Quoted in *Suggestions For Americanization Work Among Foreign-Born Women,* p. 10.

32. *The Kindergarten And Americanization,* pp. 3, 4.

33. Percentage Plans For Restriction Of Immigration: Hearings Before The Committee On Immigration and Naturalization, U.S. Congress, House of Representatives, 66th Cong., 1st sess., 12, 13, 14, 18, 19, 20 June and 25 September 1919, p. 91.

34. Gavit, *Americans By Choice*, p. 309. The passage of restrictive legislation which established quotas based upon national origins, first in 1921 and then more permanently in the Johnson-Reed Act of 1924, supplied another reason for separating the citizenship of wives from that of their husbands. In several cases native-born wives of unnaturalized immigrants found themselves excluded from returning to the United States after visits to Europe since the quote for "their" group had been filled. Each such case required a separate private bill and brought home to the Congress the need to grant women citizenship on the identical basis as men.

35. Miss W.'s career is recounted in the Bureau of Naturalization booklet, Suggestions for Securing and Holding Attendance of Foreign-Born Adults upon Public-School English and Citizenship Classes (Washington, D.C., 1922); pp. 24–25. Pp. 19–30 reprint letters the Bureau received from local directors of Americanization recounting work in their communities.

36. The critique goes back at least to Thorstein Veblen who excoriated settlement workers dedicated "to the inculcation, by precept and example, of certain punctilios of upper-class propriety in manners and customs" which they had sought to escape in their own lives. See *The Theory of the Leisure Class* (New York, 1934), p. 399. I made a similar, if less biting, point about women social experts in War and Welfare, pp. 15–19.

CRITICAL THINKING QUESTIONS

1. Discuss the purpose and goals of the Americanization movement at the beginning of the twentieth century.

2. In what ways did the Americanization movement benefit or harm the status of women in American society? How did these effects differ by social class?

3. Discuss the role of social class in the Americanization movement. In what ways did the movement perpetuate and challenge social assumptions about social class and gender?

Reading 4

The Hidden Half: A History of Native American Women's Education

Deirdre A. Almeida

In this reading, Almeida shows the ways that Native Americans have been historically placed into western-based boarding schools, where their cultural heritage has been eroded. She also discusses the role of Native American women in education and in resisting the dominance of European Americans.

NATIVE WOMEN'S MARKING OF TIME

Institutional racism was rampant in North American colonists' effort to educate Native Americans (Wright, 1992, p. 93). Educational

Source: Harvard Educational Review Vol. 67 No. 4 Winter 1997 Copyright © 1997 by the President and Fellows of Harvard College. All rights reserved.

institutions established by European colonists attempted to impose their beliefs and values on Native students, and their social, economic, and political structures onto Native American cultures and civilizations (Almeida, 1992, p. 2). Over the centuries, education has been misused to appropriate land, to destroy Native American languages and cultures, and to enslave nations of Indigenous peoples (Crow Dog, 1990; Trask,

1993). Spanish, French, and British missionary schools used education to disguise their efforts to eliminate Native American society. The U.S. government later established boarding schools that continued these efforts. Most importantly, education has been used to both justify and minimize first colonists' and later the federal government's involvement in these acts of genocide (Churchill, 1994, p. 45). This has been accomplished by eliminating any discussions of these facts from the U.S. history textbooks and from the U.S. educational system in general.

. . . Education became a key component in the plan to eliminate Native American sovereignty (Churchill, 1994, p. 139). Some of the most prestigious and enduring educational institutions, such as Harvard University and Dartmouth College, included the education of Native Americans in their charters (Wright, 1992, p. 93). Despite this history, Native American education still remains an overlooked and under-researched topic in education. The limited research that has been conducted on the history of Native American education has primarily been from non-Native scholars, the majority of whom are men (Allen, 1989; Green, 1989). Their focus has been on the development of educational systems for Native Americans and its impact on Native Americans in general, with emphasis on Native men.

Over the past ten years, Native women historians and educators have begun to draw public attention to the history of Native American women, including the influence of education on their lives and their roles within their nations. . . .

Native American historians have identified five distinct periods since the European's arrival in the Americas: Creation (the beginning of time established in Native American stories of origin, prior to European contact in 1492); Contact with Europeans (1492–1800); The Removal Era (1800–1830); The Reservation Era (1830–1929); The Reform Era (1930–1969); and Contemporary Resistance (1970–1997). This article looks at the off-reservation boarding school education of young Native American women, with a focus on the Hampton Institute of Virginia during the mid-to-late

Reservation Era, 1878–1929, and a brief discussion of the influence of off-reservation boarding schools on the lives of Native American women and their communities during the eras of Reform and Contemporary Resistance.

NATIVE AMERICAN WOMEN'S EDUCATION UNDER THE INDIAN EDUCATIONAL REFORM MOVEMENT

The Native Americans' struggle to maintain our traditional lifestyles was increased with the Western invasion by European Americans onto Native American lands from the mid-1800s to the early 1900s. The eventual reduction of Native societies through systematic genocide,[1] warfare, broken treaties, and the destruction of natural and food resources resulted in U.S. government control over Native American nations and the establishment of the reservation system (Bowker, 1993; Green, 1992).

Confinement to reservations made Native American men unable to hunt to supply their communities not only with food, but also with the materials needed for clothing, housing, and other tools and implements. For Native American women and men, the honor and respect that the hunt brought them was also lost. Also at jeopardy was the traditional form of education for Native American children. The tanning and quilling societies of the women disappeared, because clothing made of hides was replaced by government-distributed trade cloth. The training young Native American women had traditionally received from their female elders was altered greatly; in time they were forced to turn to another source for their education—the U.S. government (Green, 1992; Standing Bear, 1975).

---

[1] Systematic genocide is the deliberate destruction, in whole or in part, by a government or its agents, of a racial, sexual, religious, tribal, ethnic, or political minority. It can involve not only mass murder, but also starvation, forced deportation or removal, and political, economic, and biological subjugation. For more information on genocide and systematic genocide, see Gioseffi (1993).

The reservation system thus led to the development of a major institution of Native education, whose impact is still felt within contemporary times—the off-reservation boarding school. These schools were viewed as a means to speed up the assimilation process (Bowker, 1993, p. 24) in order to force Native Americans into a European American lifestyle (Hultgren & Molin, 1989; Standing Bear, 1975). Non-native educators won federal support and funding by promoting the idea that the best way to educate Native American children was to remove them as soon as possible from their families and communities and to place them where they only had contact with European Americans.

Native children, young adults, and, in some cases, entire families were transported from their communities to boarding schools, first in the East and later to regional federal schools in the West. This formal education system contributed enormously to the breakdown of Native families, including women's traditional roles, and led to the development of many of the social ills that still affect Native nations today, such as dysfunctional families and substance abuse (Almeida, 1992; Bowker, 1993; Green, 1989; Lomawaima, 1994; Reyhner & Eder, 1994).[2] However, the off-reservation boarding school was not a new concept in 1878. The idea that the best way to educate Native American youth was by removing them as

far as possible from their home environment dates back to colonial times and Eleazer Wheelock Moor's Charity school.[3] These boarding schools flourished during the late nineteenth century, due to the increasing conflict over land and the U.S. government's misguided policies for "handling" Native Americans.

After the Civil War, many European Americans who had actively participated in the abolitionist movement sought a new cause to champion (Hultgren & Molin, 1989, p. 18). Those who chose the issue of Indian reform dedicated themselves to achieving the Americanization of Native Americans. With the end of the Native American wars at the close of the nineteenth century, new versions of containment policies for Native Americans sprang up in the belief that the United States would best serve Native Americans by assimilating them into European American society (Hultgren & Molin, 1989; Robbins, 1992; Standing Bear, 1975).

This Indian Reform movement was made up of politicians, ministers, educators, and lawyers. Most were men, but some of their wives were among the most active reformists. They established organizations such as the Friends of the American Indian and held conferences to discuss how they could assist with the reforms needed to help Native Americans become more assimilated or, in their words, "Americanized" (Reyhner & Eder, 1994, p. 46). The Indian reformists lobbied for the General Allotment Act, a bill sponsored by Senator Henry Dawes of Massachusetts. The Dawes Act, as it is also known, advocated for the breakup of Native American communal lands, to be replaced by allotted plots of land separately owned by Native families and individuals. Private ownership of land was one of the first strategies used to force Native Americans to assimilate into a European American value system (Noriega, 1992, p. 382). The other component of the Dawes Act dealt with pro-

[2.] Native American children were removed from their families and communities at very young ages. Instead of being raised with their parents and extended family members, they grew up in an institutional setting. This resulted in the students' loss of knowledge of traditional parenting skills. Native American students attending boarding schools were subjected to corporal punishment, and were instructed to focus on the nuclear family instead of the extended family. When they became adults and had families of their own, these boarding school students relied on the style of childrearing they had experienced at boarding school, and passed it on to their children. Returning students also experienced issues of trying to fit back into their communities, often with much difficulty and internal conflicts. To cope with the frustration of a loss of identity, returning boarding school students often turned to alcohol as a means of escape. The result was generations of substances abusers and domestic violence. For more information on this, see, Bowker (1993).

[3.] The Moor's Charity School for Indians was established in 1760 by Eleazer Wheelock in Lebanon, Connecticut. Between 1761 and 1769, Wheelock enrolled approximately sixteen Native American girls at Moor's School. See Szasz (1988).

viding educational training for both males and females so that Native Americans could be educated into becoming good, civilized Christians (Lomawaima, 1994, p. 2). The Indian Reform Movement also became known as the Indian Educational Reform Movement; the establishment of off-reservation boarding schools was one of its main projects (Reyhner & Eder, 1994, p. 46).

The first school to attempt to educate adult Native American students in the East was the Hampton Normal and Agricultural Institute in Virginia. Established in 1868 to educate African Americans following the Civil War, Hampton became the first boarding school to establish an Indian education program when, in April 1878, fifteen Native American adult male war hostages were admitted at the request of Captain Richard Pratt. Hampton's founder, General Samuel Armstrong, recognized the benefits to be gained from educating Native Americans (Almeida, 1992; Hultgren & Molin, 1989). He expressed his reaction to the arrival at Hampton of the Native Americans in a letter to his wife:

> They are a new step ahead and make the school very strong and really, Kitty, they are a big card for the school and will diminish my gray hairs. There's money in them I tell you. (Samuel Chapman Armstrong to Emma Armstrong, April 19, 1878, in Williamsiana Collection)

In the late fall of 1878, Captain Pratt returned from the Dakota territories with the first group of Native American children to be educated in the off-reservation system. Included in this first group were nine girls, the first Native American females to undergo the "Americanization" process in an educational setting (Hultgren & Molin, 1989, p. 18). Pratt would eventually leave Hampton to establish the first government-sponsored, all-Native American boarding school, the Carlisle Indian Industrial School in Carlisle, Pennsylvania. By 1885, Hampton and Carlisle had served as models for 106 Native American boarding schools, many of which were established on abandoned military installations (Green, 1989, p. 12).

Native children were accustomed to being educated and taken care of by people other than their natural parents, but little had prepared them for the sheer strangeness of the boarding school, with its echoing halls and electric lighting, and a staff speaking an unintelligible language and taking unacceptable familiarities with them (Coleman, 1993, p. 79). In 1884, a Yankton female student named Gertrude Simmons, who would later become famous under her tribal name of Zitkala-Sa, entered the White's Manual Labor Institute in Wabash, Indiana. She later described her fearful arrival:

> Entering the house, I stood close against the wall. The strong glaring light in the whitewashed room dazzled my eyes. The noisy hurrying of hard shoes upon a bare wooded floor increased the whirring in my ears. My only safety seemed to be in keeping next to the wall. As I was wondering in which direction to escape from all this confusion, two warm hands grasped me firmly, and in the same motion I was tossed high in midair. A rosy-cheeked paleface woman caught me in her arms. I was both frightened and insulted by such trifling. I stared into her eyes, wishing her to let me stand on my own feet, but she jumped me up and down with increasing enthusiasm. My mother had never made a plaything of her wee daughter. Remembering this I began to cry aloud. (Zitkala-sa, 1921/1993, p. 225)

It was not unusual for Native children to be sent away to boarding school at the age of six or seven, and not to see their homes and families again until the age of seventeen or eighteen (Noriega, 1992, p. 381). The goals of these boarding schools were to teach native American students how to speak English, to teach them basic academics, and to turn them into good, hard-working Christians. The education of female students at Hampton Institute was very general compared to the technical education of the male students. The girls' industrial curriculum included making and mending garments, crocheting and knitting, as well as learning to sew by hand and machine. Household training involved washing, ironing, cooking, and table duty, plus care of their own dormitories. Beginning in 1886, female students also participated in the "Technical Round" established for male students, where they learned skills like framing a window or building a set of shelves, which the school administrators felt would be useful to them on the reservation (Hultgren & Molin, 1989, p. 28).

Another key component of the boarding schools was a work-study program known as the "outing system," which placed Native American students in the homes of European Americans during the summer months so they could be exposed to European American morals and manners and develop their English-language skills. Hampton Institute placed its students on farms and in house–holds in western Massachusetts, where they provided cheap labor, with the males working as farmhands and the females responsible for domestic work.

Some of the female students wrote favorably of their placement, saying that they were treated as a member of the family and provided opportunities to expand their knowledge and coping skills needed for survival in European American society. Lizzie Young, a Wyandotte from Oklahoma, was placed with the Bryant family of Northampton, Massachusetts, in 1891. She shared her experiences with her teachers back at Hampton Institute:

> I like my home very much, only once in awhile I get lonesome when it rains, for I do not know what to do with myself. Yesterday Mr. b. invited us down to see him play a scientific game of croquet. That was the first time I ever did see a game of that kind. . . . They are kind to me. There are just three of us in the family. . . . I do not do anything but the cooking. Another woman across the street does the washing. . . . I am learning to use the typewriter. Please excuse mistakes this time, for I am not an expert yet, but I hope I may be some day. (Letter from Lizzie Young published in *Southern Workman*, August, 1891, Indian Student files, Hampton University Archives)

However, most of the female students who went through the outing system were not as fortunate as Lizzie Young. Their placements meant long days of hard work with little time for themselves. One unidentified student wrote to her friends at Hampton of her outing experience:

> I spent my summer in Westfield, Massachusetts. . . . I used to wash, iron, make beds and sweep the parlor and sitting room once a week, and keep the house when they all go away. When I came away they gave me $10.50. I never had a regular holiday, but once that was when we went to Sunday School picnic. I never went to visit any city or interesting place . . . (Letter from student published in *Southern Workman*, January, 1890, Indian Student files, Hampton University Archives)

The boarding school further destroyed the traditional roles of Native American women, as the girls were expected to learn European American techniques of childrearing, household maintenance, and food preparation. The rationale for this instruction was not only to assist Native American women in assimilating into mainstream culture, but also to limit their work skills so that the only choices of work they had when they returned to the reservation was to be a servant in a European American home. A few of those who returned to the reservation would be hired as maids in the federal Indian agent's home (Lomawaima, 1994, p. 81).

Native American women were discouraged by their teachers and school administrators from maintaining any knowledge of their traditional Native American lifestyle and brainwashed into looking down on anyone who still lived in a traditional manner. Except for the few Native women who integrated into mainstream European American society, the majority of the female boarding school students returned to their reservations and the same lifestyle they had left. However, they found that they had become disconnected from their traditional gender roles and from their communities. It was not always easy for them, as they had to prove themselves to regain the trust of their community members, many of whom were skeptical of returning students and viewed them as the new oppressor:

> The educated Indian does not hold the respect and admiration of the old people. . . . Instead, Indian alumni had to struggle to re-establish themselves in native communities, trying to gain acceptance while introducing changes resisted by family and friends. (*Indians' Education at Hampton Institute*, p. 19.)

Returning students often accepted employment with federal Indian agencies, and many found employment as domestics in the same boarding schools that had trained them (Lomawaima, 1994, p. 81). Those who chose to assimilate into European American life changed not only their own lives, but also those of future generations, as it meant they would not pass on the traditional skills, culture, and social connections of their Native community. Attending boarding schools led many Native American women into situations of extreme isolation, and increased their dependency on the U.S. government.

In contrast, some Native American women used their boarding school education to help them lead their people to resist extinction. Armed with knowledge of European American ways and values, these women were among the central figures in the reform and resistance movements through which many Native nations, though virtual captives of the United States, would resist non-Native efforts to destroy their culture (Green, 1992, p. 69).

The boarding schools operated along these lines until 1928, when the U.S. government released the Meriam Report, which condemned the poor quality of services provided by the Bureau of Indian Affairs. It pointed out shocking conditions of boarding schools, recommended that elementary age children not be sent to boarding schools at all, and urged an increase in the number of day schools on the reservations (Reyhner & Eder, 1994, p. 50). The Meriam Report focused on educational reform within Western boarding schools, and called for improved nu-

trition and health care standards for Native American children attending these schools. It noted that "discipline of the schools were merely restrictive, not developmental, and did not encourage individual expression or responsibility" (Meriam, 1928, p. 11). It further suggested that Indian Services should devote its energies to social and economic advancements that would help Native Americans adapt to mainstream European American society, or to live on their own terms with at least a minimum standard of health and decency (Lomawaima, 1994, p. 31).

This policy of educational reform eventually lead to the Indian New Deal of 1934 and a reorganization of Native American government systems. Federal programs under the 1934 Johnson-O'Malley Act (JOM) were established to fund Native American educational programs. The Act allowed the federal government to pay states for educating Native American children in public schools (Reyhner & Eder, 1994, p. 50), and established two important concepts. First, it made it theoretically possible for Native American nations or organizations to contract for educational services with the Department of the Interior. Second, the Act reaffirmed the continuing legal responsibility of both the federal government and the states to provide education for Native Americans. These policies served to further support the boarding school approach, and during the period 1950–1975 the number of students attending off-reservation boarding schools increased. The Bureau of Indian Affairs maintained direct responsibility for the education of 52,000 Native American children. Of these, more than 35,000 were enrolled in boarding schools (Noriega, 1992, p. 385). Many of the older boarding schools were completely dilapidated and functioned more as holding pens than as schools, although a few, such as the Institute of American Indian Art in New Mexico, were very modern, having been recently constructed or refurbished (Bowker, 1993; Noriega, 1992). Despite continuous indications that the relocation experience was a disaster, for both the Native American individuals involved and their respective Native American nations, relocation programs were maintained up until 1980.

By 1980, ongoing federal pressure had resulted in the relocation to cities of slightly over half of all Native Americans, approximately 880,000 of the 1.6 million reflected in the 1980 census (Robbins, 1992, p. 99). Adjustment to urban living was often difficult for relocated Native Americans and their families, and created great pressures on women to deny their Native American identity. Many became alienated from their traditions and were rejected by Native Americans who remained on the reservation. Those who maintained contact with their relatives, both on reservations and those living in urban areas, were more successful in adjusting to a new way of life. Moreover, access to education and jobs meant that Native American women developed skills and independence that might have eluded them in the reservations' economic and social structures (Green, 1992, p. 87).

These relocation policies backfired on the U.S. government. Instead of creating a better atmosphere for assimilation, they produced a new population of educated Native American women who turned their newfound skills into tools for political and cultural activism (Green, 1992, p. 18). Nevertheless, the relocation presented Native American nations with new battles for survival. Native women met the challenge both on and off the reservations (Green, 1992; Jaimes & Halsey, 1992), though they had to make many personal sacrifices. For example, Menominee activist Ada Deer, who helped restore federal recognition to her nation, describes her experience:

> As a teenager, I saw the poverty of the people—poor housing, poor education, poor health. I thought, this isn't the way it should be. . . . I wanted to help the tribe in some way. . . . People said I was too young, too naive . . . so I dropped out of law school. That was the price I had to pay to get involved. . . . I spent six months in Washington influencing legislation and mobilizing the support of our people throughout the

country. . . . The land was restored to trust status. . . . Where did the manpower and the woman power come to accomplish this? It came from the people. (Green, 1992, p. 88)

COMING FULL CIRCLE AND LOOKING TO THE GRANDMOTHERS: CONTEMPORARY NATIVE AMERICAN WOMEN AND EDUCATION

During the late 1960s and the 1970s, Native American educators, along with Native political activists, became increasingly active in promoting the rights of Native Americans and calling for national attention to their plight (Bowker, 1993, p. 23). Native American activist groups such as the American Indian Movement (AIM) and Women of All Red Nations (WARN) grew out of the urban Native communities created by the relocation programs. These organizations and others encouraged Native Americans to stand up for their rights and to resist any further destruction of their cultures and land. AIM staged sit-ins and walk-outs in secondary and some elementary schools, where parents and students demanded greater curriculum relevance and increased Native involvement in school affairs. During this period of "Indian activism," a number of Native American educational organizations were established, including the national Indian Education Association and the Coalition of Indian Controlled School Boards (Bowker, 1993, p. 23).

The U.S. government, in another attempt to assimilate Native Americans through education, passed the 1975 Educational Assistance Act. This was the educational component of the Self-Determination Act, which was designed to provide Native American nations with more control over their reservations, including schools. The act was much criticized, especially by Native women connected to the alternative schools called "Survival Schools," who felt that the act was no more than another form of colonial domination. Through their work with the Survival Schools, this group of Native American women had come to believe the U.S. government wanted to train a selected group of Native American educators who would see themselves and their Native nations through the eyes of the colonizer. This would be the group from which the U.S. government would select Native American educators, place them in charge of Indian education, and have them carry out the 1975 Education and Self-Determination Acts (Bowker, 1993, p. 25). As Phyllis Young, an American Indian movement activist, explains:

> Aside from some cosmetic alterations like the inclusion of beadwork, traditional dance, basket weaving and some language classes, the curriculum taught in Indian schools remained exactly the same, reaching the same conclusions, indoctrinating children with exactly the same values as when the schools were staffed entirely by white people. . . . You've got to hand it to them in a way. It's really a perfect system of colonization, convincing the colonized to colonize each other in the name of "self-determination" and "liberation." (Noriega, 1992, p. 387)

Government policies under the Reagan and Bush Administrations proposed that Native American students would succeed more if they attended mainstream public schools. This led to a government effort to close all Bureau of Indian Affairs boarding schools and eventually reservation day schools, regardless of their success rates, and mainstream Native American students into public schools. Public schools have been a source of much conflict and tension for both female and male Native American students. Teachers, textbooks, and curriculum in public schools have been programmed to bring about the adoption of values such as competitiveness and individualism. Native American students come from homes and communities that value cooperation and positive interpersonal relationships. The results of this conflict, especially for female Native American students, has been high dropout rates, low achievement levels, and poor self-esteem. Public schools have often become places of discomfort for Native American youth (Bowker, 1993; DeJong, 1993).

Native American education has not been a major priority of the presidential administra-

tions of the past two decades. Currently the majority of Native American students are enrolled in public schools (Bowker, 1993, p. 28), while federal funding for Native American education continues to suffer a steady decline. At present there are 106 Bureau of Indian Affairs elementary and secondary schools and sixty tribally controlled schools.

Native American women continue to play an important role in the education of their people. Many have come to understand and seek to preserve the traditional roles women held in the past, and have sought out women elders from their families and communities to instruct them in maintaining that knowledge. Some, such as Beverly Hungry Wolf (Blackfeet) and Navajo Ruth Roessel (1981) have become authors, thereby sharing their knowledge of Native American women's traditions. Native American women have become involved with their nation's political affairs and have been elected to leadership positions. Currently, approximately 12 percent of the five hundred or so federally recognized Native American and Alaskan Native nations have female leadership (Green, 1992, p. 97).

Despite the changes in government education policy from the reservation era to contemporary times, Native American women maintain their responsibilities as the keepers of their culture, working for the revitalization of the languages, arts, and religious practices of their people, with the focus always on future generations: "It was our grandmothers who held on to what they could of our identity as a People. . . . Oftentimes the fire grew dim, but still our grandmothers persisted. We were taught that the time we are in is only borrowed from future generations" (Green, 1992, p. 93). Native women today draw on the same inner strength that sustained female Native students attending the off-reservation boarding schools of the late nineteenth and early twentieth centuries. A traditional Cheyenne saying reflects the reality of Native American women: "A people are not defeated until the hearts of its women are on the ground." As long as Native American women assert their traditional rights and assume their traditional responsibility of being the central voices of their communities, Native American nations will survive and their women's voices will remain loud and strong.

REFERENCES

ALLEN, P. G. (1989). Introduction. In P. G. Allen (Ed.), *Spider Woman's granddaughters* (pp. 1–21). Boston: Beacon Press.

ALMEIDA, D. A. (1992). *The role of western Massachusetts in development of American Indian education reform through the Hampton Institute's summer outing program (1878–1921).* Unpublished doctoral dissertation, University of Massachusetts, Amherst.

BOWKER, A. (1993). *Sisters in the blood: The education of women in Native America.* Newton, MA: WEEA.

CHURCHILL, W. (1994). *Indians are us? Culture and genocide in Native North America.* Monroe, ME: Common Courage Press.

CHURCHILL, W., & LaDUKE, W. (1992). Native North America: The political economy of radioactive America. In M. A. Jaimes (Ed.), *The state of Native America: Genocide, colonization, and resistance* (pp. 241–266). Boston: South End Press.

COLEMAN, M. (1993). *American Indian children at school, 1850–1930.* Jackson: University Press of Mississippi.

CROW DOG, M. (1990). *Lakota woman.* New York: Harper Collins.

DEJONG, D. H. (1993). *Promise of the past: A history of Indian education in the United States.* Golden, CO: North American Press.

DELORIA, E. C. (1988). *Waterlily.* Lincoln: University of Nebraska Press.

GIOSEFFI, D. (Ed.) (1993). *On prejudice: A global perspective.* New York: Anchor Books.

GREAVES, T. (Ed.) (1994). *Intellectual property rights for indigenous peoples: A source book.* Oklahoma City: Society for Applied Anthropology.

GREEN, R. (1989). "Kill the Indian and save the man": Indian education in the United States. In P. F. Molin & M. L. Hultgren (Eds.), *To lead and to serve: American Indian education at Hampton Institute 1878–1923* (pp. 9–13). Virginia Beach, VA: Virginia Foundation for the Humanities and Public Policy.

GREEN, R. (1992). *Women in American Indian society.* New York: Chelsea House.

HULTGREN, M. L., & MOLIN, P. F. (1989). *To lead and to serve: American Indian education at Hampton Institute, 1878–1923.* Virginia Beach, VA: Virginia Foundation for the Humanities and Public Policy.

HUNGRY WOLF, B. (1981). *The ways of my grandmothers.* New York: Morrow.

JAIMES, M. A., & HALSEY, T. (1992). American Indian women: At the center of indigenous resistance in North America. In M. A. Jaimes (Ed.), *The state of Native America: Genocide, colonization, and resistance* (pp. 311–344). Boston: South End Press.

LOMAWAIMA, K. T. (1994). *They call it prairie light: The story of Chilocco Indian School.* Lincoln: University of Nebraska Press.

MERIAM, L. (1928). *The problem of Indian administration: Institute for Government Research.* Baltimore: Johns Hopkins University Press.

NORIEGA, J. (1992). American Indian education in the United States: Indoctrination for subordination to colonization. In M. A. Jaimes (Ed.), *The state of Native America: Genocide, colonization and resistance* (pp. 371–402). Boston: South End Press.

REYHNER, J., & EDER, J. E. (1994). A history of Indian education. In J. Reyhner (Ed.), *Teaching American Indian students* (pp. 33–58). Norman: University of Oklahoma Press.

ROBBINS, R. L. (1992). Self-determination and subordination: The past, present, and future of American Indian governance. In M. A. Jaimes (Ed.), *The state of Native America: Genocide, colonization, and resistance* (pp. 87–121). Boston: South End Press.

ROESSEL, R. (1981). *Women in Navajo society.* Rough Rock, AZ: Navajo Resource Center.

STANDING BEAR, L. (1975). *My people the Sioux.* Lincoln: University of Nebraska Press. (Original work published 1933)

TRASK, H. K. (1993). *From a native daughter: Colonialism and sovereignty in Hawaii.* Monroe, ME: Common Courage Press.

Williamsiana Collection, Williams College Archives and Special Collections. Williams, MA: Williams College.

WRIGHT, B. (1992). American Indian and Alaska Native higher education: Towards a new century of academic achievement and cultural integrity. In P. Cahape & C. B. Howley (Eds.), *Indian nations at risk: Listening to the people* (pp. 93–96). Charleston, WV: ERIC Clearinghouse on Rural Education and Small Schools.

ZITKALA-SA (Bonnin, G.). (1993). American Indian stories. In W. G. Regier (Ed.), *Masterpieces of American Indian literature* (pp. 193–238). New York: MJF Books. (Original work published 1921)

CRITICAL THINKING QUESTIONS

1. Many people involved in the Americanization of Native Americans professed to be friends of the Indians. On what social values was their thinking based?

2. What did Native Americans gain as individuals by going to boarding schools? What did they lose as a culture?

3. What did Native American women do to resist Americanization? How has education for Native Americans changed as a result of women's activism? How might other groups use similar strategies to improve their own educational experiences?

Reading 5

Lesbian/Gay Rights and Immigration Policy: Lobbying to End the Medical Model

William B. Turner

In this article, Turner focuses on the ways that U.S. immigration law has historically restricted the entry of gay men and lesbians into the United States.

On 3 June 1977, the United States Immigration and Naturalization Service (INS) denied an immigrant visa to a Filipino woman, Zenaida Porte Rebultan, when she acknowledged that she was a lesbian. Rebultan qualified as a second-preference alien for purposes of immigration because every other member of her immediate family had already moved permanently to the United States. The INS declared her excludable, however, under section 212(a)(4) of the Immigration and Nationality Act of 1965, according to which "aliens afflicted with psychopathic personality, or sexual deviation, or a mental defect" were "ineligible to receive visas and shall be excluded from admission into the United States."[1]

Congress first enacted an exclusion directed in part at lesbian and gay aliens in 1917 and retained it in some form until 1990.[2] Never did the common terms "homosexual," "lesbian," or "gay" appear in immigration law, however. Instead, Congress invariably couched the exclusion of lesbian/gay aliens in medical terms, using psychological classifications that the Public Health Service (PHS) provided and revising the language of the exclusion to stay abreast of changing medical terminology during general revisions of immigration law in 1952 and 1965. The equation of lesbians and gay men with psychopathology apparently seemed quite logical

Source: Journal of Policy History, Vol. 7, No. 2, pp. 208–225. Copyright © 1995 The Pennsylvania State University Press. Reproduced by permission of the publisher.

to government officials who enacted, interpreted, and applied the policy.

That equation was anathema to the activists who swelled the ranks of the militant lesbian/gay rights movement in the wake of the Stonewall riots in June 1969, however. Lesbian/gay lobbyists won a major battle by convincing the American Psychiatric Association (APA) to remove "homosexuality" from its official list of mental disorders in 1973. After the 1976 presidential election, they hoped that, with their newfound access to federal policymakers under the socially liberal Carter administration, they would be able to change discriminatory policies that had rested on the assumption of psychopathology. The ban on lesbian and gay aliens was one such policy.

The INS exclusion, in itself, was hardly the most important policy for lesbian/gay lobbyists during the 1970s. No doubt they could have named more onerous sources of discrimination against lesbians and gay men in the United States. The emphasis that lesbian/gay lobbyists put on immigration policy during the first presidential administration to which they had significant access reflects in part the necessity of fighting the battles that larger events pressed on them, but it also reflects the importance of policies that rested on the presumption of psychopathology.

INS policy toward lesbian and gay aliens relied for its coherence on the congruence between the legal and medical definitions that equated lesbian/gay sexuality with mental illness. Having persuaded the APA to change the medical half of the equation, lesbian/gay lobbyists then seized their opportunity during the Carter administration to attack the legal half of the equation; although not immediately successful in eradicating the policy, they rendered it patently dated and illogical. Thus, over the long term, activists from a relatively unpopular minority effected a slow process of policy change by undermining the original rationale for the policy and lobbying where they had access to policymakers, making the policy virtually impossible for legislators to retain when revising immigration law.

THE STATUTORY BASIS FOR INS POLICY

Congress first enacted legislation that included a provision under which the INS excluded lesbians and gay men in 1917; they revised the wording of that exclusion twice, in 1952 and 1965.[3] In each instance, legislators relied on advice from the PHS in deciding on the terminology for what they considered a medically justified exclusion. The exclusion of lesbians and gay men was never the primary concern for legislators, however; in each instance, broader concerns about undesirable immigrants generally resulted in attempts to create or refine exclusions directed in part at lesbians and gay men. Defining the term "constitutional psychopathic inferiority," which appeared in the 1917 act, for example, the PHS lumped together "the constitutional psychopaths and inferiors, the moral imbeciles, the pathological liars and swindlers, the defective delinquents, many of the vagrants and cranks, and persons with abnormal sexual instincts. The dividing line between these various types is not well defined."[4]

This Progressive Era policy reflected broader fears about sexual impurity as a cause of declining morality and family stability even as rising faith in professional expertise conferred upon eugenicists and psychologists

considerable power to influence policy debates.[5] In the McCarran-Walter act of 1952, similar concerns about family stability, combined with worries about national security, contributed to the equation of "sexual perverts" with Communists during the second red scare. Thus, while revising and consolidating numerous laws dealing with immigration and naturalization, including the Internal Security Act of 1950 that expanded grounds for exclusion and deportation in the interests of national security, Congress followed the advice of PHS doctors in substituting the term "psychopathic personality" for the language of the 1917 act.[6] Thus, in both its original formulation and its first revision, the exclusion of lesbian and gay aliens was consistent with the broader motivations and attitudes toward immigration that produced the legislation in which it appeared.

By the time of the 1965 immigration reform, however, the maintenance of medical exclusions stood in contrast to the generally liberalizing motivation behind the bill. President Johnson requested the reform in order to dispense with the national-origins quota system, the racism of which had become unacceptable to many with the advent of the African-American civil rights movement. He assured members of Congress, however, that "this bill would not alter in any way the many limitations in existing law which prevent an influx of undesirables."[7] Again the PHS provided the term, "sexual deviation," that appeared in the 1965 law.[8] Even as they removed exclusions based on race, then, Congress moved to tighten the exclusion based on sexuality as psychopathology.

With this revision, beyond simply asking the PHS for the latest medical term to cover sexual behavior as psychopathology, Congress also specified that the new law aimed to resolve the ambiguity that the Ninth Circuit Court of Appeals had found in 1962, when it enjoined the application of McCarran-Walter to lesbian and gay aliens because it found the term "psychopathic personality" unconstitutionally vague.[9] As it happened, however, Congress need not have worried about this decision, because in 1967 the Supreme Court found the same term acceptable.

In the 1967 case, *Boutilier v. INS,* the plaintiff, a Canadian citizen, had applied for citizenship some twelve years after moving to the United States, where his parents and three siblings lived.[10] His initial affidavit describing an arrest for sodomy, a charge ultimately dismissed, precipitated a further investigation in which Boutilier freely admitted to repeated sexual contact with other men both before and after his arrival in the United States. A PHS doctor issued a Class A Certification finding Boutilier deportable because he had fallen within the category of "psychopathic personality" at the time of his entry, and therefore should have been excluded in the first place. The Court denied Boutilier's claim that the term "psychopathic personality" was void for vagueness. Thus, by 1967, fifty years after its initial enactment, the INS policy of excluding lesbian and gay aliens appeared well established, resting on a firm basis of both legal and medical opinion.

THE LESBIAN/GAY RIGHTS MOVEMENT AND THE MEDICAL MODEL

Among the movements of the civil rights era, the lesbian/gay rights movement was a late bloomer. Although, as John D'Emilio has shown, important organizations dedicated to lesbian/gay civil rights had existed since the early 1950s, they had little influence on public policy.[11] The Stonewall riots of 1969 mark the beginning of the modern lesbian/gay rights movement. In June of that year, patrons of the Stonewall Inn, a gay bar in New York's Greenwich Village, rioted during an otherwise routine police raid. In the aftermath of the riots, a number of advocacy groups sprang up, many of which had significant impact at the local level during the early 1970s.[12] With the conservative response to the civil rights revolution during the Nixon and Ford presidencies, however, lesbian and

gay activists' prospects for influence at the federal level seemed bleak.[13]

But advocates of lesbian/gay rights by no means lacked potential targets in places other than the federal government. High on their list of priorities was the official designation of same-sex desire as a mental illness per se. The equation of same-sex desire with psychopathology was a highly effective prop to discrimination, serving as it often did to convince lesbians and gay men themselves that they were sick.[14] Relying on direct lobbying, friends in high places, and literal disruption of meetings, lesbian/gay activists persuaded the American Psychiatric Association (APA) to remove homosexuality from its official list of mental disorders, the Diagnostic and Statistical Manual (DSM), in 1973. Beginning the next year, the National Gay Task Force (NGTF) and the Lambda Legal Defense and Education Fund, two newly formed lobbying groups, began to argue that the INS should use the APA's decision as the basis for ceasing enforcement of the exclusion of lesbian and gay aliens.[15]

LOBBYING THE CARTER ADMINISTRATION

While there seemed to be little hope for change in policies that discriminated against lesbians and gay men under Gerald Ford's administration, the presidential election of 1976 presaged greater success. Activists forced the major party candidates to address lesbian/gay rights issues, and while Ford equivocated Carter clearly expressed his support for lesbian/gay rights. Speaking to Tom Snyder during an interview for "The Tomorrow Show," Carter said, "I favor the end of harassment or abuse or discrimination against homosexuals." As he notes in his memoirs, Carter described himself as a fiscal conservative but a social liberal, giving lesbian/gay activists reason to hope that he would advance lesbian/gay rights as an area in which he could achieve significant human and civil rights gains at no financial cost.[16] Perhaps even more encouraging, Carter stated his opposition to discrimination in response to a question about Leonard Matlovich, who at the time was contesting his discharge from the Air Force for being gay.[17] Although the psychopathology argument provided part of the justification for the military's policy, Carter predicated his only reservations about ending that policy on his concerns about the potential for blackmail.

And initial signs from the Carter administration seemed to confirm activists' hopes. As part of a larger program to allow lesbian and gay lobbyists to discuss grievances with federal agencies, Marilyn Haft, assistant director of the White House Office of Public Liaison, arranged a meeting on 12 July 1977 between representatives of the INS and the NGTF. Such initiatives on the part of sympathetic White House staffers in the Carter administration were a promising sign to lobbyists. Haft, having written the ACLU's *The Rights of Gay People* and served on the board of the Gay Rights National Lobby, seemed especially likely to prove helpful.[18]

The willingness of sympathetic aides such as Haft and Assistant to the President for Public Liaison Margaret Costanza to help lesbian/gay lobbyists did not necessarily carry over into other parts of the administration, however. Leonel Castillo, newly appointed commissioner of the INS, and David Crosland, general counsel for the INS, were both present at the White House meeting, but to no avail from the lobbyists' perspective. Although Costanza asserted that the meeting had "prompted changes in Immigration procedures," representatives from the NGTF saw no changes at all stemming from the meeting with Castillo.[19]

Whatever the results in terms of policy, both lobbyists and administrators clearly established their positions on the question at this meeting. Lesbian/gay activists outlined their argument in favor of dropping the ban. Apparently assuming that the APA's decision had obviated any possible defense of "sexual deviation" as a medical classification, they fo-

cused on the requirement for exclusion on the basis of moral turpitude, citing the decriminalization of private, consensual homosexual acts in nineteen states and a New York decision finding that a conviction for homosexual conduct did not constitute sufficient grounds for refusing admission to the state bar because of moral turpitude. Further, they noted that in August 1976, after two federal district courts found that homosexual behavior failed to constitute evidence of bad moral character, the INS had stated that homosexuality was no longer grounds for denying an application for naturalization on the basis of moral turpitude. This decision created the absurd situation that an alien who was ineligible to enter the country could successfully apply for naturalization if he or she managed to slip past customs officers and border guards. Finally, the memo argued that the Supreme Court's decision in *Boutilier* did not bind the INS, citing the INS's decision that neither adultery nor fornication provided sufficient ground for deportation despite previous court rulings to the contrary.[20]

Officials at the INS and the Justice Department remained unconvinced. Both of the court rulings that the INS had disregarded came from federal district courts, and thus were binding only in limited jurisdictions, while the Supreme Court's decision in *Boutilier* applied nationally.[21] Another major problem for the lobbyists' argument lay in the fact that the court rulings that the INS disregarded were interpretations of the moral turpitude clause, not specific bans on adulterers and fornicators, whereas the Court in *Boutilier* had found just such a specific ban on "homosexuals," leaving the INS less room to revise its policies in light of changing social standards.

Part of the problem that lesbian/gay lobbyists faced in 1977 was the dearth of specific cases with which to dramatize the issue. One of the supposed benefits of medical classifications was the relative certainty they seemed to offer in implementation. As the INS had discovered, however, one peculiarity of discrimination based on sexual orientation, as

opposed to race or gender, is that discriminatory policies can be very difficult to enforce. Although PHS doctors had claimed in
1952 that their diagnostic tools would allow
them to detect even some "homosexuals"
who were unaware of their own "perversion,"
in the absence of some visible evidence or
voluntary acknowledgment, any lesbian or
gay man could sail past the INS without difficulty.[22] With lobbyists suddenly calling for
an end to the policy, the INS and the Justice
Department claimed this relative unenforce-
ability as a mitigating factor in supporting
their decision to continue the ban. They
stated that the INS had excluded only thirty-
one aliens for all medical and psychiatric
reasons between 1971 and 1978. But, as *The
New Republic* pointed out, most of those
whom INS officers detained for suspicions of
"sexual deviation" chose to leave the country
voluntarily rather than endure the potentially lengthy process of a formal examination and hearing; thus, they escaped official
notice altogether.[23]

GETTING DOWN TO CASES:
REBULTAN AND HILL

At the time that NGTF representatives met
with Castillo and White House staffers, none of
the parties knew of a particular case in which
an alien's exclusion for "sexual deviation" had
created real hardship for both the alien and
her family. This was the case of Zenaida Rebultan. When the INS denied her a visa in June
1977, Rebultan was the only member of the immediate family left in the Philippines. This situation left the entire family, especially Maria
Dionicia, Zenaida's mother, distraught. In May
1978 they contacted Congressman John McFall
(D-Calif.), who apparently tried to help, but
without success.

Both the Rebultans and the NGTF let the
issue drop for some time, until specific events
revived it with greater urgency. For the Rebultans, Zenaida's separation from the rest
of the family became increasingly disheart-

ening when Maria Dionicia fell ill in April
1979, and she began to worry that she might
never see her daughter again. This situation
spurred Stanley Rebultan, one of Zenaida's
brothers, to renew his efforts to secure a visa
for Zenaida. Beginning in May 1979, Rebultan apparently wrote to every public official
who he thought might help, including President Carter, as well as the American Psychiatric Association, and he told local lesbian/
gay groups about his sister's plight. Word of
Zenaida's situation reached administration
staffers who handled lesbian/gay issues through
activists who were organizing the 1979 National March on Washington for Lesbian and
Gay Rights.[24]

Despite certain limitations in his grasp of
English, Rebultan displayed considerable
rhetorical skill in presenting his sister's case.
Writing to Senator Alan Cranston, he stated
that Zenaida "is left behind with no one to
comfort her in time of needs. The Rebultan
Family who choosed [sic] to adopt the great
United States—the leader of Human Rights
abroad and the defender of democracy, as
their future homeland are denied the freedom
to be with one of the members of their family
just because she is a lesbian."[25] Variations on
this basic argument, in which he appealed to
the Carter administration's stand on human
rights, appear in every letter that Rebultan sent
to a U.S. official, including President Carter
himself.[26] Another argument that he failed to
develop as clearly was the obvious contradiction between the effects of the lesbian/gay exclusion in Zenaida's case and the strong
presumption built into U.S. immigration law
in favor of family reunification.[27]

Yet, even as various officials regretfully informed Stanley Rebultan that they could do
nothing for his sister, a new controversy arose
that created some hope. On 13 June 1979,
when British citizens Carl Hill and Michael
Mason arrived at the San Francisco airport
on their way to participate in the Gay Freedom Day Parade, an INS officer stopped Hill,
who sported a Gay Pride button. When Hill
acknowledged being gay, the officer detained
him pending an examination by a Public

Health Service (PHS) doctor. Hill filed suit, winning a temporary restraining order on 26 June that prevented the PHS from examining him.[28]

Charles Brydon and Lucia Valeska of the NGTF took advantage of the situation to suggest once again that the INS simply drop the exclusion policy altogether. The position that they described to Michael Egan at the Justice Department seemed much stronger than that which lobbyists had taken in 1977. *Boutilier* was no longer on point, the NGTF argued, because there the court had based its decision on the meaning of "psychopathic personality" in the McCarran-Walter Act; the 1965 revision, however, had added "sexual deviation" as a separate category. Citing the APA's 1973 decision to remove homosexuality from the Diagnostic and Statistical Manual (DSM), Brydon and Valeska argued that no basis existed for the claim that homosexuality necessarily constituted evidence of a "psychopathic personality." Further, both the Supreme Court in *Boutilier* and Congress in the 1965 Immigration Act had relied heavily on testimony from the PHS to establish that homosexuality constituted a psychopathology. The PHS, in turn, relied exclusively on the DSM for its psychiatric diagnostic categories. After Hill filed suit, the PHS began to argue that it should be relieved of responsibility for examining suspected "homosexual" aliens anyway, and the 1965 act gave the PHS sole authority to determine medical categories for exclusion. Given the INS's position that medical excludability was the sole basis for its policy on lesbian and gay aliens, and its previous decisions to change its policies on adultery and fornication administratively, there seemed to be no reason why it could not now do the same with respect to "homosexuality."[29]

Egan replied that Congress, not the PHS, had created the category "sexual deviation" and only Congress could change it. He cited the Supreme Court's opinion in *Boutilier* to the effect that, while Congress had relied on information from the PHS in creating the category, its purpose had been to establish an exclusion-ary standard rather than a diagnostic category. Thus, changes in diagnostic categories alone could not serve as the basis for a change in policy, especially given Congress's long-recognized plenary power to exclude aliens.[30]

It seemed to Brydon and Valeska at this point that officials at the INS had adopted a "'man the barricades' attitude" and intended to defend the policy at any cost.[31] To be sure, in considering how to deal with the Hill case, Philip Heymann of the Justice Department's Criminal Division developed four possible responses, none of which included simply dropping the ban.[32] But Heymann's job was to plan trial strategy for his defendant, the federal government, not to decide the merits of the INS policy.

Heymann argued, and Egan agreed, that the best option was for the INS to retract its referral of Hill to the PHS for examination, then proceed against him through the Board of Immigration Appeals; there the burden of proof would fall on Hill to refute the assertion of excludability, a near impossibility given that he had made the sworn statement to an INS officer that he was gay. In outlining this position, David Yeres, Egan's assistant, warned:

> If you choose to adopt this plan, you should be aware that the problem will not be solved by it, but merely deferred. Public Health is rewriting its regulations to prohibit the examination of suspected homosexuals and this situation is bound to reoccur [*sic*]. You suggested, and I agree, that a referral of this problem to the Congress might be appropriate.[33]

Thus, Brydon and Valeska overstated the degree of resistance at the Justice Department. The reason for the official resistance to dropping the ban stemmed from Egan's view that *Boutilier* was relevant and binding, and that Congress, rather than the PHS, was ultimately responsible for the category "sexual deviant." Further, by 20 August Egan and INS General Counsel David Crosland were providing technical assistance to Congress on legislation that would eliminate "sexual deviant" as a category for exclusion.[34] Some members of

Congress, however, agreed with the NGTF that new legislation was unnecessary because, in their view, the INS could simply change the policy on its own. INS officials continued to reject this argument.[35]

DEVELOPING AN INTERIM POLICY

Complicating matters further was the fact that Yeres was right when he wrote that the PHS was rewriting its regulations to prohibit examinations to determine "homosexuality." On 2 August Surgeon General Julius Richmond issued a memo according to which "homosexuality per se will no longer be considered a 'mental disease or defect.'" Richmond noted that "the change will reflect current and generally accepted canons of medical practice with respect to homosexuality."[36]

And here, it seemed, was the ultimate weakness in the idea of medical classification as exclusionary standard. INS administrators found themselves stuck between two conflicting policy mandates with no ready solution. They considered themselves bound by the legal term of art in the 1965 Immigration Act, but they now had no established procedure by which to make the medical determination of "sexual deviation" when the question arose. Leonel Castillo adopted an interim policy, providing that "all persons who are examined by INS officers at ports-of-entry, where the issue of homosexuality is applicable for determination as to admissibility under the Immigration and Nationality Act, will be deferred for further examination. When the legal issues are resolved, the deferred examination will be scheduled."[37] In practice, this policy supposedly meant that suspected "sexual deviants" would be allowed into the country temporarily. In announcing the policy, Castillo stated that it would not allow "sexually deviant" aliens to remain in the country indefinitely.[38]

Regardless of the fact that the new policy would allow only temporary admission to the country, Stanley Rebultan promptly cited the decision in a letter to Consul James D. Mason of the U.S. Embassy in Manila. Mason had written to Rebultan that "the Embassy will review Zenaida's application if she can submit a new psychiatric evaluation with evidence of professional therapy leading to change of behavior."[39] Rebultan would not be so easily deterred, however. He replied that

since the medical examinations conducted by the Embassy panel physician is in accordance with the guidelines established by the United States Public Health Service and the U.S. Surgeon General released a memorandum as of August 2, 1979 stating that "Homosexuality per se will no longer be considered a 'mental disease or defect,'" what is still your basis in not issuing my sister a visa?[40]

What Rebultan failed to point out here was the questionable practice of relying entirely on behavior as an indicator of psychopathology. No one had ever established that Zenaida Rebultan performed any particular behavior, whether characteristic of lesbian sexual practice or not, yet her admission to the United States was contingent on her demonstration that she would not behave according to the assumptions that her diagnosis had created in the minds of U.S. officials.[41]

IMPLEMENTATION OF THE INTERIM POLICY

Even with a visa in hand, however, Zenaida Rebultan might well have had problems getting into the country. Implementation of the new policy did not go well. On 31 August 1979 Arlie Scott, a vice president of the National Organization for Women, joined Brydon and Valeska in writing to Attorney General Benjamin Civiletti to demand that he tell the INS "to take a formal position that lesbians and gay men are no longer excludable." According to the letter, the previous week INS officers had harassed several women who tried to enter the United States from Canada in order to attend the Michigan Women's Music Festival. The officers cited INS instructions from 1952 and asked the women such questions as "Which do you enjoy more, sleeping with a man or a woman?" and "What do you do in bed?" An officer told one woman, "Well, you go back to Canada and get cured, and then you can come to the U.S. for a holiday." Another stated, "You may not enter the U.S. We are not convinced that you are not lesbians."[42] This episode demonstrates vividly the leeway that the exclusion created, especially in the absence of professional application, for reliance on personal prejudice and caprice in implementing policy.

The issue remained unresolved until late December, when the Justice Department concluded that the INS must enforce section 212(a)(4) of the 1965 act regardless of the PHS's position.[43] This decision brought the INS no peace, however. On 1 January 1980, the *New York Times* reported the case of Jaime Chavez, a Mexican tourist who INS officers detained because he was wearing makeup and an engagement ring. The INS required the airline Chavex had used to put him in a hotel room, under guard, for the night. The friends in California who Chavez was visiting, as he did every year for two weeks, hired a lawyer and persuaded Chavez to sue on the grounds that INS officers had enforced the "sexual deviant" exclusion without proper regard for Chavez's rights. Chavez spoke no English, and INS officers had persuaded him to sign a statement acknowledging his sexual orientation as well as to withdraw his application for admission to the country. The Immigration Act had empowered PHS doctors to examine aliens for purposes of medical excludability, but it gave no such authority to INS officers. As Chavez's lawyer put it, "So what you have . . . is these people at the airport being granted psychiatric licenses."[44] Again, INS officers demonstrated that they might frequently prove incapable of enforcing the exclusion in a rational manner.

On 23 January Senator Alan Cranston (D-Calif.) introduced a bill, S. 2210, that would have repealed section 212(a)(4) of the Immigration and Nationality Act. He noted

that "the practical result" of the imbroglio between the INS and the PHS "is that inexpert immigration officers acting alone will make the determination that an arriving alien is to be denied entry on the grounds of homosexuality. The Department of Justice today is preparing enforcement guidelines for immigration officers. This situation is absurd."[45] The Justice Department advised Cranston on the language of the bill, and the administration supported it as consistent with human rights policy, especially the provisions in the Helsinki Final Act that discourage regulations inhibiting the free movement of people. Administration support was lukewarm, however, and Cranston's bill made no progress in the absence of strong pressure from either the administration or lesbian/gay lobbyists, who lacked sufficient clout to demand action.[46]

Meanwhile, Heymann and Egan's strategy of taking the Hill case to the Board of Immigration Appeals paid off on 9 July 1981, when the board decided:

> An applicant for admission can be excluded from the United States as a homosexual under section 212(a)(4) of the Immigration and Nationality Act . . . absent a U.S. Public Health Service Class 'A' Certification where he has made an unsolicited, unambiguous admission that he is a homosexual and where the current U.S. Public Health Service position that homosexuality cannot be medically diagnosed is a matter of record.[47]

And so the matter rested, with hapless lesbian and gay aliens potentially subject to the whims of INS officials, for roughly two years.

Activists in San Francisco pursued the Hill case in federal court, however, winning in 1983. The Ninth Circuit court of appeals found that the statute clearly required the INS to get a Class A certification from the PHS before excluding any alien on medical grounds.[48] Thus, insofar as the PHS refused to issue such certifications for lesbian/gay aliens, those aliens could not be excluded. The month after this decision, however, in an unrelated case the Fifth Circuit court of appeals found precisely the opposite. There the court found no requirement for a PHS certification where, as with "sexual deviation," the only available source of information was the alien's own testimony.[49] Thus, whether lesbian/gay aliens could be admitted to the country came to depend on whether they arrived first in California or Texas. The Supreme Court declined its opportunity to resolve the issue by hearing an appeal of the latter case.[50]

This ambiguity remained in the law until the passage of the 1990 Immigration Act. According to the House report that accompanied it, the 1990 act

> repeals the specific disorders now listed in INA paragraphs 212(a)(1) through (5) as grounds for exclusion. These grounds represent outmoded and inflexible notions of medical diagnoses, and the Committee strongly believes they should be replaced with more enlightened and flexible alternatives that focus on the dangers that may be posed by mental and physical disorders. This bill accomplishes that goal by replacing those five grounds for exclusion with two new activities-based grounds.[51]

To be excludable under the new law, then, aliens not only must be diagnosed as mentally ill, they also must display specific behavior that will constitute a threat to property or to themselves or others.

The 1990 repeal of the ban on lesbian and gay aliens came with broad reforms of immigration law, and with little direct input from lesbian/gay lobbyists, just as its enactment and revisions had. Lesbian/gay lobbying activities were crucial to the ban's repeal, however. Although the trend toward liberalizing immigration law began in 1965, lesbians and gay men were initially excluded from it. Not until activists in a militant movement cast demands for equal treatment in terms of civil rights did they begin to have an effect, although only over the long term, on federal policy.

The removal of "homosexuality" from the *Diagnostic and Statistical Manual* failed to bring about the immediate demise of federal policies that supposedly rested on a medical justification. It is important to note in the present instance, however, that the delay stemmed in part from the simple fact that immigration law generally proved a highly contentious area throughout this period; numerous attempts at general reform failed in Congress.[52] Thus, given that lesbian/gay lobbyists could not force action on the one element of immigration law that they were most concerned with, they had to wait for a broad bill that dealt with immigration policy generally. Even so, the exclusion of lesbian and gay aliens would not have seemed to exemplify "outmoded and inflexible notions of medical diagnoses" if the diagnosis had still existed. Nor would the Surgeon General have been able to respond to a suit challenging the PHS practice of examining aliens suspected of homosexuality by announcing that such practice should cease in order to conform to prevailing medical opinion.

The seventeen-year lag between the American Psychiatric Association's decision in 1973 and the repeal of the policy in 1990 shows both the possibilities and the limitations in changing federal policy for a social movement that must rely more on logic and moral suasion than on electoral clout to pursue its agenda. With the legislative branch largely closed to a minority that was at best unknown to and at worst reviled by many members of the electorate, and an unfavorable decision from the highest court in the land, sympathetic members of the executive branch became the lesbian/gay lobbyists' best hope of ultimately changing the policy.

Over the long run, logic and moral suasion worked slowly but surely for lesbian/gay lobbyists. The obvious contradiction in federal policy that resulted from the APA's 1973 decision created the opening for later lobbying efforts and for the Surgeon General's decision in response to Hill's suit. In the context of general reform, then, the exclusion of lesbian and gay aliens seemed very hard, if not impossible, to justify without the medical model that it had once rested on.

Vanderbilt University

NOTES

1. See telegram, 13 July 1978, from the U.S. Embassy in Manila to Representative John McFall, and Department of State Information Sheet, "Classes of Aliens Ineligible to Receive Visas," enclosure to letter, 29 June 1979, from Lloyd L. DeWitt, Acting Director, Office of Public and Diplomatic Liaison, Visa Services Directorate, U.S. State Department, to Stanley Porte Rebultan (Zenaida's brother), both in file, "Gay Rights," box 7, Bob Malson files, Civil Rights Cluster, Domestic Policy Staff, Jimmy Carter Presidential Library (cited hereafter as CR/DPS JCL). Under the Immigration and Nationality Act of 1965, preference went to adult, unmarried relatives first, of United States citizens and second, of U.S. residents; Rebultan qualified, then, under the latter category.

2. Because my focus here is policy, I gloss over the significant debate among historians of sexuality about the historical specificity of "lesbian," "gay," and "homosexual" as identity categories; probably those who were attracted to others of the same gender in 1917 did not think of themselves as lesbian or gay as we would now use those terms. For an excellent discussion of this issue, see the introduction to George Chauncey's *Gay New York: Gender, Urban Culture, and the Making of the Gay Male World, 1890–1940* (New York, 1994), 12–29.

3. Accounts of immigration legislation and policy are surprisingly difficult to find. See E. P. Hutchinson, *Legislative History of American Immigration Policy, 1798–1965* (Philadelphia, 1981). More cursory, but useful, summaries appear in the legislative history included in House Report 1365 on the McCarran-Walter Act of 1952, published in *U.S. Code Congressional and Administrative News*, 82nd Cong., 2d sess., 1952, 1653–74; and Joyce Vialet and Larry Eig, "Grounds for Exclusion of Aliens Under the Immigration and Nationality Act: Historical Background and Analysis," Report to the Committee on the Judiciary, House of Representatives, 100th Cong., 2d sess., September 1988.

4. Marc Bogatin, "The Immigration and Nationality Act and the Exclusion of Homosexuals: *Boutilier v. INS* Revisited," *Cardozo Law Review* 2 (1981): 362 n. 19.

5. On immigrants as moral threats to the nation, see Linda Gordon, *Woman's Body, Woman's Right: A Social History of Birth Control in America* (New York, 1976), chap. 7, "Race Suicide"; John D'Emilio and Estelle B. Freedman, *Intimate Matters: A History of Sexuality in America* (New York, 1988), 208–15. On hereditarian and eugenic thought in the period generally, see Gordon, *Woman's Body*, 116–35; and Carl Degler, *In Search of Human Nature* (New York, 1991); see also Bogatin, "Exclusion of Homosexuals," 362 n. 19, justifying exclusion of aliens with "tainted blood." Note that the earliest federal immigration legislation (the Alien & Sedition Acts of 1798 excepted), beginning in 1882, dealt with the importation of Chinese and Japanese coolies and prostitutes; immigration and prostitution remained intimately entwined in both the public mind and in federal legislation, whether in fears of the White Slave Trade or the assumption that most johns were foreign-born men, throughout the first decades of the twentieth century. See Hutchinson, *Legislative History*, 80–158.

On the role of doctors in defining and medicalizing deviance, see Alan M. Brandt, *No Magic Bullet: A Social History of Venereal Disease in the United States Since 1880* (New York, 1987), esp. chap. 1; and Michel Foucault, *History of Sexuality, Volume I: An Introduction*, trans. Robert Hurley (1976; New York, 1990).

6. "Evolution of U.S. Immigration Policy," *Congressional Digest* 56 (October 1977): 256; John D'Emilio argues that purges of suspected "homosexuals" from the federal government during the early 1950s reflected anxiety over a perceived loss of masculinity among American men and instability in families, with "homosexuals" threatening private morality in much the same way that communists supposedly threatened the polity. See "The Homosexual Menace: The Politics of Sexuality in Cold War America," in *Passion and Power: Sexuality in History* ed. Kathy Peiss and Christina Simmons (Philadelphia, 1989), 226–40; see also Michael Rogin, "Kiss Me Deadly: Communism, Motherhood, and cold War Movies," *Representations* 6 (1984): 1–36.

7. Lyndon B. Johnson, message to Congress, 15 January 1965, *Congressional Record*, vol. 111, part 1, p. 687.

8. See transcripts for hearings on H.R. 2580, House Committee on the Judiciary, Immigration, and Naturalization Subcommittee, 89th Cong., 1st sess., 4 March 1965, 150, 152.

9. *Fleuti v. Rosenberg*, 302 F 2d 652.

10. 387 U.S. 118 (1967). The following description of the case comes from the text of this decision.

11. John D'Emilio, *Sexual Politics, Sexual Communities: The Making of a Homosexual Minority in the United States, 1940–1970* (Chicago, 1983). The commonsense presumption that before 1969 lesbians and gay men constituted a largely invisible subculture, or that legal and religious proscription served effectively to prevent significant expression of such desire, much less the development of a subculture, has become untenable in light of recent scholarship. The latest addition to a rapidly growing body of work on the subject is Chauncey, *Gay New York*.

12. The best account of the Stonewall riots is Martin Duberman's *Stonewall* (New York, 1993); for briefer accounts of the riots in the larger context of the development of the lesbian/gay rights movement, see Barry D. Adam, *The Rise of a Gay and Lesbian Movement* (Boston, 1987), 75–76; and D'Emilio, *Sexual Politics*, 231–39.

13. By characterizing the Nixon administration as conservative on civil rights issues, I have no desire to dispute Hugh Davis Graham's argument that Nixon helped to consolidate the civil rights revolution. He notes in *The Civil Rights Era: Origins and Development of National Policy, 1960–1972* (New York, 1990) that Nixon legitimated civil rights the way that Eisenhower legitimated the New Deal—by accommodating it on the margins (4). The question of motive is crucial here: Graham refers to "the relative moral indifference that characterized the political calculus of Nixon's domestic policy decisions" (475).

Clearly, political calculus from 1969 to 1974 would have dictated at best agnosticism on the subject of lesbian/gay rights because that group had yet to demonstrate any significant electoral power at the federal level (they seem to have demonstrated such power in 1992, although to what effect remains a highly contentious question). Also, one of Graham's main points is precisely that administrators in the executive branch and the permanent government can make quiet changes that the President would never claim publicly or might even oppose; see his discussion of the expanding authority of the EEOC during the Nixon administration (412–35). As I will describe below, Carter's White House aides worked on behalf of lesbian/gay rights to an extent that Carter himself could probably never have acknowledged very loudly; certainly there is no evidence to suggest that anyone in either the Nixon or Ford administrations was particularly interested in lesbian/gay rights issues. See, for example, Nixon's own discussion of civil rights in *RN: The Memoirs of Richard Nixon* (New York, 1990), 435–45; see also A. James Reichley, *Conservatives in an Age of Change: The Nixon and Ford Administrations* (Washington, D.C., 1981).

14. For two interesting perspectives on this issue, see D'Emilio, *Sexual Politics,* 116–17, 124–25, on the willingness of early homophile organizations to host speakers who told them how sick and immoral they were; and Martin Duberman, *Cures: A Gay Man's Odyssey* (New York, 1991), on Duberman's personal experience with psychoanalysis and the difficulty he had overcoming the psychoanalytic perspective on his sexuality in favor of a political one.

15. On the APA's decision and the events leading up to it, see Ronald Bayer, *Homosexuality and American Psychiatry: The Politics of Diagnosis* (New York, 1981). On lobbying the INS, see "Deviant Customs," *The New Republic,* 21 and 28 July 1979, 9.

Note that the NGTF has since changed its name to the National Gay and Lesbian Task Force, but in the text I will retain the name as it was at the time. The NGLTF is a membership organization dedicated primarily to lobbying, while the Lambda Legal Defense and Education Fund is an organization of professionals, mostly lawyers, who focus on legal issues in the courts. On the NGLTF, see the entry in *Encyclopedia of Homosexuality,* ed. Wayne R. Dynes, 2 vols. (New York, 1990), 2: 845.

16. There is extensive information, including a transcript of "The Tomorrow Show" from 19 March 1976 and a photocopy of an NGTF Action Report comparing Ford's and Carter's statements on the issue, in the file "Gay Rights," Box 7, Malson files, CR/DPS JCL. For Carter's description of himself, see *Keeping Faith: Memoirs of a President* (New York, 1982), 73–74.

17. See Mike Hippler, *Matlovich: The Good Soldier* (Boston, 1989).

18. On the meeting itself, see memo, Marilyn Haft to Margaret Costanza, 31 June 1977, "1/20/77–1/20/81," Box FG-114, White House Central File-Subject File, Jimmy Carter Library (cited hereafter as WHCF-SF JCL); roster for meeting and Bob Malson's notes, 12 July 1977, "Gay Views," Box 8, Malson files, CR/DPS JCL; on other

meetings, see, for example, "National Gay Rights Task Force—White House Meeting—3/26/77, Notes by Bob Malson," and memo, Marilyn Haft to Margaret Costanza, 25 March 1977, both in "Gay Views," For Haft's background, see letters, Haft to Women and Law Conference, 14 February 1977; and to R. Adam Debaugh, Gay Rights National Lobby, 28 June 1977, both in file, "Haft," Box FG 6-1-1, WHCF JCL.

19. Letter, 27 March 1978, Costanza to R. W. Sohns, "1/1/78–6/30/78," Box HU-8, WHCF-SF JCL; "NGTF Position Memorandum on Immigration Policy Regarding Homosexuals," 11 July 1979, "Gay Rights," Box 7, Malson files, CR/DPS JCL.

20. National Committee for Sexual Civil Liberties, "In re Petition to the Immigration and Naturalization Service for Review of its Policies on Homosexuality: Memorandum of Points and Authorities in Support of Petition," 12 July 1977, "Gay Views," Box 8, Malson files, CR/DPS JCL.

21. See letter, undated (July or August 1979), Michael J. Egan, Associate Attorney General, to C. F. Brydon and Lucia Valeska, NGTF, "Gay Rights," Box 7, Malson files, CR/DPS.

22. "Report of the Public Health Service on the Medical Aspects of H. R. 2379, a Bill to Revise the Laws Relating to Immigration, Naturalization, and Nationality, and for other Purposes," in House Report 1365 to the McCarran-Walter Act, published in *U. S. Code Congressional and Administrative News,* 82nd Cong., 2d sess., 1701.

23. *New York Times,* 12 December 1979, 16; "Deviant Customs," 8. It is worth noting here that, according to the 1988 committee report on grounds for exclusion of aliens (see note 3 above), in 1987 alone the INS refused visas to seventy-six people under paragraph (4) of section 212(a) ("psychopathic personality, sexual deviation, or mental defect"), one of the least likely grounds for exclusion. One wonders about such a large disparity between the period 1971 to 1978 and the year 1987.

24. Attached to cover sheet on letterhead of the National Logistics Office for the March, see letters from Rebultan, 12 May 1979, to Cyrus Vance; 4 June 1979, to Lloyd L DeWitt, Acting Director, Office of Public and Diplomatic Liaison, Visa Services Directorate, State Department; 20 June 1979, to Carlos P. Romulo, Philippine Ministry of Foreign Affairs; 8 July 1979, to Richard W. Murphy, U.S. Ambassador to the Republic of the Philippines. Also, letter, 12 June 1979, from Rebultan to Dr. Melvyn Sabshin, Director, American Psychiatric Association. All in "Gay Rights," Box 7, Malson files, CR/DPS JCL.

25. Letter, 12 May 1979, Rebultan to Alan Cranston, "Gay Rights," Box 7, Malson files, CR/DPS JCL.

26. See letter that refers to "your message to President Carter," 4 June 1979, Hodding Carter to Rebultan, "Gay Rights," Box 7, Malson files CR/DPS.

27. On this question, see Lundy, "Immigration Policy," 186–88.

28. "British Man Fights Immigration Policies," *Gay Community News* 7 July 1979, attachment to letter, 13 July 1979, NGTF to Bob Malson, "Gay Rights," Box 7, Malson

files, CR/DPS JCL; see also "Are Homosexuals Illegal Aliens?" *Newsweek,* 27 August 1979, 25.

29. Letter, 11 July 1979, C. F. Brydon and Lucia Valeska to Michael J. Egan, Associate Attorney General, and NGTF Position Memorandum on Immigration Policy Regarding Homosexuals, "Gay Rights," Box 7, Malson files, CR/DPS JCL.

30. Letter, undated, Egan to Brydon and Valeska, "Gay Rights," Box 7, Malson files, CR/DPS JCL.

31. Letter, 13 July 1979, Brydon and Valeska to Malson, "Gay Rights," Box 7, Malson files, CR/DPS JCL.

32. Memo, 27 July 1979, Philip B. Heymann to Michael J. Egan, "Gay Rights," Box 7, Malson files, CR/DPS JCL.

33. Memo, 31 July 1979, David Yeres to Egan, "Gay Rights," Box 7, Malson files, CR/DPS JCL.

34. Memo, 20 August 1979, David Yeres to Bill Heckman, "Gay Rights," Box 7, Malson files, CR/DPS JCL.

35. *New York Times,* 12 August 1979, 20; 27 December 1979, 16.

36. Memo, 2 August 1979, Julius Richmond to Dr. William H. Foege, Director, Centers for Disease Control, and Dr. George I. Lythcott, Administrator, Health Services Administration, "Gay Rights," Box 7, Malson files, CR/DPS JCL.

37. Memo, 10 August 1979, Leonel Castillo to Executive Group, INS, "Gay Rights," Box 7, Malson files, CR/DPS JCL.

38. *New York Times,* 15 August 1979, 14.

39. Letter, 15 August 1979, Mason to Rebultan, "Gay Rights," Box 7, Malson files, CR/DPS JCL.

40. Letter, 28 August 1979, Rebultan to Mason, "Gay Rights," Box 7, Malson files, CR/DPS JCL.

41. On the question of Zenaida's behavior, see letter from Stanley Rebultan to Secretary of State Cyrus Vance, 12 May 1979, in which he describes Zenaida as "a worthy citizen of her country with a clean Police record and a law-abiding citizen." "Gay Rights" file, Box 7, Malson files, CR/DPS JCL.

42. Letter, 31 August 1979, Brydon, Valeska, and Scott to Civiletti, "Gay Rights," Box 7, Malson files, CR/DPS JCL.

43. Memo, 6 June 1980, Stu Elizenstat and Malson to the President, "3/26/80–6/13/80," Box IM-3, WHCF-SF JCL; *New York Times,* 27 December 1979, 16.

44. *New York Times,* 1 January 1980, 40; 3 January 1980, section II, 13.

45. *Congressional Record-Senate,* vol. 126, part 1, p. 486.

46. On the administration's support for the bill, see memo, 6 June 1980, Eizenstat and Malson to the President, "3/26/80–6/13/80," Box IM-3, WHCF-SF JCL; letter, 8 April 1980, Patricia M. Derian, Assistant Secretary for Human Rights and Humanitarian Affairs, State Department, to John Shenefield, Associate Attorney General, Justice Department, "Gays [CF, O/A 728]," Box 211, Stuart Eizenstat files, JCL. On the Justice Department's concerns about the effect of the bill as written, see letters, 18 June 1980, Parker to Cranston and Kennedy, "Gays [CF, O/A 728]," Box 211, Eizenstat files, JCL.

47. *INS Reporter,* Spring–Summer–Fall 1981, 13.

48. *Hill v. United States INS* 714 F.2d 1470 (1983), 480.

49. *Matter of Longstaff* 716 F.2d 1439 (1983), 1451. To point out only one oddity of these two cases, note that the court in *Longstaff* applied to the principle of deference to administrative decisions to the INS's recent conclusion that it required no certificate, whereas the court in *Hill* applied exactly the same principle to the INS's long-standing practice of requiring certificates in all cases of medical exclusion. Compare *Longstaff,* p. 1450, to *Hill,* pp. 1477–78.

50. Vialet and Eig, "Grounds for Exclusion," 82.

51. House Report 101–187, 27 July 1989, reprinted in *U.S. Code Congressional and Administrative News,* 101st Cong., 2d sess., vol. 8, p. 6732. The old paragraphs, 1–5, required exclusion of those who were mentally retarded or insane, or had suffered "one or more attacks of insanity," as well as those "afflicted with psychopathic personality, or sexual deviation, or mental defect," and alcoholics and those addicted to narcotics. The new provisions exclude aliens with a communicable disease that may have some public health impact and those whose disorders are associated with behavior that may pose a threat to the safety, welfare, or property of the alien or others. Also, note that all health exclusions must now rest on PHS regulations, thus precluding the quandary over distinctions between medical diagnoses and legal categories of exclusion. For a discussion of the new exclusions, see Daniel Levy, "Exclusion Grounds Under the Immigration Act of 1990," *Immigration Briefings: Practical Analysis of Immigration and Nationality Issues* 91–8 (August 1991): 4–12.

52. During the Carter administration, enormous problems at the INS itself came to light even as the problem of illegal immigration and dissatisfaction with the 1965 system of legal immigration grew. See the journalistic account, John Crewsdon, *The Tarnished Door: The New Immigrants and the Transformation of America* (New York, 1983). Most attention in this period focused on the problem of revising the preference system for legal immigration and reducing the level of illegal immigration. For repeated efforts to change the law in the early 1980s, see Nancy Humel Montwieler, *The Immigration Reform Law of 1986: Analysis, Text, Legislative History* (Washington, D.C., 1987), 3–22.

CRITICAL THINKING QUESTIONS

1. Explain the medical model of homosexuality and its impact on the immigration of gay men and lesbians to the United States.

2. Explain how government policies regarding the immigration of gay men and lesbians have or have not changed during the twentieth century.

3. Why did it take seventeen years between the declassification of homosexuality as a mental illness and the repeal of the ban on gay and lesbian immigration?

Reading 6

Lifting the Ban on Gays in the Civil Service: Federal Policy Toward Gay and Lesbian Employees Since the Cold War

Gregory B. Lewis

> *In this article, Lewis discusses the ways that U.S. governmental policies have restricted the occupational opportunities of gay and lesbian workers.*

Although the military's ban on lesbians and gays has generated considerable political controversy, many people remain unaware that the federal government also prohibited the employment of gays in the civil service until 1975. This article provides a brief history of the political, bureaucratic, and judicial forces involved in the creation, implementation, and elimination of that prohibition. Though the policy apparently stretches back to the early days of the Republic, its importance exploded in the Cold War hysteria of the 1950s, when "sex perverts" in government erupted as a public policy issue that merged concerns about national security and moral purity. Under pressure from Congress, the U.S. Civil Service Commission and the Federal Bureau of Investigation (FBI) developed techniques to purge lesbians and gay men from the civil service. These bureaucratic efforts persisted long after the political issue had died down. The courts slowly undercut the government's blanket exclusion of homosexuals from federal employment, eventually demanding that the bureaucracy demonstrate a rational connection between homosexual conduct and the efficiency of the service. Although the Civil Service Commission resisted employing homosexuals for years, it institutionalized the

Source: Reprinted from *Public Administration Review,* 57, (September/October, 1997): 387–395. © 1997 by The American Society for Public Administration.

policy change in 1975, and recent progress toward guarantees of equal treatment for gay and lesbian federal employees has occurred primarily through the bureaucracy.

HOMOSEXUALS EMERGE AS A PERSONNEL POLICY CONCERN

The federal government has traditionally required that its employees be of good moral character, a standard that historically excluded known homosexuals. Regulations have long instructed the bureaucracy to deny examinations to applicants, refuse appointments to eligibles, and remove incumbent employees from their jobs for "criminal, infamous, dishonest, immoral, or notoriously disgraceful conduct" (U.S. Civil Service Commission, 1941, 37). We know of isolated dismissals for homosexuality long before the Cold War. (The Interior Department fired Walt Whitman in 1865 and the Post Office discharged the founder of the country's first homosexual political organization in 1925. See Katz, 1976).

It is not clear how actively civil servants attempted to prevent the employment of lesbians and gay men, however. A U.S. Senate report (1950, 10) charged that "some officials undoubtedly condoned the employment of homosexuals . . . particularly . . . where the perverted activities of the employee were carried on in such manner as not to create public scandal or notoriety."

By 1950, however, many in the Senate were impatient with "the false premise that what a Government employee did outside of the office on his own time, particularly if his actions did not involve his fellow employees or his work, was his own business" (U.S. Senate, 1950, 10). The problem began with a list of "admitted homosexuals and suspected perverts" sent by a Senate Appropriations subcommittee to the State Department in 1947 (Wherry, 1950, 1). In early 1950, a State Department official testified before that subcommittee that 91 "sex perverts" had been allowed to resign in the previous three years, and that some had subsequently been reemployed by other federal agencies. The Republicans launched blistering attacks on the Truman administration both for employing these people and for allowing them to resign without permanent blots on their records (although taboos on discussing homosexuality severely limited the publicity). The chairman of the Republican National Committee sent an open letter charging that "the sexual perverts who have infiltrated our Government in recent years . . . [were] perhaps as dangerous as the actual Communists" ("Perverts," 1950).

Republican Senators Wherry and Hill formed a subcommittee to study the issue and called in the experts—military investigators and the Washington, DC, morals squad. These experts "testified that moral perverts are bad national security risks . . . because of their susceptibility to blackmail on threat of exposure of their moral weakness" (Wherry, 1050, 2). This had not been the rationale for the military's ban on homosexuals during the war; indeed, "the words security risk do not appear associated with homosexuality until the late 1940s and early 1950s" (Shilts, 1993, 105), and the navy's secret Crittenden Report, a study of its policies towards homosexuals, attributes the military's concern about homosexuals as security risks to the Senate hearings on the civil service (U.S. Navy, 1957, 8).

Investigators also informed the senators that they had long lists of known or suspected

homosexuals; the navy's list included 7,859 names, with 1,740 living in the Washington, DC area, while the army had 5,000 names in that area alone. Lieutenant Blick of the Washington morals squad (which, Wherry complained, had "only four men . . . who give their full time to detecting and arresting homosexuals") was able to arrest as many as 65 homosexuals in one night, and most homosexuals could be pressured to give names of other homosexuals. Blick estimated that 5,000 homosexuals lived in Washington and that three-fourths of them worked for the government (Wherry, 1950, 5).

Wherry complained that there were inadequate safeguards to prevent reemployment of "moral weaklings" forced out of one agency, and that agencies made inadequate use of these lists of homosexuals. The Civil Service Commission responded with instructions to the agencies requiring them to submit detailed reasons for removals or resignations when those reasons could affect employees' suitability for reemployment so that the commission could prevent it if necessary. Commission Chairman Harry Mitchell also suggested that if local police departments would report all morals arrests with sufficient detail to the FBI, then the FBI could give the information to the Civil Service Commission. The commission could then pass the information on to relevant agencies to remove current employees, and the FBI could maintain the lists so that job applicants could be screened against them. Indeed, Blick testified that he was already furnishing names and fingerprints of all morals arrests to the FBI (Wherry, 1950, 9–10).

The Senate followed with a full-scale inquiry by the Hoey Committee to discover "the reasons why their [homosexuals'] employment by the government is undesirable" (U.S. Senate, 1950, 1). The committee found several reasons. The behavior of homosexuals was criminal and immoral; they lacked emotional stability because "indulgence in acts of sex perversion weakens the moral fiber"; they frequently attempted to seduce normal people, especially the young and impressionable; and they had a "tendency to gather other perverts" around them (U.S. Senate, 1950, 4).

Probably most importantly, homosexuals were seen as security risks. On the one hand, their emotional instability and moral weakness made them "vulnerable to interrogation by a skilled questioner and they seldom refuse to talk about themselves" (U.S. Senate, 1950, 5). (Berube [1990] notes that the skilled questioners had typically been military investigators in positions of authority over suspected homosexuals in the military.) On the other hand, "the pervert is easy prey to the blackmailer"(5). Although the Hoey Committee referred to rings of blackmailers exploiting homosexuals for money, it presented only one example of a homosexual betraying state secrets as a result of blackmail: Colonel Raedl in Austria in 1912. Military intelligence may have presented this as a clear case of homosexual blackmail, but most accounts of the Raedl case suggest that his motive was not blackmail but "money, which he needed to pay for a sybaritic homosexual life" (Buranelli and Buranelli, 1982, 261; see also Rowan, 1939; Dulles, 1963; Ind, 1963; Sith, 1975; and Maclean, 1978). The Hoey Committee also noted several other attempts by "Nazi and Communist agents . . . to obtain information from employees of our Government by threatening to expose their abnormal sex activities," but their language implies that these attempts were unsuccessful (U.S. Senate, 1950, 5).

The Hoey Committee was able to report marked progress since the Wherry-Hill inquiry in April 1950. Federal agencies had handled only 192 homosexual cases in the 38 months before the hearings, but they had processed 382 in the next seven months. Two thirds of the early cases had involved international agencies (the State Department and Economic Cooperation Administration), but efforts to weed out perverts had spread well into domestic agencies after the Senate investigation. FBI checks had also prevented employment for 1700 homosexual applicants between January 1947 and August 1950 (U.S. Senate, 1950, 9).

Still, the Hoey Committee called on agencies to do more to eliminate homosexuals among current employees by aggressively investigating every reasonable complaint. Arrest records were the best starting point for investigations, but there had been inadequate liaison between police and the FBI; not until the Wherry Hill inquiry had the Civil Service Commission learned the names of 457 homosexual federal employees arrested in the nation's capitol during the previous three years.

Adequate procedures . . . [were] established to correct this regrettable situation . . . The FBI obtained all available police records in the District of Columbia of persons who had been charged with perverted sex offenses and this information was furnished promptly to the Civil Service Commission and the other agencies of Government. The FBI also began furnishing to the Civil Service Commission the criminal records of persons currently arrested by the police throughout the country on charges of sex perversion who were known to be Government employees. Upon receipt of that information the Civil Service Commission transmits the data to the employing agency and later checks up with the agency to determine what, if any, action has been taken in each case (U.S. Senate, 1950, 13).

In September 1946, the secretary of the navy had rejected a proposal to turn the navy's list of homosexuals over to the FBI and other government agencies (Berube, 1990, 264), but that decision was apparently taken out of military hands in 1950.

The use of arrest records was no small problem for gay men. In the postwar years, Berube (1990, 259) reports substantial increases in arrests of lesbians and, especially, gay men for "consensual sodomy, sexual perversion, . . . public indecency, patronizing a gay bar, touching in public, or wearing the clothing of the other gender." Washington police averaged 1,000 gay-related arrests per year in the early 1950s, and Philadelphia perhaps 1,200 arrests per year (D'Emilio, 1983a). A single jurisdiction within Los Angeles County arrested 1,000 gay men a year in the early 1960s ("Consenting," 1966). In one large sample of gay men in the early 1970s, one-fourth had been arrested on sex-related charges (Weinberg and Williams, 1974, 185).

The situation for lesbian and gay employees worsened during the first 100 days of the Eisenhower administration. President Truman had instituted a loyalty program for federal employees in 1947. In 1951, he changed the standards for dismissal from "reasonable grounds for belief that the person is disloyal" (Executive Order 9835) to "reasonable doubt as to the loyalty of the person involved" (Executive Order 10241; see U.S. Civil Service Commission, 1952, 33). In 1953, Eisenhower ordered that the government could employ and retain employees only when "clearly consistent with the interests of national security" and for the first time listed sexual perversion as a condition demanding removal from the federal service (Executive Order 10450). Similar regulations applied to private sector employees needing security clearances. During the same period, state and local governments were passing similar regulations. Licensing boards restricted homosexuals from many occupations, and private employers banned homosexuals officially or unofficially. Overall, lesbians and gay men were officially barred from at least 20 percent of the nation's jobs (Berube, 1990, 269–270).

The Civil Service Commission's 1954 annual report indicated 618 dismissals under Executive Order 10450 for sexual perversion, and the commission reported 837 cases by June 1955 (Brown, 1958, 114). After 1955, political interest in employment of homosexuals seems to have died down and it becomes harder to find the number dismissed. However, this is no guarantee that the practice of firing homosexuals diminished. In Senate appropriations hearings, the Department of State reported 18 dismissals in 1959, 16 in 1960, 24 in 1961, 24 in 1962, and 45 in 1963. By 1973, when plaintiffs in a lawsuit against the Civil Service Commission requested the number of gay discharges per year, the commission refused, claiming the request was "burdensome and oppressive" (*Society for Individual Rights v. Hampton,* 63 F.R.D. 399 [1973]). We will probably never know how many gay employees were fired under this policy.

WHY DID THE CRACKDOWN ON GAYS OCCUR?

The fall of Eastern Europe to the Soviet Union and of China to the Communists, the explosion of the Soviet atom bomb, and the conviction of Alger Hiss made Americans warier about their national security, but why did that focus so much attention on homosexuals? D'Emilio (1989) suggests a fear that homosexuals, like Communists, hid their true natures, allowing them to "infiltrate" government in a way other out-groups could not. (One right-wing columnist, cited by Johnson (1994–1995, 50), charged that "an all-powerful, supersecret inner circle of highly educated, socially highly placed sexual misfits in the State Department" controlled foreign policy. Homosexuals were also easier to catch than Communists (they comprised 54 of 66 State Department employees fired under the security regulations in 1950, 119 of 154 in 1951, and 134 of 204 in 1952 (Shilts, 1993, 106) and were so unpopular that even the American Civil Liberties Union (ACLU) supported prohibitions on their employment.

The extremity of the language used to depict homosexuals suggests that more than national security was at stake, however. A 1950 White House staff memo stated that "the country is more concerned about the charges of homosexuals in the government than about Communists" (D'Emilio, 1983b, 13). Johnson argues that publicity about its dismissals of homosexuals "rendered the State Department a dirty joke" and presents a *New Yorker* cartoon in which a job applicant assures a potential employer, "It's true, sir, that the State Department let me go, but that was solely because of incompetence" (1994–1995, 47). The government fired many employees with little conceivable link to national security; the vast majority of dismissals of employees and rejections of applicants were on the basis of suitability rather than national security.

Johnson (1994–95, 46) argues that the ban on gay employees "reflected an underlying anxiety over the bureaucratization and urbanization of Washington, changes largely precipitated by the New Deal and World War II." The great increases in the size of the federal bureaucracy "offered a haven for deviants. . . . Like Communism itself, bureaucracy raised the specter of a face-less, gender-less, family-less welfare state. Homosexual civil servants were seen as the natural conclusion of this frightening trend" (51).

The dramatic social changes brought on by World War II helped build the gay community and increased the general society's perception of it (D'Emilio, 1983a; Berube, 1990). After the war, Americans had to deal with "deep anxieties . . . about the disruptive effects of World War II on family life, sexual mores, and gender norms" (Chauncey, 1993, 175). D'Emilio describes a new "politics of personal life tailored to restore a different form of domestic tranquility": a generous GI Bill of Rights, federal home mortgages, and a propaganda campaign pressuring women out of the workforce, "and extolling the virtues of marriage and childrearing" (1989, 236).

The dark side included "a genuinely national hysteria in the winter of 1949 to 1950" about sex murders of women and children, fed by grisly newspaper stories which indicated that the murderers were "men who had lost control of deviant sexual impulses" (Chauncey, 1993, 163, 161). Newspaper coverage suggested that all sexual deviates had the potential to degenerate into sexual psychopaths, and "press campaigns against sex criminals frequently turned into campaigns [and crackdowns] against homosexuals" (Chauncey, 1993, 172). Between 1947 and 1955, 21 states and the District of Columbia passed sexual psychopath laws, and "the terms child molester, homosexual, sex offender, sex psychopath, sex degenerate, sex deviate, and sometimes even communist became interchangeable in the minds of the public, legislators, and local police" (Berube, 1990, 258). The women's military services had urged fairness and restraint in dealing with lesbians during the war, but by the 1950s depicted them as "sexual vampires: manipulative, dominant perverts who greedily seduce young and innocent women" (Berube and D'Emilio, 1984, 763).

THE ROLE OF THE CIVIL SERVICE COMMISSION

The crackdown against homosexuals began in the Senate and was stoked by the political rhetoric of the 1952 election campaigns. The Civil Service Commission and the FBI expanded their efforts to purge homosexual employees in response to political demands, and the agencies dismissed gay employees when the pressure was high. When homosexual civil servants ceased to be a political issue, the commission stopped gathering information on gay dismissals leaving us with little information about the bureaucracy's continued response.

The public administration community cannot entirely escape responsibility for this period, however. No loud voices arose arguing that homosexuality had nothing to do with merit or neutral competence. Even those who attacked the loyalty-security programs had little to say about homosexuals (e.g., Brown, 1958; Bontecou, 1953). FBI Director J. Edgar Hoover played a leading role in justifying the crackdown and pursued homophile and gay liberation organizations for decades (perhaps in response to a fear that a small homophile magazine, *One*, would "out" him as a homosexual; see Shilts, 1993, 110).

Efforts to organize homosexuals to fight federal policy proved unsuccessful in the 1950s because of fear of the consequences (D'Emilio, 1983a, 62). A campaign began in the early 1960s after Frank Kameny, an astronomer with a Harvard Ph.D., lost a three year court battle to retain his job with the U.S. Army Mapping Service. With Bruce Scott, he formed the Mattachine Society of Washington and launched efforts to meet with top government officials to discuss the employment ban (D'Emilio, 1983a, 154). The society argued that homosexuals were a minority group and that federal employment policies toward gays were equivalent to racial discrimination. Kameny testified before a congressional committee in August 1963, and the society picketed the White House repeatedly in the summer of 1965 (Johnson, 1994–95, 57, 59–60).

The Mattachine Society finally achieved a meeting with a committee from the Civil Service Commission in the fall of 1965, prompting the first full justification of the policy. After the meeting, Commission Chairman John W. Macy, Jr., wrote to the Mattachine Society completely rejecting their contention that the exclusion of homosexuals constituted discrimination against an oppressed minority, and claiming that there was no such thing as a homosexual. Instead, there were only homosexual acts, and the attempt to define people with homosexual inclinations as a minority group was an attempt to excuse them from taking responsibility for their immoral actions (Macy, 1966).

Since the concern was with homosexual acts, the Civil Service Commission needed to investigate the acts in detail to determine whether the "deviate sexual behavior" was "isolated, intermittent or continuing . . . aggressive or passive," and to investigate as well a variety of aggravating and mitigating circumstances. They also sought to determine "the extent or effect of rehabilitative efforts, if any, and the admitted acceptance of, or preference for homosexual relations" (Macy, 1966, 44). Since commission policy seems to have been that any homosexual conduct disqualified an individual for federal employment, it is unclear why this level of detail was needed, but civil service investigators wanted to know names, dates, and locations of sexual contacts as well as the specific sex acts performed (Ridgeway, 1964).

According to Macy, employment of homosexuals impeded "the efficiency of the service" because of the revulsion of other employees by homosexual conduct and consequent disruption of service efficiency, the apprehension caused other employees by homosexual advances, solicitations or assaults, the unavoidable subjection of the sexual deviate to erotic stimulation through on-the-job use of common toilet, shower, and living facilities, the offense to members of the public who are required to deal with a known or admitted sexual deviate to transact Government business, the hazard that the prestige and author-

ity of a Government position will be used to foster homosexual activity, particularly among the youth, and the use of Government funds and authority in furtherance of conduct offensive both to the mores and the law of our society (Macy, 1966, 44).

As with the military's justification for its exclusionary policy, Macy did not contend that homosexuals lacked the competence to perform their work successfully. The threats to the efficiency of the service arose from the perceptions and prejudices of coworkers and the public (revulsion, apprehension, and offense). As gay employees cannot control those perceptions, the policy punishes them for others' prejudices. Macy's letter shows that he shared those prejudices and viewed homosexuals as uncontrollably driven by their perverted desires.

Macy took offense at the charge that the Civil Service Commission pried into the private sex lives of applicants or attempted to ferret out homosexual conduct. He contended that the government had no interest in "private sexual behavior between consenting adults." His definition of "truly private," however, was that "it remains undisclosed to all but the participants" (Macy, 1966, 4445). If gay people were unable to keep their sex or love lives complete secrets from everyone, they became the government's business. In anticipation of today's "don't ask, don't tell" policy, Macy argued that people who publicly proclaimed their homosexuality, especially if they argued that they were not sick or emotionally disturbed, were clearly unsuited for federal employment. "The self revelation by announcement of such private sexual behavior and preferences is itself public conduct which the Commission must consider in assaying an individual's suitability for Federal employment" (Macy, 1966, 45). In an interview three years later, the Civil Service Commission's Director of Personnel Investigations admitted that homosexual employees were no less efficient than heterosexuals, but argued that since the public still viewed homosexuals as repugnant, the commission should continue to disqualify them "in order to retain public confidence" ("Government-created," 1969, 1742).

THE ROLE OF THE COURTS

Few homosexuals fought their dismissals in court in the 1950s; those who did had little success. The courts at that time adhered to what Rosenbloom and Carroll (1995) call the "doctrine of privilege." This doctrine states that since federal employment was not a right, the government could impose essentially any conditions it chose on that employment. The one relevant protection veterans had was that they could not be dismissed unless the dismissal promoted "the efficiency of the service." However, the courts generally showed great deference to administrators in determining what affected efficiency. In *Dew v. Halaby*, 317 F.2d 582 (DC Cir. 1963), cert. dismissed, 379 U.S. 951 (1964), an air traffic controller with veterans' preference was fired when evidence emerged that he had "committed at least four unnatural acts with males . . . when he was 18 or 19," eight years prior to his firing (*Dew*, 583). A psychiatric evaluation showed that Dew was now happily married with a child, was emotionally stable, did not have a "homosexual personality disorder," and was performing successfully on his job. However, his appeals examiner concluded that to "require employees to work with persons who have committed acts that are repugnant to established and accepted standards of decency and morality can only have a disrupting effect upon the morals and efficiency of any organization" (*Dew*, 587). The appellate court saw nothing arbitrary and capricious in firing a competent employee because the civil service demanded "character as well as fitness" and his homosexual conduct, no matter how far in the past, showed a lack of character (*Dew*, 588). [1]

By the mid-1960s, many courts had begun constitutionalizing public employment cases (Rosenbloom and Carroll, 1995), a trend the *Harvard Law Review* calls a move from a "private sector" to an "individual rights" vision ("Developments," 1984). Gays were a beneficiary of this trend. When Mattachine Society cofounder and federal job applicant Bruce Scott refused to answer unspecified evidence that he was a homosexual, claiming his sexual orientation was irrelevant to his job performance, the Civil Service Commission disqualified him from federal employment based on "immoral conduct." In *Scott v. Macy*, 349 F.2d 192 (DC Cir. 1965), the Washington DC court of appeals ruled that the immoral conduct charge stigmatized Scott by disqualifying him from federal employment and jeopardizing his chance of finding employment elsewhere. This damaged his liberty interests and required the government to make a more compelling case for its actions. The court ruled for Scott, with Judge Bazelon arguing that the Civil Service Commission had to state how the alleged immoral conduct was "related to 'occupational competence or fitness'" (*Scott*, 184–185). However, the concurring opinion only called for greater specification of the immoral conduct charge, and future Chief Justice Warren Burger dissented, arguing that Congress and the executive branch had already decided that homosexual conduct established unsuitability—the Civil Service Commission need not prove it in each case. While the case pointed the direction for the future, it provided a very weak precedent.

Four years later, the Washington DC court of appeals decided the landmark case, *Norton v. Macy*, 417 F. 2d 1161 (DC Cir. 1969). DC morals squad officers arrested Norton, a NASA budget analyst, for picking up another man in a gay cruising area. Police called the NASA security chief to secretly monitor the lengthy police interrogations, then released Norton to several more hours of questioning at NASA headquarters. Although Norton denied being a homosexual, NASA fired him.

In an opinion written by Judge Bazelon, the court ruled that Norton's sexual conduct was largely irrelevant because "the notion that it could be an appropriate function of the federal bureaucracy to enforce the majority's conventional code of conduct in the private lives of its employees is at war with elementary concepts of liberty, privacy, and diversity" (*Norton*, 1165). To justify his dismissal, the government must be able to "demonstrate some 'rational basis' for its conclusion that a discharge 'will promote the efficiency of the service'" (1164).

This came to be known as the "rational nexus" test for determining whether an employee could be dismissed for homosexual or other immoral conduct. Although it was a massive step forward, it did not provide unqualified support for gay employment rights. The *Norton* decision went to great lengths to state that homosexual conduct might be grounds for dismissal in certain circumstances—blackmail risk, personal instability, offensive overtures, or notorious conduct. "Whether or not such potential consequences would justify removal, they are at least broadly relevant to 'the efficiency of the service'" (*Norton,* 1166).

In this case, however, Norton was a competent employee, there were no security concerns, his coworkers were unaware of his conduct, and he did not work with the public. The only justification his supervisor gave for firing Norton was that a repeat episode might "turn out to be embarrassing to the agency" (*Norton,* 1167). Possible embarrassment was not sufficient justification, however. "A reviewing court must at least be able to discern some reasonably foreseeable, specific connection between an employee's potentially embarrassing conduct and the efficiency of the service" (*Norton,* 1167).

In the short run, the *Norton* decision had little apparent impact on the Civil Service Commission or the courts. Both continued to find a rational nexus between homosexual conduct and the efficiency of the service based on the weakest evidence. In *Vigil v. Post Office Department,* 406 F. 2d 921 (10th Cir. 1969), the court upheld the firing of an assistant janitor, ignoring the *Norton* decision because Vigil had been convicted while Norton had not. In *Schlegel v. United States,* 416 F.2d 1372 (Ct. Cl. 1969), the court found the impact of homosexuality on the efficiency of the service to be self-evident: "Any schoolboy knows that a homosexual act is immoral, indecent, lewd, and obscene . . . If activities of this kind are allowed to be practiced in a government department, it is inevitable that the efficiency of the service will in time be adversely affected" (*Schlegel,* 1378). The concurring opinion launched an even sharper attack on the notion that poten-

tial embarrassment to the agency should not be grounds for dismissal: "In this context, the word 'embarrassment' may appear to some the understatement of 1969. . . . The presence of a known homosexual in an executive agency will bring the agency into hatred, ridicule, and contempt, to the grave detriment of its ability to perform its mission" (*Schlegel,* 1382).

THE COURTS AND THE CIVIL SERVICE COMMISSION

In the early 1970s, changing attitudes began to make the Civil Service Commission's exclusion of homosexuals less acceptable. In the wake of the sexual revolution, the Stonewall riots, and the gay liberation movement, more gays were open about their sexuality; homosexuality was no longer a taboo topic that could be dismissed without discussion. The *Washington Post* criticized the policy of the Civil Service Commission, arguing that if homosexuals possessed the necessary skills and "if they conduct themselves like other employees with reasonable circumspection and decorum, their private sexual behavior is their own business" ("Fairness," 1971). A gay rights plank was debated before the 1972 Democratic National Convention, with one speaker attacking injustices against gays, such as the $12 million the Civil Service Commission spent annually investigating gay civil servants (Shilts, 1993, 169).

The commission reluctantly recognized the change in the moral climate of the nation. In its 1971 annual report, it bemoaned "the passing of the day when 'living in sin' meant just that to most people," and regretted a recent set of court cases that limited its ability to consider the morality of the private lives of both homosexuals and heterosexuals. "This does not mean that indiscreet, promiscuous, notorious, criminal, or illegal conduct will not support disciplinary actions. It will and does" (U.S. Civil Service Commission, 1972, 49). The report indicated that the courts were upholding the principle that the government could not fire employees for being gay, but it also emphasized circumstances that would justify not hiring them.

The definitive change in commission policy came as the result of a class action suit brought in San Francisco (*Society for Individual Rights, Inc. v. Hampton*, 63 ER.D. 399 [1973]). A supply clerk, fired because his army discharge papers revealed he was gay, brought suit against the government's blanket exclusion of homosexuals. The court found that the only reason for the dismissal was "the [commission's] view that the employment of such persons will bring the government service into 'public contempt'" (400). The *Norton* decision had already found that ground to be arbitrary and capricious, and the court required the commission to demonstrate a rational connection between homosexual conduct and the efficiency of the service. "The Commission has not met—indeed, it has not even tried to meet—this standard" (*Society for Individual Rights, Inc.*, 401). The court granted class action relief because this was the only way to prohibit the commission "from continuing to ignore the plain holding of *Norton*" (401). It therefore ordered the commission to "forthwith cease excluding or discharging from government service any homosexual person whom the Commission would deem unfit for government employment solely because the employment of such a person in the government service might bring that service into contempt" (*Society for Individual Rights, Inc.*, 402).

On December 21, 1973, the commission issued a bulletin to all agencies stating that they could not "find a person unsuitable for Federal employment merely because that person is a homosexual," but that they could dismiss or refuse to hire a person whose "homosexual conduct affects job fitness—excluding from such considerations, however, unsubstantiated conclusions concerning possible embarrassment to the Federal service." Not all agencies got the message immediately. The General Accounting Office (1974) criticized the agencies' inconsistent and lax investigations: "As an example, in one case three witnesses had stated

that they suspected the subject of being a homosexual because they had observed him living with a man also believed to be a homosexual. The employing agency considered these testimonies to be inconclusive evidence since none of the witnesses had actually observed the subject committing a homosexual act." On July 3, 1975, a press release from the Civil Service Commission announced that a "significant change from past policy—resulting from court decisions and injunction [sic]—provides for applying the same standard in evaluating sexual conduct, whether heterosexual or homosexual." It continued to stress, however, that certain circumstances might justify dismissing a homosexual. The policy did not apply to the FBI or the intelligence agencies.

A major case decided the next year, however, suggested the limits of the *Norton* decision and the commission's policy change (*Singer v. U.S. Civil Service Commission*, 429 U.S. 1034 [1977]). Singer, a gay clerk-typist with the Seattle EEOC, was fired in 1972 for "flaunting" his homosexuality by being active in the gay rights movement, kissing a man in public, and applying for a marriage license. The Civil Service Commission upheld the firing because, among other reasons, "You have flaunted and broadcast your homosexual activities . . . [and] advocated for a socially repugnant concept" (*Singer*, 250). The appellate court found that neither the *Norton* nor the *Society for Individual Rights, Inc.* decisions prevented the use of homosexual conduct as a basis for dismissal in all cases. Applying a balancing test, the court ruled that "the interest of the government as an employer in promoting the efficiency of the service outweighed the interest of its employee in exercising his First Amendment Rights through publicly flaunting and broadcasting his homosexuality" (*Singer*, 256). The Supreme Court vacated the decision the following year but, because the government then dropped the case, the Court did not issue a decision explaining its logic. Subsequent cases suggest that the free speech rights of gay public employees are protected (e.g., *Van Ooteghem v. Gray*, 628 E2d 488 [5th Cir. 1980], cert. denied, 455 U.S. 909 [1982]).

ACTION BY GAY AND EMPLOYEE GROUPS

Given this level of protection, the next focus was on obtaining an executive order prohibiting discrimination on the grounds of sexual preference or orientation. In December 1979, Carter aid Anne Wexler told gay leaders that such an executive order was "under active consideration" but, according to Shilts (1993, 333), Wexler and domestic policy advisor Stuart Eisenstadt then recommended against it as politically unwise. No executive order was issued.

Instead, Eisenstadt approached Alan Campbell, the director of the U.S. Office of Personnel Management, about issuing a memorandum in place of an executive order (Campbell, 1993). Campbell's memo was essentially a gloss on 5 U.S.C. section 2302(b)(10) (prohibited personnel practice 10), which prohibits federal employees from discriminating for or against other employees or applicants "on the basis of conduct which does not adversely affect either the employee's own job performance or the performance of others." According to Campbell's memo, this meant that "applicants and employees are to be protected against inquiries into, or actions based upon, non-job-related conduct, such as religious, community or social affiliations, or sexual orientation" (Campbell, 1980). Theoretically, gay employees could fight against an adverse action that they felt was discriminatory by claiming it was a prohibited personnel practice. In practice, few cases have raised this issue.

Pressure continues for an executive order prohibiting discrimination on the basis of sexual orientation in federal employment. In the 1984 presidential campaign, several Democratic candidates discussed such an order favorably (Shilts, 1993, 453). In 1992, Vice President Quayle stated that "the Bush-Quayle administration has a good record in implementing nondiscrimination against gays and lesbians" (Freedland, 1992, A19). Many expected President Clinton to issue an executive order on nondiscrimination in the civil service. Indeed, the first page of briefing books Clinton's cabinet appointees received asked them to consider what steps they would take to protect gay and lesbian employees in their agencies from discrimination (Hattoy, 1993). The debacle of the gays in the military issue, however, indicated the political danger of an executive order.

In November 1993, openly gay congressman Barney Frank wrote to OPM Director James King requesting both clarification on "federal laws and personnel procedures regarding discrimination based on sexual orientation," and a formal notification to all federal agencies about "the state of these rules and procedures." Instead, OPM Director King responded in a letter to Frank. Rather than issuing guidance to other agencies, King stated, "I like to view OPM as a model agency and see my role as working with all of our employees to assure that we conduct ourselves in such a way that other agencies choose to adopt our methods of operation" (King, 1994). He reiterated the Campbell memo, noting that "OPM has long taken the position that [prohibited personnel practice 10] applies directly to discrimination on the basis of sexual orientation." Gay victims of discrimination could appeal through the Merit Systems Protection Board or file a grievance but could not file a complaint through the Equal Employment Opportunity Commission. Though the letter provides guidance to the courts that federal policy prohibits discrimination on the basis of sexual orientation, it was not a stirring condemnation of the practice.

Although a more explicit, government-wide nondiscrimination policy may still be years in the future, federal employee groups have been pushing for such a policy on an agency-by-agency basis. In 1988, the negotiations of the National Treasury Employees Union (NTEU) with the Department of Health and Human Services allowed union members to bring grievances charging discrimination based on sexual orientation. In 1990, the American Federation of Government Employees (AFGE) negotiated a similar agreement with the Department of Housing and Urban Development, which also extended certain benefits to domestic partners of gay and lesbian employees. Department secretary Jack Kemp refused to sign the agreement arguing that the nondiscrimination policy exceeded federal law, but the Federal Labor Relations Authority (FLRA) upheld the agreement, and a federal court upheld the FLRA on appeal. Unions have also extended some protections to gay and lesbian employees in the Internal Revenue Service, the Bureau of Alcohol, Tobacco, and Firearms, the U.S. Customs Service, and the Pension Benefit Guaranty Corporation (Freedland, 1992, A19).

Organizations of gay, lesbian, and bisexual federal employees have also emerged in recent years. Federal Lesbians and Gays (FLAG) has existed in San Francisco for several years with similar groups forming in Dallas, Los Angeles, Boston, and New York City. Recently, organization has occurred primarily in the nation's capital. Federal GLOBE (Gay, Lesbian, Bisexual Employees) functions primarily as an umbrella organization, while specific agency groups press for policy changes within their own agencies.

Partly as a result of employee pressure and partly due to sympathetic managers and department heads, several agencies now list sexual orientation in their nondiscrimination policies. These agencies include: the Department of Agriculture, the Bonneville Power Administration, the General Services Administration, Housing and Urban Development, the National Academy of Sciences, the Department of State, the Department of Transportation, the U.S. Information Agency, the White House, the Departments of Justice, Interior, and Commerce, the International Trade Commission, the Small Business Administration, Merit Systems Protection Board, and some regions of the Forest Service and the Park Service. Negotiations are ongoing in several agencies and the situation is changing rapidly. In addition, at least 18 states have policies protecting gay and lesbian employees in state and local government including: California, Connecticut, Hawaii, Illinois, Louisiana, Maine, Maryland, Massachusetts, Michigan, New Jersey, New Mexico, New York, Ohio, Pennsylvania, Rhode Island, Vermont, Washington, and Wisconsin.

CONCLUSION: WHERE DO WE STAND? WHAT'S AHEAD?

At the national level, gay men and lesbians have fared poorly when their employment rights have become political issues. When the Republicans attacked the Democrats for being soft on Communism in the 1950s, homosexuals became an easy target for both parties because "sex perverts" were so widely despised that not even the American Civil Liberties Union would stand up for them. The politicians strengthened laws and pushed the bureaucracy to enforce them, and the bureaucratic structure—especially the Civil Service Commission and the FBI—continued to enforce the exclusion of gay employees long after the political issue had died down.

Likewise, when the military's ban on gay service members became a political issue in 1993, gays were severely routed by conservative forces. This occurred despite polls suggesting that the issue would be far less controversial than it proved to be. Four Gallup polls from 1977 through 1989, for instance, showed approval for hiring gays into the armed forces rising steadily from 51 to 60 percent. Polls in 1992 generally showed a plurality of the public in favor of lifting the ban. However, polls also showed that large majorities consider homosexual acts to be immoral and that the public is less willing to allow gay people to have homosexual sex than to have equal employment rights. In that context, political support for gay employment rights is likely to be tepid and theoretical, while opposition can be both vocal and fanatic.

Gay and lesbian federal employees have had more success within the court system. While the judiciary was reluctant to infringe on administrative discretion in hiring and firing decisions in the 1950s and 1960s, their decision that administrators needed to show a rational connection between homosexual conduct and the efficiency of the service effectively ended the blanket exclusion of gays from the civil service. To date, however, no court has ruled that homosexuality or homosexual conduct is necessarily irrelevant to employment decisions. Even the key pro-gay cases (*Norton* and *Society for Individual Rights, Inc.*) have emphasized that there may be legitimate reasons for denying employment to gay men and lesbians. Most courts continue to uphold the exclusion of gays from the military and the denial of security clearances for homosexuals (or at least the courts uphold practices that make it more difficult for gays to achieve them). The Supreme Court has clearly ruled that there is no fundamental right to homosexual sodomy (*Bowers v. Hardwick*, 478 U.S. 186 [1987]). The occasional court has ruled that gays are a suspect or quasi-suspect class (*Watkins v. U.S. Army*, 875 E2d 699 [9th Cir. 1988]; *High Tech Gays v. Defense Industrial Security Clearance Office*, 895 E2d 563 [9th Cir. 1990]) and that laws or regulations having an adverse impact on them require heightened scrutiny. Those decisions have been quickly overturned, however. The Court's recent decision overturning Colorado's Amendment Two (*Romer v. Evans*, 116 S. Ct. 1620 [1996]) creates more hope for equal protection cases, but gay legal activists remain skeptical about how sympathetic the Court is to gay causes (Keen, 1996).[2]

Recent progress has come about largely through the bureaucracy. The Civil Service Commission fought implementation of the *Norton* decision for years, but its change in regulations in response to *Society for Individual Rights, Inc. v. Hampton* and OPM Director Campbell's 1980 memo probably provide the strongest protection that most gay federal employees enjoy. Those with stronger protections have obtained them largely through labor contracts or nondiscrimination policies for single agencies or single divisions within agencies. These protections have generally arisen out of negotiations between unions or gay employee groups and federal bureaucrats. (Civil servants are significantly more likely than the general public to support civil rights for gays and lesbians and less likely to feel that homosexual acts are always wrong; see Lewis, 1990). Department heads appointed by President Bush generally opposed the policy changes, while some Clinton appointees have proactively supported them. These piecemeal, agency-by-agency negotiations and policy changes may eventually provide a strong enough framework, making a presidential executive order prohibiting discrimination on the basis of sexual orientation on a government-wide basis seem a trivial policy change not worth fighting against. In the absence of clear statutory protection for gay employees, these agreements plus a general belief among federal employees that discrimination against lesbians and gay men is wrong are probably the strongest protection.

NOTES

1. The Supreme Court agreed to hear the appeal, which suggested that there were limits to the government's power to fire homosexuals, and the government dropped its case, making this the first victory of its sort. However, the Court did not clarify what employment rights homosexuals had.

2. The Court remains headed by a man who once argued that whether gay students should be allowed to organize is "akin to whether those suffering from measles have a constitutional right, in violation of quarantine regulations, to associate together and with others who do not presently have measles, in order to urge the repeal of a state law providing that measles sufferers be quarantined" (*Gay Lib v. University of Missouri*, 558 F.2d 848 [8th Cir. 1977], cert. denied, 434 U.S. 1080 [1978], 1084).

REFERENCES

BERUBE, ALLAN (1990). *Coming Out Under Fire: The History of Gay Men and Women in World War II*. New York: Free Press.

BERUBE, ALLAN, AND JOHN D'EMILIO (1984). "The Military and Lesbians during the McCarthy Years." *Signs* 9 (Summer): 759–785.

BONTECOU, ELEANOR (1953). *The Federal Loyalty-Security Program*. Ithaca, NY: Cornell University Press.

BROWN, RALPH S., JR. (1958). *Loyalty and Security: Employment Tests in the United States*. New Haven: Yale University Press.

BURANELLI, VINCENT, AND NAN BURANELLI (1982). *Spy/Counterspy: An Encyclopedia of Espionage*. New York: McGraw-Hill.

CAMPBELL, ALAN K. (1980). "Memorandum: Policy Statement on Discrimination on the Basis of Conduct Which Does Not Adversely Affect the Performance of Employees or Applicants for Employment." 12 May.

——— (1993). Telephone interview, 17 June.

CHAUNCEY, GEORGE, JR. (1993). "The Postwar Sex Crime Panic." In William Graebner, ed., *True Stories from the American Past*. New York: McGrawHill, 160–178.

"The Consenting Adult Homosexual and the Law: An Empirical Analysis of Enforcement and Administration in Los Angeles" (1966). *UCLA Law Review* 13: 643–832.

D'EMILIO, JOHN (1983a). *Sexual Politics, Sexual Communities: The Making of a Homosexual Minority in the United States, 1940–1970.* Chicago: University of Chicago Press.
—— (1983b). "The Evolution and Impact of Federal Antihomosexual Policies during the 1950s." Unpublished manuscript.
—— (1989). "The Homosexual Menace: The Politics of Sexuality in Cold War America." In Kathy Peiss and Christina Simmons, eds., *Passion and Power: Sexuality in History.* Philadelphia, PA: Temple University Press, 226–240.
"Developments in the Law: Public Employment" (1984). *Harvard Law Review* 97: 1611–1900.
DULLES, ALLEN (1963). *The Craft of Intelligence.* New York: Harper & Row.
Executive Order 9835, 12 Fed. Reg. 1935 (1947).
Executive Order 10241, 16 Fed. Reg. 3690 (1951).
Executive Order 10450 "Security Requirements for Government Employment." (1953).
"Fairness for Homosexuals." (1971). *Washington Post,* 2 February, A14.
FRANK, BARNEY (1993). Letter to OPM Director James King, 29 November.
FREEDLAND, JONATHAN (1992). "Agencies Balk at Gay Rights Policy: Park Service Limits Employment Protection to San Francisco Region." *Washington Post,* 18 September, A19.
"Government-created Employment Disabilities of the Homosexual" (1969). *Harvard Law Review* 82:1738–1751.
HATTOY, ROBERT (1993). Speech to Federal GLOBE, Washington, DC, 6 January.
IND, COLONEL ALISON (1963). *A Short History of Espionage.* New York: David McKay.
JOHNSON, DAVID K. (1994–1995). "Homosexual Citizens: Washington's Gay Community Confronts the Civil Service." *Washington History* 6 (Fall/Winter): 44–63.
KAMENY, FRANK (1993). Personal interview, 17 August.
KATZ, JONATHON (1976). *Gay American History: Lesbians and Gay Men in the U.S.A.* New York: Harper & Row.
KING, JAMES B. (1994). Letter to Congressman Barney Frank, 26 January.
LEWIS, GREGORY B. (1990). "In Search of the Machiavellian Milquetoasts: Comparing Attitudes of Bureaucrats and Ordinary People." *Public Administration Review* 50 (2): 220–227.
MACLEAN, FITZROY (1978). *Take Nine Spies.* New York: Atheneum.
MACY, JOHN W., JR. (1966). "The Issue of Homosexuality and Government Employment." Department of State Newsletter (April): 44–45.
"Perverts Called National Peril" (1950). *New York Times,* 19 April.
RIDGEWAY, JAMES (1964). "The Snoops: Private Lives and Public Service." *New Republic* (December 19): 13–18.
ROSENBLOOM, DAVID H., AND JAMES D. CARROLL (1995). "Public Personnel Administration and Law." In Jack Rabin, Thomas Vocino, W. Bartley Hildreth, and Gerald J. Miller, eds., *Handbook of Public Personnel Administration.* New York: Marcel Dekker, 71–113.

ROWAN, RICHARD WILMER (1939). *The Story of the Secret Service.* Garden City, NY: Garden City Publishing Co., Inc.
SHILTS, RANDY (1993). *Conduct Unbecoming: Gays & Lesbians in the U.S. Military.* New York: St. Martin's Press.
SITH, RONALD (1975). *Encyclopedia of Espionage.* London: New English Library.
U.S. Civil Service Commission (1941). *Civil Service Act, Rules, Statutes, Executive Orders, and Regulations.* Washington, DC: U.S. Government Printing Office.
——. (1952). *68th Annual Report.* Washington, DC: U.S. Government Printing Office.
——. (1972). *A Pace-Setting Year for Personnel Management: 88th Annual Report.* Washington, DC: U.S. Government Printing Office.
U.S. General Accounting Office (1974). *Personnel Security Investigations: Inconsistent Standards and Procedures.* B-132376. Washington, DC: U.S. Government Printing Office.
U.S. Navy (1957). "Report of the Board Appointed to Prepare and Submit Recommendations to the Secretary of the Navy for the Revision of Policies, Procedures and Directives Dealing with Homosexuals, 21 December 1956, 15 March 1957." (*The Crittenden Report*).
U.S. Senate (1950). Committee on Expenditures in the Executive Departments, Subcommittee on Investigations. *Employment of Homosexuals and Other Sex Perverts in Government.* 81st Cong., 2d sess. Document No. 241. Washington, DC: U.S. Government Printing Office.
WEINBERG, MARTIN S., AND COLIN J. WILLIAMS (1974). *Male Homosexuals: Their Problems and Adaptations.* New York: Oxford University Press.
WHERRY, KENNETH S. (1950). *Report of the Investigations of the Junior Senator of Nebraska, A Member of the Subcommittee Appointed by the Subcommittee on Appropriations for the District of Columbia, on the Infiltration of Subversives and Moral Perverts into the Executive Branch of the United States Government.* 81st Cong., 2d sess. Washington, DC: U.S. Government Printing Office.

CRITICAL THINKING QUESTIONS

1. How has federal policy approached the issue of gay and lesbian employees during the twentieth century?

2. Discuss the scope and breadth of legal protections afforded gays and lesbians in federal employment today. How effective do these legal protections appear to be?

3. Gay men and lesbians have used electoral politics, case law, and lobbying to bring about social change. Which of these approaches has been the most beneficial for this group? Why has one approach worked better than another?

Getting Involved

1. Looking at a map of your campus, research the race, gender, and, if possible, social class of the individuals for whom the buildings are named. What patterns do you see in these characteristics?

2. Look at the catalogue of history course offerings for your campus and compare it with the courses offered on another campus. (You can view these online or at your campus library.) Identify the courses that focus on the history of women, racial or ethnic minorities, gay men and lesbians, or specific social classes. Contact the professors for these courses and inquire how and when those courses were first offered on your campus.

3. Contact a national or local gay/lesbian/bisexual, civil rights, or feminist organization and ask to speak to someone about what life was like for sexual, racial, and ethnic minorities or for white women or women of color in 1900, 1930, and 1960. Ask what that organization did to achieve the level of equality they have today. Discuss with your classmates how and why things have changed for women and minorities since those times.

Site-Seeing

1. For more information on prisons and chaingangs, visit the Prison Activist Resource Center website at **http://www.prisonactivist.org.**

2. For information on heterosexist biases in current immigration laws, visit the Lesbian/Gay Immigration Rights Task Force web site at **http://qrd.tcp.com/qrd/www/world/immigration/lgirtf.html.**

3. To learn more about Native American education, visit **http://www.wambdi.bia.edu.**

Chapter 3

How Inequality Is Perpetuated: Culture and Its Impact

In every society, social life is organized around a set of beliefs, values, behaviors, and material objects that constitute a group's culture or way of life. Inequalities are deeply rooted in certain aspects of U.S. culture. For example, what people think, what they view as important or unimportant, valuable or worthless, and whom they deem to be worthwhile or expendable in society affects how they behave.

In every culture, people use material objects as symbols to convey their own importance to others. For example, some use expensive jewelry, luxury cars, and designer clothing to communicate to others that they are affluent and thus more important in a culture that values financial success. Similarly, every culture thinks of certain groups of people as more valuable to society. For example, in the United States we have a long tradition of assuming that white, middle-class, heterosexual, married men make better political leaders than members of other social groups. That is just one reason why so many politicians appear in public with their families. Moreover, just as we think of some groups as more important, we label others as less valuable, expendable, or even a burden on society. Ideas such as these are at the heart of prejudice, and it is such deeply held beliefs that work to perpetuate inequality.

People do not usually recognize that the different values placed on members of different social groups are a result of culture. Instead, they think that certain groups are naturally, perhaps even biologically or genetically, better than others. This is largely because such beliefs are all they have ever known. But the idea that certain groups of people are inherently less valuable and deserve differential treatment is inaccurate. A sociological view always looks at the world, people, and their behaviors and interactions as products of social arrangements. Our social statuses, including those upon which inequalities are based, are imbued with socially defined meanings. Although physical differences exist among people of different races and sexes, and biology may cause differences in sexuality, the fact that differential values are attached to people of varying racial or ethnic groups, sexes, and sexualities is a product of culture, not nature.

For this reason alone, examining culture is central to understanding the experiences of people who are discriminated against, how their experiences are shaped by ideas and beliefs, and how ideologies ultimately affect our very social institutions. Beliefs and values are used to shape the policies and organization of our social institutions, including the family, work, education, the economy, the law, and the media. In this way culture is translated into social institutions—the organizational foundation of society. Culture, not nature, is the foundation for society and social inequalities.

In the actual workings of any society, there is a complex relationship between culture and social structure, and to understand how these two facets of society work to sustain inequality, as well as how they accommodate social change, we must first examine how unequal treatment is built into our belief systems. One of the most difficult aspects of challenging inequalities is overcoming deeply ingrained ideas that certain unequal treatment is deserved. When one internalizes aspects of a culture, certain types of discrimination may be seen as "natural." Thus inequalities become stable parts of our lives. They are important in shaping our day-to-day experiences and are simply taken for granted.

The readings in this chapter examine how inequalities based on shared meanings of race, ethnicity, social class, gender, and sexuality are present in U.S. culture. The authors of these articles consider a broad array of cultural meanings that perpetuate inequality.

In the first article, Quindlen argues that people in the United States are reluctant to discuss issues of race. Until we are able to openly talk about our feelings, perceptions, fears, and anger, she argues, we are destined to repeat the mistakes of the past. In the United States, race has long played an important role in inequality. According to Quindlen, race continues to shape everything in our culture, often in very subtle ways. But race is not the only issue affecting our culture.

In the second article, Sidel examines the way that race, gender, and social class interact in the lives of poor women of color. She argues that the dominant culture's characterization of these women as "welfare mothers"—inherently lazy, immoral, and undeserving of aid—laid the foundation for social policy changes in the 1990s that drastically curtailed government assistance. Sidel contends that poor women of color were blamed for most social problems in the United States, and that welfare was cut at a time when the gap between the rich and the poor was widening. Rather than recognizing the prejudice in these beliefs, however, changes in welfare policy were justified on the assumption that women of color were naturally different from other social groups, and therefore less deserving of aid.

Differences in social class strongly affect the way people think about and interact with one another. Often, as with poor women, our perceptions are based more in prejudice than in fact. In the third article, Gorman examines how members of the middle and working classes in the United States perceive each other. He finds that members of each social class hold negative, stereotypical views of the other. The working class views the middle class as self-righteous "paper pushers" who do not do real work. The middle class views members of the working class as inferior, uneducated, and crude. Despite these differences in perception, neither class has an understanding of the sociological roots of the inequalities that exist between the two groups, instead believing their differences are unavoidable.

Of course, perceptions are not always based upon face-to-face interaction. Instead, they can be strongly influenced by cultural factors. Societal beliefs and values about appropriate and desirable appearance are often conveyed via the media, which present unrealistic images of how women should look. In turn, this provides young girls with a standard that is largely unattainable. In the fourth article Williams shows that judgments of individuals based on appearance are many times founded on sexist and racist ideas. When dominant groups set the standards for beauty—and consequently for social worth—certain groups are relegated to inferior status.

The fifth article in this chapter looks at these issues of appearance and how individuals' value is determined, but the author focuses on men, rather than women. Cloud argues that the media present men with unrealistic images of what their bodies should look like. When men are socialized to believe that they "can't measure up," they will often turn to radical and sometimes dangerous means of trying to meet the standards imposed on them by the media. Cloud's article demonstrates that social institutions and cultural beliefs affect all members of society, even on very basic issues such as appearance.

The sixth article presents Ferber's ideas that American men, especially white men, have been largely blamed for society's ills and, as a result, have suffered numerous setbacks. In response to such attacks, white men have developed several ways of managing their anger and perceived marginalization. These include the liberal approach of the mythopoetic men's movement and the reactionary white supremacist movement. Although at first glance these responses may seem very different from each other, Ferber argues that the ideological foundations of the two groups have much in common. Most important, both of these movements are based on essentialist perspectives that see status differences between men and women and among the races and social classes as natural. Thus, both groups conclude that traditional inequalities between social groups are natural and should not be corrected by social policies.

Many of the beliefs that women, people of color, and ethnic and sexual minorities have worked to change are deeply rooted in long-held belief systems that dominant groups can latch onto when they seek to stop or reverse social change. In the seventh article, Sappenfield and his colleagues argue that some forms of inequality, such as anti-Semitism, are centuries old and deeply rooted in cultural beliefs about religious differences. Although some forms of anti-Semitism and some anti-Semitic groups are no longer major threats in the United States, the fact remains that the threat of anti-Semitism continues. Today, alienated extremists, including those in the white supremacist movement, are willing to resort to extreme tactics, including violence. Basing their argument on reports of actual attacks, the authors argue that anti-Semitism in the United States has never been worse. Clearly, altering social beliefs and values is necessary to change behaviors, but it seems that white supremacist and certain men's groups are willing to use stereotypes and myths to maintain the privilege they have long enjoyed.

Although dominant groups often play an important role in impeding the progress of minority groups, sometimes a group's cultural reaction to oppression can hinder its members' upward mobility. The perpetuation of inequality and prejudice through many generations is the focus of the eighth article. Focusing on the educational endeavors of one Native American woman, Ridgway argues that the poor educational achievement of Native Americans is rooted, in part, in the depressed economy of the reservation. But he also recognizes that the long-standing practice by whites of removing Indian children from their families and culture in order to Americanize them has made Native Americans distrustful of the white education system. This distrust of whites, combined with the shrinking availability of federal financial aid, contributes to a low level of educational achievement among Native Americans.

Taken together, these ten articles show us that the dominant beliefs and values in American society have a significant influence on shaping the experiences of individuals as well as the structure of society itself. Culture plays out through one-on-one interactions but is also perpetuated in our social institutions, including the media, religion, welfare policy, and education, which formalize cultural ideas of what is good and bad, right and wrong. Culture, then, is the product of history, the foundation of present day society, and a major influence on the future.

Reading 1

The Problem of the Color Line

Anna Quindlen

In this article, Quindlen argues that race continues to be a central factor in social life that most Americans are hesitant to discuss openly and honestly.

Here's the riddle: why is our most important issue the one no one really wants to talk about?

Here's a riddle: why was the internationally known Princeton professor stopped for driving too slowly on a street where the speed limit was 25 miles per hour? How come a Maryland state trooper demanded to search the car of a lawyer who graduated from Harvard? And why were an accomplished actor, a Columbia administrator, a graduate student and a merchandiser for Donna Karan arrested together in New York although none of them had done anything wrong?

The answer is elementary: all of the men were black. In some twisted sense, they were the lucky ones. They were only humiliated. Not, like Rodney King, beaten bloody. Not, like Abner Louima, sodomized with a broken broomstick. Not, like Amadou Diallo, killed in a gray blizzard of bullets. [All victims of the police.]

The verdict is in. The jury has spoken. The death of Diallo, a hardworking African immigrant, was adjudged a terrible accident, not murder, not manslaughter. Louima's assailant

is in jail. Two of the officers who beat King went to prison. There have been commissions, investigations, demonstrations, public reaction, prayer vigils, op-ed pieces, television segments, classroom dialogues. And so Americans ricochet from event to event, speaking of reasonable doubt and prosecutorial competence and ignoring the big picture, the real thing, the most important issue in this country that we try not to talk about. That is, race.

"The problem of the 20th century is the problem of the color line," summed up W.E.B. Du Bois in 1903. How dispiriting to realize it is the problem of the 21st century as well. "Our truncated public discussions of race suppress the best of who and what we are as a people because they fail to confront the complexity of the issue in a candid and critical manner," wrote Cornel West, that suspiciously slow-moving Princeton professor, in his aptly titled monograph "Race Matters." But in truth there are really no public discussions of race. There are discussions of affirmative action, and single parenthood, and, in the wake of human tragedies like the Diallo killing, of police training and procedures. These are discussions designed to cause the least amount of discomfort to the smallest possible number of white people.

Police officers are just us wearing uniforms. The assumptions they make, the prejudices they carry with them, are the assumptions and prejudices of their roots, their neighborhoods, their society. These are not necessarily the excesses of the egregious bigots, but the ways in which race changes everything, often in subtle or unconscious fashion. It is an astonishing dissonance in a nation allegedly based on equality, that there is a group of our citizens who are assumed, simply by virtue of appearance, to be less. Less trustworthy. Less educated or educable. Less moral. What we need to talk about candidly is something more difficult to apprehend than 41 shots in an apartment-house vestibule. It is the unconscious racial shorthand that shapes assumptions so automatic as to be a series of psychological tics: that the black prep-school kid must be on scholarship, that the black woman with a clutch of kids is careless instead of devoted to the vocation of motherhood. Not the shouts of "nigger" but the conclusions about everything from family background to taste in music, based on color alone, which blunt the acceptance of individuality and originality that is the glory of being human.

Some of this is easy to see, and to deride. A black electrician gets on the train at night and there is the barely perceptible embrace of purses on the laps of women around him. A black lawyer stands with upraised hand and watches the cabs whiz by. A mall security guard trails the only black customer through a store. When police officers looking for drug dealers in New York threw four professional men in jail—including, ironically, the black actor who played Coalhouse Walker, harassed by bigots in the musical "Ragtime"—they became suspects by virtue of color alone. On the highways, being stopped because of race is so commonplace that there's even a clever name for it: DWB, or "driving while black." Amadou Diallo's mother is asked to accept that the police who shot her son thought his wallet was a gun. I have two teenage sons, and when they roam the streets of New York City, I never assume that they will be arrested for something they did not do, or shot, or killed. Their wallets will be seen as wallets.

Poll after poll shows a great gap in understanding, between a white America that believes things are ever so much better and a black America that thinks that is delusional. And that gap mirrors a gap more important than numbers, between what many of us believe we believe, and the subtle assumptions that creep into our consciousness, and which we are often unwilling to admit are there. For a long time we blamed this chasm on black men and women. We who are white expected them to teach us what it was like to be them, to make us comfortable, and we complained when they did not. "Why Are All the Black Kids Sitting Together in the Cafeteria?" Beverly Daniel Tatum called her book about the black experience. America is a nation riven by geographic apartheid, with precious few truly integrated neighborhoods, particularly in the suburbs. The great divide between black and white yawns wide with the distance of ignorance, and the silence of shame.

So the sophistry of the margins continues, the discussions of the LAPD or the foster-care system or the failure of black leadership. The flagrant bigotries are discussed; the psychology of how we see one another and what that does to us too often is not. The most talkative nation on earth falls silent in the face of the enormity of the failure, of being two nations across a Mason-Dixon line of incomprehension and subtle assumptions. Oscar Wilde once called homosexuality "the love that dare not speak its name." But we speak its name all the time now. Sex. Religion. Politics. We talk about them all. But what race means, in all its manifestations large and small, is too often a whisper, our great unspoken issue.

CRITICAL THINKING QUESTIONS

1. What are some of the ways that racism continues to manifest itself in the United States today?

2. Why are people reluctant to talk openly about race and racism?

3. What might be gained if people were able to talk openly about race and racism?

Reading 2

The Enemy Within: The Demonization of Poor Women

Ruth Sidel

In this article, Sidel examines the ways that race, gender, and social class interact in the lives of poor women of color, whom society often blames for the social problems it is experiencing.

They are despised, denigrated, ostracized from mainstream society. In earlier times, they were known as the "dangerous classes"; today they are labeled the "underclass." They are pictured as virtually irredeemable, lazy, dependent, living off the hard-earned money of others. They are poor single mothers. They are welfare recipients. They are the enemy within.

The demonizing of poor, single mothers has been an integral part of the recent onslaught on the safety net, meager and inadequate as it is. Poor mothers have been deemed unworthy, the "undeserving poor"; millions of welfare recipients were painted with one brush, were relegated to that area in society that is beyond the Pale. Systematic stereotyping and stigmatizing of "welfare mothers" was necessary in order to dehumanize them in the eyes of other Americans before the harsh and tenuous lifeline of Aid to Families with Dependent Children (AFDC) and the other bare-bones social programs could be shredded. The implicit and often explicit message is: if welfare recipients are so unworthy, perhaps such harsh treatment, such punishment is warranted, even necessary, in order to modify their social and reproductive behavior. Perhaps, it has been said, removing cash and other benefits, forcing mothers to work even at dead-end jobs for poverty wages, and denying aid to children of teenagers and to additional babies born while the mother is receiving

AFDC is the only way to deal with this "deviant" and "irresponsible" group. Many politicians claim, moreover, that they promote these Draconian measures against the poor as a form of "tough love," "for their own good." These cuts in assistance and services may be painful at first, this reasoning goes, and some suggest that this current generation of poor parents may have to be written off, but in the long run these harsh measures will enable the next generation to "stand on their own two feet." Congress, the tough but responsible parent, will force the poor, as though they were rebellious adolescents, to shape up, to reform their delinquent ways.

Just over a decade ago, social scientist Charles Murray, author of *Losing Ground: American Social Policy 1950–1980,* articulated the values, priorities, and underlying agenda of America's war against the poor: "Some people are better than others. They deserve more of society's rewards, of which money is only one small part. A principal function of social policy is to make sure they have the opportunity to reap those rewards. Government cannot identify the worthy, but it can protect a society in which the worthy can identify themselves," (Murray, 1984, p. 234). Thus Murray was calling for government to legitimize the existing social and economic hierarchy by safeguarding the affluence and lifestyles of those whom he has deemed "better" and more "worthy."

The rhetoric that accompanied and paved the way for the continuing assault on pro-

Source: Journal of Sociology and Social Welfare, March, 2000, Vol. 28(1), 73–84.

grams for poor women and children was fueled by a pledge made by candidate Bill Clinton during the 1992 presidential campaign to "put an end to welfare as we know it," (De-Parle, July, 1994). As Senator Daniel Patrick Moynihan, Democrat from New York, stated, "The Republicans took him at his word" and went much further. But the only real way to end welfare as we know it, Moynihan continues, is "just to dump the children on the streets," (Pear, 1995).

Prior to the repeal of Aids to Families with Dependent Children by the Personal Responsibility and Work Opportunity Reconciliation Act of 1996, the litany of criticism against poor, single women was relentless. Mother-only families were blamed for virtually all of the ills afflicting American society. Out-of-wedlock births were blamed for the "breakdown of the family," for the crime rate, drug and alcohol addiction, poverty, illiteracy, homelessness, poor school performance and the rending of the social fabric. The labeling of some citizens as "dependent"—that is, dependent on social welfare programs rather than on spouses, parents or other family members, or other, more acceptable Federal programs—has been used indiscriminately to discredit an entire group of women and children without regard to their character or their specific work and/or family history.

As the political tide turned rapidly against the poor, particularly poor women, rhetoric escalated to previously unimagined levels of hyperbole and vitriol. At a 1994 news conference called by the Mainstream Forum, a group of centrist and conservative House Democrats affiliated with the Democratic Leadership Council, the political organization President Clinton helped found and headed when he was Governor of Arkansas, Representative Nathan Deal, a Georgia Democrat, declared that welfare was dead. He went on to state, "The stench from its decaying carcass has filled the nostrils of every American," (De-Parle, May, 1994).

The very words that are being used tell us what to think and how to feel. Poor women are characterized by their "dependence," an ab-solute negative, a polar opposite from that valued American characteristic, "independence." This label presumes that *they* are "dependent," that *they* passively rely on the government for their day-to-day needs while *we,* the rest of us, are "independent," "pull ourselves up by our bootstraps," are out there "on our own." These designations leave no room for the considerable variation and complexity that characterize most people's lives, for the fact that virtually all of us are in varying degrees dependent on others and on societal supports during our adult lives—that many of us have been recipients of financial or other kinds of help from family members, that many have been helped by inheritance, by assistance in finding (and sometimes keeping) a job, by tax deductions for mortgage payments, or the Federal subsidy of farm prices or highways, or by programs such as Medicare or Unemployment Compensation or disability assistance.

Dividing people into "us" and "them" is facilitated by the resurrection of terms such as "illegitimacy" that encourage the shaming and denigration of mothers and their out-of-wedlock children, for it is far easier to refuse aid to "them," to people who engage in disgraceful, stigmatized behavior than to people who seem like "us." David Boaz, executive vice-president of the Cato Institute, a libertarian organization, even hoped to resurrect the term "bastard:" "We've made it possible for a teen-age girl to survive with no husband and no job. That used to be very difficult. If we had more stigma and lower benefits, might we end up with 100,000 bastards every year rather than a million children born to alternative families?" (Wines, April, 1995).

Poor, single mothers, particularly AFDC recipients, have been portrayed as the ultimate outsiders—marginalized as nonworkers in a society that claims belief in the work ethic, marginalized as single parents in a society that holds the two-parent, heterosexual family as the desired norm, marginalized as poor people in a society that worships success and material rewards and marginalized as people of color when in reality millions of whites live in poverty. One of the key myths in the demonizing of poor women is that most of the impoverished, single, childbearing women are black. This image of the poor, inexorably intertwined with the long-standing baggage of racist ideology, facilitates their being perceived as deviants, as the ultimate outsiders. As anthropologist Leith Mullings has stated, "Women of color, and particularly African-American women, are the focus of well-elaborated, strongly held . . . ideologies concerning race, class, and gender." She goes on to state that "the images, representation, and symbols that form ideologies often have complex meanings and associations that are not easily or readily articulated, making them difficult to challenge," (Mullings, 1994, pp. 265–89).

Historically, African-American women have been described on the one hand by the image of "'Mammy,' the religious, loyal, motherly slave . . ." and, on the other hand, by the image of "'Jezebel,' the sexually aggressive, provocative woman governed entirely by libido." As Mullings states, this Mammy/Jezebel stereotype is a variation of the widespread madonna/whore dualism but the issue of race adds an even more pernicious element to the classic stereotype. The view of African Americans as a different species, what Mullings and others have termed the "otherness of race," has "justified the attribution of excessive sexuality." That "sexuality continues to be a major theme in the discourse about race" assures that it is also a major them in the discourse about poor women. Moreover, the Mammy image, so prevalent through the first half of the twentieth century and memorialized in popular culture by the film *Gone With the Wind,* has been replaced, according to Mullings, by the image of the "emasculating matriarch," (Mullings, 1994, pp. 265–89). Therefore, whether through overt sexuality or through control within the family that supposedly robs black men of their authority and power, black women are portrayed as deviant and as the primary cause of the problems within the black family and within the black community.

Patricia Hill Collins, author of *Black Feminist Thought: Knowledge, Consciousness, and the Politics of Empowerment,* analyzes the ways in which these deeply rooted images of black women underlie and buttress the harsh treatment of poor women over the past two decades and particularly during the 1990s:

> Portraying African-American women as matriarch allows the dominant group to blame Black women for the success or failure of Black children. Assuming that Black poverty is passed on intergenerationally, via value transmission in families, an elite white male standpoint suggests that Black children lack the attention and care allegedly lavished on white, middle-class children and that diverts attention from the political and economic inequality affecting Black mothers and children and suggests that anyone can rise from poverty if he or she only received good values at home. Those African-Americans who remain poor are blamed for their own victimization (Collins, 1990, p. 74).

Since the 1994 election, attacks on other groups in the United States—particularly on criminals and potential criminals and on immigrants—have also escalated sharply. This process has included verbal denigration as well as cruel and unusual treatment of those who are traditionally perceived as outsiders. There has been harsh rhetoric against documented and undocumented immigrants, as well as attempts to deprive them of essential human services. Prisoners who are mentally ill, functionally illiterate, and otherwise usually exempt from such inhumane punishment are being executed. Chain gangs and forced labor have returned to the Alabama penal system. It is surely no accident that all of these groups are made up largely of low-income people of color. But the harshest rhetoric and most sweeping policy changes have been reserved for the poor, particularly poor women. It is the convergence of class, gender, and race that makes this sweeping attack on one segment of society possible.

This denigration of poor welfare recipients is based in large part on dichotomous thinking and on the repetition and reiteration of commonly held myths about poor women and their children. The dichotomous thinking underlying much of the so-called welfare debate divides people, primarily women, into "good" and "bad;" "workers" and "idlers;" those who abide by the traditional "family values" and those who do not; good caring mothers and those who have been characterized by Charles Murray as "rotten mothers." Even children are being characterized by this either/or language: "legitimate" versus "illegitimate" (or "bastards"); young people who become productive citizens as opposed to those who are truant, drop out of school, or engage in early childbearing and other forms of "anti-social" behavior.

As Elaine Pagels points out in her book, *The Origin of Satan,* many cultures throughout the world and over the span of recorded human history have divided people into "we" and "they," "human" and "nonhuman." The "we" is often correlated with the "human" while the "they" are envisaged as "nonhuman." Pagels claims this kind of dichotomous thinking is deeply embedded in the Judeo-Christian tradition (Pagels, 1995, xviii).

The scathing stereotyping of poor mothers has severe consequences for them, for their children, and for the society as a whole. As sociologist Erving Goffman (1963) has pointed out:

> By definition, of course we believe the person with a stigma is not quite human. On this assumption we exercise varieties of discrimination, through which we effectively, if often unthinkingly, reduce his life chances. We construct a stigma-theory, an ideology to explain his inferiority and account for the danger he represents . . . (p. 5).

Perhaps the most dehumanizing and degrading references to welfare recipients occurred on the floor of the House of Representatives on March 24, 1995 during the debate on a bill that would cut $69 billion in spending on social welfare programs over the next five years. Welfare recipients were compared to animals by two Republican members of the House. Representative John L. Mica of Florida held up a sign that said, "Don't Feed the Alligators." He explained, "We post these warnings because unnatural feeding and artificial care create dependency. When dependency sets in, these otherwise able alligators can no longer survive on their own." Mica then noted that while "people are not alligators . . . we've upset the natural order. We've created a system of dependency," (Pear, March, 1995).

Representative Barbara Cubin of Wyoming carried the analogy still further:

> The Federal Government introduced wolves into the State of Wyoming, and they put them in the pens, and they brought back elk and venison to them every day. This is what I call the wolf welfare program. The Federal Government provided everything that the wolves need for their existence. But guess what? They opened the gates and let the wolves out, and now the wolves won't go. Just like any animal in the species, any mammal, when you take away their freedom and their dignity and their ability, they can't provide for themselves . . . (Pear, March, 1995).

The persistence of myths about welfare recipients and the resistance of policy-makers to the true facts despite repeated reiteration of them by experts in the field of social welfare are noteworthy. It appears that the United States *needs* to have someone to blame, people to hate, a group to rally against. For nearly a half century Americans had a clear-cut enemy—Communism. Throughout the Cold War, there was an ideology we could despise, countries to fear, foreign leaders to demonize. We had external villains whom we could blame for many of the world's ills and whom we could identify as evil in order to define ourselves as good. With the virtual world-wide breakdown of so-called Communist countries (with the exception of Cuba and North Korea), who would be the enemy now? Whom could we distrust and despise? Who would be the devil that in comparison would make us feel righteous and worthy? Who would be the "them" to help us to feel more truly "us?"

Moreover, over the past two decades we have seen a dramatic economic shift within the U.S.—a massive concentration of wealth and income in the hands of the richest among us. In 1977, the highest fifth of all households received 44 percent of total national income, the middle three-fifths received 51.8 percent while the lowest fifth received 4.2 percent. By 1993 the income of the highest fifth rose to 48.2 percent, the highest percentage of income on record for that group; the income of the middle three-fifths dropped to 48.2 percent, the lowest share on record; and the bottom fifth only received 3.6 percent, also the lowest share ever recorded. Over the same decade and a half, the income of the top 5 percent rose from 16.8 percent to 20 percent (Center of Budget and Policy Priorities, 1994). Furthermore, according to Kevin Phillips (1994), author of *Arrogant Capital: Washington, Wall Street, and the Frustration of American Politics,* "the 100,000 American Families in the top tenth of one percent enjoy by far and away the greatest wealth and income gains in the 1980s" but despite their enormous affluence "the Clinton tax increases of 1993 did not concentrate on the high-income, high-political-influence, investment dollar rich, the people making $4 million or $17 million a year," (pp. 206–07). There is consequently a greater gap in income today between rich and poor than at any time since such data have been collected and, as Phillips points out, those profiting the most are the top tenth of one percent.

If we examine differences in wealth among the U.S. population, we see an even more dramatic differential. In 1989, the top one half of one percent (the "super-rich") owned 31.4 percent of total household wealth, an increase of five percentage points since 1983. Moreover, the top 20 percent of the population owned 84.6 percent of total wealth. Since one-fifth of Americans owned 84.6 percent of total wealth, the remaining four-fifths of Americans owned only 15.4 percent. More specifically, the top one-half of one percent owned nearly twice as much wealth (31.4%) as the bottom 80 percent of all Americans (15.4%).

Moreover, preliminary estimates indicate that between 1989 and 1992, 68 percent of the increase in total household wealth went to the richest one percent—an even greater gain than during the 1980s (Wolff, 1994, pp. 143–174).

Despite the economic boom and low unemployment rates of the 1990s, millions of families have seen their neighborhoods deteriorate, the quality of schools, public transportation, health care and other services decline, their feelings of physical insecurity rise, and their overall quality of life plummet. Whom can they blame? During the past twenty years when the working class and the middle class were losing ground, a period during which the rich and "truly rich" were increasing their income and share of the nation's wealth to what many consider obscene levels, we have seen a strategy on the part of many politicians, policy makers, and conservative strategists to encourage the middle and working classes to blame the poor and the powerless, particularly women and people of color, rather than the rich and powerful for their losses.

As Thomas and Mary Edsall, authors of *Chain Reaction: The Impact of Race, Rights, and Taxes on American Politics* (1991), point out:

> Racial polarization, in effect, helped create a political climate receptive to an economic agenda based on the conservative principle that sharply increasing incentives and rewards for those people and interests at the top of the economic pyramid and decreasing government support for those at the bottom would combine to spur economic expansion and growth . . .
>
> Insofar as those in the bottom quintile of the income distribution can be identified as disproportionately black and Hispanic—making possible the isolation of the poor as conceptually separable from the white majority—racial polarization facilitates the enactment of regressive redistributional policies. And insofar as the government programs serving those in the bottom of the income distribution simultaneously divide the poor from the working class and black from white, whose programs are highly vulnerable to conservative assault (p. 13).

Blaming the poor and powerless for America's social and economic problems is far more comforting and acceptable than blaming the rich and powerful. Blaming the poor upholds a fundamental tenet of the American Dream: that individuals can dramatically alter the course of their own lives, that they can rise in the class hierarchy on their own initiative. To maintain our own dreams of success we must blame the poor for their failure; if their failure is due to flaws in the structure of society, these same societal limitations could thwart our dreams of success. The notion that the failure of the poor is due to their characterological weaknesses enable others to blame the impoverished for their own poverty while simultaneously preserving the faith of the non-poor in the possibility of success.

The times are therefore ripe for scapegoating. Scapegoats have been used throughout history to solve societal problems. In ancient Greece human scapegoats (pharmakos) were used to ward off plagues and other calamities. In early Roman law an innocent person was allowed to take on the penalty of another who had confessed his/her own guilt. In the Old Testament ritual of Yom Kippur, a goat was symbolically burdened with the sins of the Jewish people and then sent into the wilderness to rid the nation of its iniquities. Scapegoating has become national policy in the United States. We are indeed heaping the sins of a violent and unjust society on the poor and sending them out into the wilderness.

The problems the United States must address as we move into the next century are widespread poverty amidst incredible affluence, massive hopelessness and alienation among those who feel outside of the boundaries of the society, and a deeply-felt despair among the poor and the working class that is increasingly expressed through violence. There is no question that the welfare system in particular and the society in general has not addressed these issues and, in fact, has exacerbated them—not through generosity, not through making poor people dependent on a

panoply of services but rather by not providing the essential education, job training, child care, health care, and perhaps most important, jobs by which families can support themselves at a decent standard of living. The central problem American society must deal with is not the character of poor women and the structure of the welfare system; the central problem is poverty and the multiplicity of ways that it is embedded in the structure of American society. We must recognize that people are not poor due to characterological defects but rather that the poverty that plagues so many Americans has been socially constructed and therefore must be dealt with by fundamental economic and social change.

Over three decades ago, Michael Harrington ended his powerful expose of poverty in America, *The Other America,* with the following words: "The means are at hand to fulfill the age-old dream: poverty can now be abolished. . . . How long shall we look the other way while our fellow human beings suffer? How long?" (Harrington, 1963, p. 170).

REFERENCES

Center on budget and policy priorities. (1994). *Despite economic recovery, poverty and income trends are disappointing in 1993.* Washington, D.C.

COLLINS, P. H. (1990). *Black feminist thought: Consciousness and the politics of empowerment* (p. 74). Boston: Unwin Hymen.

DEPARLE, J. (1994, July 15). The Clinton welfare bill: A long stormy journey. *New York Times,* pp. A1, A18.

DEPARLE, J. (1994, May 12). Welfare plan seeks limit on benefits. *New York Times,* p. A22.

EDSALL, T. B. AND EDSALL, M. D. (1991). *Chain reaction: The impact of race, rights, and taxes on American politics* (p. 13). New York: W. W. Norton.

GOFFMAN, E. (1963). *Stigma: Notes on the management of spoiled identity* (p. 5). New York: W. W. Norton.

HARRINGTON, M. (1963). *The other America: Poverty in the United States* (p. 170). Baltimore: Penguin.

MORRISON, T. (1974). *The bluest eye* (p. 18). New York: Pocket.

MULLINGS, L. (1994). Images, ideology and women of color. In M. B. Zinn & B. T. Dill (Eds.), *Women of color in U.S. society* (pp. 265–289). Philadelphia: Temple University Press.

MURRAY, C. (1984). *Losing ground: American social policy 1950–1980* (p. 234). New York: Basic.

PAGELS, E. (1995). *The origin of Satan* (p. xviii). New York: Random House.

PEAR, R. (1995, March 25). House backs bill undoing decades of welfare policy. *New York Times*, pp. 1, 9.

PEAR, R. (1995, May 14). Moynihan promises something different on welfare. *New York Times*, p. 22.

PHILLIPS, K. (1994). *Arrogant capital: Washington, Wall Street, and the frustration of American politics* (pp. 206–207). Boston: Little Brown.

WINES, M. (1995, April 9). Not my job. Not our job. So whose job is it? *New York Times*, Sect. 4, pp. 1, 3.

WOLFF, E. N. (1994). Trends in household wealth in the United States, 1952–83 and 1983–98. *Review of Income and Wealth, Series 40, No. 2,* 143–174.

CRITICAL THINKING QUESTIONS

1. In what ways are poor women or poor women of color deemed inferior in the United States today? Compare this with ideas about poor men and poor men of color.

2. How have social policy makers drawn upon stereotypes about poor women of color in convincing the public that social policy changes are needed?

3. When one group, such as poor women of color, is blamed for society's problems, who benefits?

Reading 3

Cross-Class Perceptions of Social Class

Thomas J. Gorman

In this article, Gorman focuses on the ways that members of the middle and working classes perceive one another, usually relying on stereotypes.

. . . Is social class still relevant to understanding the (post)modern United States? Recently, some scholars have debated the notion that American society is composed of distinct social classes (Clark and Lipset 1991; Clark et al. 1993; Pakulski 1993; Pakulski and Waters 1996; Hout et al. 1993). This debate, however, is not new; indeed, it has been going on for some time. Some research has suggested that working-class families would come to resemble the middle-class norm over time (Willmott and Young 1973). As it has turned out, later research did find indications of middle-class and working-class families living side by side, earning equivalent salaries, and frequenting similar leisure establishments (Halle 1984). Although Halle (1984) admitted that there are elements

Source: Reprinted from *Sociological Spectrum* 20, no. 1 (January–March 2000): 93–120.

of a distinct working-class life experience—job opportunities, educational level, family origin, leisure tastes, and self-esteem—he felt that the dissimilarities between the middle class and the working class have been exaggerated. The highly paid blue-collar workers he studied felt that they were "working men," differentiating themselves from white-collar college graduates they saw as paper pushers. The self-image of the "working man" was mitigated in the community by the workers' sense of being an American as well as by their high-income, expensive consumer items and nice homes.

Other researchers have explored the processes by which members of one class differentiate themselves from members of other social classes. . . . According to Lamont (1992), upper middle-class Americans tend to exclude others more on the basis of their perceived moral superiority (honesty, competence, work ethic, and friendliness) and socioeconomic superiority (professional prestige, race, income, class background, and prestigious credentials) than on their cultural superiority (intelligence, travel, language fluency, and culinary skills). She postulated that this tendency may be due to the low level of subsidies to health, education, and welfare by the U.S. government. In comparison, Lamont argued that the French do not judge social status on the basis of an individual's personal income because of the large role of the public sector in France. Another researcher (Ehrenreich, 1989) has argued that the faith and investment in higher education can be seen as an attempt by the middle class to protect itself from experiencing downward mobility in a changing economy by excluding others from the professions.

One way to explore the question of whether the working class is integrated into American society is to address the dominant ideology thesis. The income necessary to achieve the "American dream"—house, car, vacations—has historically been within reach of the working class through high-wage manufacturing jobs. Increasingly, high-wage manufacturing jobs are being lost to low-wage service and temporary or part-time positions, making it more difficult for the working class to achieve the American dream. The gulf is widening between those with a college degree in high-wage occupations and those with a high school degree in low-wage occupations (Bluestone and Harrison 1982; Ehrenreich 1989; Reich 1991).

Out of this socioeconomic transformation has come a new belief in the benefits of a college education. It is a belief, reinforced by both the media and government statistics, that a college degree will be the key factor in the future allocation of high-wage, prestigious jobs. Although hard work and rugged individualism had previously been the overriding dominant ideology in the United States, a new element has recently been added to the ideological mix—a college education. Those who work hard and get a college degree are now seen as deserving the better paying and more prestigious jobs in the occupational hierarchy. It has been ar-gued, however, that the dominant ideology, while having a mild influence over subordinate classes, sometimes has more of an impact on the dominant class (Abercrombie and Turner 1978). What are the attitudes and views of members of the working class toward higher education in general and toward college-educated, white-collar workers in particular? Do members of the working class subscribe to this new dominant ideology in the United States as much as members of the middle class or are they angry at college-educated, white-collar workers and/or alienated from American higher education? My analysis of the data in the present study helps shed light on this question. . . .

The respondents in this study are parents of school-age children. Why study parents? The attitudes of working-class parents toward white-collar college graduates have the potential to influence their children's attitudes toward higher education, their children's chances of obtaining a college degree, and their own chances of returning to school. The resistance and/or conformity of parents to the meritocratic ideology of using higher education as a means of upward mobility must be considered in any discussion of the relationship between the family and the school, or any theory of social class reproduction.

DATA COLLECTION

The sample for this study was drawn from an old, medium-sized, northeastern U.S. city (population approximately 100,000). Old City (name changed to protect confidentiality) was a magnet for immigrants during the nineteenth century; industries such as trade, transportation, foundries, lumber, and railroads dominated the landscape. These immigrants built and lived in ethnic enclaves that, to some degree, still exist today. . . .

Each interview took approximately two hours to complete and was tape recorded. All quotations in the text are verbatim, but some have been condensed for easier reading. At the end of each quotation in the text, a notation lists the respondent's age, gender, occupation and educational level, (a few respondents' occupations were changed to equivalent occupations to ensure confidentiality). . . .

My definition of social class is fairly consistent with much of the work on social class differences (Halle 1984; Lareau 1989). I coded the respondent's social class on the basis of his or her occupation. Working-class respondents in the sample held the following blue-collar/lower white-collar occupations: skilled, semiskilled, or unskilled laborers; transportation workers; and lower level sales, clerical, and service occupations. Middle-class respondents in the sample held the following white-collar occupations: professionals; middle and upper level managers; high-level civil servants; academics; high-level sales and administrative positions; or small business owners. . . .

Some caveats should be kept in mind. My research was conducted in a city; suburban residents were not included. Many of the respondents liked the city and the multicultural experiences it offers. I am quite certain that I would not find this attitude prevalent in the suburbs. It should also be kept in mind that the interviews were conducted during the ten-month period from November 1991 through September 1992. During this time, the United States was in the midst of an economic recession—affecting both blue-collar and white-collar workers—that prompted the media to carry stories extolling the benefits of riding out the recession by going to college or graduate school. The economic conditions and media accounts might have influenced particular respondents to have had positive attitudes toward higher education. It has been argued that these changes in attitude could be an outcome of deindustrialization (Weis 1990).

FINDINGS

The responses presented in this study represent the views of approximately one half of the sample; that is, one half of the middle- and working-class respondents made blatantly negative comments toward members of the other social class. The data reflect the comments made by the respondents at any point during the interviews; they do not necessarily represent comments to a single question whose responses from middle- and working-class respondents can be compared. Many members of the balance of the working-class sample, while not overtly hostile toward college-educated, white-collar workers, argued that those persons did not do "real" work. The balance of the middle-class sample did not have anything negative to say about the working class; their impression management techniques were highly refined. Indeed, a couple of middle-class respondents actually admitted during the interviews that they were not being totally honest about their true feelings toward members of the working class and, subsequently, went on to express blatantly negative attitudes toward members of the working class. Consequently, I would argue that this research understates the amount of negative attitudes found among members of the middle and working class toward each other. Still, the voices heard in this study—more than the actual percentage of respondents—give us insight into how members of the middle and working classes view themselves and each other.

Working-Class Perceptions of the Middle Class

Sennett and Cobb (1972) argued that members of the working class experience "hidden injuries of class" during their search for dignity in a capitalistic society because in such an economic system the working class are denied their fair share of two key measures of self-worth—educational credentials and occupational prestige. Working-class respondents' attitudes toward middle-class culture are shaped, in large part, by the hidden injuries of class they experienced while interacting with members of the middle class in the home, school, and workplace.

An example of the hidden injuries of class was related to me by one working-class man. He said he was at a Christmas party with people he

> had nothing in common with. One guy [made the comment] that I didn't have to worry about work, that I did manual labor. That hit a spot there. Like I could go to McDonald's, there's no difference in what I did. It made me angry that he'd say something like that because here's a guy that got a college education that he's lucky to be making $16,000 a year and I could pull down $30,000 in six months and he's going to tell me there's no difference in what I do.

This man's response to his injury was to turn against higher education—a mainstream institution—and white-collar, college-educated individuals:

> Still today I hold resentment for [people like this]. I call them "suits." I think they look down on me because I work with my hands and not sit behind a desk. I think this country would be in bad shape if everybody wanted to sit behind a desk. (34, male, unemployed bridge painter, high school)

As this man's comments suggest, members of the working class struggle to find dignity in a society that is quick to judge one's worth on the basis of income, educational credentials, and occupational prestige. There was a feeling among many working-class respondents that college-educated, white-collar workers look down on them or think they are better than them. Most of the men and women in the working-class sample felt that they were more work oriented; college-educated, white-collar workers were seen as pretentious. In describing his interactions (and injuries) with white-collar, college-educated coworkers, a maintenance worker said, "They have contests [among workers in the store] . . . it doesn't involve [me] or the people that work on the docks." Is this man integrated into the dominant culture, or is he angry, alienated, and resistant to mainstream institutions such as higher education? How did he feel about college-educated individuals?

> The way I look at it if you want to have an easy life, have money in your pocket, and do no work, go to college. That aggravates me. College makes them feel above other people intelligence wise even though they just know a few fancier words, along with that comes the fine dress and the posture. They basically get in the way. If you took [us] and you took the people who went to college and you made two little separate cities, who's going to be living right? Who's going to build the houses and the plumbing? I am right. Let's face it, the college people need people like us more than we need them. (40, male, maintenance worker, some college courses in the army)

This man rejected the notion that one needs a college degree to make it in the United States and is contemptuous of those individuals ("them") who hold college degrees and upper level white-collar occupations. Moreover, many of the working-class respondents felt that middle-class college graduates are "perpetual students"; they waste time and money in college just to get a piece of paper that does not guarantee a job. One working-class woman summarized these themes when she said,

> I have a niece who's gone through 8 years of college for an MA in art and now she's a waitress. I babysit for professional people [a child psychologist] which I think have no common sense. They drive me crazy. They're book smart and life stupid. So they know everything about child psychology. I just looked at them [and how they were raising their child] and I was like, you're doing this all wrong. This is not common sense. (31, female, inventory clerk, high school)

For such individuals, a college degree seems to be a waste of time because they know people ("us") who make as much or more money by using "common sense" as those ("them") with the "piece of paper"—the college degree.

These working-class parents also thought that they were caring and down to earth, a (cultural) essence that separates them from middle-class parents. It was not unusual for working-class parents to criticize middle-class parents for putting their careers ahead of their family lives:

> The doctor who makes $150,000 a year compared to the guy working in the same hospital buffing the floor for $6 an hour, [the doctor's] a father. The guy who's buffing the floor might be a daddy. Anybody can be a father, it takes someone special to be a daddy. (33, male, unemployed house painter, some community college courses)

A related type of response expressed pride in working-class culture. These respondents felt that those with socioeconomic advantages lack important qualities. A clerical worker said,

> Money can buy everything but not love and happiness, really. I would rather be low in money and have that happiness than be rich and miserable. I'd like to be comfortable, they don't know what to do with their money. (35, female, unemployed clerk, high school)

This type of response alleviates some of the hidden injuries of class. We hear from these working-class parents a belief that those with a socioeconomic advantage, while having financial resources, lack other qualities; working-class parents think there is a higher calling for being a parent that those with a socioeconomic advantage do not appreciate. I took these comments to be a more subtle way of voicing their negative opinions of the capitalist system. These working-class parents have not benefited from the system that gives some an advantage but take pride in being sincere, simple, genuine, unpretentious people; these attributes, they feel, are more important to pass on to their children than financial resources. They may not be rich in the capital that the system values, but these working-class parents feel that certain

aspects of their lives are superior to those with a socioeconomic advantage. A separate working-class cultural form—a counterideology (Scott 1990)—resides in the middle of this middle-class city. The anger exhibited by some of the working-class respondents in this study is symptomatic of the scars inflicted by their interactions with the members of the middle class. Members of the working class may have little respect for white-collar, college graduates, yet they realize they are in a constant struggle to win respect for their kind of work.

Social Class Interaction What makes the accounts given by working-class respondents interesting—and not explored enough by Sennett and Cobb (1972)—are the variety of settings where the hidden injuries of class took place. Many of the injuries I found were directly work related. Consider the following comments from a secretary:

> One boss used to belittle us. He was a pig. He said, "I only hired you because you graduated from high school—it doesn't take a brain surgeon to work in a job like this." I was ashamed that all I had was my associate's degree. (30, female, secretary/clerical, AAS)

The injuries experienced at work may be carried over to other situations. Although the bridge painter's comments presented earlier derive from his experiences at work, he reported how he felt interacting with college-educated, white-collar workers at a Christmas party and in the Navy. All of these feelings are hidden but constantly shape daily interactions among members of different social classes.

Even standing in a line in a quiet bank is no guarantee that (working) class resentment will not surface:

> I've walked into banks before and your yuppies look at you like you're the scum of the earth. I might be dirty. I said that to one of them. He's standing there in his suit, looking all pretty and shit. He's looking at me like I'm

a piece of scum. I said, "You think you're so hot, you want to compare apples to apples, buddy?" He held out his paycheck and I showed him mine. He shut right up. I said there is nothing wrong with an honest day's work. (33, male, unemployed house painter, a few community college courses)

This account is an example of the many attempts made by members of the working class to assert their dignity in the face of both the hidden injuries of class associated with structural (economic) realities and those individuals they see as having benefited from those realities. These injuries are the result of the interaction of social classes. Having middle-class contacts, then, not only does not guarantee that the working class will view the middle class more favorably and/or raise their educational aspirations (Kahl 1953; Halle 1984; Weis 1990) but may, in fact, increase working-class contempt for both the middle class and higher education.

Sennett and Cobb (1972) described the hidden injuries of class without talking about their genesis. What is it about the white-collar, college graduate that makes these working-class respondents angry? This is not an easy question to answer, but three foci emerge from the interviews: middle-class language, middle-class clothing, and middle-class attitudes.

Several working-class respondents voiced their resentment at attempts by middle-class, college graduates to showcase their language skills. Consider the following two comments:

My boss [is] very insulting. She talks with big words, and if you don't use a word right, she loves to insult people with that. After she says them she looks at you and says, "do you understand what I mean?" [It makes me feel] very low. (35, female, secretary, GED)

If I would have gone to college, I feel I would have been a more confident person talking to people. My neighbors, they both went to college; talking to them, no matter how old I get, I feel like an awkward little teenager stumbling about [not] knowing what I'm talking about. (27, female, unemployed clerical, high school)

Indeed, it has been argued (Lareau and Lamont 1988) that a major effect of cultural capital and its contribution to maintaining class differences is its ability to exclude others. Teenagers are excluded from important conversations. Imagine the experience of continuing to feel that way as an adult; imagine how angry that experience may make one feel.

The white-collar, college graduate's manner of dress—especially the business suit—is another aspect of middle-class behavior that made some of the working-class respondents angry. As noted above, one working-class man said, "I hold resentment for some people who wear suits. I call them 'suits.' I think they look down on me because I work with my hands and not sit behind a desk" (34, male, unemployed bridge painter, high school). Similarly, a working-class woman said, "A man comes in a three-piece suit and orders something and acts like he's better than you are. My job is not sitting behind a desk; I'm on my feet. I'm as good as he is" (43, female, waitress, less than high school).

What is it about the business suit that irritates some members of the working class? I would argue that it has less to do with the suit per se than with what the suit symbolizes. Most working-class respondents have probably worn suits at different points in their lives, but not to work. The business suit represents the ability of members of the middle class to command respect for their kind of work. The business suit in our society loudly proclaims that the wearer is involved in dignified work.

Finally, working-class respondents complained about the attitudes that college educated, white-collar workers have toward those without a college education. Which attitudes? Consider the following comments from a middle-class respondent:

If you're asking whether I categorize people, I definitely do. If someone doesn't have a college education, I definitely view them differently, which is bad. I see them as a little bit less sophisticated. I see their views as a little narrower. They don't see the whole picture, sometimes I think they don't know what they are talking about because they're talking from a limited position, especially if they're talking about issues they haven't studied. (32, female, ex-counselor [not working outside home], MA)

According to this woman, one cannot possibly be knowledgeable in an area that one has not formally studied. In turn, working-class respondents reported they were aware of, and resented, this type of "pretentious" attitude. One working-class man said, "People who go to college try to look down on people who don't or haven't attended college" (33, male, unemployed house painter, some community college courses).

Many working-class respondents felt that white-collar, college graduates did not have any basis for looking down on them because, as previously noted, working-class lifestyles were more "down-to-earth." Working-class respondents felt that they were more family oriented; the white-collar, college graduate was seen as oriented too much toward educational and career objectives. Furthermore, working-class respondents felt that they were more work-oriented; white-collar, college graduates were seen as perpetual students, afraid of a hard day's work. In short, the typical working-class respondent attributed to the white-collar, college graduate a core personality—lazy, selfish, and pretentious. The working-class respondents perceived themselves to be hard working, practical, caring, and down to earth, an essence that separates them from white-collar, college-educated people.

Class Consciousness   The working-class respondents were not class conscious in the classic Marxian sense of the concept—a class for itself—but they were aware of a group of individuals who have more opportunities, fewer constraints, and a different personality than themselves. Some working-class respondents, however, were closer than others to being class conscious in the classic sense of the concept: "Darn right, [If] you got money, money talks, bullshit walks" (34, male, electrician, some college). Similarly, another working-class man said, "You know the old adage, money talks and

bullshit walks. I think that's true, but sometimes the children do not end up getting the best education for their money" (32, male, police officer, community college courses). Here the anger is diffused and unfocused. These working-class respondents know the system is rigged but are not sure who is doing the rigging. These are the kinds of comments you find in spots where the "grumblings" (Scott 1990) of the working class can be heard: the workplace, the local tavern, and most important for this article, the home. Grumbling is difficult to police; thus, any discussion of class consciousness must deal with the issue of these hidden transcripts of resistance. In contrast, one working-class man exhibited a more focused class consciousness:

> [You] have got to have money. A good majority of the kids that went through college and are doctors and stuff come from families with money. You hear the same old story: [They] spent $50,000 to go to college so [they] deserve to have more money. Well, people who don't have money don't have that $50,000 to put into college. In what way are they equal with [me]? Money talks and you walk. That's the way it goes. The only way to survive in this world is to be born into money. You've got to have money to make money. (40, male, maintenance worker, some college courses in the army)

Some responses from working-class respondents reveal a deep understanding of American social class structure:

> If you're financially able to, and you expect your child to go to college, then [the children] tend to do what's expected of them. Poor people, when they can't even give their kids any hope of it, [the kids] end up getting into trouble. (31, female, clerk, AAS)

A truck driver felt that "children from middle-class homes just have to watch the way their parents operate. The son carries on the father. They're used to that upbringing. They're used to being in that class, in that environment" (47, truck driver, high school). Only a few of the working-class respondents used the term class during the interviews, but, as the data indicate, this does not mean that members of the American working class are totally devoid of any consciousness of their position in the social class structure. The day-to-day interactions with members of the middle class, the dominant culture, and the new dominant ideology remind them of their position. . . .

Middle Class Views of the Working Class

It is possible that the working-class respondents have little basis for their feelings toward members of the middle class, their anger and insecurity being the product of their own imaginations. The attitudes of the working-class respondents toward the middle class may, however, be a direct result of—or at least a reciprocation of—the negative attitudes and opinions that the middle class have of the working class; the negative attitudes of members of the middle class may be coming through when interacting with members of the working class. These attitudes may be directly injuring the working class and contributing to the working class's contempt for the middle class, mistrust of mainstream institutions, and uncertainty as to the fairness of the overall socioeconomic system.

The data in the present study suggest that the perceptions of working-class respondents accurately reflect an attitudinal pattern among middle-class respondents: Many members of the middle class do hold negative opinions of working-class culture. To begin with, quite a few middle-class respondents felt that working-class parents, while facing tough conditions, could motivate their children to attend college and make better lives for themselves and their children if only the parents just tried harder:

If you have money, you have options. I think it's harder but I think [the working class] can [motivate their children]. They could show their kids that if you work hard that it is possible to achieve a distant goal. (35, male, reporter, BS plus graduate courses)

And one man struggling for an answer said,

The socially disadvantaged may not have the time or . . ., no, that's such a bullshit answer. I don't know. My own gut feeling is that it doesn't preclude you from placing the value there and motivating your child. I don't deny there are other factors that come in and make that more difficult. (35, male, lawyer, law degree)

A couple of middle-class respondents, though, felt that they had advantages that the lower classes could never duplicate:

The class system in this country is getting stronger and stronger. Well, maybe it is just getting clearer to me. There is a strong privileged upper class that puts kids in an advantage. Protection from suffering is one thing. The kids that go to [the local private academy] that are going to go to [private prestigious college]. It's a whole other class that some people can't even imagine. There is a difference here in what you can get. It's very destructive. (37, male, civil service manager, MA)

Representative of a more consistent pattern, however, were the middle-class respondents who were angry because they thought blue-collar workers were overpaid. A counselor remarked, "I don't think that somebody who paints a bridge should make $50 an hour and I make $10 an hour. I don't like the inequity." (32, female, ex-counselor [not working outside home], MA).

The unemployed bridge painter would find this comment interesting. An electronics engineer (who has a PhD and manages over 40 people in a large corporation) said,

Most people who probably make the most money are the ones who never went to college. That's a sore point, really, if you talk to engineers. How many times have you called someone to fix your refrigerator [and] as soon as he walks into your house, you don't get him out without spending $100. Sometimes it's just a 1-minute thing, he just replaces a switch. I don't make $100 an hour. (43, male, engineer, PhD)

Indeed, there is an image among many of the middle-class respondents that members of the working class are, undeservedly, making a high income. These middle-class respondents may have had to pay a lot of money to get their car repaired or were charged a large service fee and came to the conclusion that most members of the working class are earning too high an income for their educational level. According to the faithful of this new dominant ideology, someone who works hard at a job is no longer deemed worthy of making as high an income as someone who works hard at a job and graduated from college. These middle-class respondents believe deeply in the new dominant ideology. A lawyer said, "I'm a strong believer that education is the basic tool and element they need to perform and exist in this world. If they [his children] said I want to pump gas, I don't need college, I would be very disappointed" (38, male, lawyer, law degree).

One woman even tried to block the thought of her children not attending college from her mind: "Right now I don't even consider that she'll [her daughter] think [about not attending college]. [With an exaggerated cry in her voice] I'm just assuming she's going to do it. [A vocational occupation?] It makes me nervous thinking about it" (38, female, nurse, 3-year nursing school). It is true that Americans were told that "to get a good job you need a good education." No mention was made, however, of needing a college degree. This is why some working-class respondents feel they were betrayed. The attitudes of members of the middle class may be linked to a contracting economy for college graduates and the fear of downward mobility (Ehrenreich 1989; Newman 1988), similar to racial tension during times of economic crisis.

Just as in working-class culture, members of the middle class have a way of distinguishing "them" from "us." The previous comment by a middle-class woman concerning the lack of sophistication exhibited by those without a college education is interesting, in that it gives us a glimpse at the criteria that some members of the middle class use in judging someone's credibility, worthiness, and, ultimately, social class.

A few middle-class respondents mentioned the language skills some working-class people use as both an irritant and another way to classify people. One middle-class man admitted, "You can definitely tell when they're not educated. Just the way they talk. They couldn't finish sentences" (31, male, social worker, AAS). A middle-class woman said,

> It does drive me crazy when I go to the stores. I hear the way people talk to their children and tell them to shut up. They use horrible English. No wonder these kids aren't ready for school; their parents are setting a horrible example. Maybe it's because their mothers are out working all day. But I think it's so sad when the children are treated that way by their parents in public. I can't imagine the way they're treated at home. (40, female, currently not working outside the home, buyer [retail], BA)

It is easy to see the criteria that this woman uses to gauge someone's educational level and social class. It is interesting that this woman made a connection between bad grammar and bad behavior; it is also interesting to remember that some working-class respondents said that people who have a college education use words as an oppressive weapon.

A couple of middle-class respondents complained that they have mundane conversations with those who have less education than themselves. A middle-class respondent found it difficult to converse with his blue-collar friend:

> Most of the time it's mundane, if I can stereotype them. Like one of my good friends, he's only got a high school education, and he sometimes talks about his work like the obvious. [His friend said], "I told them why didn't they send that out—you know what I mean, Joe?" And I'm like, all right, that seems like, second hand, old hat. I do that all the time [at work] and he's making it like it's a big thing. (26, male, middle-level sales, BA)

The job duties of this respondent's friend may seem monotonous; indeed, they may be monotonous, but they are probably important to the respondent's friend. Another middle-class man said,

> I have a lot of friends from my childhood that have less education and I think that is somewhat of a barrier in terms of communication, not that I like them any less. [One friend is interested] in motorcycles and cars and I don't have that set of interests. He has no orientation to stuff that I might like to talk about, like gardening. Things that I'm interested in are almost like, in a blue-collar sense, seen almost feminine—gardening, cooking. I like books and movies; there is a gap there. (37, male, civil service manager, MA)

Implicit in this statement are more images of working-class culture: They do not like reading books, watching movies, gardening, and cooking because these activities are not "macho." These are some subtle ways that members of the middle class distinguished educational level and social class. These are the breeding grounds for tension and conflict between members of different social classes.

Several comments provided further insight into the attitudes of members of the middle class toward members of the working class. For example, one woman said, "I wouldn't want to be a plumber. Like my mechanic says, who wants to be a wrench" (38, female, teacher, MA). That this middle-class woman thinks of someone as a "wrench" certainly gives us insight into the way she categorizes people. These are the kinds of attitudes from middle-class individuals that infuriate members of the working class. Another teacher relayed an interesting story concerning a man who worked on her roof:

> [The roofer] made a point to tell me that he had a college education and worked for the government. I felt like he was justifying himself, and it made me feel bad that he felt like he had to. I thought, gee, am I giving off these vibes that you have to be college educated to speak to me? (41, female, not currently working outside the home, teacher, MA)

She may not have directly been "giving off these vibes" but represents the dominant culture where one's self worth is now determined not only by how hard one works but also by one's educational credentials. In another case, a carpenter who has a bachelor's degree in accounting told me that he reminds his (middle-class) customers that he is a college graduate in order to, in his words, portray himself as a competent craftsperson. The college degree in our society is a powerful symbol and gatekeeper (Collins 1979).

A lawyer told me how he successfully manages to be friends with his neighbor who has a blue-collar occupation and only a high school degree:

> I've been in social contact with people in my neighborhood who I consider myself friends with, go out to a movie, have a barbecue with, who I know are somewhat defensive around me with respect to the educational differences. It's part of the relationship and we deal with it. I joke about it, they joke about it. (35, male, lawyer, law degree)

Humor is often used to manage tense situations. Having people with radically different social and educational levels in the same (community) setting can produce tensions. Halle (1984) may not have considered this aspect of the blurring of social class lines in residential sections of the United States.

Lower middle-class respondents had a slightly better understanding of what it meant to be categorized by educational level, income, and occupational status. I say slightly because some respondents who fell into this category initially had some negative comments concerning individuals who they saw as below them in social status. A social worker said,

> I've had one bad experience. I deal with a lot of lawyers. As a matter of fact, they bring up my education, too. When they get you on the stand. [They say] "What makes you qualified to sit there and say this about [their] client? What about a master's, would a master's degree ever help you?" [One lawyer] was belittling me in front of a lot of people. (31, male, social worker, AAS)

Ironically, this statement came from the same man who said that he can spot uneducated people by their lack of language skills. Thus, possessing a college degree—an AAS—can still leave one vulnerable to attacks on one's character. The associate's degree was not seen as a legitimate degree to make a professional judgment. Such accounts are indicative of a dark underside of images held by some white-collar, college graduates.

SUMMARY AND CONCLUSIONS

This research project suggests that members of the working class struggle to find dignity in a society that is quick to judge one's worth on the basis of income, educational credentials, and occupational status. Although some members of the working class sample were not angry at white-collar, college graduates, most thought that white-collar college graduates try to look down on them. There is an underlying theme behind the working-class respondents' statements: a perception that people who wear business suits think they are better than us but, in reality, we are better than them because we are down-to-earth and work at real jobs. Business suits are associated with sitting behind a desk pushing papers as opposed to real work such as painting a bridge. Basically, members of the working class hold an image of the middle class as being incompetent in negotiating everyday events and having knowledge that is not practical; there is a definite notion of "us" and "them." Two neighbors can enjoy a barbecue on a Sunday evening, but on Monday morning one is dressed in a business suit and the other is dressed in work clothes.

Today, with the economy continuing to change from a manufacturing to a service base, motivated by corporations seeking cheap foreign labor, members of the working class seek out examples to sustain their belief and pride in what they consider to be "real" work. Even though the media are filled with stories concerning the lack of high-paying blue-collar jobs, having a high income and/or knowing someone who did not attend college but who has a high income (or someone who has a college degree and a low income) tends to reinforce in some members of the working class the belief that college is a waste of time and money.

Although ambivalent about the future, many of the working-class respondents in the present study believed that high-paying blue-collar jobs are still available and that it is still possible to achieve upward mobility in the United States—regardless of one's educational level—by working hard at one's job. Working-class respondents differentiated themselves from middle-class respondents by noting they do real work, do more important work, and are more down-to-earth. Working-class respondents' attitudes toward white-collar, college graduates are based, in part, on their search for dignity in a capitalistic society. The injuries that many working-class respondents encounter in their interactions with the dominant culture—at school, in the family, in the media, and at work—lead them to lash out at white-collar college graduates. In part, this resistance to a mainstream institution and new economic realities greases the gears of social class reproduction.

An incipient class consciousness seems to be at the base of these hidden injuries of class—a class consciousness that can partially penetrate the workings of the new dominant ideology in the United States. These "penetrations," however, may ultimately lead working-class parents, like Willis's (1977) lads, to resist the achievement ideology, thereby actually helping to reproduce the social class structure. Thus, in an attempt to restore dignity by drawing on culturally valued meanings of success, the resistance to higher education exhibited by working-class parents helps solidify their social class position and may ultimately solidify their children's social class position.

Members of the middle class, for the most part, have adopted the ideology that states that one needs a college education as well as a strong work ethic to make it in American society. Many working-class respondents reject this ideology; others, at best, grudgingly accept the ideology while not feeling totally comfortable with the steps they and their children will have to take to fulfill its dictates.

It is this deeply held belief in the benefits of higher education that leads many of the middle-class respondents to judge those without a college education as unworthy of receiving a high income; some of these respondents even said they use a person's grasp of the English language (grammar and sentence construction) as a quick and easy way to determine if that person has a college background.

Additionally, some middle-class respondents revealed that they were only able to hold mundane conversations with individuals who never attended college. Working-class respondents reported that they were aware of and resented the fact that white-collar, college graduates hold these pretentious attitudes. . . .

The taken-for-granted attitude toward college attendance espoused by the middle class and the lack of self-confidence exhibited by the working class does not seem to have withered over time and place. If middle-class attitudes were going to "trickle down" to the working class, one would think it would have occurred by now. The data reported here suggest that the attitudes held by many members of the middle class, which working-class members no doubt perceive during social interaction, have an impact on the self-confidence of working-class individuals, causing some to experience self-doubt, pain, and hidden injuries.

Social class as defined by education, occupational prestige, and income still matters in American society, even within the community. The American working class may not be class conscious in the classic Marxian sense of the concept—a class for itself—but it does have a deep understanding of the inequalities between "us" and "them" based on education, income, and occupational status; the respondents in this study, it seems, do not yet know they live in a postmodern world. With educational credentials coming to define who gets high-wage jobs in American society (Reich 1991), and with access to elite colleges becoming less of a reality for the members of the working class, class resentment can only intensify.

REFERENCES

ABERCROMBIE, N., S. HILL, AND B. TURNER. 1978. "The Dominant Ideology Thesis." *British Journal of Sociology.* 29:149–70.

BLUESTONE, BARRY AND BENNET HARRISON. 1982. *The Deindustrialization of America.* New York: Basic Books.

CLARK, TERRY NICHOLS AND SEYMOUR MARTIN LIPSET. 1991. "Are Social Classes Dying?" *International Sociology* 6(4):397–410.

CLARK, TERRY NICHOLS, SEYMOUR MARTIN LIPSET, AND MICHAEL REMPEL. 1993. "The Declining Significance of Social Class." *International Sociology* 8(3):293–316.

COLLINS, RANDALL. 1979. *The Credential Society.* New York: Academic Press.

EHRENREICH, BARBARA. 1989. *Fear of Falling: The Inner Life of the Middle Class.* New York: Pantheon.

HALLE, DAVID. 1984. *America's Working Man.* Chicago: University of Chicago Press.

HOUT, MIKE, CLEM BROOKS, AND JEFF MANZA. 1993. "The Persistence of Classes in Post-Industrial Societies." *International Sociology* 8(3):259–77.

KAHL, J. A. 1953. "Educational and Occupational Aspirations of 'Common Man Boys.'" *Harvard Educational Review* 23(3):186–203.

LAMONT, MICHELLE. 1992. *Money, Morals and Manners: The Culture of the French and American Upper-Middle Class.* Chicago: University of Chicago Press.

LAREAU, ANNETTE. 1989. *Home Advantage: Social Class and Parental Intervention in Elementary Education.* London: Falmer Press.

LAREAU, ANNETTE AND MICHELLE LAMONT. 1988. "Cultural Capital: Allusions, Gaps and Glissandos in Recent Theoretical Developments." *Sociological Theory* Fall: 153–68.

NEWMAN, KATHERINE S. 1988. *Falling From Grace: The Experience of Downward Mobility in the American Middle Class.* New York: Free Press.

PAKULSKI, JAN. 1993. "The Dying of Class or Marxist Class Theory?" *International Sociology* 8(3):27–92.

PAKULSKI, JAN AND MALCOLM WATERS. 1996. *The Death of Class.* London: Sage.

REICH, ROBERT. 1991. *The Work of Nations.* New York: Alfred A. Knopf.

SCOTT, JAMES C. 1990. *Domination and the Arts of Resistance.* New Haven, CT: Yale University Press.

SENNETT, RICHARD AND JONATHON COBB. 1972. *The Hidden Injuries of Class.* New York: Vintage Books.

WEIS, LOIS. 1990. *Working Class Without Work.* New York: Routledge.

CRITICAL THINKING QUESTIONS

1. What are the differences in the ways the middle class and the working class view one another?

2. Does the middle or the working class have a more negative view of the other? Support your answer with examples.

3. How do the perceptions that members of each social class have of the other impede social change?

Reading 4

The Beauty Myth

Patricia J. Williams

> *In this reading, Williams outlines the ways that definitions of attractiveness are set by dominate groups and how such definitions—which rely heavily on racist and sexist ideas—establish hierarchies of worth.*

Professor Robert Barro must be a very handsome man. A Harvard economist and senior fellow at the Hoover Institution, he believes that "physical appearance is always a bona fide worker characteristic as long as customers and co-workers think so." In *Business Week* recently, he assailed legal decisions like *Wilson v. Southwest Airlines,* a 1981 discrimination case in which flight attendants successfully challenged practices restricting hiring to young, pretty females. In the wake of that decision and others that questioned weekly weigh-ins and age monitoring as valid employment requirements, "stewardesses" gradually came to represent a wider range of humanity: older women, wiser women, women who dare to be greater than a size 8, men and those who defy narrow conceptions of beauty—particularly ethnic and racial minorities.

Source: Reprinted from *The Nation* 266, no. 20 (June 1, 1998): 10.

"Is it not a good thing," asks Barro, "if flight attendants are selected by job skills, meaning the ability to serve people well and to carry out safety procedures efficiently, and not at all on physical appearance?" Yes, indubitably, I muse, chewing upon the question as though it were an exam.

"I would say no" answers Barro. "The only meaningful measure of productivity is the amount a worker adds to customer satisfaction and to the happiness of co-workers." Uh-oh. Clearly Barro would have flunked me if I'd had the misfortune to be in one of his classes. And since Barro was recently in the news having received a breathtaking appointment offer from Columbia University (rumored to include a salary in excess of $300,000, affirmative action for his children at the best private schools, the right to hire a couple of like-minded colleagues to keep him company—none of which was enough to lure him), I felt unusually inspired to rectify my woeful lack of economic understanding.

Back in the good old days, according to Barro, pretty stewardesses "added to the pleasure of many heterosexual male air travelers." Reducing the role of physical appearance has brought us not only flight attendants who are "much less likely to be attractive and are sometimes male" but an inefficient "redistribution of resources from more attractive to less attractive people"—a result that, Barro writes, "effectively throw[s] away national product." It's quibbling, I suppose, to wonder why national product should be so inextricably linked to the adolescent fantasies of heterosexual male air travelers. Yes, I know, selling commodities is all about manipulating dreams, and there is money to be made by tailoring Business Class to the whims of mostly male C.E.O.s whose only relaxation seems to come from watching someone in uniform bend over just so. Call me an irrational feminist fuddy-duddy, but doesn't anyone else think "product" might skyrocket if flight attendants stopped posing so anxiously and just handed over another packet of peanuts already?

Barro, moreover, embraces a pretty blinkered aesthetic standard: Beauty, like power, is treated as though it were a static thing—a "trait," he calls it, a "matter of luck." Ugliness, too, is just one of life's little givens: "Less attractive, or at least obese, women are much less likely to marry than non-obese women and tend to have husbands with sharply lower earnings. Some researchers have greeted these findings with regret. . . ." But not the upbeat Professor Barro. No sense in worrying about such "hard fact[s] of life." If we did, "ugliness would have to be protected as a disability under the Americans with Disabilities Act, and the Act would have to be extended to the marriage market. . . . Perhaps a better idea than this new intervention would be for the government to stay out of the beauty business."

It's intriguing, this elision of personal preferences and civil rights. For, in reality, far from intervening in the "business" of beauty, laws like the Americans with Disabilities Act (and decisions like *Wilson*) are meant to allow citizens who have been systematically excluded by historically documented, culturally significant biased practices (sometimes disguised as

"tastes") the freedom to go about their business. Yes, paradoxically, that freedom places certain constraints on others—employers, clients—but until recently such constraints have been deemed permissible because they are outweighed by a societal interest in fairness. One of the most vexing aspects of the clash between the new corporate global order and our civil rights laws is libertarianism's outright rejection of American notions of fairness and equality. It is ominous that well-financed right-wing politicians attack hard-won legal remedies allowing preferences for persons who have been historically excluded—because of race, color, national origin or sex—while at the same time powerful economic interests work to justify the unregulated exercise of marketplace preferences against anyone deemed substandard in appearance.

But diversity, tolerance, integration, are moral values, not commodities. Beauty, like race, has never been just skin-deep, and beauty preferences (whether for big boobs or bound feet) are every bit as politically and culturally loaded as racial ones. If, for example, a broader range of black people are today regarded as somewhat, or even just slightly, more "attractive" than at any time in our history, let's remember that it didn't come about through the hormonal dispositions of the high-flying male population of the business-as-usual class. It came about because blackness was consciously politicized as beautiful; because affirmative, corrective, legal action brought new faces into positions where gentlemen had always preferred blondes. And, as in all circumstances of sheer propinquity, the newness eventually wears off, the temptation to stare subsides. With time our differences are negotiated; we grow close to a few more of the former "others." Over time we expand our polity, our community and, yes, even our markets by looking back out into the world and finding ourselves "attracted" to more of those who remind us of our new familiars. But such expansiveness has always been the product of sustained commitment rather than free-floating desire; and when we abandon that course of deeper valuation, we shortchange ourselves and sell short our best ideals.

CRITICAL THINKING QUESTIONS

1. What is the argument in favor of the idea that workers should be attractive?

2. What is Williams' argument against the idea that workers need to be attractive?

3. How is the idea that workers should be attractive rooted in sexist and racist beliefs?

Reading 5

Never Too Buff

John Cloud

> *In this article, Cloud demonstrates how social institutions and cultural beliefs affect self-perceptions of men, and how men are willing to go to extremes to make their bodies fit social expectations.*

A new book reveals a troubling obsession: How male self-worth is increasingly tied to body image.

POP QUIZ. WHO ARE MORE LIKELY TO BE dissatisfied with the appearance of their chests, men or women? Who is more likely to be concerned about acne, your teenage son or his sister? And who is more likely to binge eat, your nephew or your niece?

If you chose the women and girls in your life, you are right only for the last question—and even then, not by the margin you might expect. About 40% of Americans who go on compulsive-eating sprees are men. Thirty-eight percent of men want bigger pecs, while only 34% of women want bigger breasts. And more boys have fretted about zits than girls, going all the way back to a 1972 study.

A groundbreaking new book declares that these numbers, along with hundreds of other statistics and interviews the authors have compiled, mean something awful has happened to American men over the past few decades. They have become obsessed with their bod-

Source: From *Time*, Vol. 155 Issue 16, April 24, 2000, pp. 64–68. © 2000 by Time Inc. Magazine Company. Reprinted by permission.

ies. Authors Harrison Pope and Katharine Phillips, professors of psychiatry at Harvard and Brown, respectively, and Roberto Olivardia, a clinical psychologist at McLean Hospital in Belmont, Mass., have a catchy name to describe this obsession—a term that will soon be doing many reps on chat shows: the Adonis Complex.

The name, which refers to the gorgeous half man, half god of mythology, may be a little too ready for *Oprah,* but the theory behind it will start a wonderful debate. Based on original research involving more than 1,000 men over the past 15 years, the book argues that many men desperately want to look like Adonis because they constantly see the "ideal," steroid-boosted bodies of actors and models and because their muscles are all they have over women today. In an age when women fly combat missions, the authors ask, "What can a modern boy or man do to distinguish himself as being 'masculine'?"

For years, of course, some men—ice skaters, body builders, George Hamilton—have fretted over aspects of their appearance. But the numbers suggest that body-image concerns have gone mainstream: nearly half of men don't like their overall appearance, in contrast to just 1 in 6 in 1972. True, men typically are fatter now, but another study found that 46% of men of normal weight think about their appearance "all the time" or "frequently." And some men—probably hundreds of thousands, if you extrapolate from small surveys—say they have passed up job and even romantic opportunities because they refuse to disrupt workouts or dine on restaurant food. In other words, an increasing number of men would rather look brawny for their girlfriends than have sex with them.

Consider what they're spending. Last year American men forked over $2 billion for gym memberships—and another $2 billion for home exercise equipment. *Men's Health* ("Rock-hard abs in six weeks!" it screams every other issue) had 250,000 subscribers in 1990; now it has 1.6 million. In 1996 alone, men underwent some 700,000 cosmetic procedures.

At least those profits are legal. Anabolic steroids—the common name for synthetic testosterone—have led to the most dramatic changes in the male form in modern history, and more and more average men want those changes for themselves. Since steroids became widely available on the black market in the 1960s, perhaps 3 million American men have swallowed or injected them—mostly in the past 15 years. A 1993 survey found that 1 Georgia high school boy in every 15 admitted having used steroids without a prescription. And the Drug Enforcement Administration reports that the percentage of all high school students who have used steroids has increased 50% in the past four years, from 1.8% to 2.8%. The abuse of steroids has so alarmed the National Institute on Drug Abuse that on Friday it launched a campaign in gyms, malls, bookstores, clubs and on the Internet to warn teenagers about the dangers. Meanwhile, teenagers in even larger numbers are buying legal but lightly regulated food supplements, some with dangerous side effects, that purport to make you bigger or leaner or stronger.

As they infiltrated the body-building world in the '70s and Hollywood a decade later, steroids created bodies for mass consumption that the world had literally never seen before.

Pope likes to chart the changes by looking at Mr. America winners, which he called up on the Internet in his office last week. "Look at this guy," Pope exclaims when he clicks on the 1943 winner, Jules Bacon. "He couldn't even win a county body-building contest today." Indeed, there are 16-year-olds working out at your gym who are as big as Bacon. Does that necessarily mean that today's body builders—including those 16-year-olds—are 'roided? Pope is careful. "The possibility exists that rare or exceptional people, those with an unusual genetic makeup or a hormonal imbalance," could achieve the muscularity and leanness of today's big body builders, he says.

But it's not likely. And Pope isn't lobbing dumbbells from an ivory tower: the professor lifts weights six days a week, from 11 a.m. to 1 p.m. (He can even mark historical occasions by his workouts: "I remember when the *Challenger* went down; I was doing a set of squats.") "We are being assaulted by images virtually impossible to attain without the use of drugs," says Pope. "So what happens when you change a million-year-old equilibrium of nature?"

A historical loop forms: steroids beget pro wrestlers—Hulk Hogan, for one, has admitted taking steroids—who inspire boys to be just like them. Steroids have changed even boys' toys. Feminists have long derided Barbie for her tiny waist and big bosom. The authors of *The Adonis Complex* see a similar problem for boys in the growth of G.I. Joe. The grunt of 1982 looks scrawny compared with G.I. Joe Extreme, introduced in the mid-'90s. The latter would have a 55-in. chest and 22-in. biceps if he were real, which simply can't be replicated in nature. Pope also points out a stunning little feature of the three-year-old video game Duke Nukem: Total Meltdown, developed by GT Interactive Software. When Duke gets tired, he can find a bottle of steroids to get him going. "Steroids give Duke a super adrenaline rush," the game manual notes.

To bolster their argument, the *Adonis* authors developed a computerized test that allows subjects to "add" muscle to a typical male body. They estimate their own size and then pick the size they would like to be and the size they think women want. Pope and his colleagues gave the test to college students and found that on average, the men wanted 28 lbs. more muscle—and thought women wanted them to have 30 lbs. more. In fact, the women who took the test picked an ideal man only slightly more muscular than average. Which goes a long way toward explaining why Leonardo DiCaprio can be a megastar in a nation that also idealizes "Stone Cold" Steve Austin.

But when younger boys took Pope's test, they revealed an even deeper sense of inadequacy about their bodies. More than half of boys ages 11 to 17 chose as their physical ideal an image possible to attain only by using steroids. So they do. Boys are a big part of the clientele at Muscle Mania (not its real name), a weight-lifting store that TIME visited last week at a strip mall in a Boston suburb. A couple of teenagers came in to ask about tribulus, one of the many over-the-counter drugs and body-building supplements the store sells, all legally.

"A FRIEND OF MINE," ONE BOY BEGINS, fooling no one, "just came off a cycle of juice, and he heard that tribulus can help you produce testosterone naturally." Patrick, 28, who runs the store and who stopped using steroids four years ago because of chest pain, tells the kid, "The s——shuts off your nuts," meaning steroids can reduce sperm production, shrink the testicles and cause impotence. Tribulus, Patrick says, can help restart natural testosterone production. The teen hands over $12 for 100 Tribulus Fuel pills. (Every day, Muscle Mania does $4,000 in sales of such products, with protein supplements and so-called fat burners leading the pack.)

Patrick says many of his teen customers, because they're short on cash, won't pay for a gym membership "until they've saved up for a cycle [of steroids]. They don't see the point without them." The saddest customers, he says, are the little boys, 12 and 13, brought in by young fathers. "The dad will say, 'How do we put some weight on this kid?' with the boy just staring at the floor. Dad is going to turn him into Hulk Hogan, even if it's against his will."

What would motivate someone to take steroids? Pope, Phillips and Olivardia say the Adonis Complex works in different ways for different men. "Michael," 32, one of their research subjects, told TIME he had always been a short kid who got picked on. He started working out at about 14, and he bought muscle magazines for advice. The pictures taunted him: he sweated, but he wasn't getting as big as the men in the pictures. Other men in his gym also made him feel bad. When he found out they were on steroids, he did two cycles himself, even though he knew they could be dangerous.

But not all men with body-image problems take steroids. Jim Davis, 29, a human-services manager, told TIME he never took them, even when training for body-building competitions. But Davis says he developed a form of obsessive-compulsive disorder around his workouts. He lifted weights six days a week for at least six years. He worked out even when injured. He adhered to a rigid regimen for every session, and if he changed it, he felt anxious all day. He began to be worried about clothes, and eventually could wear only three shirts, ones that made him look big. He still felt small. "I would sit in class at college with a coat on," he says. You may have heard this condition called bigorexia—thinking your muscles are puny when they aren't. Pope and his colleagues call it muscle dysmorphia and estimate that hundreds of thousands of men suffer from it.

Even though most boys and men never approach the compulsion of Davis or Michael (both eventually conquered it), they undoubtedly face more pressure now than in the past to conform to an impossible ideal. Rippled male bodies are used today to advertise everything that shapely female bodies advertise: not just fitness products but also dessert liqueurs, microwave ovens and luxury hotels. The authors of *The Adonis Complex* want guys to rebel against those images, or at least see them for what they are: a goal unattainable without drug use.

Feminists raised these issues for women years ago, and more recent books such as *The*

Beauty Myth were part of a backlash against the hourglass ideal. Now, says Phillips, "I actually think it may be harder for men than women to talk about these problems because it's not considered masculine to worry about such things." But maybe there is a masculine alternative: Next time WWF comes on, guys, throw the TV out the window. And order a large pizza.

CRITICAL THINKING QUESTIONS

1. What are the messages young men receive from fashion magazines about appropriate appearance?

2. What are the costs to young men who receive these messages?

3. Who benefits from these messages?

Reading 6

Racial Warriors and Weekend Warriors

Abby L. Ferber

> *In this reading, Ferber discusses the similarities between two presumably very different groups of men: those involved in the mythopoetic men's movement and white supremacists.*

THE CONSTRUCTION OF MASCULINITY IN MYTHOPOETIC AND WHITE SUPREMACIST DISCOURSE

The recent passage of Proposition 209 in California is but one sign of the broad-based attack on affirmative action programs. This proposition amends the California Constitution to read, "The state shall not discriminate against, or grant preferential treatment to, any individual or group on the basis of race, sex, color, ethnicity or national origin" (*Denver Post* 1996, 25A). Framed in this language, affirmative action is represented as a form of reverse discrimination, an attack on white males.

In both academic and mainstream circles, the idea that masculinity, especially white masculinity, is in crisis is widespread. Michael Kimmel (1987) argues that "definitions of masculinity are historically *reactive* to changing definitions of femininity" (p. 123). Because

Source: Men and Masculinities, Vol. 3 No. 1, July 2000, pp. 30–56 © 2000 Sage Publications, Inc.

men benefit most from traditional definitions and proscriptions of gender, they are less likely to initiate change. Instead, women's inroads into the workplace, increased political and economic autonomy, and questioning of male domination have historically been perceived as threats to male privilege. Since the 1960s and the second wave of the women's movement, many males have responded with fear, anger, and feelings of loss. As Susan Faludi (1991) argues in her wide-ranging book *Backlash*,

> "backlashes" . . . have always been triggered by the perception—accurate or not—that women are making great strides . . . efforts that have been interpreted time and again by men—especially men grappling with real threats to their economic and social well-being on other fronts—as spelling their own masculine doom. (p. xix)

A similar argument can be advanced in terms of race. Since the rise of the Civil Rights movement and the destruction of many legal barriers to racial integration and equality, a strong white reaction has been brewing, and occasionally, explodes. Many white males feel under attack by movements for both gender and racial equality. As Michael Omi (1991) explains, the Civil Rights movement and the subsequent shift in racial politics

> ushered in a period of desegregation efforts, "equal opportunity" mandates, and other state reforms. By the early seventies, however, a "backlash" could be discerned to the institutionalization of these reforms and to the political realignments set in motion in the 1960s. (p. 78)

Charles Gallagher (1995) found that backlash and anger characterize the feelings of many white college students. He concludes "that many whites see themselves as victims of the multicultural, pc, feminist onslaught [and this] would be laughable if it were not for the sense of mental crisis and the reactionary backlash that underpin these beliefs" (p. 169). Central to this backlash is a sense of confusion over the meanings of both masculinity and whiteness, triggered by the perceived loss of white, male privilege (Gallagher 1995; Steinberg 1995). Both the contemporary white supremacist movement and the mythopoetic movement have been able to attract some of these disillusioned white males, who now believe that their interests are not being represented. As Ezekiel (1995) describes the sentiments of white supremacist activists, "White rule in America has ended, members feel. A new world they do not like has pushed aside the traditional one they think they remember" (p. xxv).

Identities once taken for granted as secure and stable are in flux, challenged by the Civil Rights movement, women's movement, and gay and lesbian movements.

> As a result, many middle-class, white, middle-aged heterosexual men—among the most privileged groups in the history of the world—do not experience themselves as powerful. Ironically, although these men are everywhere in power, that aggregate power of that group does not translate into an individual sense of feeling empowered. In fact, this group feels quite powerless. (Kimmel and Kaufman 1995, 18)

As David Wellman argues, the declining position and wages of all Americans means that white men are correct when they perceive themselves to be losing ground. In fact, the United States is experiencing greater income inequality than ever before. As a result of both cultural and structural changes, white men do not see themselves as possessing power and are increasingly joining social movements to represent their interests. Rather than exploring the real sources of economic dislocation in the United States today, many of these movements instead blame the losses of white men on women and minorities.

This article will explore contemporary white male backlash by comparing the discourses of two movements usually assumed to have little in common: the mythopoetic men's movement and the contemporary white supremacist movement. While their differences are obvious, I argue that they are similar in important ways, and with consequences.

Faludi (1991) observes that a backlash is not an organized response and that "the lack of orchestration, the absence of a single string-puller, only makes it harder to see" (p. xxii). It is this lack of formal connections that often prevents us from seeing the similarities or ties among disparate movements. While it may not be overt or obvious, analyses of each movement have argued that they represent a backlash to feminism and the changing meanings of gender (Ferber 1998b; Kimmel 1995; Messner 1997). Reading these two discourses alongside each other gives us a fuller picture of the current climate of backlash and highlights new implications, different from those derived from looking at either discourse individually.

On the surface, the white supremacist movement presents itself as primarily concerned with race relations. Scholars studying the movement have explored its racist and anti-Semitic ideologies, but there has been little discussion of the role of gender in its ideology. The mythopoetic movement, on the other hand, is about gender, masculinity in particular. However, sympathetic observers point out that the movement is centrally concerned with helping men to rediscover their "deep" masculinity, which, in contrast to hypermasculinity, aims to help men become more in touch with their feelings and emotions, to examine negative and narrow social definitions of masculinity, to balance their masculine and feminine sides, and to become better fathers and husbands. The goals of the mythopoetic movement are certainly laudable and seem well-intentioned, in sharp contrast with the motivations of the white supremacist movement, easily recognized as despicable to most casual observers. It is for this reason that it is all the more surprising to find such striking similarities in their discourses.

It is not my intention to downplay the very real differences between the two movements but instead to examine certain key assumptions and analyses they share. To find such similar concerns at the roots of such diverse movements, with such purportedly different objectives, is revealing. I believe this is an important exercise whose implications suggest that male anxiety and fear over changing gendered expectations are widespread, and resonate strongly even in very diverse locations. New social movements attract men to the extent that they capitalize on these concerns, and concerns over other important issues, including race relations, affirmative action, immigration, teenage delinquency, the collapse of the nuclear family, adolescent disdain for authority, and corporate downsizing, are all rearticulated in gendered terms. Diverse social problems are being rewritten as problems resulting from changing gender expectations, demasculinization, feminism, and so forth. And this phenomenon is not limited to these two movements; it can be seen at work in various social movements, including, most obviously, the Promise Keepers, as well as other discourses of the religious right.

Within the context of a broader backlash, I see these two discourses as reinforcing broader discourses about gender; my comparison will emphasize the connections between white supremacist and mythopoetic ideologies, revealing their shared assumptions and foundations. This analysis, then, will not only allow us to look at these two movements in new ways but will shed light on our broader understanding of the construction of gender and the fears and anxieties of white men in contemporary America.

READING WHITE MASCULINITY

I focus here on the discourses of each of these movements. I am more interested in the ideas about gender formulated in these discourses than the members themselves. It is the literature that carries the ideas and messages of these movements to a far wider audience.

As Kimmel (1995) points out, "The mythopoetic men's movement [is] as much a textual phenomenon as it [is] a ritual process" (p. 4). The mythopoetic men's movement formed around certain key texts, especially Robert Bly's *Iron John: A Book About Men* (1990). The movement's gatherings and retreats are a means of making the messages of the texts real for people, a means of gathering men together to discuss the ideas and issues generated within the written works. For the white supremacist movement as well, written works bind together a range of people and organizations. As Ezekiel (1995) found in his study of members of the movement, "The agreement on basic ideas is the glue that holds the movement together . . . the ideas are important to the members. The white racist movement is about an idea" (p. xxix). It is in the written texts that we find the most comprehensive and persistent explication of these ideas.

How many people do these ideas actually reach? The Intelligence Project of the Southern Poverty Law Center, established to monitor hate group activity, identified 462 white supremacist hate groups in existence through-out the United States in 1997 (Intelligence Project of The Southern Poverty Law Center 1998, 6). It is difficult to estimate the membership of these groups, which is often concealed. Daniels conservatively estimates the general membership in white supremacist organizations to be around forty thousand, while Ezekiel reports that hard-core members number twenty-three thousand to twenty-five thousand. Another 150 thousand purchase movement literature and take part in activities, however, and an additional 450 thousand actually read the movement literature, even though they do not purchase it themselves (Daniels 1997; Ezekiel 1995). The Anti-Defamation League (1988) estimates that fifty white supremacist periodicals continue to publish, and there are at least 2000 "hate sites" on the Internet (p. 1; Roberts 1997).

At its peak, it was estimated that approximately one hundred thousand men participated in some sort of mythopoetic event (Schwalbe 1996, p. 4). Robert Bly's book *Iron John* spent months among the top ten national best-sellers. These two discourses, then, reach a far wider audience than only those men (and some women) who consider themselves members of these movements. From this perspective, these discourses reach huge numbers of people and have far wider implications than only what they mean for those actively involved in the movements.

Schwalbe (1996) argues that

by reviving and injecting these ideas into the culture, the mythopoetic movement has altered the course of gender politics in the late twentieth century. Even those vehemently opposed to ideas associated with the mythopoetic movement have had to respond to those ideas. It is the power of these ideas, in the cultural and economic context of late twentieth century Western society, that makes the mythopoetic movement important. (p. 5)

It is the power of these ideas that concerns me, and they are even more powerful when similar messages are voiced from numerous divergent corners of the cultural landscape. . . .

THE MOVEMENTS

The Mythopoetic Men's Movement

Beginning even before the 1990 publication of *Iron John,* retreats, workshops, and conferences were being organized across the country. As Kimmel (1995) observes, men "were trooping off to the woods on weekend retreats to drum, chant, be initiated, bond, and otherwise discover their inner wildmen or retrieve their deep masculinity" (p. 4).

The mythopoetic men's movement is a world of and for men. Its leaders, authors, and followers are all men. Workshop attendees are overwhelmingly white, middle class, middle aged, heterosexual men. While race is not an overt feature of their ideology, they nevertheless appeal primarily to white men.

Bly argues that men are experiencing an identity crisis; numerous forces, especially men's lack of relationships with their fathers, have prevented men from discovering their deep masculinity. According to Bly, men can only get in touch with their true being with other men. Throughout the discourse, as well as in retreats and workshops, men are encouraged to reclaim their authentic masculinity through initiation ceremonies, rituals, stories, and myths, guided by other men.

The mythopoetic movement is about reenvisioning masculinity; the term *mythopoetic,* according to Shepherd Bliss (1995), "refers to remythologizing. It means re-making, so the mythopoetic approach means revisioning masculinity for our time" (p. 293).

Aaron Kipnis (1995) argues that the mythopoetic movement seeks to replace the violent warrior imagery of toxic masculinity with an "image of men who dance, make music, protect nature, and love women" (p. 277). Bliss (1995) describes the "Deep Masculine" as "generative, earthy, nurturing, playful, forceful, and zany," in contrast to "Toxic Masculinity," which "poisons through means such as neglect, abuse, and violence" (p. 302).

The White Supremacist Movement

The white supremacist movement is also overwhelmingly a movement of and for white men. Despite the efforts of some organizations to increase the number of women involved, white men make up the bulk of the membership of the movement and serve as the writers, publishers, and editors of white supremacist discourse (Blee 1996). Ezekiel (1995) notes that the organizations he observed remain almost exclusively male, and tasks within the organizations are strictly segregated by gender. He notes, "A few women are around, never as speakers or leaders; usually they are wives, who cook and listen. Highly traditional ideas of sex roles, and fears of losing male dominance, fill the conversation and speeches" (p. xxvii). Reading white supremacy alongside mythopoetic discourse reveals that it is not just a racist, anti-Semitic movement, but a patriarchal one as well.

Most white supremacist organizations share a number of unquestioned beliefs. They believe that races are essentially and eternally different, not only in terms of visible characteristics, but also behaviorally and culturally, and that races are ranked hierarchically based on these supposedly innate differences. They believe the white race is superior and responsible for all of the advances of Western civilization. They also mobilize against a common threat: they believe the white race faces the threat of genocide, orchestrated by Jews and carried out by blacks and other nonwhites. White supremacist discourse asserts that this genocidal plan is being carried out through forced race mixing, which will result in the mongrelization, and therefore annihilation, of the white race. Interracial sexuality is defined as the "ultimate abomination," and images of white women stolen away by black men are the ever present symbol of that threat (Ridgeway 1990, 19). In stark contrast to the images of active, sexually independent women put forth by the women's movement, white supremacist discourse depicts white women as passive victims at the hands of Jews and blacks, and in dire need of white men's protection. The protection of white womanhood comes to symbolize the protection of the race; thus, gender relations occupy a central place in the discourse.

While the contemporary white supremacist movement is concerned with rearticulating a white identity in response to the challenges of racial and ethnic social movements, this white identity is most certainly a gendered identity. Both the white supremacist and the mythopoetic movements represent responses to the second wave of the feminist movement and the challenges it has presented to traditional gender identities. Responding to what is perceived as a threat to what were once believed to be stable identities, both movements are primarily concerned with rearticulating white male identity and privilege. Both movements appeal to similar constituencies of white males who feel vulnerable, victimized, and uncertain about the meaning of masculinity in contemporary society; the white supremacist movement attempts to redeem a specifically white, racial masculinity, whereas the mythopoetic movement couches its version of masculinity in nonracial terms. Nevertheless, their visions of masculinity and their analyses of the problems faced by men share much in common.

ESSENTIAL MASCULINITY

Gender is a social construction. The definitions and meanings of gender vary both historically and cross-culturally. Biologist Ruth Hubbard argues that biology and culture interact and points out that biology is not destiny; humans are not born with wings or fins, yet we fly and sail (Butler 1993; Hubbard 1990; Nicholson 1994; Scott 1988). As Kimmel (1994) explains, masculinity is a "constantly changing collection of meanings that we construct . . . manhood is neither static nor timeless; it is historical. Manhood is not the manifestation of an inner essence; it is socially constructed. . . . Manhood means different things at different times to different people" (p. 120).

Despite decades of scholarship demonstrating that gender is a social construction, both the mythopoetic and white supremacist movements reassert an essentialist notion of gender identity. Essentialism is the centerpiece of both ideologies, and their other similarities revolve around this shared central assumption. Ken Clatterbaugh (1995) explains that essentialism assumes that "social differences such as those between men and women, people of different races, or social classes are due to intrinsic biological or psychic differences between the members of the different groups" (p. 49). These differences are believed to be innate and immutable, and are seen as more significant than environmental factors in explaining differences among people.

As Kimmel (1987) points out,

> The search for a transcendent, timeless definition of manhood is itself a sociological phenomenon—we tend to search for the timeless and eternal during moments of crisis, those points of transition when old definitions no longer work and new definitions are yet to be firmly established. (p. 120)

Partly due to the challenges of the women's movement and minority social movements to traditional notions of gender and race, these identities are in flux. Michael Messner (1995) argues that, "Like it or not, men today must deal, on some level, with gender as a problematic construct, rather than as a natural, taken-for-granted reality" (p. 97). Both mythopoetic and white supremacist discourse respond by reasserting essentialist notions. When men feel that their identity as men is under attack, "essentialist views of gender will be attractive. Such views provide more than a way to explain gender; they make it morally defensible, since only nature is held accountable" (Schwalbe 1996, 66).

There are, nevertheless, differences between the two essentialist revisions of masculinity. Both respond in different ways to our culture's definition of hegemonic masculinity, an ideal based on an image of white, middle- or upper-class, heterosexual men. This image serves as the ideal that all men are expected to live up to, and against which all men are measured, but that few can achieve. Kimmel (1994) writes,

> The hegemonic definition of manhood is a man in power, a man with power, and a man of power. We equate manhood with being strong, successful, capable, reliable, in control. The very definitions of manhood we have developed in our culture maintain the power that some men have over other men and that men have over women. (p. 125)

Both movements suggest that men today are betrayed by such ideals, but in very different ways: white supremacists argue that white men are prevented from achieving this ideal, while the mythopoets argue that the definitions themselves are problematic.

The white supremacist movement promises its recruits that it will enable them to prove themselves real men according to the vision of hegemonic masculinity. They argue that white men have been unfairly prevented from achieving this ideal (by Jews, nonwhites, and women) and denied their rightful position of power. Join the white supremacist movement, they reassure, and regain the powerful masculinity that should be yours. Key to achieving this vision of masculinity is reasserting control over women and other men.

The mythopoetic movement, on the other hand, to some extent challenges hegemonic masculinity, at least the part of it that says men must be unfeeling, must never show emotion, must be independent, violent, and dedicated to competitive work. They argue that men must explore their wounds and emotions. Yet, rather than exploring masculinity as a social construction, they argue that those aspects they despise represent "toxic" masculinity, or hypermasculinity, not the real, true, deep masculinity that men must discover. In *Knights Without Armor*, Aaron Kipnis (1992) presents a "New Male Manifesto," where he states, "A man doesn't have to live up to any narrow, societal image of manhood. . . . Masculinity does not require the denial of deep feeling. . . . Violence springs from desperation and fear rather than from authentic manhood."

Like the white supremacist movement, mythopoets present their movement as men's salvation—join our retreats, read our books, and find your real masculine self. Unfortunately, this deep masculinity nevertheless retains many other features of hegemonic masculinity, as we shall see. Both movements, then, promise to help men discover their true masculinity and prove to the world that they are real men.

Despite these differences, the similarities are striking. To enable men to discover their masculinity, both movements are concerned with creating community among men, "drawing men together . . . breaking isolation . . . for the development of community" (Bliss 1995, 296). Both see men as out of touch with their true masculinity. Kimmel and Kaufman (1995) argue that the "central assumption" of mythopoetic discourse is that of an essential male and female nature (p. 25). Scholars observe that *Iron John* is filled with sweeping generalizations "about what 'men' are, feel, or need. Most of them have no basis in evidence or argument at all" (Connell 1995, 81). Masculinity is characterized as unchanging and universal, merely needing to be recovered. Beneke (1995) notes that "'Deep masculinity' is a pancultural, transhistorical essence, built into the male psyche and (presumably) biology, which is men's true, 'deepest' identity" (p. 154). As Bly (1990) writes, "The structure at the bottom of the male psyche is still as firm as it was twenty thousand years ago" (p. 230). Describing the process by which a boy becomes a man, Bly (1996) concludes, "That is the way it has been for hundreds of years" (p. 127). Mythopoetic authors Moore and Gillette (1992) claim that masculinity has "remained largely unchanged for millions of years," because it is "hard wired" and "genetically transmitted" (p. 33).

Men and women are depicted as opposites possessing complementary natures. Bly (1990) writes that we must "recognize opposites . . . rejoice that they exist . . . male and female

make up one pair" (pp. 174–75). As Clatterbaugh (1995) observes, "mythopoetics see the masculine and feminine as opposite . . . men have little or nothing to gain from women's teachings" (p. 51). Not only do men and women possess essential natures, then, but these natures are dichotomous and timeless.

Reliance on Jungian archetypes grounds the essentialism of mythopoetic discourse. According to this doctrine, all humans possess archetypes,

inborn potentials for the patterning of psychic energy . . . [they] lead us to think, feel, and act in particular ways. Archetypes are the products of species evolution . . . [and] certain archetypes tend to dominate in men, while others dominate in women. . . . Women and men are thus predisposed to think, feel, and act differently because their psyches, like their bodies, are built differently. Men, by virtue of their masculine archetypes, are inclined to impose order on the world, defend territory, provide for others, give of themselves to others, and love women. Women are inclined by their feminine archetypes to perceive the connectedness of all things, establish intimate ties with others, nurture others, bear children, and love men. (Schwalbe 1996, 37)

Schwalbe refers to this as loose essentialism, rather than strict essentialism, because these potentialities are shaped by experience, so that men and women may end up acting very differently or similarly. However, most essentialist theories can be characterized this way, because they tend to offer to solve the contemporary problems that they suggest have resulted from straying away from our essentialist identities. There is usually room left for environmental factors to distort what is assumed to be the work of nature.

Like mythopoetic discourse, white supremacist discourse rearticulates essentialist notions of identity. The discourse insists that racial and gender differences are essential and immutable, secured by either God or genetics. While race is the most overt preoccupation of the white supremacist movement, gender identity remains central to the discourse and is intertwined with the construction of racial identities. While whiteness is repeatedly defined in terms of visible, physical differences in appearance, differences in intelligence, morality, character, and culture are all posited as racially determined. As *The NSV Report* (National Socialist Vanguard) proclaims, "Racists believe that values and ideals are a manifestation of race and are thus biologically inherited" (*NSV Report* 1991, 3). Physical characteristics and culture are linked here, both determined by race and unchanging.

Gender differences are also posited as inherent. While supremacist discourse, like mythopoetic discourse, often relies on stories of the past to demonstrate the immutability of these natures. For example, a *White Power* article explains that "our ancestors wisely realized that women were different from men not just biologically, but psychologically and emotionally as well. They recognized that the sexes had distinct but complementary roles to play in society . . . ordained by natural law" (*White Power* no. 105, 4). As in mythopoetic discourse, sexual difference is depicted as oppositional and complementary.

Rather than revealing race and gender as biological essences, these discourses demonstrate Judith Butler's (1993) assertion that identities are constructed through reiterative and citational practices (p. 2). The construction of identity is not a singular act or gesture but rather a process—or performance, as Butler calls it—that must be continually repeated. The elaboration of racial and gender difference must "repeat itself in order to establish the illusion of its own uniformity and identity" (Butler 1991, 24). Contrary to their claims, these discourses actually construct gender.

These identities are always at risk and never secure. The endless repetition through which these identities are constructed suggests that they require this repetition for their existence; they are neither innate nor essential. It is at this historical juncture, when both racial and gender identities are increasingly revealed to be unstable, that those who have the most invested in these categories and their hierarchical construction react by reasserting their unwavering foundations.

WHITE MEN UNDER ATTACK

Both movements argue that their existence is necessary to protect men (and for white supremacists, only white men), who are depicted as under attack in contemporary society. As suggested by the title of David Duke's National Association for the Advancement of White People, women and minorities have organizations to protect their interests, why not white men?

These sentiments are overt throughout white supremacist publications. As an article in the *White Patriot* asserts, "the White people of America have become an oppressed majority. Our people suffer from discrimination in the awarding of employment, promotions, scholarships, and college entrances" (*White Patriot* no. 56, 6). Similarly, an *Instauration* article echoes, "we are now becoming a minority in a land which we tore from the vines and tangle of the wilderness" (*Instauration* 1985, 14).

As these passages suggest, the contemporary white supremacist movement depicts the white race, and men in particular, as under attack. In *The Racist Mind*, Raphael S. Ezekiel (1995) suggests, "white rule in America has ended, members feel. A new world they do not like has pushed aside the traditional one they think they remember" (p. xxv). Trivializing and dismissing the enduring reality of both race and gender oppression, white masculinity is often depicted as the new minority, the only truly oppressed group.

Issues such as affirmative action, which have increasingly been reframed in the terms of "reverse racism," are rallied around to garner support. For example, *The NSV Report* contends that affirmative action is not really about giving jobs to disadvantaged minorities but part of a bigger conspiracy against white men:

A White man goes to a government employment office. He is on the bottom of the totem pole by Federal law. All non-Whites get first crack at all the jobs. The government does not want White men to have the money to raise a White family. It is called keeping the White birth rate as low as possible. The government would rather keep a White woman employed rather than a White man because this keeps the White woman out of the home and on the job. (*NSV Report* 1989, 1)

Both movements encourage men to see themselves as victims, depicting men as under attack in today's world and arguing that "those who hold the reins of power pile abuse, distortion, ridicule and hatred" on white men (begging the question, Who then holds the reins of power?) (*Instauration* 1985, 14).

According to Bly (1996),

The ridicule of masculinity that has poured out of comic strips, from Dagwood Bumstead to Homer Simpson, from sitcoms and Letterman monologues, and from university classrooms, has had a profoundly damaging effect on young men. Gender feminists have contributed to this problem, encouraging stereotypes of masculinity that would be totally unacceptable if directed toward any other group . . . the new equation, male equals bad, has given rise to a loss of identity for a whole generation of men. (p. 129)

Both movements attack women and minorities for playing the "victim" role, arguing that it is a ruse used against white men, the "real" victims. "How obvious it is," Bliss (1995) explains, "once we look—men die eight years younger than women in the U.S. today: they have higher rates of cancer, heart attacks, and suicide. More substance abuse, risk-taking, and automobile accidents" (p. 303).

Kipnis (1995) argues that "male-bashing is de rigueur in today's academy" and describes feminism as "male-denigrating. . . . After decades of unrestrained male-bashing, men have good cause for anger toward the women's movement. This is not backlash; it is a legitimate response to abuse of academic, social, media, and literary power" (pp. 278–80).

These descriptions depict women and feminism as in power everywhere: "Feminist attitudes breed many double standards for men. They now affect almost every social institution," argues Kipnis (1995), providing a laundry list of problems plaguing men:

in many schools, over 5 percent of boys are given behavior modification drugs to get them to conform to a regimented, feminized school environment. The vast majority of teachers and counselors who refer them to psychiatrists for this treatment are women. . . . At last count there were over 600 academic women's studies programs, yet not a single one examining . . . men in our society. There are about 15,000 courses devoted to women's studies, yet only 91 courses on men's studies . . . in this increasingly antimale academic environment. In many instances, male-affirming voices on campus are actually repressed by feminists . . . indoctrination still takes precedent. (pp. 282–83)

Kipnis describes a conspiratorial environment where women are in control and patriarchy is a relic of the past.

Wherever patriarchy is referred to, it is in the past tense. For example, Bly (1996) admits, "We know that women paid a huge price in self-respect, in violence, in slavery, in shame, in the old paternal society. Almost no woman in the world wants to return to that" (pp. 113–14). Elsewhere Bly (1995) explains, "None of us wants to reestablish patriarchy" (p. 272).

We find in both discourses a reversal of the reality of inequality. Both movements assert that the days of white male power are over and that the playing field has been leveled. Within this framework, then, any attempts to aid women or minorities are seen as giving them unfair advantages, and perceived as unfair attacks against white males. Whether affirmative action or women's studies programs, they are depicted as attempts to privilege women and minorities. Because they assume that white men receive no power or privilege in contemporary society, they reverse the balance of power, seeing all attempts to remedy inequality as actually attacks against white men, as instances of reverse discrimination. Kipnis (1992) suggests it is now men who must fight for equal rights. In his "New Male Manifesto," he declares, "Men deserve the same rights as women for custody of children, economic support, government aid, education, health care, and protection from abuse."

Sociologists, however, continue to document white male privilege (Coppock, Haydon, and Richter 1995; Wellman 1997). While some men (white, middle/upper class, heterosexual, able bodied) are more privileged than others, generally speaking, all men have greater access to valued resources in our society than women as a group. As Coppock et al. (1995) painstakingly demonstrate, "the proclamation of 'post-feminism' has occurred at precisely the same moment as acclaimed feminist studies demonstrate that not only have women's real advancements been limited, but also that there has been a backlash against feminism of international significance" (p. 3). They point out that "criticising feminism for oppressing men has become positively fashionable" (p. 5). That is precisely what we find in these two discourses.

The reality of power relations is further eclipsed with the mythopoets' emphasis on wounding. For example, Kipnis (1995) writes,

> Concerning wounds and power, it is valuable that feminists have raised our consciousness about the gender-specific wounds of women. In fact postfeminist men actively support women's demands for social, political, and economic equality. It is a given. We also, however, express similar concerns for men and boys. . . . Blatantly missing from feminist analysis of gender entitlements is an understanding of the disproportionate, gender-specific ways in which males suffer, are disempowered, and are at risk for abuse and neglect. Why fault the men's movement for merely recapitulating the same gender sensitivity feminism developed toward women? (p. 280)

Inequality and power are erased, and instead both men and women are said to be "wounded." According to this logic, both men and women must explore their wounds and "reconcile" with each other.

Numerous mythopoetic authors, including Bliss, Diamond, and Kipnis, write about reconciliation, and retreats have been held for men and women to come together and reconcile. As Bliss (1995) explains it,

> Women's and men's movements are maturing toward a movement of men and women for Gender Reconciliation. Some of the adherents of the original women's and men's movements remain stuck in the early stages of blame, anger, shame. . . . Together men and women can end sexism, which injures both genders. . . . We need to be allies, partners, even when we differ. (p. 306)

There is no patriarchy, only sexism, which is equally harmful to women and men. There is no power, only differences that must be reconciled. Elsewhere, Bliss (1995) argues for "gender reconciliation designed to end the sexism which injures both men and women. Since 'both are victims,' . . . rather than fight against each other, 'it seems more sensible for them to join in a common struggle'" (pp. 302–3). Here, structural power imbalances are reduced to a matter of miscommunication, to psychological obstacles to be worked through.

Responding to criticism that the mythopoets dismiss gender inequality, Bly (1995) responds, "I agree that men, white men particularly, have claimed for themselves a place of privilege that forces women to accept mistreatment in hundreds of ways. . . . The question is what to do about this arrogance." He goes on to explain that the answer is for men to experience and explore their own "deep grief" (p. 272). Here, power is rewritten as a personality characteristic: arrogance. And again, the answer is that men must explore their own wounds. In a similar vein, Kipnis (1995) argues, "The social tolerance for all forms of abuse toward males is one of the primary causes of male rage and violence" (p. 282). The only time male violence is acknowledged, it is said to be a result of the abuse that males themselves have suffered. Men here are relieved of any responsibility, and they are unveiled as the true victims.

Both Bliss (1995) and Diamond (1995) refer to a favored thirteenth-century poem by

Rumi: "Out beyond ideas of wrongdoing and rightdoing,/there is a field. I'll meet you there." Bliss pleads, "Let us get beyond blame and shame to meet each other in such a clearing" (p. 305). Erasing any notions of right and wrong, refusing to accept any responsibility for privilege and inequality, these authors seek to "reconcile" men's and women's "differences." Like Promise Keepers' language of "racial reconciliation," the language erases all relations of power and reduces inequality to a misunderstanding.

While Kipnis (1995) argues that "it is important to create a forum where . . . proactive male perspectives are not paranoically distorted as implicitly antifeminism" (p. 275), the mythopoetic movement is *not* that forum. This discourse is clearly antifeminist, and the "pro-male" language distorts this fact. Like the white supremacist movement, the mythopoetic movement presents itself as not "anti" anyone, simply pro-male. They simply love and seek to protect their own kind. This logic mirrors white supremacist logic, evident in a *Western Guardian* article that argues that the purpose of the white supremacist movement is merely "the restoration of a healthy interest in and love of the achievements of White Western man" (*Western Guardian* 1980). Another publication proclaims that the social problems they address have "very little to do with the black man rising . . . rather it is about the white man falling" (*Instauration* 1980, 14). The language used here is part of a broader effort to remake the image of the movement. Rather than be seen as haters, white supremacists are attempting to present themselves simply as defenders of the white race. In many articles, they insist that they hate no one but simply wish to promote and protect the white race, and white men in particular, today's truly oppressed.

The *NSV Report* argues,

> Racism is a natural and healthy instinct instilled by genetic inheritance in normal people, regardless of race. A program of total geographic separation of the races is a form of racism in which all people are with their own races and there is no hate involved. (*NSV Report* 1991, 2)

Here, they attempt to twist language to define racism as something normal and healthy, simply a form of love for one's own race.

An article in *White Power* clearly demonstrates just what their message of love is really about:

> Perhaps the cruelest hoax is the liberal lie of telling the Negro he's the equal of the White man and expecting to make an instant White man out of him by sending him to college, giving him a federal handout. . . . Let's have the honesty and decency to recognize the Negro for what he is, and not make impossible demands of him. . . . This has nothing to do with "hate" or "bigotry." I love my dog, for example, but I'm not about to recognize her as my equal. (*White Power* 1973, 3–6)

Here, the recognition of essential difference as rooted in nature absolves white supremacists of any responsibility, so that they can argue that they do not hate anyone, they are merely recognizing and respecting the natural order.

Messner (1997) concludes that

> relatively privileged men may be attracted to the mythopoetic men's movement because, on the one hand, it acknowledges and validates their painful "wounds." . . . On the other hand, and unlike feminism, it does not confront men with the reality of how their own privileges are based on the continued subordination of women and other men. (pp. 23–24)

Certainly this helps to explain some of the appeal of both movements and highlights important shared aspects of their discourse.

DEMASCULINIZATION AND FEMINIZATION

Both mythopoetic and white supremacist discourse suggests that misery and destruction result when men and women try to deny their essential natures, and they argue that this is precisely what has been occurring in contemporary America.

Both discourses argue that contemporary social problems are due to the women's movement and the breakdown of traditional gender roles. For example, Bly (1996) points out

> Some of the areas in which the women's movement, as we know it, has increased some of the less desirable sides of the new society. . . . There has been an increase in neglect of the young. . . . The spokeswomen for "leaving the house" feminism bear some responsibility for telling a woman that she could follow her career for years and still have a child. (p. 171)

The women's movement is blamed for distorting the natural gender order and, according to both discourses, this has led to the demasculinization of men.

What is wrong with America? Men have become wimps.

> The male of the past twenty years has become more thoughtful, more gentle. But by this process he has not become more free. He's a nice boy who pleases not only his mother but also the young woman he is living with. (Bly 1990, 2)

And as Schwalbe (1996) observes, "Some of the men believed that in being taught to be nice boys—to please their mothers or other powerful people in their lives—they were forced to stuff many masculine impulses into their shadows" (p. 59).

The problems facing us today, then, are a result of this demasculinization, which both Bly and the white supremacists trace to the widespread questioning of authority during the 1960s and the rise of new social movements. Now, men are no longer willing to stand up and assert their masculinity.

> "If his wife or girlfriend, furious, shouts that he is 'chauvinist,' a 'sexist,' a 'man,' he doesn't fight back, but just takes it." In short, the new man turns out to be a wimp; he is the problem, not the solution, and manhood needs to be rescued from such sensitive Mama's boys. (Kimmel and Kaufman 1995, 20–21)

Elsewhere, Bly (1990) argues that men have become "nonhierarchical," "passive," "tamed," and "domesticated" (p. 61). The natural order has been reversed, the hierarchy threatened: "Young men for various reasons wanted their women harder, and women began to desire softer men. It seemed like a nice arrangement for a while, but we've lived with it long enough now to see that it isn't working" (p. 4).

Bliss (1995) believes that men have become feminized and argues, "Rather than trying to imitate women or become 'honorary women,' the path I suggest is to overcome Toxic Masculinity and recover the Deep Masculine, which lies at the base of each man" (p. 303). Similarly, Kipnis (1992) proclaims, "Men do not need to become more like women in order to reconnect with soul." Each movement exhibits anxiety over men becoming more like women. As we have seen, both discourses construct an essentialist male/female dichotomy, where men and women are seen in oppositional terms, and any threat to masculinity is perceived as a threat to sexual difference, feminizing men.

This demasculinization is believed to have social consequences. Shame turns a man into a wimp, unwilling to defend himself or his masculinity, and "a man who cannot defend his own space cannot defend women and children" (Bly 1990, 156).

Like mythopoetic discourse, white supremacist discourse sees contemporary society as sick and blames this decline on the demasculinization of white men. As the *New Order* explains,

> The racial and political ills from which our Race suffers today are merely symptoms of a more profound *spiritual sickness.* . . . *We live in a society which is completely out of harmony with the natural world* . . . the relationships between the races, between the sexes and between the generations—*everything* is out of sync with natural order. . . . *Because of the unnatural, anti natural society they live in and the lives they lead, White people have lost touch with the biological community to which they belong—their racial community.* (*White Power* no. 104, 1)

Again mirroring mythopoetic discourse, the demasculinization of white men is defined as the root of our problems.

As a typical article laments,

> Northern European males have traditionally tended throughout history to be dominant by nature, but . . . they are becoming submissive and passive. This phenomenon is especially obvious in the declining strength of their opposition to the interracial sexual transgressions of non-Northern European males with Northern European females. [Northern European men] repress the natural inborn tendencies of exclusivity which played an important role in preserving the biological integrity of their race during its evolution. Many carry their altruism to the point of even seeming to approve of, and to encourage, the sexual trespasses of non-Northern European males upon Northern European females whom their more vigorous and race-conscious ancestors would have defended from such defilements with their very lives. (*Instauration* 1985, 8)

This author mourns the destruction of what he sees as the natural roles of men and women, attacking contemporary white men as no longer "real men" willing to prove their masculinity by protecting their women.

Contemporary society, by questioning the inevitability of racial and gender differences, is necessarily diseased. The root of our social ills is said to lie in movements for racial and gender equality, which have distorted our true natures. In an article entitled "Sexuality in a Sick Society," and subtitled, "The changing relationship between men and women is leading to ominous racial consequences for the West," we are told that feminism and the sexual revolution have lead to the

> demasculinization of the Western male, [and] together with the reaction of the Western female to this, [it] is a cause for grave concern . . . [men] are constrained from expressing their maleness in any of the ways which were natural in the past. One of the most important of those ways was protecting a mate. . . . All the brave, new talk about marriage today being a partner-

> ship of equals does not change the basic, biological natures of men and women. Those natures have fitted them for complimentary roles, not for the same role . . . [but now he is no longer] the master in his house. (*National Vanguard* 1983, 17)

Like the mythopoetic movement, white supremacist discourse also targets the women's movement as a threat, here to both traditional race and gender relations. As a *White Power* article asserts,

> the "Women's Movement" which evolved out of the social turmoil of the 1960s . . . seem[ed] to be less interested in securing equal rights for women than in turning men and women into unnatural rivals, each struggling against the other for supremacy instead of working together. (*White Power* no. 105, 4)

A *National Vanguard* article warns that

> as Northern males have continued to become more wimpish, the result of the media-created image of the "new male"—more pacifist, less authoritarian, more "sensitive," less competitive, more androgynous, less possessive—the controlled media, the homosexual lobby, and the feminist movement have cheered . . . the number of effeminate males has increased greatly—not just the sexual inverts, who actually have taken pseudo-female sexual roles, but even more the legions of sissies and weaklings, of flabby, limp-wristed, non-aggressive, non-physical, indecisive, slackjawed, fearful males. (*National Vanguard* 1983, 17)

The "unnatural" feminization of white men is blamed for leading to interracial sexuality and the supposed Jewish goal of genocide of the white race. The demasculinization of white men, then, is blamed for the destruction of the race.

Throughout both discourses, contemporary social problems are blamed on the supposed demasculinization of white males by women and feminism. Both movements believe that the questioning of traditional gender roles and identities has led men to become more like women, breaking down the natural order of essential sexual difference. Both movements argue that men can no longer stand up and protect women and the community (for white supremacists, the racial community), and so chaos and social disorder prevail. Both movements offer themselves as alternatives to help men rediscover their masculinity and save the community.

SHAME

Throughout both discourses, shame is presented as a primary tool relied on to demasculinize and attack (white) men. Both movements seek to redeem masculinity and help men overcome the shame leveled against them: "many young men . . . are ashamed of being men. . . . To be ashamed of your gender is not healthful for anyone" (Bly 1995, 274).

Once again, women, and especially the women's movement, are targeted for the downfall of manhood. As one retreat leader explains,

> Men feel hung out to dry by the women's movement. A lot of men feel that they, personally, are being held responsible for everything that's macho and wrong in the world today. . . . They've been feeling very bad about themselves, and so they're overjoyed to recover their maleness and feel proud about themselves as men. (Kimmel and Kaufman 1995, 40)

Bly reveals,

> Blaming is not new. Mothers have felt blamed for centuries, and parents in general feel blamed unjustly by teenagers. But the virulent new kind of blaming that we see today is sanctioned by thousands, if not millions, of well-educated people and has become a standard part of all intellectual debate in the last forty years. (p. 172)

Here, Bly is equating the unjust blame of parents and mothers with the blame leveled against patriarchy and white privilege by the women's and minority movements. In doing this, he trivializes the concerns of these movements, dismisses their claims, and ignores the fundamental issues of power they raise. He sympathizes with white males, whom he sees as unfairly under attack. As he writes, "Men in general are not good enough, fathers are not thoughtful enough, sons are not pacific enough, men don't express their feelings enough: there's a lot of 'not enough.' But some harsh criticisms are softening" (p. 173).

As these passages indicate, shame and guilt play a prominent role: Bly believes that men are made to feel ashamed and guilty for being men. Clatterbaugh (1995) explains that, according to Bly, "men have been shamed into losing touch with the masculine side, thus becoming soft, feminine, and passive" (p. 50). "'Femininity' . . . softens and deadens their masculine life-affirming potential" (Messner 1997, 17). According to Bly, this is unavoidable as long as women continue to raise sons in the absence of fathers. "Women cannot help, given their natures, but shame the son" (Clatterbaugh 1995, 50). It is female nature to degrade a boy's masculinity, so a woman cannot raise a boy to be a man. Bly explains that when a woman raises a boy alone, "he may in some way have no male face, or he may have no face at all. The old men initiators, by contrast . . . helped boys to see their genuine face or being" (Messner 1995, 102). Boys can only become men with the help of other men. Female essence is so different that it hinders masculinity. When boys are shamed, they cannot become real men, and they are kept from knowing their true masculinity.

Shame also plays a central role in white supremacist discourse. For example, a *Thunderbolt* article asserts in its title that "'Destroy Racism' Means Mongrelize Whites."

> The time has come for White Americans everywhere to understand what this monstrous fight against "Racism" actually is. It is a diabolical movement to implant such a deep seated guilt

complex within our people that we willingly will join the march behind the Judas goat into the abyss of racial suicide!! (*Thunderbolt* 1975, 3)

Here, as in mythopoetic discourse, it is argued that guilt and shame are primary weapons used to demasculinize men.

The Turner Diaries (Pierce 1978), a futuristic novel describing white supremacist terrorism and a race war for world domination, presents a picture of society where white women and young girls are constantly raped and attacked by black men, but no one ever protests out of fear of being branded a racist. For example, the character Turner describes the following scene:

> Two grinning black soldiers forced their way through the throng in front of the tent and went inside, dragging a terrified, sobbing White girl about 14 years old between them. The raping queue moved forward another space. I ran over to a White officer [and] began angrily protesting what was happening, but [he] turned shamefacedly away from me and hurried off in the opposite direction. Two White soldiers nearby cast their eyes downward and disappeared between two tents. No one wanted to be suspected of "racism." (p. 187)

Throughout the novel, shame and guilt are used to immobilize white men. Like the terms *sexist* and *chauvinist* for the mythopoets, the term *racist* is presented as a tool used to control white men.

While white men are never depicted engaging in interracial sexuality, they are, nevertheless, held responsible for much of the interracial sexuality between white women and black men. For example, this is demonstrated by a photograph in *National Vanguard* of a black man and white woman, nude from the waist up, embracing. The caption beneath the photograph reads, "SHAME of White men in their loss of control over their women. This German girl is one of thousands who have sought sexual fulfillment with blacks in Jamaica" (*National Vanguard*

1983, 17). White women are depicted as being forced to turn to black men for sexual fulfillment, suggesting that white men are demasculinized and have failed to hold on to their women.

THE SOLUTION

Men must put an end to the shame by reclaiming their masculinity and usurping women's power. In *Iron John*, the boy does this by stealing the key from under his mother's pillow. Power is stolen back from women.

According to both discourses, all of society is threatened when masculinity is lost. Society can only be saved if men reclaim their authority and reassert their masculinity. "Men thus need a movement to reconnect with the 'Zeus energy' that they have lost. And 'Zeus energy is male authority accepted for the good of the community'" (Messner 1995, 103; Bly 1990, 22).

Through the use of myths, Bly and others lead men in search of this "deep masculinity." Men are invited to reclaim their lost masculinity by attending mythopoetic retreats and workshops. Male initiation ceremonies and gatherings are designed to substitute for the absent father and restore masculinity. "At weekend retreats . . . they can feel a sense of intimacy and connectedness to other wounded and searching men. They can discover the depths of their manhood" (Kimmel and Kaufman 1995, 24). These retreats and the discourse draw on male initiation rituals over thousands of years to establish the permanence and essence of manhood.

The discourse argues that these rituals require separation from women and the world of women. As Kimmel and Kaufman (1995) argue, "the demonstration of manhood becomes associated with a relentless repudiation of the feminine," reasserting the oppositional nature of sexual difference (p. 24).

White supremacist discourse, like mythopoetic discourse, turns to the past for its vision of a healthy society. Stories about the past are offered as evidence to bolster the assertions of inherent racial and gender differences. White supremacist discourse is filled with stories about the past, yet these stories are never simple retellings of some static history. Historical memory is thoroughly political, reflecting the interests and position of those who write it. The process of excavating the past is, instead, the construction of the past. Both depict a past where men were secure in their masculinity and the hierarchical gender order remained firmly entrenched.

For example, one article presents a picture of the past to redefine white masculinity:

[In the past,] when a father had some authority over his daughter, and a husband over his wife, another male approached either at his peril. Not only did female dependence carry with it the need for protection, but it also stimulated in the male the desire to provide that protection. The entire community was behind the man who drew his sword or his gun in defense of his womenfolk. (*National Vanguard* 1983, 17)

This picture of the past attempts to encourage white men to reclaim their rightful role as patriarchs who will protect white women from the advances of nonwhite men.

Like mythopoetic discourse, white supremacist discourse venerates the past by honoring "fathers" and male ancestors. White supremacists argue that we must turn to the rules and laws of our fathers, and our fathers' times, to solve the problems of the present.

The road to social deterioration runs by the way of continued breeding with inferior racial stocks. . . . Our forefathers established laws in the South which forbade socializing between the races as well as interracial marriage. . . . Still there remains social customs that, if followed to the letter as laid down by our forefathers, would still stop interracial contacts and the disgusting racially mixed couples we see on our streets today. (*Thunderbolt* 1979, 9)

Another article argues,

If our desires to pursue the beliefs and practices of our fathers and our fathers' fathers are to be ignored and disregarded . . . then the hour has come for us to declare our independence. . . . Let us prepare once again to build a land in which the temples of our fathers will be honored. (*Instauration* 1985, 14)

White supremacist discourse, then, offers itself as the only solution to restoring the natural order.

It is the goal of the New Order to attack the spiritual syphilis which is eating away at the soul of our Race . . . and to destroy the infection by massive doses of the proper antidote—the pure, undiluted medicine of the National Socialist world view. . . . We will create a new society in which Nature and her laws are honored and venerated. (*White Power* no. 104, 1)

For both movements, restoring what they see as the natural gender order is the key to solving what they see as our most pressing social problems. A *National Vanguard* article highlights this, warning, "Unless a healthy relationship between the sexes is reestablished in the West, the White race certainly will not survive" (*National Vanguard* 1983, 21–22).

The fate of the white race, then, hinges on the need for real white men to act. A *New Order* article argues that "the world is in trouble now only because the White man is divided, confused and misled. Once he is united, inspired by a great ideal and led by real men, his world will again become livable, safe and happy" (*New Order* 1979, 8).

The white supremacist project, then, is primarily concerned with forging a new white male identity and restoring the "natural relationship that existed between the sexes in earlier times" (*National Vanguard* 1983, 21).

For both movements, the solution is for white men to come together and reclaim their masculinity. As a recruitment pamphlet for the Knights of the Ku Klux Klan explains, "*The*

KKK is a fraternal movement. We are actually building today our new Community of White racial brotherhood."

CONCLUSION

While the mythopoetic men's movement and the white supremacist movement are very different, with different tactics and purportedly different goals, they have much in common. They both construct masculinity as an essence; they both posit the demasculinization of white men as a primary cause of the problems facing our society today; they both blame women and the women's movement for that demasculinization; and they both posit a conspiratorial, politically correct environment where men are under attack. For both movements, men today are no longer in touch with their true natures, and this natural order must be restored if we are to combat the ills that plague us. Both movements offer themselves as the solution, claiming to help men rediscover their true masculinity, reclaim authority, protect the community, and solve our social ills.

Schwalbe (1996) observes that "what was special about mythopoetic activity, and what made it especially appealing, was the gender angle: the chance to bond around a common interest in redefining 'man' as an identity signifying moral goodness" (p. 30). Both movements are primarily concerned with revalidating male identity. As Schwalbe continues,

> Mythopoetic men's work . . . was, to a large extent, identity work, specifically, the remaking of 'man' as a moral identity. One reason this identity had to be remade was that the mythopoetic men felt it had been damaged by feminist criticism, some of which held that men were by nature brutish, insensitive, destructive, violent, competitive, untrustworthy, and emotionally inept. . . . The whole mythopoetic movement might even be described as a big identity reconstruction project. (p. 102)

The same is true for the white supremacist movement. I have argued elsewhere that its central project is the reconstruction of white masculinity (Ferber 1995, 1998b).

It is in this respect that both of these movements are part of a backlash against the women's movement, changing ideas about gender, and other social movements that have destabilized taken-for-granted notions of identity. Both the mythopoetic and white supremacist movements seek to reassert traditional notions of authentic masculinity and reclaim and maintain white male authority and privilege.

Given the very obvious differences between these two movements, the similarities are all the more striking. Messner (1997) suggests that men are attracted to the mythopoetic movement because "it is so congruent with shifts that are already taking place within current constructions of hegemonic masculinity . . . mythopoetic discourse appears congruent with the contemporary resurgence of belief in essential differences between women and men" (p. 18). Both movements may be appealing today not because they are extreme or outrageous but because they resonate with widely held assumptions about essential gender and racial identity, which have been increasingly subject to interrogation.

While race is not central to the mythopoetic movement's ideology, both movements appeal to privileged white men who feel they have been denied what they were taught they were entitled to. For the mythopoets, this birthright is framed in terms of masculinity; for the white supremacists, it is a specifically white masculinity. Whether racialized or not, both movements' visions of masculinity are similar.

The most significant feature of each construction of masculinity is its essentialist nature. Kimmel (1994) argues that the "idea that manhood is socially constructed and historically shifting should not be understood as a loss, that something is being taken away from men. In fact, it gives us something extraordinarily valuable—agency, the capacity to act" (p. 120). Yet, it is precisely this agency that both movements seek to deny. Both movements appeal to white men tired of being blamed for gender and racial inequality, especially given their own declining class position. Both discourses provide them with easy outs: on one hand, if men are violent or abusive, it is because they have been wounded; on the other hand, men should, by nature, be in power. Relegating behavior to the realm of human nature relieves us of responsibility—if it is nature, it cannot be changed, or so we assume. How can we possibly blame someone for acting according to their nature? Recognizing race and gender as social constructs, however, requires that we accept responsibility for these categorizations and the consequences once assumed to follow.

We should hardly be surprised to find such similarities between these two movements. In his article, "The Contemporary 'Crisis' of Masculinity in Historical Perspective," Kimmel (1987) explores crises of masculinity in late seventeenth- and early eighteenth-century England and in the late nineteenth- and early twentieth-century United States. He argues that broad structural changes precipitate women's demands for greater equality, which then trigger crises of masculinity. In each of these periods, like today, women's attempts to increase autonomy are perceived as threatening taken-for-granted assumptions about the nature of sexual difference, provoking a crisis of masculinity. And during each of these periods, a male backlash emerged to seek a return to what it had constructed as the "natural order." As Kimmel (1987) observes, "Opponents of increasing economic, political, and social equality between men and women almost always resort to arguments about the 'natural order of things' as counters to progressive social trends" (p. 143). Both the mythopoetic men's movement and the white supremacist movement should be situated within this broader trend, the recurring attempt to make socially constructed identities and relations of inequality appear inevitable and rooted in nature.

REFERENCES

Anti-Defamation League. 1988. *Hate groups in America: A record of bigotry and violence.* New York: Author.

BENEKE, T. 1995. Deep masculinity as social construct: Foucault, Bly and masculinity. In *The politics of manhood,* edited by M. S. Kimmel, 151–63. Philadelphia: Temple University Press.

———. 1996. Becoming a racist: Women in contemporary Ku Klux Klan and neo-Nazi groups. *Gender & Society* 10 (6): 680–702.

BLISS, S. 1995. Mythopoetic men's movements. In *The politics of manhood,* edited by M. S. Kimmel, 292–307. Philadelphia: Temple University Press.

BLY, R. 1990. *Iron John: A book about men.* Reading, MA: Addison-Wesley.

———. 1995. Thoughts on reading this book. In *The politics of manhood,* edited by M. S. Kimmel 271–74. Philadelphia: Temple University Press.

———. 1996. *The sibling society.* New York: Vintage.

BUTLER, J. 1991. Imitation and gender insubordination. In *Inside/out: Lesbian theories, gay theories,* edited by D. Fuss, 13–31. London: Routledge.

———. 1993. *Bodies that matter: On the discursive limits of sex.* New York: Routledge.

CLATTERBAUGH, K. 1995. Mythopoetic foundations and new age patriarchy. In *The politics of manhood,* edited by M. S. Kimmel, 44–63. Philadelphia: Temple University Press.

CONNELL, B. 1995. Men at bay: The "men's movement" and its newest best-sellers. In *The politics of manhood,* edited by M. S. Kimmel, 75–88. Philadelphia: Temple University Press.

COPPOCK, V., D. HAYDON AND I. RICHTER. 1995. *The illusions of "postfeminism": New women, old myths.* London: Taylor and Francis.

DANIELS, J. 1997. *White lies: Race, gender and sexuality in white supremacist discourse.* New York: Routledge.

Denver Post. 1996. Affirmative action foes see new era. 8 November, 25A.

DIAMOND, J. 1995. Twenty-five years in the men's movement. In *The politics of manhood,* edited by M. S. Kimmel, 313–20. Philadelphia: Temple University Press.

EZEKIEL, R. S. 1995. *The racist mind: Portraits of American Neo-Nazis and Klansmen.* New York: Viking.

FALUDI, S. 1991. *Backlash: The undeclared war against American women.* New York: Crown.

FERBER, A. L. 1995. "Shame of white men": Interracial sexuality and the construction of white masculinity in contemporary white supremacist discourse. *Masculinities* 3 (2): 1–24.

———. 1998b. *White man falling: Race, gender and white supremacy.* Lanham, MA: Rowman and Littlefield.

GALLAGHER, C. 1995. White reconstruction in the university. *Socialist Review* 24 (1&2): 165–87.

HUBBARD, RUTH. 1990. *The politics of women's biology.* New Brunswick, NJ: Rutgers University Press.

Intelligence Project of The Southern Poverty Law Center. 1998. *Intelligence report* 89 (Winter).

KIMMEL, M. S. 1987. The contemporary "crisis" of masculinity in historical perspective. In *The making of masculinities: The new men's studies,* edited by H. Brod, 121–53. Boston: Allen and Unwin.

———. 1994. Masculinity as homophobia: Fear, shame, and silence in the construction of gender identity. In *Theorizing masculinities,* edited by H. Brod and M. Kaufman, 119–41. Thousand Oaks, CA: Sage.

———. 1995. *The Politics of manhood: Profeminist men respond to the mythopoetic men's movement (and the mythopoetic leaders answer).* Philadelphia: Temple University Press.

KIMMEL, M. S., AND M. KAUFMAN. 1995. Weekend warriors: The new men's movement. In *The politics of manhood,* edited by M. S. Kimmel, 15–43. Philadelphia: Temple University Press.

KIPNIS, A. 1992. *Knights without armor.* New York: Putnam.

———. 1995. The postfeminist men's movement. In *The politics of manhood,* edited by M. S. Kimmel, 275–86. Philadelphia: Temple University Press.

MESSNER, M. A. 1995. "Changing men" and feminist politics in the United States. In *The politics of manhood,* edited by M. S. Kimmel, 97–111. Philadelphia: Temple University Press.

———. 1997. *Politics of masculinities: Men in movements.* Thousand Oaks, CA: Sage.

MOORE, R., AND D. GILLETTE. 1992. *The king within: Accessing the king in the male psyche.* New York: William Morrow.

NICHOLSON, L. 1994. Interpreting gender. *Signs: Journal of Women in Culture and Society* 20: 79–105.

OMI, M. 1991. Shifting the blame: Racial ideology and politics in the post-civil rights era. *Critical Sociology* 18 (3): 77–98.

PIERCE, W. 1978. *The Turner diaries.* Hillsboro, VA: National Vanguard Books.

RIDGEWAY, J. 1990. *Blood in the face.* New York: Thunder's Mouth Press.

ROBERTS, R. M. 1997. Assault on "cyberhate" launched. *Denver Post,* 30 November.

SCHWALBE, M. 1996. *Unlocking the iron cage.* New York: Oxford University Press.

SCOTT, J. W. 1988. Deconstructing equality-versus-difference: Or, the uses of poststructuralist theory for feminism. *Feminist Studies* 14 (1): 33–50.

STEINBERG, S. 1995. *Turning back: The retreat from racial justice in American thought and policy.* Boston: Beacon.

WELLMAN, D. 1997. Minstrel shows, affirmative action talk, and angry white men: Marking racial otherness in the 1990s. In *Displacing whiteness: Essays in social and cultural criticism,* edited by R. Frankenberg, 311–31. Durham, NC: Duke University Press.

BIBLIOGRAPHY OF WHITE SUPREMACIST PUBLICATIONS

Crusader. n.d. Metairie, LA: Knights of the Ku Klux Klan.

The Fiery Cross. 1979. Edited by Robert Shelton. Swartz, LA: The United Klans of America (UKA).

Instauration. 1985. Edited by Wilmot Robertson. Cape Canaveral, FL: Howard Allen Enterprises, Inc.

The National Alliance Bulletin. 1978–80. Edited by William Pierce. Mill Point, WV: National Alliance.

The National Socialist. 1982–83. The World Union of National Socialists.

National Vanguard. 1978–84. Edited by William Pierce. Mill Point, WV: National Alliance.

New Order. 1979–83. Edited by Gerhard Lauck. Lincoln, NE: National Socialist German Workers Party.

The Northlander. 1978. No information available.

N S Bulletin. 1974–83. Edited by Matt Koehl. Arlington, VA and New Berlin, WI: National Socialist White People's Party (*The New Order* after 1982.)

N S KAMPFRUF/N S Mobilizer. 1974–83. Edited by Russel R. Veh. National Socialist League.

The NSV Report. 1983–93. Edited by Rick Cooper and Dan Stewart. National Socialist Vanguard.

The Spotlight. 1986. Edited by Willis A. Carto. Liberty Lobby.

The Thunderbolt. 1974–84. Edited by J. B. Stoner and Edward Fields. National States Rights Party.

The Torch. 1977–79. Edited by Thomas Robb. The White People's Committee to Restore God's Laws, a division of the Church of Jesus Christ.

Voice of German Americans. 1977–80. Editor and publisher unknown.

The Western Guardian. 1980. Roanoke, VA: Western Guard America.

White Patriot. 1979–84. Edited by Thomas Robb. Knights of the Ku Klux Klan.

White Power. 1969–78. Edited by Matt Koehl. Arlington, VA and New Berlin, WI: National Socialist White People's Party.

CRITICAL THINKING QUESTIONS

1. What are the similarities and differences in the basic beliefs of the mythopoetic men's movement and the white supremacist movement?

2. What is the relation between these two movements and the gains of the feminist and the civil rights movements?

3. What is the likelihood that these two movements will form an alliance to work toward their common goals? Support your answer with evidence from the belief system of each group.

Reading 7

The Hardening Face of Anti-Semitism

Mark Sappenfield, James N. Thurman, William Echikson,
Corinna Schuler, Tom Regan, and Peter Grier

> *In this reading, Sappenfield and his associates examine the history of anti-Semitism in the*
> *United States and argue that this form of prejudice is stronger today than ever before.*

Public prejudices have faded, but extremist violence grows.

A CHRISTIAN SCIENCE MONITOR ROUNDUP

The followers of Judaism have been discriminated against and attacked for their faith since the earliest times of antiquity. But Tuesday's shootings in a Jewish community center in Los Angeles may be emblematic of something new: the hardening face of modern anti-Semitism.

Among the general public, anti-Semitism has declined significantly over the decades. But among the alienated extremists willing to resort to violence, symbols of the Jewish community are becoming primary targets, say experts who track the problem.

While largely an American phenomenon, these alienated extremists are attracting followers in other nations, from Australia to Austria.

"If you look at the organized white-supremacist movement, anti-Semitism has never been higher," says Mark Potok of the Southern Poverty Law Center in Montgomery, Ala. "Jews have not been the No. 1 enemy of these groups historically, but now they are."

The suspect in the 1999 Jewish community center shootings, Buford Furrow Jr., al-

Source: Reprinted from *Christian Science Monitor* 91, no. 181 (August 13, 1999): p. 1.

legedly told federal law-enforcement officials he carried out the attack because he wanted to "send a message to America" by killing Jews.

It would be wrong to make too much of his motivation, experts caution. A person who would target small children is by definition deeply troubled.

And overall, anti-Semitism is far from the deep and troubling stain on the world that it once was. In the United States, anti-Semitic acts have been on a slow decline throughout most of the 1990s, according to Anti-Defamation League statistics, despite a slight 2 percent rise last year. The ADL counted 1,611 anti-Semitic incidents in the US in 1998, up from 1,571 the year before.

The percentage of Americans who harbor anti-Jewish views is now 12, according to ADL statistics. While that still seems far too high, it is lower than the comparable figure from 1964 of 29 percent.

To read too much into the activity of a few extremists would be to play into their hands.

"Their goal is to stir up hatred and create religious and ethnic divisions we've tried so hard to overcome in the last couple of decades," says Jonathan Sarna, an expert in American Jewish history at Brandeis University in Waltham, Mass.

There have been several changes in the character of anti-Semitic activity, however, say Mr. Sarna and other experts.

One is the increased likelihood that Jewish institutions, not just individuals, will be attacked. There have been several synagogue bombings on the West Coast recently, as well as community-center shootings.

The other is a heightened level of violence. "There are a growing number of cases where people are physically harmed" instead of just property damaged, says Chris Freeman of the Center for Democratic Renewal, an Atlanta-based civil rights group that monitors far-right extremists. "That is a trend we are seeing."

ROOTS OF HATRED

This stems from the rise of organized hatred in America. Whether it goes by the name of Aryan Nations, or The Order, or Christian Identity, it bears similar characteristics: An alienated fringe of extremists unite on the Internet and in the name of their own brand of Christianity, are increasingly willing to take desperate steps to promote their doctrine of hate.

The theology, if it can be called that, of these groups often holds that Jews, blacks, and other traditional scapegoats are "mud people" or the spawn of the devil, and that they must be eliminated from the earth if true Christianity is ever to return.

These groups take a dash of neo-Nazi thinking, a pinch from the Ku Klux Klan, and a dose of myths from the 1930s that have been totally discredited—such as the belief that banking is controlled by a Jewish conspiracy—and mix them together into a combustible product.

Today, the Christian Identity movement is in many ways the glue that holds the radical right together, says Mr. Potok.

"It is Bible-based, and it has had some success making inroads into the Christian fundamentalist movement," he says.

Its violence stems from its beliefs, the kind of people it attracts, and the tactics leaders adopt to gain attention.

"What's happening is that there are people who are willing to take a page from international terrorism, saying, 'We don't need a movement. We just need a few people who are willing to go to the wall,'" says Abraham

Cooper, a rabbi and associate dean of the Simon Wiesenthal Center in Los Angeles.

The Internet is a natural fit with these groups, say experts. It allows small, isolated groups to feel they are part of larger communities. Surfing the Web appeals to loners and being a loner is often a necessary, though not sufficient, condition to membership in a Christian hate group.

In a twisted way, the Internet is attracting a new and more dangerous kind of anti-Semite—"a younger, better educated hater," says Tamar Galatzan, a lawyer with the Anti-Defamation League in Los Angeles.

Anti-Semitism is hardly a new phenomenon, of course. Since antiquity Jews have been an obvious choice of adversary for some in Christianity, due to a shared lineage of the two religions, and the fact that both consider themselves chosen people of God. "It's a basic Christian story, and one of the real blemishes on Christianity," says Krister Stendahl, retired dean of the Harvard Divinity School in Cambridge, Mass.

When Christians became the preeminent religious group in the Byzantine Empire under Constantine in the 4th century, they began persecuting the Jews, Mr. Stendahl says.

At the turn of the 19th century, people who had trouble transitioning to the new industrialized world saw Jews doing well and turned to their ancient scapegoat to blame them for all that was wrong, says David Biale, a professor of Jewish history at the University of California at Davis.

That is a predecessor of American anti-Semitism today, which came over with immigrants.

The Christian Identity movement per se is a largely American phenomenon. But echoes of its beliefs can be found in many other nations—including some that have dark histories of widespread persecution of Jews.

ATTACKS IN ARGENTINA

Take Argentina, for instance. Many Nazi leaders fled to Argentina after Hitler's defeat and the exposure of the Holocaust. "Hitler's anti-Semitism isn't dead. It's just mutating," says Sergio Widder, the Buenos Aires-based Latin American representative of the Simon Wiesenthal Center.

Mr. Widder has no exact figures on the rise of incidents, but says there is a growing trend of anti-Semitism in his region. Argentina now has 15 neo-Nazi Web sites, all of which have appeared in the past two years. A neo-Nazi Congress has been proposed for April 2000 in Chile.

Even Canada—a nation not traditionally associated with hate groups—has seen a rise in anti-Semitic incidents. Such acts rose 14 percent in Canada, from 212 in 1997 to 240 in 1998, according to the League for Human Rights of the B'nai Brith Canada.

"After two consecutive years of declining incidents, anti-Semitism and hate again appear to be on the rise again . . . the incidents of anti-Semitism in Canada have become more diffuse in nature and the faces of hate are becoming harder to identify," says Lawrence Hart, the national president of the B'nai Brith Canada.

Throughout Europe, actual violent attacks against Jewish targets have decreased in the past few years. And indigenous anti-Semitism, whether of the far right or left, seems on the decline.

Now, ironically, the danger comes from the US, where the combination of easy access to firearms and the rise of hate groups could cross the Atlantic.

"We're seeing a lot of the violent material placed on the Internet by American groups being copied here in Europe," says Shimon Samuels, director of the European branch of the Simon Wiesenthal Center in Paris. "Today, that's the real danger."

Today's relative calm is quite a change from the 1980s. Far-left European terrorists then combined with Palestinian groups to produce a deadly mixture. In 1979, they bombed a Paris synagogue on Rue Copernic.

From then through 1982, Mr. Samuels says 79 shootings took place in Europe. Rabbi Mayer attended the Rue Copernic synagogue as a child and says the attack changed Jewish life on the continent. "Before, we never even thought about security," he says. "Afterwards, we never have forgotten about security."

COLD-WAR EFFECT

The collapse of the cold war took the steam out of French left-wing terror organizations such as Action Directe and Germany's Baader Meinhof. And the tentative peace between the Palestine Liberation Organization and Israel reduced the threat of Middle Eastern terrorism. "The far left has been decimated," says Samuels. "Only a few Trotskyites are left hanging around."

The Right experienced no such neutron bombs. During the early 1990s, anti-immigrant and anti-Semitic nationalist groups such as France's National Front and Germany's Republikaners made dangerous electoral inroads.

France's Jean-Marie Le Pen, who once said the Holocaust was a mere "detail" during World War II, got 15 percent in a presidential vote. Similar parties remain strong in Belgium's Flanders and Austria, among other places. But in recent elections, German far-right scores have fallen off and the French National Right has split into weaker factions.

The biggest danger comes from skinheads and neo-Nazi groups. "We are not so afraid of the parliamentary extreme right, but of the military extreme right," says Samuels. "Most of these movements here are inspired by North America and the hate groups there that preach a racial holy war."

Last year, he convinced French police to arrest 17 skinheads who had taken a Canadian hate site on the Internet and adapted it for use in France under the label Charlemagne Hammerskins, making threats to kill prominent French Jews.

Another danger comes from Muslim extremists. In recent years, Arab fundamentalists have congregated in Britain.

Algerian fundamentalists also are visible in both France and Germany and have begun recruiting local Arab immigrants into terror groups. Unlike their American counterparts, European skinheads have difficulty obtaining guns. Strict firearm laws exist throughout Europe. "There's still anti-Semitism here," says Rabbi David Meyer of Beth Hillel Synagogue in Brussels. "There's just less access to weapons."

Most anti-Jewish attacks in the West consist of desecrating Jewish cemeteries. Samuels counts 100 such attacks throughout Europe last year and says they're more common in Eastern rather than Western Europe.

When he returned to visit his parents' graves in London last year, he was shocked to find that a quarter of the cemetery was de-stroyed. "I've worked fighting against anti-Semitism all my life," he says. "This was the first time it had touched me personally."

CRITICAL THINKING QUESTIONS

1. What are the historical roots of anti-Semitism?
2. How is anti-Semitism communicated and carried out in the United States today?
3. How is anti-Semitism related to the gains of the women's, civil rights, and gay/lesbian movements?

Reading 8

Overcoming Reservations about Leaving the Reservation

Michael Ridgway

In this article, Ridgway examines the ways that the culture and economics of Native American reservations contribute to low educational achievement levels and how this in turn has contributed to the generally poor status of Native Americans.

For Many Native Americans, 'Non-Indian Education' Is Something They Just 'Don't Want'

BROOKINGS, S.D.—As Clarice Mesteth loaded her life into a car last summer and headed 300 miles from home in the Pine Ridge Indian Reservation, fear churned in her gut.

The 25-year-old Oglala Sioux woman had embarked upon a journey rare among American Indians, one that too often ends in failure when it is undertaken at all—a journey to college.

Source: Reprinted from *Community College Week* 10, no. 15 (February 23, 1998): 11.

But Mesteth, now in her second semester at South Dakota State University here, is determined to beat the enormous odds against her and return home clutching a bachelor's degree.

"When you leave the . . . reservation, it's like you're naked," she explains. "But I can't drop out of college, because this is my future."

Statistically speaking, Mesteth is an anomaly. The vast majority of American Indians never set foot on a college campus. And many who do end up dropping out.

Fewer than 7 percent of American Indians here in South Dakota earn a four-year degree, according to the U.S. Census Bureau. That's far fewer than any other minority group.

And while American Indians make up about 8 percent of the state's population, they represent just 2 percent of students at public universities, state figures show.

Those numbers disturb educators and tribal officials, who view education at the state's six public universities, four community colleges and three tribal colleges as a tool to enrich this state's poorest residents.

Retention figures also are troubling. A 1995 sampling of students showed that fewer than half of American Indians enrolled at public universities came back the following year.

ECONOMICS AND ISOLATION

State educators say that the reservations' grim economics and traditional culture account for much of the lagging American Indian participation in higher education. With staggering unemployment and low wages, few reservation families can afford college degrees.

On the Rosebud Indian Reservation, for example, unemployment has soared to 95 percent. The few Indians who work, earn an average income that is less than half the state average.

Tribes offer some financial aid to students but do not cover many college costs. And as federal money shrinks, tribes are finding it more difficult to help students at all.

"There's a perception that Native American students get a free ride through college," says Velva-Lu White, South Dakota State University's Native American adviser. "But that's not true. Any Indian who hits this university is very special, just by the fact that they made it here."

Those who do journey to a college campus often discover a landscape littered with cultural hurdles. Universities are starkly different from reservations, and for many Indians, the change proves too much.

When Mesteth began class at South Dakota State last fall, she felt the burden of being Indian in a predominantly white population.

"It was like I didn't have anything in common with these people," she said. "When I first got here, I didn't think there was another Native American here. I felt like people were looking at me."

Mesteth's reaction is fairly typical, said Francine Hall, minority achievement director Northern State University.

"A lot of students come from a reservation, and on the reservation you're isolated and you're in the majority," she said. "But they come into higher education as a small .percentage of the population, and it's a culture shock."

Indian attitudes toward education, marred by a tyrannical past, have also hindered their progress in academics, said Eldon Lawrence, president of Sisseton-Wahpeton Community College.

"Education historically was used as a weapon to kill our culture," he said. "Non-Indian education educates us away from our culture, it assimilates us. Indians don't want that."

Only recently have Indians begun to see education as a tool for taking charge of their future, but many still are wary, he said.

ASSISTANCE AND MOTIVATION

Both universities and tribes have begun efforts to boost Indian enrollment in higher education. The five tribal colleges in South Dakota have been instrumental, giving students a way to pursue an education without leaving the reservation.

"Our college offers a link to higher education, because we're situated right with the people," said Lawrence. "We're getting people who never would have thought of enrolling in a college."

The tribal colleges also help ease Indian students into state universities. At local colleges, Indian students can adjust to college life without the cultural chaos.

That has better prepared students for studying at larger public Universities, said Stephanie Charging Eagle, director of Black

Hills State's Indian studies program. In fact, students who transfer from a tribal college to a state university are much less likely to drop out, she said.

Indian Studies departments on state campuses also have helped smooth the transition from reservation to university. The courses on Indian heritage and history give students a cultural anchor while studying at large public universities, Hall said.

"Indian students can take classes about things they're familiar with, and they acquire the academic behaviors that will help them in college," she said.

Many of the universities also provide advisers and assistance programs that help Indian students adjust. White, South Dakota State's Indian adviser, guides students through the financial-aid maze and cultural perplexities. But mostly, she's there to listen as students try to gather their bearings.

South Dakota State also has set aside an emergency fund that pays small amounts to cash-strapped students for gas, child care and groceries. Sometimes, a tank of gas can mean the difference between a dropout and a college graduate, White said.

Both educators and tribes agree that more educated tribal members are needed badly to turn the tide of poverty on reservations. With jobs scarce on most reservations, many Indians see little motivation to earn a degree that will put them in debt.

But some see the professional opportunities, particularly in health care and education, that now are filled largely by whites.

"Ninety-nine point nine percent of the students here are going back to the reservation, and they're going back to help," White said. "They're not going to school for the larger home, the new car or the money in the bank. They realize they can help more with an education."

That's precisely why Janelle Andrade left her home on the Pine Ridge Reservation to study for a degree in social work at SDSU.

"There's a lot of hopelessness on the reservation," said Andrade, an Oglala Sioux. "Indians need to see other Indians in professional positions. They need to know that we're capable of succeeding."

CRITICAL THINKING QUESTIONS

1. In this article, Clarice Mesteth says that "When you leave the . . . reservation, it's like you're dead." What does she mean by this? How does this feeling make it more difficult for Native Americans than whites to complete college? What other ethnic groups might experience similar feelings? Explain.

2. In this article, Ridgway contends that Native Americans, as a group, tend to distrust education. Why? What have educators done to gain their trust? What more could they do?

3. In your opinion, what role should education play in helping Native Americans overcome poverty? In what ways does education have the potential to preserve or further eradicate their cultural heritage?

Getting Involved

1. Talk to teenage boys and teenage girls about how they look, how they would like to look, and where they got ideas about how they should look. Take notes as you talk with them, and discuss your findings with your classmates.

2. When you are out socially with a racially mixed group of friends or classmates, casually introduce to the conversation a topic related to race, such as the number of minorities at your school or an incident that has been in the media. Observe the reactions you get from your friends. Do they discuss the issue as freely as they would any other topic you might raise? Why or why not?

3. Contact the Jewish Community Center, B'nai B'rith, or another Jewish group in your area and make arrangements to interview the director about her or his perceptions of the forms that anti-Semitic prejudice and discrimination take in your community.

Site-Seeing

1. To learn more about the mythopoetic men's movement, visit **http://www.widesky.org/** and **http://www.menstuff.org/**.

2. For more information on Native American education, visit **http://www.collegefund.org/**.

3. To learn more about anti-Semitism in the United States, visit the Anti-Defamation League's web site at **http://adl.org/backgrounders/Anti_Semitism_us.html**.

Chapter 4

Barriers to Equality

As we have already seen in the first three chapters, today's inequalities are commonly rooted in historical practices and cultural beliefs and are often perpetuated through face-to-face interaction. However, the real reason prejudice and discrimination continue is that they have become part of many of our social institutions—the major building blocks of society.

Even when individuals no longer hold prejudices against particular groups, institutionalized discrimination can be one of the most difficult barriers to surmount. Institutionalized discrimination refers to the organizational practices and prescribed ways of accomplishing tasks within society's institutions that systematically disadvantage particular groups on the basis of race, ethnicity, social class, gender, sexuality, or any other group status.

Institutionalized discrimination continues to be a serious problem in U.S. society, yet it can be extremely difficult to detect. Indeed, many people are completely unaware of some of the more common institutional barriers that certain social groups must overcome in their quest for equal treatment. To take a more in-depth look at some of the ways that institutionalized discrimination affects people today, we have divided this chapter into four parts, which examine institutionalized discrimination in social institutions that have an immediate, direct impact on people's lives and inequality: the economy, health care, education, and the legal and criminal justice systems. In an era when many people believe that equality of opportunity has been achieved in U.S. society, it is especially important to understand the hurdles that minority groups continue to face.

We turn first to institutionalized discrimination in the economy. The remaining three barriers are introduced later in the chapter.

ECONOMIC BARRIERS TO EQUALITY

The economy, as an institution, structures people's access to property, employment, housing, government assistance, and other means of meeting their basic needs and gaining upward mobility. Yet, as the articles in this section of the chapter demonstrate, access to these resources is unequal because barriers to equality are built right into the economy itself.

In the first article, Conley argues that the poorer economic status of many African-Americans today is due, in part, to the fact that they lack assets, such as houses or business holdings, that whites enjoy. Despite decades of affirmative action in education, employment, and housing, African-Americans continue to be restrained in their quest for upward mobility by redlining—a banking practice in which lenders refuse to issue mortgages or home improvement loans in certain neighborhoods—and by white flight—the migration of whites from cities, which are increasingly populated by people of color, to the predominately white suburbs. One result is the devaluation of the property that African-Americans have been able to acquire. Conley argues that the low socioeconomic status of African-Americans is rooted in centuries-old practices of discrimination in jobs, education, and housing that goes back to the time of slavery. To remedy the inequality between African-Americans and whites, Conley argues for a number of changes in social policy, including compensating African-Americans today for the toll that slavery, prejudice, and discrimination have taken upon them as a group.

Just as African-Americans have suffered economic barriers to equality, the second article in this subsection delineates one way that Native Americans have been prevented from escaping poverty. Indeed, they are more likely to be unemployed and to have higher rates of poverty than any other racial or ethnic group (Feagin and Feagin 1996). Yet, as McCarthy explains, the Bureau of Indian Affairs—a government agency that administers services for and government relations with Native Americans—has mismanaged trust funds set up for them by the U.S. government.

Poverty is a social problem that affects racial and ethnic minorities and women more often than it does whites or men, and although it exists in rural areas, it is, by definition, more concentrated in urban areas. One of the dilemmas that poor people confront daily is whether to spend their limited funds on food, housing, medicine, or any of their other requirements for survival.

In the 1960s, the U.S. government established a number of social programs to alleviate poverty. Among those programs was the Department of Housing and Urban Development (HUD), which was to build low-income housing and provide rent subsidies to low-income people. In the third article in the economic section, Norquist charts the decline of low-cost housing and argues that the federal programs designed to provide low-income housing have been disastrous for cities and urban residents. He argues that federally funded public housing suffers from poor targeting, design, and management as well as from periodic corruption and scandal. Programs such as HUD and the Bureau of Indian Affairs, which were established by the government to alleviate the effects of inequality, have actually played a major role in perpetuating poverty.

The one social policy of the 1960s that may have been expected to have the greatest impact on alleviating poverty and inequality was the Civil Rights Act of 1964. This federal law prohibits segregation in employment and in public accommodations and facilities. In the fourth article, Grossman argues that the Civil Rights Act failed to deliver economic opportunities for African-Americans. He contends that the workplace for African-Americans continues to be a hostile environment in which prejudice and discrimination continue, although in more subtle forms than in the past. For example, even when companies recruit African-American employees, they are more likely to be rejected by hiring officials who believe they will not "fit" in the corporate culture. And once hired, they are less likely than whites to be promoted into upper management positions. With such difficulties in being hired and promoted, it is little wonder that African-Americans continue to lag behind whites where money is concerned. Prejudice and discriminatory practices continue to be a part of the economy that have proven more difficult to change than the law.

The Civil Rights Act of 1964 was passed because of the hard work of activists in the civil rights movement, most of whom were African-American. But the Act was never intended to pertain only to that minority group. Nonetheless, in the fifth article, Yaffe argues that in Los Angeles County, equal employment in the local government workforce has been historically defined as a "Black-White" issue. He contends that Hispanics are now the only major racial or ethnic group to be under-represented in all segments of the local government workforce. Yaffe argues that Hispanics have been excluded from important political and economic decision-making processes by whites and African-Americans, both of whom are motivated by a desire to preserve their own power and privilege. Yaffe contends that to rationalize their practices, officials continue to cite two myths: that Hispanics have lower levels of education than do other minority groups, and that the Hispanic population is largely made up of illegal immigrants. Yaffe's article shows us how institutionalized discrimination is intertwined with prejudiced beliefs and how the two can combine to make it particularly difficult for certain groups to overcome the barriers to full participation in society.

Not all inequality is perpetuated by such obvious contests over wealth, power, or status. As Larson argues in the sixth article, the workforce in the United States has become subject to a new trend, known as "outsourcing," or the hiring of temporary workers to replace regular employees. The main reason employers have turned to temporary employees, or "temps," is that they save money when they no longer have to pay fringe benefits such as vacation, sick leave, health insurance, or retirement. The problem, Larson argues, is that the U.S. economy is trending toward the use of "temps," so even when employees would like the security and fringe benefits of a regular job, they are finding it harder to obtain them. Larson says that outsourcing has had a particularly negative effect on women and children and contends that the trend toward temporary employment is likely to continue. Workers, Larson argues, must learn to adapt to these new workplace demands by becoming smarter consumers. For example, they must demand that companies provide flexibility in fringe benefits such as health insurance or retirement accounts, allowing workers to carry them from one job to the next. However, even if such arrangements are eventually instituted, workers will no longer enjoy the employment security that their parents once did, making upward mobility more tenuous for them than for previous generations.

The trend toward outsourcing came only three decades after racial and ethnic minorities and women won the legal right to be protected from discrimination against in the workforce. Women have made important employment gains, both in the number of previously male-dominated jobs and professions they have entered and in their movement into the upper echelons of management. But have women come as far as people seem to think they have?

In the seventh article, Brett and Stroh compare the career paths of 1,000 managers and their spouses and find that women's management careers often lag behind those of men in terms of salary increases and promotions. The managers in their study had, on average, comparable educational achievement and workplace experience and a similar low level of workplace interruptions due to illness or other factors. The authors argue that the reasons for women's lower workplace achievement include fewer opportunities to relocate for career advancement, a lower value placed on the education and skills women bring to the job, and less frequent placement in high-profile positions that are more likely to lead to promotion. Moreover, women managers' salaries lag behind men's because they are paid, on average, thousands of dollars less annually for working overtime and because, when they seek employment at other corporations, they are offered salaries far below those of men with comparable educations, skills, and work experience. Brett and Stroh argue that one way to entice women to compete for upper-level management positions is for employers to offer conditions that allow for a better balance between the demands of work and home. They argue that with equal opportunities and compensation, women will one day reach upper-level management in numbers comparable with those of men.

But what about women who are unable or unwilling to devote long hours to their careers because they have children and need or wish to devote considerable time to raising them? In the eighth article, Williams points out that nonparents of both sexes are doing well in economic terms, but that mothers are more likely to be poor, in large part because the demands of caring for their children make it difficult to gain well-paying jobs. Williams maintains that the demands placed on employees are based on the assumption that workers are male—that is, that workers do not get pregnant and do not have primary responsibility for the home or children. The key to breaking this pattern of feminine poverty, she maintains, is to reorganize the workplace to accommodate the demands that mothers face in the home.

Williams' argument that the workplace is organized around assumptions that workers are men is similar to a point made by Yared in the ninth article in the economics section. The author focuses on the story of an acclaimed teacher who was assumed to be heterosexual until he publicly planned a commitment ceremony with his male partner. When the community learned that the teacher was gay, angry parents demanded that he resign or be fired. Yared uses this story to focus on the stresses that gay employees face, the lack of protection that they contend with in many areas, and the toll that discrimination can take on individuals when they are not legally protected from such treatment.

Finally, in the last article in this section, Gagné and Tewksbury examine the pressures to conform to traditional gender ideals that masculine-to-feminine transgenders—including transsexuals and cross-dressers—face. (Cross-dressers are men who occasionally dress and go out in public as women, but who live as men and do not wish to become women.) In addition to strong interpersonal pressures to act like "real men," the transgendered individuals the authors interviewed talked about difficulties on the job, which ranged from harassment from co-workers to being fired. In the United States, only a few cities provide workplace or other civil rights protections for transgendered individuals. In this way, transgenders face workplace discrimination similar to that experienced by sexual minorities. But unlike gay men, lesbians, and bisexuals, many transgenders—specifically transsexuals—are required to live full time as the gender they wish to be for one year before they can legally change their identity or surgically alter their bodies. Because of this requirement, unlike sexual minorities, transgenders are unable to control information about their minority status.

Collectively, the articles in this section demonstrate just some of the ways in which unequal opportunities have been institutionalized in the U.S. economy. In some instances, individuals are targeted by prejudiced people whose discrimination is made possible when the law fails to protect workers. The failure of the law to ensure equality of workplace opportunity is, itself, a form of institutionalized discrimination. More often, however, such discrimination is less obvious. Whether it includes the government's mismanagement of Indian trust funds, the demise of affordable housing, or the failure to hire or promote minorities and women, the articles in this section demonstrate that discrimination is built into our economy through the institutions to which people are expected to turn in order to support themselves or achieve upward mobility. Until these and other forms of institutional discrimination are eliminated, we can expect to see inequalities of opportunity that result, invariably, in unjust, unequal results.

REFERENCE

FEAGIN, JOE R. AND CLAIRECE BOOHER FEAGIN. 1996. *Racial and Ethnic Relations*, 5th Edition. Upper
Saddle River, NJ: Prentice-Hall.

Reading 1

40 Acres and a Mule

Dalton Conley

> *In this article, Conley details the causes and consequences of long-standing traditions that
> have restricted the economic opportunities of African-Americans. The author also proposes a
> number of solutions to poverty for African-Americans.*

In 1965, the last of a series of laws that capped
the civil rights movement was passed in the
United States. No one expected socioeconomic conditions for African Americans to
improve straightaway as a result of "equal opportunity." However, a generation later, it
might be more reasonable to expect substantial progress toward racial equity to have been
made. Still today, blacks are half as likely to
graduate from college as whites, twice as likely
to be unemployed, and earn about 55 percent
of what whites make. As bad as these statistics
sound, they represent improvements since the
1960s; what is more, they obscure the real nature of racial inequality in the United States
today: property and class.

In fact, if there were one statistic that captured the persistence of racial inequality in the
post-civil rights United States, it would be net
worth—also known as wealth, equity, or assets.
If you want to know your net worth, all you have
to do is add up everything you own and sub-
tract your total amount of outstanding debt.
When we do this for white and minority households across America, incredible differences
emerge: Overall, the typical white family enjoys

a net worth that is around ten times that of its
non-white counterpart. Latinos—a very diverse
group—overall fare slightly better than African
Americans but still fall far short of whites on
this indicator. To make matters worse, this "equity inequity" has grown in the decades since
the heralded civil rights triumphs of the 1960s.

The wealth gap cannot be explained by income differences alone. That is, even when we
compare black and white families at the same
income levels, asset gaps remain large. For instance, at the lower end of the economic spectrum (incomes less than $15,000 per year), the
median African American family has a net
worth of zero, while the equivalent white family holds $10,000 of equity. Likewise, among
the often-heralded new black middle class, the
situation is not much better. The typical white
family that earns $40,000 per year enjoys a nest
egg of around $80,000. Its African American
counterpart has less than half that amount.

CONSEQUENCES OF ASSET INEQUITY

The consequences of this racial wealth gap
are not benign; rather, wealth differences account for many of the racial differences in socioeconomic achievement that have persisted

Source: Reprinted from *National Forum* 80, no. 2 (Spring
2000) 21–24.

in this era since the Civil Rights Movement. Just comparing blacks and whites, blacks are less likely to graduate from college, earn less, and are more likely to rely on welfare. However, when we compare African Americans and whites who are coming from similar socioeconomic backgrounds in terms of income and wealth, we find that African American children are more likely to graduate from high school than whites are and are just as likely to complete college. Likewise, we find that the wage gap between blacks and whites disappears and that African Americans are just as likely as Anglos to be working full-time. Among the poor, it is a lack of assets that explains the higher propensities of blacks to rely on welfare. In short, the economic problems of African Americans rest in the realm of property relations, not in the labor market.

Stacey Jones, an African American woman with a graduate degree and a solidly middle-class job, typifies the bind in which many minority parents find themselves. "I find it hard to locate a decent school in Atlanta for my children without resorting to parochial education because I am, in effect, priced out of home-buying in good school districts." She explains, "This, in turn, makes it difficult for me to pay more for housing, since I am spending a good deal of my income on education for my children." This is the dilemma of the black middle class, a growing group that is often touted as a badge of racial progress. A lack of assets means living from paycheck to paycheck, being trapped in a job or a neighborhood that is less beneficial in the long run, or not being able to send one's children to the top colleges because one lacks the asset cushion to facilitate change. Income provides for day-to-day, week-to-week expenses. In the contemporary United States, wealth is the stuff that upward mobility is made of.

For the minority poor, the situation is even more precarious. The $10,000 in equity that impoverished white families enjoy would certainly come in handy when the inevitable economic downturn puts a family member out of work or when a medical crisis strikes. With no asset cushion to speak of and a weak U.S. welfare state, minorities who are hit with such a blow—and they are not uncommon—would much more quickly slip into the sand pit of alternative living arrangements, family break-ups, and, of course, welfare dependency.

Aside from the purely financial benefits that wealth provides families and children, assets may also have other, less tangible effects. These are best illustrated by the efforts of the philanthropist Eugene Lang. In 1980, he returned to the Bronx neighborhood where he had grown up to give a speech to sixth-graders. Lang was awestruck by the urban blight that had infected his old stomping ground. In face of such devastation, he tore up his speech on the importance of education and hard work. Instead, he promised each of those sixth-graders that if they completed high school, he would personally pay their college tuition. He did not change their weekly income or their neighborhood conditions; what he essentially did was provide them an asset in the form of a promissory note (as well as some after-school tutoring). The result was that in a neighborhood where a majority of students dropped out of high school and almost nobody attended college, a full fifty-four of those sixty-one students finished high school, and more than half went on to pursue higher education.

The result of viewing racial inequality through the lens of assets is that equal opportunity and equal conditions cannot be viewed as separate or as alternative. They are one and the same when viewed across generations. Namely, whether or not my parents enjoy the American dream of the house, the car, and the private pension is one of the best predictors of whether or not I will have a chance to achieve the same. This last point hints at the origin of the wealth gap. Simply put, equity inequity is, in part, the result of the head start that whites have enjoyed in accumulating and passing on assets. In short, it takes money to make money, as the old adage goes. Whites not only earn more now, they also have always earned more than African Americans—a lot more. Wealth differences, in turn, feed upon these long-term income differences. Some economists estimate that up to 80 percent of lifetime wealth accumulation results from gifts in one form or another from past generations of relatives (more conservative estimates put the figure at around 50 percent). These gifts can range from the down payment on a first home, to a free college education, to a bequest upon the death of a parent. Over the long run, small initial differences in wealth holdings spin out of control.

SOME HISTORY

However, as if lower wages and initial wealth levels were not enough, there have long been institutional restraints on black property accumulation. After the emancipation of slaves, blacks were promised "40 acres and a mule" by the Freedmen's Bureau, a government agency set up to integrate the former slaves into the world of wage labor. However, of the total number of confiscated plantations, the lion's share went to white northerners, who hired the former slaves to cultivate them, inaugurating the system of sharecropping that would keep blacks asset-poor for many decades. While legally and politically different from slavery, the end result was the same. For blacks who tried to escape sharecropping, formidable obstacles existed as well. In many southern states, African Americans who tried to set up their own businesses were stopped by "black codes" that required African Americans (but not whites) to pay exorbitant licensing fees. Similarly, if former slaves tried to go West with the promise of free land by virtue of the Homestead Act, they were likely to find that their claims to title were not legally enforceable in some areas.

During the twentieth century, barriers to black property accumulation remained formidable. For instance, the Home Owners' Loan Corporation (HOLC) of the United States government helped many white homeowners avoid default during the Great Depression; however, the same cannot be said for black homeowners. In fact, it was this agency that instituted the technique of "redlining," in which the highest-risk neighborhoods would be assigned a red (no-loan)

rating. Black neighborhoods invariably received this designation, a practice that private banks adopted, too. Meanwhile, the U.S. public pension system, Social Security (originally Old Age Insurance), excluded most black workers because it exempted the agricultural and service sectors. The result was that a greater proportion of black assets had to be spent on supporting elderly family members, and less could be passed on to the next generations.

After the Great Depression, the situation was no better. The Federal Housing Authority (FHA), established in 1937, in combination with the Veterans Administration (VA) home-lending program that was part of the Serviceman's Readjustment Act of 1944, made homeownership possible for millions of Americans after World War II by underwriting low-interest, long-term loans for first-time home buyers. But African Americans were systematically shut out of participation in these programs because loans were channeled to suburbs and away from the central cities, where blacks predominantly resided.

Since the 1960s, occasional efforts have been made to promote minority-asset accumulation, but they have not amounted to much. For instance, in the wake of the urban unrest of the late 1960s, there was much talk of fostering "black capitalism." Black capitalism boils down to educational programs to bolster the business skills and entrepreneurial spirit in the minority community. Black capitalism never took off, however, and was replaced by "community development" strategies to foster minority property accumulation during the 1970s. In this approach, a nonprofit group called a community development corporation (CDC) acts to attract capital to an economically depressed, predominantly minority, inner-city neighborhood. Today's equivalents are the community development banks that form part of the "enterprise" or "empowerment" zones proposed by Jack Kemp and implemented on a limited basis by George Bush and Bill Clinton.

A more radical policy alternative to fostering black capitalism or community development calls for reparations for black Americans. Espoused by black separatist organizations in the 1960s, the argument for reparations became particularly refined during the 1970s. One researcher used 1790–1860 slave prices as indicators for the value of slave capital. He then converted the prices into an income stream upon which he applied compound interest, calculated since the slavery era. The figure he came up with matched what the Republic of New Africa (RNA), a prominent separatist group, was asking for.

EFFECTS OF "WHITE FLIGHT"

Recently, President Clinton made it illegal for banks to redline. The bad news is that simply providing African Americans with the opportunity—or even the means—to become homeowners will not be enough. The problem is that homes in black neighborhoods do not accrue value at the same rate as those in predominantly white areas. Property has the particular attribute of quantifying the social value of ideas or objects. A diamond or a misprinted stamp or a Van Gogh has no inherent productive value. Its value stems only from the price that our culture is willing to pay for it in the marketplace. In this vein, when a neighborhood's housing values precipitously decline as the proportion of black residents rises, the price changes provide a record of the social value of "blackness" on the part of society.

The devaluation of black neighborhoods is partially a result of white fears of a decline in property values and the "white flight" that ensues. In other words, there is a causal loop: As long as whites are a significant majority and have the ability to decide where they will live, they will have an economic incentive to flee integrated neighborhoods, thus perpetuating the vicious cycle. Aside from any personal ideology, it is in the economic interest of white homeowners to sell off when they anticipate that the neighborhood has reached a racial "tipping point" for

fear that others will make the same calculation and sell off first, causing them to lose money on their homes.

In this way, both blacks and whites are trapped into reproducing current residential patterns. As a result, even if African Americans were allowed equal access to the home-buying market and if interest rates were prescribed by law to be the same for blacks and whites, African Americans would still be at a disadvantage in terms of housing equity because whites could flee, depressing values for those who remained. Remedies for this situation are difficult to come by. Politically, any policy limiting the market (restricting the ability of white homeowners to sell, for instance) would fly in the face of the notion of individual choice that is so central to American ideology; furthermore, from an economic point of view it is not in the interest of whites, whose housing is generally worth more precisely because it is not in a black neighborhood. In this way, race and class can reinforce each other. Another unlikely option is to limit the proportion of blacks in any given neighborhood to 15 percent, thereby eliminating the fear of racial tipping. However, this encroaches on black property rights.

POLICY OPTIONS

A third solution is to provide "integration insurance." This form of insurance would protect property owners from any rundown in prices that resulted from a rash in selling as a neighborhood tips from white to black. With this policy in place, the economic incentive to pull out when a neighborhood starts to integrate would be eliminated; ideally the insurance policy would never need to be cashed in. The difficulty lies in the details, of course, especially the task of factoring out changes in prices that may be resulting from other forces.

Other policy options to promote wealth equity include a national wealth tax: At the end of each calendar or fiscal year, each individual would use a checklist to assess his assets and liabilities and would be required to pay the government a certain percentage of that net worth if it exceeded a certain deduction. The resulting funds would be redistributed to the asset-poor.

Another idea would be to loosen the asset restrictions currently built into the welfare system. If welfare recipients were able to save without being penalized for their asset accumulation, public assistance might truly become a safety net instead of a way of life. Likewise, by selling public housing to its residents (who are predominantly black) in a program not unlike the VA or FHA programs instituted after World War II, the government could create a whole new class of urban homeowners with a stake in the American dream.

Another interesting idea that has been proposed is the creation of Individual Development Accounts (IDAs) that foster savings among the asset-poor through matching funds. If such programs target individuals and communities that are both income- and asset-deprived, they will inevitably favor minorities while being ostensibly color-blind. The good news is that home ownership, savings, and asset accumulation are values that are universally espoused these days by both the left and right because it is generally agreed that stakeholders make better citizens.

Rather than redistribute wealth, another policy option entails making it matter less through the implementation of a color-blind, class-based affirmative-action policy in the areas of schooling and work. Current American affirmative-action policies, which give historically oppressed minorities a leg up in college admissions and in the labor market, are under increasing assault. Such practices have been outlawed through plebiscite or court order in a rapidly rising number of U.S. states. If affirmative action is to survive at all, it will be under a different guise. "Affirmative-asset" policy is one solution. This entails "positively discriminating" on the basis of social-class background—as measured by income and wealth. Such a policy would blunt several of the criticisms of the current policy. First, it would not be based on race at all, or on "group rights" of any kind, something that is anathema to the American ideology of individualism. Asset-poor blacks and whites would receive a boost. Second, because parental net worth is not as obvious as skin color, such a policy would be less stigmatizing to the beneficiaries. Currently, even minorities who have not benefited personally from affirmative action are often "labeled" as having gotten where they are on account of government largesse. Third, basing preferential treatment on economic background would address the claim that affirmative action mainly benefits those minorities who need it the least, the middle and upper classes who were going to go to college and get good jobs anyway. By contrast, using an income and wealth formula, the "truly disadvantaged" would be aided.

Of course, the best course of action would be to opt for both policies—those to foster black property accumulation as well as a revised affirmative action program. Whether or not Americans will pursue either is, of course, another matter. However, one thing is for sure; until the United States does take some action along these lines, rising stock markets will only worsen divisions; America is still two societies, "separate and unequal."

CRITICAL THINKING QUESTIONS

1. The author specifies a number of reasons why African-Americans are, on average, poorer than white Americans. What are they?

2. In what ways have the structural barriers to upward mobility for African-Americans been consciously and unconsciously created by white society?

3. In what ways would compensation to African-Americans remedy the harmful long-term effects of slavery? Do you think this policy will ever be enacted? Why or why not?

Reading 2

A Busted Trust

Colman McCarthy

As financiers, Elouise Cobell and Paul Homan have been watching over money at opposite poles of the banking universe. Cobell is one of some 10,000 Blackfeet living on an impoverished 1.5 million acres east of Glacier National Park. She chairs the Blackfeet National Bank in Browning, Montana. Indiana-owned and -run, it has $18 million in assets and fifteen employees. Homan's thirty-year career includes the presidency of the multibillion-dollar Riggs National Bank in Washington, DC, and service as deputy comptroller in the Bush Administration.

For more than three years, the toil of these dissimilar bankers has converged on one question: Where's the money? In one of the nation's most calamitous and enduring financial debacles, Indian trust funds have been mismanaged by the bungling Interior Department's Bureau of Indian Affairs. A case prompted by the mismanagement, in which Cobell is the lead plaintiff, is set to go to trial June 10 before federal district judge Royce Lamberth in Washington, DC.

As many as 500,000 Native Americans—going back to the 1880s—have had money or land held in trust for them by the BIA. Income was earned on the sale or lease of property or revenues from oil, timber or cattle companies. In 1994 the agency, cornered by a few members of Congress, confessed that it couldn't account for $2.4 billion of Indian money. Tens of thousands of records were lost or destroyed. Accounts lacked addresses or Social Security numbers. Antiquated file cards were scattered throughout dozens of BIA offices. At hearings on March 3, Senator Ben Nighthorse Campbell, chairman of the Committee on In-

dian Affairs, displayed photos of how trust fund records were kept. "These are essentially bank records," he said, "water damaged, kept in trashbags, disintegrating boxes, next to paint cans, mop buckets and road signs." Homan, who had been appointed as a special trustee for the Indian accounts, has described the situation as "one of the worst messes that I've seen."

On February 22 Judge Lamberth held two Cabinet secretaries—Bruce Babbitt of Interior and Robert Rubin of Treasury—in civil contempt of court. In a seventy-six-page lambasting, Lamberth said the pair "cannot be trusted." They have been engaging "in a shocking pattern of deception of the court," he said, adding, "I have never seen more egregious misconduct by the federal government."

Babbitt is the latest of the Great White Fathers to speak with forked tongue. His pattern of deceit continued when, unctuously vowing to the Senate on March 3 to "do my best," he boasted that he was the first Interior Secretary in a hundred years to attempt "a serious correction" of the "deplorable situation." The facts tell a different story. Since 1993 ten Congressional hearings have been held on trust fund issues. Babbitt had testified at none. Indian groups reported that Babbitt has consistently stonewalled requests for meetings. He opposed the creation of the special trustee and then, after Homan was appointed, worked to subvert his work by underfunding and understaffing his office. In January Homan, who had visited more than twenty Indian reservations to learn the depths of the problem and was universally admired by Cobell and such allies as the Native American Rights Fund, resigned in frustration.

Cobell, a MacArthur genius award winner in 1997, is from a family of nine children. In her

Source: Reprinted from *The Nation* 268, no. 23 (June 21, 1999): 24.

girlhood, she walked to a one-room school. Noting that 80 percent of the Blackfeet tribe live below the poverty level, she tells stories of destitute Indians denied access to their money or knowledge of what they are due. When I interviewed Cobell near the time of the Lamberth ruling, she pointed out that "our county—Glacier County—is the eleventh poorest" in the United States. "It is hard to get people out of poverty when they have nowhere to go," she said. "Even in the bank, we experience it. A lot of people lack the equity to do something. That's why I'm working so hard on this trust fund issue. If we can get people to the point where trust mortgages flow easily, and they understand they can leverage that to go into homes or businesses, then you have a lot of opportunities."

"I run a bank," she says. "I understand how other people's money is managed. The BIA is not a bank. It doesn't have people who are qualified to be bankers."

CRITICAL THINKING QUESTIONS

1. According to the article, in what ways is the Bureau of Indian Affairs meant to help Native Americans?

2. How might the lives of Native Americans, as a group, be improved with the money for which the Bureau of Indian Affairs has failed to account?

3. What standard accounting practices might help to account for the money the authors report as missing? Is the failure to use these procedures a form of institutionalized discrimination? Why or why not?

Reading 3

How the Government Killed Affordable Housing

John O. Norquist

> *In this article Norquist summarizes the lack of affordable housing in the United States and the ways the federal government has failed to address these problems and enacted policies to make matters worse.*

Federal intervention in housing has been a disaster for cities and the people who live in them. After a succession of fiascos associated with attempts to eradicate slums, build housing for the poor, and pursue other seemingly noble goals, it should be obvious that government efforts often make urban conditions worse rather than better. Not every government effort is destined to fail. In Milwaukee, where I serve as mayor, we have achieved success with some housing endeavors. But the efforts that have brought genuine benefits have usually been *locally initiated* and have tried simply to help the private market work better, rather than assuming that a bureaucracy can competently build or operate the places that people call home.

The sorry consequences of federal involvement in housing can be seen in the decline of

Source: The American Enterprise, Vol. 9, Issue 4 (July/Aug 1998) pp. 68–70.

low-cost housing. Up to the 1950s, American cities offered people without much money a variety of choices in shelter. Not all of that housing was pretty or spacious. But the options were numerous, and included walk-ups, apartments over stores, triplexes, duplexes, single-family houses, apartments over garages, flats in back, boardinghouses, tenements, low-rent hotels, and row houses.

Many of the customers for these places were immigrants, most of whom eventually moved on to something much better. Though much of this housing fell short of today's standards, it allowed people to save their money while still being sheltered in an urban setting.

Efficient, low-income housing grew organically in cities. For instance, at the turn of the century it was common for people to live above the shops on a commercial street. Tenants attracted to these apartments worked in the establishments below or on streets nearby. Sometimes the apartments above shops were occupied by the shop owners themselves.

In Milwaukee, German and Polish immigrants with peasant backgrounds placed an extremely high value on home ownership. Their self-denial and inventiveness is demonstrated by the "Polish flat."

The Polish flat was a modest three- or four-room cottage built with the first money these immigrants saved. As the mortgage was paid off, the owner of the cottage typically would raise it on posts four or five feet high in order to construct a semi-basement living space, with a separate entrance, below. Sometimes this space was occupied by newly arrived, income-earning members of the owner's family or extended family; sometimes it was let to boarders. As soon as additional income allowed, the timbers in the basement were replaced by brick walls. Rooms were added to the upper floor. Sometimes cottages were lifted off their foundations and rolled through the neighborhood to be joined to the homes of their kin. You could tell the Polish families that had made it in Milwaukee—they no longer used the basement for income, and had converted their duplex to a single-family house.

In Milwaukee and other big cities, there were sometimes gaps in the urban housing market. The incredibly rapid urbanization of the United States during the industrial revolution caused the gears of the housing market to grind painfully at times in an effort to keep up, particularly in the major destination of immigrants, New York City.

In 1890, muckraking journalist Jacob Riis produced *How the Other Half Lives,* documenting the unhealthy living conditions of some of New York's tenements. Riis's book focused public attention on real problems, resulting in valuable improvements in immunization programs and water, sewer, and sanitation services. But a detrimental consequence of the book was the vilification of such urban housing forms as New York's tenements and Boston's triplexes.

Reformers spread the notion of a housing shortage, claiming that the market had failed. New York, Chicago, and other cities began to create public housing, at first paying for it themselves. Cities built only what they could afford, and thus built to a human scale. In 1920 in Milwaukee, money was appropriated for cooperative home building, which consisted of two- or three-story apartment buildings. These buildings had an institutional look, but unlike later federally funded housing many of these buildings are still in service and attractive to tenants.

While cities tried to patch perceived housing gaps, state and federal bureaucrats and planners began to damn the urban neighborhoods that were playing such a valuable role in assimilating immigrants and low-income citizens. Of the poor but marvelously functional and upwardly mobile Polish neighborhoods of Milwaukee, one state health official said:

"The 12th and 14th wards are more than any others the regions of the modern cave dwellers. . . . The basements are occupied from choice and long fixed habit, as well as, in some cases, to reduce the cost of living. In many cases well-to-do owners of the property are found living in the basement when the first floor rooms are vacant. The only excuse for such living is ignorance. . . . In fact, the basement has a musty, sour, human smell that they like."

Such prejudice fueled many state and federal improvement programs for cities. The exalted ideals of reformers crushed the humble dreams of the immigrants. "Lot coverage restrictions gradually eliminated new construction of the rear house and the Polish Flat," report researchers Judith Kenny and Thomas Hubka. As a consequence, home ownership became more difficult.

In 1930, the Hoover administration developed a model zoning ordinance that emphasized separation of houses from commercial and industrial activity. This was a response to some legitimate concerns raised by people living near noxious factories, stockyards, and rendering plants. But the result is the familiar pattern we see today in suburbs—offices in one parking pod, retail in another, light industrial in another, and housing on cul-de-sacs, isolated from everything.

Neighborhoods have no corner stores or anything else within walking distance, except identical housing. Nearly overnight, with the widespread adoption of these codes, the corner store with living space overhead ceased to be built in the United States. Main Street, with its mixed uses and pedestrian orientation, became a historical rather than contemporary form.

Separated, single-use zoning hurts U.S. cities. If governments would get rid of some of their prohibitions on combining commercial and residential uses, developers could build low-cost housing on top of venues like video stores, supermarkets, fast-food outlets, or drugstores. Developers will respond, as they have in Japan, Western Europe, and Canada as well as a few U.S. cities like Charleston, South Carolina, and San Francisco.

In 1937, as part of the New Deal, Congress established the United States Housing Authority to create more public housing. Most of it was two-story and three-story construction, widely scattered. Early public housing simply

shadowed the natural housing market, supplementing a market disrupted by depression and then war. By 1950 federal public housing—intended to be a temporary program during a time of economic distress—had outlived its usefulness. The small federal bureaucracy could have been easily dismantled. Instead, aided by Congress, it looked for and found a new clientele.

Housing bureaucrats adopted the migration of poor African Americans to big cities as a cause. Before the gears of urban housing markets could click into place, giving low-income blacks housing strategies like immigrants before them, the federal government jumped in with sterile high-rises, separated from the urban fabric by lawns and parking lots.

This resulted in such infamous projects as Pruitt-Igoe in St. Louis, where 12,000 African Americans with incomes at or below poverty level were warehoused in a high-rise apartment complex and expected to create a community. They didn't. Pruitt-Igoe, Robert Taylor Homes in Chicago, and scores of similar projects were complete disasters.

From coast to coast, cities used federal urban-renewal grants and, later, Urban Development Action Grants to eliminate the blight of low-cost hotels and apartments. Removing blight really meant putting people without means on the streets and onto government dependence. After World War II, journalist Pete Hamill rented a one-room apartment in New York for $8 a month, which, even in today's inflated dollars, would be a low outlay, about $100. That kind of opportunity was available in U.S. cities before urban renewal removed it. By tearing down low-cost housing, the government forced private providers out of the low-end housing market, thus creating both a permanent public-housing clientele and, eventually, homelessness.

After much of the low-cost housing had been destroyed, the federal government began a single-room-occupancy program to increase the supply of one-person dwellings. For nearly 200 years the market had produced low-cost housing in a variety of forms, shapes, and sizes. Now the only low-cost housing is produced by the government. And considering the tax subsidies involved, it is not low-cost.

What's wrong with federally funded public housing other than poor targeting, poor design, poor management, and periodic scandal? Just one thing: It's not needed. The United States does not have a housing shortage. Rather, it has a distorted housing market. The federal government, by focusing on below-market public housing in city neighborhoods, has smothered market mechanisms that would attract private-sector investment. This has made it easy for lenders to "redline" those neighborhoods. In his book *HUD Scandals,* Irving Welfeld points out how illogical it is to have the government build "affordable housing": "If the poor cannot afford food, we earmark assistance and give them food stamps. We don't create farms that grow only 'affordable food' or build 'affordable food' supermarkets where only the poor can shop."

The housing problems of cities have been aggravated by government agencies like the Federal Housing Authority (FHA), which has insured almost $200 billion in mortgage loans for detached, single-family, new construction. The FHA diverted capital from the urban housing market by focusing almost exclusively on new single-family homes in the suburbs.

And for most of its existence, the FHA has been unnecessary. Mortgage insurance has been widely available in the private market since the mid-1950s. Yet the private companies providing it have to compete every day with the federal government.

The federal Department of Housing and Urban Development (HUD) is another problem agency. It has 11,000 full-time employees (that's more than 100 federal bureaucrats for every central city in the U.S.). It administers dozens of programs that add billions of dollars to the national debt each year. And most of these programs aim to solve problems that have actually been created by government.

Congress hasn't helped in any of this. Over the years it has directed housing programs to

sprint one way, stop, turn around, and sprint the other way. Until 1949 low- and middle-income workers were public housing's clients. For the next 25 years policies wavered back and forth, but gradually excluded all wage-earners except those with the lowest incomes. In the mid-1970s Congress "tried to turn the clock back to the good old days" and appeal to a broader range of incomes. Not surprisingly, it was too late to induce "role-model" families to live in what had become shabby, crime-ridden projects. In the 1980s the tide turned back to providing services only for people with the very lowest incomes.

After high-rise projects failed miserably as family housing, local housing authorities began to convert them to elderly housing. In Milwaukee, these changes were working well. In the 1970s, however, HUD told local housing authorities that the agency's rules required that elderly people live with people with disabilities. Under HUD's rules, however, *disabled* included people with drug or alcohol addictions. Often these people had criminal records. Not only did they have to be housed in the same buildings with elderly people; it required placing them *on the same floors.* A conspiracy theorist might think this was a calculated attempt to drive law-abiding citizens out of federally subsidized housing in order to turn it into an extension of the crowded federal prison system.

As a state senator in 1987, I visited a high-rise housing unit on the west side of Milwaukee. The elderly residents cried as they pleaded with me to help get the drug addicts and criminals off their floors. I told Milwaukee Congressman Gerald Kleczka I wanted the law changed. After continued pressure from Kleczka and from Wisconsin's U.S. Senators, and over the opposition of HUD bureaucrats and advocacy-group extremists, the rules were finally changed years later, during the Clinton administration.

Private landlords still provide most of the low-cost housing in the United States, and much of what they supply is in pretty good shape. Some is not. That's where building-code enforcement has traditionally stepped in. Court-enforced penalties may be the only way to deal with genuine slumlords. But experience has taught our Milwaukee building inspectors that people who own and manage residential property may perform poorly simply because they don't know better.

Milwaukee's inspectors were using up valuable time chasing the same code violators who were renting to the same bad tenants over and over. Then deputy building inspector Marty Collins had the idea for the Landlord Training Program, in which building inspectors teach landlords how legally to screen against bad tenants—those with a history of damaging property, engaging in criminal activity, or not paying the rent. The inspectors also teach that well-kept property attracts reliable tenants. The program provides tips to landlords on how to comply more easily with code requirements. Equally important, the program gives building inspectors an opportunity to learn from landlords.

More than 30 percent of Milwaukee's landlords have completed the program. Code violations among those who have received training are down substantially. Also, landlords are helping the police reduce illegal drug use and related crime.

Milwaukee's building inspectors, police, and neighborhood groups together devised the Drug Abatement Program which encourages landlords to evict suspected drug sellers immediately, even if this means passing up the opportunity to stage a big drug raid. Why? Because people, especially children, who live near a suspected drug house need quick relief from the threat to their lives and property. As soon as drug activity is suspected, the landlord is informed and asked to evict. Police monitor the suspects if they move to another location in Milwaukee. Statistical review shows that drug sellers generally stop after being confronted; they know that the police and that cooperating landlords have them on watch lists.

People already living in public housing should be allowed to stay as long as they follow the rules. But the federal government should stop producing new public housing. Over time, the private market can produce low-cost housing much more efficiently. The presence of public housing, both through its buildings and through rent subsidies, distorts the low-cost housing market by chasing away private investors and raising rents.

The federal government should also reduce its mortgage subsidies, whether they are made through the Federal National Mortgage Agency, the FHA, or the mortgage-interest tax deduction. In 1994, income earners in the top 20 percent received $63 billion in housing subsidies; those in the bottom 20 percent received $18.7 billion, and the middle 60 percent received $21.9 billion. The current mortgage interest deduction could be capped at the level of interest required to finance a half-million-dollar home. Over time, as housing prices increase, the deduction would have a decreasing impact on housing decisions.

There are many bad policies that need to be discontinued and bad habits that must be broken. If we heed the lessons from this century's experience with housing problems and urban deterioration, we can make stronger, healthier cities which will work better for everyone, including people of modest means.

CRITICAL THINKING QUESTIONS

1. How has the U.S. Department of Housing and Urban Development contributed to the problem of affordable housing for low-income people? What has it done to alleviate this problem?

2. How is access to adequate housing related to poor people's efforts to succeed in life? In your opinion, is access to adequate, affordable housing a right the government should help less fortunate people achieve? Why or why not?

3. Would poor people have better access to affordable housing if the government stayed out of the real estate business? Explain.

Reading 4

Race in the Workplace

Robert J. Grossman

> *In this article, Grossman explores the effects of the 1964 Civil Rights Act and how the intentions of the legislation have largely failed to be realized.*

It's been more than 35 years since the champions of the civil rights movement gained one of their crowning achievements—the passage of the Civil Rights Act of 1964. Many hoped the law would spur a new era of opportunity for minorities.

But many workplace experts say that once-bright outlook on the future has yet to materialize for the black members of the nation's workforce.

To be sure, there are some encouraging developments. For example, in 1964 there was not a single Fortune 500 company headed up by a black executive; now there are three—A. Barry Rand at Avis Rent-A-Car, Lloyd Ward at Maytag Corp. and Franklin Raines at Fannie Mae. And even more black managers are in the pipeline—like Kenneth Chenault, American Express's president and chief operating officer, who is expected to take over as CEO in 2001.

However, even with these high-profile examples, the overall statistics are sobering: Combined, blacks and Hispanics account for less than 2 percent of executive positions in the United States.

The numbers leave people like George Gamble unimpressed. Gamble, director of the International Institute for Diversity and Cross-Cultural Management at the University

of Houston, says, "What's going on in corporate America is deceitful. A few minority CEOs—like at Maytag and American Express—get exposure and people think things are better. But in the trenches it's a different ballgame."

To get a truer picture, Gamble says, speak to average workers. "They'll say 'things have not gotten better for us,' that 'The company I'm working for has allowed a couple of people to make it so they can say we're diverse. But the system continues to be terribly unjust. The masses haven't benefited, and there's only so much this company is going to do.'"

Ted Childs, IBM's vice president for global workforce diversity in Armonk, N.Y., sees a brighter side. "Race relations have improved significantly since passage of the Civil Rights Act of 1964," he says. "When I joined IBM in 1967, we didn't have a lot of African American managers or executives. If someone became a second-level manager out there, I'd hear about it. Now we've reached the point where I don't know all the African American executives. That's an extraordinary example of progress."

But Nat Alston, vice president of HR at the State Employees Credit Union of Maryland and vice president of the National Association of African Americans in HR (NAAAHR), contends the conditions experienced by black employees today are no different from what he experienced 30 years ago when he started in HR. "They would say it's no different, and I think that demonstrates that we haven't made meaningful progress at all. We've seen America get comfortable with its prejudices. It's like the Cold War, with Russia and the U.S. living under peaceful co-existence."

Leroy Warren, chair of the National Association for the Advancement of Colored People's (NAACP) Federal Task Force on Discrimination in the Workplace, agrees. "It's not much better than 20 years ago. What you hear is progress, but the reality is we're still in the same rut." At best, he says the nation has "moved ahead a few inches."

Are these merely the comments of a disaffected few? Apparently not. "African Americans' opinions on how things were going in business have not improved at all," says John P. Fernandez, president of ARMC Consultants in Philadelphia and the author of a study of workplace race relations over the past 20 years.

SOBERING STATISTICS

At issue is whether the glass is half full, as IBM's Childs perceives, or 95 percent empty, as the NAACP's Warren sees it. The record suggests that Warren may be closer to the mark.

For example, as a whole, black employees still haven't achieved financial parity with whites, according to data from the U.S. Bureau of Labor Statistics (BLS):

In 1983, 25 percent of working blacks were clustered in low-paying service and unskilled jobs. By 1999, that number had dropped only slightly, to 22 percent of working blacks.

For every dollar a white man earned in 1979 (the first year for which figures are available), a black man on average earned 76 cents. Two decades later, in 1999, the numbers were identical.

In 1979, black women earned 57 cents for every dollar a white male earned; by 1999 that figure had risen, but to only 64 cents on the dollar.

"There's still a huge gap and it hasn't improved over the last 20 years," says Steve Hip-

pie, a BLS economist in Washington, D.C. "African Americans are in lower-paying, lower-skill occupations. Even though African American women have seen a little increase in earning power, it's still very low."

The gap between the races also shows up in the unemployment rolls. According to BLS data, blacks were twice as likely as whites to be unemployed in 1999—a ratio that has remained unchanged since the 1970s. In 1999, black teens were 2.5 times more likely to be unemployed than white teens; again, the ratio is comparable to the 1970s.

Similarly, advancement for black employees in professions has moved slowly. Between 1983 (the first year for which statistics are available) and 1999, blacks consistently made up about 11 percent of the total U.S. workforce. Yet in 1983, only 3 percent of engineers and 3 percent of attorneys were black. In 1999, blacks made up 5 percent of engineers and 5 percent of attorneys. In 1983, 3 percent of physicians were black, rising to 5 percent to 6 percent in 1999. Over the years, blacks in marketing advertising and public relations rose from 3 percent to 5 percent, and blacks in financial management went from 4 percent to 7 percent.

Blacks who have made it into the managerial arena seem to have stalled at the lower levels or have been relegated to less mobile staff positions, Alston says. "We look good in the numbers, but when you look at the landscape and see where they're concentrated, it's not a good representation," he says. "We don't see enough in marketing or finance."

Representation of blacks in the human resources field is marginally better. In HR, the percentage of blacks serving in personnel and labor relations positions grew from 4.9 percent in 1983 to 7.5 percent in 1997, according to BLS. But, as with other professions, plateauing at mid-level remains an issue. "African Americans are making it in [HR] middle management, and some are advancing to the VP level," says NAAAHR president Tom Vines in Washington, D.C. "But in terms of reaching senior VP or chief HR officer, it's still a challenge."

'A HOSTILE CULTURE'

Why haven't blacks fared better in the workplace, despite the passage of a law more than three decades ago that was designed to protect their interests and help them avoid prejudicial treatment? Some say that, in spite of the Civil Rights Act of 1964, discrimination and prejudice remain in the workplace, albeit in more subtle forms.

Mary-Jane Sinclair, a former HR executive and consultant in Morristown, N.J., says racial bias can range from "a sense of discomfort all the way up to aggressive prejudice—and it's more prevalent than anyone would want to say it is. This still is a society that is not open to people who are different from those in its dominant culture."

She believes that "organizations try to do the right thing by recruiting more minorities. But when the people come in they face a hostile culture."

Sinclair has seen cases where whites told racist jokes, where the letters "KKK" mysteriously and repeatedly appeared on a worker's computer screen. E-mail jokes—at best in bad taste, at worst blatantly racist—are common. According to Sinclair, if you ask black employees, they'll say, "This company tries hard, but it ain't happening."

"There's a persistence of racism which says it's institutionalized," says Sharon Parker, president of the American Institute for Managing Diversity Inc., a nonprofit research organization in Atlanta. "It's about our policies, practices, beliefs and the formal ways we do things in our work lives that put up barriers to full participation. It's partly conscious and partly subconscious. On the conscious level, there's this politically correct attitude which drives it underground, making it harder to detect."

"It's mostly underground, not right on the surface," agrees Herbert Wong, a Cambridge, Mass., consultant who has worked with 210 organizations on diversity and EEO issues. He says HR professionals tell him that racial tensions often are unacknowledged but lurk in the shadows around issues that they're asked to investigate and mediate.

"It hasn't changed that much since the '60s," says Lisa Willis-Johnson, chair of the Society for Human Resource Management's Workplace Diversity Committee and director of HR and administrative services for the Mid-Ohio Regional Planning Commission in Columbus. "Today it's still with us but there's more cover. The blatant part is down; the subtle part has risen. The code words still exist. It's easy to say, 'This person won't fit into our culture.' In hiring and promotion discussions, decision-makers can visualize the progress of the non-minority but not the minority. The benefit of the doubt isn't there for the minority candidate."

However, Willis-Johnson believes there are still some areas where blatant discrimination flourishes in the open. In those places, "they'll tell you up front they won't hire you because of your color and say, 'I'm going to tell you this and if you sue me, I'll deny it.'"

But most shut-outs are more sophisticated. "Now you get the job, but you don't move ahead," observes Rejeana Pendleton, diversity manager at Carrier Corp., the heating, air conditioning and refrigeration company based in Syracuse, N.Y. "You're not developed; you're not part of succession planning and don't get assigned to the high visibility projects."

The tendency to unfavorably stereotype blacks has become more "refined" but is still there, agrees Fernandez. "In the early 1970s, stereotypes were more open—like 'They're lazy.' Now it's more subtle. Whites will say, 'They don't have particular skills, they're not qualified,' or what have you."

PERCEPTIONS IN BLACK AND WHITE

A factor that makes it difficult to effectively address racial issues in the workplace is that black and white employees see blacks' career progress, or lack of it, through different lenses, says Fernandez. In his book *Race, Gender & Rhetoric* (McGraw Hill, 1998), he reports on attitudes and perceptions of both blacks and whites in the workplace from 1975 to 1995.

In his studies—based on surveys, interviews and training programs—Fernandez found that, in 1972, 88 percent of blacks believed that they had to be better performers than whites to get ahead. In 1995, 89 percent believed so. Thirty-three percent of whites believed it in 1972; 30 percent in 1995.

Consistently, in the 20-year-period ending in 1995, between 75 percent and 85 percent of blacks believed that people of color had to be better than whites to get ahead.

Perhaps even more disturbing, in 1972, 56 percent of whites said blacks would file undeserved charges of discrimination if they lost their jobs. In 1995, that number rose to 59 percent.

WHAT COMES NEXT?

What does the future hold for race relations in the United States? Childs says the playing field still is not level, but he points out that a growing number of blacks are assuming corporate leadership positions and he predicts continuing improvements. "We have reached a point where the people who have been advocating for African Americans over the years are in the picking mode instead of the telling mode. This may be the last 10 yards of the game."

In contrast, Warren offers harsh criticism of the tortoise-like progress achieved by Childs and the rest of the corporate diversity establishment, whom he labels "accommodationists."

"You're getting nothing but paid mercenaries in these jobs, people drawing a check," Warren says. "They say, 'I got what I got, and I don't give a damn what my kids wind up with.'"

Meanwhile, corporations are too preoccupied with mergers and acquisitions and overall financial performance to devote much time to race relations, says Vines. "Shareholder value is what investors and CEOs are looking at rather than representation of minorities in their workplaces and fostering improved relations and morale."

As a result, says Tracy Brown, president of Person to Person Consulting in Dallas, the discussion of race in the workplace often surfaces only when a problem arises. She says organizations are more likely to respond to the stick than the carrot "like Texaco and Denny's. They were forced to do something because they ran afoul of the law." (The oil company and the restaurant chain both faced negative press coverage and legal difficulties over allegations about their treatment of blacks.)

"We throw money at looking good rather than doing good," Brown says. "We don't care about the root causes; we don't want to correct our behavior. Most people are spending their energy trying to avoid getting into trouble."

CRITICAL THINKING QUESTIONS

1. According to Grossman, what employment gains have African-Americans made since the passage of the Civil Rights Act of 1964? In what areas do they continue to lag behind whites?

2. What barriers to employment equity for African-Americans does Grossman identify?

3. Why has the Civil Rights Act of 1964 failed to achieve full employment equity for African-Americans? How has the law been circumvented, and what might minority groups do to overcome the continued barriers to equality that they face?

Reading 5

Institutional and Racial Barriers to Employment Equity for Hispanics

Jerry Yaffe

> *In this reading, Yaffe discusses the hiring policies and practices of Los Angeles County and the efforts of African-Americans to keep minority issues defined in "black and white" terms. The problem is that Hispanics are the largest minority group in the community, yet they continue to be under-represented in county government jobs.*

If free and equal individuals are to retain their dignity as moral agents then . . . the institutions of society need to be founded on a public principle of justice as fairness.

    J. Rawls (1972, as quoted in Ranson & Stewert, 1989, p. 13)

. . . This article explores the conditions under which a regional government has failed to act legally, morally, effectively, and objectively in carrying out its obligations for implementing equal employment policies and programs for assuring a legitimate and equitable application of civil rights laws for Hispanics in the LACO [Los Angeles County] government workforce. Underlying their failure to set adequate goals and improvement in results for equal employment of Hispanics, officials have rationalized 25 years of civil rights failures by citing an alleged lack of educated and qualified Hispanics in the labor force. Thus, by omission or commission, they have chosen to placate Black employees and vindicate their own lack of commitment and priorities to equal opportunities for Hispanics. In an interview about Hispanic underrepresentation in the county government workforce, the county's former affirmative action officer (a representative of the board of supervisors)

Source: Reprinted from *Hispanic Journal of Behavioral Sciences* 16, no. 3 (August 1994): 211–229.

stated that "recruitment of blacks would suffer if Latinos were hired at the rate that the Latino [employee] Association wants" (Merina, 1987, p. 5B).

Every county government review and audit of affirmative action progress since 1964 confirms that every minority except Hispanics has (progressively) achieved or far exceeded a reasonable representation in the county government workforce (various LACO reports and audits, 1965–1992; Yaffe, 1994b). The historical belief in and government rationalization of a lack of an educated and qualified Hispanic labor pool has been communicated and propagated by both government officials and Black employees. It is accepted at face value because it provides one of many elements county officials can use to avoid accountability for their failure to achieve a reasonable workforce representation for Hispanics.

The current research discloses that the claim of an uneducated Hispanic labor pool is unfounded and unsupported by educational data. An analysis of educational and graduation data reveals that on all secondary and postsecondary levels (since 1979) Hispanics have not only exceeded the number of Black graduates but in several cases exceeded the actual number of combined non-Hispanic minority graduates in LACO. In addressing the current or potential availability of qualified Hispanics (high school and college graduates), research and public documents ordinarily make reference to comparative (ethnic and racial group) graduation rates to explain the low Hispanic representation in the labor pool requiring high school or college graduation. These references do not critique or decipher these statistics, but instead accept their alleged validity. This practice only strengthens the belief in the spurious validity of an uneducated and undereducated Hispanic labor pool as a barrier to hiring and promotional opportunities.

To fully understand the complex decision-making processes in LACO, I will make an effort to place my perspectives and conclusions in the context of their actual social, political, and organizational state. Because of the propensity to embrace a myth of a deficit in Hispanic individual and group educational achievement, government officials have expected and thus required only perfunctory efforts and results that stress Hispanic recruitment and hiring and remove promotional barriers for existing employees. Affirmative action goals and timetables for Hispanics traditionally have had little relationship to incremental reduction, or elimination, of the degree of underrepresentation and the prevention of its reoccurrence. Local government remains unaffected or ignorant of the reality of educational achievements of Hispanics, choosing to minimize the actual number of graduates or simply to disregard these trends. To acknowledge these realities would counter their belief in the rationale of a lack of qualified Hispanics and thereby force government officials to confront their protracted and systematic discrimination against Hispanics.

I present documentation that reveals these political and workforce patterns. These conditions and conclusions are reinforced by an analysis of the actual numbers (not comparative rates) of minority high school and college graduates in LACO, an analysis of population patterns in the region, and an analysis of minority representation in the county government workforce between 1977 and 1991. Data are also included on minority college graduates for the

entire state, which traditionally have served as an important and expansive source for the county's labor force requirements.

What will become evident is that the LACO government has for over 20 years been a, if not the, dominant factor in the exclusion of Hispanics from entering the county government workforce. When Hispanics are hired, the LACO government has served as an obstacle to equitable promotional opportunities. Although invested with the power, authority, and responsibility for implementing legal equal employment requirements, this local governmental body appears to have abdicated both its moral and legal responsibilities for including and assuring equal employment opportunities and civil rights guarantees for all minorities.

Second, their inertia has aided in perpetuating the myth of the lack of a qualified and educated Hispanic labor pool from which to recruit Hispanics to assure a more diverse and representative county government workforce. Both federal and state equal employment legislation is clearly inclusive of national origin and ethnic groups. The county's own affirmative action policy also includes Hispanics as a protected group. From a governance standpoint, there is no question about these legislative facts. There is also no question regarding the obligation of local government to assure that Hispanics are not singularly excluded from civil rights and equal opportunity guarantees.

Typically, the political climate in LACO has for several decades fostered a perception of the Hispanic population as an "immigrant" population (frequently illegal), illiterate and uneducated, and passive and accommodating. By ignoring, allowing, or contributing to these perceptions in equal employment implementation and programs, LACO government has illustrated its failure as an elected body to serve as either a symbol or an advocate of civil and equal rights, or to function as an enlightened and reformed administration. In the area of equal employment opportunity, county government traditions exemplify indifference, institutional discrimination, and feigned impotency. These practices are antithetical to the very requirements of a diverse and democratic society and to what civil rights laws were intended to overcome. . . .

THE LOS ANGELES DEMOGRAPHIC ENVIRONMENT

Hispanics or Latinos (the collective ethnic designation that includes Mexican Americans, Central and South Americans, Cubans and Puerto Ricans, and others) are an ethnic group unquestionably included in all civil rights and equal employment entitlement. Prohibitions against employment discrimination, in addition to race and gender, also include discrimination against ethnic minorities or members with a common national origin (e.g., Latinos or Hispanics). In terms of required compliance to civil rights and equal employment legislation and provisions, local government is accountable both as an employer and as a contractor receiving federal and state funds.

In California, Hispanics in 1990 numbered 7,687,938 residents (25.8% of the total state population). In the seven-county Southern California region, Hispanics accounted for an average of 31.3% (5,361,834) of the combined population of 17,138,848. The Hispanic population in LACO (3,351,242—the most populated county in this region, the state, and the nation—accounted for 37.8% of the total county population. Since 1960 Hispanics in LACO have increased at an annual rate of approximately 0.8% to 0.9%. They are now (1994) the largest single racial or ethnic constituency and the largest minority in the county population. . . .

HISPANICS IN THE COUNTY GOVERNMENT WORKFORCE

Hispanics have been underrepresented in the county government workforce since the inception of the Civil Rights Act of 1964. When confronted in the past, county officials publicly took a stance against workforce discrimination and only made perfunctory efforts toward correcting these patterns of underrepresentation. Concurrently, they actually conceded even further workforce positions (new hires and promotions) to already overrepresented groups to placate non-Hispanic agendas. For each of the following benchmark years, Blacks, Asians, and Filipinas either increased proportionally or experienced actual (numerical) increases in representation (or both) in spite of being (and remaining) above parity for a given period. On the other hand . . . regardless of proportional or actual increases, Hispanics have remained severely and perpetually underrepresented.

In spite of an increasing Hispanic population in LACO, and regardless of the actual numbers and positive trends in available Hispanic graduates, all other racial and ethnic representation in the county government workforce has increased significantly, above the group's representation in the general population. In 1980 Hispanic representation was 3.8% below 1970 population parity. In 1990 their representation was 7.2% below 1980 parity. For projected 2000, Hispanics under current conditions will be 10.7% below 1990 parity, and even slightly below (0.7%) 1980 parity. The underrepresentation is even more pronounced on management and professional levels and for Hispanic women when gender, race, and ethnicity are examined. What seems evident is that, regardless of reasonable, comprehensive, and codified (formal) affirmative action policies, discrimination remains prevalent (the status quo). This is due in large part because the "implementation" of those policies in and by government has been predicated more on informal and politicized responses and concerns in addition to ethnocentric and divisive definitions of entitlements.

Regardless of demographic changes and educational achievements, Hispanic representation in the county government workforce has been decreasing at an increasing rate. In the overall workforce, Whites experienced a decline in parity and have also "sacrificed" positions to Blacks, Asians, and Filipinos since the 1970s. However, White disparity is steadily decreasing (−15.2% in 1977, −11.9% in 1987, and −3.8% in 1991). In 1991 Whites experienced a lower disparity (compared to 1987) and were a smaller proportion of the workforce, but occupied more positions in 1991 over 1987. For Hispanics, most actual or proportional incremental increases were so negligible that Hispanics still remained the only underrepresented group since 1969. Blacks cite their minimal annual proportional increases in representation; however, they fail to cite the fact that they have remained significantly overrepresented since 1964 and have consistently increased in real numbers since that time.

For Hispanics, the dramatic population increases and the increasing disparity over the years make most county affirmative action plans obsolete on their inception. Unless a plan takes into account the degree of disparity and increases in population, they have no realistic corrective value and predictably fall short of achieving the goal of creating a diverse and representative workforce. A deceptive assortment of rates, relative percentages, and actual numerical increases have also been used depending on the desired effects and the audience served. Although percentages can increase, increases in actual positions may be minimal and may present a deceptive or exaggerated picture of progress.

HISPANIC EDUCATIONAL ATTAINMENT

. . . Even prior to 1977, Black county government employees have been the most consistently and severely overrepresented—in some cases by as much as 250%. They have also gone public in their offensive endeavors against any increase in Hispanic workforce representation, citing the existence of a lack of qualified Hispanics.

Between 1980 and 1991, the total actual number of Hispanic high school graduates exceeded the number for each individual major ethnic/racial minority in LACO. Further, the number of Hispanic high school graduates

also was greater than the combined number of graduates for all other minorities during this period. Hispanic graduates for these years numbered 152,941, compared to the 133,623 combined graduates for other minorities (Black graduates numbered 71,847, Asians produced 52,631 graduates, and Filipinos 9,145). . . .

The data for Hispanic college graduates in LACO show similar patterns. For the years 1979 through 1991 for community college graduates (an associate's degree), the number of Hispanic graduates (17,989) has exceeded that of Blacks (13,225), Asians (11,009), and Filipinos (497). Although the trends are erratic for all ethnic groups except Filipinos, they do show an upward progression for Hispanics and Asians, and a downward trend for Blacks.

Similar erratic patterns can be found between the years 1979–1991 for bachelor's, master's, doctorate, and professional degrees. But again, . . . the overall 1979 to 1991 trend shows that Hispanic graduates of these degrees exceeded Blacks and Filipinos and were 7,680 graduates below Asian graduates. Again, trends would indicate that Hispanics should continue this upward progression over the coming years. What is also significant is that Hispanics exceeded Blacks in virtually every separate degree category for the 12-year period.

In California during this same period, Hispanic graduates exceeded Black graduates in all college degree categories. Hispanic graduates numbered 139,639 and consisted of the following: associate's (46,167), bachelor's (71,757), master's (16,074), doctorate (1,438), and professional (4,203). Black graduates numbered a total of 83,080: associate's (27,484), bachelor's (39,082), master's (12,632), doctorate (1,150), and professional (2,732).

ANALYSIS AND COMMENTARY

Hispanics in LACO have been disenfranchised from the political processes and outcomes that guarantee the same civil rights for other minorities. They are confronted and confounded by two patterns of restrictive entitlement. The first is a historical prerogative of control and power established by Anglo-European dominance, the second is a Black-defined exclusive equal employment and affirmative action entitlement emanating from the civil rights movement of the 1960s. For both Blacks and Anglos, these processes have juxtaposed to provide each group with a desirable, offensive, and convenient rationale to explain the lack of an educated and qualified Hispanic labor pool. Each group seeks to protect its political dominance and economic gains—an Anglo power structure to regulate and perpetuate its own power base and the more recent Black focus on an unlimited and unregulated equal employment entitlement.

But, as the data reveals, there is no lack of an educated or qualified Hispanic labor pool (either in the past, present, or in the predictable future). For Black county government employees, the lower representation in the population and a lower number of Black high school and college graduates have sustained a significantly higher representation in the county government workforce. In the case of Hispanics, the significantly higher population base and the higher number of secondary and postsecondary graduates have been disregarded to assure that Hispanics do not achieve a reasonable workforce representation.

The common variable in both of these arrangements has been the predominantly Anglo gatekeepers—those who control the region's political, decision-making, and governing processes. A most conspicuous conclusion is that the severe and historic underrepresentation of Hispanics in this county government workforce can be accounted for only by politicized efforts to restrict and exclude Hispanics from the benefits of public employment. In spite of civil rights laws and requirements and the county's own comprehensive formal affirmative action policies that take into account national origin and ethnic minority status, in reality, Hispanics in LACO remain the invisible and ignored stepchildren of equal employment efforts.

This continuous discrimination and under-representation of Hispanics could only reach its present level with the concurrent neglect by elected officials. Should these perceptions of equal employment continue (and it appears they will), a reasonable Hispanic equity will never become a reality. Local government refuses to place a priority on these issues and will sabotage any efforts for reform (Cobb & Elder, 1971, pp. 906–907). "No society has ever funded its own overthrow" (as quoted in Hardy-Fanta, 1993, p. 162).

The continued preference for politicized, informal, and discriminatory decisions regarding employment opportunities almost guarantees the failure of needed reforms. It also reinforces the perceptions of many Hispanics that they are the forgotten 40% as far as local government is concerned. As long as county officials remain oblivious to the ramifications of their informal and antagonistic decisions on equal employment, disparities and inequities will increase and the hope of any effective and constructive solutions will blend into some distant, unknown, and uncontrollable future.

If county government officials continue these practices and Hispanic county government employees are unable to obtain recourse and remedies, then civil rights and equal employment in local government in the 21st century shall be sculptured on the failure of governance and on racism from these latter decades of the 20th century. The opportunity to experience the rewards of education and the betterment of one's lifestyle will continue to remain elusive for Hispanics.

Hispanic population growth (both proportional and numerical) and the continuing patterns of Hispanic educational attainment are realities that Los Angeles government and society must accept and to which they must positively adapt. Intensified interminority conflict and, ultimately, confrontations between Hispanic activists (seeking reform) and county government officials are inevitable outcomes of the abdication of responsibility by elected and appointed officials. Rather than preventing and rising above ethnic and racial dissension, LACO's informal policies and protected practices almost guarantee that the negative competitive patterns of racial and ethnic relations will only intensify potential dilemmas.

Government is no more important than the people it is empowered by and required to serve. Whether viewed from the standpoint of American political and democratic ideals and values, with a moral and enlightened conception of justice and equality, or from a strict and literal interpretation of civil rights law, employment equity and affirmative action cannot, nor are they meant to, accrue to one group at the expense of another.

REFERENCES

COBB, R. W., & ELDER, C. D. (1971). The politics of agenda-building: An alternative perspective for modern democratic theory. *Journal of Politics,* 33(4), 892–915.

HARDY-FANTA, C. (1993). *Latina politices, Latino politics.* Philadelphia: Temple University Press.

MERINA, V. (1987, December 10). New drive for county jobs set by Latino group. *Los Angeles Times,* pp. 3B, 5B.

YAFFE, J. (1994b). Twenty-five years of underrepresentation: Hispanics in the county work force. *Local Government Studies* (UR), 20, 113–130.

CRITICAL THINKING QUESTIONS

1. What are the arguments put forth by employers and black leaders to justify the under-representation of Hispanics in public employment? Are these arguments valid? Explain.

2. What compels African-Americans and Hispanics to compete for jobs? What might both groups gain by cooperating with each other? What might each lose by cooperating with the other?

3. Is the treatment of Hispanics by African-Americans that Yaffe describes a form of institutionalized discrimination? Or is it just a form of marketplace competition for jobs? Explain.

Reading 6

Temps Are Here to Stay

Jan Larson

In this article, Larson focuses on the increasing use of temporary employees by American businesses, a practice that has negative consequences for workers, and especially for women with children.

The term "temp" brings to mind a replacement receptionist who answers phones and sorts the mail while a salaried employee is on vacation or medical leave. But this is only one of many ways of describing today's contingent work force. The term describes millions of people who, for whatever reason, do not have a sense of permanence about their jobs.

Source: American Demographics, January 1996, Volume 18, Issue 2, p. 26–31. Used by permission of the author.

Estimating the size of the nation's contingent work force is like asking a group of scientists when and where the next California earthquake will hit. It all depends. "There is no agreement among scientists about what constitutes a contingent worker or how many there are," says Heidi Hartmann, author of a number of studies on contingent workers and director of the Washington, D.C.–based nonprofit Institute for Women's Policy Research.

The job may be tough, but researchers are scrambling to find the answers. They are counting the number of contingent workers, describing their varied life and work situations, and assessing employee attitudes toward contingent work. Managers are eager for this information because the use of temporary workers, also known as "outsourcing," is one of the hottest trends in business. Two-thirds of surveyed executives of large corporations expect to use more temporary help in the next three years, according to a 1995 study conducted by the staffing service Office Team in Menlo Park, California. The reason is that more managers are using temporary workers as a competitive tool, rather than a simple means of cost control.

Outsourcing such tasks as building maintenance or fleet management is relatively common. But according to a survey by the global accounting firm Arthur Andersen & Company, a growing number of companies are hiring outsiders to take care of central business functions like tax, payroll, and pension management. "Companies are recognizing the need to focus relentlessly on their core competencies," says Dennis Torkko of Andersen's contract services practice. Contingent workers can take care of non-core but essential business functions, he says. As this trend grows, more business managers will view skilled labor as something they can lease with an option to buy.

ESTIMATES VARY

The word "contingent" is fraught with uncertainty. The term has been used to describe a variety of employment situations, including part-time work, self-employment, employment in the business services industry, and work situations of a tenuous nature. Depending on the definition and data used, contingent work force estimates range from less than 2 percent of the working population to an impressive 16 percent-plus. That's a difference of between 2 million and 19 million workers.

The lowest estimate is published by the Federal Reserve Bank of Chicago, at 1.9 million. The Bureau of Labor Statistics (BLS) publishes three estimates based on the results of a first-time supplement to the bureau's monthly Current Population Survey conducted in February 1995. The lowest number (2.7 million) derives from a narrow definition that includes only wage and salary workers who had been in their jobs one year or less and who anticipated those jobs would last an additional year or less.

The second BLS definition adds self-employed and independent contractors who consider their jobs less than long-term, which bumps up the tally to about 3 percent of workers (3.4 million). The third and broadest BLS estimate includes any worker who considered his or her job temporary, resulting in a total of 5 percent, or 6 million.

Some observers consider the numbers low; they say that the BLS definitions are too narrow. Hartmann's 1995 study of the economic impact of contingent work on women and their families found that in 1990, more than 19 million workers, or 16 percent, held contingent jobs. This number was based on the Census Bureau's 1987 and 1990 Surveys of income and Program Participation.

The number of contingent workers grew 5 percent between 1987 and 1990, according to Hartmann's study, compared with an overall work force gain of less than 4 percent. One easily identifiable portion of contingent workers, those employed by the personnel-supply services industry, is clearly outpacing other industries. Personnel services employment increased 25 percent between 1990 and 1993, compared with 1 percent for total employment, according to BLS data.

Whatever their numbers, contingent workers are no longer limited to clerical duties. They include pink-, blue-, and white-collar workers, according to Lewis Segal and Daniel Sullivan, senior economists at the Federal Reserve Bank of Chicago. Their research focuses on the personnel-supply industry—the largest employer of contingent workers—and is based on BLS and 1990 census data, which show that approximately 2 million workers are currently employed in the personnel-services industry.

Nationally, manufacturing employment has been declining. But the share of temporary workers who hold blue-collar jobs grew from 9 percent in 1983 to 23 percent in 1993. This indicates that manufacturers have moved away from periodically hiring and laying off workers, and toward filling more of their variable employment needs with contingent workers on a routine basis. The number of white-collar professional temporary workers has also grown. But the faster gains in blue-collar employment mean that white-collar temps have lost share, from 34 percent in 1983 to 27 percent in 1993.

The share of temp workers in "pink collar" or clerical jobs has remained stable, at about one-third. Women continue to dominate this portion of the industry, but men are entering it at a faster rate and gaining share. In 1993, 38 percent of all personnel-supply service workers were men, up from 25 percent in 1983, according to Segal and Sullivan. Data from the National Association of Temporary and Staffing Services (NATSS) in Alexandria, Virginia, confirm that male participation in the temp work force is growing.

The temporary work force is aging along with the total labor force; 52 percent of contingent workers were aged 35 or older in 1994, up from 43 percent in 1989, Yet they remain much younger than the overall work force. Between 31 and 42 percent of all types of contingent workers were aged 16 to 24 in 1995, according to the BLS estimates, compared with 14 percent of noncontingent workers. And between 12 and 14 percent of contingent workers aged 25 to 64 are not high school graduates, compared with 10 percent of noncontingent workers. The share of temporary workers with a high school diploma or less increased from 18 percent in 1989 to 27 percent in 1994, according to NATSS.

Youth and lack of higher education would appear to explain part of the wage gap between contingent and noncontingent workers. But contingent workers tend to earn less than their permanent counterparts even after adjusting for age, sex, race, and education, according to Segal and Sullivan's research. Pink-collar temporary workers earn 10 percent less than comparable permanent workers. The

wage differential is even greater for blue-collar workers, who earn 34 percent less in contingent jobs than in permanent ones. The exception is among white-collar contingent workers, who earn 2 percent more than noncontingent workers. Highly skilled professionals, executives, and technicians who work as consultants on a project basis can often command fees well in excess of staff salaries.

EARNINGS AND BENEFITS

Contingent workers worry about things that "regular" employees take for granted. Dave Reichard, a contract worker for a technical services firm in Escatawpa, Mississippi, worries about health insurance. His firm offers access to group health insurance, but Reichard says it's "pretty expensive." He and his wife have four children, one income, and a monthly insurance tab of $145. Reichard would like to start his own computer services business, but doesn't know where he'd find affordable insurance. "I have to be concerned with my insurance, because I would be on my own," he says.

Insurance isn't Reichard's only concern. He's wondering if he'll ever be able to retire. By the time he pays for insurance, rent on his home, and other daily living expenses, there's not much left.

The proportion of contingent workers with health insurance from any source ranges from 57 to 65 percent, according to the BLS, compared with 82 percent of noncontingent workers. And contingent workers who do have health insurance are much less likely to get it through an employer. This indicates a growing need for affordable private options, says Audrey Freedman, an economist and management consultant based in New York City, who coined the term "contingent workers"—in the mid-1980s. "Nobody is really specializing in portable benefits that workers can carry from employer to employer. If entirely self-financed, health insurance is portable, but it's also high-priced," says Freedman.

The same problem exists in the area of financial planning. Contingent workers don't have access to standard employer-provided pension plans, so they have to do it themselves. Businesses that can help people plan their retirement will be tapping into a growing market. So will those that help workers plan their work lives.

Child care is the top concern for women employed as contingent workers, says Hartmann of the Institute for Women's Policy Research. She has found that one in four women contingent workers has young children, compared with 16 percent of women who work full-time for a single employer. One explanation is that contingent workers tend to be younger.

Flexibility is a key advantage for hiring contingent workers, but the workers themselves also need flexibility from those who provide them with services. Pay-by-the-day, drop-in day care can offer a sense of security to parents whose erratic work schedules prevent them from taking out long-term contracts.

What many contingent workers really want is to become noncontingent. For four weeks in 1994, Joyce Hall, a home-health-care worker in Fresno, California, was a contingent worker in the temporary-services industry. When her temporary employer offered to make the position permanent, Hall eagerly made the switch. She increased her earnings and gained health benefits and a 401K plan. "The benefits are really important, as well as the pay," says Hall.

She is not alone. Over half (54 percent) of NATSS survey respondents say they took temporary work because they were between jobs and needed the money. Fifty-six percent of the personnel-supply workers studied by Segal and Sullivan say they took a temporary job for economic reasons. The BLS estimates that between 56 and 64 percent of contingent workers would prefer a more permanent arrangement.

VARIETY AND FLEXIBILITY

Employers may be reluctant to end contingent arrangements, says consultant Freedman. She insists that the contingent arrangement is the natural evolution of businesses seeking new ways to remain competitive in a demanding environment. But the arrangement may be less attractive to workers. Fewer than one-third of the temporary workers Segal and Sullivan studied were still in temporary positions a year later; more than half had gotten permanent positions.

Some temps like the arrangement. For college students, semi-retirees, and those free of financial worries, contingent work may be the optimal choice. Thirty-one percent of those responding to the 1994 NATSS survey say they like the "diversity and challenge of working on different assignments," and the same share say they work as temps because it gives them "the flexibility and time to pursue nonwork interests."

Maureen Briggs lives and works in Honolulu. Although her primary occupation is teaching English as a second language, Briggs has worked as a temporary employee for nearly three years. In 1995, NATSS named her national temporary employee of the year. "Working as a temp fills in the gaps in my teaching schedule," says Briggs, who is a contract instructor for Hawaii Pacific University. Briggs pursued temporary work when she moved to Hawaii to finish her college education.

Previous career experience as a public relations and retail marketing director in the banking industry has helped Briggs land a number of temporary jobs with law firms and she enjoys the constant change of pace, but has been pleased when firms invite her back for other assignments.

Briggs works as a temp because it fits her lifestyle. She enjoys traveling and doesn't want a full-time job to stand in the way of her teaching career. She has turned down many full-time job offers and the retirement and health benefits they'd provide. "For me, it's a matter of weighing your priorities," she says.

Despite the many pros for both employers and employees, contingent employment as a business strategy may have a less certain future than proponents suggest. While the average annual growth rate in personnel-services employment charted by Segal and Sullivan of the Federal Reserve Bank of Chicago between

1973 and 1994 was 11 percent, it has fluctuated from a decline of 10 percent in 1982 to a high of 30 percent in 1984. "It's a fast-growing part of the work force now," says Segal. "But it's a little risky to say it's going to become the modal type of employment." In fact, Segal suggests that this type of arrangement is a cyclical trend. Currently, it is on an upswing, but it's bound to fluctuate in the future.

William Bridges, author of *Jobshift,* sees promise in the "de-jobbing" of America. He sees a society in which people are not tied to restrictive job descriptions but enjoy the freedom to simply get the work done. At the other extreme, the April 1994 issue of *Reason* magazine decries the "myth of a contingent work force" as one invented "to advance the political agenda of unions."

Most Americans probably don't care whether it's called a job, or whether the arrangement benefits employers, unions, or anyone but themselves. As long as it provides them with the wherewithal to keep a roof over their heads, put food on the table, and pay the bills, workers will adapt to their surroundings and do whatever they have to do. But if employers no longer provide them with health insurance or a regular schedule, workers have to change their habits when they become consumers. That shift, will create opportunities for many businesses.

CRITICAL THINKING QUESTIONS

1. What do employees see as the short-term and long-term advantages and disadvantages of being a temporary worker, as opposed to having a more permanent job?

2. How does the growing use of temporary workers hinder the advances of racial and ethnic groups and women?

3. Is outsourcing a form of institutionalized discrimination against the poor and working class? Why or why not?

Reading 7

Women in Management: How Far Have We Come and What Needs to Be Done as We Approach 2000?

Jeanne M. Brett and Linda K. Stroh

In this article, Brett and Stroh explore the different career achievements of male and female managers, as well as the reasons for women's lower levels of status and pay.

As we approach the year 2000, it is both heartening and appropriate to reflect on the progress women have made in business. It is equally valuable, although a lot less

Source: Reprinted from *Journal of Management Inquiry* 8, no. 4 (December 1999): 392–398.

heartening, to assess the goals that remain to be realized before the career experiences of male and female managers will be similar. In particular, female managers still lag significantly behind male managers in income, relocation opportunities, the benefits of pursuing an external labor market strategy, and their ability to balance work and family responsibilities. This article is about our research that has led us to this conclusion. It is also about what is to be done and who is to do it.

PROGRESS IN REACHING OUR GOALS

We have been particularly interested in dual-career couples, by which we mean mixed-sex couples who are married or cohabiting, both of whom are employed for pay outside the home. In the couples we study, one spouse is typically a manager in a large organization that has an internal labor market and clearly identified career paths. In such organizations, managers work for future remuneration, rewards, and career opportunities, as well as current benefits. We study their success in realizing those opportunities.

As we have investigated this issue, our primary sample has been 1,000 geographically mobile managers employed by 20 Fortune 500 organizations and their spouses. We collected survey data from them in 1989 and again in 1992. About 22% of the sample is female, 78% is male. Of the males, 86% are married and 62% of them have children at home. In contrast, 45% of the females are married and 20% of the females have children at home. Roughly 21% of males and females have graduate degrees. Males averaged 37 years of age, and females averaged 34 years of age. Each of the companies for which these managers worked has multiple sites and transfer on average 250 managers each year. Eight industries are represented: pharmaceuticals and hospital supplies, communications, consumer products, professional and financial services, retailing, hospitality, chemicals, and manufacturing.

Income Disparities

One of the first questions we researched was whether female managers' careers progress at the same rate as male managers' careers

(Stroh, Brett, & Reilly, 1992). Given that the men and women in the study appeared indistinguishable with respect to work experience, education, functional area, and industry, we anticipated that the men and women's financial compensation would increase at approximately the same rate. In fact, the gap was significant. The male managers had increased their salaries by 65% during the prior 5-year period, whereas the female managers had increased their salaries by only 54%. Their self-reported rates of promotion were the same; however, on average, the women had relocated 2.3 times for their careers, whereas the men had relocated 2.7 times. In other words, the males' larger increases appeared to be related to their having been offered and/or accepted more relocations.

Perhaps, we thought, the reason for the male-female difference was that the women in our study (despite having relocated) were not really on a career track but a "mommy track" (Schwartz, 1989). Support for this possibility was available in empirical studies that indicate that women with children reduce their working hours in countries like Sweden and Norway, which support such a coping mechanism (Kalleberg & Rosenfeld, 1990), and their job involvement in countries where such support is lacking (Schwartz, 1989). The "mommy track" explanation (the label given by the media for the slow career path, described by Schwartz in her 1989 *Harvard Business Review* article) did not apply to our study participants however, because we found that only 17% of the women in the dual-career households had children. Furthermore, their career experiences were not significantly different from those of the female managers in the study without children or those who were single.

We had already ruled out human capital as an explanation for the gap in income. The female managers were as well educated as the males, had been in the workforce for as long, and had not been entering and leaving the workforce any more often than the male managers in the study. The dual-career female managers were also earning the same proportion of family income as the dual-career male managers (81%). We also considered and ruled out the possibility that the female managers were employed disproportionately in lower paying industries.

Given these similarities in human capital why then, were so many of these women paid disproportionately less than their male counterparts? The literature on career development has identified "stretch assignments" as a key factor distinguishing women who make it to the top (Ohlott, Ruderman, & McCauley, 1994; Ragins, Townsend, & Mattis, 1998; Tharenou, Latimer, & Conroy, 1994). Stretch assignments that are high-profile, in a "hot" area of the company, and that are a particularly good fit with the woman's skills are the best investment in future career growth. In these jobs, the women capture attention through their hard work, innovative problem solving, and sheer initiative in the face of conservative corporate norms, thereby generating a base of support beyond their immediate bosses and work groups. With one of the assignments on a woman's resume, other developmental opportunities such as assignments with clear budgetary responsibility, assignments at corporate headquarters, assignments in a line or major operations position appear rather than having to be sought out. Those who pass these corporate hurdles often get a chance to prove their worth in a general management assignment and move into top management. The first step is to get the first high-profile assignment. Ragins and her colleagues (1998), reviewing the experiences of 461 female executives, conclude that the burden for identifying and then obtaining these key assignments falls on the woman. Male counterparts, instead, are more likely to be approached by senior management and offered key assignments.

The critical difference between the successful women managers in Ragins et al.'s (1998) study and the less successful women in our study may have been that they initially got that high-profile job in a hot area of the company. One of the ways to obtain such an assignment may be to be willing to relocate for the company. This led us into our next avenue of research.

Relocation Opportunities

We found that male and female managers do not relocate at the same rate (Brett, Stroh, & Reilly, 1993). Maybe, we speculated, self-selection was affecting the women's salary progression. Evidence pointed in this direction because salary progression was significantly correlated with the relocation rate. . . . However, we found that although female managers were no less willing to relocate than the males and were not turning down offers, their rate of transfers was slightly less.

In a subsequent study, we found that dual-career dads (men with children and wives who worked outside the home) were considered for relocation about as frequently as male managers in traditional marriages (in which the wife did not work) and men without children (Brett & Stroh, 1995), but unlike the men in traditional marriages and the men without children, the dual-career dads withdrew their names from consideration for transfers significantly more often (30% vs. 19% for the comparison group).

Juxtaposing these two studies, the differences in the career relocation opportunities and, subsequently, the salaries of the male and female managers became starkly obvious. The male managers, including the dads, were in control of their careers. Even though they opted out of some relocation opportunities, they continued to be considered for future relocations. The female managers were considered for fewer transfer opportunities and, consequently, seemed to have less control over their careers. The data suggested not only that the males were being given more opportunities but also that they were using greater discretion in how they handled the opportunities they were given. Future research might investigate whether a manager does more damage to his or her career by withdrawing from an opportunity to relocate than by turning down an offer once it is given.

Benefits of an External Labor Market Strategy

The compensation of managers who leave their organizations to accept employment elsewhere is higher overall than the compensation of employees who are promoted within one organization throughout their careers (Pfeffer & Baron, 1988; Sonnenfeld & Peiperl, 1988; Sonnenfeld, Peiperl, & Kotter, 1988). Perhaps, we reasoned, female managers are less likely than male managers to "jump ship" and seek employment in the external labor market. If so, that could begin to explain the differences in the career experiences and, consequently, the compensation of male and female managers.

Our results were surprising (Brett & Stroh, 1997). We discovered that female managers were as likely as male managers to seek employment in the external labor market, but there were minimal or no benefits to them in doing so. Unlike the male managers, who benefited greatly from accepting employment in other organizations, women who changed organizations received no greater compensation than their female peers who stayed behind and pursued an internal labor market strategy. We speculated but could not prove that the cause of some of the differences in benefits may be discrimination in the external labor market. Another possible explanation is that men may be better connected to networks that help them navigate the external labor market. Further research on why the benefits are unequal is needed. The result, however, is that female managers who seek better employment through the external labor market gain less than their male peers who follow that strategy and no more than their female peers who do not leave their organizations.

Closely related to this problem is the negative effect having a family has on a woman's career progression. The following section addresses this important issue.

Balancing Work and Family Responsibilities

In general, marriage and parenting have negative effects (salary and promotions) on women in management and positive effects on men (Tharenou, Latimer, & Conroy, 1994). Getting to the top in corporate America requires an enormous commitment to work. In many organizations, this means putting in extraordinary hours. For example, in our study of dual- and single-earner male managers (Stroh & Brett, 1996), we found that the dual earners (the men whose spouses worked outside the home) were working an average of 51 hours each week, whereas the single men were averaging 53 hours.

In another, more recent study of managers with masters of management degrees (Brett, Medvic, & Stroh, 1999), we found that male and female managers in a variety of major industries worked an average of 56 hours per week and, proportionately, the men were working longer hours than the women. Among the men who worked 40-plus-hour workweeks, the average workweek was 56.7 hours, versus 52.6 hours for the women.

Our study (Brett et al., 1999) also revealed some interesting distinctions between the men and the women, especially among those who worked 61 or more hours per week. Among the men whose workweek was 51 to 60 hours, average annual compensation was $149,000, whereas the figure for the women was $127,000. Among the men who worked 61 or more hours per week, however, the figure jumped a significant $55,000. For the women the pay-off for greater hours was a negligible $4,000.

Several corporate changes have contributed to what appears to be the significant net increase in the number of hours managers spend working. One of the most significant of these changes is the downsizing of managerial ranks without commensurate reengineering of jobs that occurred in the 1980s and early 1990s. Then came the economic expansion of the 1990s. The rapid global expansion of markets could not be met by growth in managerial ranks.

Another significant change that may be increasing managers' workloads, and, as a result, making it more difficult than ever to balance work and family responsibilities, is the restructuring of organizations that focuses decision making on groups. Group decision making has many benefits, including broader perspectives on issues and better acceptance and implementation of decisions. On the downside, however, it takes longer. Managers are spending more hours in meetings and have less time available to work on individual tasks.

Yet, another environmental change that is resulting in managers working longer hours is the shift in managerial focus to a service orientation. In many organizations, time spent on returning phone calls and responding to queries means there is less time to read and write reports (yet more reports to write) and less time to plan for meetings and analyze and execute decisions.

In Schor's (1992) book, *The Overworked American: The Unexpected Decline of Leisure,* it is suggested that the entry of women and minorities into middle management may have caused social contagion of work hours. New entrants to groups typically try to blend in with old hands, so they do not question what appear to be norms. Old hands, not to be overshadowed by zealous new entrants, extend the norms. In this way, social contagion contributes to not just the transmission of norms but also to their contagion.

Finally, no discussion of the escalation of managerial work hours can be complete without an evaluation of Hochschild's (1997) hypothesis that managers and others working extremely long hours are using work as an emotional refuge from home. We tested Hochschild's thesis with our data set of managers with MBA degrees (Brett et al., 1999). We considered family involvement, family satisfaction, and the stress of family life on work. We found no evidence that those working the longest hours were the least satisfied with their home lives. In fact, we found that female

managers working 51 or more hours per week felt they had better control over their work-family interface than female managers working fewer hours per week, leading us to conclude that these women may have been trying to do too much.

Whatever the cause of the escalation in managerial hours of work, no one disputes that the escalation is real. Unfortunately, just at the time when more and more women qualify for higher-level management positions, the job of balancing work and family becomes harder because of the expectations for long hours. The net result is that increasing numbers of women feel they must choose between making a commitment to their careers and having families. For the many women who aspire to top management positions, this means forsaking marriage and having children. For others, it means turning down high-level positions. These women's choices not only pose problems for their own career development but also for the organizations that have nurtured their careers. Organizations at the end of the 1990s are desperate for managers. Having high-potential women managers leave organizations for organizations that have a better work/family balance is a huge loss of firm-specific human capital that most organizations cannot afford.

WHAT CAN BE DONE: GOALS FOR 2000 AND BEYOND

Undeniably, women have achieved much greater recognition and visibility in the higher ranks of American corporations in the past 25 years than in any other period of American history. Yet, as the results of our research make all too evident, there is still a way to go. Women are still not receiving starting salaries equal to men's or equal compensation as they reach the higher rungs of the corporate ladder. Women who work longer hours are not rewarded comparably to men who are also working these hours. Women are not being offered the same plum opportunities to relocate domestically and internationally as men. They also are not being compensated as much as men on the external labor market. In short, women with the human capital credentials equal to men nevertheless lag behind the men in opportunity and compensation. To achieve these broad goals requires first that several interim goals be met.

Equality in Salaries

Women who do not start out at the same salary level as men with comparable credentials have to play catch-up for the rest of their careers. This is exactly what many women have been doing. Part of the reason so many women start out earning less than men is that women tend to be employed in female ghettos: social work, clinical psychology, and teaching, all of which pay poorly relative to the level of education required. When women do work in traditionally male fields, such as management, 10 out of 11 leave for traditional female fields (Gutek, 1993). Furthermore, although women hold 49% of the positions in the executive, managerial, and professional labor force, they overwhelmingly hold more lower level positions. Only 3.8% of corporate officers are women and only 11% of directors of Fortune 500 companies are women (Catalyst Census of Women Corporate Officers and Top Earners, 1998).

The key to making equality in starting salaries a reality is education. An advanced degree in business is the single most important credential that a woman can have. An investment in advanced education makes a woman's application for a management job credible. When women present educational credentials that are comparable with those of male job candidates, it is much more difficult to discriminate. Moreover, when all the proper controls are in place, including prior experience and industry, there is seldom a difference between males and females in their top initial job offers after receiving an advanced degree. The difference, however, shows up in the offers taken.

Many women feel, with justification, that following a career track means forsaking their personal lives. This will have to change before significant numbers of women will accept the high-paying management positions that will result in their starting salaries—as well as their long-term compensation—being comparable to men's. As we previously mentioned, to ensure that their salaries are comparable throughout their working lives, women must not only be offered, but must be willing to take, high-profile jobs in "hot" areas of the company.

Equal Consideration for Relocation Opportunities

With the globalization of the business environment and the heightened connection between business and government that characterizes the end of the 20th century, international experience has become crucial for movement to the top of many organizations. Opportunities for women to relocate are limited with respect to domestic but especially international assignments. Yet, in our study (Brett & Stroh, 1995), we found that many of the stereotypical perceptions related to who is and who is not willing to relocate were myths. For example, male spouses of female managers were found to be no less willing to relocate internationally than female spouses of male managers (dispelling the myth that male spouses are more reluctant to follow their managerial wives on an international assignment than female spouses are to follow their male spouses). The problem of what to do about a trailing spouse on international assignments is no more serious for a female than a male manager. Yet, women are still rarely offered an international career opportunity (Stroh, Varma, & Valy, in press). Our study also showed that female managers were no less willing to accept an international assignment than were male managers.

Based on the findings of a more recent study (Stroh et al., in press), companies that were once overtly resistant to sending women overseas appear to be overcoming some of this resistance. Although the supervisors in this study showed progress in attitudes toward female expatriates (relative to previous research), this study found supervisors still maintained traditional beliefs and prejudices that resulted in some reluctance to select women for global assignments. In the years ahead, companies will need to work harder to communicate their policies and procedures for selecting managers for international assignments to ensure that these policies are fair to both male and female candidates and to reverse myths and misperceptions about women expatriates. According to Adler (1997), women are systematically passed over for international assignments because of beliefs that they will make ineffective managers in cultures where women have not traditionally held positions of power or authority in business or government. Yet, Adler (1997) and Stroh et al. (in press) find that women on international assignments are effective on these assignments, whereas both men and women who lack corporate backing are equally as likely to fall.

Equality in the Internal and External Market

Another area in which parity has not been achieved is in the opportunities available to men and women in the external labor market. Women are turning to the external labor market even more frequently than men according to our research; yet, at least from the perspective of compensation, they are not receiving the benefits men receive from doing so. What might women do? First, they should ensure that they have well-honed negotiating skills so that they are effective bargainers in the external job market. Second, they should make sure they are linked into professional networks that are not just female networks. Women's networks tend to be tightly coupled, whereas men's networks are loosely coupled. Loosely coupled networks are more extensive and provide more opportunities regarding job leads. A woman's network should extend to include headhunters. To the extent that the headhunter field is dominated by men and in many industries access to the

top-level jobs is controlled by headhunters, women, yet again, are at a disadvantage. As more women themselves become headhunters, women managers' access to top-level management positions should improve. In the meantime, companies should consider insisting that headhunters propose equal numbers of men and women for a position.

Companies also can ensure that everyone is aware of internal labor market advancement opportunities. Supervisors should be encouraged to publicize openings as well as encourage the brightest and best subordinates to apply for such openings. Of course, the incentives are normally just the opposite. Supervisors, wishing to avoid disruption of their own businesses, may not want to lose their brightest and best to another area of the corporation. There also may be motivational problems due to subordinates by-passing their supervisors up the corporate ladder. High-level mentors who are not threatened by rising stars may help publicize internal job openings. Making sure that women managers are well represented in groups identified as high potentials will also generate widespread visibility throughout the organization for women. Most important, selection must be based on credentials, not sex or age. Decoupling career opportunities from age or sex and linking them to experience and credentials enables male and female managers to change the pace of their careers depending on developments in their families. Similarly, managers who withdraw their names from consideration for a job requiring relocation should not be penalized. The conditions that lead to this decision one year may not be present the next.

Ability to Balance Work and Family Responsibilities

Almost all of our studies underscore the challenges facing women especially, but men too, as they try to juggle their work and family lives. What can managers do to facilitate the balance between work and family? Managers are usually rather proficient in managing the family side of their lives. Family needs are mostly predictable, and advanced planning works well. Managers typically have sufficient financial resources to cover predictable family demands. They understand the need to buffer themselves against the unpredictable with everything from back-up child care to mitten and scarf inventories.

However, there is still a lot organizations can do. Managing is a major time and energy commitment. Companies need to determine ways to ensure that high quality is maintained, extraordinary hours are not a day-to-day expectation, and that qualified, committed female managers are hired, promoted, and retained. One way to do this is by reengineering managerial positions, focusing on the job to be done, rather than on "face-time" in the office. Simply shifting norms from face-time to work-time should enable managers to work more efficiently and have more time for families. The result of such an effort might be managerial jobs in which advanced planning is the rule and last-minute fire fighting might be sanctioned, and in which performance evaluation might be tipped in favor of managers who deal responsibly with work and family rather than those who sidestep family obligations. Workdays that extend far into the night or through the weekend might be viewed as time spent only by the poor performer or the inefficient worker.

BEYOND 2000

The beginning of the new millennium is an appropriate time for corporations and managers to initiate new strategies of career development. If the economic boom of the late 1990s rides out the fiscal crisis in Asia, corporations will have no choice but to initiate new strategies to hire, develop, and retain managers. Economic expansion that generates a tight labor market can only benefit women managers. Even in the face of structural discrimination, business necessity will force organizations to reach out to their women

managers. It will be up to the women managers to take advantage of these opportunities as they materialize and to push for the restructuring of jobs to make balancing work and family possible.

REFERENCES

ADLER, N. (1997). *International dimensions of organizational behavior.* Cincinnati, OH: Southwestern Publishing.

BRETT, J. M., MEDVIC, V., & STROH, L. K. (1999). The overworked American manager. Unpublished manuscript, Northwestern University.

BRETT, J. M., & STROH, L. K. (1995). Willingness to relocate internationally. *Human Resource Management Journal,* 34(3), 405–424.

BRETT, J. M., & STROH, L. K. (1997). Jumping ship: Who does better on the external labor market? *Journal of Applied Psychology,* 82(3), 331–341.

BRETT, J. M., & STROH, L. K., & REILLY, A. H. (1993). Pulling up roots in the 1990s: Who's willing to relocate? *Journal of Organizational Behavior,* 14, 49–60.

Catalyst census of women corporate officers and top earners [Online]. (1998). Available: http://www.catalyst.org.

GUTEK, B. A. (1993). Changing status of women in management. *Applied Psychology: An International Review,* 42(4), 301–312.

HOCHSCHILD, A.R. (1997). *The time bind.* New York: Metropolitan Books.

KALLEBERG, A. L., & ROSENFELD, R. A. (1990). Work in the family and in the labor market: A cross-national, reciprocal analysis. *Journal of Marriage and the Family,* 52, 331–346.

OHLOTT, P. J., RUDERMAN, M. N., & McCAULEY, C. D. (1994). Gender differences in managers' developmental job experiences. *Academy of Management Journal,* 37, 46–67.

PFEFFER, J., & BARON, J. N. (1988). Taking the workers back out: Recent trends in the structuring of employment. In B. M. Staw & L. L. Cummings (Eds.), *Research in organization behavior* (pp. 257–303). Greenwich, CT: JAI.

RAGINS, B., TOWNSEND, B., & MATTIS, M. (1998). Gender gap in the executive suite: CEOs and female executives report on breaking the glass ceiling. *Academy of Management Executive,* 12(1), 28–42.

SCHOR, J. B. (1992). *The overworked American: The unexpected decline of leisure.* New York: Basic Books.

SCHWARTZ, F. N. (1989). Management women and the facts of life. *Harvard Business Review,* 1, 65–76.

SONNENFELD, J. A., & PEIPERL, M. A. (1988). Staffing policy as a strategic response: A typology of career systems. *Academy of Management Review,* 13, 588–600.

SONNENFELD, J. A., PEIPERL, M. A., & KOTTER, J.P. (1988). Strategic determinants of managerial labor markets: A career systems view. *Human Resources Management,* 27, 360–388.

STROH, L. K., & BRETT, J. M. (1996). The dual earner daddy penalty in salary progression. *Human Resource Management*, 35(2), 1–21.

STROH, L. K., BRETT, J. M., & REILLY, A. H. (1992). All the right stuff: A comparison of female and male managers' career progression. *Journal of Applied Psychology*, 77(3), 251–260.

STROH, L. K., VARMA, A., & VALY, S. (in press). Women and expatriation: Revisiting Alder's findings. In M. J. Davidson & R. J. Burke (Eds.), *Women in management: Current research issues II*. London: Paul Chapman.

THARENOU, P., LATIMER, S., & CONROY, D. (1994). How do you make it to the top? An examination of influences on women's and men's managerial advancement. *Academy of Management Journal*, 37, 899–931.

CRITICAL THINKING QUESTIONS

1. In what ways do the career paths of men and women managers differ?

2. What reasons do the authors give for women managers' lower levels of career achievement?

3. What structural changes would need to be achieved to ensure that women and men managers have equal opportunities for career successes? What has prevented these changes from being made?

Reading 8

Designing Mom-Size Jobs

Joan Williams

In this article, Williams discusses the challenges that working mothers confront, including the workplace assumption that employees are free to put their jobs ahead of responsibilities at home.

The US Census Bureau reported recently that for the first time, in a majority of American families, both parents work. Does this mean women are moving ever-closer to equality?

It does not. The data on workforce participation mask the rising "family gap" between the wages of mothers and other adults. The negative impact of women's income of having children increased in the 1980s; it's increasing still in many income groups.

In our economy of mothers and others, nonmothers—of both sexes—are doing fine. But mothers remain a pocket of poverty. Eighty percent of the poor in this country are mothers and their children.

To break this cycle, we need to change the ways we organize work. In good jobs today, we define the ideal worker as someone who works

Source: Reprinted from *The Christian Science Monitor* 92, no. 250 (November 17, 2000): 11 with permission from the author.

full-time and overtime "as needed" for 40 years straight.

This ideal is designed around men. Women need time off for childbirth; and in the US, they still do three-fourths of the child care.

Defining our work ideals around men excludes most mothers. New data show that 2 out of 3 work under 40 hours a week during key years of career advancement. Even fewer—less than 10 percent—work substantial overtime. Jobs that require large amounts of overtime, from auto worker to corporate lawyer, exclude mothers almost completely.

Workforce participation may be up, but many mothers are in dead-end jobs, and very few reach the top.

We need to discuss the economic arrangements that leave more than 95 percent of upper-level management, and most good blue-collar jobs, in the hands of men.

CRITICAL THINKING QUESTIONS

1. Why do mothers have generally fewer economic resources than men and fewer than women who are not parents?

2. How would creating more "mom-size" jobs help women's career opportunities? What groups of women would most likely be helped by such jobs?

3. How might "mom-size" jobs hurt women's career opportunities? What groups of women would be most likely to have their careers adversely affected by such institutional changes?

Reading 9

Where Are the Civil Rights for Gay and Lesbian Teachers?

Christine Yared

> *In this reading, Yared discusses the case of an award-winning teacher who was pressured to resign when the public learned that he was gay. The author uses this case to illustrate the difficult situations gay and lesbian employees can encounter when their sexuality becomes public knowledge.*

. . . Byron Center is a small town, outside of Grand Rapids. In 1993, Gerry Crane was hired to revive a floundering music program at the public high school in Byron Center. During the first two years, Crane received exceptional reviews. He was described as "the teacher who built the music program," "one of the best teachers on staff" and "a good role model for our students."

In the summer of 1995, Crane and his partner Randy began to plan their October commitment ceremony. In September, someone in Byron Center learned about the ceremony and word spread to school officials, parents and students. At the November school board meeting, angry parents attended the meeting and demanded that the gay teacher either resign or be fired.

In the months that followed, Crane endured pain and stress on a daily basis. Many parents removed their children from his classes. Crane continued to teach while the value of his life as a gay man was being publicly debated in the local, state, and national media. Fear prevented many of his colleagues and others in the community from providing public support for him.

At the December 1995 school board meeting attended by about 700, the school board issued a scathing statement that read in part, "individuals who espouse homosexuality do not constitute proper role models as teachers." The board concluded with a warning to Crane that it would continue to "investigate and monitor" the situation and "take appropriate and lawful action when justified."

During the balance of the school year, Crane experienced the "investigate and monitor" portion of the statement in the form of harassment. For example, a school official released a list of the names and addresses of

Source: Reprinted from *Human Rights: Journal of the Section of Individual Rights & Responsibilities* 24, no. 3 (Summer 1997) 22–24.

Crane's students to facilitate a propaganda campaign. The parents of Crane's students received a booklet and video, *Gay Rights/Special Rights: Inside the Homosexual Agenda*. The video explained that the "homosexual agenda" is harmful to the nation's school children. The video contains selected scenes from gay pride celebrations in large cities highlighting transvestites and gays clothed in leather. Parents continued to remove students from his classes.

While parents, educators, and clergy worked aggressively to undermine his career and character, Crane mustered the strength to go into a hostile work environment each day and teach. Throughout the struggle, Crane and his partner exhibited courage, integrity, and grace. At the end of the school year, however, Crane evaluated his options and concluded that like a poison, the hatred and fear were spreading and dangerous.

In July 1996, he entered into a settlement agreement with the school district that included one year's salary, health benefits and a letter of reference. In exchange, Crane agreed not to sue or seek employment in the district.

Five months later on December 27, 1996, Crane collapsed and went into a coma. Seven days later at age 32, he died. After conducting an autopsy, the forensic pathologist concluded that Gerry Crane died because of a floppy heart valve, a congenital condition that is usually not fatal. The doctor further concluded that the stress of his public struggle to maintain his job could have led to his death, stating, "It may have put him over the edge."

Gay teachers work in fear that a student, parent, or school official will discover their orientation. The ramifications for gay teachers who are "out" or "outed" are serious. The teacher's health is at risk as a result of both likely harassment and physical violence. In addition, in most school districts the teacher's career is also at risk. Gay teachers who remain "closeted" will also experience stress, anxiety, and depression as they attempt to hide their sexual orientation and family life from those in their work environment.

In 1990, the Gay, Lesbian, and Straight Teachers Network (GLSTN) was founded. GLSTN's mission is to ensure that each member of every school community is valued and respected, regardless of sexual orientation. Yet, it is important to understand that for gay teachers (and heterosexual supportive teachers), the mere decision to join an organization such as GLSTN is fraught with fear.

Litigants have been unsuccessful in using federal legislation to support a claim of employment discrimination based on sexual orientation. Title VII of the Civil Rights Act of 1964 prohibits employment discrimination based on race, color, religion, sex and national origin. . . . Courts have held that Title VII does not prohibit discrimination based on sexual orientation. . . .

The reasoning supporting this position has included reference to the failure of the bills that have been introduced in Congress over the years to amend the Civil Rights Act of 1964 to prohibit discrimination based on sexual orientation. . . . In addition, the courts have dismissed claims of employment discrimination based on sexual orientation. . . .

The majority of the states have adopted [this] federal view. Michigan's civil rights legislation extends protection beyond federal criteria and precludes discrimination based on height, weight, and marital status. . . . Yet when faced with the issue of applying the Michigan law to a case involving sexual orientation, the court relied solely on federal precedent interpreting the federal law, and held that the Michigan law does not extend to discrimination based on sexual orientation.

While the courts discuss the need to examine these cases in light of interference with the educational process, the courts are unwilling to uphold a claim of discrimination even where the educational environment is not affected.

In *Acanfora v. Board of Education* . . . (1974), the plaintiff claimed that he was wrongfully transferred from a[n] eighth grade teaching position to a non-teaching position after the school learned that he was gay. The Maryland District Court concluded that the transfer was justified not because the teacher was gay, but because students and parents knew that he was gay. The Court framed the First Amendment issue as "whether the speech is likely to incite or produce imminent effects deleterious to the educational process." (*Acanfora*, 359 F. Supp. 843.) The court explained that publicity undertaken by a known homosexual teacher:

> . . . does not best serve the purposes of sexual adjustment maturation and student-parent relationships in the educational context. These questions are charged with emotion and of such a delicate and sensitive nature that the injection of controversy tends to breed misunderstanding, alarm and anxiety. *Acanfora* at 856.

Thus, the teacher's First Amendment rights are dependent upon the ability of the students and parents to process the information that one of the teachers is gay. In *Acanfora*, the teacher voluntarily discussed his claim of employment discrimination with the media. While observers may conclude that the Court's action in *Acanfora* related to his media interviews, in *Rowland v. Mad River Local School Dist.*, . . . (1984), the U.S. Supreme Court upheld sexual orientation-based discrimination where the teacher revealed her sexuality during private discussions with school employees.

In *Rowland*, the Court found that the discrimination was constitutional even though the jury concluded that knowledge of the teacher's bisexuality did not interfere with the school's operation in any way. The facts in *Rowland* were summarized by Justice Brennan in his dissenting opinion: "Petitioner's first mention of her bisexuality at school apparently came in response to friendly but repeated questions from her secretary as to why petitioner seemed in a particularly "good mood" one day. When petitioner eventually responded that she was in love with a woman, the secretary apparently was upset by the unexpected answer, and reported it to petitioner's principal. On another occasion, petitioner was confronted by an angry mother who wanted to know why petitioner was counseling her to accept her son's expressed homosexuality when such conduct was "against the Bible." Petitioner did not inform the mother of her own preferences, but did inform her vice principal, because she was "uneasy" that if the mother complained her own "job would be at stake" . . . Finally, petitioner mentioned her bisexuality to some of her fellow teachers, first simply in the course of her friendships with them and later to enlist their support when it became clear that she would be disciplined for her bisexuality. (*Rowland*, U.S. at 1017.)

Justice Brennan further described the first conversation as being a natural result of the teacher's bisexuality "in the same way that coworkers generally know whom their fellow employees are dating or to whom they are married." (*Rowland*, U.S. at 1018.)

In challenging the logic underlying the majority's decision . . . Justice Brennan reasoned "the jury was entitled to make rational inferences and apply its common-sense knowledge of the world, which includes the knowledge that most teachers are openly heterosexual and yet go undisciplined for that sexual preference." (*Rowland*, U.S. at 1018.)

In addition, the courts have upheld discrimination based on sexual orientation even where the record was void of evidence that the teacher was gay. In *Jantz v. Muci*, . . . (1993), a teacher alleged that he was not hired because the school concluded that he was gay. The record stated that the teacher was married, with two children, and that he did not admit to being gay. The discrimination was based on the secretary's statement that the principal found the applicant to have "homosexual tendencies." (*Jantz*, 759 at 1545.)

In *Jantz*, the 10th Circuit Court relied on the U.S. Supreme Court decision upholding the constitutionality of Georgia's criminal sodomy law in *Bowers v. Hardwick*, . . . (1986). Consequently, courts are using an opinion that addresses homosexual and heterosexual conduct to justify discrimination based on a person's status or perceived status as a homosexual.

Nine states, the District of Columbia, and numerous cities have passed legislation prohibiting employment discrimination based on sexual orientation. Since most of these laws were passed in the 1990s it is not clear whether the laws will provide adequate protection for gay teachers. It is troubling to note that five of the nine state laws contain language limiting the application of the civil rights legislation. For example, in Massachusetts the civil rights law states that the provision should not be considered an endorsement or approval of homosexuality or bisexuality and should not be construed as legitimizing marriages between same-sex couples. (The Vermont, Connecticut, and California laws also contain a same-sex marriage exception.)

Would this law protect a gay teacher who is fired after she brings her partner to a faculty holiday party where the invitation includes "spouses"? Would this law protect a gay teacher in Connecticut who is fired for "flaunting" his sexuality by wearing a wedding band (which includes the symbolic gay pink triangle)? The Connecticut civil rights law states in part that the Act shall not be read:

(1) to mean the State of Connecticut condones homosexuality or bisexuality or any equivalent lifestyle, or

(2) to authorize the promotion of homosexuality or bisexuality in educational institutions or require the teaching in educational institutions of homosexuality or bisexuality as an acceptable lifestyle. . . .

(5) to establish sexual orientation as a specific and separate cultural classification in society. . . .

By the standards of many, wearing the "gay" ring could be interpreted to be promoting homosexuality in the educational institution. Assume further that the gay teacher walks to the snack machines in the school and opens his wallet in front of a group of students to obtain money for a drink. Another teacher walks by and notices that the gay teacher has a picture of himself with his partner in his wallet. The teacher reports that the gay teacher is confusing the teenagers by "flaunting" his sexuality. Armed with a homophobic teacher, a confused student, and an angry parent as witnesses, the "ring and photograph" stories could support a conclusion that the gay teacher is attempting to "promote homosexuality in the school."

Imagine a civil rights bill addressing discrimination based on race, sex, and disability that contained language explaining that the bill is not intended to "promote minorities, women or the disabled in the school."

The issue of civil rights for gay teachers is also critical for youth. According to statistics provided by GLSTN, 30 percent of all completed teen suicides are by gay and lesbian youth. The physical and emotional development of gay youth and of youth (gay or straight) who have gay and lesbian parents, relatives and friends is dependent on a positive climate for gay teachers. Our laws currently facilitate and nurture an educational system where schools are able to use tax money to speak about respect while modeling bigotry.

Gerry Crane's public struggle and death mirrors the many private, symbolic and actual deaths that gays and lesbians experience and fear on a daily basis. While his story may energize some gay activists, for many teachers his story will lead them to remain in the closet with increased anxiety.

In *Romer v. Evans,* . . . (1996), the U.S. Supreme Court held that a state referendum precluding legislative, executive, or judicial action providing legal protection based on a person's sexual orientation violated the equal protection clause since it infringed on the fundamental right of gays and lesbians to participate in the political process. The majority in *Romer* specifically rejected the state's rationale for the law, "to respect for other citizens' freedom of association, and in particular the liberties of landlords or employers who have personal or religious objections to homosexuality."

While the gay teacher cases do not typically involve the application of a broad state law, the school districts often justify their action based on personal and religious objections of parents. The reasoning in *Romer* may thus be helpful in challenging alleged government interests based on emotion.

While activists need to lobby for laws decriminalizing sodomy and adding sexual orientation into existing civil rights legislation, lawyers litigating these cases should aggressively seek change by relying on existing free speech, free association, and equal protection balancing tests. Litigants must incorporate into the lawsuits data provided by the social scientists and human service professionals to dispel myths about homosexuality and educate society about the needs of children who are gay or who come from gay families. The legal profession should take the lead in securing civil rights for gay teachers.

CRITICAL THINKING QUESTIONS

1. What assumptions did parents and the community make about Gerry Crane before the summer of 1995? What did they think about his teaching?

2. What were the reasons the community gave for demanding that the teacher be fired? Were these at all related by his ability to teach?

3. How is the situation of gay and lesbian employees similar to and different from that of racial minorities before the Civil Rights Act of 1964 and today?

Reading 10

Conformity Pressures and Gender Resistance among Transgendered Individuals

Patricia Gagné and Richard Tewksbury

In this article, Gagné and Tewksbury explore the personal and public pressures to conform to mainstream ideas about gender that transsexuals and cross-dressers encounter when they make their transgenderism known to others.

Research on transgendered individuals has tended to come from medical, psychiatric, or deviance perspectives, with little attention to the so-

Source: Reprinted from *Social Problems* 45, no. 1 (February 1998). © 1998 by the University of California Press and The Society for the Study of Social Problems, Inc.

This research was funded, in part, by grants from the following: The Society for the Psychological Study of Social Issues, the Foundation for the Scientific Study of Sexuality, and a Project Completion Grant from the Office of the Vice President for Research and Development at the University of Louisville. The authors wish to thank Judith Lorber, Deanna McGaughey, and four anonymous reviewers for their assistance with this article. Direct correspondence to Patricia Gagné, Department of Sociology, University of Louisville, Louisville, Kentucky 40292. E-mail: plgagn01@ulkyvm.louisville.edu

cial context in which these individuals exist or their efforts to resist normative expectations of sex and gender. Based upon in-depth interviews with 65 masculine-to-feminine transgendered individuals, this research examines gender as a social institution. Focusing on the pressures experienced by individuals to maintain binary enactments of gender, we demonstrate how the institution of gender is taken for granted as a presumably natural aspect of social life. Social pressures to conform, experienced as desires for relationship maintenance and self-preservation, as well as the overwhelming need to actualize an identity that does not fit within the binary system of sex and gender, illuminate the gender resistance and conformity exhibited among the individuals in our sample. Our analysis is rooted in an expanded Foucauldian perspective incorporating the theoretical insights of contemporary feminists who consider social actors as active agents in the development and enactment of everyday resistance. Transgenderism is a discursive act that both challenges and reifies the binary gender system. As such, it provides important lessons about the power dynamics of gender and how such systems may and may not be resisted.

Social scientists have demonstrated the pervasiveness of gender as a central organizing factor in all societies. As a system, gender is taken for granted, often completely overlooked, until the norms of gender presentation, interaction, or organization are inadvertently violated or deliberately challenged (Lorber 1994). While some believe gender is rooted in our biological make-up (e.g., Wilson 1975), as a system it receives constant surveillance and is policed continually through social interactions that socialize new members of society (see Richardson 1988) and sanction those who violate the rules (Bullough and Bullough 1993; Chesler 1989; Schur 1984). It exists at both individual and group levels, where women and men "do gender" and others decode, interpret, and categorize individuals based upon presented gender cues (West and Zimmerman 1987). At the organizational level gender exists to categorize individuals and assign them meanings and roles (Kanter 1977). At the institutional level (e.g., in the economy, family, religion, law, politics, and medicine), gender determines individuals' roles, statuses, rights, and responsibilities (see Richardson 1988).

Western industrial and post-industrial cultures share the ideological presumption that gender will correlate with the sex assigned at birth. Individuals who seek to challenge this binary system of gender through enactments of androgynous gender or by crossing gender boundaries, including masculine women and feminine men, are likely to be stigmatized, ostracized, and labeled mentally ill (see Gagné and Tewksbury 1996). "Transgen-

der" is a term that refers to a spectrum of individuals who express gender in ways that deviate from the gender binary, and includes transsexuals, cross-dressers, and others (Tewksbury and Gagné 1996). These terms will be defined more fully below.) Transgendered individuals, in fact all gender deviants, lose legitimacy as social actors because, as a society, "we have no social place for a person who is neither a woman nor a man" (Lorber 1994:96). So while gender is an internalized sense of self, it is also a social institution that, in western societies, demands conformity to a binary system where males present themselves as masculine men and females as feminine women.

Not all individuals' internalized sense of gender fits within the binary system. Feminine men and masculine women are pressured to conform to the binary system, either by concealing their gender "deviance" or by transforming their presentations and physical selves to conform to notions of the "opposite" sex and gender category. Further, a binary system offers few cultural resources to assist individuals in developing an alternative gender identity and understanding themselves as alternatively gendered. There is not only no social space for such individuals, there is no way of being known except as highly stigmatized social deviants. Nonetheless, such alternatively gendered individuals find ways to challenge and resist the gender binary, even as their conformity is compelled. Their efforts both destabilize and reify the gender binary.

THEORETICAL FRAMEWORK

Individuals "do" gender, but accountability in gender presentation is a "feature of social relationships, and its idiom derives from the institutional arena in which those relationships come to life" (West and Fenstermaker 1995:21). Gender is neither fixed nor static, but like all social institutions, it is resistant to change. It is neither passively accepted nor rejected outright by individuals in society. Individuals are active in the creation of an internalized gender identity (Kohlberg 1966), they maintain gender identity and construct and re-invent gendered presentations (Davis 1995).

Resistance and acquiescence to normative gender are inherent aspects of the social world. Even individuals whose gender identities do not fit within normative expectations have a clear understanding of the dominant belief system, for it is against that system that they react (Gagné, Tewksbury, and McGaughey 1997). Despite the institutionalized nature of gender, its enactment has been analyzed from a Foucauldian perspective as a cultural statement (Bordo 1989; Davis 1995). Following this tradition, we analyze the ways that transgendered individuals both resist and conform to normative gender through their enactments of alternative gender identities.

Drawing from the theoretical model proposed by Davis (1995) in her analysis of women's involvement with cosmetic surgery, we look upon transgenderism as a discursive act in which the transgendered individual is an active agent in the establishment of an alternative gender identity and the presentation of an alternatively gendered self (see also Smith 1990). Unlike Davis, however, we view the presentation of alternative gender as an act of everyday resistance (see Collins 1990). Transgenderism is an expression of self that resists the assumption that gender correlates with sex. At the same time, transgendered individuals are caught in a moral dilemma of wanting to challenge the binary system of gender, while at the same time wishing to "pass" and be accepted as the other sex in order to avoid stigma, ostracism, and physical danger (see also Bartky 1990). . . .

Using a Foucauldian perspective to examine the acts of resistance and conformity of 65 masculine-to-feminine transgendered individuals, we use transgenderism to understand and analyze the gendered dynamics of social power. To accomplish this, we examine: 1) the agency of individuals who try to challenge the assumption that gender is congruent with the sex assigned at birth; 2) the social pressures experienced by such individuals to "do gender and do it right"; and 3) the ways that transgendered individuals both destabilize and reinforce the binary system of gender. At the individual level, gender may (or may not) be successfully renegotiated. But, through acts of gender resistance, transgendered individuals challenge and destabilize the binary system of gender, while simultaneously and inadvertently reinforcing it as an institution.

METHODS

We completed semi-structured, in-depth, tape-recorded interviews with 65 masculine-to-feminine individuals from several points along the transgender spectrum. For purposes of categorization, we relied on each respondent's self-proclaimed identity. Included are individuals who self-identify as pre-operative (N = 27), post-operative (N = 10), and non-operative (N = 4) transsexual. These are people who believe themselves to be female and who wish to, or do, live full-time as women. Pre-operative transsexuals are those who desire to, but have not yet had sex reassignment surgery (SRS); post-operative transsexuals have had SRS; while non-operative transsexuals live full-time or nearly full-time as women but do not desire SRS. Some have availed themselves of other medical and cosmetic procedures, including female hormones, breast implants, and electrolysis, while others change their gender presentations without bodily alteration. . . .

Our sample also includes nineteen cross-dressers. All but one of the transsexuals in our study had self-identified as a cross-dresser at some time preceding the development of a transsexual identity, and four cross-dressers in our sample were exploring the possibility they might be transsexual. . . .

A small number of persons (N = 5) who cross-dressed and had no desire for SRS referred to themselves in more politically oriented terms. While there are subtle differences in politics, all of these people have used trans-

genderism to consciously challenge binary assumptions about sex, gender, and sexuality.
Their intent, unlike cross-dressers, is not to
"pass" as women, but to challenge the idea that
gender is a "natural" expression of sex. . . .

To maximize reliability, the first author conducted all but one interview. Where distance
precluded a face-to-face meeting, interviews
were conducted over the telephone. They were
organized so that, after providing background
information on age, education, occupational
history, and family, respondents were encouraged to tell their life stories as they pertained to
their transgendered feelings and experiences.
Interviews ranged from 45 minutes to eight
hours in length, averaging about three hours.

Interviews were transcribed in full. Data
were coded following principles of analytic
induction (Charmaz 1983) in multiple readings, with each focused on a narrow range of
conceptual categories (e.g., pressures in interactions with significant others, or legal,
economic, religious, and medical pressures
to conform).

FINDINGS

Among non-political transgendered respondents, one of the clearest findings was a belief in the existence of a gendered self
separate and distinct from embodied representations. While the overwhelming majority
adhered to the belief that males should be
masculine, females should be feminine, and
that identity as a gay male should be avoided,
gender identity was an internalized sense of
self that was not always congruent with the
sex assigned at birth. These individuals believed that gender identity was not a natural
outgrowth of sex, but that enactments of a
feminine self—whether permanent or temporary—needed to be convincing, giving the
impression that gender was indicative of
anatomy. Although the individuals in our
sample had feminine traits and, in the case
of transsexuals, believed themselves to be
women, before accepting a transgender

identity they believed they needed to hide
their transgender behavior and attempted to
conceal their feminine traits and behaviors
from others. . . .

To make sense of the incongruity between
their anatomy and gender identity, several
transsexuals adhered to biological theories,
and many believed the sex and genders to be
opposites. Some believed that it was possible
for males to be born with female brains. Others simply explained that they were women
with male bodies:

> I wanted to be a girl. I always thought that I
> had the wrong body. I don't know, I think it's a
> birth defect. That's my personal feeling, be-
> cause there's nothing in my early childhood
> that I can remember that would have caused
> this. (pre-operative transsexual, living full time
> as a woman)

The individuals in our sample expressed different levels of femininity and desires to enact
a feminine self, suggesting considerable gender diversity among individuals who were classified as male at birth. Nonetheless, the
overwhelming majority declined to radically
challenge the notion that gender must express
the sex assigned at birth. Instead, the majority
modified the definitions of the gender binary
by arguing either that they really were women,
despite the physical evidence regarding their
sex, or that they had a feminine self that
needed to be expressed on occasional, temporary bases. Only five argued that expressions of
gender should be free of biological prescriptions and societal constraints. Clearly, conformity was far more prevalent than resistance.

Transgendered individuals' modified adherence to the gender binary is central to
our research. First, it speaks to their perceptions of the gendered world. Second, it
raises the issue of individual agency and creativity in making sense of the self as a feminine man or a male who is a woman. Third,
it suggests that transgendered individuals do
not accept the physical self as indicative of
gendered identity; instead, they view the
body as malleable, or a text upon which they

may inscribe an internalized sense of self (see Smith 1990). Nonetheless, these beliefs raise the issue of the extent to which one can revolt against social institutions, including gender, without being expelled as a member of society or having one's acts of rebellion coopted back into the system. . . .

Because non-political, transgendered individuals deeply believe that males should be masculine and females feminine, those in our sample experienced a feminine self that could not be expressed, except when the body was adorned and presented as that of a woman. Dressing or living as a woman allowed the freedom to express one's femininity but, because achieving femininity involved interaction with others, it had to be done convincingly and at least semi-publicly.

Our sample experienced the pressures to conform to traditional masculinity as intense and pervasive. They learned early in life that it was their obligation to enact masculine presentations of gender. Nonetheless, while most tried to conform to societal demands, all yearned to be able to be themselves on either permanent or temporary bases (see Mason-Schrock 1996; Turner 1976). . . .

While coming out was fraught with fears of physical danger and rejection (see Gagné, et al. 1997), such revelations expanded the spaces where transgendered individuals could "be themselves." Such interactions, however, produced pressures to transform completely and convincingly from social manhood to womanhood. Restricting feminine presentations to private settings concealed transgenderism, but then public interactions were premised on the presentation of a false self. Once a feminine presentation was perfected, the impression that sex and gender were congruent was maintained. Nonetheless, during periods of transition, while cross-dressers endeavored to "pass" as women, or transsexuals learned to live as women, their public (or quasi-public) presence in society disrupted the gender binary in two ways, challenging the idea that gender is a "natural" outgrowth of biological sex, and creating public recognition of the presence of a "third gender" category.

Conformity Pressures and Gender Resistance

Pressures to conform to traditional masculinity were most commonly situated in interpersonal interactions with others who expected conformity to the binary system of gender. In direct interaction with others, these pressures were experienced as fear of rejection and desire for self-preservation. At the institutional level, however, individuals were not only rejected, but faced erasure as social actors if they did not conform to the institutionalized norms for transgendered individuals. That is, as individuals who were neither women nor men, they had no legal, economic, or social standing in society (see Lorber 1994). Nonetheless, transgendered individuals were not blind conformists. Instead, they actively sought opportunities (especially semi-public events), to enact the feminine self, even while they attempted to conceal such activities or to "purge" themselves of transgendered proclivities. In the end, for each person in our sample, the need to come to terms with and publicly proclaim an alternative gender identity outweighed the fear of rejection and desire for self-preservation. . . .

In the following sections, we examine pressures to conform, analyzing them in light of transgendered individuals' desires to maintain relationships, preserve their own economic security and physical well-being, avoid social erasure, and achieve a comfortable identity. Although these issues push individuals toward conflicting ends of a binary system, the commonality is that all are pressures to *stay within the binary*. Open transitions from one gender to the other challenge the assumption that gender is a natural outgrowth of sex. Nonetheless, to the extent that gender rebels can be pressured to perfect their presentations of alternative gender to more closely approximate the "opposite" sex, the binary system is preserved, with those known as transgendered relegated to the third gender category of "unnatural" or deviant (Segal 1997).

Fear of Rejection and Resistance to Conformity. Early in life, and in the initial stages of coming out as a transgendered individual, fear of rejection is a conformity pressure focused on relationships with family, friends, and colleagues. Beginning in early childhood, and continuing throughout their lives, individuals learn to expect rejection, stigmatization, and the loss of relationships, should they violate gender norms. Fear of rejection acts as a pressure to establish and maintain "proper" gender in order to preserve personal relationships. Most transgendered individuals, at least for extended periods of time prior to proclaiming a transformed identity, place greater value on preserving relationships with significant others, (primarily parents, partners, and children) than on accurate self-identification and presentation of self. Conformity, while distressing, offers valued rewards in interactions and social integration. The result is repression of the authentic self in the interest of preserving valued relationships. In childhood, this fear of rejection centers on the maintenance of primary relationships; in adulthood, it expands to include economic relationships and avoidance of danger in the public domain.

As young children and adolescents, the people we interviewed quickly learned that to cross-dress or act feminine was inappropriate and intolerable. Therefore, they learned to hide their transgendered activities and feminine characteristics and attempted to become appropriately masculine:

> Some of my earliest memories, I didn't know it was transsexual. I just didn't feel like a male. Everyone was telling me I was and I felt I had to act that way, but I just didn't feel that way and I felt it was something very, very wrong. I guess it was social pressure, and I just tried to act the way someone expected me to, and it just went on for a long time. (pre-operative transsexual)

Being a feminine male meant being labeled abnormal, weird, sick, or homosexual. Boys were scolded, shamed, sent to psychiatrists, and sometimes beaten by their parents for wanting to do feminine things: "I would paint my toenails on occasion. My father caught me one time and beat the hell out of me for it." As children, our respondents reported being called "fucking queers," having their dolls taken away because "you're a little boy, and little boys don't sleep with dolls," and otherwise having any expression of a desire to enact feminine appearance, behaviors, or roles sanctioned: "I was being beat up, called sissy, and I really didn't know why at the time." Although the reasons for such sanctions were not necessarily understood, they learned that feminine aspects of self would have to be kept hidden.

Threatened with physical and verbal assault, and fearing the rejection of parents, siblings, peers, and others, many children learned to give the appearance of conformity, often isolating themselves as much as possible from those around them. For example, one pre-operative transsexual told us about her efforts, as a young boy, to conform:

> I'd go fishing. I tried to play football. That didn't work. I couldn't take it. . . . Instead of trying to hide [my femininity], I became a loner.

Some adopted a hypermasculine persona that endured into adulthood. They played contact sports, joined the military, got married, and for long periods of time refused to do anything even remotely feminine. But the desire to enact femininity always came back; while they gave the appearance of conformity, it was not genuine.

All of the transgendered individuals understood the social expectation that sex and gender be congruent but, as young children they had difficulty figuring out how they—as boys who wished to be (or thought they actually were) girls—could fit into society. To be accepted they needed to conform, and for many that was difficult. Making sense of the self was an interactive process, dependent upon emergent cultural categories and meanings, as well as the individual's strong need to express a feminine self (Davis 1995). A post-operative transsexual exemplified the hidden resistance, search for identity, and dependence upon cultural resources in the establishment and manifestation of identity:

As I got older, throughout elementary school, I really started to get the wrath of the peers at school. I certainly would not tell anybody about my feelings or express my desires. . . . It was like I was cross-dressing and I really didn't understand and I knew I was alone in the world. . . . Then the *Mike Douglas Show* had somebody on there [who] had a sex change operation. . . . and it was at that point in time that I realized that other people had my problem and there was a solution to it. From that day forward, I knew I had to have SRS.

Maintaining adult relationships with significant others also pressured individuals to conceal and try to rid themselves of transgenderism. Pressures to conform to the gender binary were social facts, situated in direct interaction with others. In part, fear of rejection came from a lifetime of being taunted, beaten, and stigmatized for not "acting right." Although some transgendered individuals preserved important relationships, many lost family members and friends, or at the least, relationships suffered in quality and intimacy. For many, maintaining marital relationships was the most stressful issue. Long-term, committed relationships problematized the formation and presentation of a transformed gender identity. Despite the stigma and fear of rejection, our respondents tried to identify and present themselves in feminine ways. Striving to maintain adult relationships, transgendered individuals moved from attempting to give the outward appearance of conformity (as in childhood) to trying to strike a balance between the authentic self and the self known to others.

Disclosing one's transgenderism is a uniquely stressful experience (see Gagné, et al., 1997) for both the transgendered individual and the recipient of the news. Informing a spouse or partner of one's transgenderism elicits a wide array of reactions. Acceptance or tolerance tended to be more common among the wives of cross-dressers than of transsexuals. Although far from universal, acceptance was typically conditioned on preventing children, relatives, neighbors, and business associates from knowing. While some wives assisted their husbands

in perfecting feminine presentations, most insisted that cross-dressing be separated from other family members, public interactions with others, and the couple's sexual relations. Among cross-dressers, the greatest pressure experienced from accepting or tolerant wives was to be discrete and pass well enough in public to avoid detection. Maintaining the marital relationship depended upon ensuring that the husband's transgenderism did not become public knowledge:

[My wife's] known about it for all but two years of our marriage and it bothers her. . . . We had quite a talk about a year ago about how she reacted to all this. She said, 'In honesty, it bothers me as much today as it did when I first found out.' But, she'll go out with me occasionally. Her concern is that I'm going to be looked at. Because my wife and I have been married so long and we're so well-known as a couple, if we're out in public, somebody could see me that knows and wouldn't have a clue to who I was. You put me next to [my] wife and you're going to get two and two is four real fast. She's worried about recognition. (married cross-dresser)

When this couple's adult daughters moved back into their home, the wife became increasingly concerned about them learning about their father's cross-dressing, particularly because they had a tendency to borrow their mother's clothing. Husband and wife wore different sizes, but kept both wardrobes in the same closet. The husband suggested that keeping the cross-dressing a secret was more stressful to his wife than telling their daughters. Pressured to conceal transgenderism, this cross-dresser resisted absolute conformity to the wife's hope that the cross-dressing would stop, or that it would be kept segmented from the rest of their lives. Although the transgenderism was concealed, through persistent resistance this cross-dresser created increasingly wider spaces in which the feminine self could be enacted. When told about the transgenderism, the daughters' reaction was, "It's fine by us." Since then, the daughters have gone out in public with their father's feminine self, making this cross-dresser feel "validated."

Transgendered individuals who were married or had children placed a great deal of emphasis on their desire to maintain relationships with wives and children and fulfill their roles as husbands and fathers. Most balanced the need to actualize a feminine self against the need to maintain family relationships. Transsexuals found the maintenance of relationships more difficult than cross-dressers. Even when transsexuals offered to limit their transgendered explorations to highly privatized cross-dressing, as a compromise between actualizing a "true self" and maintaining the relationship, they often met with hostility and rejection. For example, one divorced pre-operative transsexual, involved in a failed marriage for years, told of her desire to maintain a relationship with her children, fulfill her responsibilities as a father, and help her wife become self-sufficient before openly pursuing a transgendered identity:

Divorce is something I argued against for years. Especially when there's children involved. . . . I got [my son] through college, got [my daughter] through high school, and got the wife through college and half-way through her masters. Really amazing feat.

While apparently conforming to the gender binary, this person secretly cross-dressed whenever the family was away. After ensuring the wife and children's self-sufficiency, she felt the need to more openly pursue her own identity issues. She told us about coming out to her wife as a cross-dresser who would limit transgendered activities to wearing nightgowns to bed and cross-dressing when the family was out of town. Her open gender resistance met with rejection: "I was moved out of the bedroom. . . . She couldn't tolerate it because, 'You're trying to make me a lesbian.' That's the automatic response, and she wouldn't have any of that." Ultimately, when this transsexual told her children of her desire to live as a woman, she was forced from the home, rejected by her daughter, and minimally tolerated by her son.

Wives' outright rejection of transgenderism tended to be based upon gender ideologies rooted in religious beliefs, fears that the husband wanted to become a woman, and homophobia. Because most individuals wanted to maintain relations with their wives and children, they experienced strong pressures to purge, hide their transgenderism, and maintain a masculine persona within the marriage. Many transgendered individuals worried they might be gay, and wives equated cross-dressing and femininity with male homosexuality. Other wives feared that their husbands would become women, thus transforming the relationship to one of lesbianism. Clearly, these fears were based in assumptions about sex, gender, sexuality, and the role requirements of women and men within marital relationships.

Even during periods of conditional acceptance, social distancing by others, or threatened or actual rejection, transgendered individuals worked to maintain their relationships while making social space for their feminine selves. Many mixed conformity with resistance in a cyclical pattern—conformity - resistance - revelation - repression—until resolving the issue through compromise or ending the relationship. Some purged, throwing out all their feminine accouterments and promising never to cross-dress again. Such resolutions were almost always short-lived. For example, one pre-operative transsexual, divorced after twenty-eight years of marriage, described telling her wife about her cross-dressing approximately four years into their marriage:

Just the frustration, the guilt, the loneliness of [cross-dressing], which I . . . didn't understand. I was lonely to a frustration level where I felt like I had to confess . . . I told her that first time. She was angry, of course. During the course of that conversation I promised to quit. I went outside and burned what few clothes I had. . . . I remember that it was at least a year before I really felt like she was civil again to me. In the course of the next twenty-four years, I promised to quit. That would last, we're talking days, not any length of time at all. . . . It would build up to such a frustration level again, months and months down the road, that I would tell her again.

Although interactional pressures to conform were intense, and transgendered individuals sought to maintain relationships with wives and children, masculine role obligations brought additional pressures. In order to maintain any semblance of a relationship with wives and children, even if they were estranged, respondents felt the need to fulfill their roles as husbands, fathers, and providers. To do that, they had to separate transgenderism from their jobs and other vestiges of their public lives. For example, one cross-dresser, separated at the time of our interview, and whose marriage ultimately ended in divorce, explained:

> I have to be realistic. I have a job. My employer has certain expectations. I have a mortgage and a car payment and two kids and my wife. I can't take the pay cut.

Another pre-operative transsexual, still married and living with her wife at the time of our interview, explained her desire to continue to provide for her family while her wife gained job skills and until the children grew up and left home. The situation was difficult. Understanding her loved ones' reactions was exhausting. At home, she dressed as a woman, although during our visit, her children called her "dad." . . . She explained the conflict she experienced between her wife's pressure to make her conform, her own desires to maintain relationships and fulfill her roles as husband, father, and provider, and her quest for complete transformation to her true self:

> [My wife] doesn't realize how close she's coming to driving me away. She refuses to call me [by my feminine name]. She doesn't call me by my old name, either. She refers to me only as 'he.'

Over time, many in our sample accepted rejection and placed their identity needs above their desire to maintain relationships. Still, they blamed themselves for the rejection and often sought ways to mend old relationships or help others cope with the loss.

Throughout their lives, our respondents had to choose between repressing their authentic selves or risking the loss of important statuses, roles, and relationships. They had to choose between conforming to or resisting the gender binary. Such pressures were powerful forces, limiting the formation and presentation of alternative identities. Summarizing how and why she hid her feelings and repressed what she knew to be her true identity for many years, one pre-operative transsexual explained: "The things that held me back would have been my commitment to family and job, that feeling that I had to maintain a certain degree of acceptability in order to protect my family and my job." Maintaining a "degree of acceptability" in the family of procreation was central to maintaining legitimacy as a social actor, just as it was in the family of origin and in other arenas defined as central to maintaining a sense of community and self.

Transgendered adults strived to maintain relationships with parents and siblings. When possible, the majority hid their transgenderism from their families of origin, sometimes to prevent what they thought would be the inevitable rejection, and others to protect aging parents from the shock: "My mother has rarely seen me, and that is by my choice. Because of her condition, I don't want that responsibility resting on me if it were to cause her to have another stroke or heart attack" (pre-operative transsexual).

Among those living full time as women (or who were publicly known to be transgendered), concealing transgenderism from family members meant breaking off relations and losing an important potential source of validation. Often this involved moving away, limiting contact, or dressing more androgynously in family members' presence. Most respondents, however, did whatever they could to maintain relationships with families of origin. Still, rejection was the norm; they were told not to call or come home, written out of wills, and generally abandoned and rejected. Those rejected or ostracized by family members were hurt, but they placed identity issues above relationship maintenance and sought to fill their lives with "family members of choice." Those able to maintain relationships with their families of origin felt confirmed in their newly emergent gender identities when family members accepted or tolerated them. For example, one post-operative transsexual talked about being able to explore childhood issues and memories with her mother:

> I called Mom and said, 'Would you like to come down to [my sister's]? I've got some questions I would like to ask you.' She came down. She walked in the door and she liked to fell out. This was the first time she had ever seen her son dressed. . . .

For those who defined spirituality or religion as central to their lives and identities, rejection by church members or the church itself was particularly common and troublesome. Nonetheless, individuals worked to find ways to maintain church membership and their relationships with church leaders and members while disclosing their transgenderism. Several came out to their pastors or priests and explained that they would like to begin coming to church as women. Negative reactions predominated. . . .

Most of those who defined religion as important attended churches that very strongly supported a binary conceptualization of sex and gender and defined homosexuality and transgenderism as sinful. Nonetheless, the desire to maintain such church memberships and to be accepted by others of similar faith was strong. Those who were asked to leave the church or told not to come back felt a strong sense of loss, even though they found new churches to attend and faiths in which to participate. Losses that resulted from resistance were painful, even when they entailed relationships that most strongly encouraged conformity.

In each of the examples given, transgendered individuals were under enormous pressure to conform to traditional gender presentations for males. While they often gave the appearance of conformity, in each instance, they devised ways to express themselves, either secretly as children or married

adults, or more openly, as when they informed wives, parents, and children of their transgenderism and negotiated the conditions under which they could enact their feminine selves. Those rejected by families or excluded from participation in their religious faith developed "families of choice" or cultivated more open, accepting religious traditions. Even with these pressures to conform and their own desires to be "normal" and to "purge" themselves of transgenderism, the people in our sample devised ways to resist and survive the strong sanctions of the gender binary.

Self-Preservation Pressures

Self-preservation pressures are social forces compelling individuals to conform to the gender binary in order to maintain their physical and economic security. Unlike the stigma and rejection that emanate from interpersonal relationships, self-preservation issues may pressure transgendered individuals either to conform to traditional manhood or to transition to complete, convincing womanhood. Physical safety pressures included fear of physical or verbal assault. Such fears were occasionally confirmed by actual events, but more often by others' stories of experiencing violence and harassment. Economic pressures included difficulties in finding and keeping employment. Among those who publicly transformed from men to full-time transgenderism or womanhood, job loss was very common.

Economic Self-Preservation.   In industrial and post-industrial societies maintaining employment and economic well-being is important to individual survival. Further, one's job or career can be an important component of identity. Particularly for those individuals wishing to live full-time as women, transition required economic resources that were often threatened when public transformation began. While on-the-job transformations did not inhibit the inherent ability to perform job duties, employers' fears of stigma and the disruption that came from the reactions of other employees, customers, clients, and the general public frequently resulted in demotion and job loss. Economic and employment difficulties varied, depending on the type and stage of individual transformation. Generally speaking, most transsexuals and gender radicals in our sample had lost or voluntarily left the jobs they held when they began to transition and were either unemployed or underemployed when we met them. By contrast, cross-dressers, who tended to separate their transgenderism from their jobs, continued to be fully employed at the jobs for which they were educated or trained.

Transgendered individuals trying to transition on the job often faced unanticipated dilemmas and complex issues. Determining the best way to inform an employer of the desire to transition was difficult; anticipated rejection caused great anxiety and often postponement of full transformation. One pre-operative transsexual, who lived part-time as a woman, explained her reluctance to live full-time as a woman: "I couldn't deal with the rejection of it, the shame of it, losing my job, things like that. If I could just do it, [have surgery and transform overnight] I would do it." Those who chose no transition to full-time womanhood occasionally left their jobs voluntarily or used involuntary unemployment (e.g., layoffs) as opportunities to learn new skills, begin new careers, or transition in college. When individuals left one job, began transition to full-time womanhood, and sought new employment, they often found jobs that paid less, had less prestige, and offered less security.

More common than such opportunistic transitions, transsexuals attempted to begin living full-time as women on the job. The most understanding employers expected full-time immediate transformation. Unlike the pressures at home, that tended to be cyclical, those at work were more linear. Either the individual was fired or pressured to quit, or she was pressured to transform quickly and convincingly. For example, one employer of a pre-operative transsexual reacted to the employee telling him she wanted to transition on the job by saying, "'We're not going to see that other person [her

masculine self] again are we?' [She said], 'No.' [The employer] said, 'Fine. Go for it.'" Another self-identified pre-operative transsexual, still exploring gender issues and trying to determine how much femininity she needed to incorporate into her identity and persona to feel comfortable, met with support when she informed her employer. Nonetheless, the support turned into pressure to transform to a full feminine self and to stop living between genders:

After you come out to people, they almost expect it and they want to see [the feminine self]. And like my boss, he wanted a date to begin with that I would change to being female. And I told him, "I don't want to give you a date because there may not be a date. I might be in the middle ground for a little while and then one day I might go into a little more make-up and a little more dressing." . . . The bathroom issue came up and he was scared that people were going to get all freaked out if I started using the women's bathroom, and if a woman read me and got uncomfortable, they might complain to the police or someone and I could get arrested. . . . He said, "Give me a date that you're going to do this. . . . [We're] going to try and make a bathroom for you." . . . And so I just picked a date. It got closer and closer and I was like, "I don't think I'm ready." . . . My boss came up and said, "You've got your bathroom. When are you coming in dressed?" I said, "I may not be ready even though that bathroom exists." . . . He said, "You know, we did this on the premise that you were going to do this."

Living outside the binary—as a male who had told others she was a woman, even though she did not present as a woman—made even accepting, supportive others uncomfortable. For many, the binary is all that is known or conceivable regarding sex and gender. Consequently, encountering those who resist, or worse, seem to challenge the binary is confusing and frightening. As a result, living outside the binary was extremely difficult and potentially dangerous for all who tried it.

Even tolerant employers limited transgendered employees' interaction with the public until they were able to pass convincingly as women. Some individuals were reassigned to jobs where contact with the public would be limited or eliminated. One was placed on involuntary paid leave and told she could not return to work until she had completed SRS. After recovering from surgery, she was offered a severance package to terminate her employment. While relieved to finally be able to openly express her feminine self, she expressed deep remorse at the loss of her career and that aspect of her identity.

While some acceptance or tolerance by coworkers and employers occurred, rejection and harassment were more common: "I was literally crucified on the job there everyday. It just finally got to where I couldn't take it anymore and I just walked off the job one day" (post-operative transsexual). Others were not harassed, but simply fired:

> When I was starting hormones, and as my chest started to develop, my boss started giving me these looks and finally asked me into the office. . . . Two days later I was called back into the office and the first thing he said was, "This is not because you're a transsexual, but you are being fired." (pre-operative transsexual)

For those unable to maintain employment during transition, finding another job could be arduous. Individuals either needed to come out as a transgendered individual, reconstruct a work history as a female, or account for their lack of employment history. Most began seeking jobs in their original areas of expertise but, as their economic situations worsened, accepted work doing almost anything. Being unable to conceal one's past as a man made getting and keeping even menial jobs difficult. When transgendered individuals could find jobs, they often had difficulty keeping them because they had not yet perfected their ability to pass as women. Those in a period of gender exploration, or who desired to enact a gendered self that was neither man nor woman, faced ubiquitous pressure to be one or the other. Those who knew they were women but could not yet pass faced economic pressures to perfect their feminine presentations. For example, a pre-operative transsexual lost her job as an administrator for a large insurance company when she requested permission to transition on the job. After being fired, she found a job at a convenience store where she began working as a man. After proving her ability to do the job, she came out to her boss and requested permission to come to work as a woman. After several weeks of coming to work as her feminine self, she again faced the question of how she could survive if she was to be herself:

> [The first few days] I thought things went pretty good. [Then] complaint after complaint after complaint to the manager. . . . Customers coming in and some people reading me and they're getting complaints. . . . [My boss] said, 'First of all . . . it's not your work. I wish I had ten people that worked the way you do. But I've got to terminate you for the good of the store.'

The economic institution, like the family and religion, demands conformity to the gender binary. Still, even knowing their economic security would be threatened, transsexuals sought the freedom to be their feminine selves on the job. The pressure to transform convincingly was simply another expression of the pressure to conform to, and not resist, the gender binary.

Physical Self-Preservation Pressures. Self-preservation includes significant pressures that arise from individuals' attempts to avoid violence. Violence permeates American society, and marginalized members bear the heaviest share of violent victimization. As persons marginalized by both mainstream society and other marginalized (e.g., gay) communities, persons known (or accidentally discovered) to be transgendered are at a heightened risk of harassment and violent attack.

There have been well-publicized instances of assaults and murders of transgendered individuals across the country, with some of the most extensive coverage in the gay and transgender media. While information about assaults, murders, and violation of civil rights is frequently circulated in order to generate moral outrage and social protest, fear is often the outcome, creating another pressure to either conceal transgenderism or to transform convincingly to the other gender.

Similar to transsexuals' experiences on the job, those individuals who publicly presented an alternative gender commonly reported harassment. However, the public often reacted with threats and physical assault. While verbal harassment was problematic, transgendered individuals' greatest concerns involved physical safety:

> I went to the movie theater and some young punk about thirteen years old comes waltzing up to me yelling at the top of his voice, 'Faggot!' I'm sure it was to show off to some of his buddies, 'Hi, Fag. How ya doin'? Want a date? Are you queer?' I was scared. I was petrified. (non-operative transsexual who lived full-time as a woman)

All our respondents recognized that being unable to "pass" increased the likelihood of harassment, threats, or attack while in public:

> I was walking to the store and there was a large group of people that were standing in a huddled circle. I walked past and there was a lot of comments. By the time I crossed the street, I felt a sharp pain in my back and realized that someone had thrown a rock and hit me in the back with it. I basically had to crawl into the store. (pre-operative transsexual, who knew from experience that she was not yet able to pass)

Her life was later threatened by her neighbors and she was physically assaulted while in the process of moving from her neighborhood.

Even those who believed they could pass reported having feared for their safety. As fears of an attack for transgenderism relaxed, fears of being assaulted as women increased. When individuals transformed from masculine to feminine gender presentations, their perceptions of vulnerability increased. Those who went out in public commonly reported taking extra safety measures, such as parking their cars in well-lighted areas, getting their keys out before

arriving at their cars or doors, walking in pairs or groups, or restricting their nighttime activities. For "passable" pre- and non-operative transsexuals, the fear of sexual assault was compounded by anxiety that the incongruity between sex and gender would be discovered:

> Dressed as I am, I have the same problems women have being attacked. . . . Then I have the added problem, assuming the attacker is somebody that has very low standards all the way around, when he does find out I'm not what he thought I was, there's an added problem of him taking his vengeance out on me for that reason. (non-operative transsexual who had little difficulty passing)

Transgendered individuals who have not had sex reassignment surgery who successfully pass as the other sex are presumed to have genitals congruent with the gender they present. Relying on assumptions that gender is indicative of sex, they socially construct, in the minds of others, the presence of appropriately sexed bodies. Those attempting to pass without SRS fear that, if their secret is discovered, they will be in even greater danger than women. Reports of murders, assaults, harassment, and civil rights violations made many of our respondents fearful of going out in public. Those who overcame their fear were concerned first with protecting themselves by passing as women; second, with protecting the secret of their socially constructed genitals; and third, with protecting themselves from the dangers all women face. Thus, fears of violence and concerns with physical self-preservation pressured individuals to conform to binary conceptualizations and presentations of sex and gender. Despite these fears, transgendered individuals devised ways to go out in public and to be recognized and validated as their feminine selves.

Identity Achievement Pressures

The desire to understand, achieve, and publicly express an authentically real self motivated transgendered individuals to risk relationships, jobs, and physical safety. Initially, most repressed their transgenderism. Tentatively, they sought ways to enact their feminine selves, most commonly within their understandings of the binary system of gender. Most believed that, to be feminine, they must look like or be women. Transgendered individuals' understandings of themselves and their ability to formulate alternative identities depended upon existing cultural categories as well as institutional pressures to be one gender or the other. Like the individual pressured by her boss to make a complete transformation, transgendered individuals seldom have the freedom to live between genders. In the process of coming out to oneself and formulating a clear understanding of self, individuals' understandings and identities are coopted into existing, if emergent, cultural categories. The individual cannot understand the self outside a cultural context, nor can she or he be recognized as an ungendered person.

Although there is an attempt to move outside binary understandings of sex and gender, as individuals rebel against pressures to enact traditional masculinity, they move into a state where they must construct an alternative gender identity—one that is recognizable within the dominant cultural discourse on gender and existing institutionalized categories. Most transgendered individuals lack the cultural resources necessary to live between genders or outside the gender binary, though many were innovative in sidestepping some of the gendered requirements of most institutions.

Social Erasure.   When participating in everyday activities, (driving a car or cashing a check), cross-dressers, non- and pre-operative transsexuals, and gender radicals confronted the incongruity between the sex assignment on their driver's license or other identification and the feminine gender they enacted. Those willing to undergo medical scrutiny, and who subsequently were diagnosed as transsexual, could receive documentation to legally change the assigned sex on some, if not all, their legal documents. (Laws regarding the documentation necessary to change sex categories on legal documents, as well as regulating which documents may be changed, vary from state to state.) Those wishing to avoid medical diagnosis or intervention had greater difficulty, but were innovative in changing their legal sex from one category to the only other available. A common strategy among pre-operative transsexuals in our sample was to file for a legal name change. Upon receiving legal documentation of the change to a feminine name, they applied for a new driver's license. Several reported that clerks responsible for altering the driver's license inquired whether the individual wished to have the sex changed as well. Such documentation provided greater security for those needing legal documentation to prove their identity, but of course, also placed them at risk should the truth about their socially constructed genitals be discovered. Further, the ability to enact feminine presentations as a man (e.g., by wearing a skirt and a beard) was dangerous and the option of being assigned into a category as a male woman was impossible.

Legal transformations were expected to be complete and permanent, and thus were not available to cross-dressers or those wishing to live between genders or as both genders. Those exploring gender, temporarily enacting a feminine self, living between genders, or wishing to forego medical and legal reassignment had more difficulty than transsexuals willing to have their identities verified and validated through medical and legal channels; nonetheless, the former were innovative in their resistance. Cross-dressers told us about the extreme care they exercised while driving, primarily because they feared the reactions of officers demanding to see their (male) driver's licenses. Many individuals informally shortened their birth names to facilitate living between genders: James became Jamie, Patrick, Pat, and Richard, Ricki. Of course, not all had the luxury of adopting names that allowed such gender versatility. Some retired individuals lived most of their lives as women, going out in public as their masculine selves only to transact business. Those wishing to preserve a social place for themselves, and to avoid erasure within institutions that required them to be one gender or the other, had to either conceal their transgenderism (like cautious-driving cross-dressers) or to completely and permanently transform themselves to the other gender category. Living between genders was possible, but the loss of statuses—as employees, family members, church members, and citizens—eroded their social positions, potentially leading to their erasure as social actors.

As transgendered individuals begin to come out to themselves, they search for ways to understand who they are, in part, by seeking others similar to themselves and searching for socially recognized identity categories (see Gagné et al. 1997). Not only are they marginalized and stigmatized, but as "not women/not men," they lose their positions within family and community, important sources of identity verification and validation in society. Adopting a transgendered identity allows those whose gender falls outside the binary to find a social place, albeit in a highly stigmatized and marginalized status, within a community of perceived similar others. Once alternatively gendered individuals adopt a transgendered identity, however, they are pressured to adhere to the norms and values associated with their new social status. Resistance to the gender binary has conformity pressures of its own.

Community Pressures.   Aside from the individual's desire to realize and achieve a true sense of self, the pressure to actualize a socially recognizable identity emanates from society and the transgender community itself. Within the masculine-to-feminine transgender community there were only two non-deviant ways of presenting oneself: as an individual desirous of passing as a woman or as a woman. Most commonly, those who could not pass as women were relegated to subordinate positions within both mainstream and transgendered communities. Those new to transgenderism were encouraged to perfect their feminine presentations, while those unable to pass were informally sanctioned and ostracized within local transgender support groups and organizations. Common to support group meetings and national conferences were sessions by pro-

fessionals offering advice on make-up, clothing, body language, walk, and voice. Newsletter advice columns on similar matters written by transgendered individuals were common. Within mainstream society, as well as the gay/lesbian community, transgendered individuals have been marginalized and ostracized. In their effort to achieve social legitimacy and respectability within mainstream society, most try to attain acceptance by "passing" and downplaying their gender "difference." . . .

Community is central to formation and maintenance of alternative identity (Taylor and Whittier 1992). While those who adopt a transgender identity and work to perfect feminine presentations are marginalized, they do receive the support of community members; those who fall outside the gender binary are marginalized as deviants within the transgender community and pressured to conform to traditional notions of feminine presentation. Nonetheless, individuals whose physical characteristics (e.g., height, muscularity) made it difficult or impossible to pass as women continued to attend support group meetings and devise other social spaces where they could enact a feminine self. In our interactions within the transgender community, however, we noted that although more passable individuals were cordial to those who could not pass while in private settings, they often refused to be seen with them in public, often fearing that such association would make themselves more detectable.

When immersed in a community of like-minded others, the perceived norms of that community can be very powerful, and in the case of transgenderism, could be defining elements in identity transformation. When the community of presumably similar and accepting others suggests that membership is conditioned upon achieving certain characteristics and behaviors, new members have a tendency to accept the judgments and perspectives of existing members. When individuals exploring transgenderism and searching for a comfortable identity and style of presentation first locate and initiate interactions with a transgender community, they often believe that they have found the only few others who "truly understand" and accept them for who they are. Therefore, being accepted by these others is highly valued, and the norms that structure this newly discovered community become important. Perhaps more importantly, the community's values and belief system are believed to be correct and to deserve conformity.

Realizing that others are not likely to be tolerant or accepting, the search for support focuses on the transgender community. Consequently, messages that convey rejection or marginalization may hasten identity development. Pressures took the form of suggestions that individuals adhere to the support group's norm of coming to meetings cross-dressed and explore the limits of their transgenderism by considering transsexualism as a potential identity option. Those with a strong desire to be treated in a feminine manner, recognizing that support might be withheld when transition is less than complete, experienced strong pressures to identify as a transgendered person and achieve a convincing feminine presentation. For example, upon first finding and interacting within the transgender community, an individual who at the time defined herself as a cross-dresser reported that transsexuals in her support group began pushing her to explore transsexualism:

> They immediately . . . encouraged me to even start more intensively working through this, thinking about it, reading up, getting more knowledge about the transvestite and transsexual community and to get more knowledge about both of them. And they encouraged me to get more experience, living on weekends and what not to see what kind of effect that would have.

Today she identifies as a non-operative transsexual. Although many support groups accept and support cross-dressers, the transgender community generally defines transsexuals as somehow more "real" than cross-dressers, and their issues take higher priority. Further, because many cross-dressers eventually re-identified

as transsexuals, there was underlying, often unspoken, pressure on cross-dressers to test the limits of their transgenderism.

Transgendered individuals are agents in the creation of an alternative self, but not in a social context or community of their own making. They are pressured by, and react against, institutional constraints and dominant ideologies about masculinity, femininity, sex, and gender. As individuals explore alternative gender identities and presentations, facing social stigma and erasure from mainstream society and pressure to pass from the community, the goal of the overwhelming majority becomes recognition and treatment as a woman, the only acceptable way to enact a feminine self in a binary system. Although most in our sample originally resisted the dictates of the gender binary, the achievement of an identity that is recognized by others requires conformity to the binary system. What once seemed possible only via resistance, in the end is only attainable through conformity.

In addition to the acceptance and legitimation individuals receive from the community and others, being feminine and treated as a woman entails a freedom from the internalized constraints of masculinity, a chance to experience a wider array of emotions, and an opportunity to relax and be themselves: "The shackles of pretending to be something I'm not are gone. I don't have to be macho, tough . . . I can be soft, I can cry. I can feel" (pre-operative transsexual). Most respondents' gender belief systems were affected by a lifetime of socialization and negative reactions from others when they attempted to elicit feminine treatment without full transformation:

> You have to understand that I was a child of the 50s and 60s. That whole part of me had to be segmented off. Men didn't cook. Men didn't clean. Men didn't cry. Men weren't spontaneous in their affections. There was a whole part of men that was pushed back. (post-operative transsexual)

But they did not passively internalize and accept dominant ideologies about masculinity. They sought ways to express a feminine self, albeit within an emergent cultural system that suggested that feminine men must either be homosexuals or women. While masculinity was seen as constraining, achieving femininity and having it verified by others meant obtaining gender freedom and a different perspective of the social world. Escaping into a feminine persona was an active, creative way of expressing a sense of self that society expected would be repressed.

In addition to the perceived emotional and behavioral freedoms, romantic and sexual interactions were also altered. Respondents reported that they enjoyed having men treat them as "ladies." Transgendered individuals most frequently sought out others who would interact with them according to traditional masculine norms. Although as individuals they rejected the compulsory congruence of sex and gender, their enactments of new gender within the binary system lets them achieve a new identity and have it recognized and validated by others:

> This older man took me home and he treated me very much in a feminine role, and that felt so comfortable. He treated me the way I saw men treating their wives. The way he talked to me, he was the leader. He'd say, 'Let's do this now,' and kind of guide me along. (post-operative transsexual)

Such masculine attentions, defined as ideal to receive, were the sorts of acts transgendered individuals found uncomfortable to perform when they were presenting themselves as men. They did not reject masculinity as part of the gender binary; they simply expressed a preference for being accepted as feminine by others. They accepted the binary system; it was only their original placement within the binary that disturbed and dismayed most respondents.

Lorber (1994:85) asserts: "The final rite of passage is not only passing as a visibly and legally identifiable gendered person with a bonafide kinship status but passing as a *sexual* person" (emphasis in original). In this way, a primary focus of identity achievement is to thoroughly fulfill the roles and emotional experiences associated with femininity. Among our sample, this

focus was so strong that when anatomical males, presenting themselves as men, engaged in sexual activity with males, they universally found such interactions distasteful. However, when anatomical males presented themselves as women and were accepted and treated as such, even when their partners knew them to be male, they tended to report the gendered aspects of sexual interactions as enjoyable, whether they were with females or males. Even if they found the actual sexual activity distasteful, they enjoyed being treated as women and found that sexual interactions verified them as women. For example, one post-operative transsexual lesbian described her first sexual interaction as a woman with a female (before she had undergone SRS):

> Even though I did not really find this person very attractive, she was forceful and she was directive and taking more of a leading role and telling me what to do and how to be. . . . I didn't feel masculine with her. She accepted that female part of me. I didn't have to be male with her. Being sexual with her was very different. It was easy to think of it as other than male-female.

Similarly, a self-identified heterosexual, pre-operative transsexual who lives full time as a woman said, "I want a man that wants me as a woman. If he doesn't want me as a woman, I have no desire for him." And a self-identified bisexual, post-operative transsexual explained: "I believe I would like to play the traditional female role, whether it's with a man or a woman. I guess I would like to have my femininity confirmed."

For transsexuals, one of the greatest barriers to confirmation as sexual women was the presence of male genitalia. For most transgendered individuals, finding intimate and sexual partners who accepted and loved them for themselves was, to say the least, difficult. Many transsexuals postponed looking for an intimate partner and avoided finding one, feeling they could not become involved sexually until they had undergone sex reassignment surgery and were "complete" as women:

I'm happy the way I am now. The only problem is basically I cannot please a man sexually and I cannot live in the regular life, the life everybody else lives. I can't date men that don't know about me because I don't have the right equipment. (pre-operative transsexual)

Despite the acceptance some anatomical males may have received as women, the lack of the "right equipment" was perceived by some as a pressure to alter their bodies to meet gendered expectations. To achieve true womanhood, they needed to conceal a transgendered past, except as they perceived that others needed to know.

CONCLUSION

The binary gender system of western industrial and post-industrial societies interprets the body as a predictor of who the person will be. Such assumptions begin at birth, and with prenatal testing, may start even before the body's formation is completed. The body, then, is an integral aspect of the self, presented to the world and to which the social world reacts. For transgendered individuals, however, the body often announces a self that does not exist.

Transgendered individuals' consciousness of self is limited to possibilities available within the dominant discourse and those emergent in transgender subcultures. It is against the former that they react, and within the confines of both that they actualize a true self. Constrained by the fear of rejection and the desire for self-preservation, transgendered individuals initially formulate understandings of themselves within the gender binary, frequently believing their gender identity to be something "very, very wrong." As a result, they try to repress the feminine self and force themselves to conform to masculine expectations, or to avoid interactions with others when they believe their masculine presentations will fail. Ultimately, however, the individuals in our sample were compelled forward by the need to enact, and ultimately actualize, an alternatively gendered authentic self. Initially they enacted femininity secretively. Over time,

they created ever-widening social spaces for these performances. But gender, and by consequence gender identity, may only be achieved in interaction with others. To actualize an authentic self, transgendered individuals must come out to significant others, interact with others in public, and achieve the alternative gender within kinship, religious, legal, economic, and other salient statuses. In order to avoid social erasure, they must express themselves within a recognizable idiom.

Transgendered individuals provide important lessons on the power dynamics of gender, as well as the possibility of resistance to the binary gender system's encroachment into the consciousness and identity of social actors. The presentation of alternative gender is an act of resistance to the expectation that sex determines gender. Although many conform to binary expectations that feminine individuals will be female, by actively transforming from one gender to the other, they create the social presence of a third gender category, in this case women who were or are male. But this alternative gender discourse is neither "subservient to power or raised up against it" (Foucault 1990:100). The overwhelming majority of the transgendered individuals we interviewed only wanted the freedom to be themselves and be accepted as who they were. They placed a high premium on trying to preserve relationships while devising ways to be themselves. Theirs was not an open rebellion against the institution of gender; rather, their acts of resistance were quests to find room to be themselves within a system that made no space for them. Their desires to maintain relationships and to survive, both physically and economically, and to join a community of potentially accepting others, led them to refine their definitions of self to fit within recognized, albeit highly marginalized, transgender categories and try to quickly perfect their feminine presentations. To the extent their gender resistance received public notice, it challenged the social dictum that sex determines gender. Through their refusal to enact masculine presentations of self, transgendered individuals successfully challenge the social recognition of two and only two gender categories. Cross-dressers, transsexuals, and other types of trans-gendered individuals are now routinely recognized, if still highly marginalized, in western society.

Nonetheless, because the attempt to actualize an identity and associated acts of resistance transpire in a social context not of their own making, transgendered individuals are limited in their ability to enact an alternatively gendered self that is not recognizable within the institutionalized gender idiom. While there are a few gender radicals who live as openly transgendered individuals and enact gender presentations that are neither masculine nor feminine, our research demonstrates the ubiquity of the binary system's dictate that all social actors "do gender and do it right," as well as the limited impact of gender resistance.

While the possibility of immediate, radical transformation of the gender binary is doubtful, our research suggests that the gender binary, imposed upon all individuals in all facets of life, is susceptible to acts of everyday resistance. While transgendered individuals form a small minority, their creative insistence on actualizing an authentic self whose gender differs from the sex assigned at birth, presents a challenge to the dictate that sex "causes," or is "naturally" or biologically linked to gender. Instead, the experiences of transgendered individuals suggest that gender is a continuum that does not always correlate with sex in accordance with traditional expectations. A significant minority of the population experiences a gendered self that does not fit within, and is not able to conform to, normative expectations of sex and gender. It is through the creative insistence of such individuals that the freedom to actualize an authentic self will be safeguarded.

REFERENCES

BARTKY, SANDRA. 1990. Femininity and Domination: Studies in the Phenomenology of Oppression. New York: Routledge.

BORDO, SUSAN. 1989. "The body and the reproduction of femininity: A feminist appropriation of Foucault." In Gender/Body/Knowledge, eds., Alison Jaggar and Susan Bordo, 13–33 New Brunswick, New Jersey: Rutgers University Press.

BULLOUGH, VERN L., and BONNIE BULLOUGH. 1993. Cross Dressing, Sex, and Gender. Philadelphia: University of Pennsylvania Press.

CHARMAZ, KATHY. 1983. "The grounded theory method: An explication and interpretation." In Contemporary Field Research, ed., Robert Emerson, 109–126. Boston, Massachusetts: Little, and Brown.

CHESLER, PHYLLIS. 1989. Women and Madness. New York: Harcourt Brace Jovanovich.

DAVIS, KATHY. 1995. Reshaping the Female Body: The Dilemma of Cosmetic Surgery. New York: Routledge.

FOUCAULT, MICHEL. 1990. The History of Sexuality: An Introduction, Volume I. New York: Vintage Books.

GAGNÉ, PATRICIA, AND RICHARD TEWKSBURY. 1996. "No 'man's' land: Transgenderism and the stigma of the feminine man." In Advances in Gender Research, Vol. 1, eds., Marcia Texler Segal and Vasilikie Demos, 115–156. Greenwich, Connecticut: JAI Press.

GAGNÉ, PATRICIA, RICHARD TEWKSBURY, AND DEANNA McGAUGHEY. 1997. "Coming out and crossing over: Identity formation and proclamation in a transgender community." Gender & Society 11:478–508.

COLLINS, PATRICIA HILL. 1990. Black Feminist Thought: Knowledge, Consciousness, and the Politics of Empowerment. London: HarperCollinsAcademic.

KANTER, ROSABETH MOSS. 1977. Men and Women of the Corporation. New York: Basic Books.

KOHLBERG, LAWRENCE. 1966. "A cognitive-developmental analysis of children's sex-role concepts and attitudes." In The Development of Sex Differences, ed., Eleanor E. Maccoby, 93–120. Stanford, California: Stanford University Press.

LORBER, JUDITH. 1994. Paradoxes of Gender. New Haven, Connecticut: Yale University Press.

MASON-SCHROCK, DOUG. 1996. "Transsexuals' narrative construction of a 'true self.'" Social Psychology Quarterly 59:176–192.

RICHARDSON, LAUREL. 1988. The Dynamics of Sex and Gender: A Sociological Perspective. New York: Harper Collins.

SCHUR, EDWIN M. 1984. Labeling Women Deviant: Gender, Stigma, and Social Control. Philadelphia: Temple University Press.

SEGAL, EDWIN. 1997. Personal communication.

SMITH, DOROTHY. 1990. Texts, Facts and Femininity: Exploring the Relations of Ruling. New York: Routledge.

TAYLOR, VERTA, AND NANCY WHITTIER. 1992. "Collective identity and social movement communities: Lesbian feminist mobilization." In Frontiers in Social Movement Theory, eds. Aldon D. Morris and Carol McClurg Mueller, 104–129. New Haven, Connecticut: Yale University Press.

TEWKSBURY, RICHARD, AND PATRICIA GAGNÉ. 1996. "Transgenderists: Products of non-normative intersections of sex, gender and sexuality." The Journal of Men's Studies 5:105–129.

TURNER, RALPH H. 1976. "The real self: From institution to impulse." American Journal of Sociology 81:989–1014.

WEST, CANDACE, AND SARAH FENSTERMAKER. 1995. "Doing difference." Gender and Society 9:8–37.

WEST, CANDACE, AND DON ZIMMERMAN. 1987. "Doing gender." Gender and Society 1:125–151.

WILSON, EDWARD O. 1975. Sociobiology: The New Synthesis. Cambridge, Massachusetts: Harvard University Press.

CRITICAL THINKING QUESTIONS

1. Gagné and Tewksbury argue that our society is governed by a "gender binary." Explain what this means and how it pressures everyone (not just transgenders) to conform to gender norms.

2. Compare and contrast the institutional barriers to full participation in society that transgenders face with those encountered by gay men and lesbians.

3. In your opinion, should transgenders attempt to align themselves politically with gay men, lesbians, and bisexuals in order to gain legal protection from discrimination? Should they align themselves with women or the civil rights movement? Why or why not?

Getting Involved

1. Locate a public housing community in your area. Go there with a friend or two and drive or walk around. Make note of the race and gender of the people you see there. Describe the physical condition of the housing and the public areas surrounding it, including lawns, parking lots, playgrounds, and trash facilities. If you feel comfortable doing so, ask residents about the quality of their individual units and their opinion of the quality of maintenance in the community as a whole.

2. Contact a temporary agency in your area and inquire about placement opportunities for yourself, as well as the availability of fringe benefits such as vacation and sick leave, health insurance, and retirement benefits.

3. Look through your university's directory and make note—judging according to names—the gender of individuals who hold positions as president, vice-president, provost, and dean. Go to the library at your university and ask to see the public records that list the salaries of these officials. What patterns do you see in these upper-level management positions at your university, and in the compensation of these administrators?

Site-Seeing

1. For more information on fair housing, visit **http://www.fairhousing.com.**

2. To learn more about issues facing Native Americans, visit **http://www.doi.gov/ bureau-indian-affairs.html.**

3. For more information on equal employment opportunities, visit **http:// www.eeoc.gov/index.html.**

4. To learn more about barriers that women face in gaining access to upper-level management positions, go to **http://www.va.gov.1vaemployee/gccinfo.htm.**

INSTITUTIONAL BARRIERS TO EQUALITY IN HEALTH CARE

People without access to health care are at an economic disadvantage. Without health insurance or the means to pay a physician, people put off going to a doctor until what might have been an easily treated ailment becomes a serious—even life-threatening—condition. With regular checkups, medication, and proper medical care, chronic illnesses such as high blood pressure or diabetes can be managed relatively easily, and acute diseases such as cancer or tuberculosis can be detected and treated early. Unequal access to health care means that poor people get less care than those who are well insured. Moreover, because they are over-represented among the poor, people in certain racial and ethnic categories, such as Native Americans, African-Americans, and Hispanics, on average die younger than whites and are more likely to see their children die within the first two years of life.

Unequal access to health care is only part of the problem. Poor people often live in inadequate housing, eat inadequate diets, and are subject to a number of environmental factors—such as pollution, lead paint, and violence—that put their health and lives at risk. Even when the poor, racial and ethnic minorities, women, or gay men and lesbians seek health care, doctors and nurses are likely to evaluate their health care needs on the basis of commonly held stereotypes and to overlook social factors affecting their health. All of this means that inequalities in health care are unavoidable because they are institutionalized.

As the six articles in the health care section show, health is not simply a matter of one's physical makeup or genetic heritage. Rather, the physical well-being, quality of life, ability to work, and indeed, even the length of a person's life, are significantly affected by the health care industry.

Unequal access to health care is the theme of the first article in this section. Josefson summarizes a study conducted at an emergency room in Atlanta, Georgia, where researchers compared the pain relief offered to patients with similar injuries. The study found that black patients were significantly more likely to receive no medication for pain, regardless of their ability to pay for care. The study shows how racial bias unconsciously affects the way that health care workers treat their patients and the quality of care that patients receive.

Treatment for pain is only one way in which prejudice and discrimination are entrenched in the health care system. In the second article, Rich presents statistics to document African-American men's poorer health, higher rates of preventable deaths, and inferior access to health care, as compared to other groups. Rich clearly documents a long history of racism in the institution of health care, as well as the role African-American men and women played in developing their own institutions of medical education and care. The author argues that improving the health of African-American men will depend upon improving access to medical insurance, eliminating the biases that alienate black men from seeking health care, increasing the number of African-American health care providers, and developing health care approaches that recognize the unique needs and challenges faced by African-American men.

When considering health and health care, we often think first about doctors and hospitals. But a number of other social factors—access to clean drinking water and nutritious food, for example—also have significant effects on health and well-being. In the third article, Sharfstein and Sandel explain the negative effects that homelessness and inadequate, unsafe, or overcrowded housing can have on the health of poor children. The authors provide statistics on the number of families living in inadequate housing, and they document the increased health care needs of poorly housed children as well as the difficulties these children have in completing school. Sharfstein and Sandel argue that medical insurance companies should pay for certain repairs to inadequate housing, such as the removal of lead paint. They maintain that the government needs to be more aggressive in ensuring that all children have access to safe, adequate places to live. In the long run, poor people would not be the only ones to benefit from such practices, they argue. Insurance companies would save money on claims, and more affluent people and their employers would save money on health insurance premiums.

The failure of government programs to efficiently and effectively provide poor people with adequate housing, food, or medical care is often based on the belief that providing aid will make them lazy. In this way, Scharfstein and Sandel show just one way that beliefs become institutionalized in government policy, which affects the nation's health and well-being. Similarly, beliefs affect the health of certain social groups, in part because they influence people's willingness to seek medical care, and in part because they affect the ways that care is provided. These beliefs affect even dominant social groups, including white, middle-class, heterosexual men. In the fourth article in the health section, Courtenay notes that, on average, men die younger than women. He argues that men associate health care with femininity just as they associate toughness, robustness, health, and not needing a doctor with masculinity. These cultural ideas are reinforced, according to Courtenay, by a number of social institutions, including medicine, which fails to deliver health education and health care in ways that appeal to men.

Courtenay argues that health care as an institution has failed to address the needs of men, but Gannon, in the fifth article in this section, maintains that the medical establishment has taken too close an interest in women's bodies. Medicine, she argues, has deemed as pathological certain normal female biological functions, thereby institutionalizing ideas about good and bad, right and wrong, when it comes to women and reproduction. By drawing upon a review of the medical literature, Gannon first explains how medicine exercises power over women by labeling certain events in the normal life course, such as menstruation and menopause, as illnesses. She further demonstrates that despite a scientific failure to show that commonly prescribed treatments work or are even needed, doctors continue to believe that women's reproductive cycles need to be medically managed and treated. Through the medical management of women's bodies, Gannon argues that the health care profession maintains its power, prestige, and profits. Rather than maintaining that doctors deliberately misdiagnose women, Gannon shows the power that commonly held beliefs hold over a profession that claims to believe scientific evidence over unproven myths. In this way, the author powerfully demonstrates how sexist beliefs have become institutionalized into health care policy.

Just as beliefs about what is natural or good have influenced health care policy, stereotypes and prejudice affect one-on-one interactions between health care providers and their patients. In the last article in the health care section, Stevens and Hall draw on interviews with lesbians to explore the experiences of this stigmatized group with receiving health care. The authors find that lesbians are frequently reluctant to seek health care because they are fearful of the treatment they will receive if providers learn of their sexual orientation. The authors provide quotations from the women in their sample to demonstrate some of the ways—including inferior treatment, rough handling, and a refusal to provide care—in which lesbians face discrimination in health care. When such discrimination is left unchecked, it becomes part of the medical institution. Because such behavior is unethical, it is extremely difficult to document.

The health care institution is critical to everyone's well-being, the quality of our day-to-day lives, and our very survival. As the articles in this section demonstrate, health care is not immune to institutionalized forms of discrimination. If anything, it presents itself as being above accusations of prejudice and discrimination by relying on claims that it adheres to scientific standards to determine the quality and content of the care providers give. Yet the articles in this section show just some of the ways that scientific standards are sidestepped and ethics overlooked when prejudices are deeply held and discriminatory treatment is firmly entrenched.

Reading 11

Pain Relief in US Emergency Rooms Is Related to Patients' Race

Deborah Josefson

In this article, Josefson reports on a study that found that African-Americans receive less pain relief in emergency rooms than do white patients.

Patients from ethnic minorities seen in emergency rooms are relatively undertreated for pain, according to a new study (*Annals of Emergency Medicine* 2000; 35:11–6, 77–81).

Doctors at Emory University School of Medicine, Atlanta, Georgia, conducted a retrospective analysis of the medical charts of 217 patients who had presented with long bone fractures to a single urban emergency department over 40 months.

Of the total, 127 patients were black and 90 were white. The patients had similar injuries and similar complaints of pain. Overall, 43% of the black patients received no pain medication whereas only 26% of white patients went untreated for pain.

This is the second study to uncover a racial bias in the prescribing of pain relief. An earlier study conducted by the same authors at the University of California School of Medicine in Los Angeles found that Hispanic patients were also less likely to receive adequate pain relief in the emergency room.

Commenting on the research, Dr. Knox Todd, lead author of the latest report, said: "Patient ethnicity affects decision making, independent of objective clinical criteria." He implied that the racial bias in offering analgesia is not due to differences in pain assessment by physicians or in its reporting by patients. Ingrained racial stereotypes may insidiously and unconsciously make their way into medical practice.

In an accompanying editorial Dr. Marcus Martin of the University of Virginia said that his clinical experience suggested that ethnic differences in pain tolerance and expression existed and that pain relief is sometimes withheld because doctors feared drug seeking and substance misuse behaviours in subsets of patients.

Source: Reprinted from *BMJ: British Medical Journal* 7228 (January 15, 2000) 139.

Some patients may also be viewed as histrionic and less deserving of pain relief. The manner in which an injury was sustained also plays a part in the prescription of pain relief. For instance, patients who are injured during police fights or during drunken brawls may be considered less deserving of pain relief than those injured during skiing accidents. He called for additional studies to be performed to see if some patients act in a manner that appears less convincing than others, causing physicians to disbelieve their complaints of pain.

Dr. Knox and colleagues are calling for standardised criteria for pain assessment to eliminate the racial bias. They concluded: "Efforts to alter pain management practice may be more successful using interventions that target administration of medications and standardise pain assessments, including using clinical guidelines that couple pain ratings with specific recommendations for analgesic use."

In another accompanying editorial, Dr. Louis Goldfrank, director of the New York University School of Medicine's emergency medicine training programme, called for an "affirmative action approach" to solving racial bias.

CRITICAL THINKING QUESTIONS

1. According to Josefson, how are white and African-American emergency room patients treated differently? What would account for the differences in medical treatment received by people from different racial or ethnic groups?

2. Why is it important to study differences in medical treatment by race, ethnicity, social class, or gender?

3. If you were the director of a large hospital, what programs would you put in place to reduce prejudice and discrimination in the provision of medical care? What resistance might you encounter in establishing these programs? Explain.

Reading 12

The Health of African American Men

John A. Rich

In this article, Rich explores the generally lower level of health experienced by African-American men. He explains some of the social reasons for racial differences in health and discusses some possible remedies to this problem.

African American men in the United States suffer a disproportionate burden of preventable morbidity and mortality. According to 1997 data from the National Center for Health Statistics, black males had the highest age-adjusted death rate of any group, at

Source: Reprinted from *Annals of the American Academy of Political & Social Science* 569, (May 2000): 149–159.

921 deaths per 100,000, a rate that is 60 percent higher than the death rate for white males and 90 percent higher than the overall death rate. While the life expectancy at birth for black males increased 1.1 years between 1996 and 1997 and reached a record high of 67.2 years in 1997, it still lagged 7.1 years behind the life expectancy for white males and 9.3 years behind the overall life expectancy

for all groups. The difference in life expectancy between black males and white males was primarily due to higher death rates in black males for five conditions: heart disease, cancer, homicide, human immunodeficiency virus (HIV) infection, and perinatal conditions (Centers for Disease Control and Prevention 1999b).

Men between the ages of 15 and 44 also have a high death rate from preventable diseases. However, young black men suffer a greater burden of preventable causes of death than white men in the same age group. In 1997, the three leading causes of death for all males between the ages of 15 and 24 were, in order, accidents, homicide, and suicide. However, the leading cause of death for young black men aged 15–24 was homicide, followed by accidents and suicide. The death rate from homicide for these men was five times the rate for white males. For 25- to 44-year-old males of all races, accidents, heart disease, and suicide ranked as the top three causes of death. Among black men between the ages of 25 and 44, HIV stands as the leading cause of death, followed by heart disease, accidents, and homicide. The death rate from HIV in this group is four times the rate among similarly aged white men (Centers for Disease Control and Prevention 1999a).

Black men also suffer higher rates of preventable illness such as sexually transmitted diseases. Nationally, gonorrhea rates among black males aged 15–19 are 77 times the rates for similarly aged white males. Syphilis and chlamydia rates show similar disparities (Centers for Disease Control and Prevention 1997). Despite this disproportionate burden of disease, young men in this age group are the least likely to have health insurance and the least likely to seek preventive health services. Data from the National Ambulatory Medical Care Survey show that men aged 15–24 have lower physician visit rates than any other gender and age group and that black patients aged 15–24 have the lowest rates of any race-age group. However, black patients in this age group are more likely to seek care in an emergency room (McCraig 1999).

The reasons for increased risk of preventable disease among African American men are multifactorial. Black men have higher rates of poverty and unemployment than any other group. Current mortality data clearly demonstrate that all cause mortality and disease rates are inversely related to socioeconomic status. Courtenay and others have documented the relationship between unhealthy behaviors and constructions of manhood. They argue that risk-taking behavior provides a way in which marginalized men attempt to establish themselves as men, in the absence of more mainstream ways to demonstrate power. African American men, perceiving themselves as powerless, may more likely think to engage in risk behavior as an assertion of manhood. Yet when data on the health status of black men are reported in the popular media, important explanatory factors are rarely included, leading to the further propagation of negative stereotypes of black men (Courtenay 1998, in press). Larger structural barriers such as racism and class bias further alienate men of color from health care resources that might affect unhealthy behaviors (Williams and Collins 1995; Williams, Lavizzo-Mourey, and Warren 1994). In the sections that follow, I examine several specific health issues and their disproportionate prevalence among black men.

VIOLENCE

Homicide is the leading cause of death for young black men aged 15–34. In 1996 in the United States, 5626 black men in this age group died as homicide victims. In 1989, the lifetime chances of a black man's dying as a result of homicide were 1 in 27, compared to 1 in 205 for white men. In 1992, despite making up only 1.3 percent of the nation's population, black males aged 16–24 experienced 17.2 percent of the nation's homicides. This is equivalent to a homicide rate of 114.9 per 100,000 for this group. Black males in 1992 were nearly 14 times more likely to be victims of homicide than the general population (Bastian and Taylor 1994).

The impact of nonfatal violence among young black men is much less appreciated. Nonfatal injury accounts for significant morbidity and occurs 100 times more frequently than fatal violence. In 1992, among young black males aged 12–24, there was one violent victimization for every eight black males. These episodes of nonfatal violence have serious consequences. Some young men are left with crippling disabilities that remove them from the workforce and destroy their chances for future meaningful work. Others are left with significant emotional disability due to post-traumatic stress disorder.

The truth of young black men as victims of violence is often overshadowed by depictions of their roles as perpetrators. Most young black male victims are injured by other young black men; U.S. Justice Department statistics show that the vast majority of interpersonal violence for blacks and whites is intraracial. In 1992, among the victims of violence aged 16–24 who could determine the characteristics of their assailants, 82 percent of the victimizations of black males and 71 percent of the victimizations of white males involved an offender or offenders of the same race (Bastian and Taylor 1994).

Post-traumatic stress disorder is a trauma-related syndrome, characterized by extreme hyperstimulation, nightmares, depression, hypervigilence, and flashbacks to the traumatic experience. It has been little studied in young men in the inner city but may contribute to significant disability, substance use, and possibly even recurrent violence (Breslau et al. 1991; Campbell and Schwarz 1996; Fitzpatrick and Boldizar 1993). Young men who are injured in the inner city may be left feeling vulnerable when they return to their neighborhoods. Plagued by symptoms of anxiety and hyperstimulation even in environments that previously seemed safe to them, some may feel compelled to arm themselves with guns or knives, doubting the ability or desire of the police to protect them or to apprehend their assailants. Others may turn to alcohol or other drugs such as marijuana in an attempt to self-treat their anxiety. The combination of these reactions related to the symptoms of trauma has the potential to increase a young man's risk of violence.

Victims of violent injury are more likely to suffer a recurrent violent injury. In a study of victims of violence in Detroit, Sims et al. (1989) found that 44 percent of patients suffered a recurrent injury within a five-year period. Over that same period, 20 percent died, due to both violence and substance abuse. Goins, Thompson, and Simpkins (1992) found a recurrence rate of 48 percent in a Baltimore study. They also found an association between unemployment and recurrent violence, suggesting that efforts aimed at reducing the rate of unemployment might help to lower episodes of violent injury.

While some have suggested that this increased rate of reinjury is due to the return of these young men to illicit or dangerous activities or their attempting to exact revenge upon their assailants, our own work suggests something more complex. Young men who live in economically hostile environments and who are injured may feel compelled to attempt retribution not out of anger but out of a perceived need to show their strength and thereby avoid future victimization. This reaction to assault in a social environment that is perceived as very hostile is common and may be resistant to traditional conflict resolution approaches. In the language of these young men, the need to avoid being a "sucker" is deeply rooted in their adoption of societal notions of what it means to "be a man" but also in their ideas about the consequences of being perceived as weak or vulnerable. Some terms ("punk," "chump," and "buster") have similar meanings and represent a central notion of what it means to live in the world as a young black man in the inner city (Rich and Stone 1996). While some young men are injured due to their involvement in gangs or in the illicit economy, many more (and this fact is supported by police data) are injured as a result of interpersonal conflicts, perceived jealousy, and conflicts inflamed by the presence of drugs or alcohol.

The public health approach to violence recognizes that it is a broad issue and not isolated to the individual. In fact, more progressive approaches to violence address the whole individual, including mind, body, and spirit. Such approaches, by capitalizing on the capacity and resilience of young people, are more likely to have a lasting effect than those that focus on a single behavior.

However, despite the recent tendency to regard violence as a public health problem, amenable to a more holistic approach, recently observed decreases in violence have been accompanied by dramatic increases in the number of young black men in prison. Given what we know about the effects of trauma and violence on young men and the lack of economic opportunity in communities of color, young men who spend significant amounts of time in jail would be expected to have high rates of substance abuse, homelessness, and recidivism to jail. Jails rarely possess the resources to provide adequate drug treatment services and mental health support. Overcrowding, more and more the rule in American prisons, exposes newly incarcerated young men to even more stress and to violence played out in a more controlled environment. Many young men dread these incarcerations, which are fast becoming a rite of passage in the inner city, tremendously traumatic and lacking in adequate health services.

HIV AND AIDS

Acquired immunodeficiency syndrome (AIDS) is the leading cause of death for black men between the ages of 25 and 44, and the rate of HIV infection is rising in black men at a higher rate than in any other group (Centers for Disease Control and Prevention 1998a). While 35 percent of these infections result from the use of intravenous drugs and the sharing of infected needles, a substantial proportion of them are sexually transmitted. Of these, the largest proportion (38 percent) has

resulted from men having sex with men. In 7 percent of the sexually transmitted cases, the infection was attributed to heterosexual contact, and in 12 percent of the cases, no risk factor was identified. This high proportion of cases in which no risk factor can be identified is significantly higher for black men than for any other group, perhaps indicating that black men are reluctant to acknowledge risk behaviors even when diagnosed with AIDS. Blinded seroprevalence data about HIV infections also indicate that black men are at a high risk of new HIV infection.

These data point to the necessity of finding effective ways to change the behavior of young black men. National studies conducted between 1988 and 1995 among urban adolescent males have shown that while black adolescents' attitudes about premarital sex became more conservative, their behavior did not change (Leighton et al. 1998). In addition, AIDS education did not lead to any changes in sexual activity by black males, although this change did occur among nonblack males. All types of HIV risk behavior must be emphasized in educational approaches to stem the epidemic in black men. Even those behaviors that are heavily stigmatized in communities of color, such as men having sex with other men and intravenous drug use, must be openly and honestly dealt with. Young men who are struggling to understand their sexual preferences may be unable to identify with resources that characterize them as gay or bisexual. It is therefore important that resources be developed that address the unique cultural, religious, and political meanings that certain behaviors hold in the black community.

MENTAL HEALTH

Many of the mental health problems that young black men experience are related to the unique stresses they experience as a result of poverty, racism, and past trauma. In general, young black men have higher levels of stress and anxiety due to a lack of meaningful employment opportunities. The stresses of balancing multiple life pressures, often without material or social capital, may lead to feelings of hopelessness and desperation. Add to this the impact of trauma in the form of losing friends and family to violence, and we have the makings of a mental health crisis.

Over the past decade, there has been a substantial increase in suicide rates not only among black males but among young black males in particular (Centers for Disease Control and Prevention 1998b). While the suicide rate for young black men is still lower than the rate for their white counterparts, this rate is increasing more rapidly than for any other group. Insufficient data are available to help us understand the reasons for this change, but it is likely to be due to the stresses previously detailed combined with a lack of access to mental health services. Some of the suicides are by young men who are struggling with their sexual identities, since we know that a major contributor to suicides in young people is the feeling of alienation brought on by their emerging sexual preferences. Given that homosexuality is particularly stigmatized in African American communities, this alienation may be felt in an extreme manner by inner-city young black males.

Substance-abuse behaviors also provide some insight into the emotional health of young black men in the urban environment. While alcohol use rates are higher among white males than black males, young black men have a particularly high rate of marijuana use, and this rate seems to be on the increase (McCraig 1999). This is in contrast with cocaine use, which seems to be decreasing in all U.S. populations. While many use marijuana because of its much highlighted role in the pop culture, using it mainly during social interactions, a significant number of others use this drug to self-treat symptoms of anxiety. In addition, there is growing concern that marijuana use may lead to the use of more serious substances such as alcohol, cocaine, and pos-

sibly even heroin. Given that these substances are not effective in treating symptoms of anxiety and given the illicit nature of marijuana, use of this drug may lead to even more interaction with the police and the criminal justice system and increases in life stress.

While less easily quantified than specific diseases, racism and oppression stand as a constant backdrop against which these men live their lives. Harvard psychiatrist Chester Pierce (1970) has written eloquently about the notion that microaggression, that is, small racial insults experienced on a daily basis by people of color, has an aggregate effect that is equivalent to or greater than so-called macroaggression, such as beatings or lynching. Clearly, because of the widely held stereotypes that have been applied to young black men, they are likely to experience microaggression, such as being followed by security guards in stores, arrested or harassed by the police, denied frontline employment, and treated poorly in the health care system. To the extent that the effects of these insults are additive to the other stresses of life, they may take a particular toll on the health of black men.

CANCER

Black men have a higher death rate from cancer than do other groups. Prostate cancer in particular has a disproportionate incidence among African American men. African American men have the highest incidence of prostate cancer in the world, and the rate is twice that of white men. Black men have an age-adjusted death rate from all cancers that is 50 percent higher than that for white men, despite similar or lower incidence rates for some cancers. This disproportionate death rate relates in large part to a lack of access to health care since many of these cancers can be prevented or, if detected early, limited in the harm that they cause. In addition, lifestyle factors, such as smoking, sedentary lifestyle, and diet, are linked to higher rates of cancer. To the extent that significant life stresses and lack of access to health care inhibit lifestyle changes, impoverished men of color are even less likely to adopt healthier behaviors. Community-based efforts to increase prostate screening rates for black men have met with some success; similar efforts are necessary to address other high-mortality cancers such as lung and colorectal cancers.

CARDIOVASCULAR DISEASE

Similar to cancer, black men have a higher death rate due to cardiovascular disease than any other group. Once again, the increased mortality seen here is due in part to factors that are associated with the black race, such as poverty and lack of access to health care, rather than caused by race itself. In fact, men with lower incomes are more likely to die of cardiovascular disease, regardless of race. Recently identified biases in the health care system no doubt contribute to this also. Recent studies have shown that physicians are less likely to refer black patients for certain diagnostic or therapeutic cardiac procedures, independent of their socioeconomic status (Schulman et al. 1999). Lack of access to effective primary health care, combined with lifestyle issues such as smoking, diet, and lack of exercise, renders black men at the highest risk of death due to cardiovascular disease.

ACCESS TO HEALTH CARE AND HEALTH CARE UTILIZATION

Young men of color are less likely than others to have access to effective health care services. Young people between the ages of 18 and 24 in the United States are the least likely group to have insurance coverage. Black and Latino men are also disproportionately represented among the uninsured in some states. Fully 25 percent report having no in-

surance (Hoffman 1998). Young black and Latino men in particular, because of their socioeconomic position, are less likely to qualify for public sources of insurance such as Medicaid. Even though, in some states, Medicaid eligibility has been greatly expanded in the past few years, young men over the age of 18 qualify only if they are classified "long-term unemployed," defined as having been unable to find work for a period of two years or more. Otherwise, nondisabled young men cannot access Medicaid.

Most Americans, who have health insurance, obtain insurance through their workplaces. Those who occupy unskilled and nonunion jobs are less likely to be offered insurance coverage. Such insurance is prohibitively expensive for any lower-income or working-class individual to purchase on the open market. The socioeconomic position of young urban black men, with higher rates of unemployment and lower-skilled jobs, means that they have less access to health insurance. Even those who qualify for coverage may not know that they are eligible since they may lack critical information about access to health care.

Finally, even for those young men who are fortunate enough to have health insurance through their jobs or through public coverage, the current health care environment, marked by managed care competition, may limit their access to appropriate care. Fierce competition within the health care market has relegated prevention to the back burner. Decisions about the kinds of services most relevant to these men, such as community-based outreach and preventive mental health, are often made on financial grounds, and little justification is seen for outreach to the most disenfranchised groups. As a result, young black men may have insurance but still face barriers to effective preventive care.

Lack of health insurance leads to several problematic health-seeking behaviors. Young men may defer necessary care for nonemergent problems because of concern that they will be unable to pay. Consequently, they may receive care in settings such as emergency rooms or urgent care clinics that are less well equipped to deal with preventive health. Encounters in acute and emergency settings tend to be less satisfying since patients are faced with harried staff and long waiting times. Such experiences may further alienate this group from seeking care, particularly preventive health care, the mainstay of future health and wellness.

Even for those with health insurance or with the ability to obtain free care, access to culturally appropriate providers may not exist. Health care providers are not immune to general societal stereotypes of young black men. Providers who hold these unconscious preconceptions may interact with these patients based upon preconceived notions, further alienating them. Anecdotally, numerous young black men have related that providers have assumed that they were involved with gangs, sold or used drugs, or had particular attitudes, based solely upon their appearance. A young black man who was an innocent victim of random street violence related being lectured by a white provider about the need to "change [his] lifestyle" without even asking the youth about the circumstances of his injury.

Recent research supports the notion that providers unconsciously consider race when making treatment decisions in the application of expensive technologies like cardiac surgery and kidney transplantation. Schulman and colleagues (1999) found that physicians viewing videotapes of actors depicting patients with heart disease, all of whom were scripted to have the same symptoms, test results, occupation, and socioeconomic status, recommended certain high-technology cardiac diagnostic studies less often for black patients and for women. If, in the face of such highly data-driven decisions, providers consider race, then it is likely that in interfacing with young black men, racial stereotypes as well as other deeply held notions influence the interaction. This finding is of particular concern given that the vast majority of physicians are white, even in areas where the population is much more diverse.

MEDICAL EDUCATION

Medical education for African Americans began in organized fashion in 1868 with the founding of Howard Medical School, which graduated its first M.D. graduates in 1871. While, during the decade that followed, 12 more schools sprang up to educate black doctors, only two, Howard and Meharry Medical College, in Nashville, Tennessee, ultimately survived. The *Flexner Report,* a Carnegie Foundation–sponsored report on the state of medical education in the United States, led to the closure of inadequate medical programs, both predominantly black and white. Therefore, those two predominantly black institutions were responsible for training the vast majority of black physicians through the 1960s (Organ and Kosiba 1987; Epps, Johnson, and Vaughan 1994). Two additional predominantly black medical schools now exist, Charles R. Drew University of Medicine and Science, in Los Angeles, and Morehouse School of Medicine, in Atlanta. In addition, a number of physicians of color are trained at majority institutions.

The view of the future of African Americans in medicine is uncertain. While it is well documented that physicians of color are more likely than their majority counterparts to practice in underserved areas, fewer blacks are matriculating at U.S. medical schools. Data collected by the Association of American Medical Colleges (AAMC) indicate that, between 1969 and 1975, the enrollment of underrepresented minorities in American medical schools increased from 3.1 to 8.1 percent. Howard and Meharry went from training 75 percent of black medical students in 1969 to only 20 percent in 1979. However, since peaking at 8.1 percent in 1975, minority enrollment in medical schools has begun to decrease. This is particularly true for black males. While organizations like the AAMC have developed innovative programs to increase the enrollment of people of color in medical school, it is clear that broader interventions designed to increase the number of black men in college and who pursue health-related careers are necessary.

CONCLUSION

By virtue of social inequality, racial bias, and lack of adequate access to health care, African American men have a worse health status than other groups. Some of these health outcomes can be traced to poverty and historical racial discrimination, while others more clearly emanate from health behaviors and risk taking. Simultaneously, African American men have, as a group, made a significant contribution to the health of black and white Americans alike.

The future health of African American men will depend upon improving their access to health care that addresses health behaviors in their social context while also providing access to primary care and appropriate technologies. Concerned African American men have the ability and power to affect the health of their communities by influencing their peers to alter unhealthy behaviors and seek regular medical care, while also teaching them to advocate for their health needs. Furthermore, increasing the representation of African Americans, particularly men, in medical school and other health professions will be critical to improving the health of people of color. But these outcomes will depend upon increasing the number of underrepresented groups in higher education and improving the lot of African American boys in primary and secondary education.

REFERENCES

BASTIAN, LISA D. AND BRUCE M. TAYLOR. 1994. *Young Black Male Victims*. Washington, DC: Bureau of Justice Statistics.

BRESLAU, N., G. C. DAVIS, P. ANDRESKI, AND E. PETERSON. 1991. Traumatic Events and Posttraumatic Stress Disorder in an Urban Population of Young Adults. *Archives of General Psychiatry* 48:216–22.

CAMPBELL, CARLA. AND DONALD F. SCHWARZ. 1996. Prevalence and Impact of Exposure to Interpersonal Violence Among Suburban and Urban Middle School Students. *Pediatrics* 98(3, pt. 1):396–402.

Centers for Disease Control and Prevention. 1997. *Sexually Transmitted Disease Surveillance Report*. Atlanta, GA: U.S. Department of Health and Human Services, Centers for Disease Control and Prevention.

———. 1998a *HIV/AIDS Surveillance Report*. Atlanta, GA: U.S. Department of Health and Human Services, Centers for Disease Control and Prevention.

———. 1998b. *Suicide Among Black Youths—United States, 1980–1995*. Atlanta, GA: U.S. Department of Health and Human Services, Centers for Disease Control and Prevention.

———. 1999a. *National Vital Statistics Report*. Vol. 47. No. 19. Atlanta, GA: U.S. Department of Health and Human Services, Centers for Disease Control and Prevention.

———. 1999b. *National Vital Statistics Reports*. Atlanta, GA: U.S. Department of Health and Human Services, Centers for Disease Control and Prevention.

———. In press. Constructions of Masculinity and Their Influence on Men's Well-Being: A Theory of Gender and Health. *Social Science and Medicine*.

EPPS, C. H., D. G. JOHNSON, AND A. L. VAUGHAN. 1994. *African American Medical Pioneers*. Rockville, MD: Betz.

FITZPATRICK, K. AND J. BOLDIZAR. 1993. The Prevalence and Consequences of Exposure to Violence Among African-American Youth. *Journal of the American Academy of Child and Adolescent Psychiatry* 32:424–30.

GOINS, WENDELL A., JONATHAN THOMPSON, AND CUTHBERT SIMPKINS. 1992. Recurrent Intentional Injury. *Journal of the National Medical Association* 84(5):431–35.

HOFFMAN, CATHERINE. 1998. *Uninsured in America: A Chart Book: The Kaiser Commission on Medicaid and the Uninsured*. Menlo Park, CA: Henry J. Kaiser Family Foundation.

LEIGHTON, K., F. SONENSTEIN, L. D. LINDBERG, C. H. BRADNER, S. BOGGESS, AND J. H. PLECK. 1998. Understanding Changes in Sexual Activity Among Young Metropolitan Men: 1979–1995. *Family Planning Perspectives* 30(6):256–62.

MCCRAIG, LINDA F. 1999. *National Hospital Ambulatory Medical Care Survey: 1997 Outpatient Department Summary*. Atlanta, GA: U.S. Department of Health and Human Services, Centers for Disease Control and Prevention.

ORGAN, CALUDE H., Jr. AND MARGARET M. KOSIBA, eds. 1987. *A Century of Black Surgeons*. Vol. 2. Norman, OK: Transcript Press.

PIERCE, CHESTER. 1970. *Offensive Mechanisms. In The Black Seventies*, ed. F. Barbour. Boston: Porter Sergent.

RICH, JOHN A. AND DAVID A. STONE. 1996. The Experience of Violent Injury for Young African American Men: The Meaning of Being a "Sucker." *Journal of General Internal Medicine* 11:77–82.

SCHULMAN, KEVIN A., JESSE A. BERLIN, WILLIAM HARLESS, JON F. KERNER, SHYRL SISTRUNK, BERNARD GERSH, ROSS DUBE, CHRISTOPHER TALEGHANI, JENNIFER E. BURKE, SANKEY WILLIAMS, JOHN E.

EISENBERG, and JOSE J. ESCARCE. 1999. The Effect of Race and Sex on Physicians' Recommendations for Cardiac Catheterization. *New England Journal of Medicine* 340(8):618–26.

SIMS, DEBORAH W., BRACK A. BIVINS, FAROUCK N. OBEID, H. MATILOA HORST, VICTOR J. SORENSEN, and JOHN J. FATH. 1989. Urban Trauma: A Chronic Recurrent Disease. *Journal of Trauma* 29(7):940–47.

WILLIAMS, DAVID R. and CHIQUITA COLLINS. 1995. U.S. Socioeconomic and Racial Differences in Health: Patterns and Explanations. *Annual Review of Sociology* 21:349–86.

WILLIAMS, DAVID R., RISA LAVIZZO-MOUREY, and REUBEN C. WARREN. 1994. The Concept of Race and Health Status in America. *Public Health Report* 109:26–41.

CRITICAL THINKING QUESTIONS

1. What are the major differences between the health status of African-American men and white men?

2. What historical and cultural factors contribute to the different levels of health of men of different racial or ethnic groups?

3. What changes in social policies, programs, and institutions would need to be made to bring the health status of African-American men up to the status of white men?

Reading 13

Inadequate Housing: A Health Crisis for the Children of the Poor

Joshua Sharfstein, M.D. and Megan Sandel, M.D.

In this article, the authors discuss the negative effects that inadequate, unsafe, or overcrowded housing, as well as homelessness, can have on the health of poor children.

Millions of American children who live in substandard housing are subjected to conditions that put them at great risk for health problems and injuries.

Each year, doctors care for children whose life-threatening asthma attacks are made worse by sleeping in bedrooms infested with cockroaches. Doctors also tend to the wounds of toddlers who sustain major injuries because they live in unsafe apartments. Medical professionals chart the slow recovery of school children who have learning disabilities brought on by poisonous exposure to lead.

And doctors are called upon to treat the numerous ailments of homeless children as they wind their way through the shelter system. Often, the best solution to a child's

Source: Journal of Housing and Community Development. 1998 Vol. 55, Issue 1, (July/August): 14–24.

chronic health problems is decent, safe, and sanitary housing. Even when poor housing is the cause of a child's illness, however, many families have to wait months—and sometimes years—for safer, subsidized housing.

For approximately 10 million families, housing is too expensive, substandard or both. HUD considers housing to be affordable if it consumes less than 30 percent of a family's income. According to the 1993 American Housing Survey (AHS), however, nearly three out of four families spend more than 30 percent of their incomes for rent and more than one-third of very low-income families spend more than 70 percent of their incomes for rent.

Housing is considered severely physically inadequate if it "lacks complete plumbing or a complete kitchen, has inadequate heating, has structural or maintenance problems and/or lacks adequate electricity," according to HUD standards. The 1993 AHS study showed that more than 1.2 million households lived in housing with severe or moderate physical problems, and 700,000 poor renter households suffered in overcrowded living conditions. Families with children have some of the most acute housing needs.

Low-income households that receive some form of housing assistance—either public housing or assisted housing programs—fare better than those who receive no assistance. More than half of poor renters with housing expenses less than 30 percent of their incomes lived in subsidized housing in 1993. Unfortunately, there is no guarantee of assistance, and the vast majority of eligible families cannot participate in assistance programs.

Asthma causes the airways of the lungs to become irritated and swollen enough to cause difficulty breathing. If uncontrolled, asthma can progress to the point where the airways are swollen shut. Indeed, asthma kills hundreds of American children each year.

Doctors often can treat asthma attacks with medication, but prevention requires changes at home, such as removing or decreasing common irritating factors (smoke, cold, dust mites, and cockroaches).

Asthma is the most common chronic childhood illness, affecting an estimated 11 to 12 percent of black children and 8 to 9 percent of white children in inner cities. In the last decade, the incidence of this common illness has increased by 29 percent. The hospitalization rate for people affected by asthma is almost three times as high for black children under the age of 5, compared to their white counterparts. The mortality rate is significantly higher for black children, as well. This racial difference has been explained, in large part, by poor access to a regular source of health care.

Substandard housing triggers asthma attacks by exposing residents to irritants, such as smoke, cockroaches, dust mites, mold, rats and mice. In allergic children, long-term exposure to these substances can be life-threatening. Dry heat and lack of heat also can cause dangerous asthma flares.

Inadequate housing and overcrowding are commonly associated with infestations of cockroaches, rats and mice. Studies have estimated that almost half of poor children live in housing overrun with such pests, compared to only 12 percent of nonpoor children.

There is mounting evidence that cockroach exposure causes the worsening of children's asthma. A 1997 study found that children allergic to cockroaches who were exposed to them at home suffered:

- 3.4 times more hospitalizations than other asthma patients,
- 78 percent more unscheduled visits to health care clinicians,
- more wheezing and labored breathing, and
- more absences from school.

In another study, children living in urban areas were 4.4 times more likely to have cockroach allergen in their bedrooms than children from suburban areas, and poor children were 4.2 times more likely to be exposed to cockroaches at home than the nonpoor.

Children with asthma also are put at risk for more severe disease by other factors associated with inadequate housing, including dust mites found in old carpeting. The common dust mite has been implicated as a cause for the world-wide increase in asthma. As many as one in four children living in poor housing have inadequate heat or hot water—other factors linking poor housing with asthma attacks.

In addition to asthma, poor housing and crowding can lead to increased rates of infection with such respiratory viruses as the Respiratory Syncytial Virus. Infection with this virus can threaten the life of former premature babies and can predispose other children to asthma.

Water damage in run-down housing may expose young residents to *stachybotroys atra,* a fungus whose toxin has been linked to fatal hemorrhage in the lungs of infants.

For all these reasons—cockroaches, mold, dust, infections and overcrowding—inadequate housing can, literally, take a child's breath away.

Accidents are the leading cause of death among children 1 to 14 years of age. Though accidents associated with motor vehicles are the most common, accidents associated with housing (falls, burns, drownings and fires) are almost as common. Such accidents associated with problems in housing result in more than 5,000 deaths annually, and more than 1.4 million injuries each year.

Considering burns and fires alone, more than 54,000 Americans are admitted to the hospital. An estimated lifetime cost from fire and burn injuries from one year has been as high as $3.8 billion.

Tap water temperatures and home heating systems often are associated with burns that occur in housing. It has long been established that hot water heater temperature settings have been associated with the increased incidence and severity of burns.

In one study, more than 98 percent of poor families did not know what temperature their hot water should be to prevent burns. Further, many poor families have no way of knowing or controlling their hot water settings in their apartments.

Reports of home heating burns are extremely common, either from wood stoves, kerosene heaters, floor furnaces or exposed home radiators. These burns can cause serious lifelong injury. In 1993, approximately 1,800 children visited emergency rooms for burns related to non-vehicle radiators alone.

In a study conducted in an inner-city housing development in Chicago between 1991 and 1994, it was shown that a majority of radiator burns were caused by uncovered radiators. In all buildings where the affected children lived, there were steam radiator systems, with temperatures ranging from 180 degrees to 230 degrees Fahrenheit. Seventy-nine percent of the buildings in which an incident involving a burned child occurred were found to be missing radiator covers, insulation over radiator pipes, or both.

Many children slept in beds located too close to radiators. Often, this was due to overcrowded conditions.

Steam radiators are very common in older buildings in Chicago. There are no regulations requiring covering of radiators in private or public housing. For many poor parents, options to move are unavailable, and many of their children are in danger of severe, and sometimes repeated, burns.

Fires are the third leading cause of death among children under the age of 14, after motor vehicle accidents and drownings. About three-quarters of the deaths from fires are from house fires, some 2,000 deaths a year occur among children aged 15 and under. The largest group of these children are under the age of four. Fires are a particular risk for poor families, whether from higher-risk faulty heating systems or from the use of wood stoves or kerosene heat.

It has been shown that simple smoke detector use can decrease substantially the risk of dying in a fire. Despite the fact that smoke detectors are required by law, about one-third of households had no smoke detectors in 1988, according to a survey that appeared in the *American Journal of Public Health.*

In a 1993 study conducted in New Mexico, death by fire was strongly associated with certain types of homes. Residents who lived in mobile homes had three times the mortality rate from fires than those who lived in standard homes or apartments. Homes without plumbing carried more than 10 times the fatality risk. Since 82 percent of children killed by fires die at the scene, perhaps the best intervention to prevent deaths is to improve housing conditions, rather than to build better hospital burn units.

Due to the unaffordability of housing, many poor children are trapped in unsafe neighborhoods or living arrangements. In a study done in Washington, D.C., 45 percent of first and second graders had witnessed a mugging, 47 percent had seen a shooting, 31 percent had seen a stabbing, and 39 percent had seen a dead body.

In a survey done at Boston City Hospital, 10 percent of children in the primary care clinic had witnessed a stabbing or shooting by age six. Half of these incidents had occurred within the children's homes and half had occurred on the streets in their neighborhoods. This exposure to violence can have long-term effects, including post traumatic stress disorder, psychotic episodes and suicidal tendencies.

Violence at home is a particular threat. Women often stay in abusive relationships because they are financially dependent on the batterer.

Faced with no alternative other than entering a shelter—an option that sometimes exposes children to health and social risks—many mothers stay in violent relationships. While the long-term consequences of child abuse are well-known, recent evidence has shown that witnessing violence at home may cause children to have many of the same terrible psychological and developmental problems.

Lead poisoning has long been recognized as a threat to children's health. As early as ancient Greek times, it was known that ingesting large amounts of lead caused severe abdominal pain and even seizures.

The relationship between housing conditions and lead poisoning also dates back more than a century.

As early as 1894, cases of childhood lead poisoning were being attributed to children eating lead paint off the porches in Brisbane, Australia. It also has been known for many years that children absorb more lead after ingestion than adults.

Lead damages many different parts of the human body. Sudden poisoning can cause abdominal pain, constipation, fatigue, anemia, nerve damage, and altered brain function, which can lead to coma and seizures. Long-term exposure can harm the blood, the brain, the kidneys, and the reproductive organs.

Of special concern in children are the long-term effects of lead on the developing brain. Researchers have noted that children with high levels of lead in the umbilical cord had lower mental developmental scores and problems with fine motor and interactional/linguistic skills.

Even in children who appear otherwise healthy, teachers rate children with higher lead levels as having poorer speech and language processing, disordered classroom behavior, more daydreaming, and an inability to follow directions.

Another study found that children with increased lead levels in their teeth were seven times more likely to drop out of high school and more than five times more likely to have a reading disability.

Housing conditions are the most frequent cause of childhood lead poisoning. Most commonly, children ingest lead from lead-containing paint—mostly in older, often deteriorating, housing stock. Besides paint, lead in the soil and water around houses are other possible sources of exposure.

According to a national study that examined many different aspects of American health from 1991–1994, lead levels are high in children living in housing built before 1946, and even higher if housing was built between 1946 and 1973. This study found that 5.9 percent of all American children 1 to 2 years of age have blood lead levels greater than 10, placing them at risk. The Centers for Disease Control estimated that about 1 million children between 1 and 5 years old have elevated blood lead levels.

Living in older housing may place children more at risk. Lead is now banned from household paint, plumbing systems, and food and drink cans (as well as gasoline). In a random telephone survey of children across the country, children under the age of 7 were found to be more likely to have an elevated lead level if they lived in housing built before 1960, in a rental home, in the northeast, or lived in a low income household.

An estimated 14 million children in the at-risk age group of 0 to 6 years old still live in housing built before 1960 with the highest concentration of lead paint. Poor and minority children are more likely to face increased risk, but in absolute terms, the majority of at-risk children are white.

Some legal changes have been responsible for a significant decline in lead exposure over the last 25 years. By the mid 1980s, the Environmental Protection Agency (EPA) had required that lead be eliminated from gasoline. In addition, the Occupational Safety and Health Administration had lowered acceptable lead levels in the workplace by 75 percent, the Consumer Product Safety Commission had limited lead in paint to 0.06 percent, and lead solder in water pipes had been banned.

As early as 1961, city officials in Baltimore instituted a program to remove lead from homes. This caused controversy over whether the cost of lead removal was excessive. For many years afterwards, laws on lead in housing had remained largely regional and scarce.

In 1992, Congress passed the Residential Lead-Based Paint Hazard Reduction Act (Title X), legislation that required sellers to tell buyers of lead hazards prior to purchase. Still, only 9.1 percent of pre-1960 homes have been tested for lead.

Lead removal legislation can be found in Massachusetts, where the state's Lead Law requires the institution of strict control measures or removal of lead paint from all homes built before 1978 when children younger than six move in. The city of Boston also offers grants and low-interest loans to assist landlords with the cost of lead removal. Many landlords are leery of the cost of lead removal, which can exceed the annual income from tenant rents.

As a result, discrimination against families with children can prevent families from finding safe housing. Newer, lead-free apartments often are too expensive for poor families. Many parents have no choice but to live in homeless shelters or put their children at risk for permanent brain damage.

The General Accounting Office estimated in 1989 that 41,000 to 107,000 children are homeless on any given day, with 39,000 to 296,000 more in "doubled up" or shared housing.

Most information on the effects of homelessness is related to children in shelters, because they are the only accessible population. Many other children live in cars or "doubled up" with friends or family. Some studies have suggested that residential instability, either from homelessness or other housing problems, put these children at twice the risk of becoming homeless adults.

While nearly 70 percent of homeless families who live in shelters are only there for three months or less, one in four families are homeless from three months to three years.

While longer periods of homelessness can be more detrimental to a child's health, any length of homelessness can be associated with many short-term and long-term effects.

Children who are homeless are at significantly increased risk of infections compared with other children, even housed poor children. In one study, homeless children had a 42 percent chance of having an upper respiratory infection. The general population of children had a 22 percent chance of having an upper respiratory infection. Multiple respiratory and ear infections can lead to hearing problems, language delays, and even poor school performance. Other contagious infections, such as diarrhea, have been shown to be more than five times more frequent in children living in shelters.

Homeless children may contract even more serious infections, like tuberculosis—a lung infection that requires months of expensive medicines and can affect the entire body if it goes untreated. In addition, children in shelters have high rates of such breathing problems as asthma.

Homeless families often want for food. One study documented that 21 percent of children in shelters felt they did not get enough to eat in the last four days or more of every month because of lack of money.

This lack of food can have long-term effects, especially iron deficiency anemia—a disease that is associated with behavioral problems and decreased cognitive development. Homeless children are seven times more likely to be iron deficient than housed children.

Perhaps the most disturbing of the effects homelessness has on children are the delays in their development, like walking, talking and playing.

In one study, half of children in shelters had one or more developmental delay. Similarly, 45 percent of school age children in homeless shelters were found to need special education evaluation, yet only 22 percent actually received this important testing or placement.

Moreover, about half of children in shelters missed one week of school in three months and 20 percent missed more than three weeks in three months, which is significantly more than poor housed children. Children who change shelters often must change schools, too, disrupting continuity in learning.

The psychological health of children also can be devastated by homelessness. Half of all children in shelters show signs of anxiety and depression. When compared to poor housed children, homeless children show significant behavioral disturbances, like tantrums and aggressive behavior.

Since the very word homelessness implies transiency, it makes sense that many homeless children lack a regular place for health care. This has many results, the most frightening of which is lack of immunizations against such deadly diseases as polio, whooping cough, and meningitis. Children in shelters have shown as high as a 70 percent rate of delay in immunizations in comparison to 22 percent among poor housed children.

Many homeless families are unable to visit or even identify a regular clinic. In some homeless shelters, more than 44 percent of families use the emergency room or clinics in hospitals as their only source of health care.

One of the most preventable health hazards for children is injury. In one survey of homeless mothers, 20 percent responded that their children needed to be seen at an emergency room for an injury or fall. Six percent of children reported either a fracture or a fall (being "knocked unconscious") and 14 percent reported having had a burn serious enough for a scar to form. These injuries needlessly endanger homeless children.

There is a common connection between inadequate housing and malnutrition. Often, children whose parents must spend a large proportion of their income on rent do not get enough food.

Evidence of this trade-off comes from a 1992 government survey that demonstrated that families receiving rent assistance paid approximately 30 percent of their income for rent. Poor families who were eligible but were not receiving assistance (such as those on the waiting list), however, paid more than 40 percent for rent. Thus, they spent less of their income on food.

Frighteningly, additional evidence reveals that families receiving welfare benefits in cities like Boston can spend more than 75 percent of their income for rent.

The trade-off between food and housing expenses is particularly acute during winter months. In a recent study, researchers at Boston City Hospital analyzed data on more than 11,000 children between 6 months and 2 years of age. The researchers found that growth was decreased in the three months following the coldest months of the year.

The researchers also found that families who were without heat or were threatened with utility turnoff in the previous winter were twice as likely as other families to report their children were hungry or at risk for hunger.

Among poor families, housing subsidies may prevent malnutrition by allowing families to spend more of their small income for food. A 1995 study compared the rate of malnutrition among poor children whose families already received subsidized housing with the rate among children of families on the waiting list.

The results were dramatic. Almost one in five children on the housing waiting list had indicators of stunted growth, compared to about one in 30 children who lived in subsidized housing. The authors noted that "the biologic consequences of poor growth for children may include a negative influence on future school performance."

Subsidized housing also has been linked to a lower rate of iron deficiency anemia. Children who do not receive housing assistance are 50 percent more likely to be iron deficient than children of families receiving housing subsidy.

Inadequate housing threatens the health of all children, but it only significantly harms the health of some. When children have a chronic disease, they live in a precarious balance between sickness and health.

All of the consequences of poor housing affect children with chronic disease even more dramatically.

Government agencies that inspect housing for adequacy also should be able to assess asthma risk factors and respond quickly when a child's health is threatened. An asthma intervention team should be developed by cities and hospitals to reduce the risks of very hazardous living situations.

Medical insurance should pay for asthma-related cleanup of inadequate housing. At a minimum, all insurance programs should cover the cost of replacing bed and sheet covers, and periodic anti-pest, anti-mold, and dust-mite treatment.

Significant public financing is needed to insure that homes and apartments with young children are made safe from lead hazards.

Medical insurance should pay for radiator covers, fire alarms, and window guards. Landlords who maintain apartments with risks to children should be prosecuted to the fullest extent of the law.

Fuel assistance during winter months should be guaranteed to poor families to reduce the trade-off between "heating" and "eating." Food stamp allotment should be increased during winter months in cold areas.

Homelessness is not compatible with a safe and nurturing childhood. The United States should endeavor to end this threat to children by significantly expanding housing access. All homeless families should immediately qualify for housing assistance with the goal of placement within one month.

Quality housing should be considered a health issue. As such, affordable and adequate housing through public housing units and certificates should be guaranteed to poor children and their families. The Section 8 housing voucher program should be expanded significantly to allow parents to find safe and affordable housing.

Vouchers should be targeted to the poorest families who have the most to lose from inadequate housing and the most to gain from control over their environment.

Proposed changes in housing developments and programs should be evaluated, in part, based upon their likely effects on children's health. Contracts should consider not just cost, but the implications of building materials for asthma, injuries and lead poisoning.

Residents should have full access to legal aid to be able to obtain what is often their legal right—housing that is free of lead, free of infestation, and free of causes of severe asthma and allergies. Federal, state and local governments should fund legal aid programs to help parents fight for their legal right to a safe home for their children.

Public housing developments should take the lead by assessing the health needs of their families around such areas as asthma prevention, injuries and lead poisoning. Health care institutions, which often have significant resources, should collaborate with public housing organizations to identify the health needs of families.

Housing authorities should be responsive to children whose health is compromised by poor housing.

CRITICAL THINKING QUESTIONS

1. In what ways does inadequate housing negatively affect the health of children?

2. What are the long-term health-related and social consequences of inadequate housing for children?

3. In your opinion, should health insurance companies be required to pay for home repairs that are known to cause illness in children? Why or why not? Who should ensure that all children grow up in safe, adequate housing? Explain.

Reading 14

Constructions of Masculinity and Their Influence on Men's Well-Being: A Theory of Gender and Health

Will H. Courtenay

In this article, Courtenay explores some of the cultural and institutional reasons that men tend to live shorter lives than women.

Men in the United States, on average, die nearly 7 years younger than women and have higher death rates for all 15 leading causes of death (Department of Health and Human Services [DHHS], 1996). Men's age-adjusted death rate for heart disease, for example, is 2 times higher than women's, and men's cancer death rate is 1½ times higher (DHHS, 1996). The incidence of 7 out of 10 of the most common infectious diseases is higher among men than women (CDC, 1997). Men are also more likely than women to suffer severe chronic conditions and fatal diseases (Verbrugge and Wingard, 1987), and to suffer them at an earlier age. Nearly three out of four persons who die from heart attacks before age 65 are men (American Heart Association, 1995). Furthermore, men's health shows few signs of improving—their cancer death rates have increased more than 20% over the past 35 years; the rates for women have remained unchanged during the same period (American Cancer Society, 1994).

A variety of factors influence and are associated with health and longevity, including economic status, ethnicity and access to care (Laveist; Pappas and Doyal). However, these factors cannot explain gender differences in health and longevity. For instance, while lack of adequate health care, poor nutrition and substandard housing all contribute to the

Source: Reprinted from *Social Science & Medicine* 50, no. 10 (May 16, 2000) 1385–1401.

health problems of African Americans (Gibbs, 1988), they cannot account for cancer death rates that are 2 times higher among African American men than among African American women (National Institutes of Health [NIH], 1992). Health behaviours, however, do help to explain gender differences in health and longevity. Many health scientists contend that health behaviours are among the most important factors influencing health, and that modifying health behaviours is "the most effective way" to prevent disease (Woolf et al., 1996, p. xxxvii). Although not all health professionals and scholars would agree, the evidence supporting this belief is compelling. According to a former U.S. surgeon general, a wealth of scientific data have "confirmed the importance . . . of health behaviours in preventing disease" and "suggest that efforts directed at improving these behaviours are more likely to reduce morbidity and mortality in the United States than anything else we do" (Koop, 1996, p. viii). An independent scientific panel established by the U.S. government that has evaluated thousands of research studies recently estimated that half of all deaths in the United States could be prevented through changes in personal health practices (U.S. Preventive Services Task Force [USPSTF], 1996). Similar conclusions have been reached by other health experts reviewing hundreds of studies (Woolf et al., 1996). These findings provide strong evidence of risk reduction through preventive practice; they are among the factors that have recently revolutionised the U.S. health care system, a system that increasingly emphasises interventions that can effectively contain health care costs through disease prevention (USPSTF, 1996). These findings also recently led the U.S. assistant secretary for health to claim that "it is particularly pertinent to highlight the health consequences of behaviour" (Lee, 1996, p. v).

Many sociocultural factors are associated with and influence health-related behaviour. Gender is one of the most important of these factors. Women engage in far more health-promoting behaviours than men and have more healthy lifestyle patterns (Walker; Kandrack; Lonnquist; Rossi, 1992; Courtenay, 1998a; Courtenay and Courtenay, 1999). Being a woman may, in fact, be the strongest predictor of preventive and health-promoting behaviour (Mechanic; Brown and Ratner). Government health surveillance systems are providing increasing evidence of gender differences in specific behaviours associated with risk among nationally representative samples. Data from one such system indicate that the prevalence of risk behaviours among adults is more common among men than women for all but 3 of 14 (nonsex-specific) behaviours, including smoking, drinking and driving, using safety belts, getting health screenings, and awareness of medical conditions (Powell-Griner et al., 1997). Compared to men, women nationally are making the most beneficial changes in their exercise habits (Caspersen and Merritt, 1995), are less likely to be overweight (Powell-Griner et al., 1997 and National), and are more likely to consume vitamin and mineral supplements (Slesinski et al., 1996). Among adults in South Carolina, women are more likely than men to practice a cluster of healthy behaviours (Shi, 1998). Among California college students, men are more likely than women to engage in 20 of 26 specific high-risk behaviours (Patrick et al., 1997). A recent, extensive review of large studies, national data, and metanalyses summarises evidence of sex differences in behaviours that significantly influence health and longevity (Courtenay, in press a). This review systematically demonstrates that males of all ages are more likely than females to engage in over 30 behaviours that increase the risk of disease, injury and death.

Findings are generally similar for health care visits. Although gender differences in utilisation generally begin to disappear when the health problem is more serious (Verbrugge; Waldron and Mor), adult men make far fewer health care visits than women do, independent of reproductive health care visits (Verbrugge; Verbrugge and Kandrack). According to the U.S. Department of Health and Human Services (1998), among persons *with health problems,* men are significantly more likely than women to have had no recent physician contacts, regardless of income or ethnicity; poor men are twice as likely as poor women to have had no recent contact, and high-income men are 2½ times as likely.

Despite their enormous health effects, few researchers or theorists have offered explanations for these gender differences in behaviour, or for their implications for men's health (Verbrugge; Sabo and Courtenay, 1998a). Early feminist scholars were among the first to engender health, noting, for example, the absence of women as subjects in health research and the use of males as the standard for health. The result, however, has been an exclusive emphasis on women, and "gender and health" has become synonymous with "women's health" (e.g. Bayne-Smith, 1996). Although health science of this century has frequently used males as study subjects, research typically neglects to examine men and the health risks associated with men's gender. Little is known about *why* men engage in less healthy lifestyles and adopt fewer health-promoting beliefs and behaviours. The health risks associated with men's gender or masculinity have remained largely unproblematic and taken for granted. The consistent, underlying presumption in medical literature is that what it means to be a man in America has no bearing on how men work, drink, drive, fight, or take risks. Even in studies that address health risks more common to men than women, the discussion of men's greater risks and of the influence of men's gender is often conspicuously absent. Instead, the "gender" that is associated with greater risk remains unnamed (e.g., Donner-meyer and Park, 1995). Left unquestioned, men's shorter life span is often presumed to be natural and inevitable.

This paper proposes a relational theory of men's health from a social constructionist and feminist perspective. It provides an introduction to social contructionist perspectives on gender and a brief critique of gender role theory before illustrating how health beliefs and behaviour are used in constructing gender in North America, and how masculinity and health are constructed within a relational context. It further examines how men construct various forms of masculinity—or masculinities—and how these different enactments of gender, as well as differing social structural influences, contribute to differential health risks among men in the United States.

HEALTH AND THE SOCIAL CONSTRUCTION OF GENDER

Constructionism and Theories of Gender

Previous explanations of masculinity and men's health have focused primarily on the hazardous influences of "*the* male sex role" (Goldberg; Nathanson; Harrison; Verbrugge and Harrison). These explanations relied on theories of gender socialisation that have since been widely criticised (Deaux; Gerson; Kimmel; Pleck; West; Epstein; Messerschmidt and Connell). The sex role theory of socialisation, still commonly employed in analyses of gender, has been criticised for implying that gender represents "two fixed, static and mutually exclusive role containers" (Kimmel, 1986, p. 521) and for assuming that women and men have innate psychological needs for gender-stereotypic traits (Pleck, 1987). Sex role theory also fosters the notion of a singular female or male personality, a notion that has been effectively dis-

puted, and obscures the various forms of femininity and masculinity that women and men can and do demonstrate (Connell, 1995).

From a constructionist perspective, women and men think and act in the ways that they do, not because of their role identities or psychological traits, but because of concepts about femininity and masculinity that they adopt from their culture (Pleck et al., 1994a). Gender is not two static categories, but rather "a set of socially constructed relationships which are produced and reproduced through people's actions" (Gerson and Peiss, 1985, p. 327); it is constructed by dynamic, dialectic relationships (Connell, 1995). Gender is "something that one does, and *does* recurrently, in interaction with others" (West and Zimmerman, 1987, p. 140; italics theirs); it is achieved or demonstrated and is better understood as a verb than as a noun (Kaschak; Bohan and Crawford). Most importantly, gender does not reside in the person, but rather in social transactions defined as gendered (Bohan and Crawford). From this perspective, gender is viewed as a dynamic, social structure.

Gender Stereotypes

Gender is constructed from cultural and subjective meanings that constantly shift and vary, depending on the time and place (Kimmel, 1995). Gender stereotypes are among the meanings used by society in the construction of gender, and are characteristics that are generally believed to be typical either of women or of men. There is very high agreement in our society about what are considered to be typically feminine and typically masculine characteristics (Williams; Golombok and Street). These stereotypes provide collective, organised—and dichotomous—meanings of gender and often become widely shared beliefs about who women and men innately *are* (Pleck, 1987). People are encouraged to conform to stereotypic beliefs and behaviours, and commonly do conform to and adopt dominant norms of femininity and masculinity (Eagly; Deaux and Bohan). Conforming to what is expected of them further reinforces self-fulfilling prophecies of such behaviour (Geis and Crawford).

Research indicates that men and boys experience comparatively greater social pressure than women and girls to endorse gendered societal prescriptions—such as the strongly endorsed *health-related* beliefs that men are independent, self-reliant, strong, robust and tough (Williams; Golombok and Martin). It is, therefore, not surprising that their behaviour and their beliefs about gender are more stereotypic than those of women and girls (Katz; Rice; Street and Levant). From a social constructionist perspective, however, men and boys are not passive victims of a socially prescribed role, nor are they simply conditioned or socialised by their cultures. Men and boys are active agents in constructing and reconstructing dominant norms of masculinity. This concept of agency—the part individuals play in exerting power and producing effects in their lives—is central to constructionism (Courtenay, 1999a).

Health Beliefs and Behaviours: Resources for Constructing Gender

The activities that men and women engage in, and their gendered cognitions, are a form of currency in transactions that are continually enacted in the demonstration of gender. Previous authors have examined how a variety of activities are used as resources in constructing and reconstructing gender; these activities include language (Perry and Crawford); work (Connell, 1995); sports (Connell and Messner); crime (Messerschmidt, 1993); and sex (Vance, 1995). The very manner in which women and men do these activities contributes both to the defining of one's self as gendered and to social conventions of gender.

Health-related beliefs and behaviours can similarly be understood as a means of constructing or demonstrating gender. In this way, the health behaviours and beliefs that people adopt simultaneously define and enact representations of gender. Health beliefs and

behaviours, like language, can be understood as "a set of strategies for negotiating the social landscape" (Crawford, 1995, p. 17), or tools for constructing gender. Like crime, health behaviour "may be invoked as a practice through which masculinities (and men and women) are differentiated from one another" (Messerschmidt, 1993, p. 85). The findings from one small study examining gender differences and health led the author to conclude that "the doing of health is a form of doing gender" (Saltonstall, 1993, p. 12). In this regard, "health actions are social acts" and "can be seen as a form of practice which constructs . . . 'the person' in the same way that other social and cultural activities do" (Saltonstall, 1993, p. 12).

The social experiences of women and men provide a template that guides their beliefs and behaviour (Kimmel, 1995). The various social transactions, institutional structures and contexts that women and men encounter elicit different demonstrations of health beliefs and behaviours, and provide different opportunities to conduct this particular form of demonstrating gender. If these social experiences and demonstrated beliefs or behaviours had no bearing on the health of women and men, they would be of no relevance here. This, however, is not the case. The social practices required for demonstrating femininity and masculinity are associated with very different health advantages and risks (Courtenay, 1998a and Courtenay, 1999). Unlike the presumably innocent effects of wearing lipstick or wearing a tie, the use of health-related beliefs and behaviours to define oneself as a woman or a man has a profound impact on one's health and longevity.

THEORISING MASCULINITY IN THE CONTEXT OF HEALTH

As Messerschmidt (1993, p. 62) notes in regard to the study of gender and crime, a comprehensive feminist theory of health must similarly include men "not by treating men as the normal subjects, but by articulating the gendered content of men's behaviour". The following sections provide a relational analysis of men's gendered health behaviour based on constructionist and feminist theories, and examine how cultural dictates, everyday interactions and social and institutional structures help to sustain and reproduce men's health risks.

Gender, Power and the Social Construction of the "Stronger" Sex

A discussion of power and social inequality is necessary to understand the broader context of men's adoption of unhealthy behaviour—as well as to address the social structures that both foster unhealthy behaviour among men and undermine men's attempts to adopt healthier habits. Gender is negotiated in part through relationships of power. Microlevel power practices (Pyke, 1996) contribute to structuring the social transactions of everyday life, transactions that help to sustain and reproduce broader structures of power and inequality. These power relationships are located in and constituted in, among other practices, the practice of health behaviour. The systematic subordination of women and lower-status men—or patriarchy—is made possible, in part, through these gendered demonstrations of health and health behaviour. In this way, males use health beliefs and behaviours to demonstrate dominant—and hegemonic—masculine ideals that clearly establish them as men. Hegemonic masculinity is the idealised form of masculinity at a given place and time (Connell, 1995). It is the socially dominant gender construction that subordinates femininities as well as other forms of masculinity, and reflects and shapes men's social relationships with women and other men; it represents power and authority. Today in the United States, hegemonic masculinity is embodied in heterosexual, highly educated, European American men of upper-class economic status.

The fact that there are a variety of health risks associated with being a man, in no way implies that men do not hold power. Indeed, it is in the pursuit of power and privilege that men are often led to harm themselves (Clatterbaugh, 1997). The social practices that undermine men's health are often the instruments men use in the structuring and acquisition of power. Men's acquisition of power requires, for example, that men suppress their needs and refuse to admit to or acknowledge their pain (Kaufman, 1994). Additional health-related beliefs and behaviours that can be used in the demonstration of hegemonic masculinity include the denial of weakness or vulnerability, emotional and physical control, the appearance of being strong and robust, dismissal of any need for help, a ceaseless interest in sex, the display of aggressive behaviour and physical dominance. These health-related demonstrations of gender and power represent forms of microlevel power practices, practices that are "part of a system that affirms and (re)constitutes broader relations of inequality" (Pyke, 1996, p. 546). In exhibiting or enacting hegemonic ideals with health behaviours, men reinforce strongly held cultural beliefs that men are more powerful and less vulnerable than women; that men's bodies are structurally more efficient than and superior to women's bodies; that asking for help and caring for one's health are feminine; and that the most powerful men among men are those for whom health and safety are irrelevant.

It has been demonstrated elsewhere (Courtenay, 1998a; Courtenay, in press b; and Courtenay, 1999) that the resources available in the United States for constructing masculinities are largely unhealthy. Men and boys often use these resources and reject healthy beliefs and behaviours in order to demonstrate and achieve manhood. By dismissing their health care needs, men are constructing gender. When a man brags, "I haven't been to a doctor in years," he is simultaneously describing a health practice and situating himself in a masculine arena. Similarly, men are demonstrating dominant norms of masculinity when they refuse to take sick leave from work, when they insist that they need little sleep, and when they boast that drinking does not impair their driving. Men also construct masculinities by embracing risk. A man may define the degree of his masculinity, for example, by driving dangerously or performing risky sports—and displaying these behaviours like badges of honor. In these ways, masculinities are defined *against* positive health behaviours and beliefs.

To carry out any one positive health behaviour, a man may need to reject multiple constructions of masculinity. For example, the application of sunscreen to prevent skin cancer—the most rapidly increasing cancer in the United States (CDC, 1995a)—may require the rejection of a variety of social constructions: masculine men are unconcerned about health matters; masculine men are invulnerable to disease; the application of lotions to the body is a feminine pastime; masculine men don't "pamper" or "fuss" over their bodies; and "rugged good looks" are produced with a tan. In *not* applying sunscreen, a man may be simultaneously demonstrating gender and an unhealthy practice. The facts that 1½ times more men than women nationally believe that one looks better with a tan (American Academy of Dermatology, 1997), that men are significantly less likely to use sunscreen (Mermelstein; Courtenay, 1998a and Courtenay), and that the skin cancer death rate is twice as high for men as for women (CDC, 1995b), may be a testament to the level of support among men for endorsing these constructions.

When a man does experience an illness or disability, the gender ramifications are often great. Illness "can reduce a man's status in masculine hierarchies, shift his power relations with women, and raise his self-doubts about masculinity" (Charmaz, 1995, p. 268). The friend of a U.S. senator recently cautioned him against publicly discussing his diagnosis of prostate cancer, contending that "some men might see [his] willingness to go public with his private struggle as a sign of weakness" (Jaffe, 1997, p. 134). In efforts to preserve their masculinity, one researcher found that men with chronic illnesses often

worked diligently to hide their disabilities: a man with diabetes, unable to maneuver both his wheelchair and a cafeteria tray, would skip lunch and risk a coma rather than request assistance; a middle-aged man declined offers of easier jobs to prove that he was still capable of strenuous work; an executive concealed dialysis treatments by telling others that he was away attending meetings (Charmaz, 1995).

Femininities and Men's Health

It is not only the endorsement of hegemonic ideals but also the rejection of feminine ideals that contributes to the construction of masculinities and to the systematic oppression of women and less powerful men. Rejecting what is constructed as feminine is essential for demonstrating hegemonic masculinity in a sexist and gender-dichotomous society. Men and boys who attempt to engage in social action that demonstrates feminine norms of gender risk being relegated to the subordinated masculinity of "wimp" or "sissy." A gay man who grew up on Indiana farms said he would have been ridiculed as a "sissy" had he done the (risk-free) tasks of cooking, baking, and sewing that he preferred: "My uncle would have started it and it would have spread out from there. Even my grandfather would say, 'Oh, you don't want to do that. That's girl stuff.'" (Fellows, 1996, p. 12). Health care utilisation and positive health beliefs or behaviours are also socially constructed as forms of idealised femininity (Courtenay, 1998a; Courtenay and Courtenay, 1999). They are, therefore, potentially feminising influences that men must oppose with varying degrees of force, depending on what other resources are accessible or are being utilisied in the construction of masculinities. Forgoing health care is a means of rejecting "girl stuff."

Men's denial and disregard of physical discomfort, risk and health care needs are all means of demonstrating difference from women, who are presumed to embody these "feminine" characteristics. These behaviours serve both as proof of men's superiority over women and as proof of their ranking among "real" men. A man's success in adopting (socially feminised) health-promoting behaviour, like his failure to engage in (socially masculinised) physically risky behaviour, can undermine his ranking among men and relegate him to a subordinated status. That men and boys construct masculinities in opposition to the healthy beliefs and behaviours of women—and less masculine (i.e., "feminised") men and boys—is clearly apparent in their discourse, as evidenced by the remarks of one firefighter: "When you go out to fires, you will work yourself into the ground. Just so nobody else thinks you're a puss" (Delsohn, 1996, p. 95). Similarly, one author, the chief editor of a major publishing company, recently revealed his concern about disclosing his pain to others after a radical prostatectomy: "I was reluctant to complain further [to hospital staff], for fear of being thought a sissy" (Korda, 1996, p. 148). In prison, men criticise fellow prisoners who "complain too much" about sickness or pain or make frequent health care visits, as displaying signs of "softness" (Courtenay and Sabo, in press).

Differences Among Men

Contemporary feminist theorists are as concerned about differences among men (and among women) as they are about differences between women and men. As (Messerschmidt, 1993, p. 87) notes, "'Boys will be boys' differently, depending upon their position in social structures and, therefore, upon their access to power and resources." Although men may endorse similar masculine ideals, different men may enact these ideals in different ways. For example, although most young men in the United States may agree that a man should be "tough" (Courtenay, 1998a), *how* each man demonstrates being tough—and how demonstrating toughness affects him physically—will be influenced by his age, ethnicity, social class and sexuality. Depending upon these factors, a man may use a gun, his fists, his sexuality, a mountain bike, physical labor, a car or the re-

lentless pursuit of financial strength to construct this particular aspect of masculinity.

Social class positioning "both constrains and enables certain forms of gendered social action" (Messerschmidt, 1993, p. 94) and influences which unhealthy behaviours are used to demonstrate masculinity. Demonstrating masculinities with fearless, high-risk behaviours may entail skydiving for an upper-class man, mountain climbing for a middle-class man, racing hot rods for a working-class man and street fighting for a poor urban man. Many working-class masculinities that are constructed as exemplary—as in the case of firemen—require the dismissal of fear, and feats of physical endurance and strength, that often put these men at risk of injury and death. The avoidance of health care is another form of social action that allows some men to maintain their status and to avoid being relegated to a subordinated position in relation to physicians and health professionals, as well as other men. For an upper-middle-class business executive, refusing to see a physician can be a means of maintaining his position of power. Prisoners can similarly maintain their status by disregarding their health care needs: "When you got stabbed you usually bandaged yourself up . . . To go to the doctor would appear that you are soft" (Courtenay and Sabo, in press).

The construction of health and gender does not occur in isolation from other forms of social action that demonstrate differences among men. Health practices may be used simultaneously to enact multiple social constructions, such as ethnicity, social class and sexuality. The use of health beliefs and behaviours to construct the interacting social structures of masculinity and ethnicity is illustrated in this passage by a Chicano novelist:

A macho doesn't show weakness. Grit your teeth, take the pain, bear it alone. Be tough. You feel like letting it out? Well, then let's get drunk with our *compadres* . . . Drinking buddies who have a contest to see who can consume the most beer, or the most shots of tequila, are trying to prove their maleness (Anaya, 1996, p. 63).

Too often, factors such as ethnicity, economic status and sexuality are simply treated by health scientists as variables to be controlled for in statistical analyses. However, the social structuring of ethnicity, sexuality and economic status is intimately and systematically related to the social structuring of gender and power. These various social structures are constructed concurrently and are intertwined. When European American working-class boys speed recklessly through a poor African American neighborhood, not wearing safety belts and yelling epithets out their windows, they are using health risk behaviours—among other behaviours—in the simultaneous construction of gender, power, class and ethnicity; when they continue these behaviours in a nearby gay neighbourhood, they are further reproducing gender, power and normative heterosexuality. Similarly, poor health beliefs and behaviours are used by men and boys to construct masculinities in conjunction with the use of other behaviours such as crime (Messerschmidt, 1993), work (Pyke, 1996) and being "cool" (Majors and Billson, 1992). Committing criminal acts may be insufficient to win a young man inclusion in a street gang; he may also be required to prove his manhood by demonstrating his willingness to ignore pain or to engage in physical fighting.

Making a Difference: The Negotiation of Power and Status

Just as men exercise varying degrees of power over women, so they exercise varying degrees of power among themselves. "Masculinities are configurations of social practices produced not only in relation to femininities but also in relation to one another" (Pyke, 1996, p. 531). Dominant masculinities subordinate lower-status, marginalised masculinities—such as those of gay, rural or lower-class men. As Connell (1995, p. 76) notes, "To recognise more than one kind of masculinity is only a first step"; "we must also recognise the relations between the different kinds of masculinity: relations of alliance, dominance and

subordination. These relationships are constructed through practices that exclude and include, that intimidate, exploit, and so on" (Connell, 1995, p. 37). In negotiating this perilous landscape of masculinities, the male body is often used as a vehicle. The comments of one man in prison illustrate how the male body can be used in structuring gender and power:

> I have been shot and stabbed. Each time I wore bandages like a badge of honor . . . Each situation made me feel a little more tougher than the next guy . . . Being that I had survived, these things made me feel bigger because I could imagine that the average person couldn't go through a shoot out or a knife fight, survive and get right back into the action like it was nothing. The perception that I had constructed in my mind was that most people were discouraged after almost facing death, but the really bad ones could look death in the eye with little or no compunction (Courtenay and Sabo, in press).

Physical dominance and violence are easily accessible resources for structuring, negotiating and sustaining masculinities, particularly among men who because of their social positioning lack less dangerous means.

The health risks associated with any form of masculinity will differ depending on whether a man is enacting a hegemonic, subordinated, marginalised, complicit or resistant form. When men and boys are denied access to the social power and resources necessary for constructing hegemonic masculinity, they must seek other resources for constructing gender that validate their masculinity (Messerschmidt, 1993). Disadvantages resulting from such factors as ethnicity, economic status, educational level and sexual orientation marginalise certain men and augment the relevance of enacting other forms of masculinity.

Rejecting health behaviours that are socially constructed as feminine, embracing risk and demonstrating fearlessness are readily accessible means of enacting masculinity. Messerschmidt (1993, p. 110) notes that "participation in street violence, a more frequent practice when other hegemonic masculine ideals are unavailable (e.g., a job in the paid-labor market), demonstrates to closest friends that one is 'a man'"—or as one young man reported, "If somebody picks on you or something, and you don't fight back, they'll call you a chicken. But . . . if you fight back . . . you're cool" (Majors and Billson, 1992, p. 26). Among some African American men and boys, "toughness, violence and disregard of death and danger become the hallmark of survival in a world that does not respond to reasonable efforts to belong and achieve" (Majors and Billson, 1992, p. 34). The results of one small study suggest that toughness and aggression are indeed means for young inner-city African American men to gain status in communities where few other means of doing so are available: "If a young man is a 'tough guy,' peers respect him . . . The highest value is placed on individuals who defend themselves swiftly, even if by doing so they place themselves in danger" (Rich and Stone, 1996, p. 81). Gay and bisexual men or boys may also attempt to compensate by endangering themselves or by adopting physically dominant behaviours rather than being relegated to a lower-status position. As one man put it, "I really hated football, but I tried to play because it would make me more of a man" (Fellows, 1996, p. 40). Gay men may also refuse to engage in behaviour that reduces the risk of contracting AIDS when that behaviour contradicts dominant norms of masculinity: "Real men ignore precautions for AIDS risk reduction, seek many sexual partners, and reject depleasuring the penis. Abstinence, safer sex, and safer drug use compromise manhood" (Levine, 1998; pp. 146–147).

Marginalised men may also attempt to compensate for their subordinated status by defying hegemonic masculinity and constructing alternative forms of masculinity. As Pyke (1996, p. 531) explains, men "with their masculine identity and self-esteem undermined by their subordinate order-taking position in relation to higher-status males" can and do use other resources to "reconstruct their position as embodying *true* masculinity" (emphasis added).

Other authors have variously referred to these alternative enactments of gender as *oppositional* (Messerschmidt, 1993), *compulsive* (Majors and Billson, 1992), *compensatory* (Pyke, 1996), or *protest* (Connell, 1995) masculinities. These "hypermasculine" constructions are frequently dangerous or self-destructive (Meinecke, 1981). Majors and Billson (1992, p. 34) suggest that compulsive masculinity can "lead toward smoking, drug and alcohol abuse, fighting, sexual conquests, dominance and crime". Pyke (1996, p. 538) describes lower-class men who "ostentatiously pursued drugs, alcohol and sexual carousing . . . [to compensate] for their subordinated status in the hierarchy of their everyday work worlds". Similarly, working-class men can and do "use the physical endurance and tolerance of discomfort required of their manual labor as signifying true masculinity, [as] an alternative to the hegemonic form" (Pyke, 1996, p. 531). When the demonstration of the (dominant) heterosexist ideal is not an option—as among gay men—dismissing the risks associated with high numbers of sexual partners or unprotected anal intercourse can serve for some men as a means of demonstrating a protest masculinity. In describing coming out gay, one young man said, "Rage, rage, rage! Let's do everything you've denied yourself for 25 years. Let's get into it and have a good time sexually" (Connell, 1995, p. 153).

It is important to note that although these hypermasculinities may aspire to or be complicit in the reconstruction of an idealised form of masculinity, they are not hegemonic. The fact that some inner-city African American men are successful in being "tough" or "cool," and that some gay men refuse to have protected sex, does not mean that these men are enacting hegemonic masculinity. On the contrary, for marginalised men, "the claim to power that is central in hegemonic masculinity is constantly negated" (Connell, 1995, p. 116).

Like unhealthy behaviours, dominant or idealised beliefs about manhood also provide the means for demonstrating gender. These signifiers of "true" masculinity are readily accessible to men who may otherwise have limited social resources for constructing masculinity. In fact, among young men nationally, lower educational level, lower family income and African American ethnicity are all associated with traditional, dominant norms of masculinity (Courtenay, 1998a). The stronger endorsement of traditional masculine ideology among African American men than among non-African American men is a consistent finding (Pleck; Levant and Levant). Among African American men, the endorsement of dominant norms of masculinity is stronger for both younger and nonprofessional men than it is for older, professional men (Hunter and Harris).

Gay and bisexual men may also adopt culturally sanctioned beliefs about masculinity to compensate for their subordinated and less privileged social position. National data indicate that young men in the United States who are not exclusively heterosexual hold more traditional or dominant beliefs about masculinity than young men who are exclusively heterosexual (Courtenay, 1998a). Although this finding may at first glance appear counterintuitive, it is consistent with a constructionist and relational theory of men's health. The endorsement of hypermasculine beliefs can be understood as a means for gay and bisexual men to prove to others that, despite their sexual preferences, they are still "real" men. Diaz (1998) also maintains that gay Latino men are more compelled to demonstrate dominant norms of masculinity than nongay Latino men.

A growing body of research provides evidence that men who endorse dominant norms of masculinity engage in poorer health behaviours and have greater health risks than their peers with less traditional beliefs (Neff; Pleck; Eisler and O'Neil, Good & Holmes, 1995). One recent longitudinal study of 1,676 young men in the United States, aged 15 to 23 years is among the few nationally representative studies to examine the influence of masculinity on health behaviour over time. When a variety of psychosocial factors were controlled for, beliefs about masculinity emerged as the strongest predictor of risk-taking behaviour 2½ years later. Dominant norms of masculinity—the most traditional beliefs about

manhood adopted by young men—predicted the highest level of risk taking and of involvement in behaviours such as cigarette smoking, high-risk sexual activity and use of alcohol and other drugs.

This feminist structural framework for understanding men's health may help to explain the many health differences found among men, based on their ethnicity, socioeconomic status and education (DHHS, 1998). It may help to explain, for example, why men with the least education are twice as likely to smoke cigarettes as the most highly educated men, and nearly 3 times more likely to report frequent heavy alcohol use; and why their death rate for injuries is nearly 3½ times higher and (among those 25 to 44 years of age) their death rate for homicide is 7 times higher (DHHS, 1998).

Rethinking Compulsive, Oppositional, Compensatory and Protest Masculinities

The terms *compulsive, oppositional, compensatory* and *protest* masculinities can be somewhat misleading. *Most* men are compulsive in demonstrating masculinity, which, as Connell (1995) notes, is continually contested. Furthermore, *most* masculinities that men demonstrate in the United States are oppositional or compensatory; relatively few men construct the hegemonic masculine ideal. This is not to suggest, however, that hegemonic masculinity is not profoundly influential. On the contrary, hegemonic masculinity is a ubiquitous aspect of North American life. Most men necessarily demonstrate alternative masculinities in relation to hegemonic masculinity that variously aspire to, conspire with or attempt to resist, diminish or otherwise undermine hegemonic masculinity. They do this not only in relation to other men perceived to embody hegemonic ideals, but also in relation to institutionalised, hegemonic social structures—including the government and media, the judicial system, corporate and technological industries and academia. However, to suggest that only certain men are compulsive in demonstrating dominant norms of masculinity is to risk further marginalising the subordinated masculinities of lower-class, non-European American, nonheterosexual men. Masculinity *requires* compulsive practice, because it can be contested and undermined at any moment.

Whichever term one chooses to use to describe masculinities that resist (or undermine) hegemonic masculinity, it is critical to distinguish among various forms of resistant masculinity. In terms of men's health, the risks associated with enacting gender can differ greatly among different forms of resistant masculinity. Gay men who identify as *radical fairies* (Rose, 1997) and pacifists provide two examples of men who actively undermine hegemonic masculinity. These men are enacting very different resistant masculinities than those enacted by inner-city gang members, who are constructing an alternate *yet still authoritative and dominant* form of masculinity. Indeed, when lower-class men who lack access to cultural or economic resources attempt to demonstrate power and authority through the use of physical violence, it could be argued that they are not enacting a "compensatory" form of masculinity, but rather a form of *situational or interpersonal hegemony*. Furthermore, the resistant masculinities demonstrated by pacifists, radical fairies and inner-city gang members lead to very different levels and categories of health risk; the masculinities enacted by radical fairies and pacifists may in fact reduce their risks, unlike those forms requiring the use of physical dominance or violence.

Further Contextualising Men's Health

As Messerschmidt (1993, p. 83) notes, "Although men attempt to express hegemonic masculinity through speech, dress, physical appearance, activities and relations with others, these social signs of masculinity are associated with the specific context of one's actions and are self-regulated within that context." Because masculinity is continually contested, it must be renegotiated in each context that a man encounters. A man or boy will enact gender and health differently in different contexts. On the football field, a college student may use exposure to injury and denial of pain to demonstrate masculinity, while at parties he may use excessive drinking to achieve the same end. A man may consider the expression of emotional or physical pain to be unacceptable with other men, but acceptable with a spouse or girlfriend. In some contexts, such as a prison setting (Courtenay and Sabo, in press), the hierarchies of masculinities are unique to that particular context.

Farm life provides a context within which to examine the negotiation of one form of rural masculinity. Growing up on a farm, much of what boys learn to do to demonstrate hegemonic masculinity requires them to adopt risky or unhealthy behaviours, such as operating heavy equipment before they are old enough to do so safely. As two rural men said, "if you're over ten, you'd better be out doing men's work, driving a tractor and that kind of thing" (Fellows, 1996, p. 173); and, "my brother Tony and I started driving the pickup on the farm at age six, as soon as we could reach the pedals. We also learned how to drive a tractor" (Fellows, 1996, p. 305). Another rural man describes similar expectations: "if you were a guy . . . you were born to be a total, typical, straight male—to play sports, to hunt, to do everything a guy was supposed to do" (Fellows, 1996, p. 307). The ways to enact masculinity are dictated in part by cultural norms, such as the belief held by most Pennsylvanians that "farmers *embody* the virtues of independence and self-sufficiency" (Willits et al., 1990, p. 572; emphasis added). Farmers who attempt to demonstrate this cultural ideal of masculinity undermine their health—and there are many such farmers. Among Wisconsin residents who had suffered agricultural injuries—most of whom were men—farmers were the most likely to delay seeking health care; half of them waited for over 2 hours and one in four waited 24 hours (Stueland et al., 1995). Long (1993) described a farmer who caught his finger in equipment while harvesting his wheat field; he pulled his finger out—severing it—

wrapped his hand in a handkerchief, and finished his work for the day before seeking medical care.

It has been emphasised elsewhere (Courtenay and Sabo and Rich) that the negotiation of masculinity in certain contexts can present men with unique health paradoxes, particularly in regard to physical dominance and the use of violence. The perception both among some men in prison (Courtenay and Sabo, in press) and some inner city African American men Rich and Stone (1996) is that failing to fight back makes a man vulnerable to even more extreme victimisation than does retaliating. This health paradox is reflected in the "protective, though violent, posture" described by Rich and Stone (1996, p. 81): "If you appear weak, others will try to victimise you . . . if you show yourself to be strong (by retaliating), then you are perceived as strong and you will be safe" (pp. 80–81). Although these men may neither actively resist nor embrace hegemonic masculinity, they are complicit in its reconstruction.

Institutional Structures, Masculinities and Men's Health

The institutionalised social structures that men encounter elicit different demonstrations of health-related beliefs and behaviours, and provide different opportunities to conduct this particular means of demonstrating gender. These structures—including the government and the military, corporations, technological industries, the judicial system, academia, health care system and the media—help to sustain gendered health risks by cultivating stereotypic forms of gender enactments and by providing different resources for demonstrating gender to women than they provide to men. Institutional structures, by and large, foster unhealthy beliefs and behaviours among men, and undermine men's attempts to adopt healthier habits (Courtenay, 1998a and Courtenay, 1999).

The workforce is one such structure. The work that men do is the most dangerous work.

Mining, construction, timber cutting and fishing have the highest injury death rates in the United States, while the largest number of total injury deaths occur in construction, transportation, agriculture, farming, foresting and fishing—all of which are jobs held primarily by men (Bureau and National). Consequently—although they comprise only half (56%) of the U.S. workforce—men account for nearly all (94%) fatal injuries on the job (NIOSH, 1993). Furthermore, as one small study found, positive health-related activities often conflict with the work activities expected of men—and work is typically given precedence, as evidenced by one man's comments: "I'd do more [to be healthy], but I can't with my job hours. My boss at the lab would kill me" (Saltonstall, 1993, p. 11). When a corporate law firm requires its employees to work 12- to 14-hr days, it is limiting access to health care for its (primarily male) attorneys.

Although they have a profound influence on men's health, institutional structures are not simply imposed on men any more than a prescribed male sex role is simply imposed on men. "Social structures do not exist autonomously from humans; rather . . . as we engage in social action, we simultaneously help create the social structures that facilitate/limit social practice" (Messerschmidt, 1993, p. 62). Men are agents of social practice. When men demonstrate gender "correctly," in the ways that are socially prescribed, they "simultaneously sustain, reproduce and render legitimate the institutional arrangements that are based on sex category" (West and Zimmerman, 1987, p. 146). In a continuous cycle, definitions of gender influence social structures, which guide human interactions and social action, which in turn reinforce gendered social structures. This ongoing process results in a gender division and a differential exposure that inhibits both women and men from learning behaviours, skills and capacities considered characteristic of the "opposite" gender (West and Epstein). Men sustain and reproduce institutional structures in part for the privileges that they derive from preserving existing power structures. The businessman who works tirelessly, denies his stress, and dismisses his physical needs for sleep and a healthy diet often does so because he expects to be rewarded with money, power, position and prestige. Thus, although they are increasing their health risks, men who achieve these hegemonic ideals are compensated with social acceptance; with diminished anxiety about their manhood; and with the rewards that such normative, masculine demonstrations provide in a patriarchal society.

In these regards, men also contribute to the construction of a health care system that ignores their gendered health concerns. Indeed, they are often the very researchers and scientists who have ignored men's gendered health risks. As Assistant Surgeon General Susan Blumenthal, who directed the Office on Women's Health at the U.S. Public Health Service, noted recently, "Men need to become advocates and speak passionately about their health, but they may be concerned that speaking out will reveal weakness, not strength" (Jaffe, 1997, p. 136. As Coward (1984, p. 229) notes, men have kept their bodies from being the subjects of analysis: "Men's bodies and sexuality are taken for granted, exempted from scrutiny, whereas women's are extensively defined and overexposed. Sexual and social meanings are imposed on women's bodies, not men's . . . men have left themselves out of the picture because a body defined is a body controlled".

The Medical Institution and Its Constructions of Gender and Health

Connell (1993) identifies three institutions that are particularly relevant in the contemporary organisation of gender: the state, the workplace/labor market and the family. The health care system and its allied health fields represent a particularly important structural influence in the construction of gender and health. In the case of cardiovascular disease, for example, it is often noted that the fact that women are less likely than men to be routinely tested or

treated for symptoms can foster unrealistic perceptions of risk among women (Steingart and Wenger). Rarely, however, have the ways in which health care contributes to social constructions of men's health been examined. Recently, it has been argued that sociologists, medical researchers and other health professionals have all contributed to cultural portrayals of men as healthy and women as the "sicker" gender (Gijsbers van Wijk et al., 1991); to strongly held beliefs that men's bodies are structurally more efficient than and superior to women's bodies (Courtenay, 1998a); and to the "invisibility" of men's poor health status (Annandale and Clark, 1996).

As Nathanson (1977, p. 148) noted two decades ago, sex differences in health and health-related behaviour arise "out of a medical model that has singled out women for special professional attention"; "women are encouraged and trained to define their life problems in medical terms and to seek professional help for them" (p. 149). While the personal practice of participating in health care is constructed as feminine, the institutional practice of conducting, researching or providing health care is constructed as masculine and defined as a domain of masculine power. Physicians, who are primarily men, maintain power and control over the bodies of men who are not physicians and the bodies of women—as well as over male and female health professionals in lesser positions of power, such as nurses and orderlies. In these ways, the health care system does not simply adapt to men's "natural" masculinity; rather, it actively constructs gendered health behaviour and negotiated among various forms of masculinity. Medical, sociological and feminist approaches to addressing gender and health have all contributed to the devaluing of women's bodies and to the privileging of men's bodies, as two feminist authors have noted recently (Annandale and Clark, 1996).

Historically, women but not men in the United States have been encouraged to pay attention to their health (Nathanson; Lonnquist; Signorielli; Oakley; Annandale and Reagan, 1997). According to Reagan (1997), who recently analysed decades of cancer education in the United States, these educational efforts have been directed primarily at women. Although many counseling and psychological interventions with men have been recommended in the past two decades (Courtenay, in press c), very rarely are these interventions designed to reduce men's health risks (Courtenay, 1998c). Men also receive significantly less physician time in their health visits than women do (Blanchard; Waitzkin and Weisman), and generally receive fewer services and dispositions than women (Verbrugge and Steiner, 1985). Men are provided with fewer and briefer explanations—both simple and technical—in medical encounters (Waitzkin; Hall and Weisman). During checkups, they receive less advice from physicians about changing risk factors for disease than women do (Friedman et al., 1994). Only 29% of physicians routinely provide age-appropriate instruction on performing self-examinations for testicular cancer, compared to the 86% who provide instruction to women on performing breast examinations (Misener and Fuller, 1995). A recent review revealed that no study has ever found that women received less information from physicians than men, which led the authors to conclude that the findings "may reflect sexism in medical encounters, but this may act to the advantage of female patients, who have a more informative and positive experience than is typical for male patients" (Roter and Hall, 1997, p. 44).

A variety of scientific methodologic factors and research methods—developed and conducted primarily by men—have also contributed to the model of deficient women's bodies (Courtenay, 1998a and Courtenay, 1999). For example, the use of behavioural indices of health—such as bed rest and health care utilisation—both pathologises women's health and underestimates the significance of men's health problems. These indices confound our understanding of morbidity, because they actually represent how men and women *cope* with illness rather than representing their true health status (Gijsbers van Wijk et al., 1991); thus they obscure what may be greater illness among men (Verbrugge, 1987 and Kandrack, 1991). The assumption underlying these and other indices of health is that male behaviour is the normative or hidden referent; consequently, researchers and theorists alike presume that women are in poorer health because women get more bed rest than men do and see physicians more often. The terms applied to these behaviours—behaviours that can be considered health promoting—further pathologise women's health: women's *excess* bed rest and women's *over*utilisation of health services. These terms simultaneously transform curative actions into indicators of illness, make women's health problematic, and reinforce men's position in providing the standard of health or health behaviour.

Given that women are unquestionably less susceptible to serious illness and live longer than men, it would seem that women should provide the standard against which men's health and men's health behaviour are measured. If this were the case, we would be compelled instead to confront men's *inadequate* bed rest and men's *under*utilisation of health care. However, the social forces that maintain women's health as problematic are strong. When morbidity statistics and women's greater propensity for illness are challenged as an artifact of research, for example, the conventional reading of this challenge further pathologises women's health by suggesting that women "aren't really ill at all, they're only inventing it" (Oakley, 1994, p. 431). In contrast, the interpretation that men really *are* ill and they are simply denying it is rarely proposed. It was recently argued that a cultural perception of men's health problems as nonexistent is required both to construct women's bodies as deficient and to reinforce women's disadvantaged social position (Annandale and Clark, 1996). To maintain this construction, "women 'cannot' be well and . . . men cannot be ill; they are 'needed' to be well to construe women as sick" (Annandale and Clark, 1996, p. 32). By dismissing their health needs and taking physical risks, men are legitimising themselves as the "stronger" sex.

Despite countless examples in research, literature and daily life, the poor health beliefs and behaviours that men use to demonstrate gender remain largely invisible—a testament to the potency of the social construction of men's resiliency and health. Medical and epidemiologic examinations of health and health behaviour consistently fail to take into account gender, apart from biologic sex. For example, while men's greater use of substances is well known, the reasons *why* men are more likely to use substances are poorly understood and rarely addressed. Similarly, although injury and death due to recreation, risk taking and violence are always associated with being male, epidemiologic and medical findings are consistently presented as if *gender* were of no particular relevance (Courtenay, 1999b). Few health scientists, sociologists and theorists identify masculinities—and rarely even male sex—as a risk factor; fewer still have attempted to identify what it is about men, exactly, that leads them to engage in behaviours that seriously threaten their health. Instead, mens' risk taking and violence are taken for granted.

The failure of medical and epidemiologic researchers to study and explain men's risk taking and violence perpetuates the false, yet widespread, cultural assumption that risk-taking and violent behaviours are natural to, or inherent in, men. Similarly, cultural assumptions that men simply don't (read inherently) seek help prevent society from defining men's underutilisation of health services as a problem. Although it too is taken for granted, there is nothing natural about the fact that men make fewer health visits than women. Early in their lives, most adolescent girls in the United States are *taught* the importance of regular physical exams and are introduced to them as a part of being a woman; adolescent boys are not taught that physical exams are part of being a man. Furthermore, for many men, it is their wives, girlfriends and mothers who monitor their health and schedule any medical appointments that they have. Men who want to take greater responsibility for their health will need not only to cross gendered boundaries, but also to learn new skills. Gendered health perspectives that address social structural issues and masculinity are similarly absent from health science research and literature. Such perspectives could, for example, utilise a gendered approach to examining men's work and their far greater exposure to industrial carcinogens as a possible explanation for their greater risk of cancer as compared to women.

The Social Construction of Disease

Depression provides one example of how the health care system contributes to the social construction of disease. Despite suicide rates that are 4 to 12 times higher for men than for women (DHHS, 1994), according to Warren (1983), early documentation on the prevalence of depression among women based on self-reporting has resulted in an emphasis on treating women for depression and suggested an immunity to depression among men. Although young men account for nearly seven of eight suicides among those 15 to 24 yr old (DHHS, 1996)—an age group in which suicide is the third leading cause of death—a recent large study based exclusively on self-report data concluded that depression is a "more critical" health problem for college women than for college men (Sax, 1997, p. 261). This study fails to take into account men's suicides in this age group. It also disregards decades of research that have consistently found a lack of significant sex differences in *diagnosable* depression among college students (Nolen—Hoeksema, 1987, and Courtenay, 1998).

Treatment rates are also used as indicators of morbidity. However, because depressed men have been found to be more likely than depressed women to not seek help (Chino and Keepasis, 1984), treatment rates are likewise an inaccurate measure of depression. Gender-biased diagnostic decisions of mental health clinicians also contribute to inaccuracies in morbidity statistics (Ford; Waisberg; Fernbach and Adler). One recent large and well-constructed study found that clinicians were less likely to identify the presence of depression in men than in women, and that they failed to diagnose nearly two thirds of the depressed men (Potts et al., 1991).

Although the failure among clinicians to diagnose depression in men contributes to men's low treatment rates, men's own unwillingness to seek help contributes to the social construction of their invulnerability to depression. Indeed, in response to depression, men are more likely than women to rely on themselves, to withdraw socially, to try to talk themselves out of depression, or to convince themselves that depression is "stupid" (Warren, 1983; Chino & Funabiki, 1984; and O'Neil, 1985). Nearly half of men over age 49 nationally who reported experiencing an extended depression did not discuss it with anyone (American Medical Association, 1991). Instead, men tend to engage in private activities, including drinking and drug use, designed to distract themselves or to alleviate their depression (Chino and Nolen). Denial of depression is one of the means men use to demonstrate masculinities and to avoid assignment to a lower-status position relative to women and other men. As Warren (1983, p. 151) notes, "The linkage between depression and femininity may provide men with the strongest motivation to hide their depression from others," and, "Because depression is frequently accompanied by feelings of powerlessness and diminished control, men may construe depression as a sign of failure."

CONCLUSION

Research consistently demonstrates that women in the United States adopt healthier beliefs and personal health practices than men. A wealth of scientific data suggests that this distinction accounts in no small part for the fact that women suffer less severe chronic conditions and live nearly 7 years longer than men. From a social constructionist perspective, this distinction can be understood as being among the many differences that women and men are expected to demonstrate.

If men want to demonstrate dominant ideals of manhood as defined in North American society, they must adhere to cultural definitions of masculine beliefs and behaviours and actively reject what is feminine. The resources available in the United States for constructing masculinities—and the signifiers of "true" masculinity—are largely unhealthy. Men and boys do indeed use these resources and adopt unhealthy beliefs and behaviours in order to demonstrate manhood. Although nothing strictly prohibits a man from demonstrating masculinities differently, to do so would require that he cross over socially constructed gender boundaries, and risk reproach and sometimes physical danger for failing to demonstrate gender correctly. By successfully using unhealthy beliefs and behaviours to demonstrate idealised forms of masculinity, men are able to assume positions of power—relative to women and less powerful men—in a patriarchal society that rewards this accomplishment. By dismissing their health needs and taking risks, men legitimise themselves as the "stronger" sex. In this way, men's use of unhealthy beliefs and behaviours helps to sustain and reproduce social inequality and the social structures that, in turn, reinforce and reward men's poor health habits.

It should be noted that some men do defy social prescriptions of masculinity and adopt healthy behaviours, such as getting annual physicals and eating healthy foods. But although these men are constructing a form of masculinity, it is not among the dominant forms that are encouraged in men, nor is it among the forms adopted by most men. It should also be noted that women can and do adopt unhealthy beliefs and behaviours to demonstrate femininities, as in the case of unhealthy dieting to attain a culturally defined body ideal of slimness. However, as has been demonstrated elsewhere (Courtenay, 1998a and Courtenay, 1999b), the striving for cultural standards of femininity leads women to engage primarily in healthy, not unhealthy, behaviours.

This relational theory of gender and men's health will undoubtedly meet with resistance from many quarters. As a society, we all work diligently at maintaining constructions of women's health as deficient, of the female body as inferior, of men's health as ideal, and of the male body as structurally efficient and superior. From a feminist perspective, these constructions can be viewed as preserving existing power structures and the many privileges enjoyed by men in the United States. Naming and confronting men's poor health status and unhealthy beliefs and behaviours may well improve their physical well-being, but it will necessarily undermine men's privileged position and threaten their power and authority in relation to women.

REFERENCES

ADLER, D.A., DRAKE, R.E. AND TEAGUE, G.B., 1990. Clinicians' practices in personality assessment: does gender influence the use of DSM-III axis II? *Comprehensive Psychiatry* 31 2, pp. 125–133.

American Academy of Dermatology, 1997. "It Can't Happen to Me": *Americans Not As Safe From the Sun As They Think They Are* American Academy of Dermatology, Schaumburg, IL.

American Heart Association, 1995. *Heart and Stroke Facts: 1995 Statistical Supplement* American Heart Association, Dallas TX.

American Medical Association, 1991, October. Results of 9/91 Gallup survey on older men's health perceptions and behaviours (News Release). American Medical Association, Chicago, IL.

ANAYA, R., 1996. "I'm the king": the macho image. In: Gonzales, R. Editor, 1996, *Muy Macho* Doubleday, New York, pp. 57–73.

ANNANDALE, E. AND CLARK, J., 1996. What is gender? Feminist theory and the sociology of human reproduction. *Sociology of Health and Illness* 18 1, pp. 17–44.

BAYNE-SMITH, M. Editor, 1996. *Race, Gender, and Health* Sage Publications, Thousands Oaks, CA.

BLANCHARD, C.G., RUCKDESCHEL, J.C., BLANCHARD, E.B., ARENA, J.G., SAUNDERS, N.L. AND MALLOY, E.D., 1983. Interactions between oncologists and patients during rounds. *Annals of Internal Medicine* 99, pp. 694–699.

BOHAN, J.S., 1993. Regarding gender: essentialism, constructionism and feminist psychology. *Psychology of Women Quarterly* 17, pp. 5–21.

BROWN, J.S. AND MCCREEDY, M., 1986. The Hale elderly: health behaviour and its correlates. *Research in Nursing and Health* 9, pp. 317–329.

Bureau of Labor Statistics, 1991. *National Census of Fatal Occupational Injuries, 1993* Bureau of Labor Statistics, Washington, DC.

CASPERSEN, C.J. AND MERRITT, R.K., 1995. Physical activity trends among 26 states, 1986–1990. *Medicine and Science in Sports and Exercise* 27 5, pp. 713–720. Abstract

Centers for Disease Control, 1995. *Skin Cancer Prevention and Early Detection: At-a-Glance* Centers for Disease Control, Atlanta, GA.

Centers for Disease Control, 1995b. Deaths from melanoma—United States, 1973–1992. Morbidity and Mortality Weekly Report, 44 (44), 337, 343–347.

Centers for Disease Control, 1997. Demographic differences in notifiable infectious disease morbidity—United States, 1992–1994. Morbidity and Mortality Weekly Report, 46 (28), 637–641.

CHARMAZ, K., 1995. Identity dilemmas of chronically ill men. In: Sabo, D. and Gordon, D.F. Editors, 1995. *Men's Health and Illness: Gender, Power and the Body* Sage Publications, Thousand Oaks, CA, pp. 266–291.

CHINO, A.F. AND FUNABIKI, D., 1984. A cross-validation of sex differences in the expression of depression. *Sex Roles* 11, pp. 175–187.

CLATTERBAUGH, K., 1997. *Contemporary Perspectives on Masculinity: Men, Women and Politics in Modern Society* (2nd ed.), Westview Press, Boulder, CO.

CONNELL, R.W., 1992. Masculinity, violence and war. In: Kimmel, M.S. and Messner, M.A. Editors, 1992. *Men's Lives* (2nd ed. ed.), Macmillan, New York, pp. 176–183.

CONNELL, R.W., 1993. The big picture: masculinities in recent world history. *Theory and Society* 22, pp. 597–623.

CONNELL, R.W., 1995. *Masculinities* University of California Press, Berkeley, CA.

COURTENAY, W.H., 1998a. Better to die than cry? A longitudinal and constructionist study of masculinity and the health risk behaviour of young American men. (University of California at Berkeley). Dissertation Abstracts International, 59(08A), (Publication number 9902042).

COURTENAY, W.H., 1998b. College men's health: an overview and a call to action. *Journal of American College Health* 46 6, pp. 279–290.

COURTENAY, W.H., 1998c. Communication strategies for improving men's health: the 6-point HEALTH plan. Wellness Management, 14(1), 1, 3–4.

COURTENAY, W.H., 1999a. Situating men's health in the negotiation of masculinities. *The Society for the Psychological Study of Men and Masculinity Bulletin (the American Psychological Association)* 4 2, pp. 10–12.

COURTENAY, W.H., 1999b. *Youth* violence? Let's call it what it is. *Journal of American College Health* 48 3, pp. 141–142.

COURTENAY, W.H. Behavioural factors associated with disease, injury, and death among men: evidence and implications for prevention. Journal of Men's Studies (in press a).

COURTENAY, W.H. Engendering health: a social constructionist examination of men's health beliefs and behaviours. Psychology of Men and Masculinity (in press b).

COURTENAY, W.H. Social work, counseling, and psychotherapeutic interventions with men and boys: a bibliography. Men and Masculinities (in press c).

COURTENAY, W.H. SABO, D. Preventive health strategies for men in prison. In: Sabo, D., Kupers, T., and London, W. (Eds.), Confronting Prison Masculinities: The Gendered Politics of Punishment. Temple University Press, Philadelphia, PA (in press).

COWARD, R., 1984. *Female Desire: Women's Sexuality Today* Paladin Publishing, London.

CRAWFORD, M., 1995. *Talking Difference: On Gender and Language* Sage Publications, Thousand Oaks, CA.

DEAUX, K., 1984. From individual differences to social categories: an analysis of a decade's research on gender. *American Psychologist* 39 2, pp. 105–116.

DELSOHN, S., 1996. *The Fire Inside: Firefighters Talk About Their Lives* HarperCollins Publishers, New York.

Department of Health and Human Services, 1994. *Mortality, Part A: Vital Statistics of the United States, 1990* vol. II Public Health Service, Hyattsville, MD.

Department of Health and Human Services, 1996. Report of final mortality statistics, 1994. Monthly Vital Statistics Report, 45 (3, Supplement). Public Health Service, Hyattsville, MD.

Department of Health and Human Services, 1998. *Health, United States, 1998: Socioeconomic Status and Health Chartbook* National Center for Health Statistics, Hyattsville, MD.

DIAZ, R.M., 1998. *Latino Gay Men and Hiv: Culture, Sexuality and Risk Behaviour* Routledge, New York.

DONNERMEYER, J.J. AND PARK, D.S., 1995. Alcohol use among rural adolescents: predictive and situational factors. *International Journal of the Addictions* 30 4, pp. 459–479. Abstract

DOYAL, L., 1995. *What Makes Women Sick: Gender and the Political Economy of Health* Rutgers University Press, New Brunswick, NJ.

EAGLY, A.H., 1983. Gender and social influence: a social psychological analysis. *American Psychologist* 38, pp. 971–981.

EISLER, R.M., 1995. The relationship between Masculine Gender Role Stress and men's health risk: the validation of a construct. In: Levant, R.F. and Pollack, W.S. Editors, 1995. *A New Psychology of Men* BasicBooks, New York, pp. 207–225.

EPSTEIN, C.F., 1988. *Deceptive Distinctions: Sex, Gender and the Social Order* Yale University Press, New Haven, CT.

FELLOWS, W., 1996. *Farm Boys: Lives of Gay Men from the Rural Midwest* The University of Wisconsin Press, Madison, WI.

FERNBACH, B.E., WINSTEAD, B.A. AND DERLEGA, V.J., 1989. Sex differences in diagnosis and treatment recommendations for antisocial personality and somatisation disorders. *Journal of Social and Clinical Psychology* 8, pp. 238–255.

FORD, J.R. AND WIDIGER, T.A., 1989. Sex bias in the diagnosis of histrionic and antisocial personality disorders. *Journal of Consulting and Clinical Psychology* 57, pp. 301–305.

FRIEDMAN, C., BROWNSON, R.C., PETERSON, D.E. AND WILKERSON, J.C., 1994. Physician advice to reduce chronic disease risk factors. *American Journal of Preventive Medicine* 10 6, pp. 367–371.

GEIS, F.L., 1993. Self-fulfilling prophecies: a social psychological view of gender. In: Beall, A.E. and Sternberg, R.J. Editors, 1993. *The Psychology of Gender* Guilford Press, New York, pp. 9–54.

GERSON, J.M. AND PEISS, K., 1985. Boundaries, negotiation, consciousness: reconceptualising gender relations. *Social Problems* 32 4, pp. 317–331.

GIBBS, J.T., 1988. Health and mental health of young black males. In: Gibbs, J.T. Editor, 1988. *Young, Black and Male in America: An Endangered Species* Auburn House, New York, pp. 219–257.

GIJSBERS VAN WIJK, C.M.T., VLIET VAN, K.P., KOLK, K.P. AND EVERAERD, W.T., 1991. Symptom sensitivity and sex differences in physical morbidity: a review of health surveys in the United States and the Netherlands. *Women and Health* 17, pp. 91–124.

GOLDBERG, H., 1976. *The Hazards of Being Male: Surviving the Myth of Masculine Privilege* Nash Publishing, Plainview, NY.

GOLOMBOK, S. AND FIVUSH, R., 1994. *Gender Development* Cambridge University Press, Cambridge, MA.

HALL, J.A., ROTER, D.L. AND KATZ, N.R., 1988. Meta-analysis of correlates of provider behaviour in medical encounters. *Medical Care* 26, pp. 657–675.

HARRIS, I., TORRES, J.B. AND ALLENDER, D., 1994. The responses of African American men to dominant norms of masculinity within the United States. *Sex Roles* 31, pp. 703–719.

HARRISON, J.B., 1978. Warning: the male sex role may be dangerous to your health. *Journal of Social Issues* 34 1, pp. 65–86.

HARRISON, J., CHIN, J. AND FICARROTO, T., 1992. Warning: the male sex role may be dangerous to your health. In: Kimmel, M.S. and Messner, M.A. Editors, 1992. *Men's Lives* (2nd ed. ed.), pp. 271–285.

HUNTER, A.G. AND DAVID, J.E., 1992. Constructing gender: an exploration of Afro-American men's conceptualisation of manhood. *Gender and Society* 6, pp. 464–479.

JAFFE, H., 1997. Dying for dollars. *Men's Health*, 12, 132–137, 186–187.

KANDRACK, M., GRANT, K.R. AND SEGALL, A., 1991. Gender differences in health related behaviour: some unanswered questions. *Social Science and Medicine* 32 5, pp. 579–590. GEOBASE

KASCHAK, E., 1992. *Engendered Lives: A New Psychology of Women's Experience* BasicBooks, New York.

KATZ, P.A. AND KSANSNAK, K.R., 1994. Developmental aspects of gender role flexibility and traditionality in middle childhood and adolescence. *Developmental Psychology* 30 2, pp. 272–282.

KAUFMAN, M., 1994. Men, feminism, and men's contradictory experiences of power. In: Brod, H. and Kaufman, M. Editors, 1994. *Theorising Masculinities* Sage Publications, Thousand Oaks, CA, pp. 142–163.

KIMMEL, M.S., 1986. Introduction: toward men's studies. *American Behavioural Scientist* 29 5, pp. 517–529.

KIMMEL, M., 1986. *Manhood in America: A Cultural History* Free Press, New York.

KOOP, C.E., 1996. Foreword. In: Woolf, S.H., Jonas, S. and Lawrence, R.S. Editors, 1996. *Health Promotion and Disease Prevention in Clinical Practice* Williams and Wilkins, Baltimore, MD, pp. 7–9.

KORDA, M., 1996. *Man to Man: Surviving Prostate Cancer* Random House, New York.

LAVEIST, T.A., 1993. Segregation, poverty and empowerment: health consequences for African Americans. *Milbank Quarterly* 71 1, pp. 41–64.

LEE, P.R., 1996. Foreword. In: *U.S. Preventive Services Task Force, Guide to Clinical Preventive Services* (2nd ed. ed.), Williams and Wilkins, Baltimore, MD, p. 5.

LEVANT, R.F. AND MAJORS, R.G., 1998. Masculinity ideology among African American and European American college women and men. *Journal of Gender, Culture and Health* 2 1, pp. 33–43.

LEVANT, R.F., MAJORS, R.G. AND KELLEY, M.L., 1998. Masculinity ideology among young African American and European American women and men in different regions of the United States. *Cultural Diversity and Ethnic Minority Psychology* 4 3, pp. 227–236.

LEVINE, M., 1998. *Gay Macho: The Life and Death of the Homosexual Clone* New York University Press, New York.

LONG, K.A., 1993. The concept of health: rural perspectives. *Nursing Clinics of North America* 28 1, pp. 123–130.

LONNQUIST, L.E., WEISS, G.L. AND LARSEN, D.L., 1992. Health value and gender in predicting health protective behaviour. *Women and Health* 19 2/3, pp. 69–85.

MAJORS, R. AND BILLSON, J.M., 1992. *Cool Pose: The Dilemmas of Black Manhood in America* Touchstone, New York.

MARTIN, C.L., 1995. Stereotypes about children with traditional and nontraditional gender roles. *Sex Roles* 33 11/12, pp. 727–751.

MECHANIC, D. AND CLEARY, P.D., 1980. Factors associated with the maintenance of positive health behaviour. *Preventive Medicine* 9, pp. 805–814.

MEINECKE, C.E., 1981. Socialised to die younger? Hypermasculinity and men's health. *The Personnel and Guidance Journal* 60, pp. 241–245.

MERMELSTEIN, R.J. AND RIESENBERG, L.A., 1992. Changing knowledge and attitudes about skin cancer risk factors in adolescents. *Health Psychology* 11 6, pp. 371–376.

MESSERSCHMIDT, J.W., 1993. *Masculinities and Crime: Critique and Reconceptualisation of Theory* Rowman and Littlefield Publishers, Lanham, MD.

MESSNER, M.A. AND SABO, D.F., 1994. *Sex, Violence and Power in Sports: Rethinking Masculinity* The Crossing Press, Freedom, CA.

MISENER, T.R. AND FULLER, S.G., 1995. Testicular versus breast and colorectal cancer screen: early detection practices of primary care physicians. *Cancer Practice* 3 5, pp. 310–316.

MOR, V., MASTERSON-ALLEN S., GOLDBERG, R., GUADAGNOLI, E. AND WOOL, M.S., 1990. Prediagnostic symptom recognition and help seeking among cancer patients. *Journal of Community Health* 15 4, pp. 253–261.

NATHANSON, C., 1977. Sex roles as variables in preventive health behaviour. *Journal of Community Health* 3 2, pp. 142–155.

National Institute for Occupational Safety and Health, 1993. *Fatal injuries to workers in the United States, 1980–1989: a decade of surveillance* National Institute for Occupational Safety and Health, Cincinnati, OH (DHHS [NIOSH] No. 93–108).

National Institutes of Health, 1992. *Cancer statistics review: 1973–1989* U.S. Government Printing Office, Washington, DC (NIH Publication No. 92-2789).

National Institutes of Health, 1998. *Clinical Guidelines on the Identification, Evaluation and Treatment of Overweight and Obesity in Adults* National Heart, Lung and Blood Institute, Rockville, Office, Washington, DC (NIH Publication No. 92-2789).

NEFF, J.A., PRIHODA, T.J. AND HOPPE, S.K., 1991. "Machismo," self-esteem, education and high maximum drinking among Anglo, Black and Mexican-American male drinkers. *Journal of Studies on Alcohol* 52, pp. 458–463.

NOLEN-HOEKSEMA, S., 1987. Sex differences in unipolar depression: evidence and theory. *Psychological Bulletin* 101 2, pp. 259–282.

OAKLEY, A., 1994. Who cares for health? Social relations, gender and the public health. *Journal of Epidemiology and Community Health* 48, pp. 427–434. Abstract

O'NEIL, J.M., GOOD, G.E. AND HOLMES, S., 1995. Fifteen years of theory and research on men's gender role conflict: new paradigms for empirical research. In: Levant, R.F. and Pollack, W.S. Editors, 1995. *A New Psychology of Men* BasicBooks, New York, pp. 164–206.

O'NEIL, M.K., LANCEE, W.J. AND FREEMAN, J.J., 1985. Sex differences in depressed university students. *Social Psychiatry* 20, pp. 186–190.

PAPPAS, G., QUEEN, S., HADDEN, W. AND FISHER, G., 1993. The increasing disparity in mortality between socioeconomic groups in the United States, 1960 and 1986. *New England Journal of Medicine* 239 2, pp. 103–109.

PATRICK, M.S., COVIN, J.R., FULOP, M., CALFAS, K. AND LOVATO, C., 1997. Health risk behaviours among California college students. *Journal of American College Health* 45, pp. 265–272.

PERRY, L.A., TURNER, L.H. AND STERK, H.M. Editors, 1992. *Constructing and Reconstructing Gender: The Links Among Communication, Language and Gender* State University of New York Press, Albany, NY.

PLECK, J.H., 1987. *The Myth of Masculinity* (3rd ed.), M.I.T. Press, Cambridge, MA.

PLECK, J.H., SONENSTEIN, F.L. AND KU, L.C., 1994. Problem behaviours and masculinity ideology in adolescent males. In: Ketterlinus, R.D. and Lamb, M.E. Editors, 1994. *Adolescent Problem Behaviours: Issues and Research* Lawrence Erlbaum, Hillsdale, NJ, pp. 165–186.

PLECK, J.H., SONENSTEIN, F.L. AND KU, L.C., 1994. Attitudes toward male roles among adolescent males: a discriminant validity analysis. *Sex Roles* 30 7/8, pp. 481–501.

POTTS, M.K., BURNAM, M.A. AND WELLS, K.B., 1991. Gender differences in depression detection: a comparison of clinician diagnosis and standardised assessment. *Psychological Assessment* 3, pp. 609–615.

POWELL-GRINER, E., ANDERSON, J.E., MURPHY, W., 1997. State-and sex-specific prevalence of selected characteristics—behavioural risk factor surveillance system, 1994 and 1995. Morbidity and Mortality Weekly Report, Centers for Disease Control, Surveillance Summaries, 46 (3) 1–31.

PYKE, K.D., 1996. Class-based masculinities: the interdependence of gender, class and interpersonal power. *Gender and Society* 10, pp. 527–549.

RATNER, P.A., BOTTORFF, J.L., JOHNSON, J.L. AND HAYDUK, L.A., 1994. The interaction effects of gender within the health promotion model. *Research in Nursing and Health* 17, pp. 341–350.

REAGAN, L.J., 1997. Engendering the dread disease: women, men and cancer. *American Journal of Public Health* 87 (11), 1779–1187.

RICE, T.W. AND COATES, D.L., 1995. Gender role attitudes in the southern United States. *Gender and Society* 9 6, pp. 744–756.

RICH, J.A. AND STONE, D.A., 1996. The experience of violent injury for young African-American men: the meaning of being a "sucker". *Journal of General Internal Medicine* 11, pp. 77–82.

ROSE, B. EDITOR, 1997. *A Radical Fairy's Seedbed: The Collected Series* Nomenus, San Francisco.

ROSSI, J.S., 1992, March. Stages of change for 15 health risk behaviours in an HMO population. Paper presented at the 13th annual scientific sessions of the Society of Behavioural Medicine, New York.

ROTER, D.L. AND HALL, J.A., 1997. *Doctors Talking with Patients/Patients Talking with Doctors: Improving Communication in Medical Visits* Auburn House, Westport, CT.

SABO, D. AND GORDON, D.F. Editors, 1995. *Men's Health and Illness: Gender, Power and the Body* Sage Publications, Thousand Oaks, CA.

SALTONSTALL, R., 1993. Healthy bodies, social bodies: men's and women's concepts and practices of health in everyday life. *Social Science and Medicine* 36 1, pp. 7–14.

SAX, L., 1997. Health trends among college freshmen. *Journal of American College Health* 45 6, pp. 252–262.

SLESINSKI, M.J., SUBAR, A.F. AND KAHLE, L.L., 1996. Dietary intake of fat, fiber and other nutrients is related to the use of vitamin and mineral supplements in the United States: the 1992 National Health Interview Survey. *Journal of Nutrition* 126 12, pp. 3001–3008. Abstract

SHI, L., 1998. Sociodemographic characteristics and individual health behaviours. *Southern Medical Journal* 91 10, pp. 933–941. Abstract

SIGNORIELLI, N., 1993. *Mass Media Images and Impact on Health: A Sourcebook* Greenwood Press, Westport, CT.

STEINGART, R.M., PACKER, M., HAMM, P., COGLIANESE, M.E., GERSH, B., GELTMAN, E.M., SOLLANO, J., KATZ, S., MOYE, L., BASTA, L.L., LEWIS, S.J., GOTTLIEB, S.S., BERNSTEIN, V., MCEWAN, P., JACOBSON, K., BROWN, E.J., KUKIN, M.L., KANTROWITZ, N.E. AND PFEFFER, M.A., 1991. Sex differences in the management of coronary artery disease. *New England Journal of Medicine* 325 4, pp. 226–230.

STREET, S., KIMMEL, E.B. AND KROMREY, J.D., 1995. Revisiting university student gender role perceptions. *Sex Roles* 33 3/4, pp. 183–201.

STUELAND, D., MICKEL, S.H., CLEVELAND, D.A., ROTHFUSZ, R.R., ZOCH, T. AND STAMAS, P., 1995. The relationship of farm residency status to demographic and service characteristics of agricultural injury victims in central Wisconsin. *The Journal of Rural Health* 11 2, pp. 98–105.

U.S. Preventive Services Task Force, 1996. *Guide to Clinical Preventive Services* (2nd ed.), Williams and Wilkins, Baltimore, MD.

VANCE, C.S., 1995. Social construction theory and sexuality. In: Berger, M., Wallis, B. and Watson, S. Editors, 1995. *Constructing Masculinity* Routledge, New York, pp. 37–48.

VERBRUGGE, L.M., 1985. Gender and health: an update on hypotheses and evidence. *Journal of Health and Social Behaviour* 26, pp. 156–182.

VERBRUGGE, L.M., 1988. Unveiling higher morbidity for men: the story. In: Riley, M.W. Editor, 1988. *Social Structures and Human Lives* Sage Publications, Thousand Oaks, CA, pp. 138–160.

VERBRUGGE, L.M. AND STEINER, R.P., 1985. Prescribing drugs to men and women. *Health Psychology* 4 1, pp. 79–98.

VERBRUGGE, L.M. AND WINGARD, D.L., 1987. Sex differentials in health and mortality. *Women and Health* 12 2, pp. 103–145.

WAISBERG, J. AND PAGE, S., 1988. Gender role nonconformity and perception of mental illness. *Women and Health* 14, pp. 3–16.

WAITZKIN, H., 1984. Doctor–patient communication: clinical implications of social scientific research. *Journal of the American Medical Association* 252, pp. 2441–2446.

WALDRON, I., 1988. Gender and health-related behaviour. In: Gochman, D.S. Editor, 1988. *Health Behaviour: Emerging Research Perspectives* Plenum, New York, pp. 193–208.

WALKER, S.N., VOLKAN, K., SECHRIST, K.R. AND PENDER, N.J., 1988. Health promoting life-styles of older adults: comparisons with young and middle-aged adults, correlates and patterns. *Advances in Nursing Science* 11, pp. 76–90.

WARREN, L.W., 1983. Male intolerance of depression: a review with implications for psychotherapy. *Clinical Psychology Review*, 3, pp. 147–156.

WENGER, N.K., 1994. Coronary heart disease in women: gender differences in diagnostic evaluation. *Journal of the American Medical Women's Association* 49, pp. 181–185.

WEISMAN, C.S. AND TEITELBAUM, M.A., 1989. Women and health care communication. *Patient Education and Counseling* 13, pp. 183–199.

WEST, C. AND ZIMMERMAN, D.H., 1987. Doing gender. *Gender and Society* 1 2, pp. 125–151.

WILLIAMS, J.E. AND BEST, D.L., 1990. *Measuring Sex Stereotypes: A Multination Study* Sage Publications, Thousand Oaks, CA.

WILLITS, F.K., BEALER, R.C. AND TIMBERS, V.L., 1990. Popular images of 'rurality': data from a Pennsylvania survey. *Rural Sociology* 55 4, pp. 559–578. GEOBASE

WOOLF, S.H., JONAS, S. AND LAWRENCE, R.S. Editors, 1996. *Health Promotion and Disease Prevention in Clinical Practice* Williams and Wilkins, Baltimore, MD.

CRITICAL THINKING QUESTIONS

1. What are the social and cultural reasons that men generally die at a younger age than women?

2. What cultural reasons contribute to the lower level of health care utilization of men? How does the health care industry contribute to men's reluctance to seek health care?

3. If you were the director of the county health department, what programs would you put in place to increase men's utilization of health care?

4. Compare and contrast the problems that Courtenay addresses about health care for men with those that Gannon addresses about health care for women in the next article. If underutilization of care is a problem for men, and over-medicalization is a problem for women, how might the institution of medicine address these problems?

Reading 15

The Impact of Medical and Sexual Politics on Women's Health

Linda Gannon

> *In this article, Gannon explores the ways that the institution of medicine has defined women's bodies and health issues as pathological. She discusses negative consequences of this view, as well as the ways that sexist cultural beliefs have created this situation.*

Women's hormones undergo rather dramatic changes at puberty, during the menstrual cycle, during pregnancy and labor, and at menopause. Patriarchal politics determine which of these 'raging hormones' are designated as 'healthy' and which as 'unhealthy'. Consider the similarities and differences between the beginning (puberty) and end (menopause) of women's fertility. Both are accompanied by dramatic changes in hormones, and both are accompanied in some

Source: Feminism & Psychology © 1998 SAGE (London, Thousand Oaks and New Delhi), Vol. 8(3): 285–302.

women by varying degrees of physical and psychological distress. Puberty, although signaling the beginning of risk for breast cancer and endometriosis, worry and concern over birth control, and physical and social problems associated with possible pregnancy is, nonetheless, viewed with indulgence, applause and celebration. The transient emotional, physical and behavioral manifestations—the insolence, acne and lack of coordination—are viewed as temporary, as part of growing up, as a necessary and inevitable life transition. Menopause, on the other hand, is seen as a time of decay, deterioration, illness and loss.

The emotional, physical and behavioral manifestations are considered damaging and permanent. The hormonal changes are interpreted, not as an inevitable and natural life transition, but as the cause of illness, disease and death. The 'cost' to the woman who 'buys' this view of menopause is a diminishing self-esteem, unnecessary and potentially dangerous medical 'treatment,' and acquiescing in the control of her health by a misogynist medical profession.

A similar contrast can be made between pregnancy and the menstrual cycle. Pregnancy is accompanied by far greater hormonal fluctuations and is more consistently reported by women to be a difficult time in terms of emotional liability and physical changes than is the menstrual cycle. However, according to patriarchal politics, pregnancy is good, the craving for pickles and ice cream is cute, the discomfort associated with size and water retention is 'worth it'. A salient gender-distinguishing feature, pregnancy is the ultimate state of womanhood under patriarchy and is, consequently, encouraged. In contrast, a craving for chocolate and water retention prior to menses are said to be symbols of underlying neuroticism. The 'raging hormones' of the menstrual cycle are used as an excuse to disqualify women as competition in the workplace and reinforce their status as semi-invalids. The mood changes prior to menses experienced by some women have been labeled a 'mental disorder' (Premenstrual Dysphoric Disorder) by the American Psychiatric Association (1994). Imagine, if you can, labeling the behavioral and mood changes of pregnancy a mental disorder. Other than anatomical differences, menstruation is probably the single, most salient biological phenomenon that distinguishes women and men. As such, menstruation and the hormonal fluctuations of the menstrual cycle are a readily available symbol for women's inferiority. For patriarchy to persist and thrive, women's essential role must be biologically based and culturally mundane: reproduction fulfills these criteria. Unfortunately, for women to be physically and psychologically healthy, they cannot subscribe to the belief that only 30 years of their lives are important and worthwhile.

THE INTERTWINING OF BIOLOGY AND PSYCHOLOGY: FOR WOMEN ONLY

Historically, one misogynist interpretation of biological sex differences has been that men are 'above their biology' and women 'are their biology' (Lorber, 1994; Oakley, 1993). Smith-Rosenberg (1985) provides numerous 19th-century examples of women being defined, essentially, as pairs of ovaries: "'A woman's system is affected,' health reformer J.H. Kellogg commented as late as 1895, "we may almost say dominated, by the influence of these two little glands...'" (Smith-Rosenberg, 1985: 184). The 20th century brought little improvement. The linkage of women and children in protective laws and legislation and in medicine by combining obstetrics and gynecology in one specialty, paved the way (Stevens, 1971). Although the world wars relieved some of the pressure to stay home and reproduce, these reprieves were transient. The primary difference between the 19th- and 20th-century accounts is that, in the 19th century, a woman's uterus and ovaries were the essence of her psychological and physical well-being whereas, today, the focus is hormones (Ehrenreich and English, 1978). Two targets of patriarchy's biological determinism have been and continue to be the influence of the hormonal environment on sexuality and mood (or depression). These will be considered in some detail, first, in the context of the hormonal changes associated with the menstrual cycle and, second, in the context of the hormonal changes associated with menopause. The discrepancy between the empirical data and 'medical opinion' is blatant, providing clear examples of the pervasive influence of patriarchal values and beliefs on doing 'science.'

The Menstrual Cycle as Illness

A major focal point for describing women as victims of 'raging hormones' has been the menstrual cycle. Several years ago, I reviewed the research studies published in the previous

25 years designed to evaluate the influence of the hormonal fluctuations accompanying the menstrual cycle (Gannon, 1985). The dependent variables were diverse and included pain, swelling, anxiety, hostility, depression, anger, confusion, confidence, exam performance, accidents, memory, inductive reasoning, creativity and reaction time. Although menstrual cycle phase effects on numerous psychological and behavioral variables are obviously present in women suffering from various forms of menstrual cycle dysfunction, there was little evidence in support of a menstrual cycle influence on any of the variables studied in random samples of normal women. The results of more recent studies are consistent with these conclusions (e.g. Meuwissen and Over, 1992; Steiner, 1992).

Scientists, however, have continued to pursue verification of biological determinism in women by seeking causal links between hormonal status and any one of a number of behaviors. A popular target has been sexuality and a common methodology has been to study changes in sexual parameters across the menstrual cycle. Schreiner-Engel et al. (1981) evaluated 30 women at three points in their cycles; the phases were confirmed by hormonal analysis, and the dependent variables included both subjective and physiological measures. Sexual arousal and hormonal levels were found to be unrelated. A study similar in design was published a year later (Hoon et al., 1982) with phase determined by basal temperature and arousal measured both subjectively and physiologically; no significant phase effects were found. Bancroft et al. (1983), after conducting yet another similar study, reported similar results. Again, in 1991, Slob et al. conducted a similar study with the addition of a comparison between those women using and those not using oral contraceptives; the results did not support the hypothesized relationship between sexuality and hormones. Most recently, Meuwissen and Over (1992) reported the results of three studies: they found no menstrual cycle phase effects for subjective or physiological sexual arousal nor for processes believed to mediate sexual arousal including mood state,

recency of sexual experience and vividness of imagery. Repetition and redundancy characterize this body of research. Perhaps, if the results had been supportive of patriarchal ideology, one of these studies would have been sufficient. Readers are not bombarded year after year with studies which document the lack of association between testosterone levels and sexual behavior in men.

A similar persistence of a patriarchal stereotype can be noted in the study of mood variation in women. As with sexuality, a basic assumption has been that hormones are a primary determinant of women's mood: the premenstrual phase is 'a time of regression, of an increased libido, poorly controlled by a weakened ego, and of a recurrence of neuroses, originally established at the time of puberty' (Tuch, 1975: 388). Koeske (1980) has criticized this area of research as being characterized by the following: (1) the dependent variables are consistently negative (hostility, anxiety, depression) and the implicit assumption is that any variability in these is related to chemical imbalances; (2) researchers have consistently neglected to control for the potentially potent effects of environmental and/or stressful variables on the dependent variables and on cycle length; and (3) researchers have failed to separate beliefs and stereotypes about cycle-related emotionality from the causes of that emotionality. Extensive reviews by both Gannon (1985) and Koeske (1980) concluded that the empirical research has not supported a relationship between mood and the menstrual cycle in the general population. Although research interest in this area has diminished considerably in the last decade, the results of several recent studies are consistent with these early conclusions: differences in symptom reporting among distinct cultures (Van den Akker et al., 1995) and variation between cycles within individuals (Walker, 1994) imply that changes in mood and/or behavior across phases of the menstrual cycle are most likely due to learned and cultural factors and not to hormonal fluctuations.

Feminists have criticized the claim that science is an 'objective' and 'value-free' endeavor (Oakley, 1993; Tuana, 1989). The perpetuation of the myth of 'menstrual cycle determinism' in spite of 40 years of research to the contrary legitimizes the criticism. The fact that women's hormones are still, today, in spite of continued demonstrations to the contrary, being given considerable importance as a determinant of inferior or pathological behavior, emotion and performance is evidence for the continuing strength of patriarchal and medical politics exerting influence over the values and beliefs of 'science'. The American Psychiatric Association has renewed the interest by inventing the Premenstrual Dysphoric Disorder. This new diagnosis is included in the 1994 *Diagnostic and Statistical Manual of Mental Disorders*. Feminist groups were vehemently opposed to this psychiatric category arguing that it would allow any menstruating woman to be categorized as mentally disordered. The diagnosis could subsequently provide the legal basis for educational and occupational discrimination. Although the 'medical imperialism' of the Premenstrual Dysphoric Disorder diagnosis is obvious, the sexual politics only become evident with the realization that a parallel diagnostic category for men is not included in spite of a long tradition of animal and human research documenting an association between testosterone and aggression (Archer, 1991; Olweus et al., 1980; Rubinow and Schmidt, 1996).

Although the jargon has changed in the last 20 years, the politics have not. Between 1975 and 1994, there have been no significant advances in understanding the causes or in developing treatments for the changes in mood that occur with the menstrual cycle in some women. The only essential change has been in assessment. Researchers have reported that approximately 50 percent of the women reporting premenstrual syndrome (or Premenstrual Dysphoric Disorder) have this diagnosis confirmed with two or three cycles of daily, prospective records (Gannon, 1989); women who exhibit high levels of distress the week prior to menstruation with the remainder of the cycle being symptom-free are diagnosed with PMS. Those women who do not 'qualify' are generally women who experience high levels of distress on a more-or-less continuous

basis; they are generally dismissed as attention seekers, hysterics or hypochondriacs. Perhaps these women attribute their distress to the menstrual cycle because, by doing so, they feel more hope for relief than they would if they blamed their distress on the consequences of patriarchy—poverty, occupational discrimination or a violent husband.

The Menopause as Illness

The primary theoretical model for conceptualizing menopausal changes has been a biomedical one. Within this context, all of the negative changes stereotypically associated with menopause and aging—hot flashes, profuse sweating, headaches, increased weight, dryness and thinning of the vaginal walls, increased incidence of vaginal infections, loss of breast firmness, dizziness, sensations of cold in the hands and feet, irritability, depression, insomnia, pruritus of the sexual organs, constipation, atherosclerosis, osteoporosis and incontinence (Weideger, 1977)—are attributed to the hormonal changes associated with menopause and are assumed to be effectively treated with hormonal replacement therapy (HRT). Much of the research cited in support of this model suffers from basic methodological flaws: (1) the endogenous hormonal differences between naturally menopausal women and castrated women are ignored; (2) the etiology of symptoms is (inappropriately) inferred from treatment effectiveness; (3) causes are inferred from observational studies; (4) hormonal status is assumed rather than measured; (5) results from studies evaluating the treatment effectiveness of estrogen alone are offered as a rationale for treatment with estrogen and progesterone; and (6) the duration of experimental treatment studies is inadequate to assess potentially serious side-effects.

Nonetheless, studies meeting basic, scientific methodological criteria include those assessing the covariation between certain experiences and hormonal levels (e.g. Abe et al., 1977), studies comparing experiences of women in different phases of menopause (e.g. Ballinger,

1975, 1976), and the effectiveness of treating complaints of menopausal women with exogenous estrogen (Gerdes et al., 1982; e.g. Utian, 1972). . . . The results of investigations across disciplines have been surprisingly consistent and indicate that hot flashes, night sweats, vaginal changes and, to a lesser extent, bone density covary with hormonal levels and menopausal status and are effectively modified with hormone therapy. Other changes—fatigue, depression, tension, insomnia, libido, irritability, headaches and weight gain—do not covary with hormonal levels or menopausal status, nor do they respond to hormone treatment. These data have been consistently replicated, leading social science researchers to propose alternative, non-medical models (Gannon, 1997; Hunter, 1990; Kahn and Holt, 1987) as bases for understanding menopause. These women-focused or feminist models emphasize historical, role, stress and cultural causes, as opposed to hormonal ones, for mid-life problems and changes.

The relationship between sexuality and hormones in women has been studied by comparing pre- and postmenopausal women. In this context, a woman's sexual decline during and after menopause has been assumed to be a direct consequence of declining levels of estrogen. However, attempting to understand *why* sexuality decreases may be premature since it is not clear that sexuality does, in fact, decrease coincidentally with or subsequent to menopause. In 1953, Kinsey et al. reported that in their sample of 127 postmenopausal women who had been sexually active prior to menopause, 39 percent reported no change in sexual activities and responses, 13 percent stated their responses had increased while 48 percent believed their responses had decreased. The authors noted that, for those women who reported diminished sexual activity, the change was essentially due to their partners' declining interest in sex. Later surveys confirmed this considerable variability in the direction and magnitude of the changes in sexual activity of women as they proceed through menopause (Kahn and Holt, 1987; Runciman, 1978). In a peri- and postmenopausal sample of women studied by Leiblum and Swartzman (1986),

62 percent maintained that sexual interest and comfort increased following menopause. In surveys, Hunter (1980) and Hallstrom and Samuelson (1980), again, noted considerable variability in postmenopausal sexuality and reported that sexual activity in postmenopausal women was more highly correlated with factors other than menopausal status, most notably the availability of a partner, adequacy of emotional support from spouse, alcoholism in spouse and psychological problems. In spite of this evidence that in only a minority of women does sexuality decrease with menopause, many professionals continue to assume that the decreasing estrogen levels associated with menopause necessarily result in a diminished sexuality in the postmenopausal woman. Three unproven assumptions—(1) postmenopausal women have hormonally caused sexual difficulties, (2) an active sex life is a criterion of health and well-being in aging persons (Corby and Zarit, 1983), and (3) hormone supplements restore lost sexuality—conveniently lead to the conclusion that postmenopausal women need to ingest hormones to be 'normal' and 'healthy'.

Numerous studies evaluating the impact of hormone supplements on sexual parameters in postmenopausal women have been published. In 1990, Walling et al. reviewed studies testing the effects of hormone replacement therapy on sexual outcomes in postmenopausal women. Their review can be summarized as follows: (1) estrogen supplements were superior to placebo for problems with vaginal lubrication but estrogen was not effective for increasing sexual frequency, satisfaction or desire; (2) estrogen combined with progesterone was not associated with improvement in any measure of sexuality; (3) although several studies evaluating estrogen combined with androgens found these drugs to effectively treat 'loss of desire' and dysparneuia, none utilized placebo-control groups. Since sexual parameters are notoriously subject to placebo effects, this research cannot be construed as evidence for effectiveness.

Both women and men produce less of their respective hormones as they age, both experience similar changes in sexuality and for neither gender is there empirical support to link hormones and sexuality (Gannon, 1994). Why is it recommended that middle-aged and elderly women take estrogen supplements in order to remain sexual while it is not recommended that men of similar age take androgens? This is yet another manifestation of 'biology is destiny'—for women. A patriarchal medical establishment is, by definition, less likely to pathologize and medicalize men's lives. A recent article in *Scientific American* (Hoberman and Yesalis, 1995) traced the history of testosterone treatment in men. In the early 20th century, men were treated for a variety of problems including sexual difficulties with extracts from animal testicles. The authors characterize this practice as having been based in 'primitive beliefs' and absurd according to current standards and knowledge. Yet today women are encouraged to swallow the urine of pregnant mares in order to retain their femininity and sense of well-being.

A biological basis for mood variation in women has been sought in the context of the hormonal changes of menopause. For at least a century, the medical profession has associated menopause with depression. According to Formanek (1990), the 1888 Surgeon-General's Catalogue directs readers interested in menopause to 'See also: insanity in women'. In 1909, the German psychiatrist Kraepelin coined the term 'involutional melancholia'. 'Its onset was gradual during the climacterium; it was marked by hypochondriasis, pessimism, and irritability and led to a full-blown depressive syndrome. Prominent symptoms included agitation, restlessness, anxiety and apprehension, occasionally bizarre guilt and worthlessness' (Formanek, 1990: p. 28). Fortunately, the longevity and persistence of patriarchal propaganda cannot be taken as evidence for its verity. Data from large surveys of women of menopausal age reliably indicate that depression does not vary predictably with menopausal status (Ballinger, 1975, 1976; Kaufert and Gilbert, 1986; Leiblum and Swartzman, 1986; Lennon, 1987; McKinlay and Jeffreys, 1974; McKinlay et al., 1987). Furthermore, studies aimed at

demonstrating relationships between menopausal hormonal levels and psychological states have consistently failed. An early study by Abe and colleagues (1977) found no significant relationships between the severity of psychological symptoms and serum levels of estrogen, progesterone, follicle stimulating hormone and luteinizing hormone in menopausal women. Similarly Castrogiovanni et al. (1982), in a study evaluating plasma levels of hormones and various mood and personality variables in menopausal women, reported no significant associations; the hormonal profile of those depressed was identical to that of those not depressed.

Although hormone therapy has been advocated as a cure for psychological difficulties occurring coincidentally with menopause (Wilson, 1966), there is virtually no empirical support for this recommendation. Depression is notoriously sensitive to placebo effects and spontaneous remission. Consequently, treatment effectiveness can be demonstrated only through the use of double-blind, cross-over, placebo-controlled research. The first study satisfying these strict requirements was reported by Utian (1972). He compared the effectiveness of exogenous estrogen to placebo treatment in women experiencing natural and surgical menopause. Symptoms of depression, irritability, insomnia and palpitations responded significantly both to estrogen and placebo therapies. In spite of the repeated replication of these results in the last 20 years (George et al., 1973; Gerdes et al., 1982; Poller et al., 1980), physicians continue to prescribe hormone therapy for psychological problems: 'estrogen replacement therapy enables postmenopausal women to sleep better, wake rested, perform better, and feel less irritable and depressed' (Brenner, 1988: 7S). In support of this statement, Brenner cites Thomson and Oswald (1977) who did, indeed, find estrogen to relieve depression and anxiety but not as effectively as did a placebo.

And, if a menopausal woman finds that HRT does not cure her depression, *she* is to blame according to Ferin et al. (1993). They suggest that HRT may not cure psychological problems in all menopausal women because some women have always been mad: 'psychological symptoms are not always alleviated [by HRT]. Many of the symptoms that appear around the climacteric have deep roots in the distant past . . .' (1993: 102). In such cases, they recommend tranquilizers be added to the pharmacy. Again, social, interpersonal, economic and occupational causes of women's distress in a patriarchal society are not considered.

Perhaps one of the clearest examples of the mutually enhancing forces of medical and sexual politics on etiological models of depression forms a recent paper by Schmidt and Rubinow (1991). These authors argue for the existence and formal recognition of 'menopause-related affective syndrome'. They attempt to justify their argument with 'science' by claiming that mood symptoms occur with declining levels of estradiol, citing one study of castrated women. They further argue that mood disturbances in menopausal women are effectively treated with hormone replacement therapy, citing only research which had failed to use control groups. They are impressed by the historical precedents and cite 'evidence' from 1890:

> The connection between the reproductive nerve centers and the higher psychical centers in the brain is so intimate, and the effect of menstruation on the vascular system is so marked, that a priori we should expect menstrual derangement to cause corresponding disturbances in the brain, both through the nervous and vascular systems (1991: 844).

The authors use this Victorian view of menopause as evidence for the persistence of scientific attention to menopausal psychological problems, and then interpret this persistence, per se, as evidence for the syndrome. (Interestingly, feminists have cited the same historical quotes as evidence of historical medical misogyny [Smith-Rosenberg, 1985].) Schmidt and Rubinow do acknowledge the considerable research which has failed to identify increased depression associated with menopause and those studies which have documented significant relationships between

contextual factors (poverty, discrimination, violence) and mood/behavior changes at all ages, including menopause. Yet, they conclude, 'However, this evidence is far from conclusive in refuting the existence of a menopause-related affective syndrome' (1991: 846). Only because of the political agenda does a syndrome that has never been empirically, clinically or epidemiologically validated *need* to be refuted.

Despite the research evidence, biologically based scientists and physicians continue to characterize menopause as a time of deterioration and decay, a time of physical and psychological trauma caused by the diminishing levels of estrogen and alleviated by the taking of estrogen (Schmidt and Rubinow, 1991). The US Federal Drug Administration (*Physician's Desk Reference*, 1997) has ruled that estrogen may only legitimately be prescribed for hot flashes, atrophic vaginitis and osteoporosis; similarly, the indications for HRT provided by the *British National Formulary* (1997) are vaginal atrophy, vasomotor instability and early menopause (either natural or surgical). Yet popular magazines and self-help books, television programs and pharmaceutical advertising continue to quote 'medical experts' who advocate HRT for alleviating cardiovascular disease, depression, marital discord, sagging breasts and wrinkled skin, and for increasing a 'sense of well being' (e.g. Stoppard, 1994). Similarly, the medical profession promotes HRT as effective treatment or prevention for physical conditions, such as cardiovascular disorders (e.g. L'Hermite, 1990), in spite of a glaring lack of adequate research support (Gannon, 1997). Clearly, both the pharmaceutical and medical industries have financial interests in all women over 50 taking a drug every day. And, added to the profit motive is the influence of sexual politics which is apparent in the intertwining of biology and psychology for women, but not for men. Memory problems, fatigue, wrinkles and loss of libido are, in women, said to result from diminishing levels of hormones, but, in men, these problems are assumed to be due to, not lowering levels of testosterone, but from natural aging, boredom, loneliness and, of course, the lack of an understanding and compassionate wife (Coney, 1994; Sarrel, 1990).

Patriarchy, in order to survive as such, must keep women as separate, as other, and the easiest way to achieve this is to emphasize the observable differences—those that are biological. Not only are women defined throughout their reproductive years as sources of sexual gratification and as mothers, but at menopause, when they are finally relieved of these demands, and perhaps have the opportunity for new challenges, they are told they have a deficiency disease. They are then encouraged to take hormone supplements in order to retain their beauty and sexuality—though there is no evidence that they have lost these, nor that hormone supplements enhance them.

Why, in spite of the repeated evidence that hormones do not consistently, predictably or significantly impact women's sexuality, are studies investigating the impact of varying levels of hormones associated with the menstrual cycle and menopause still funded and published? Why are these empirical studies not accepted by empiricists? Science claims to have triumphed over mysticism and primitive beliefs by applying 'objective' scientific methods to determine the existence of, the parameters of, and the causes and consequences of phenomena. While concurring with feminist claims that science is heavily value laden and determined, I would suggest that even scientists do not accept or believe the conclusions of their own work when these conclusions contradict strongly held stereotypes. These abuses and misuses of the scientific method are exaggerated and mystified when men do research on women in a misogynist society.

Schmidt and Rubinow conclude that 'the use of excessively stringent criteria for severity may result in failure to identify clinically significant mood disturbances during menopause' (1991: 847). And this is precisely what feminists predict and fear—that by creating sex-specific disorders, all members of that sex will be formally or informally diagnosed with the disorder. Thus women will suffer from Premenstrual Dysphoric Disorder from the age of 12 to the age of 50 and will then suffer from menopause-related affective syndrome. In this way, women who proceed 'normally' with respect to their productive lives, will be labeled as ill. Medical politics are served in that a large segment of the population is encouraged to pathologize normal and healthy behavior, to attribute causation to biology, and to interpret health issues related to age and lifestyle as medical problems requiring medical treatment. Sexual politics is served in that menopausal affective syndrome is but one of many instances of the persistence of the dominant culture ensuring their continued control—women, but not men, are victims of their biology. The medicalization of women is presented under the guise of 'concern for' and, 'attention to' women's health while ensuring the continued inferior status of women because they *require* concern and attention.

THE IDEOLOGY OF OBGYN MEDICINE

The very foundation of the OBGYN specialty is the epitome of medical imperialism. Obstetrics and gynecology would have little business if puberty, menstruation, pregnancy, labor, birth and menopause had not been transformed from natural life events to illnesses requiring regular medical attention (Conrad and Schneider, 1980)....

... [The] intrusion of medical politics is extensive and is legitimized by the existence of the OBGYN specialty. The interaction with sexual politics has (at least) three manifestations. First, by defining certain life events as healthy (pregnancy), others as unhealthy (menopause), women may be subtly coerced and manipulated into conforming to patriarchy's version of the *real* woman, i.e. to venerate pregnancy and accept the disease model of menopause. Second, medical personnel often perceive women patients as inherently dependent and lacking in intelligence and common sense—a view that rationalizes paternalistic attitudes and advice. Under the guise of 'treatment', physicians often instruct women patients on values, morals and sexual behavior (e.g. Foster, 1995; Miles, 1991; Szasz, 1980). And third, when a woman chooses not to comply with medical advice, she is often labeled paranoid, sentimental, uninformed, misguided and/or self-defeating. For example, the compliance with HRT among menopausal and postmenopausal women has been a disappointment to medical and pharmaceutical professionals (Berman et al., 1996) and has elicited patronizing responses: 'Women may not be as informed or as knowledgeable about menopause as they think they are' (Andrews, 1995: 1); 'Doubtless many women do not obtain the benefits of estrogen therapy because of *unfounded* fears of complications and side effects' (Belchetz, 1994: 1069; emphasis added). Perhaps the ultimate example of misogynist reactions to noncompliance comes from Studd (1989: 508) who recommends prophylactic oophorectomy [surgical removal of the ovaries] for healthy middle-aged women in order to prevent the possibility of ovarian cancer: 'the only worthwhile argument against prophylactic oophorectomy . . . [is] a sentimental desire to keep her ovaries. . . .'.

The methods by which patriarchy's version of womanhood is imposed are numerous and varied, subtle and direct. When a woman is angry, she is often assumed to be premenstrual. When a man is aggressive or violent, he is assumed to have been provoked, to have had a stressful day, or to be protecting himself or his family; he is not thought to have too much testosterone. If we were to accept women's anger as a legitimate response to economic, social and political oppression, we would not assume that she is premenstrual every time she raises her voice. If we were to view men's aggressiveness as a symptom of excessive testosterone, we would require hormonal monitoring of those men who control nuclear weapons. Rather than attribute Saddam Hussein's brutality to familial, historical and cultural factors, we would be concerned about excessively high levels of testosterone.

Ideological underpinnings are not always obvious within the 'objective' terminology of science. Consider the following description of menopause:

> I think of the menopause as a deficiency disease, like diabetes. . . . Most women develop some symptoms whether they are aware of them or not, so I prescribe estrogens for virtually all menopausal women for an indefinite period (cited in Seaman and Seaman, 1977: 293).

The terms 'deficiency' 'disease' and 'diabetes' sound like science, and therefore invite the expectation of 'facts'. Although the language is meant to convey superior wisdom and an attitude of concern, not-so-subtle implications are that the author knows his patients better than they know themselves and that he is willing to prescribe potentially dangerous drugs to treat symptoms that exist only in *his* fantasy.

And, consider my description of menopause:

> After approximately 30 years of menstrual cycles in order to provide transitory fertility, ovarian serenity is restored, estrogen once again becomes stable and levels return to normal, menstruation ceases. The woman experiences release from reproductive pressures and is able to participate fully in her career, social, and family activities as she need no longer be concerned about the problems associated with menstruation, birth control and pregnancy and is no longer at a heightened risk for endometriosis, uterine fibroids, and breast cancer.[1]

Both descriptions are opinions, subjective interpretations of a physiological process. There is no 'hard' evidence to support or refute either. The disease version is gaining more acceptance only because our society has conferred expert status, and therefore power, on the medical profession, and because their version is consistent with the traditional and unfortunate stereotype of women in a patriarchal culture. By defining menopause as an illness, all middle-aged and old women are characterized as ill— a Y-chromosome has become a necessity for well-being. Medical politics are served by defining natural life events and social/political problems as biologically determined and requiring medical intervention; sexual politics are served by applying these theories to women, but not to men.

Hansen and Osborne (1995) examined pharmaceutical advertising in medical journals as a possible source of patriarchal images of women. They suggest that the portrayal of women as helpless, depressed and incompetent reinforces the cultural stereotype of women as inferior and vulnerable. Similarly, the pharmaceutical advertising in the OBGYN journals is consistent with patriarchal ideology. Advertising for oral contraceptives typically portrays a beautiful, feminine woman, perhaps in a sun-dress on a beach. Ads for products to aid pregnancy tend to be somewhat old-fashioned and Victorian; the women are happy and content, hugely pregnant, yet beautiful and feminine. Advertisements for HRT are of two types: one portrays the woman who *needs* HRT—tired, wrinkled, depressed, inactive, with a mean, ugly expression; the other portrays those women who are taking HRT—a happy grandmother back on the job doing laundry and cooking (Coney, 1994).

One of the more interesting and revealing aspects of the OBGYN specialty is the relative importance placed on the various topics subsumed by the discipline. In a recent study (Gannon et al., 1997), we analyzed the content of all articles published in 1970, 1975, 1980, 1985, 1990 and 1993 in the three major OBGYN journals (two US journals and one British journal). In accord with the cultural developments and popular media topics in the last two decades, we had hypothesized a decreased emphasis on pregnancy, birth and the fetus and an increased focus on menopause and sexually transmitted diseases (STDs). Surprisingly, the relative emphasis on various topics remained essentially unchanged over the last two decades. The percentage of articles on menopause remained low and varied from 1 to 3 percent, as did those on STDs, varying between 1 and 2 percent. On the other hand, 30 percent were concerned with pregnancy. In a second analysis, we combined menstruation, gynecological disorders, menopause, surgical menopause, hysterectomy and sexually transmitted diseases

into a 'women's health' category while pregnancy, birth/labor, fetus, neonate, postpartum, fertility and reproductive technology formed the 'reproduction' category. We found articles focusing on 'women's health' to comprise less than a quarter of those devoted to 'reproduction' and this ratio changed little over the years of the study. We concluded that:

> . . . rather than responding to current medical needs based on changing social needs and lifestyles, the obstetrics/gynecology specialty has ignored the health and well-being requirements of nonpregnant and non-fertile women. The social values and attitudes toward women inferred from the priorities evident in these data are ideologically consistent with the view that woman's primary role is that of reproduction. The implied importance of certain themes, in conjunction with the neglect of others, may serve to perpetuate the politically oppressive view of women as biologically motivated and determined (Gannon et al., 1997: 43).

CONCLUSIONS

Basic to the study of women's psychological and physical well-being is an understanding and appreciation of the powerful and pervasive political motivation underlying the definition and treatment of women's health concerns. The politics inherent in the medical ideology operating in patriarchal society provide a basic structure by defining a healthy woman as one who fulfills her biological destiny—one who is able and willing to bear and raise children—and by inventing illness and remedy for the woman who is unwilling or unable to conform. Sexual politics ensure that biological sex differences are emphasized, exaggerated and consistently interpreted in a general context of women being inferior to men. In a mutually interactive and enhancing manner, medical and sexual politics render women biologically determined and serve to limit women's roles to those that serve patriarchal values.

The medicalization of women is a natural outgrowth of biological determinism. Women in the 19th century were described as a person built around a womb; they were advised not to tax their brains since this could interfere with their reproductive functioning. Today, the focus has changed from the womb to hormones but the ideology remains. In both centuries, medical politics dictate locating explanations for moods and behavior in biology while ignoring social and political explanations. A woman is said to be depressed because she has PMS or is beginning menopause while ignoring the fact that she lives in a household in which she is treated as a slave or is physically abused and/or lives in a society in which she is deprived basic human rights. Medicine as a social and political tool of biological determinism thrives under patriarchy by encouraging women to ascribe gender inequality to biology rather than to the social, economic and political arenas (Kaufert, 1982; Strong, 1979).

NOTES

The author would like to thank Tracy Luchetta for her helpful comments on earlier drafts of this manuscript.
1. Although breast cancer risk continues to increase with age, the *rate* of increase slows after menopause.

REFERENCES

ABE, T., FURUHASHI, N., YAMAYA, Y., WADA, Y., HOSHIAI, A. AND SUZUKI, M. (1977) 'Correlation between Climacteric Symptoms and Serum Levels of Estradiol, Progesterone, Follicle-Stimulating Hormone, and Lutenizing Hormone', *American Journal of Obstetrics and Gynecology* 129: 65–7.

American Psychiatric Association (1994) *Diagnostic and Statistical Manual of Mental Disorders (4th edn)*, Washington, DC: American Psychiatric Association.

ANDREWS, W.C. (1995) 'The Transitional Years and Beyond', *Obstetrics and Gynecology* 85: 1–5.

ARCHER, J. (1991) 'The Influence of Testosterone on Human Aggression', *British Journal of Psychology* 82: 1–28.

BALLINGER, C.B. (1975) 'Psychiatric Morbidity and the Menopause: Screening of General Population Sample', *British Medical Journal* 3: 344–6.

BALLINGER, C.B. (1976) 'Subjective Sleep Disturbance at Menopause', *Journal of Psychosomatic Research* 20: 509–13.

BANCROFT, J., SANDERS, D., DAVIDSON, D. AND WARNER, P. (1983) 'Mood, Sexuality, Hormones, and the Menstrual Cycle, III: Sexuality and the Role of Androgens', *Psychosomatic Medicine* 45: 509–16.

BELCHETZ, P.E. (1994) 'Hormonal Treatment of Postmenopausal Women', *New England Journal of Medicine* 330: 1062–71.

BERMAN, R.S., EPSTEIN, R.S. AND LYDICK, E.G. (1996) 'Compliance of Women in Taking Estrogen Replacement Therapy', *Journal of Women's Health* 5: 213–20.

BRENNER, P.F. (1988) 'The Menopausal Syndrome', *Obstetrics and Gynecology* 72: 6S–11S.

British National Formulary (1997) London: British Medical Association and the Royal Pharmaceutical Society.

CASTROGIOVANNI, P., DE LUCA, I.B., TETI, G., CORRADI, I., MOGGI, G., ZECCA, R., MURRU, S., SILVESTRI, D. AND FIORETTI, P. (1982) 'Depressive States during the Menopause: A Preliminary Study of Endocrinological, Socioeconomical and Personality Factors', in P. Fioretti, L. Martini, G.B. Mills and S.S.C. Yen (eds) *The Menopause: Clinical, Endocrinological, and Pathophysiological Aspects*. New York: Academic Press.

CONEY, S. (1994) *The Menopause Industry*. Alameda, CA: Hunter House.

CONRAD, P. AND SCHNEIDER, J.W. (1980) *Deviance and Medicalization: From Badness to Sickness*. St. Louis: C.V. Mosby.

CORBY, N. AND ZARIT, J.M. (1983) 'Old and Alone: The Unmarried in Later Life', in R.B. Weg (ed.) *Sexuality in the Later Years: Roles and Behavior*, New York: Academic Press.

EHRENREICH, B. AND ENGLISH, D. (1978) *For Her Own Good: 150 Years of the Experts' Advice to Women*. Garden City: Anchor Books.

FERIN, M., JEWELEWICZ, R. AND WARREN, M. (1993) *The Menstrual Cycle: Physiology, Reproductive Disorders, and Infertility*. New York: Oxford University Press.

FORMANEK, R. (1990) 'Continuity and Change and "the Change of Life": Premodern Views of the Menopause', in R. Formanek (ed.) *The Meanings of Menopause: Historical, Medical, and Clinical Perspectives*. Hillsdale, NJ: Analytic Press.

FOSTER, P. (1995) *Women and the Health Care Industry*. Buckingham: Open University Press.

GANNON, L. (1985) *Menstrual Disorders and Menopause: Biological, Psychological, and Cultural Research*. New York: Praeger.

GANNON, L. (1989) 'Dysmenorrhoea, Premenstrual Syndrome and the Menopause', in S. Pearce and J. Wardle (eds) *The Practice of Behavioural Medicine*. Oxford: British Psychological Society.

GANNON, L. (1994) 'Sexuality and Menopause', in P.Y.L. Choi and P. Nicolson (eds) *Female Sexuality: Psychology, Biology and Social Context*. London: Harvester Wheatsheaf.

GANNON, L. (1997) 'Perspectives on Biological, Social and Psychological Phenomena in Middle- and Old-Age Women: Interference or Intervention?', in S. Clancy and L. DiLalla (eds) *Assessment and Intervention Issues across the Life-span*. New York: Lawrence Erlbaum.

GANNON, L., STEVENS, J. AND STECKER, T. (1997) 'A Content Analysis of Obstetrics/Gynecology Scholarship: Implications for Women's Health', *Women and Health* 26: 43–57.

GEORGE, G.C.W., UTIAN, W.H. BEUMONT, P.J.V. AND BEARDWOOD, C.J. (1973) 'Effect of Exogenous Oestrogens on Minor Psychiatric Symptoms in Postmenopausal Women', *South African Medical Journal* 47: 2387–8.

GERDES, L.C., ETPHIL, D.L., SONNENDECKER, E.W.W. AND POLAKOW, E.S. (1982) 'Psychological Changes Effected by Estrogen-Progesterone and Clonidine Treatment in Climacteric Women', *American Journal of Obstetrics and Gynecology* 142: 98–104.

HALLSTROM, T. AND SAMUELSON, S. (1980) 'Changes in Women's Sexual Desire in Middle Age: The Longitudinal Study of Women in Gothenburg', *Archives of Sexual Behavior* 19: 259–68.

HANSEN, F.J. AND OSBORNE, D. (1995) 'Portrayal of Women and Elderly Patients in Psychotropic Drug Advertisements', *Women and Therapy* 16: 129–41.

HOBERMAN, J.M. AND YESALIS, C.E. (1995) 'The History of Synthetic Testosterone', *Scientific American* February: 76–81.

HOON, P.W., BRUCE, K. AND KINCHLOE, B. (1982) 'Does the Menstrual Cycle Play a Role in Sexual Arousal?' *Psychophysiology* 19: 21–7.

HUNTER, M. (1980) *Your Menopause: Prepare Now for a Positive Future.* London: Pandora.

KAHN, A. AND HOLT, L. (1987) *Menopause: The Best Years of Your Life?* London: Bloomsbury.

KAUFERT, P. (1982) 'Anthropology and the Menopause: The Development of a Theoretical Framework', *Maturitas* 4: 181–93.

KAUFERT, P. AND GILBERT, P. (1986) 'The Context of Menopause: Psychotropic Drug Use and Menopausal Status', *Social Science and Medicine* 23: 747–55.

KINSEY, A.C., POMEROY, W.B., MARTIN, C.E. AND GEBHARD, P.H. (1953) *Sexual Behavior in the Human Female.* Philadelphia, PA: W.B. Saunders.

KOESKE, R.K. (1980) 'Theoretical Perspectives on Menstrual Cycle Research: The Relevance of Attributional Approaches for the Perception and Explanation of Premenstrual Emotionality', in A.J. Dan, E.A. Graham and C.P. Beecher (eds) *The Menstrual Cycle, Volume 1: A Synthesis of Interdisciplinary Research.* New York: Springer Publishing.

LEIBLUM, S.R. AND SWARTZMAN, L.D. (1986) 'Women's Attitudes Toward the Menopause: An Update', *Maturitas* 8: 47–56.

LENNON, M.C. (1987) 'Is Menopause Depressing? An Investigation of the Perspectives', *Sex Roles* 17: 1–16.

L'HERMITE, M. (1990) 'Risks of Estrogens and Progestogens', *Maturitas* 12: 215–46.

LORBER, J. (1994) *Paradoxes of Gender.* New Haven, CT: Yale University Press.

McKINLAY, J.B., McKINLAY, S.J. AND BRAMBILLA, D. (1987) 'The Relative Contributions of Endocrine Changes and Social Circumstances to Depression in Mid-Aged Women', *Journal of Health and Social Behavior* 28: 345–63.

McKINLAY, S.J., AND JEFFREYS, M. (1974) 'The Menopausal Syndrome', *British Journal of Preventative and Social Medicine* 28: 108–15.

MEUWISSEN, I. AND OVER, R. (1992) 'Sexual Arousal Phases of the Human Menstrual Cycle', *Archives of Sexual Behavior* 21: 101–20.

MILES, A. (1991) *Women, Health and Medicine.* Milton Keynes: Open University Press.

OAKLEY, A. (1993) *Essays on Women, Medicine, and Health.* Edinburgh: Edinburgh University Press.

OLWEUS, D., MATTSSON, A., SCHALLING, D. AND LOW, H. (1980) 'Testosterone, Aggression, Physical, and Personality Dimensions in Normal Adolescent Males', *Psychosomatic Medicine* 42: 253–69.

Physicians' Desk Reference (1997) Montvale, NJ: Medical Economics Company.

POLLER, L., THOMSON, J.M. AND COOPE, J. (1980) 'A Double-Blind Cross-Over Study of Piperazine Oestrone Sulphate and Placebo with Coagulation Studies', *British Journal of Obstetrics and Gynecology* 87: 718–25.

RUBINOW, D.R. AND SCHMIDT, P.J. (1996) 'Androgens, Brain, and Behavior', *American Journal of Psychiatry* 153: 974–84.

RUNCIMAN, I. (1978) 'Sexual Problems in the Senior World', in R.L. Solnick (ed.) *Sexuality and Aging.* Los Angeles: Southern California Press.

SARREL, P.M. (1990) 'Sexuality and Menopause', *Obstetrics and Gynecology* 75: 26S–35S.

SCHMIDT, P.J. AND RUBINOW, D.R. (1991) 'Menopause-Related Affective Disorders: A Justification for Further Study', *American Journal of Psychiatry* 148: 844–52.

SCHREINER-ENGEL, P., SCHIANI, R.C., SMITH, H. AND WHITE, D. (1981) 'Sexual Arousability and the Menstrual Cycle', *Psychosomatic Medicine* 43: 199–213.

SEAMAN, B. AND SEAMAN, G. (1977) *Women and the Crisis in Sex Hormones.* New York: Rawson Associates.

SLOB, A.K., ERNSTE, M. AND VAN DER WERFFTEN BOSCH, J.J. (1991) 'Menstrual Cycle Phase and Sexual Arousability in Women', *Archives of Sexual Behavior* 20: 567–77.

SMITH-ROSENBERG, C. (1985) 'Puberty to Menopause: The Cycle of Femininity in Nineteenth-Century America', in C. Smith-Rosenberg (ed.) *Disorderly Conduct.* New York: Knopf.

STEINER, M. (1992) 'Female-Specific Mood Disorders', *Clinical Obstetrics and Gynecology* 35: 599–611.

STEVENS, R. (1971) *American Medicine and the Public Interest.* New Haven, CT: Yale University Press.

STOPPARD, M. (1994) *Menopause.* London: Carroll and Brown.

STRONG, P.M. (1979) 'Sociological Imperialism and the Progression of Medicine', *Social Science and Medicine* 13A: 199–215.

STUDD, J. (1989) 'Prophylactic Oophorectomy', *British Journal of Obstetrics and Gynecology* 96: 506–9.

SZASZ, T. (1980) *Sex by Prescription.* New York: Anchor Press/Doubleday.

THOMSON, J. AND OSWALD, I. (1977) 'Effect of Oestrogen on the Sleep, Mood, and Anxiety of Menopausal Women', *British Medical Journal* 2: 317–19.

TUANA, N. (1989) *Feminism and Science.* Bloomington: Indiana University Press.

TUCH, R.H. (1975) 'The Relationship between a Mother's Menstrual Status and her Response to Illness in her Child', *Psychosomatic Medicine* 37: 388–94.

UTIAN, W.H. (1972) 'The Mental Tonic Effect of Oestrogens Administered to Oophorectomized Females', *South African Medical Journal* 46: 1079–82.

VAN DEN AKKER, O.B.A., EVES, F.F., SERVICE, S. AND LENNON, B. (1995) 'Menstrual Cycle Symptom Reporting in Three British Ethnic Groups', *Social Science and Medicine* 40: 1417–23.

WALKER, A. (1994) 'Mood and Well-Being in Consecutive Menstrual Cycles: Methodological and Theoretical Implications', *Psychology of Women Quarterly* 18: 271–90.

WALLING, M., ANDERSEN, B.L. AND JOHNSON, S.R. (1990) 'Hormonal Replacement Therapy for Postmenopausal Women: A Review of Sexual Outcomes and Related Gynecologic Effects', *Archives of Sexual Behavior* 19: 119–37.

WEIDEGER, P. (1977) *Menstruation and Menopause.* New York: Knopf.

WILSON, R. (1966) *Feminine Forever.* New York: M. Evans.

CRITICAL THINKING QUESTIONS

1. What aspects of women's health have been defined as pathologies? What is the basis for defining some female functions as problematic and others as normal and worth going through?

2. What are the advantages and disadvantages to women when medicine defines their health as needing intervention? What are the advantages and disadvantages to health care providers when medicine defines women's health as needing treatment?

3. Gannon argues that health care providers ignore scientific evidence in order to provide the care that they believe women need. In your opinion, is the evidence she gives to support her argument convincing? Why or why not? If you believe her argument, how is it possible that health care providers, whose careers are based on science, could ignore the findings of medical research?

Reading 16

Stigma, Health Beliefs and Experiences with Health Care in Lesbian Women

Patricia E. Stevens and Joanne M. Hall

> *In this article, Stevens and Hall discuss the negative experiences lesbian women encounter when accessing health care.*

Nursing claims as its distinguishing core the concept of care (Leininger, 1984). Authentic presence in interaction, in which the nurse is aware of and open to each client as a unique and worthwhile being, is essential for nursing to offer humanizing care (Patterson & Zderad,

Source: Image: Journal of Nursing Scholarship, 1988, 20(2), 69–73.

1976). If each human being is a valued "whole," authentic, humanizing care necessitates that nurses broaden and deepen their knowledge about specific client populations. Good and Good (1981) suggest that illness and wellness be conceived of as a coherent network of meaning and experience that is linked to the deep semantic and value structures of a cultural aggregate. To offer culturally sensitive care to lesbians in a way that allows them to feel respected and regarded, nurses need an understanding of the cultural experience of being lesbian, a knowledge of what illness and wellness mean for them and a comprehension of their experience in health care interactions.

For lesbian women, the cultural meanings of illness and wellness are linked to lesbian identity, which is an immutable quality that permeates and differentiates the self. Lesbian identity is not limited to sexual activity but is a totality that encompasses a primary orientation toward women and a way of being that is women-relating (Ponse, 1978). As a cultural group lesbians share developmental experiences (Cass, 1979; Dank, 1971; Di Angi, 1982; Kus, 1985), value orientations, community identification (Ponse), argot (Warren, 1980), characteristic family construction (Krestan & Bepko, 1980) and literature, art and music (Nixon & Berson, 1978).

REVIEW OF THE LITERATURE

Culture is the symbolic system of a people. Wellness and illness, a group's subjective perception of health (Tripp-Reimer, 1984), are patterns of behavior having significance in cultural terms. What it means to be well or ill in a particular cultural context is negotiated by the members within the belief system of that group. The accumulated wisdom and experience of groups yield informal bodies of codified knowledge about wellness and illness called folk theories (Fabrega, 1979).

The concept of health includes the capacities and activities of individuals in cultural enterprises (Smith, 1981). It is a multidimensional process involving the well-being of whole persons in the context of their psychosocial and cultural environment (Ahmed, Kolker, & Coelho, 1979). Value orientations differentiate cultural groups and affect the ways that health, illness and health care are viewed by members of a group (Hartog & Hartog, 1983).

A core element in the cultural experience of lesbians is the phenomenon of stigmatization. There is abundant historical and sociological evidence that lesbians are viewed negatively in this society, encountering discrimination, social distancing, antilocution and defensiveness. They sustain the damage of others' anger, hostility, fear, anxiety, aversion, excitement and ambivalence (Aguero, Bloch, & Byrne, 1984; Hudson & Ricketts, 1980; Irwin & Thompson, 1978; Laner & Laner, 1980; Levitt & Klassen, 1974; Millham, San Miguel, & Kellogg, 1976; Minnigerode, 1976; Morin, 1981; Nungesser, 1983; Nyberg & Alston, 1977; Weinberger & Millham, 1979).

Goffman (1963) defined the stigmatized as having an identity "spoiled" by a discrediting attribute, which leads to their disqualification from full social acceptance. The concept of stigma requires a relational perspective because only in interaction does stigma become apparent. According to Goffman, there are two groups of stigmatized individuals, the "discredited," whose stigmatizing feature is immediately apparent to others, and the "discreditable," whose attribute may be concealed but is at risk of disclosure in social situations. In dealing with stigma, the task for the "discredited" is to minimize the impact of the stigmatizing feature during social interaction, whereas the task for the "discreditable" is to manage information so that others do not become aware of their discrediting attribute.

Lesbian identity has been conceptualized by numerous sources as a "discreditable" stigma (Fein & Nuehring, 1981; Jandt & Darsey, 1981; Plummer, 1975). Therefore, the "mark" of lesbian identity conspicuously affects interactive outcomes (Jones et al., 1984). Lesbians cannot take for granted that they share the world with others who hold congruent values, interpretations and behaviors; nor can they assume that they will be evaluated according to their own personal qualities. They must always consider the implications of their stigmatized lesbian identity as they anticipate their participation in all areas of life including health care. While self-disclosure is generally considered to be necessary in the formation of authentic interpersonal relationships (Jourard, 1971), the potential negative consequences in the behavior of others often act as effective deterrents to self-disclosure by lesbian women (Brooks, 1981).

Persons formulate ideas of themselves and take action in light of what they encounter in the action of others (Blumer, 1969). Cues about lesbian identity—the "mark"—(Becker, 1973; Fein & Nuehring, 1981) may be available in interactions even though they are not stated or confirmed. The beliefs of lesbians about their degree of identifiability is a basis on which they interpret the responses of others toward them. Self-schemata, the cognitive generalizations that organize the processing of self-related experience (Markus, 1977), are linked to an individual's sense of well-being and health. The degree to which illness and wellness may be assumed to correlate with stigmatized identity is related to the perceptions of lesbians about how identifiable they are to others.

There is a dearth of research regarding lesbian folk theories about health, lesbian identifiability and lesbians' experiences interacting with health care providers. Brooks (1981) found that stress tended to be lower for those who believed that only other lesbian/gay people could identify them as lesbians and higher for those who felt visible to the larger society. Ponse (1978) and Painter (1981) described lesbian folk theories about the ability of lesbians to recognize each other in social interaction. Unfortunately there are no studies about the perceptions of lesbians about how recognizable they are within society as a whole. The few studies that have been done on the interaction of lesbians with health care providers suggest that lesbians found them to be judgmental, nonsupportive and negatively responsive when the identity of the lesbians was known (Chafetz, Sampson, Beck, & West, 1974; Smith, Johnson, & Guenther, 1985). Many wished that they could be open about their lesbian identity in health care situations but never were, fearing that it would hinder the quality of health care (Glascock, 1983; Johnson, Guenther, Laube, & Keettel, 1981). The status of the research in this area means that those who care for lesbians must rely on common sense and intuition with all the potential pitfalls of myth, speculation and antipathy entailed in such an approach (Chafetz et al., 1974).

The present study was undertaken in an attempt to begin to fill these gaps in knowledge. The purposes were (a) to investigate the perceptions of lesbians of their identifiability and the ways in which they feel their identity is communicated to others; (b) to investigate the cultural beliefs of lesbians about wellness and illness; (c) to hypothesize about relationships between health and identifiability in lesbian women, and (d) to investigate the experience of lesbians in interaction with health care providers.

METHODS

. . . Twenty-five self-identified lesbians participated in interviews lasting approximately two hours. Their confidentiality was protected throughout the process. They were solicited through a snowball design by flyers and by word of mouth from the lesbian community in Iowa City, Iowa. Most were college educated, white and employed. Ages ranged from 21 to 58 years with a mean of 30 years. A potential bias in this self-selected sample was inclusion of a majority of women who were more vocal, who openly disclosed and accepted their lesbian identity. However, such a sample is desirable for qualitative research because spokespersons are sought, rather than a random, representative sample (Agar, 1980). . . .

FINDINGS

Identifiability

Identifiability was defined as the belief that one is known to others as a lesbian without a verbal disclosure. There was a range of belief about personal identifiability: 48 percent of the participants thought they were clearly recognizable to everyone as lesbians; 32 percent thought that other lesbians could tell that they were lesbian, while the general public could not; and 20 percent thought that nobody could tell. Their opinions about the identifiability of lesbians as a whole were similar.

About half of these women believed that, in social interactions, their lesbian identity was readily apparent to all. It has been assumed in the literature that the task for lesbians in managing stigma is to conceal information so that others do not become aware of the attribute. However, the present findings suggest that at least some women perceive themselves to be readily recognized as lesbians so that their task becomes minimizing the negative impact of the stigma. Consequently, a lesbian's perceived social vulnerability is related to her beliefs about her own identifiability.

The means by which the participants believed lesbians were identifiable to others formed a gestalt of physical appearance, personality, interaction and association. Participants thought themselves to be more androgynous in appearance. They believed themselves to be differentiated from other women by a more purposeful carriage; a less "affected," more natural walk; a stronger, more athletic body; open, definite body gestures; and a more casual mode of dress and hair style. They believed that their degree of independence, self-reliance, assertiveness, confidence, persistence and strength of will distinguished them, making them recognizable as lesbians. They referred also to the perception that some men feel intimidated by them and are more likely to conclude that they are lesbians.

The participants believed that lesbians are marked also by their interactional style and patterns of association. They believed it was noticeable that they do not defer to men, do not form intimate relationships with men and, in general, pay less attention to them. In contrast, they felt lesbians establish more eye contact with other women, stand and sit closer to women, are more likely to touch women as they socialize and ordinarily associate more with women. Speaking about and affiliating with such political concerns as feminism and minority rights helped to identify them as lesbians as did talking about women partners and friends, rather than husbands and boyfriends. A verbal style that sought clarification and offered criticism was also indicated as a distinguishing factor. Participants believed that a constellation of physical, psychological and social factors—as opposed to a single characteristic—combined to distinguish them. These results suggest that for those women who believe they can conceal their lesbian identity and avoid stigmatization, comprehensive management of that information involves vigilance about the intimate details of who they are, how they act, how they look, what they say, who they are with and where they are. Such a task is extremely complex and not replicated in the experience of nonlesbian women.

Health Benefits

Participants conceptualized health in a wholistic fashion, discussing wellness as a composite of emotional, physical and social elements and envisioning health strengths in lesbians as well as serious health concerns. They focused on independence and self-reliance as the primary components of wellness. A positive self-concept, an affirming attitude toward life, purposeful work toward emotional health and an ability to manage stress were frequently cited as the participants identified the healthiest things about themselves as lesbians. There was consensus about a number of physical health strengths including athleticism, involvement in physical exercise and good nutrition. Social factors identified as common to lesbians and sources of well-being were group cohesiveness that lends social support, ethical responsibility that prompts political action and a tendency to value mutuality in relationships. A predilection for alternative healing strategies such as massage, homeopathy, chiropractic, and accupuncture as well as the avoidance of mainstream [medicine] were also viewed positively.

Substance abuse was frequently mentioned. Some participants remarked positively that many lesbians are recovering from substance abuse or simply choosing not to use drugs or alcohol. Others focused on the belief that abuse of substances is more likely to occur in lesbians than in nonlesbian women and is of serious concern.

These women were distressed about aging, viewing it as a loss of physical, economic and social autonomy and as an impairment of athletic capabilities, all of which were so vitally important to their definition of wellness. They feared being dependent on others as they grow older yet isolated from social support. Most had contemplated being old and anticipated alienation, seeing no present social structures supportive of older lesbians. They also feared increasing involvement in the mainstream . . . health care system because of an overwhelming mistrust of its ability to care adequately and safely for lesbians.

Another health concern identified specifically was the stress of socioeconomic discrimination suffered by women, particularly lesbian women. They described its impact on them much as Adam (1978) did, when he theorized that structural limitations are placed on the alternatives open to stigmatized individuals, so that one dominant group maximizes its life chances by minimizing those of another group . . .

Identifiability in Relations to Health

These lesbian women conceived of the concepts of both identifiability and health as an amalgam of physical, psychological and social components. Several hallmarks of lesbian health were also primary qualities that they believed identified them as lesbians. It may be hypothesized that the challenge of coping with stigma engenders a strong self-concept and underlies many of the attributes of lesbian health, but the factor of identifiability mediates the process. The means by which a lesbian believes her identity to be revealed may affect how she values such aspects of herself as body image, associations and personality characteristics. Her attitude toward the degree of identifiability she attributes to herself may be related to the degree of self-affirmation that she has as a lesbian. Her sense of control over the disclosure of her lesbian identity may be related to the level of stress that she experiences. For example, both the woman who believes that she can conceal her lesbian identity and the

woman who behaves as though she is highly identifiable may experience a sense of control and thereby reduce stress.

Interactions with Health Care Providers

Experience in health care interactions was also related to stigmatized identity. Participants discussed health care contacts in which they were known to be lesbians. They identified circumstances in which they were identifiable to health care providers by their behavior, interaction, appearance and associations or by verbal disclosure of lesbian identity. The majority (72%) recounted negative responses from health care providers after their identity was known. They described being responded to with ostracism, invasive personal questioning, shock, embarrassment, unfriendliness, pity, condescension and fear. They reported instances in which nurses did not answer their call lights and doctors stopped talking to them. They felt that their partners had been mistreated; their confidentiality breached. Rough physical handling and derogatory comments were also perceived as being related directly to their disclosures. Of the respondents, 36 percent described situations in which they had had to terminate the interaction or not return to that provider because of events following disclosure. A few of their comments serve to illustrate:

> As soon as I said I was a lesbian, the nurses started giving me disgusted looks. They were nasty to my partner. They rough-housed me. They were not gentle like they would be to a straight woman. They treated me like I was "one of those," like they might catch something.

> The reaction was a subtle thing, an air of pity and fear. A wall went up. I read the shocked facial expressions, and they were saying, "That's too bad." But they made no remarks. They just acted real nervous.

> One of the doctors I told turned completely different colors. He left the office saying he had to get equipment and returned with two nurses like he had to have protection from me.

In the course of the discussion with the counselor, it became more like voyeurism than therapy. She was obviously curious about the life-style and asked a lot of inappropriate sexual questions.

I was in the hospital and the nurses would never come down to my room. I was told later that they had specifically talked about not wanting to care for me because I was a lesbian. I was surprised. I am always surprised when these things actually happen.

Negatively perceived interactions occurred in a variety of settings including hospitals, emergency rooms and community clinics. Of particular distress to these lesbians were interactions that involved gynecological health care. They felt harassed by persistent questioning about birth control and pregnancy. As two women put it:

When you go for a pap test they always ask if you are sexually active. If you say no, they don't believe you. If you say yes, you get badgered about how you should use birth control. If you are stuck with the birth control lecture you disclose just to avoid all that. But I've never done it voluntarily. I've always felt forced to disclose.

When I was having abdominal pain, they asked me at the emergency room if I was pregnant. When I told them I was sure I was not pregnant, they kept asking me over and over until I got angry and said, "No, I can't be pregnant, I'm a lesbian."

Questions asked by health care providers assumed that their female clients were heterosexual, their partners were male and their sexual activity involved intercourse. Overwhelmingly, participants found that there was no routine, comfortable way to let health care providers know that heterosexual assumptions were not applicable to them as lesbians. To avoid being referred to persistently as something they were not, to avoid upbraiding about irrelevant issues and to obtain pertinent health teaching, many participants felt forced to "make an announcement" of their lesbian identity.

Every participant identified circumstances in which it would be important for her providers to know about her lesbian identity so that they might deliver optimal, comprehensive care. For instance, several feared being hospitalized for a serious condition in which visitation and treatment decisions were relegated to "immediate family" and said that they would definitely disclose in this situation so that their partner or a significant friend could be involved in their health care.

Nearly all (96%) of the women in this study anticipated situations in which it could be harmful to them if their health care provider were to know that they were lesbian. Although they believed that there was frequent specific health care situations in which they wanted to disclose, they described having to assess each individual encounter for both potential antilesbian sentiment and personal vulnerability. In potentially harmful situations, if they were identifiable, they would attempt to minimize the impact of their lesbian identity during health care interactions. On the other hand, if they were to believe that they were not identifiable, they would not disclose and would attempt to manage the information so that health care providers would not become aware that they were lesbian. Their sensitivity to these risks seemed to have developed over a lifetime of dealing with the larger stigmatizing society.

Society says it is not okay to be a lesbian. We face rejection based on that all the time. Not having access to health care in which it is safe to disclose is just a small part of the larger picture.

When they disclosed or were otherwise identifiable in an unsafe health care situation, they feared danger, infliction of pain, inadequate care, withdrawal of concern for their welfare and pathological assumption, "where your health problem is seen as a pathological extension of the fact that you are lesbian." Several women addressed these fears:

I think some caregivers leave that room of margin. They put limits on how far they will go to help lesbians, just decide to give you only the minimum care.

You'd get poorer care if they knew you were lesbian. If they thought it was bad they wouldn't care if you didn't get well. They could relax during surgery. They could give you bad drugs.

If the environment isn't safe for disclosure, I'm not going to be taken care of. I might even get hurt.

It would be very damaging if you got into interactions with health care providers in which you are considered deviant. Some people have very negative, very violent reactions. I don't think they can separate from their personal prejudices. It is like putting your life in someone's hands who really hates you.

The most dominant feature of positive health care experiences reported by these women was the perception that providers accepted the knowledge of their clients' lesbian identity as a matter of routine. This was demonstrated by providers' treating them "like anybody else" and maintaining a calm, supportive demeanor. These lesbian women wanted to feel accepted, respected and welcomed by health care providers. They did not want to be questioned when they chose to have their lesbian partners included as their significant others in health care interactions. They felt more comfortable with women and appreciated the availability of female health care providers.

Lesbians take action in light of what they encounter in the behavior of others. Given their negative experiences in interaction with health care providers and their fearful perceptions that harm could befall them, 84 percent described a general reluctance to seek health care. According to the participants, dispelling heterosexual assumption and eliminating prejudicial attitude and action is the responsibility of health care providers so that health care can be made more accessible to lesbians. They suggested the use of inclusive language and the education of providers about lesbian culture and health concerns to accomplish these goals. With empathy and accurate information about lesbians, participants felt it would be possible for health care providers to overcome their negative responses. However, they wanted providers to have dealt with the issue before that moment when it comes to providing care to them.

CONCLUSION

Lesbians share common beliefs and experiences with identifiability, health and health care. They often do not feel comfortable seeking health care, have experienced nonempathetic responses when they did and even feel at risk of harm in some health care situations. The commitment of nursing to wholism and advocacy in the care of women and vulnerable cultural groups and lesbians' preference for female providers makes nursing a logical health care profession to facilitate lesbians' positive involvement in health care. Only when the recipients of care can report feeling respect and regard from caregivers is that commitment to care genuinely fulfilled. This study points out a burden of responsibility for nursing as a profession and for nurses as individual clinicians, educators and researchers to evaluate the adequacy of its knowledge base and reassess the quality of health care offered to lesbian women.

REFERENCES

ADAM, B. (1978). The survival of domination: Inferiorization and everyday life. New York: Elsevier.

AGAR, M. (1980). The professional stranger: An informal introduction to ethnography. New York: Academic Press.

AGUERO, J. E., BLOCH, L. & BYRNE, D. (1984). The relationship among sexual beliefs, attitudes, experience and homophobia. Journal of Homosexuality, 10(1–2), 95–107.

AHMED, P. I., KOLKER, A., & COELHO, G. V. (1979). Toward a new definition of health. In P.I. Ahmed & G. V. Coelho (Eds.), Toward a new definition of health: Psychosocial approaches (pp. 7–21). New York: Plenum Press.

BECKER, H. S. (1973). Outsiders: Studies in the sociology of deviance. New York: The Free Press.

BLUMER, H. (1969). Symbolic interactionism: Perspective and method. Englewood Cliffs, NJ: Prentice-Hall.

BROOKS, V. (1981). Minority stress and lesbian women. New York: D. C. Heath.

CASS, V. (1979). Homosexual identity formation: A theoretical model. Journal of Homosexuality 4(3), 219–235.

CHATETZ, J., SAMPSON, P., BECK, P., & WEST, J. (1974). A study of homosexual women. Social Work, 19(6), 714–723.

DANK, B. (1971). Coming out in the gay world. Psychiatry, 34, 180–197.

DI ANGI, P. R. (1982). Grieving and the acceptance of the homosexual identity. Issues in Mental Health Nursing, 4, 101–113.

FABREGA, H., JR. (1979). Disease and illness from a biocultural standpoint. In P. I. Ahmed & G. V. Coelho (Eds.), Toward a new definition of health: Psychosocial dimensions (pp. 23–50). New York: Plenum Press.

FEIN, S. B., & NUEHRING, E. M. (1981). Intrapsychic effects of stigma: A process of breakdown and reconstruction of social reality. Journal of Homosexuality, 7(1), 3–13.

GLASCOCK, E. (1983). Lesbians growing older: Self-identification, coming out, and health concerns. Paper presented at the American Public Health Association Annual Meeting, Dallas.

GOFFMAN, E. (1963). Stigma: Notes on the management of spoiled identity. Englewood Cliffs, NJ: Prentice-Hall.

GOOD, B. J., & GOOD, M.D. (1981). The meaning of symptoms: A cultural hermeneutical model for clinical practice. In L. Eisenberg & A. Kleinman (Eds.), The relevance of social science for medicine (pp. 165–196). New York: D. Reidel.

HARTOG J., & HARTOG, E. A. (1983). Cultural aspects of health and illness behavior in hospitals. Western Journal of Medicine, 139(6), 910–916.

HUDSON, W. W., & RICKETTS, W. A. (1980). A strategy for the measurement of homophobia. Journal of Homosexuality, 5(4), 357–372.

IRWIN, P., & THOMPSON, N. L. (1978). Acceptance of the rights of homosexuals: A social profile. Journal of Homosexuality, 3(2), 107–121.

JANDT, F. E., & DARSEY, J. (1981). Coming out as a communication process. In J. Chesebro (Ed.), Gayspeak: Gay male and lesbian communication (pp. 12–27). New York: Pilgrim Press.

JOHNSON, S., GUENTHER, S., LAUBE, D., & KEETTEL, W. (1981). Factors influencing lesbian gynecologic care: A preliminary study. American Journal of Obstetrics and Gynecology, 140(1), 20–28.

JONES, E. E., FARINA, A., HASTORF, A. H., MARKUS, H., MILLER, D. T., SCOTT, R. A., & FRENCH, R. DE S. (1984). Social stigma: The psychology of marked relationships. New York: W. H. Freeman.

JOURARD, S. (1971). Self-disclosure: An experimental analysis of the transparent self. New York: Wiley-Interscience.

KRESTAN, J., & BEPKO, C. S. (1980). The problem of fusion in the lesbian relationship. Family Process, 19, 277–289.

KUS, R. (1985). Stages of coming out: An ethnographic approach. Western Journal of Nursing Research, 7(2), 177–198.

LANER, M. R., & LANER, R. H. (1980). Sexual preference or personal style? Why lesbians are disliked. Journal of Homosexuality, 5(4), 339–356.

LEININGER, M. (1984). Care: The essence of nursing and health. Thorofare, NJ: Charles B. Slack.

LEVITT, E. E., & KLASSEN, A. D. (1974). Public attitudes toward homosexuality: Part of the 1970 national survey by the Institute of Sex Research. Journal of Homosexuality, 1(1), 29–43.

MARKUS, H. (1977). Self-schemata and processing information about the self. Journal of Personality and Social Psychology, 35(2), 63–79.

MILLHAM, J., SAN MIGUEL, C. L., & KELLOGG, R. (1976). A factor-analytic conceptualization of attitudes toward male and female homosexuals. Journal of Homosexuality, 2(1), 3–10.

MINNIGERODE, F. A. (1976). Attitudes toward homosexuality: Feminist attitudes and sexual conservatism. Sex Roles, 2(4), 347–352.

MORIN, S. F. (1981). Psychology and the gay community: An overview. Journal of Social Issues, 34(3), 1–6.

NIXON, J., & BERSON, G. (1978). Women's music. In G. Vida (Ed.), Our right to love: A lesbian resource book (pp. 252–255). Englewood Cliffs, NJ: Prentice-Hall.

NUNGESSER, L. G. (1983). Homosexual acts, actors and identities. New York: Praeger Publishers.

NYBERG, K. L., & ALSTON, J. P. (1977). Analysis of public attitudes toward homosexual behavior. Journal of Homosexuality, 2(2), 99–107.

PAINTER, D. S. (1981). Recognition among lesbians in straight settings. In J. Chesebro (Ed.), Gayspeak: Gay male and lesbian communication (pp. 68–79). New York: Pilgrim Press.

PATERSON, J., & ZDERAD, L. (1976). Humanistic nursing. New York: John Wiley & Sons.

PLUMMER, K. (1975). Sexual stigma: An interactionist account. Boston, MA: Routledge and Kegan Paul.

PONSE, B. (1978). Identities in the lesbian world: The social construction of self. Westport, CT: Greenwood Press.

SMITH, E., JOHNSON, S., & GUENTHER, S. (1985). Health care attitudes and experiences during gynecologic care among lesbians and bisexuals. American Journal of Public Health, 75(9), 1085–1087.

SMITH, J. (1981). The idea of health: A philosophical inquiry. Advances in Nursing Science, 3(3), 43–50.

TRIPP-REIMER, T. (1984). Reconceptualizing the construct of health: Integrating emic and etic perspectives. Research in Nursing and Health, 7, 101–109.

WARREN, C. A. B. (1980). Homosexuality and stigma. In J. Marmor (Ed.), Homosexual behavior (pp. 123–141). New York: Basic Books.

WEINBERGER, L. E., & MILLHAM, J. (1979). Attitudinal homophobia and support of traditional sex roles. Journal of Homosexuality, 4(3), 237–245.

CRITICAL THINKING QUESTIONS

1. Why do lesbians seek health care less often than heterosexual women?

2. In what ways is the health care that lesbians receive inappropriate to their needs? In what ways do health care providers discriminate against known or suspected lesbians?

3. What changes in the institution of medicine are needed to correct the problems that lesbians face in getting appropriate, high quality health care?

Getting Involved

1. Contact the public health department in your community and get information on the location and hours of the nearest off-campus public clinic in your area. Go to the clinic and tell the receptionist that you are observing waiting rooms for a college class. Make note of the race and gender of the individuals in the waiting room, as well as the length of time that each person waits before being called in to see a care provider. If you feel comfortable doing so, talk to the people in the waiting room to learn opinions about the clinic, its doctors and nurses, and the quality of care they receive.

2. Contact the public health department in your community and request statistics on lead poisoning, as well as information on any programs the department might have in place to address this problem and statistics on the people they have helped. What are the rates at which African-Americans, Hispanics, other people of color, and whites are known to have experienced lead poisoning? What are the rates at which they have received assistance with removing lead paint from their homes? How do these rates compare to the racial and ethnic make-up of your community?

3. Contact your local Red Cross office and ask for a copy of the forms individuals are required to fill out when they volunteer to donate blood. Examine the questions. Are there any that discriminate against individuals on the basis of sexual activity or sexual orientation? Explain. Once you have examined the questions, contact the Red Cross and ask an official there about any questions you think might be discriminatory. Discuss your findings with classmates.

Site Seeing

1. For more information on the health issues facing African-Americans, visit **http://www.kenyada.com/aahealthissues.htm.**

2. For information about women's health provided by women, visit the Boston Women's Health Collective web site at **http://www.ourbodiesourselves.org.**

3. To learn more about the connections between poverty and poor health, visit the Almanac of Policy Issues at **http://www.policyalmanac.org/social_welfare/poverty.shtml.**

4. To learn more about the health issues facing gay men, lesbians, bisexuals, and transgenders, visit **http://www.-hsl.mcmaster.ca/tomflem/gay.html.**

EDUCATIONAL BARRIERS TO EQUALITY

In the United States, one of the best ways to get ahead in life is to get a good education. Graduating from college is strongly related to access to jobs that offer more security, better pay, and more fringe benefits than those available with a high school education or less. Moreover, graduating from one of the nation's elite colleges—such as Harvard, Yale, or Stanford—usually brings even greater rewards. However, getting into college depends on earning a high school diploma or a General Equivalency Diploma (GED); and getting into a good college depends on graduating at the top of the class of a good high school.

As the articles in this section discuss, not all people in the United States have access to a good primary or secondary education. Without equal access to a good education early in life, admissions to colleges and universities will continue to be determined by social factors such as race or social class. That is because race and social class correlate with the quality of education one receives more than do individual talent, intelligence, and motivation. Moreover, what people learn, even in good schools, is likely to continue to be influenced by gender, while the quality of their interactions with teachers and peers is influenced by race, social class, gender, and their perceived sexual orientation. Without equality of opportunity in education, schools in the United States continue to do much to perpetuate inequality among social groups, even while they help certain individuals get ahead in life. Education, then, is clearly organized in ways that perpetuate inequality.

Throughout the last half of the twentieth century and in the beginning of the twenty-first century, a number of social policies were implemented to reduce institutional barriers to education. The first of these was the U.S. Supreme Court's 1954 *Brown v. Board of Education* decision, which ruled that segregation in public schools is unconstitutional. In the wake of this decision, the National Guard was called upon to protect African-American children from white mobs who attacked black students when they tried to integrate white schools. Ultimately, school districts were forced to provide equal access to children of all racial and ethnic backgrounds, thus formally and legally ending racial segregation. But the end of official racial segregation gave rise to another form of unequal access to schools, in which discrimination on the basis of race is unintended, but very real.

Because people live in segregated neighborhoods, a common practice used to achieve racial balance in public schools has been busing—transporting white children to predominately African-American schools, and black children to predominately white facilities. When it was first implemented, busing prompted strong, often violent reactions by many white parents. Those parents who had the means to move out of their urban neighborhoods relocated to the suburbs, beyond the reach of busing. The result is that today, on average, poorer parents live in central urban areas and more affluent parents live in the suburbs. Thus urban schools now tend to be racially integrated because poor parents include those who are white as well as people of color. However, schools are now economically segregated, with the children of well-off parents attending predominately white suburban schools and the children of poorer parents going to racially mixed urban schools. The two issues—race and social class—are clearly and closely intertwined.

As Renwick explains in the first article in this section, the courts in the United States have largely abandoned busing, leaving those interested in integrating schools to search for other ways to reduce segregation and inequality in education. Renwick explores the history of integration efforts, as well as the conservative backlash against busing and other desegregation programs. She notes that one solution to segregation in public schools would be to integrate the neighborhoods in which children live, but that desegregating housing is a long and complex process that more affluent people are likely to resist.

In the second article, Meeks and her colleagues consider four types of programs that have been implemented to various degrees throughout the United States. Proponents believe that these programs will help to equalize educational opportunities. The authors critique several of these programs, including magnet schools, vouchers, private education, and home schooling, and argue that all of them have the effect of increasing racial and class-based segregation in schools. Meeks and her colleagues maintain that with each of these approaches, children from single-parent and other disadvantaged families are left to public schools, while children from two-parent or more affluent homes avail themselves of private and parochial schools. With lower enrollments in public schools, disadvantaged children will be left with fewer resources and fewer parents to pressure the government to improve public education.

The quality of the education students receive varies greatly among schools, but even students who attend the same school receive unequal treatment. Social scientists and feminist scholars have long documented the ways in which girls are discriminated against in public education. Whether they are discouraged from taking mathematics and science courses, provided inferior access to sports and recreational opportunities, or simply not taken seriously as students, research has established a long history of discrimination against girls in school. As a result of this research and the activism of feminists, a number of social policy changes opened opportunities for girls and women, including Title IX of the Educational Amendments of 1972. Title IX bans sex discrimination in schools receiving federal aid. As a result of this and other social policies, girls now have much greater access to a challenging and rewarding education than ever before.

Girls' progress in education has prompted a debate among social scientists. Some argue that discrimination against girls still exists, albeit in more subtle and hard-to-detect forms. But others maintain that with so many changes to enhance opportunities for girls, boys have suffered in school and are now the subjects of discrimination.

In the third article, Sadker argues that important gender differences still remain in students' educational achievement and experiences, with girls still being denied opportunities equal to those of boys. Sadker organizes his argument using a Top Ten list format, and provides strong evidence to suggest that, although girls have made progress, U.S. schools have a long way to go before gender equity in the classroom is achieved. On the other hand, the author of the fourth article, "Back-Seat Boys," reports on a number of difficulties facing boys in today's schools, including the greater likelihood that they will be medicated for hyperactivity. The author argues that the same attention that has been paid to improving the educational experiences of girls should be devoted to boys. In an inset article, the author focuses on the compound problems that African-American boys are likely to have in school, as well as one program designed to address their needs. That article illustrates the effects of the intersection of institutionalized discrimination—in this instance on the basis of gender, race, and social class.

Getting an education can be extremely difficult for students who are labeled as different, particularly when that difference carries with it social stigmas. In the last article in this section, McIntosh reports on the toll harassment took on one student when his teachers learned he was gay. Even when the student reported his teachers' harassment to school administrators, they did nothing to protect him. Indeed, in that particular school district, as in most, administrators were completely within their legal rights, since gay men, lesbians, bisexuals, and transgenders have no right to be protected from harassment in school or at work. In some ways, this article harkens back to the days when racial and sex discrimination were openly practiced. The effects of discrimination seen in this article are very similar to those long experienced by racial and ethnic minorities and by women.

Together, the articles in this section demonstrate just some of the ways that the educational system in the United States does as much to perpetuate inequality among social groups as it does to help individuals get ahead. Individual African-Americans, Hispanics, Native Americans, poor people, women, gay men, and lesbians have shown that it is possible to overcome prejudice and interpersonal discrimination by finding ways to get the educations they deserve. But individual success stories belie the institutional patterns of discrimination discussed in this collection of articles. If it is true, as many people assume, that the keys to getting ahead in the United States include working hard and getting a good education, equality of opportunity demands that the institutionalized discrimination woven into the very fabric of our educational system be dismantled.

Reading 17

Busing Rolls to a Stop

Lucille Renwick

In this article, Renwick explores the history of school integration efforts, including busing and newer desegregation programs.

As Courts Give up on School Desegregation, Activists Look for New Strategies.

Since the seventies, Boston has been an icon of the passions evoked by the government's attempt to desegregate schools, but today it is emblematic of a new trend in American race relations. Gone are the angry crowds from South Boston and Charlestown hurling rocks at

Source: Reprinted from *The Nation* 269, no. 16 (November 15, 1999): 17–19.

buses full of black students, yet the forces allied against court-ordered integration have finally won a quiet victory. Last year, a US Appeals Court judge ruled that the prestigious Boston Latin High School violated a prospective white student's constitutional rights when it denied her admission, so the city adopted a race-blind admissions policy for its elite schools. Then, under pressure from another lawsuit on behalf of white students, the Boston School Committee agreed in July of this year to abandon the last vestiges of its citywide busing program.

According to the Justice Department, since the seventies, forty-two school desegregation orders, affecting forty-five school districts, have been lifted. Judges in Boston, Tampa, Denver, Buffalo, St. Louis and dozens of other municipalities have been either considering ending or have already halted court-supervised school integration. Courts that once ordered school districts to integrate are now declaring school systems "unitary"—meaning they have eliminated the effects of racial discrimination—and returning them to the control of local school boards. "We're going to have very few desegregation orders standing in our cities in the next five years," says Gary Orfield, a professor at Harvard University's Graduate School of Education and an expert on school integration. "Many of them have already settled, are going to be settled or the cities are going to be sued."

While organizations like the NAACP Legal Defense and Educational Fund continue to fight for desegregation programs, opposition from the courts seem unrelenting. In several cities where desegregation programs have been dismantled, educators and policy-makers have devised new approaches to redress racial imbalances without directly invoking race—focusing instead, for example, on mixing poor kids with those from well-to-do backgrounds, or channeling more funds into city schools. But as race-based programs dissolve, school re-segregation is on the rise.

Sudden as it seems, the end of desegregation has been coming for quite some time. It began during the Reagan and Bush administrations, with the ascent of conservative judges who viewed desegregation orders with suspicion. Together, Reagan and Bush appointed more than 60 percent of the country's district court judges, nearly 70 percent of appellate judges and five of the nine Supreme Court Justices. This set the stage for a series of Supreme Court rulings between 1992 and 1995 easing the way for school districts to protest court mandates and to be declared free of judicial scrutiny. The rulings allow judges to end judicial oversight if a school board has made a "good faith" commitment and has succeeded "to the extent practicable" in establishing racial balance, even if it has come nowhere close to achieving it. "The present position of the Court has basically legitimated de facto segregation," says Cheryl Hams, a law professor at UCLA.

Under Reagan and Bush, the Justice Department and individual judges urged school districts to request release from desegregation orders. "In practice, the tenor, at least in some cases, has been: Even though nobody has even raised this issue, I'm going to end this," says Jay Heubert, an associate professor of education and law at Columbia University's Teachers College, who spent five years as a civil rights lawyer at the Justice Department under Reagan. "And this is not responsible, judicious behavior. It's also not the kind of initiative that courts take in most other cases."

The courts have not, for the most part, been sympathetic to the argument that race-based programs are necessary because discrimination still exists. For example, in Delaware in 1995, after the four districts of the Wilmington school system forced a trial to end nearly two decades of federal court supervision of schools, US District Court Judge Sue Robinson, a Bush appointee, decided that the school system had done its job toward integration. The city's black students complained about racial inequality in enrollment in college prep and honors courses and about race-based tracking to lower-level courses, but Judge Robinson saw this not as an effect of discrimination but as an example of social and economic forces beyond the school system's control. She concluded that Wilmington had at least done something during its years of court-ordered integration, whether or not it worked.

Yet the demise of desegregation can't be entirely blamed on a right-wing conspiracy. Another important factor has to do with how the programs were received—by white and black parents alike. In many cities, busing proved an inadequate remedy, because wealthy white parents chose to flee cities rather than send their kids to integrated schools. In Boston, the desegregation plan was applied only within the city limits (with the exception of a voluntary city-to-suburb alternative, called METCO, which still stands), and white families who could afford it flocked to the suburbs. When busing began, Boston schools were 60 percent white; today, the 64,000-student school district is 49 percent African-American, 26 percent Hispanic, 10 percent Asian-American or other ethnic groups and 15 percent white.

There was also a less than enthusiastic response from some black parents. Despite the additional resources black children received in predominantly white schools, many black parents grew tired of their children being forced to travel hours to and from school. Wary of the idea that their kids just needed to be exposed to white classmates to do well, they began to demand better-funded schools in their own neighborhoods. In Seattle many black parents were among those who pushed to have the voluntary busing program scrapped, because little had been done to improve achievement among black students. Seattle ended its busing program in 1996 and agreed to funnel more resources to schools in poorer, predominantly minority communities. Frustrated with public schools, increasing numbers of African-Americans are also founding Afrocentric schools in their neighborhoods; about 400 now exist in the United States, according to Molefi Kete Asante of Temple University.

Does this mean that Americans of all races want to give up on integration? Not exactly. A 1998 poll by Public Agenda found that both black and white parents felt that raising student achievement and academic standards was more important than integration. However, the poll also revealed that 80 percent of black parents and two-thirds of white parents say it is important to them that their own child's school be racially integrated. A more recent Public Agenda report showed strong support for voluntary initiatives that would bring city and suburban students together.

Unlike voluntary programs, however, court-ordered desegregation programs were able to achieve racial integration on a large scale. And without them, minority and white students are increasingly isolated from each other. "We've become far more diverse and racially and ethnically mixed as a nation, but terribly segregated in our schools and in our neighborhoods," says Orfield. "So we're left with very segregated, very impoverished schools now." A recent study by Orfield and John Yun documented the trend toward resegregation since the eighties. More schools are on either end of the spectrum: either mostly students of color or predominantly white. African-American and Hispanic students are attending schools with smaller numbers of white students. About a third of African-American children attend public schools with 90–100 percent minority enrollment. Fewer African-Americans attend predominantly white schools than a decade ago, especially in the South, the study found.

Among the alternative measures being considered in the wake of desegregation is a plan in Indianapolis that attempts to address the housing segregation that public schools reflect. Officials from the Indianapolis Housing Agency, the state and the Justice Department are working together to assist low-income and minority families in finding affordable housing in the suburbs.

But since remedying housing segregation is a long and complex process, others argue that the primary focus should now be on creating more equitable and better-directed school funding. Noreen Connell, executive director of the Educational Priorities Panel in New York, points to an alarming disparity in the funding of urban versus suburban schools. New York City schools, for example, are more than $1,000 below the rest of the state average in per pupil annual spending. That's why the Campaign for Fiscal Equity is now suing New York, contending that the state's school financing formula robs poor kids of their constitutional right to a "sound, basic education." Similar lawsuits in New Jersey, Connecticut and elsewhere have forced states to address funding disparities [see David L. Kirp, "New Hope for Failing Schools," June 1, 1998]. The New York lawsuit is unusual, though, in that it invokes civil rights law to argue that since 74 percent of New York's minority students are in New York City, the state's underfunding of city schools has a racially discriminatory impact.

Yet injecting money into high-poverty schools does not in itself solve the problem of school quality, according to Richard Kahlenberg, a senior fellow at the Century Foundation. School quality also depends on the people who make up the community-parents, students, teachers. If they are poor and undereducated the likelihood is that schools will still suffer. Kahlenberg contends that greater equality and opportunity can be achieved through economic desegregation—combining poor and middle-income students in the same school. After all, as Orfield points out, desegregation was as helpful in mixing students of different class backgrounds as of different racial backgrounds. A 1986 study by the Education Department found that students from poor families attending middle-class schools did better than middle-class students attending high-poverty schools. "You're not only desegregating the students, you're also desegregating the money," Kathlenberg says.

He points to La Crosse, Wisconsin—which instituted economic desegregation in 1992 by redrawing elementary school zones to spread out the number of students receiving free lunch (an indicator of poverty)—and to San Francisco, which replaced its racial desegregation plan with one that takes into account students' economic status, English proficiency, achievement and race (the San Francisco plan is pending court approval). Emphasizing economic disadvantage can eliminate issues of race that might not survive legal challenges, Kahlenberg contends. But it benefits Hispanic and African-American children, who are disproportionately poor, and still provides greater diversity.

In cities like Boston, however, where more than 70 percent of students qualify for free or subsidized lunch, efforts toward economic integration are futile unless suburbs are drawn in, which is not likely to happen. That's why many activists argue that the pragmatic strategy is to document inequalities in resources among schools and fight the necessary battles to rectify them. According to Elizabeth Reilinger, chairwoman of the Boston School Committee, when the lawsuits arose they had already been

reconsidering the race-based assignment strategy. In the post-business era, the school committee will build three elementary schools in Roxbury, Dorchester and Matapan, largely minority areas of Boston where few or no elementary schools currently exist. The committee "tried to insure an equitable allocation of resources in schools . . . especially in minority areas that got the least amount of resources," Reilinger says.

Unfortunately, these neighborhood schools won't solve the problem of low school quality in poor areas. And many who support efforts to reallocate resources also contend that business should be maintained as the simpler, more straightforward remedy to segregation. William Taylor, vice chair of the Citizens Commission on Civil Rights, notes the situation in St. Louis, where a settlement was reached that required suburban districts to accept students of color until they had 25 percent minority enrollment. "These kids graduate from high schools and go on to college at significantly higher rates than kids who go to racially and socio-economically segregated schools," Taylor says.

Another major challenge today is eliminating segregation inside schools, rather than among them, says Dennis Parker, an attorney with the NAACP Legal Defense and Educational Fund who has defended court-ordered desegregation plans. Many supposedly integrated schools with high minority enrollments have a mostly white college-prep track—with gifted and talented programs and Advanced Placement courses—and a low-level track that serves mostly minority children. African-American boys, in particular, end up in special-education classes in disproportionate numbers. The NAACP fund has brought up this issue in several cases, with little success in court.

Perhaps it was naive to believe that the antidiscrimination laws of the sixties by themselves would protect minority students from being denied opportunities. Certainly these programs did not prevent power and money from following white children who were already well-off. But desegregation at least allowed minority children access to the same schools their white counterparts enjoyed, and attempted to address the problem of racial discrimination in education. "We're going to reach a point where we will realize how much we've eroded the successes and gains integration has made," says Orfield. "Unless we get equal resources and funding to the poorest schools, there will never be equal education. Even with those resources for all schools there will still be some inequalities. Desegregation was working to change that."

CRITICAL THINKING QUESTIONS

1. Why was busing first instituted and then later abandoned by school districts?

2. What alternatives to busing are available in the effort to achieve racial integration of schools?

3. Do you believe racial integration of schools benefits individual students? Does it benefit society? Explain.

Reading 18

Racial Desegregation

Loretta F. Meeks, Wendell A. Meeks, and Claudia A. Warren

In this article, the authors introduce and critique four alternative programs designed to equalize educational opportunities in the United States.

MAGNET SCHOOLS, VOUCHERS, PRIVATIZATION, AND HOME SCHOOLING

The control and welfare of urban schools continues to occupy the attention of mayors, governors, state legislatures, and local citizens. Public funding, media scrutiny, and the school's reflection of society are primary contributors to this ongoing interest. The changing demographics of the urban setting and its effect on public policy have launched education into broader political, economic, and legal arenas. The major change in the education of urban students began with the 1954 ruling by the United States Supreme Court in *Brown v. Board of Education*. At that time, the Supreme Court recognized, through a unanimous 9-0 decision,

Source: This article first appeared in The *Christian Science Monitor,* 8/13/99, Vol. 91 (181), and is reproduced with permission. Copyright © 1999 The Christian Science Monitor (www.csmonitor.com). All rights reserved.

the significance of the fiscal, sociological, and psychological role of the public school and its significance to our democratic existence.

The empirical findings from Myrdal (1944) were the foundations of the psychological argument convincing the Court that segregation did in fact have a negative effect on African American students' potential for success (Orlich, 1991) and that there can be no equitable system of separate but equal schooling. Although the detrimental effects of segregation appeared clear to the Court a decade preceding the civil rights movement, neither *Brown* (1954) nor *Brown* (1955) provided prescriptive strategies to incorporate desegregation or to eliminate segregation. Some see this as synonymous with legalizing freedom but not abolishing slavery. However great, this omission has left a generation to continue to grapple with achieving a goal that has far-reaching underpinnings exacerbated by unforeseen circumstances, such as a changing national demographic, pervasiveness of racial separatism, unequal patterns of poverty, the political divisiveness of this educational issue, and the shift in the country's economic base from national to global.

Today, the United States is experiencing a shift in the demographic configurations of its cities and schools. Minority populations are growing at a faster pace than the majority. Some urban school districts have greater numbers of minority students than majority students, and the numbers of affected districts is predicted to increase (Stringfield, 1997). Neighborhood segregation and the imbalance of wealth, which influence the racial divide in this country, are factors that have not changed significantly since the inception of *Brown*. Reports indicate that the per capita cost of public schools is increasing, whereas scores on achievement measures are decreasing. In addition, the United States is evidencing a shift in its global positioning. It is no longer the monolithic power from previous decades but, rather, one of several major economic entities in a global market. The authors of *Brown* could not have anticipated these issues.

Although *Brown* continues to uphold the moral principles of desegregation, the legal significance is being debated and is eroding with current policies supported or ignored by the Court. The current Court has intentionally or unintentionally made no rulings on desegregation cases in nearly 10 years (Russo, Harris, & Sandidge, 1994). This failure to provide the legal framework for school reform may have given decision makers too much latitude, which many interpret to nullify the effects of Brown.

Since Brown, race has been a constant factor for parents in the selection of schools for their children. Brown and Hunter (1995) reported that, although 95% of White parents surveyed had no objection to their children attending a school in which a few of the children are Black, the proportion of objecting Whites grew steadily as a school population became increasingly Black. This resentment led to "White flight," leaving the urban schools primarily minority.

Although public perception of integration is clearly more positive now than nearly 50 years ago, the realization of legalized desegregation as a means toward this end has not been as readily endorsed. Court-ordered desegregation was accepted as a remedy for the "deliberate speed" implementation mandate for almost three decades, but now the federal courts are relieving most urban schools from court-ordered supervision of all efforts to desegregate schools.

The contradictory messages regarding the effects of desegregation from both races—perception of White parents that desegregated schools benefit Black students more so than Whites and the growing discontent of Blacks that desegregation has not had the intended positive effect on academic success for Black students—have led to the incorporation of politically inspired initiatives into the public educational arena. Consequently, the basis for assessment of these initiatives has primarily been political rather than educational because parent and student satisfaction are replacing traditional measures of educational achievement and program effectiveness. Even less empirical attention has been given to the effects on multicultural and exceptional populations (McKinney, 1996; Ramirez, 1998).

With the apparent end of court-ordered desegregation, the avenues of escape for White parents from enrolling their children in largely minority and poor schools have been identified as choice options. The most prevalent of these include magnet schools; vouchers; privatization of public schools or private, for-profit schools; and home schooling. These choice options initiated in the 1970s present an alternative to forced busing. They are particularly significant for middle-class families who cannot afford to reside in affluent neighborhoods with well-financed, predominently White schools nor afford the tuition of private schools (Glenn, 1998). Proponents of both political parties see some form of choice option as being the most efficient route to needed educational reform.

If the central focus of *Brown* (1954) was to create a school environment conducive to learning for all students, the central question in analyzing the choice option movement is whether this premise is still at the forefront of policy making and school options. Have the alternatives to traditional education promoted in the past decade lived up to their promise? The discussion that follows scrutinizes the alternatives based on this question.

ALTERNATIVE CHOICES

Magnet Schools

Magnet schools are defined as a selective, academically demanding public elementary or secondary school with superior facilities and programs that are more readily received by White citizens than is forced busing (Dejnozka & Kapel, 1991). They were established under the administrations of Presidents Richard Nixon and Ronald Reagan as a mechanism of a choice option for parents in lieu of forced busing to desegregate public schools. The assumption was that middle-class White parents could be lured back to inner-city schools with the assurance of an innovative and focused curriculum with locally tailored extras and that the financial base influenced by this infusion of students would revitalize the school. Magnet schools typically offer a nontraditional curriculum, incorporating thematic learning and technology that are governed by the school district and local school board (Metz, 1986).

The number of students enrolled in magnet schools has tripled in the past decade (Steel & Levine, 1994). Between 1985 and 1993, the federal Magnet School Assistance Program spent $739 million in school districts promoting magnet schools (Steele & Eaton, 1996). Typically, program offerings include an emphasis on basic skills, language immersion, humanities, and instructional approaches such as open classrooms, individualized instruction, and enriched curricula as well as career or vocational education, the arts, and gifted-talented programs. In other words, magnet schools specialize in programs that cater to the population that will support and control them. One important aspect of magnet schools is internal control that involves parents and teachers. The expectation is that the school will be responsive to its constituency because this group is in control. These schools are governed by administrative policies dictated through internal leadership.

According to Goldhaber (1997), the assumptions underlying the selection of a magnet school include the following: (a) All parents will be well informed regarding the benefits for enrollment in the school; (b) representation will be broad in policy development and management of the school; (c) the location will be centralized, supposedly assuring access for all populations; and (d) the selection or enrollment process will be equitable, thus promoting an inclusive population. Specifically, magnet schools should appeal to a broad base of parents and be accessible to a similar base of students. If these assumptions are not met, magnet schools can mimic the segregated neighborhood schools predating the *Brown* era.

Although the practical, economic impetus for magnet schools is clear, from an inclusion perspective, the intent of magnet schools seems suspect. Archbald (1996) notes, "Variables related to parent socioeconomic status and proximity to magnet schools were found to be significant predictors of magnet school enrollment" (p. 152). This is further evidenced by Orfield and Eaton's (1996) study of magnet schools in Kansas City, Missouri that showed the following:

- Magnet schools did little for integration.
- Magnet programs tend to help desegregate schools in middle-class communities with school districts and sizable minority and White populations.
- Magnet schools have less effect in large cities where Whites have fled to the suburbs.

In districts dominated by minorities, White students typically comprise 32% of the magnet school population. When analyzing the demographics of magnet school populations, Archbald's (1996) finding that neighborhoods with higher levels of educational attainment find magnet schools to be more attractive is also significant. White parents in Buffalo, Boston, and Charlotte have successfully challenged the concept of the magnet schools selection process by race to use this scheme to fashion desegregated schools (Hunter & Brown, 1991).

Although magnet schools purport to offer a superior curricular program, issues of accountability and quality controls for magnet schools continue to plague the U.S. Department of Education as researchers find that 453 of the 1,068 schools that received federal grants between 1989 and 1991 did not have objectives compatible with those defined by the government for a magnet school (Waldrip, Marks, & Estes, 1993). Consequently, the data resulting from empirical studies documenting achievement gains for magnet schools compared with the traditional public schools are conflicting.

The effect of these schools on minorities and special needs populations in urban settings also needs further study (Ramirez, 1998). Sociological and psychosocial factors impede this type of research, yet these issues must be addressed.

Vouchers

Vouchers are individual scholarships to parents that can be used to defray the cost of a child's tuition at any school—public or private, religious or secular—so long as that voucher is awarded on the basis of neutral secular criteria (Lewin, 1999). This plan provides public monies to parents to pay or supplement the cost of schooling. Parents rather than the government determine the schooling options for children financed by public funds. From the very beginning, constitutional challenges of vouchers have been at the forefront of discussions regarding their place in the educational arena. The challenge centers on the interpretation of the Establishment Clause of the First Amendment that prohibits public funds from being spent on religious activities or teaching.

The economist Milton Friedman introduced the concept of vouchers in the mid-1950s when he urged that competition would strengthen public education. His ideas were revived in the 1980s and 1990s when education became a central political theme and vouchers were promoted as parental choice. Public schools were portrayed as ineffective and in serious need of advancement. Vouchers provided the government a means to address public education externally rather than internally, pursuing alternatives rather than solutions. This strategy would "fix" public schools by providing competition for them, and competition would spark improvement because school survival would be linked to public popularity.

The assumption underlying vouchers is that parents, not the government, should have control over the selection of schools for their children. Gallup poll results indicate that the percentage of parents in favor of having this option is steadily increasing, especially among Black parents (Rose & Gallup, 1998). In the educational arena, the belief is common that parents are their child's best teacher, so the proposition that parents are the group best equipped to select an educational experience for their children also seems reasonable. According to proponents, this would be the natural result of providing parents with an opportunity to actively advocate for schools that are effective versus those that are ineffective. Theoretically, effective schools would be deemed as those schools that provide the greatest opportunity for achievement and have a history of proven achievement gains. Achievement results, not school demographics, would be the ultimate determiner of school selection. Therefore, the premise for vouchers is that all parents can choose schools based on academic success. Neither race nor socioeconomic makeup of the school would be a primary factor in selection increasing the opportunities for equitable access.

An essential question is the following: How do parents interpret school effectiveness? Rose and Gallup's (1998) results indicated that when parents were asked to rate factors that contribute to effective schools, more parents ranked good citizenship as a result of schooling higher than scores on standardized tests, the typical measure of academic achievement. This finding contradicts the media's portrayal of poor performance on tests as the community's reason for dissatisfaction with public schools. Also, it contradicts voucher proponents' claim that a demand for higher test scores is the major reason that they embrace a voucher system. The Gallup findings also contradict the primary goals of public school education if one defines good citizenship as promoting moral values.

When Black parents support the voucher system as a means for effective schools, is good citizenship their litmus test for success or are they seeking an alternative from the deprivation inherent in urban schools? Are the expectations for the two groups the same or is the voucher movement merely assuming similarity in goals? Is the movement an avenue to circumvent the policies of *Brown* by exploiting the dissatisfaction of poor, predominantly minority parents who have been discriminated by our economy to achieve the goal of creating a publicly funded, private school system free of public control and oversight (Molnar, Farrell, Johnson, & Sapp, 1996)?

The presumption that choice options are a remedy for public schools may also be flawed. Based on final evaluation findings from the Milwaukee Parental Choice Program, the first publicly funded voucher program, no conclusive evidence supports the academic superiority of one system versus the other (Witte, Stern, & Thorn, 1995). Although other researchers have questioned the research model (Greene, Peterson, & Du, 1999), the lack of evidence to support the voucher system cannot be dismissed.

A study frequently cited in support of vouchers was conducted in 1988 (National Center for Education Statistics, 1988). The study's sample included more than 20,000 eighth graders nationwide. Follow-up studies of these students were conducted in the 10th and 12th grades. Higher graduation rates and academic performance were found in favor of students attending private schools. Another significant finding was that private school students in the study started at a higher academic base, and their parents had substantially higher incomes than those in the public school sample. Goldhaber's (1997) analysis of this data found no significant effect in academic achievement when these factors were controlled.

The results do not lend support to the premise that race is not a primary factor in school selection, and Goldhaber (1997) suggests that race and socioeconomic status are primary factors in parents' selection of schools. Results such as these validate opponents' fears regarding vouchers' potential for greater economic and racial stratification of the schools.

Public support is currently against vouchers (Rose, Gallup, & Elam, 1997). Voters in Washington State defeated a voucher initiative by a 2-1 margin. Similar defeats were evidenced in Oregon, Colorado, and California. More recently, the state courts have struck down a total of six private or religious school voucher plans in Maine, Vermont, Pennsylvania, and Ohio. The country's two teacher unions, the National Education Association (NEA) and the American Federation of Teachers (AFT), vehemently oppose vouchers. The Court's position is presently unclear. Although lower courts have ruled that an expanded Milwaukee Parental Choice plan that would include religious schools violated the state constitution, the Wisconsin Supreme Court upheld the constitutionality of the plan in June 1998. The Court declined to hear the case in November, thus allowing the lower court's ruling to stand.

Cleveland's attempt to incorporate a choice plan that would allow poor students in Grades K-3 to attend religious and secular private schools with public money was supported by a trial judge and then appealed and first ruled unconstitutional by the Ohio Court of Appeals and then reversed, allowing students already selected to participate but barring any future selections. The decision to disallow further enrollment was appealed to the court that ruled to allow the continuation of the voucher program for the time being. The court did not deliver a ruling on the constitutionality of vouchers in this decision.

Florida's Choice Plan was thrown out and ruled unconstitutional. The judge concluded that the mandate violated the law that provides a free education through a system of public schools. Under Florida's voucher law, students at public schools that earn a failing grade 2 years out of 4 could ask for tax dollars to pay for private school tuition. Vouchers would be worth between $3,000 and $4,000, depending on the deficiency of the schools' scores.

Typically, the amounts of money awarded in vouchers do not cover the entire cost of the choice option school. Parents would have to pay as much as one half of the remaining costs. On the surface, this may appear as an option for all socioeconomic levels, but realistically it is not. Middle- to high-income parents' benefits would be far greater than representative urban parents.

Privatization and Charter Schools

A third and most recent alternative to public schools that evolved during the latter part of the 20th century is the move toward privatization, engaging private enterprise in the management and operation of schools. The contracting strategy of privatization is the most popular, in which the public sector remains the financier of the school but delegates production or provision of services to the private sector (Murphy, 1996). The resulting schools from this approach are called charter schools. Although similar in intent, charter schools are different from magnet schools in that they are privately owned and managed by that entity rather than the local school board. They are chartered to produce achievement gains with state and federal funding based on the delivery of results and operate as tuition-free public schools. They were fueled by the nation's perception of the high cost and inefficiency of government and a renewed interest in private-market values (Murphy, 1996). Assumptions that emulating organizational models of the private sector and educational models of other industrialized countries that boast of high academic achievements can enhance education belie the move toward privatization.

During the beginning of the movement toward charter schools, many perceived them as a perfect complement to vouchers. Currently, with the popularity of the concept and the extremely controversial nature of vouchers, proponents of charter schools make a clear distinction between the two. Charter schools can be sponsored by one of three entities: the State Board for Charter Schools, the State Board of Education, or the local school boards. Supporters are broad in political and financial base, educational expertise, and philosophy. Although the AFT and NEA oppose vouchers, they support charter schools with reservations—that they are limited in number and governed by comparable standards as public schools.

Some believe that charter schools are the precursors of the government's abandonment of public school funding. Olson's (2000) report of charter schools charged that there are free marketers who believe that government should stop financing education entirely, and who view vouchers as one step in that direction; rural communities that are trying to stave off the consolidation of local schools by converting them to charter schools; teachers and parents who are teaming up with philanthropists to put innovative ideas into practice; and religious schools that are looking to vouchers as a way to shore up their enrollments and financial future. (p. 3)

According to Olson (2000), at least a dozen for-profit companies (led by the New York City-based Edison Schools, Inc.) are trying to make money by running charter schools because charter schools are sweeping the nation. Today, there are nearly 1,700 across 36 states. A key concern is that accountability approaches across these states vary significantly.

President Clinton, a strong supporter of charter schools, recognizes that differences in standards of accountability are a major problem for schools. He notes,

> . . . not every state has had the right kind of accountability for charter schools. . . . Some states have laws that are so loose that no matter whether the charter schools are doing their jobs or not, they just get to stay open, and I think even worse, some states have laws that are so restrictive, it's almost impossible to open a charter school in the first place. (Clinton, 2000)

Educational and political supporters are claiming charter schools to be the panacea of choice options for the prevailing ills of public schools. This support is evident by federal funds as well as rhetoric demanding that every state should give parents the power to choose the right public school for their children. They claim that charter schools, vouchers, and other new means of providing education will produce higher achievement; encourage innovation; promote equity by giving poor families, in particular, more options; and foster accountability by enabling dissatisfied consumers to vote with their feet (Olson, 2000). Further evidence of their increased popularity is the establishment of a $4.4 million federal grant program to support their growth.

Charter schools are varied in design and accountability. Although some use traditional methods, many replicate curricular innovations similar to those seen in magnet schools and other public schools. Barring the dissimilarity of curricular approaches, one aspect is the same: All charter schools promise academic results through the charter, contract, or desolation [abandonment] of the schools. However, nationwide, closures have been relatively rare (Archer, 2000). Archer (2000) reports that only 59 charter schools had shut down by last fall, representing a failure rate of just fewer than 4%, and most closures have resulted from severe mismanagement or financial crises not because of concerns over academic achievement.

Currently, there are 19 charter schools in Illinois. The surrounding states of Michigan and Missouri have 93 and 18 charter schools, respectively. The Multiple States Charter School study conducted by the Center for School Change at the University of Minnesota reviewed data from 31 charter schools in the following eight states: Arizona, California, Colorado, Georgia, Massachusetts, Michigan, Minnesota, and Texas. Published results of the study indicate that 68% of the schools appear to be making gains. No comparative analysis was made between charter school students and regular public school students. To address the issue of whether private industry has the answers to the current educational dilemma, comparative studies with public schools are needed.

Although parent satisfaction with charter schools is high, the question remains of whether the original intent of charter schools to produce greater academic gains than public schools remains unanswered. There is no conclusive answer; therefore, further research is warranted.

Home Schooling

The last alternative to be discussed is home schooling. Home schooled or home educated, the teaching of one's own children at home is steadily becoming an accepted and respected alternative to public school education. Duffy (1998) reports recent estimates of home-schooled students to be about slightly more than a million.

Home schooling is not new, but the recognition of the phenomenon as a legitimate option to public school is receiving renewed attention. Also new is its position in the desegregation controversy. The right to home school is not questioned but, rather, the effect on public schools is the focus of discussions.

Researchers cite parents' concerns for safety, security, morality, and educational quality as primary reasons for home schooling (Dahm, 1996). Parents want decision-making authority to determine their child's teacher, classmates, and curriculum with access to extracurricular activities of the public schools.

Opponents of home schooling (e.g., Gorder, 1996; Mayberry, Knowles, Ray, & Marlow, 1995; Ramirez, 1998) cite issues regarding accreditation, parents' lack of formal training for teaching, comparable facilities and resources for schooling, lack of opportunity for socialization, and the deflection of students from public school as detractors. A primary area of concern is the lack of standardization of home schooling laws across states.

Duffy (1998) reports that the typical home schooling family is White and Protestant with two parents, three children, and above-average income and education. The mother is the primary instructor and religion is likely to be the most important—although seldom the only—reason for home schooling. Home schooling is typically not an option for urban parents primarily because of the same problems that plague urban schools (e.g., poverty, lower levels of parental education, parental involvement in the educational process). A single parent—primarily the mother—who is also the principal wage earner heads most urban families. Rather than a choice issue, however, home-schooled students do present another opportunity to divert funds from urban schools. Currently, with the percentages of home-schooled students being proportionally low, the threat appears minimal. But as the trend grows in popularity, the competition will be more evident.

The Supreme Court's position on home schooling is as uncertain as its stance on the other alternatives. No case has been tried in the past 25 years. The last case tried in the early 1970s (*Wisconsin v. Yoder*, 1972) provided only a limited ruling in support of Amish students not attending a public high school.

Although prominent educators such as Holt (1983) advocate home schooling, little empirical research is available regarding academic achievement and comparative data with non-home-schooled students. Supporters attribute this to the general distrust of educators of home schooling with traditional research; however, if it is to be legitimized as an educational alternative, this scrutinization must be forthcoming. Without adequate evidence of academic superiority over public schools, the choice of home schooling as an alternative to public school instruction must be questioned.

CONCLUSION

The most prominent issues in the 20th century regarding American education were school quality and desegregation. It appears that, almost 50 years after the *Brown* decision, these issues continue to be dominant concerns in education. Whereas during the 20th century much of the discussion was focused inside the educational community, this community has now expanded to include all stakeholders, including parents, businesses, and the general public. With the inclusion of these participants, the reform of education has become a public forum and a political agenda.

Choice is a valued principle of democracy. The foundations of our political, economic, and legal systems are driven by this principle. In each of these areas, however, the presumption is that choice will be influenced by a thorough investigation of facts followed by objective reasoning. If not, what is perceived as choice may become biased assessments or personal preferences.

The origin of the argument for choice options for public schools was a response to desegregation and based on the assumption that schools were ineffective and unresponsive to the varying needs of the population. The problems identified with the system were internal, requiring systemic changes at many levels. There is no evidence that choice option programs recognize or make any attempt to address this key factor. Rather, these options are focused on creating a separate system that will avoid the ills of its predecessor rather than address them. Consequently, an analysis of the problems that they attempt to avoid is critical to urban education.

Educational issues that confront urban public schools are low test scores, poor graduation rates, poor attendance, inequality, discipline, overcrowdingness, lack of parent involvement, violence, and poor teaching. Few studies have shown that, when the same populations of the public schools are provided the current choice options, these issues are significantly influenced. These alternatives are providing an avenue for those that are dissatisfied with the current system to abandon it in lieu of a better choice. The literature has shown that there are inequities in income and education for those that are electing to take this route to school reform; therefore, one can conclude that these options are not flawless.

In 1983, the government's report "A Nation at Risk" analyzed the status of education in this country, and many accepted its findings as representative of the nation's educational system. More than 25 years later, many of its primary findings still have not been addressed. The choice option debate has not added to the resolution of any of these findings, but it may have diverted our attention away from the real issues in education.

If educational choices are not motivated by reasoning due to validated progress of choice options, it is reasonable to speculate that bias or personal preference is motivating these decisions. If this is the case, the effect of choice options on desegregation is clear. The proposed solutions are attempts to separate from the traditional public schools and to maintain an equal funding base, curriculum, and accreditation in favor not of school reform but more so the creation of a separate system. Parents who separate from the traditional system supposedly leave these same problems for another generation. Funding alternatives naturally deplete resources from the primary system. You cannot make one system equitable without making another more inequitable. This concept was struck down and found ineffective, unfair, and unconstitutional more than 50 years ago.

REFERENCES

ARCHBALD, D. (1996). SES and demographic predictors of magnet school enrollment. *Journal of Research and Development in Education,* 29(3), 152–162.

ARCHER, J. (2000, May 17). *Education Week.*

BROWN, F., & HUNTER, R. C. (1995). Introduction privatization of public school services. *Education and Urban Society,* 27(2), 107–113.

Brown v. Board of Education, 347 U.S. 483 (1954).

Brown v. Board of Education, 335 U.S. 294 (1955).

CLINTON, W. J. (2000, May 4). [Speech].

DAHM, L. (1996). Education at home with help from school. *Educational Leadership,* 54, 68–71.

DEJNOZKA, E. L., & KAPEL, D. E. (1991). *American Educator's Encyclopedia.* Westport, CT: Greenwood.

DUFFY, J. (1998). Home schooling: A controversial alternative. *Principal,* 77, 23–26.

GLENN, C. L. (1998). Public school choice: Searching for direction. *Principal.* 77(5). 10–12.

GOLDHABER, D. D. (1997). School choice as education reform. *Phi Delta Kappan,* 79, 143–147.

GORDER, C. (1996). *Home schools: An alternative.* Mesa, AZ: Blue Bird Publishing.

GREENE, J. P., PETERSON, P. E., & Du, J. (1999). Effectiveness of school choice: The Milwaukee experiment. *Education and Urban Society,* 31(2), 190–213.

HOLT, J., (1983). Schools and home schoolers: A fruitful partnership. *Phi Delta Kappan,* 64, 391–394.

LEWIN, N. (1999). Are vouchers constitutional? *Policy Review,* 93, 5–8.

MAYBERRY, M., KNOWLES, J., RAY, B. B., & MARLOW, S. (1995). *Home schooling: Parents as educators.* Thousand Oaks, CA: Corwin Press.

MCKINNEY, J. R. (1996). Public school choice and desegregation. *Journal of Law & Education,* 25, 649–660.

METZ, M. H. (1986). *Different by design: The context and character of three magnet schools.* New York: Routledge Kegan Paul.

MOLNAR, A., FARRELL, W. C., JR., JOHNSON, J. A., JR., & SAPP, M. (1996). Research, politics, and the school choice agenda. *Phi Delta Kappan,* 78, 240–243.

MURPHY, J. (1996). Why privatization signals a sea of change in schooling. *Education Leadership,* 54, 60–62.

MYRDAL, G. (1944). *An American dilemma: The Negro Problem and modern democracy.* New York: Harper.

National Center for Education Statistics. (1988). *Private schools in the United States: A statistical profile, with comparison to public schools.* Washington, DC: Office of Educational Research and Development.

OLSON, L. (2000, April 26). Redefining public schools. *Education Week.*

ORFIELD, G., & EATON, S. E. (1996). *Dismantling desegregation: The quiet reversal of* Brown v. Board of Education. New York: The New Press.

ORLICH, D. C. (1991). *Brown v. Board of Education:* Time for a reassessment. Phi Delta Kappan, 72, 631–632.

Programs for Educational Opportunity (1995). *Equity, excellence and school reform: A new paradigm for desegregation.* Ann Arbor, MI: Author.

RAMIREZ, A. (1998). Vouchers and voodoo economics. *Educational Leadership,* 56, 36–39.

ROSE, L. C., GALLUP, A. M. AND ELAM, S. M. (1997). The 29th annual Phi Delta Kappa/Gallop poll of the public's attitudes toward the public schools. *Phi Delta Kappan,* 79(1), 41–58.

ROSE, L. C., GALLUP, A. M. (1998). The 30th Annual Phi Delta Kappa/Gallop Poll of the public's attitudes toward the public schools. *Phi Delta Kappan,* 80, 41–56.

RUSSO, C. J., HARRIS, J. J., III, & SANDIDGE, R. F. (1994). *Brown v. Board of Education* at 40: A legal history of equal educational opportunities in American public education. *Journal of Negro Education,* 63, 297–309.

SAKS, J. B. (1997). The voucher debate. *The American School Board Journal,* 184, 24–28.

STRINGFIELD, S. (1997). Research on effective instruction for at-risk students: Implications for the St. Louis public schools. *Journal of Negro Education,* 66, 258–288.

STEEL, L. & LEVINE. R. H. (1994). *Educational innovation in multiracial contexts. The growth of magnet schools in American education.* Washington, DC: U.S. Department of Education.

STEELE, L., & EATON, M. (1996). *Reducing, eliminating, and preventing minority isolation in American schools: The impact of the Magnet Schools Assistance Program.* Washington, DC: American Institutes for Research.

U.S. Department of Education. (1983). *A nation at risk.* Washington, DC: Government Printing Office.

WALDRIP, D. R., MARKS, W. L., & ESTES, N. (1993). *Magnet school policy studies and evaluations.* Houston, TX: International Research Institute on Educational Choice.

Wisconsin vs. Yoder. 406 U.S. 205 (1972).

WITTE, J. F., STERR, T. D., & THORN, C. A. (1995). *Fifth year report: Milwaukee parental choice program.* Madison, WI: Department of Political Science and the Robert M. LaFollette Institute of Public Affairs, University of Wisconsin-Madison.

CRITICAL THINKING QUESTIONS

1. For individual students, what are the advantages of magnet schools, vouchers, private education, and home schooling?

2. How are poor children or those living in single-parent households harmed by magnet schools, vouchers, private education, and home schooling?

3. What programs can you foresee that will reduce inequalities in education? Who is likely to be helped by such programs? Who, if anyone, is likely to be harmed? Explain.

Reading 19

Gender Equity: Still Knocking at the Classroom Door

David Sadker

> *In this article, Sadker uses a "top ten" list format to summarize the differences in educational achievements of girls and boys. He argues that educational disparities between the genders continue to be significant in our society.*

Although we have come far in ensuring that girls and boys receive equal treatment and opportunity in school, we still have a long way to go.

Gender equity? Oh, yes, that was big a few years ago. Today, girl's home economics and boys' shop are gone.

Girls get better grades. Girls are more likely to get into college, whereas boys are more likely to get into trouble. Why all this attention to girls? Boys are the ones in trouble.

Title IX? Wasn't that repealed?

Many educators are confused about gender equity. Is it still a problem? Is it more about political correctness than about educational effectiveness? Wasn't that battle fought and won years ago? Until 1980, Ivy League schools such as Columbia University did not even admit women. Today, the majority of college students are women. Perhaps we should declare victory and move on.

Source: Reprinted from *Educational Leadership* 56, no. 7 (April 1999): 22–26 with permission of the author.

Michael Kazin, in his forthcoming book *America Divided: The Civil War of the 1960s* (Oxford University Press, 1999), helps educators understand the cultural context surrounding educational equity. Kazin writes that in the war between liberals and conservatives that characterized the 1960s, the conservatives actually won most battles. Today's cultural landscape is littered with their mantras, now part of the national conventional wisdom: Government is too big, taxes are too high, affirmative action is unfair, business is overregulated, and school choice will improve education. But conservatives did not win all the battles. Kazin believes that the decade's most successful social crusade was feminism, a movement that restructured U.S. society.

Commentators now proclaim on the airwaves that gender bias no longer exists, except for the men who are victimized by feminists. Their efforts are not without success: Today the word feminist carries as many negative as positive connotations. So what is an educator to believe?

Those who believe in gender equity face an uphill struggle. Each time I begin a training program to help educators detect and eliminate bias from their classroom teaching, I am reminded of what some call gender blindness (Bailey, Scantlebury, & Letts, 1997, p. 29). Often I show a videotape with subtle, if pervasive, gender bias. Asked to evaluate the tape, most teachers miss the bias. After practicing some rudimentary coding of classroom interactions, we go back to the tape. Surprise, surprise! Now the gender bias is overwhelming. No longer political or personal, the bias has become a research reality, their reality, and the teachers are motivated to create equitable teaching strategies. But why the initial gender block?

In *Failing at Fairness,* Myra Sadker and I described "a syntax of sexism so elusive that most teachers and students were completely unaware of its influence" (1995, p. 2). Teacher education and staff development programs do little to prepare teachers to see the subtle, unintentional, but damaging gender bias that still characterizes classrooms.

But subtlety is not the only reason for the persistence of inequity. A false sense of accomplishment has also taken root. We have made wonderful advances, especially in the area of access to schools, courses, and careers. Although bias is less problematic today, it still permeates and influences our classrooms.

What is the salient and current research on gender progress and problems in schools? What are the disturbing cultural developments that have distoned and politicized educational equity? To answer these questions, I will borrow a device used by a late night television host: a top 10 list.

The Top 10 Gender Bias Updates

Update #10: Segregation still thrives in U.S. schools. Title IX has breached the walls of the Citadel and the Virginia Military Institute,

and females are now admitted to all tax-supported educational institutions. Too often, however, courses of study and careers remain gender-specific.

- The majority of females major in English, French, Spanish, music, drama, and dance, whereas males populate computer science, physics, and engineering programs.

- A recent study of 14 school-to-work programs revealed that over 90 percent of females cluster in a few traditional careers: allied health careers, teaching and education, graphic arts, and office technology (American Association of University Women Educational Foundation, 1998, p. 88).

- Although almost half of medical and law students are female, they are concentrated in a few "female friendly" (and lower-paying) specialties (Sadker & Sadker, 1995, p. 194).

Update #9: Public schools are now creating single-gender classes and schools. More than a century ago, most schools were gender-segregated. Some private schools still are. And the research on their effectiveness, at least for the girls, is compelling, if not universally accepted. In response to this research and to the pressures of assertive parents (usually of girls), public school districts have openly and sometimes surreptitiously created their own single-gender classes or schools. Is this a positive or a negative development?

If we were to carefully implement and research a limited trial of single-gender public schools and classes, the findings could improve public coed schools for boys as well as for girls. However, the current approach has the potential to fractionalize our society. In short, creating single-gender classes and schools is not a substitute for ensuring equitable public education for all our students.

Update #8: Gender-related safety and health concerns continue to plague females. One hundred years ago, the argument against female education centered on health. Doctors warned that education redirected blood initially destined for the ovaries to the brain. The result: Educated women would be less likely to reproduce and more likely to go insane. The doctors' prescription: Keep girls out of school. Bizarre, but a sign of how people viewed female health issues. Today, our attention turns to more genuine and pressing health risks.

- Twenty percent of school-age girls report being physically or sexually abused, and 80 percent report experiencing some form of sexual harassment.

- Although research shows that physical activity leads to higher self-esteem and lifelong health benefits, girls are only half as likely as boys to participate in physical education.

Update #7: The dropout rate is not what we think it is. Most educators know that boys repeat grades and drop out of school at higher rates than girls. However, few realize that girls who repeat a grade are more likely to drop out of school than male grade repeaters. When girls drop out of school, often because of pregnancy, they are less likely to return and complete school than boys. In 1995, for example, approximately one-third of Hispanic females between 16 and 24 had not completed school and had not passed a high school equivalency test. Boys drop out with a "crash," whereas girls drop out more quietly, more quickly, and more permanently.

Update #6: For girls, gifted programs are often "early in and early out." Elementary school gifted programs identify girls in equal or in greater numbers than boys. However, by 10th grade, girls begin to drop out of these programs at a higher rate than boys. Boys are more likely to take math and science gifted programs, whereas girls populate gifted programs that focus on language arts. For both girls and boys, gifted programs often reinforce gender segregation.

Update #5: Gender bias also affects males. Because men earn more money, manage most organizations, and dominate both government offices and sports arenas, many Americans assume that men are the victors in the great gender divide. In fact, sexism harms—and Title IX

protects—both genders. Boys are stereotyped into gender roles earlier and more rigidly than females. Three out of four boys report that they were targets of sexual harassment—usually taunts challenging their masculinity. Males who express an interest in careers typically thought of as "feminine" also encounter social pressures. The percentage of males in elementary teaching, for instance, is smaller today than when Title IX came out a quarter of a century ago.

Although females receive lower grades on many high-stakes tests, males receive lower course grades (American Association of University Women Educational Foundation, 1998, pp. 27–33). Males are less likely to have close friends and are more likely to endure alienation and loneliness throughout life. Males, after all, experience higher mortality rates through accidents, violence, and suicide. From schoolyard shootings to low humanities enrollments, boys act according to negative male stereotypes, and educators need to discourage this influence.

Update #4: Classroom interactions between teachers and students put males in the spotlight and relegate females to the sidelines. Studies of teacher discourse underscore male dominance in the classroom. Teachers unconsciously make males the center of instruction and give them more frequent and focused attention. Although some boys do not want this attention, and some girls may not notice or may even desire this lack of attention (Feldhusen & Willard-Hold, 1993), the impact on both genders can be costly. Increased teacher attention contributes to enhanced student performance. Girls lose out in this equation. African American girls, for example, are assertive and outgoing when they enter school, yet they grow more passive and quiet through the school years (American Association of University Women Educational Foundation, 1998, p. 49). Boys reap the benefits of a more intense educational climate.

Update #3: The math and science gender gap is getting smaller. The idea that boys outperform girls in math and science has received national attention, and that attention is paying off.

- During the 1990s, female enrollment increased in many math and science courses. Honors as well as advanced placement courses showed enrollment gains.

- Girls are now more likely than boys to take biology and chemistry courses, whereas physics is still a male domain. Boys, however, are more likely to take all three core sciences—physics, chemistry, and biology (American Association of University Women Educational Foundation, 1998, p. 13).

- Tests continue to reflect a gender gap, particularly high-stakes tests like the SAT. Although the gap has decreased in recent years, males continue to outscore females on both the math and verbal sections of the SAT. Boys outscore girls on math and science achievement tests, whereas females outscore males on the verbal section of the ACT. Although girls take more advanced placement exams in all courses except math, science, and computers, boys earn higher advanced placement scores and are more likely to receive college credit (American Association of University Women Educational Foundation, 1998, pp. 35–41).

Update #2: A new gender gap exists in technology. Certainly, the greatest change in education in recent years is the technology explosion, with the majority of U.S. schools now connected to the Internet. But boys are more wired into this revolution than girls are.

- Boys enter school with more computer experience than girls, and girls know it. Girls rate themselves significantly lower on computer ability.

- Stereotyping is alive and well in the tech world. Girls are more likely to enroll in word processing and clerical courses, whereas boys are more likely to enroll in advanced computer science and computer design classes. Both print and Internet resources continue to promote sex stereotyping, with males portrayed in powerful and prestigious technological positions (Knupfer, 1998).

Update #1: Some political forces are intent on reversing many gains in educational equity made during the past decade. Thirty years ago, when Myra and I first began to research

gender bias, we thought that the task was pretty straightforward. First we would objectively analyze schools to see whether bias really existed. If we found bias, we would then document the inequities and work on solutions. We thought that armed with knowledge, people would want to change. Not so simple.

Educational equity is a political issue. Ultraconservatives have created "educational research" to discredit the decades of studies documenting gender bias in schools. The Women's Freedom Network is one such group that sponsors attacks not only on the research but also on the integrity and motivations of the researchers. With generous private funding and contracts with talk show hosts, news commentators, and even mainline periodicals, these "media experts" launch their attacks.

In the past, the enemies of equity spoke more openly about their beliefs: the "natural" roles of men and women, the "biological destinies" of each, even biblical references to explain the "second-class" status of females. A new day requires new tactics. The Internet and the media do not evaluate the qualifications of researchers. As a result, individuals who make up in colorful commentary what they lack in research qualifications attack the lifework of competent researchers. I regret the ultimate cost that such tactics have on the lives of children.

Cultural Support of Sexism

After practicing techniques to identify the subtle gender bias embedded in her classroom behavior, a teacher education student at the University of Wisconsin wrote:

> I really didn't think [gender bias] was very prevalent, particularly because it can be so subtle. I especially didn't think I would ever do it. But . . . I had also called on the boys more, not realizing. They were being quiet, instead of noisy, and I called on them to reward them they could pick out the next book. Yet the girls had been good the entire time, yet I hadn't called on them, at all. (Lundeberg, 1997, p. 59)

What is unusual about the story is not that the student could not see the bias; rather, it is that she was enrolled in a teacher education program that included such fundamental research in her training.

In a recent national study of mathematics and science methods professors, Campbell and Sanders (1997) found that two-thirds of education professors spent less than two hours teaching about gender equity and that they rarely provided practical classroom strategies to neutralize bias. More than half the professors were satisfied with this limited treatment. Why has teacher education been so slow to teach about and respond to gender bias?

One explanation may be the social resistance to feminism, female concerns, and even gender studies. In one study, students taking 17 different courses received a Sociology of Gender course syllabus developed and taught by a fictitious Wendy Barker. The students rated the syllabus. Many students indicated that the course was imbued with bias, promoted a political agenda, and contained exams and papers that were too subjective. Although all students showed a bias against the female instructor, the bias was strongest among male students. When a similar group of students received the same syllabus, this time developed and taught by William Barker, a fictitious male, the evaluations were more positive. Now the course was rated as less biased, the work appeared fair and reasonable, and the instructor was credible and available to students. Taught by a male, the same course seemed more comprehensive and attractive to students (Moore & Trahan, 1997).

Many female administrators, teachers, professors, and counselors share similar experiences, believing that they must work harder simply to be considered equal. Males have an unspoken, often unconscious, sense of entitlement, which is reflected in their belief that they influence school policy. Female teachers do not express similar feelings of power and influence (Lee, Loeb, & Marks, 1995). No wonder, then, that political forces can exploit female alienation and cultural resistance to feminism to promote their social agenda.

What are educators to do? Individual educators, teachers, and administrators need to ensure that instructional strategies and curricular innovations benefit all our children. Twenty-five years after Title IX, we must celebrate our progress and recommit ourselves to finishing the job.

GENDER EQUITY ON COLLEGE CAMPUSES

Years ago, most U.S. colleges and universities were single-sex. Now women are dominating college campuses that used to be all-male—in both numbers and achievements. Even at the Massachusetts Institute of Technology, a traditionally male-dominated university, this year's incoming class is 43 percent women, the highest percentage in its history. Consider these facts:

- Nearly 60 percent of all college students are women.
- In 1999, women will earn 57 percent of all bachelor's degrees, compared with 43 percent in 1970 and less than 24 percent in 1950.
- By 2008, women will outnumber men in undergraduate and graduate programs by 9.2 million to 6.9 million.
- Among full-time workers, women with BA degrees make only $4,708 more on average than men with only high school diplomas. They make $20,000 less than men with college degrees.
- Between October 1995 and October 1996, boys accounted for 58 percent of U.S. dropouts.—Statistics compiled by Carol Tell from *U.S. News & World Report* (available at http://www.usnews.com).

REFERENCES

American Association of University Women Educational Foundation. (1998). *Gender gaps: Where our schools fail our children*. Washington DC: Author.
BAILEY, B. L., SCANTLEBURY, K., & LETTS, W. J. (1997, January/February). It's not my style: Using dis-

claimers to ignore issues in science. *Journal of Teacher Education*, (48)1, 29–35.

CAMPBELL, P. B., & SANDERS, J. (1997, January/February). Uninformed but interested: Findings of a national survey on gender equity in preservice teacher education. *Journal of Teacher Education*, 48 (1), 69–75.

FELDHUSEN, F. F., & WILLARD-HOLT, C. (1993). Gender differences in classroom interactions and career aspirations of gifted students. *Contemporary Educational Psychology*, 18, 355–362.

KAZIN, M. (1999). *America divided: The Civil War of the 1960s.* Oxford, England: Oxford University Press.

KNUPFER, N. N. (1998, Winter). Gender divisions across technology advertisements and the implications for educational equity. *Theory Into Practice*, 37(1), 54–63.

LEE, V. E., LOEB, S., & MARKS, H. M. (1995, May). Gender differences in secondary school teachers' control over classroom and school policy. *American Journal of Education*, 103, 259–301.

LUNDEBERG, M. A. (1997, January/February). You guys are overreacting: Teaching prospective teachers

about subtle gender bias. *Journal of Teacher Education*, 48(1), 55–61.

MOORE, M., & TRAHAN, R. (1997, December). Biased and political: Student perceptions of females teaching about gender. *College Student Journal*, 31,434–444.

SADKER, M., & SADKER, D. (1995) *Failing at fairness: How our schools cheat girls.* New York: Touchstone Press.

CRITICAL THINKING QUESTIONS

1. In what ways has progress been made toward gender equity in education?

2. Where do gender barriers to equal education remain?

3. What needs to be done to achieve gender equity in education? Who is likely to oppose such programs? Why?

Reading 20

Back-Seat Boys

This article focuses on the lack of attention given to boys' education. The author argues that the same resources and attention that have helped girls to improve their academic achievement should also be devoted to boys.

Walk the halls of most American schools and you can easily spot them.

Members of their ranks are the most likely to drop out—and to excel in important areas. Increasingly, they're targeted as troublemakers at the same time that many are tapped as leaders. They're likely to be first to shout out a response to a teacher's question—even as they're recommended more frequently for special education or treatment to address disruptive behavior. They own the top echelons of SAT math scores—but are less likely to go on to college.

THEY'RE BOYS

To look casually at boys' performance in school at the turn of the century is to wonder if this is the same group girls were struggling to gain equal footing with just a decade-plus ago. The push to help girls "catch up"—spurred by a 1992 report that said schools were shortchanging girls—spotlighted everything from how often teachers call on girls to a need to engage them more in math and science classes.

Since then, girls have made strides in a number of areas. But the growing awareness of gender issues in the classroom—in addition to Columbine and a spate of other violent actions by boys—has turned more attention to the male side of the classroom. And academic struggles there are prompting questions about whether schools are meeting the needs of boys—as well as calls for a new sense of gender equity that focuses equally on boys and girls.

"We developed an increased consciousness of how girls learn, but didn't believe boys needed that," says William Pollack, a psychologist at Harvard Medical School and co-director of the Center for Men at McLean Hospital in Belmont, Mass. "No one thought there was a problem with boys. We weren't seeing that boys beneath the top level were starting to drop slowly," says Dr. Pollack, who recently published *Real Boys' Voices* [New York: Random House, 2000].

BOYS NEED MORE ATTENTION?

The subject has sparked heated battles between those who say the focus on girls was needed to address longstanding imbalances and others who argue that such initiatives have come at boys' expense.

"In the current environment, boys aren't seen as needing help," says Christina Hoff Sommers, a scholar with the American Enterprise Institute in Washington and author of the book *The War on Boys* [New York: Simon & Schuster, 2000]. "We have had 15 years of efforts to help girls academically. That was based on a distorted picture that underestimated the problems of boys. We need to do for boys what we have done for girls."

Regardless of where they stand on which gender has the better deal, most observers agree that certain evidence points to trouble among the crowd long assumed to have the upper hand. Boys generally get lower grades, though they still outpace girls in areas where they have traditionally held a lead.

Seventeen-year-old males, for example, scored five points ahead in math and eight points ahead in science on a 1996 national assessment, according to the United States Education Department.

But while girls are catching up in math and science, the same is not true for boys in the key skills of reading and writing, where girls have led for a number of years.

In 1996, 17-year-old girls bested boys by 14 points in reading assessments and 17 points in writing. The average 11th-grade boy was writing with the proficiency of the average eighth-grade girl.

Boys are also twice as likely to be tagged "learning disabled" and are "substantially" more likely to be suspended or drop out, according to Pollack. They also far outnumber girls in being diagnosed for such things as attention-deficit disorder.

TIME TO REASSESS OLD ASSUMPTIONS

To some observers, such facts are reason enough to reassess what's happening in the classroom. "Many aspects of American schools are not sympathetic to boys," says Eli Newberger, who wrote *The Men They Will Become* [Perseus Press, 1999] and is a professor of pediatrics at Harvard Medical School. "Their robust behavior, physicality, and translation of anxiety into inattention is frequently pathologized and demonized."

Behavior is a big part of the current debate. Teachers tend to hold up girls as models in the classroom because many girls do teacher-pleasing things like finishing their homework on time, sitting still, doing neater work. Perhaps equally important, they are rarely seen as threatening to a teacher.

School days that are tightly scheduled from start to finish also cast a negative light on restlessness and rambunctiousness that tend to accompany boys. And traditional outlets that help active students let off steam, such as physical education and recess, have long been on the decline in schools.

HIGH ENERGY LEVELS

To Richard Melvoin, head of Belmont Hill School, a boys school in Belmont, Mass., removing daily time for activity "is almost criminal. . . . It's ignoring who boys are."

Mr. Melvoin says that it's important to be alert to relatively minor adjustments that can be effective in helping boys succeed in school.

He cites a math teacher at Belmont Hill who has "walk around" quizzes, requiring boys to move to different parts of the classroom to complete their work. Students also get morning breaks and participate in a strong athletic program.

"In middle school, boys have a different energy level," he says. "We need to be mindful of that, and accept it. It's not evil. In the elementary level, if kids are told they're supposed to sit and be quiet, boys can't do that. If we can work with it, we do a lot better."

Diane Hulse, who heads the middle school at all-boys Collegiate School in New York and has done comparative research on single-sex and co-ed schooling, concurs. She says that teachers at Collegiate have developed a distinct structure for classes, though they draw on techniques that have become popular for both boys and girls, such as group learning.

"Boys can be very competitive with each other, and we want them to develop alternative learning strategies where they're mutually supportive," she says.

To keep groups focused, teachers will assign group members individual tasks: to take notes, to keep everyone on track, to present results to the class. Teachers offer minilessons within the regular class period to keep the pace up, and give boys opportunities to move around or to build things as part of the learning process.

Hulse notes that successfully running such classes demands well-trained and skillful teachers. And, she says, it is crucial that those teachers set a high standard for boys' performance.

At Project Boys, a summer program for inner-city boys that Collegiate runs in cooperation with New York's Fresh Air Fund, Hulse says seventh-graders who had rarely seen themselves as academic material became engaged by Shakespeare's "Othello," their interest piqued by the characters and language.

"Boys often don't have the bar set high for them, and boys respond well to high expectations. We're not stressing them, but saying 'You can do this, you can think it through,'"

she says, noting that boys in the program come back for a second year talking about the difference it made in their attitude toward school. "The most important part of that is giving them support and coaching to get there."

The need may be particularly acute with minority boys. Indeed, a new study by the National Urban League indicates that black males are often the victim of low expectations, and show up more often in special education and less often in advanced-placement classes.

BOYS MAY GET LESS RESPECT

Carole Shmurak, a former high school teacher and now professor of education at Central Connecticut State College in New Britain, is in the midst of studying an urban middle school in Connecticut that is testing all-girl and all-boy classes. The intent was to boost girls' performance, but the ones who benefited in terms of test scores were boys.

In suburban schools she has observed, Dr. Shmurak has more often seen the behavior that has long concerned advocates for girls: boys getting called on frequently and dominating the computers. But the different treatment of boys and girls in schools she has observed in urban schools in Connecticut left her amazed. "If I am going to an urban school, I'm much better off being a girl," she says. "Teachers treat me with more respect, and are less likely to yell."

MOVING AWAY FROM EITHER/OR

To some extent, Shmurak says, her research has moved her away from centering the issue around gender. Indeed, a number of experts say the best outcome of the current discussion about boys would be to move the focus away from what benefits boys or girls toward what is best for all students.

"If you're talking about education, the best is one that provides the greatest flexibility for both boys and girls," says Susan Bailey, executive director of the Wellesley Centers for Women in

Massachusetts and a contributor to the 1992 report on girls.

What shifted Shmurak's focus was looking at the experience of 50 girls from ninth grade till they graduated from college. Half the group attended single-sex high schools, and half co-ed schools.

"The more I got to know the girls, that focus [on single-sex or co-ed schooling] became less relevant," Shmurak says. "I concluded that what's important is going to a small school with dedicated faculty and small class sizes."

TEACHING BOYS THAT 'ALL THE ANSWERS ARE WITHIN'

To Ray Johnson, boys would benefit from more movement in school—and a new sense of what it means to be male.

"There's always pressure on boys to be 'the man,'" with its connotations of power and conquest, says Mr. Johnson, principal of the Paul Robeson Academy in Detroit.

But boys can learn from a different model—one that values learning. Old-style teaching—sitting still, learning passively—works against achievement, particularly for boys, says Mr. Johnson, whose public, coeducational K-8 school is Afrocentric in curriculum and almost entirely African-American in enrollment. And according to a new National Urban League study, black males are particularly at risk of failing because of low expectations and overrepresentation in special education.

"I marvel at how boys even exist in many of these schools," he says. "I couldn't sit through that litany of stuff, on and on. There's no opportunity to have constructive engagement and movement throughout the day."

He notes that people who get candy are often ones who can sit and be quiet. "That's cool, if I'm already in a culture that says this is the way I [a girl] ought to be anyway," Johnson says. "But [as a boy] I'm restless, because in the external environment, music is going all the time," and many of the messages are in sharp contrast to what school offers as a model.

Johnson, whose school has a long waiting list of urban and suburban families, says it's crucial to teach kids other models in ways that reach them. At Paul Robeson they learn, for example, to meditate for brief periods. "I want to focus on the internal locus of control, rather than a Pavlovian response," he says, noting that the school doesn't use bells. "Values need to be character-driven, from the inside out. We start this in preschool, so by the time they're 12, they know all the answers are within them. It helps kids discover their capacities."

Johnson also sets great store by having many male role models in the school, either as teachers or as mentors. Boys learn to embrace each other and teachers on greeting. "Boys get a chance to see new ways of behaving, and it offers a counter to the World Wrestling Federation," he says.

Engagement on every level is what counts. Struggling students often are assigned as mentors to younger kids, and thus boost their own self-esteem and learning. The school has more than 40 programs to engage kids beyond academics, be it baton-twirling, baseball, drum corps, or chess club.

The key, Johnson says, is to tap into what boys want to be able to do. "They want to be involved. You need to create programs where they can give back in realistic, relevant ways."

CRITICAL THINKING QUESTIONS

1. In what ways does the author argue that boys are discriminated against in schools?

2. How, according to the author, is this discrimination related to educational advances made on behalf of girls and women?

3. How do race and social class interact with gender to determine how students are treated in classrooms? Is one of these social statuses more important than the others in determining how students are treated? Or is the treatment a person receives the result of the combination of the statuses (e.g., poor, African-American, female) she or he represents? Explain.

Reading 21

Triumph Over Trauma

Sabrina McIntosh

In this article, McIntosh focuses on the gay student's experiences with harassment in school.

Forced out of two high schools, George Loomis fights for other gay students.

George Loomis was an above-average high school student. He was active in student government and even served as the student representative on the Visalia [Calif.] Unified School District board of trustees. His grade point average was above 3.5. Then last October, Juan Garcia, his Spanish teacher at Golden West High School, turned to him and spoke.

"He looked at me and said, 'Only two kinds of men wear earrings, pirates and faggots, and there isn't any water around here.' After that he started calling me 'pirate,'" Loomis, 18, recalls. "He said that during class, in front of all the other students. I was humiliated."

Loomis didn't reply to the teacher's comment. But that single joke unleashed a torrent of abuse that eventually drove Loomis from school. Other students followed the teacher's example, and for months Loomis was the victim of name-calling and personal attacks.

Loomis is not alone in his plight with school educators, says Jim Anderson, a spokesman for the Gay, Lesbian, and Straight Education Network. "Sadly, far too many students face harassment, not only from other students but from the administration and teachers," Anderson says. "In our National School Climate Survey, 36% of lesbian and gay students reported hearing antigay epithets from faculty or school staff." GLSEN and other groups have been working to reduce those numbers. Parents, Families, and Friends

of Lesbians and Gays announced in August that it was launching a program called "From Our House to the Schoolhouse" to educate teachers about antigay harassment. And legislation took effect this year in California to protect students harassed because they are gay.

That legislation arrived too late to help Loomis. "I was spit on and yelled at. It was horrible," he says. "I would come home and cry. It finally got to be too much." When Loomis found the courage to go to principal Bob Cesena, he did not get the result he wanted. "He told me it was unfair of me to go over my teacher's head and that I had to work it out with Mr. Garcia," Loomis says.

The school district will not comment on any of Loomis's statements, although they don't deny that Garcia made the comment. "The events happened when the student was still a minor, and it is our policy not to discuss anything that involves minor students," says district official Anthony Escobar.

Rather than face the teacher again, Loomis retained an attorney and asked for compensation from the district for doctor's visits and the counseling he underwent as a result of the harassment. His request was denied.

"I was sent to a school psychologist who told me if I wanted to be safe, I would have to leave school and go to an independent study program," Loomis said. "[School officials] said they would not protect me from this."

Loomis left the school in December and began the independent study program, for which he attended class at another high school for an hour a week and completed his schoolwork at home. His problems did not end there, however.

"I was working at a portrait studio," Loomis says. "One day a counselor from that school came in with someone. I was standing near her when she said, 'That boy's a faggot.'" When Loomis went back to school, he confronted the counselor. "I went into her office and said I had heard what she said," he recalls. "She immediately denied saying it. Then I told her I had the name and phone number of another customer who had heard it too. That's when she changed her story. She said she was sorry if she offended me and that she'd been talking about another student."

The counselor then called in the principal, whom Loomis says told him he had violated the terms of his independent study contract and would have to go to adult school. Loomis started the adult school program in January.

The district's silence about his case is not keeping Loomis quiet. He feels he will be of more use to the gay rights cause by becoming an activist. "When we go to the store, people recognize him," says Loomis's partner, Aaron Jura, 19. "This whole thing is a tragedy. The system works for everyone else, but a gay person is totally left out."

Loomis's ordeal put a strain on his relationship with his family. While he is still close to a few relatives, many won't talk to him. In fact, when a family member was married recently, Loomis was not invited to the wedding.

The harassment affected his educational future as well. When he was kicked out of school, he lost any chance of being accepted to a University of California campus. He is looking instead to attend California State University, Fresno, on a scholarship.

"I had already been interviewed by U.C., Berkeley," Loomis says. "They called me for the interview after finding out about my grades and student government experience. U.C. campuses don't take students who had to go to independent study or adult school. I've lost out on that dream. I don't want anyone else to lose their dreams."

For more on programs designed to end antigay harassment in schools, go to **www. advocate.com.**

CRITICAL THINKING QUESTIONS

1. What rights do gay and lesbian students have in schools?

2. What are teachers and administrators expected to do when they learn they have a gay or lesbian student? When they learn that other students or teachers are harassing a gay or lesbian student?

3. Compare and contrast the experiences of gay and lesbian students today with the experiences of African-American students in the 1950s and 1960s, when the integration of schools began.

Getting Involved

1. Get a copy of your university course catalog. Look at the courses offered in the education department. What courses are taught that might help future teachers reduce their own biases and discriminatory treatment of students in their classrooms? What additional courses do you think might help to reduce classroom prejudice and discrimination?

2. Ask your friends whether they have a class that is centered on discussion more than lecture. Get permission from the professor of that class to visit. Tell her or him you need to observe a class for another course. Observe the class and record the number of times the professor calls on students, documenting the sex and race of each student called on. How does this pattern correspond with the overall demographics of the class. Also take notes on how the professor responds to the comments and questions of students, based on their race and gender. For example, do some students get more praise than others? What patterns do you see in who is and is not called on and responses to comments and questions.

3. Select a professor from your university (a sociology professor if possible) and make an appointment to see him or her. Talk with the professor about how he or she handles issues of sexual diversity in the classroom. Also do this with professors who teach women's studies, black studies, and if you have any courses in gay/lesbian studies, a professor who teaches in that program. Take notes on the answers they provide. Compare and contrast their answers. What do you think accounts for similarities and differences that you see in these responses?

Site-Seeing

1. To learn more about racial discrimination in education, visit the web site of the U.S. Department of Education, Office of Civil Rights at **http://www.ed.gov/offices/OCR/**.

2. To better understand the issues behind the debate over school vouchers, visit the web site sponsored by Ohio University at **http://www.ohiou.edu/esl/project/voucher/index.html**.

3. To learn more about efforts to reform education in the United States, visit the web site sponsored by The Center for Education Reform at **http://www.edreform.com**.

CRIMINAL JUSTICE AND LEGAL BARRIERS TO EQUALITY

The founders of the United States recognized the importance of the legal system in ensuring citizens their right to life, liberty, and the pursuit of happiness. For that reason, the Fourteenth Amendment to the U.S. Constitution guarantees citizens equal protection under the law. Despite this guarantee, however, the law is applied differently to individuals on the basis of race and ethnicity, social class, gender, and sexuality. The articles in this section explore just some of the ways that this occurs every day in the United States.

In the last decade, the number of inmates in jails and prisons in the United States nearly doubled. By the end of the twentieth century, a higher percentage of the U.S. population was in prison than was incarcerated in Russia, a society long known for its harsh criminal justice system. Still, many in the United States believe strongly that if you commit a crime, you must do time in prison. This strong anti-crime sentiment might be more reasonable if the criminal justice system equitably enforced laws against all groups, and if the law itself were unbiased.

In the United States, African-Americans make up about 13 percent of the population, yet they are arrested for about a third of all crimes and represent more than 40 percent of all prisoners (U.S. Department of Commerce, 1998). At first glance, it might appear that African-Americans commit more crimes than whites or other minority groups. But, as some of the articles in this section demonstrate, several factors contribute to the over-representation of African-Americans and other people of color among those arrested and incarcerated. In the first article, Prescott summarizes the findings of a study that found that minorities are more likely than whites to be stopped and searched by police. In this practice, known as "racial profiling," police exercise their discretion over whom to stop, and whether to warn or arrest an offender. Once arrested, Prescott reports, minorities are subjected to the discretion of judges, who have a great deal of latitude in the sentences they mete out to defendants. As a result, Prescott reports, African-Americans receive prison sentences that are twice as long as those of whites with similar criminal histories.

When individuals of any race or ethnicity are detained, they are subject to the power and authority of the arresting officer. In the second article in this section, the author discusses the all too common abuse of power by police officers who, the author argues, are more likely to beat people of color than whites. The author focuses on several cases, including that of Abner Louima, a Haitian immigrant who was wrongfully arrested, beaten, brutally sodomized with a plunger handle, and nearly killed by officers. Two of the officers responsible for Louima's torture were convicted of a crime. The article also discusses the case of Rodney King, an African-American whose brutal beating at the hands of several police officers was captured on video tape. Despite this evidence, the officers who beat King were acquitted of all criminal charges, although some were later convicted of violating his civil rights. By drawing on these and other cases and the ways they were handled, the author demonstrates just some of the ways that elected officials condone and support police brutality.

Equal protection under the law depends, in part, on the assumption that anyone charged with a crime will receive a fair trial. To get a fair trial, defendants need an attorney who will fight hard to defend their legal rights. Whether or not a suspect goes to prison is determined as much by his or her ability to afford a good attorney as by the individual's guilt or innocence. The United States Supreme Court mandates that poor defendants have the right to a court-appointed attorney if they cannot afford one themselves. However, as the author of the third article demonstrates, U.S. politicians, wishing to appear tough on crime, have voted to cut the funding for public defenders. As a result, court-appointed attorneys now urge more of their clients to plea bargain—admit guilt in exchange for a lighter sentence than they would receive if convicted after a trial. This means that even clients who are innocent are likely to face prison time because their attorneys, under pressure to reduce the number of cases they must handle, lack the time or resources to defend them adequately. In the fourth article, Berlow expands upon this argument. Focusing on a Georgia attorney who, at one time, contracted with the county to represent all of their poor criminal defendants, Berlow discusses how a lack of resources for public defenders has jeopardized the Sixth Amendment—the right to a speedy trial and the right to be represented by an attorney. Without adequate legal representation, poor defendants, including disproportionate numbers of people of color, are more likely to plea bargain even if they are innocent, and to be convicted when their cases go to trial. On the other hand, more affluent defendants, who can afford private attorneys, private investigators, and expert witnesses, have a better chance of getting all their evidence before a jury and of being acquitted, whether they are innocent or not.

Of course, not all people who suffer injustice in the justice system are alleged criminals. Some are victims. Because of discrimination built into the criminal justice system, certain victims are likely to receive inadequate protection and help from law enforcement officers. Each year, nearly 2 million women suffer beatings and other forms of abuse at the hands of their intimate partners (Bachman & Saltzman, 1995; Straus & Gelles, 1990). Yet when they turn to the police and courts for protection, many find the system lacking. Although better protection is still needed, over the last three decades a number of improvements—including emergency protective orders and preferred or mandatory arrest policies—have been made in the criminal justice system's response to the abuse of women. But these changes have been slow to reach rural areas. In the fifth article, Websdale draws upon interviews with battered women, social workers, judges, and police officers to document rural battered women's experiences with abuse. Websdale argues that this institutionalized discrimination, combined with cultural beliefs about men's right to control women, results in a rural patriarchy. Within this patriarchal system, women find it difficult to get police protection and encounter similar difficulties getting judges to enforce the law against men who abuse them.

Just as biases are institutionalized in the criminal justice system, discrimination remains an inherent aspect of the civil law, as well. In the sixth article in this section, Arnup draws upon actual court cases to explain some of the legal problems that lesbian and gay parents encounter when seeking custody or visitation of their own children. As the author explains, the biases that gay men and lesbians face in these family matters are built into the law, rather than resulting from a failure to address the parental rights of sexual minorities. Similarly, in the seventh article, Miller discusses many of the other ways in which discrimination against gay men and lesbian women is institutionalized in the law. Drawing upon laws and court decisions that prohibit gays and lesbians from legally marrying, serving openly in the military, or serving as Boy Scout leaders, Miller argues that sexual minorities live under a system of legal institutionalized segregation, often referred to as apartheid.

Taken together, the articles in this section show us just some of the ways that racial and ethnic minorities, poor people, women, and sexual minorities are likely to be discriminated against in the criminal justice system and the law. The unfair targeting of certain racial and ethnic minorities for scrutiny and arrest means that they are more likely to be brought to trial than are whites who commit the same crimes. Similarly, with inadequate representation, poor people are more likely to admit guilt or be convicted than are those who can afford a private attorney, and thus more likely to serve time in prison. At the same time, the articles in this section also demonstrate how biases against women are built into the criminal justice system, just as discrimination against gay men, lesbians, and other sexual minorities is an institutionalized part of civil law. Clearly the law and the criminal justice system have a long way to go before the barriers to guaranteed equal protection under the law are eradicated.

REFERENCES

BACHMAN, R., AND L.E. SALTZMAN. 1995. *Violence Against Women: Estimates from the Redesigned Survey.* BJS Publication No. 154-348. Washington, DC: U.S. Department of Justice, Bureau of Justice Statistics.

STRAUS, MURRAY A. AND RICHARD J. GELLES. 1990. *Physical Violence in American Families: Risk Factors and Adaptations to Violence in 8,145 Families.* New Brunswick, NJ:Transaction.

Reading 22

New Facts on Racial Profiling

Jeffrey Prescott

In this article, Prescott examines the practice of racial profiling as it is practiced by law enforcement officers and agencies.

For years, activists, community leaders, and ordinary citizens have said minorities in this country are treated unfairly by police and the criminal-justice system. Now, a flood of recent studies and reports are proving them correct.

Last week, the Leadership Conference on Civil Rights released a report suggesting that African-American and Hispanic citizens are treated more harshly than their white counterparts at all levels of the criminal-justice system, from arrests to likelihood and length of imprisonment. And on April 25, a groundbreaking study financed by the Justice Department examining the juvenile justice system reached the same stark conclusion.

These reports, among others, join a growing body of evidence on race and police practices, particularly racial profiling.

Law-enforcement agencies have generally responded to accusations of profiling by arguing for its rationality. Because blacks commit crimes at a higher rate than whites, the argument goes, profiling is justified. A more subtle explanation for profiling suggests that since poverty-stricken communities feel the impact of crime most severely, and because these areas are also composed disproportionately of minorities, use of race as a factor in selecting potential lawbreakers is an inevitable byproduct of sound police practices.

Extensive new research on profiling, however, has exposed this rationale as a myth. In the April 25 juvenile-justice report, minorities were at least twice as likely as whites to be sentenced to prison, even comparing youth with similar criminal histories.

Similarly, a recent General Accounting Office study showed that minorities were far more likely than whites to face intrusive searches by US Customs.

In fact, Customs Service searches did not correlate with the likelihood of discovering contraband. In at least one category, the disparity was startling: The report found that black women were 9 times more likely to be x-rayed after a frisk or pat-down in 1997 and 1998, but actually "were less than half as likely to be found carrying contraband as white women."

Source: This article first appeared in *The Christian Science Monitor* 92, no. 118 (May 10, 2000):8. © by author.

New York Attorney General Eliot Spitzer's study of the "stop and frisk" practices in New York City, using a complex statistical model, found that 50 percent of all police stops were of black New Yorkers, though African-Americans account for only 25 percent of the city's population. Even taking into account the demographics of each police precinct and the crime rate by race, the report found black New Yorkers were still twice as likely to be stopped and frisked as whites.

These data support one obvious conclusion: Race is not a rational factor to use in law enforcement. When people of color are targeted for stops and searches, police are no more likely—in some cases, much less likely—to find them breaking the law. But by focusing on skin color, the police create a self-fulfilling prophesy, as minorities will be "over policed" compared with their white counterparts. The disparity by race in arrests, convictions, and jail sentences will be exacerbated—and perhaps feed stereotypes that created the disparity in the first place. Deteriorating police and community relations, of course, are the destructive byproduct of this depressing formula.

The need for law-enforcement agencies to collect and make public data about their work is most important in repairing damage done by racial profiling. Strong public interest in evaluating the work of police and duplicating the recent research can help root out irrational or pernicious police practices.

In New Jersey, a lawsuit was necessary to start the process; other states and cities are considering laws to require data collection. The Traffic Stops Statistics Study Act (2000) has been introduced in Congress to provide for collection and analysis of data on traffic violations nationwide. Society gets the type of policing it demands. It is our civic responsibility to make certain political leaders react constructively to these new findings, support further research, and demand law enforcement that focuses on individual suspicion—not group stereotypes.

CRITICAL THINKING QUESTIONS

1. What is racial profiling? How do law enforcement agencies rationalize the need to practice racial profiling?
2. Where in the criminal justice process are minorities subject to racial profiling? How does this affect their opportunities in life?
3. What other practices could law enforcement agencies use to maximize their efforts to reduce crime without using racial profiling? Why do they continue to use racial profiling rather than implementing practices that are unbiased?

Reading 23

Police Brutality Must End

This article explores the issue of police brutality and the greater likelihood that racial minorities will experience excessive force at the hands of law enforcement agents.

Police brutality is a fact of American life. In major cities across the country, officers are abusing their authority in the most flagrant ways.

Source: Reprinted by permission of *The Progressive* 64, no. 4 (April 2000):8–9. www.progressive.org

New York City and Los Angeles are the epicenters of this crisis.

When the New York City officers who shot and killed Amadou Diallo were acquitted in late February, Mayor Rudolph Giuliani responded to the verdict with the words, "Probably until the day I die, I will always give police officers the benefit of the doubt."

But what about giving other people the same benefit?

Diallo, an African immigrant, was unarmed, but the police said they acted in self-defense when they unloaded forty-one shots at him. Two days after the verdict, Malcolm Ferguson, also unarmed, was killed while struggling with a police officer in the same Bronx neighborhood where Diallo was shot.

Throughout his time as mayor, Giuliani has shown his disdain for civil rights and his eagerness to impose law and order at all costs. When Giuliani took office in 1994, he instituted his "zero tolerance" policy, which led to a huge increase in arrests for such crimes as playing music too loudly, biking on the sidewalk, and public drinking. Some officers got the message that it was OK to rough people up—especially people of color.

"Many of the people allegedly kicked or beaten by police were not criminal suspects but people who had simply questioned police authority or had minor disagreements with officers," Amnesty International said in a 1996 report "Police Brutality and Excessive Force in the New York City Police Department." "Nearly all the victims in the cases of deaths in custody and police shootings reviewed by Amnesty International were from racial minorities—particularly African Americans, Latinos, and Asians."

Diallo's murder and the grotesque abuse of Haitian immigrant Abner Louima [who was beaten and sodomized with a plunger handle] in 1997 are only the most notorious examples of the brutality behind the N.Y.P.D. badge. Other incidents have occurred with alarming regularity.

In Los Angeles, infamous for the Rodney King case, [he was videotaped being beaten and kicked by several police officers] a new, smoldering scandal has singed an elite anti-gang unit and threatens to consume the entire police department. The L.A.P.D. had a unit called Community Resources Against Street Hoodlums, or C.R.A.S.H. Formed in

the late 1970s, it patrolled the Rampart section of Los Angeles, a low-income area with a large immigrant population, and a home to gangs.

Rampart officer Rafael Perez—who was accused of stealing eight pounds of cocaine in police custody—cooperated with authorities. He claimed that his fellow officers frequently framed suspects and hid wrongful shootings. [They were later convicted.]

In 1998, when investigators searched Perez's house, they saw a plaque that was decorated with a playing card imprinted with a red heart that had two bullets through it. "Uh, that plaque that you probably saw at my house. . . . Do you know what that plaque is even about?" Perez said to the internal police investigators, according to a transcript obtained by the *Los Angeles Times*. "[A sergeant] gave me that plaque for the Ovando shooting. That's what that is. We give plaques when you get involved in shootings. Uh, if the guy dies, the card is a black No. 2. If he stays alive, it's a red No. 2." (Perez had admitted to shooting, then framing, Javier Ovando, an unarmed man, with another officer. The victim was paralyzed as a result of the shooting and sentenced to twenty-three years in prison as a result of the frame-up.)

"Is it more prestigious to get one that is black than red?" Detective Mark Thompson asked Perez.

"Yeah. I mean, you know, the black one signifies that a guy died," he answered.

According to the *Los Angeles Times*, "So-called shooting parties at which officers drank beer and were awarded plaques for wounding or killing people were quasi-official events sometimes held at the Los Angeles Police Academy and attended by supervisors, according to four officers who worked in the Ramparts Division's anti-gang unit. The officers—all of whom asked not to be identified—said similar plaques were awarded to anti-gang officers in the L.A.P.D.'s 77th Street Division, and to officers in other units."

But police brutality is not confined to New York and Los Angeles. In 1998, Human Rights Watch published a 440-page report "Shielded From Justice: Police Brutality and Accountability in the United States." It examined fourteen U.S. cities (Atlanta, Boston, Chicago, Detroit, Indianapolis, Los Angeles, Minneapolis, New Orleans, New York, Philadelphia, Portland, Providence, San Francisco, and Washington) from 1995 to 1998. It concluded that "police brutality is persistent in all of these cities; that systems to deal with abuse have had similar failings in all the cities; and that, in each city examined, complainants face enormous barriers in seeking administrative punishment or criminal prosecution of officers who have committed human rights violations."

The evidence of excessive force is all around us:

In Houston in July 1998, Pedro Oregon was shot during a drug raid on his home. He was an unarmed Mexican national. The police officers were fired following protests from the Hispanic community.

In Kansas City, Missouri, in November 1998, thirteen-year-old Timothy Wilson, a black child, died from a gun wound after six officers saw him driving recklessly and chased him.

In Hartford, Connecticut, in April 1999, fourteen-year-old Aquan Salmon, an unarmed suspect in a robbery, and also African American, died after being shot in the back by a police officer.

And in early March of this year, Louisville, Kentucky, was reeling from days of community protests and counter-protests by the police department after Mayor David L. Armstrong fired police chief Eugene Sherrard. Chief Sherrard had approved medals of valor for two police officers who used twenty-two bullets to shoot at and kill an unarmed black man suspected of stealing a car. The officers were later cleared in a grand jury inquiry, but their action was denounced by black leaders.

Human Rights Watch makes the following sensible recommendations:

- federal aid to police departments should be contingent on regular reports concerning excessive force "and on improvements in oversight and discipline";
- police and political leaders should create "a policy of zero tolerance for abuse";
- police departments should establish means of identifying officers who are at risk of using excessive force and should remove those who commit abuses;
- civilian review agencies should have adequate power to rein in the police;
- each state should hire a special prosecutor for police cases.

Not all, not most, police officers are brutal. And many cities, from Boston to San Diego, have reduced crime by taking an enlightened approach, one that stresses community policing and good relations with the citizenry. They have had as much success reducing crime as New York City has, without trampling on civil liberties. Departments around the country should be looking to this civilized approach—and discard the N.Y.P.D. and L.A.P.D. models.

Police cannot become a law unto themselves. Those who act illegally must be forced, through criminal prosecution, to pay for their crimes. And we must hold the officials in charge accountable: the police chief, the mayor, the district attorney.

We deserve to be treated as citizens, not as subjects—or suspects.

CRITICAL THINKING QUESTIONS

1. What is police brutality? Why is this more likely to happen to certain racial and ethnic minorities than whites?

2. In what ways does the criminal justice system support and encourage police brutality?

3. Do you agree that a "zero tolerance" policy on crime encourages police to use excessive force? Why or why not? In your opinion, what social policies might be more effective than "zero tolerance" in reducing crime? Explain.

Reading 24

Too Poor to Be Defended

In this article, the author explains how strong anticrime sentiments have led to a reduction in the resources provided for public defenders, which seriously impedes the likelihood that poor criminal defendants will receive justice.

The right of indigent criminal defendants to a lawyer is increasingly in jeopardy.

IN AMERICA'S fiercely adversarial legal system, a good lawyer is essential. Ask O.J. Simpson. In a landmark case 35 years ago, *Gideon v Wainwright*, a unanimous Supreme Court ruled that indigent defendants must be provided with a lawyer at state expense because there could be no fair trial in a serious criminal case without one. "This seems to us to be an obvious truth," wrote Justice Hugo Black in his opinion. At the time, the decision was hailed as a triumph for justice, an example of America's commitment to the ideal of equality before the law.

This is the image most Americans still have of their criminal-justice system—the fairest in the world, in which any defendant, no matter how poor, gets a smart-aleck lawyer who, too often manages to get the culprit off on a technicality. Nothing could be further from the truth. About 80% of people accused of a felony have to depend on a publicly-provided lawyer; but over the past two decades the eagerness of politicians to look harsh on crime, their reluctance to pay for public defenders, and a series of Supreme Court judgments restricting the grounds for appeal have made a mockery of Gideon. Today many indigent defendants, including those facing long terms of imprisonment or even death, are treated to a "meet 'em and plead 'em" defense—a brief consultation in which a harried or incompetent lawyer en-

courages them to plead guilty or, if that fails, struggles through a short trial in which the defense is massively outgunned by a more experienced, better-paid and better-prepared prosecutor.

"We have a wealth-based system of justice," says Stephen Bright, the director of the Atlanta-based Southern Centre for Human Rights, a legal-aid and advocacy group. "For the wealthy, it's gold-plated. For the average poor person, it's like being herded to the slaughterhouse. In many places the adversary system barely exists for the poor."

Many lawyers, of course, have made heroic efforts for particular defendants for little or no pay, but the charity of lawyers can be relied on to handle only a tiny fraction of cases. As spending on police, prosecutors and prisons has steadily climbed in the past decade, increasing the number of people charged and imprisoned, spending on indigent defense has not kept pace, overwhelming an already hard-pressed system.

A rise in the hourly rate paid to defence lawyers preparing a case in the federal courts, approved by Congress in 1986, has still not been implemented in 77 of the country's 94 federal districts because Congress itself refuses to appropriate any additional money. At $45 an hour, many defence lawyers practising in the federal courts are not paid enough to cover their hourly overhead costs for maintaining a law office, according to the federal government's own calculations. Even in those districts where the rise has been implemented, the maximum $75-an-hour fee allowed is less than half the $150-$200 an hour the average private lawyer would receive.

At state level, where the vast majority of criminal trials are held, the situation is often far worse. In Louisville, Kentucky, salaried lawyers in the public defender's office handle a staggering 750 cases a year. In Virginia, private lawyers are paid a maximum fee of $265 for felony cases that carry a sentence of up to 20 years and $575 if the potential penalty is more than 20 years. Alabama pays defence lawyers a mere $20 an hour, up to a maximum of $1,000, to prepare for a death-penalty case. Mississippi pays a maximum of $1,000, above overhead expenses, for work in the courtroom during a death-penalty trial. Other states pay more, but few approach the fees that would be paid by individuals with the means to hire their own lawyers. The amounts public defenders are allowed to spend on investigation or expert witnesses—widely available to prosecutors—are often severely restricted and sometimes not allowed at all.

In addition to the sheer lack of money, the methods of appointing and paying defense lawyers are also open to abuse. This varies from state to state and even from county to county within some states. In many state jurisdictions, trial judges appoint defence lawyers on a case-by-case basis and set the level of their fees. These fees can sometimes be so low that no lawyers can be found to accept the job. In that event, judges can force lawyers practicing in the area to take turns defending indigent clients, whether or not the lawyers have any criminal-law experience. "This is like forcing a podiatrist to do brain surgery," observes Paul Petterson, indigent-defence coordinator for the National Association of Criminal Defence Lawyers (NACDL).

Even when there are lawyers willing to take on indigent cases, judges often appoint cronies, or those they know will not vigorously contest a case. Most state judges are elected or subject to recall votes. Faced with crowded lists, they have little incentive to bend over backwards to ensure that the hundreds of impoverished defendants who pass through their courts, many accused of heinous crimes, are represented by well-paid or zealous lawyers.

Judges in Houston, Texas, have repeatedly appointed one local lawyer who is famous for hurrying through trials like "greased lightning" to represent indigent defendants. Ten of his clients have been sentenced to death. During one death-penalty case, he fell asleep on several occasions. Nevertheless, the death sentence was upheld on appeal and the defendant has since been executed.

A second approach is to contract out to a single lawyer or group of lawyers all a county's defence work. Too often this means the contract goes to the lowest bidder. In 1993 one Georgia county cut the cost of its indigent-defence budget by awarding the contract to a lawyer who, at $25,000 a year, bid almost $20,000 less than the other two bidders. In the next three years the contracted defender tried only one felony case in front of a jury, while entering guilty pleas in 213 other cases.

The most reliable method used to provide lawyers for poor defendants is to appoint salaried public defenders. But public-defender offices are often grossly underfunded. Training programmes for defenders are scarce. Inexperienced lawyers fresh out of law school are often buried under a gigantic caseload, as in Louisville. The amount spent on defender offices is typically one-third or less than spent on the teams of prosecutors they face.

It is hardly surprising that many poor defendants receive less than sterling representation. Mr. Bright's files are stuffed with examples of people whose public defenders were either grossly negligent or ignorant. This can be a disaster for any defendant. The innocent face wrongful conviction. However, even the guilty may suffer because their lawyer failed to raise mitigating factors which, by law, entitle them to a milder sentence. Once, wrongful convictions because of lawyer error stood a good chance of being overturned on appeal, especially in death-penalty cases. But Congress and the Supreme Court have recently made appeals far more difficult.

In 1996 Congress eliminated all federal funding for death-penalty resource centres, which had handled or advised on most death-penalty appeals. Most of these centers have since closed. The same year Congress also passed an anti-terrorism law which included strict new procedural rules that make it much more difficult to mount an appeal in a death-penalty case, even when new evidence is found.

The Supreme Court has ruled that appeals based on lawyer error must prove not only that a defence lawyer was incompetent, but that his incompetence changed the outcome of the trial. Proving such a negative is often impossible. Lower courts have used this ruling to uphold convictions, even in death-penalty cases, in which the defence lawyer was drunk, asleep during the trial or completely ignorant of the relevant law. As a result, most wrongly convicted poor defendants now face a catch-22: to prove their original lawyer incompe-

tent, they must find a highly competent lawyer to navigate the bigger appeal hurdles recently erected, although behind bars they are in an even worse position to do that.

Providing poor defendants with proper legal representation would cost money, but it is affordable. The estimated spending on indigent defence is less than 2% of total national spending on law enforcement, and only about 10% of spending on all judicial and legal services. Some states, such as Minnesota and Colorado, have found the money for a reasonably financed public-defender programme. Criminal legal aid is also starved of support in many other countries, but some, such as Britain and the Scandinavian countries, can find the money to do the job well.

Reading 25

Requiem for a Public Defender

Alan Berlow

In this article, Berlow focuses on the life and work of one public defender to make the point that the constitutional right of poor criminal defendants to be represented by an attorney is in serious jeopardy.

A long, dreary corridor of black-marbled linoleum serves as a makeshift waiting room for defendants scheduled to be tried at the Spalding County Courthouse in Griffin, Georgia, 40 miles south of Atlanta. More than 50 men and women, mostly black, stand along a pale yellow wall or sit on a dark oak bench, waiting to talk to a heavyset lawyer with a silver beard, a handlebar mustache, and square wire-rimmed glasses, who suddenly pokes his head from a doorway, a cigarette dangling from his lips. "Lashawn Reid, front and center," he barks,

Source: Reprinted with permission from *The American Prospect,* June 5, 2000, Vol. 11, No. 14 Princeton, NJ: New Prospect Inc. All rights reserved.

and a young woman charged with burglary rises from the bench. She enters a tiny office guarded by an armed sheriff, where attorney Johnny B. Mostiler—his hands sparkling with six gold, diamond, and onyx rings, his wrists with three gold bracelets—pulls a utility drawer from an aluminum desk and crushes his cigarette into a pile of butts in the paper clip tray.

For the past 10 years, the gruff-talking, chain-smoking Mostiler was Spalding County's only public defender, which meant that if you were poor and accused of a serious crime, sooner or later you'd probably be sitting down with him. Most of his clients didn't get to sit with him for very long, however, because with as many as 900 felony cases a year, Mostiler was a very, very busy man. The 53-year-old attorney, who died of a massive heart attack on April 1, was perhaps the archetype of what many public defenders refer to as "meet 'em, greet 'em, and plead 'em" lawyers: attorneys who dispense with huge numbers of cases in a minimal amount of time.

At the time of his death, Mostiler—who spent only 60 percent of his time handling the county's business and the rest on his private clients—was processing more than seven times the number of indigent cases the American Bar Association (ABA) believes is manageable. In concrete terms, that meant he was turning over one case every 100 minutes, less time than a private attorney might devote to a simple traffic violation. Lashawn Reid's fate was settled in less than five minutes. She agreed to plead guilty and is serving three years in prison.

Johnny Mostiler never conformed to the stereotype of the public defender—the ragged, sleep-deprived idealist, toiling away on behalf of the downtrodden for a few dollars a year. Decked out in his flashy jewelry and a black cowboy hat, he arrived at the Spalding Courthouse in a mustard green 1972 Cadillac El Dorado convertible; he easily took home well over $100,000 a year. But for thousands of poor people, the Johnny Mostilers of the world may represent the future face of indigent defense in America.

CRIMINAL DEFENSE

Mostiler was one of a growing breed of what are known as "contract attorneys." Though unknown until the early 1980s, contract attorneys now increasingly represent a legal way for budget-conscious county commissioners to control costs while fulfilling the Supreme Court's mandate under *Gideon v. Wainwright* (1963) to provide an attorney to anyone accused of a crime who is too poor to hire one. Rates of arrest, indictment, and incarceration have doubled in the past decade due to the war on drugs, increased police and prosecuto-

rial budgets, and tougher sentencing laws. More indictments have meant more bills for defense attorneys, costs traditionally borne by states and counties that have rarely shown much enthusiasm for spending taxpayer money to defend those they want to lock up.

Enter the contract attorney. In 1990 Mostiler convinced Spalding County's commissioners that they were wasting money paying as many as 20 court-appointed attorneys $50 an hour to handle indigent cases without knowing exactly how many hours those attorneys would bill during any given year. Mostiler proposed instead that the commissioners pay him a flat fee to handle all of the county's indigent cases, regardless of the number. That way the county would have to deal with only one lawyer, and it would know its final bill at the start of the fiscal year rather than at the end. "The pay wasn't great, but it was steady and regular," Mostiler explained when I first met him last summer. "That's why I took it on. And I thought I could save the county some money." Mostiler estimated that in a decade as Spalding's public defender, he saved the county more than $1 million.

Spalding County's commissioners clearly like the system Mostiler devised. But what about Mostiler's clients? Is the average indigent defendant's Sixth Amendment right to counsel better served by Mostiler, who was paid an average of $189 per case, than by the court-appointed attorney who made $325 per case 10 years ago? More to the point, can any attorney look after a county's fiscal interests and also seek justice for the 900 men and women the state is trying to put away?

One of those who says it can't be done is Michael Mears of the Georgia Indigent Defense Council, a state agency charged with improving the criminal-justice system for the state's poorest citizens. Mears, whose office subsidized Mostiler's contract and assisted him on complex death penalty cases, considered Mostiler a competent attorney, but doesn't think anyone can do justice to 900 felonies a year. "It is absolutely mind-boggling that he could juggle that number of cases," Mears said in an interview last fall, arguing that an attorney handling 900 felonies a year would have to choose which cases to focus on and which to neglect. "There are only so many hours in the day. I don't care what the case is; a defendant is entitled to sit down with his attorney and go over the case and discuss his options."

The National Association of Criminal Defense Lawyers, which represents some 10,000 criminal lawyers, has condemned the use of fixed-price contracts. It says they're designed "to process the maximum number of defendants at the lowest cost, without regard to truth, justice or innocence." A new report by the U.S. Justice Department's Bureau of Justice Assistance (BJA) says contract systems can work if case loads are limited and competent attorneys are hired with support staff, such as investigators. But the report says the worst of the contract systems "place cost containment before quality," rely heavily on unqualified lawyers, fail to employ investigators and expert witnesses, and "create incentives to plead cases out early rather than go to trial."

No one seems to have a clear idea how many low-bid contract attorneys are practicing in the United States. The ABA has reported that at least half the states make some use of them. But Nancy Gist, director of BJA, which dispenses nearly $2 billion a year in grants to state and local criminal-justice agencies (of which less than .5 percent end up in indigent defense), says the contractors are only one manifestation of a "crisis" in indigent defense.

Gist estimates that "hundreds of thousands" of indigents nationwide receive ineffective legal counsel each year, whether they are represented by contractors, lawyers appointed by judges, or full-time public defender offices that may simply be underfunded and understaffed. "A gross injustice is being done every day across this country with respect to the rights of criminal indigent defendants," says Gist. "It would be fair to say that the level of quality representation provided indigent defendants is uneven and frequently abysmal."

Gist's boss, Attorney General Janet Reno, has wrung her hands over the problem, noting that defenders are the worst-financed portion of the justice system (indigent defense gets about 2 percent of combined state and federal criminal-justice expenditures) and that the widespread reliance on bargain-basement lawyers will "inevitably erode the community's sense of justice." She and the head of the Justice Department's criminal division, James K. Robinson, have both talked about a "comprehensive plan" for improving indigent defense nationwide. But it turns out to be little more than an inoffensive collection of educational and hortatory measures designed to encourage states and localities to do what many have steadfastly refused to do since the Sixth Amendment was adopted in 1791: empower it.

Chief Justice William H. Rehnquist, meanwhile, has made the case that federally funded public defenders should be better paid, arguing that the absurdly low hourly rate "is seriously hampering the ability of judges to recruit attorneys to provide effective representation." But if finding competent lawyers is a problem at the federal level, where fees average $53 an hour, one can only imagine what kind of attorneys are working in state courts, where attorneys are commonly paid between $30 and $40 an hour. In one Montana county, a contractor earned $18 an hour.

MASS JUSTICE

With 900 felony cases a year assigned just to Mostiler—who worked with one half-time associate—one might think the Spalding County Courthouse would be a cyclone of trial activity. In fact, the court operates at a fairly leisurely pace, setting aside only six weeks each year for its entire felony docket. Although Mostiler had 150 cases set for trial during a two-week court session last summer, nearly every one was disposed of through a plea bargain. Sitting in his courthouse cubicle, smoking one Tourney cigarette after another, the blue-eyed, dimple-cheeked lawyer described the process matter-of-factly. "We'll enter pleas all week, at a rate of about 10 to 12 every 45 minutes," he said, noting that a large number of pleas were entered at the last minute because "defendants don't get the fear of God in them 'til a trial is coming up."

While Mostiler worked out plea agreements in his smoke-filled cubicle one morning, I sat a few feet away in the third-floor courtroom of Johnnie L. Caldwell, a steely-eyed and indefatigably humorless judge who dispensed justice to some of Mostiler's diverse clientele: men and women accused of everything from aggravated assault to dog fighting, armed robbery, child molestation, kidnapping, sodomy, distribution of pornography, stalking, and possession of any number of controlled substances. At one point in the proceedings, no less than 16 defendants, all dressed in dark green prison garb, some with legs shackled, were lined up beneath Caldwell's dais. All had agreed to plead guilty. The ruddy-faced judge admonished them to respond loudly, then asked if they agreed to waive their rights to a jury trial, to remain silent, and to subpoena witnesses (all did), after which he read out their sentences and called for the next batch of criminals.

Mostiler's first courtroom appearance during the two-week summer session involved Melishia Renee Gosha, a doe-eyed 15 year old with a tight ponytail, who showed up in court without a single family member or friend to support her. One year earlier, Gosha had allegedly fired two .38 caliber bullets into the back of her great-aunt's head after an argument over use of the family car. Gosha's "day in court" lasted all of 10 minutes, from the prosecution's summary of her offense, to her waiver of her right to a trial by jury and guilty plea, to Judge Paschal A. English's sentence: life in prison. Another attorney might have contested Gosha's being tried as an adult for an offense committed when she was 14, or might have taken the case to trial, hoping that a psychologist or some other expert witness might convince jurors that mitigating factors—mental illness, a deprived childhood, or possible abuse by her guardian, for example—warranted a more lenient sentence.

But Mostiler stood by the guilty plea, insisting that Gosha had no viable defense and got the best deal possible under the circumstances. He said the plea spared the defendant and the victim's family a lot of trauma, and that District Attorney Bill McBroom agreed to drop a gun possession charge that could have gotten Gosha an additional 15 years and thereby delayed the date she would be eligible for parole.

In his chambers, Judge English, who tries cases in four Georgia counties, acknowledged that an attorney with greater resources for expert witnesses or investigators might have been able to create a bleak enough picture of Gosha's home life to have gotten her a better deal than life, but he adamantly defended Mostiler. "I've seen high-profile lawyers come through here at $25,000 and $50,000 per client who do half the job of Johnny Mostiler. I don't think anyone gives better representation than Mr. Mostiler." What English didn't say was that attorneys like Mostiler also provide judges like him with an invaluable service: They keep court dockets clear and on budget by holding trials, hearings, and procedural delays to an absolute minimum.

THE "EFFICIENCY" OF THE CONTRACT SYSTEM

Contract lawyers and those who rely on a heavy load of court assignments for their livelihoods are notorious for their aversion to trials, which are both costly and time-consuming. As case loads increase, studies show, so do guilty pleas because lawyers have no time or interest in researching cases, holding hearings, or filing motions. William Wheeler, the low-bid contractor in McDuffe County, Georgia, entered 262 guilty pleas for his clients between 1993 and 1995, trying only 14 cases and filing only seven motions. Eduardo Falla, the chief contract attorney in Flathead County, Montana, didn't present a single case to a jury between 1994 and 1999, and filed no motions to suppress evidence or have cases dismissed. In

California, contract lawyer Jack Suter testified last year in a civil action brought by a former member of his firm that although his office handles well over 1,000 felonies each year, he hadn't tried more than one case since 1996. A single attorney handled all of the firm's misdemeanors—more than 3,500 a year—nearly nine times the cap of 400 cases recommended by the ABA. Contract lawyers in Jones County, Mississippi, themselves became so disgusted with the system that they filed suit, urging a court to find that they were providing ineffective counsel.

Rod Uphoff—who runs a legal clinic at the University of Oklahoma, in a state that relies almost entirely on low-bid contractors—cited one attorney who handled several hundred felonies and several hundred misdemeanors on a part-time basis for $20,000. "He said he went down to court every Thursday and would take care of 14 or 15 cases every week. He said, 'We're very efficient.'" Uphoff believes such "efficiencies" lead to innocent people serving time. As a defendant, says Uphoff, "I'm forced to plead guilty because my lawyer is saying, 'If you don't plead, you're likely to go to prison for five to 10 years, and they're offering you six months.' So the client says, 'I'll take the six months because I don't want to run the risk of a much more serious penalty.' I can tell you, from my experience, that's what is happening under the contract system."

Even if they don't press innocent clients to plead guilty, one of the nation's leading criminal-defense experts, Professor Richard Klein of Touro College's Law Center, suggests that a client familiar with the reputation of an attorney such as Mostiler might feel compelled to plead rather than go to trial. "If I'm a defendant, and I'm offered a plea, and I know my lawyer hasn't done any work on my case because I know he's got 899 other cases, what am I going to do? I'd be a fool to go to trial with a lawyer who's not going to do any work, regardless of my guilt or innocence or the strength of the DA's case."

Mostiler told me he never forced a client to accept a plea bargain and that his clients always made the final decision whether or not to go to trial. At the same time, he said, he typically tried no more than seven cases a year, while his associate Rosamund Braunrot said she probably tried another eight or nine. Together, that's less than 2 percent of the firm's case load. Nevertheless, even Mostiler's harshest critics acknowledged that he could be a formidable advocate in front of a jury.

District Attorney McBroom complained bitterly about the amount of money Mostiler was paid, but had nothing but praise for the defender's oratorical and trial skills. Last September I saw Mostiler convince a jury to spare the life of Areguss Clark, who brutally shot and killed his fiancée's father in the Spalding hospital emergency room where he also shot his fiancée in the head, rendering her a barely conscious quadriplegic. Clark got life without parole. In 1998 Mostiler pulled another rabbit from his hat when he won a life sentence for Wendell White, who was videotaped by police as he murdered a former lover's six-month-old son by smashing his head to the ground. In a business where success can mean keeping your client out of Georgia's electric chair, these were impressive victories.

IMPRISONING THE INNOCENT

Over a Styrofoam tray of deep-fried chicken gizzards from the Big Chic restaurant, Mostiler defended his law practice one sunny afternoon, explaining how he'd deliberately created his unconventional persona when he'd set up shop in Griffin, fresh out of the University of Georgia School of Law, because it was a very competitive environment and he needed to stand out. "I'm known as the guy who defends all the criminals," he said, acknowledging that he wasn't the most popular man in town. Labeling himself "the last Democrat in Spalding County," he said he was one of the few people there who didn't own a firearm—"I just don't believe in it." He called Supreme Court Justice Thurgood Marshall one of his heroes and argued that Ronald Reagan "gutted" the public defender program. Mostiler had little patience for critics of his law practice.

"I'm proud to say I'm an indigent defender," he told me. "I feel a great responsibility in my job, not just for my client, but for everybody's rights." Mostiler said he fought hard on behalf of all those he represented. "You won't find anyone in Spalding County who'll say I'm a bad lawyer or that I don't represent people well. I couldn't maintain a substantial civil practice if people thought I was a bad lawyer."

Though he acknowledged that he'd had 40 complaints filed against him alleging inadequate counsel, he said all of them were thrown out. His brow furrowed, Mostiler dismissed suggestions that he'd taken on too many cases, arguing that most of them "deal with repeat offenders" who have no justifiable issues, and that his full-time investigator, a paralegal, and attorney Braunrot helped him work out the prodigious number of plea agreements. As for his own contacts with clients, Mostiler said he personally interviewed "10 to 12 clients a day at the jail." The lawyer visitation log at the Spalding County Jail suggested a somewhat different picture, however. It showed that during the nine-month period from January 5 to September 20, 1999, Mostiler paid only 26 visits to the jail, about three per month. During the same period, his private investigator made 43 visits, and Braunrot visited the jail 20 times.

One former client, Johnel Edward Taylor, complained that the first time he spoke with Mostiler was the day before his trial in December 1998. Taylor was sentenced to life in prison for a murder he says he didn't commit. He has since filed an appeal alleging ineffective assistance of counsel.

Whether or not Taylor has a legitimate claim (Mostiler told me only that Taylor's case was "one I shouldn't have lost"), there is mounting evidence, much of it provided by new DNA testing, that a sizeable number of innocent people have been convicted and incarcerated. Since 1976, 87 innocent people have been discovered on death row alone, and a 1996 Justice Department report suggested that the actual number of innocents in U.S. prisons facing lesser sentences is many times greater. That report found that in one sample of 8,000 primary suspects, 2,000 had their cases thrown out on the basis of DNA evidence. The report also concluded that one of the major reasons for wrongful convictions is attorney error and incompetence. Needless to say, the likelihood of making a case for an innocent defendant declines precipitously if the lawyer has no time to work on it and has no one investigating the state's evidence.

For Scott Wallace, director of defender services at the National Legal Aid and Defender Association, which represents 13,000 public defenders, the issue is not whether an attorney like Mostiler can win one of two spectacular cases at trial, but whether he has the time and resources to secure equal justice under the Constitution for 900 discrete individuals. Wallace is convinced that none of the clients represented by high-volume contractors can receive truly effective counsel, but he also says the contractors are only part of the problem. "In every courtroom where there's a shyster lawyer who is spending five minutes per felony case, there is a judge who sees it and a prosecutor who sees it, and [they don't] complain. For low-bid contracts to flourish, it requires lawyers who are willing to do bad work solely to earn a living through high volume; it takes local county officials who are willing to turn a blind eye and don't care about the quality of indigent defense, and it takes legislators who appropriate money. Those are the silent coconspirators in this process." It also requires a citizenry complacent about the denial of due-process rights to a huge segment of the population.

The Supreme Court has only exacerbated the problem by setting a standard of competence for attorneys so ridiculously low that trained circus bears very nearly qualify. As a result, lower courts have found no constitutional violation, even when lawyers have slept through trials or have come to court drunk or high on drugs. And since state bar associations have largely abdicated responsibility for disciplining incompetent lawyers, the indigent defendant who is strapped with a lousy lawyer, more often than not, is simply out of luck. Meanwhile, many state criminal-justice systems view lawyers who try to stand up for their clients as troublemakers who must be weeded out. In several instances, contract attorneys have been fired for protesting that huge case loads have prevented them from effectively representing clients. When one court-appointed attorney, Steven J. Benjamin, told a Virginia judge that the court's fee cap of $840 to defend a murder suspect forced him to choose between his need to make a living and his ethical obligation to represent his client, the judge called in all the attorneys to whom he assigned cases and advised those who held similar views to find another line of work. The complaints ceased. Benjamin went on to prove his client's innocence in a spectacular trial in which he also identified the actual murderer. He no longer accepts court-assigned cases.

Several state courts have ruled that contract and other defender programs were unconstitutional because they had insufficient staff and too many cases, and more legal challenges are no doubt in order. What is really needed, however, is an end to both low-bid contracting and to judicial appointments of indigent defenders—which create unconscionable conflicts between a lawyer's loyalty to his client and his sense of obligation to the judge paying his salary—as well as creation of fully funded, full-time public defenders' offices. Several states have linked the budgets of defense and prosecution offices (in Oklahoma, the defense is guaranteed 75 percent of what the prosecution gets). Such systems may mean that both sides lack sufficient resources, but they at least stand for the principle of equalizing justice.

Legislation introduced recently by Democratic Senator Patrick Leahy of Vermont would put an end to court-appointed attorneys in death penalty cases, provide an incentive for states to increase indigent-defense spending,

and establish standards of competence for capital defenders. But it's unlikely many Republicans will go along with such an intrusion on what they view as a sacred state right to continue providing incompetent attorneys to the poor. The Leahy bill is a response to the fact that 87 innocent people have been identified on death rows nationwide as well as to Illinois Governor George Ryan's recent moratorium on executions in his state, where 13 innocents were found on death row. But the death row cases should be viewed as a wake-up call that there is something fundamentally wrong with the operation of the criminal-justice system. If conservatives like George Will and Pat Robertson can now agree that it's unsavory to have states condemning innocent people to death and that something should be done to prevent these travesties in the future, then it should not require a great leap, at least in principle, to convince people that it is also wrong to imprison innocent people for lesser crimes than capital murder and that those people also have a right to competent lawyers. Attorney General Janet Reno has remarked that "if we do not adequately support criminal defense for poor Americans, people will think that you only get justice if you can afford to pay a lawyer." The problem is getting from the principle that the Sixth Amendment is not just for those who can afford it, to an agreement on how to pay for it.

CRITICAL THINKING QUESTIONS

1. Why are public defenders more likely than private attorneys to have clients that plea bargain?

2. How are tough anticrime sentiments related to reductions in funding for public defenders? Who benefits when funding for public defenders is reduced? Who is harmed?

3. In what ways does the public defender system in U.S. courts help to perpetuate racial and class-based inequalities? Explain.

Reading 26

An Ethnographic Assessment of the Policing of Domestic Violence in Rural Eastern Kentucky

Neil Websdale

In this article, Websdale draws on interviews with battered women, police, judges, and shelter workers to outline the ways that poor rural communities have failed to address adequately the needs of battered women. The author argues that a lack of resources and long-standing cultural tradition leave women at high risk of violence.

INTRODUCTION

As Dobash and Dobash (1992) have argued, the last two decades have seen a marked growth in our awareness about domestic violence. They attribute this growth to the battered women's movement and to feminist demands for change. We now have various studies that, by drawing upon the experiences of battered women, capture the nature and extent of interpersonal violence against women (Dobash and Dobash, 1979; Pagelow, 1981; Russell, 1990; Pizzey, 1974; Pahl; 1985, Stanko, 1991).

Studies of rural domestic violence and its policing have not appeared systematically in the research literature of criminology, social science, or gender studies. Indeed, there is no clear-cut definition of "rural." The 1990 U.S. Census estimates the population of rural counties in the United States to be 61,690,238. For the U.S. Census Bureau, rural areas consist of communities of less than 2,500 people. For my purposes, people live in a rural setting if they reside in the countryside or a relatively small town, with a population of less than 5,000. I also understand rural to refer to certain types of communities where people know each

other's business, come into more regular contact with each other, and share a larger core of values than is true of people in urban areas.

In this exploratory article, I raise questions about the marginalization of rural women, the violence they experience, and the inadequacy of the police response to that violence. . . .

THEORIES OF DOMESTIC VIOLENCE AND ITS POLICING

Feminists have theorized male violence within families as part of the wider structure of patriarchy (see Dobash and Dobash, 1979 and 1992; Radford and Russell, 1992; Hanmer and Saunders, 1984; Pahl, 1985; Russell, 1990). Sylvia Walby (1990: 20) uses the term patriarchy to refer to the domination, oppression, and exploitation of women by men. Walby situates male violence within a nexus of relations that includes: (1) the reluctance of the patriarchal state to confront violence against women or provide women with sufficient funds to live independently of violent men, (2) sexuality, (3) the cultural depiction of women as objects of the male gaze, (4) the gendering of the capitalist economy, and (5) the disproportionate share of unpaid work performed by women within the patriarchal household.

Source: Reprinted with permission from *Social Justice* Vol. 22, No. 1 1995. socialjustice@aol.com

Historically, the most common police response has been to treat "domestics" as non-criminal problems, to be "resolved" within the family (Tong, 1984). Stanko (1989) observes that domestic altercations produce arrests that do not elicit much recognition from police officers' peers. However, according to Sherman (1992a), the arrest of batterers increased during the 1980s, as part of a much "broader revolution" in the policing of domestic violence that dates back to the 1970s. The use of mandatory arrest laws increased after the Minneapolis "experiment" in which researchers found that the arrest of batterers correlated with a reduction in recidivism (Sherman and Berk, 1984). A number of other federally funded studies in urban areas (Miami, Milwaukee, Colorado Springs, Omaha, and Charlotte) largely failed to replicate the Minneapolis findings and consequently cast doubt upon the effectiveness of mandatory arrest (see also Sherman, 1992a: 104–109; 1992b).

Feminists have been skeptical of this "broad revolution" in the policing of battering and have argued that the failure to intervene and/or arrest batterers is one way in which the patriarchal oppression of women is reproduced (see Edwards, 1989; Hanmer, Radford, and Stanko, 1989). Rather than focusing on the pros and cons of mandatory arrest, feminists argue that until the structure of patriarchy is changed, any change in police response will have a limited effect on levels of intra-familial violence.

A BLIND SPOT IN EXISTING RESEARCH ON DOMESTIC VIOLENCE AND ITS POLICING

Nearly all the research on domestic violence and its policing has been limited to urban areas. This bias does not simply reflect the urban orientation of mainstream criminology; rather, it reflects the much wider marginalization of rural social problems. Impoverished rural women constitute an acutely marginalized group. The failure to confront the batter-

ing of these women and the police response to that violence is akin to the failure of traditional disciplines such as history and the social sciences to address women's lives and issues as legitimate subject matter. This article addresses domestic violence and its policing in rural eastern Kentucky as integral components of the structure and practices of patriarchy.

STATEMENT OF PROPOSITIONS: LAYING THE GROUNDWORK FOR A THEORY OF DOMESTIC VIOLENCE AND ITS POLICING IN RURAL AREAS

The intense isolation experienced by many rural women results from a variety of factors. This isolation increases their vulnerability to intra-familial violence. I identify three forms of isolation that differentially influence rural domestic violence and policing: physical, socio-cultural, and institutional.

Proposition One: Physical Isolation. The physical isolation of the rural milieu provides opportunities for batterers to engage in particular forms of abusive behavior. Similar control strategies would either be more visible or less effective in urban areas. This isolation also makes it difficult for battered women to leave or otherwise resist violent men.

Proposition Two: Socio-Cultural Isolation. Rural family life, gender roles, and patriarchal ideology generate acute forms of socio-cultural isolation that render rural women particularly vulnerable to domestic violence and passive policing.

Proposition Three: Isolation from Potentially Supportive Institutions. Rural battered women experience acute difficulties in using the limited but potentially supportive services of the state. These acute difficulties and limited state provisions tend to reproduce, in a complex and often contradictory fashion, the power relations of rural patriarchy.

THE UTILITY OF THE KENTUCKY CASE STUDY: MOVING FROM PROPOSITIONS TO THEORY

The research literature on rural crime is both inadequate and undertheorized. Bachman (1992), using data from the National Crime Victimization Survey (NCVS) covering the period from 1973 to 1990, usefully points out that the crimes of rape, robbery, aggravated assault, and simple assault are far less prevalent in rural areas. She also notes that in rural areas, the NCVS data suggest that violent crime is more likely to be perpetrated by offenders known to the victim. This information is helpful insofar as it directs attention to "known offender" violence in rural areas. However, much remains to be done on known-offender violence within rural families. As noted, my ethnography moves in this direction.

METHODOLOGICAL APPROACH

Cultural anthropologists use the term ethnography to refer to a method employed to describe an unfamiliar culture. The researcher often immerses him or herself in that unfamiliar culture through participant observation. In this way the researcher can study a different way of life, in part by living out or at least closely observing daily life. The proximity of the researcher to the minutiae of cultural life ideally enhances the level of understanding the researcher acquires. Though there are many problems with ethnographic research, the details need not concern us here (see Reinharz, 1992: 65–75). . . .

The core of my ethnographic research in eastern Kentucky consists of 50 focused interviews. I conducted interviews while living in a small town in the Appalachian hills. In addition to the interviews, I rode with police officers and observed them as they dealt with a small number of domestic altercations. Likewise, I became familiar with the leaders and organizers of the Kentucky Domestic Violence Association. This organization also employed me in my capacity as a sociologist to evaluate a federally funded program that was being conducted in half the shelters in Kentucky. I also spent time observing domestic cases in the local courts. Finally, I worked closely with several people who ran groups for men who battered their partners. . . .

RURAL VOICES AND THEORETICAL THEMES

Below I develop a number of theoretical themes from the propositions. I employ the ethnographic material and other sources to clarify and highlight these themes.

Theme One: Physical Isolation

The physical isolation of the rural milieu provides opportunities for batterers to engage in particular forms of abusive behavior. Similar control strategies would either be more visible or less effective in urban areas. This isolation also makes it difficult for battered women to leave or otherwise resist violent men.

Geographical Isolation   The most consistent factor in women's description of their lives was isolation. Even if battered women lived in small towns and worked outside the home, they still reported great isolation and loneliness. It is important to bear in mind that the geographical isolation experienced by battered women may stem from the batterer's calculated decision to reside in the country. In other words, the isolation may be a product of abuse, as well as a physical setting conducive to abuse.

Abusers' tactics fed off this isolation and were all the more effective because of it. Physical isolation provides space for batterers' strategies and also limits women's resistance. The batterers' strategies, according to the women, included removing the phone receiver (for example, when leaving for work) so that she could not contact the outside world by phone; locking the thermostat, especially in winter, as a form of torture; disabling motor vehicles to reduce or eliminate the possibility of her leaving the residence; destroying motor vehicles; closely monitoring the odometer reading on motor vehicles (a simple yet effective form of control due to the lack of alternate means of transportation); driving recklessly to intimidate his partner; discharging firearms in public (for example, at a battered woman's pet) in an intimidating manner to scare or otherwise distress her. Simply put, batterers can get away with different control tactics in rural areas, primarily because of the isolation. These tactics might still be used in urban areas, but they would either have less impact or be more visible.

If rural battered women are more isolated and depend more upon the batterer, they may be more vulnerable to extreme battery. Kalmuss and Strauss (1982) used national survey data to argue that the more dependent a battered woman is on her batterer, the more likely she is to endure more extreme violence.

In my interviews, battered women reported how difficult it was to leave an abusive home that is located several miles from the nearest paved road. Though it may be possible for her to walk to the paved road, attempting to take her children along makes the task much more difficult. If we add to this the fact that there is no public transport that services the paved road, the act of leaving the violent home in an isolated rural area becomes more difficult than leaving a similar abode in an urban setting. The extended length of time it might take a rural battered woman to leave her abuser makes the danger she is exposed to correspondingly greater. The act of leaving is a form of resistance that can evoke extreme violence on the part of abusers. Many of the murders of women by their violent partners take place during or shortly after leaving them. There are numerous other geographical considerations in

rural areas that vary by region of the country. For example, weather conditions may influence the way battered women strategize against their abusive partners and negotiate geographical isolation.

Living in a rural area, Barbara relied heavily on her vehicle to transport her children to school and herself to work. One night her abusive ex-husband set her car on fire and destroyed it.

> **BARBARA:** He did not want me to have a car. That way I would have to stay home. I would have no choice. And he knew I would have no choice.

June lived in a very remote rural area and had no vehicle. The victim of extreme physical abuse, including a shooting, she reported that she would have filed charges against her abusive husband if she had had a vehicle to get to the courthouse.

> **N.W.:** Did you ever bring charges against him?
>
> **JUNE:** I never had no way to get over to do nothin'. I never had no vehicle.

Communication Difficulties Since telephone subscription rates are significantly lower in rural communities, it is likely to be more difficult for battered women to call the police when an act of violence is committed against them. In urban counties in Kentucky, subscription rates run as high as 98%. In the counties in the case study, roughly two to three households in 10 did not have a phone. Similarly, if a neighbor's house is far away, then calling police from the neighbor's residence will be more problematic.

Since batterers employ tactics that compound isolation (including disabling cars, checking the odometer, and forbidding women to drive), the chances of reaching a phone by driving may also be reduced. Of the 25 battered women I interviewed, three did not have telephones at their residence and another three were prevented from using the phone by the batterer. In other words, 76% had phones they could use to call the police.

June did not have a phone at her Mule County house. After incidents of abuse she walked to a telephone box and called her mother, who lived in Rhino County. Her mother then called the Mule County sheriff's department. This happened on at least six occasions. This delay in calling the police meant that officers attended the scene much later, often when the assaultive behavior was over. This tardiness influenced the officers' perception of the seriousness of the calls. According to June, the officers' typical response in this situation was, "If there isn't anything goin' on now, there isn't anything we can do."

We know little about the relationship between rural women seeking the services of spouse-abuse shelters and telephone access. Rural residences without phones may be the reservoirs of an alarming amount of domestic violence that never sees the light of day.

Rural Isolation and Police Response Time
In many cases of rural domestic violence, the distance separating responding police officers from incidents is considerable. Even assuming that the officers are trained, willing, and able to travel to the scene immediately, this distance will mean that it will take longer for a police officer to attend. In her study of Raven Ridge, Gagne (1992: 410) provides a limited amount of ethnographic evidence showing that the response time of police to domestics was at least an hour. When they did arrive, officers sat in their cars and beeped their horns rather than approach the house. The reported reason for the reticence of officers was their perception that many officers had been shot during domestics. As Gagne points out, more officers are accidentally shot by other officers than they are by the participants in a domestic disturbance.

Tardy police responses may compound the sense of desperation and isolation that rural battered women feel. Saltiel et al. (1992), focusing on fear of vandalism, theft,

and burglary in rural areas, note that it may be the general presence of police in rural public space, rather than their response time to specific incidents, that allays fears of victimization. My ethnographic research suggests that the general presence of police in rural areas will do little to allay battered women's fears of violence in the private sphere. Long response times may also increase a battered woman's sense of disillusionment with the police and make it less likely that she will call them in the future. The longer response time may also add to the number of injuries and fatalities from domestic violence.

Individual state troopers in eastern Kentucky often patrol several counties on their shift. This makes it very difficult for the trooper to reach the scene of domestic violence in much less than 30 minutes. On many occasions, the response time is much greater. Sheriffs have acquired a very poor reputation among battered women in the region for not attending domestic calls at all. Of the 25 women interviewed, 18 expressed varying degrees of dissatisfaction with the police. In most of these cases, the tardiness of the police was commonly seen as problematic. Only three women were satisfied with the police response in their cases.

On the surface, the Kentucky State police are the best trained to deal with domestics. They display a greater awareness of the liability issues, a firmer grasp of how to deal with Emergency Protective Orders, and are more alive to the dangers of false arrest. This awareness probably derives from their training and the fact that they see their jobs more as careers than do sheriffs and their deputies. Nevertheless, because of the wide area they patrol, the state police often attend a very different situation than that attended by the municipal police in Lovelace. State trooper Davis talked of the difficulties associated with responding to domestic calls in rural regions.

DAVIS: You're on one end of the county [Dolphin] and there's no road like this [wide, well surfaced] . . . and . . . you're called to the opposite end of Rhino County.

A domestic in progress. As hard as you can run, lights and siren, you're looking at best of 40 minutes. That's hard runnin', that's 100 plus most of the way.

In Lovelace, the municipal police appeared to respond to domestic calls within a minute or two, especially if an assault was in progress. This was the view of Chief Jones, his officers that I interviewed, and the women who ran the local spouse-abuse shelter. In small towns in rural regions where municipal police are committed to attending domestics quickly, the response time may be significantly less than it is in urban areas. However, in most rural regions in the study, battered women identified a number of other factors that affected police response to domestics. These other factors, discussed below, militated against a fast response by police agencies and especially undermined the potentially fast response of municipal police.

Theoretical Theme Two: Socio-Cultural Isolation

Rural family life, gender roles, and patriarchal ideology generate acute forms of socio-cultural isolation, which render rural women particularly vulnerable to domestic violence and passive policing.

Marriage and the Family in Rural Areas   For feminists, marriage and family life lie at the heart of the subordination of women. Marriage rates are higher among rural women than urban women (Bushy, 1993: 188). In rural areas there is a much more traditional division of labor between men and women (Fassinger and Schwarzweller, 1984; Gagne, 1992). Men are seen as providers and women have an intense and highly privatized relationship with domestic production. As both Gagne (1992: 395–398) and Bushy (1993: 191) note, rural women seem to be more strongly associated with domestic activities such as child rearing and housework.

Given the often longstanding social relationships between people in rural areas, informal social controls can strongly influence social life. These informal controls may work to pressure battered women not to report domestic violence, since such disclosure might affect the standing of the family in the community and adversely affect business or trade.

Another informal cultural control mechanism is the proximity of extended family, especially if it is the abuser's family and is hostile to the interests of the battered woman. If the victim lives with or near the family she was born into, her parents or other family members may act against her abusive partner.

Roxy was forced into what her abusive husband saw at the appropriate place for a wife. She gave up work at his insistence, after he had eventually found a job. She found that her new economic dependence, combined with her rural isolation, intensified her fears. Her husband bought a gun and used it to intimidate her.

> **ROXY:** He kept tellin' me, when he first bought his gun: "I bought this just for you." . . . It just got worse, because when he saw that I really had to depend on him for everything, he was a complete ass.

The proximity of the abuser's extended family can compound the sense of isolation and work against the interests of battered women in rural areas. Virginia's resistance was limited by the proximity of her abuser's large and influential extended family, which wanted to keep Virginia's and her partner's children in the extended family circle.

> **VIRGINIA:** In order for him to keep his kids, they would do anything they had to. A lot of people would tell me one thing like leave him, you know you don't deserve that, and a lot of them wouldn't open their mouth because there's too much of his blood in the county.

Employment Though rural women have traditionally been limited to the private sphere of domestic production, many have moved into the public sphere of wage labor. When this has happened, rural women have earned roughly 50% of the wage made by rural men. This compares unfavorably with urban women, who have earned roughly two-thirds of the urban male wage (Bushy, 1993: 189). The limited earning potential of rural women negatively affects their ability to leave violent partners. Bushy suggests that rural women, more than urban women, may experience greater conflict with their partners over seeking employment outside the home. This fits with rural patriarchal ideology, which emphasizes women's place in the home.

According to Stewart and Payne (1991), of all persons employed in Kentucky in 1990, over 48% were women (820,713 out of 1,704,731). As in the United States in general, Kentucky women are clustered in certain occupations that tend to pay poorly. For example, in 1990, 42.7% worked in the service sector and 23.4% in wholesale/retail. The most significant predictor of income in Kentucky is gender. In 1989, 76.5% of Kentucky women had incomes of less than $15,000. Among Kentucky men, 51.3% had incomes greater than $15,000. Perhaps the most striking income disparities between men and women in Kentucky emerge when years of schooling are controlled for. With the same number of years of schooling, Kentucky men still earn between $8,000 and $10,000 per annum more than women. These disparities hold true at the lowest levels of schooling. For example, with eight or fewer years of schooling, the difference between men and women in Kentucky is still around $10,000. This stands in marked contrast to national figures, which indicate that at lower levels of schooling, gender disparities approximate to $5,000 per annum (U.S. Bureau of Census, 1991, cited by Macionis, 1993: 453). Women in Kentucky, with fewer years of schooling, are particularly hard hit by low wages. This fact is especially significant, since many of the battered women I interviewed received few years of schooling and experienced abject poverty.

Patriarchal Ideology and the Attitudes of Rural Police Officers It is more likely that rural police officers, particularly those who were raised in the rural cultural milieu, will view the family as a private and insular patriarchal unit (see also Gagne, 1992: 410–411). This may mean that police in those areas are less willing to intervene in domestics and less inclined to arrest husbands, who they feel should be in a dominant position in the family. Ronnie, an officer with the Lovelace municipal police, put it as follows: "In one sense I feel that at times we are sticking our nose where it doesn't belong."

The shared understandings, common interests, collusion, and outright misogyny of officers and batterers significantly affect the outcome of police intervention. The attitudes of rural police officers toward battered women and the battering situation as a whole tend to mirror wider rural patriarchal constructions about the social position of women. According to Sally, local police failed miserably to take domestic violence seriously.

N.W.: So the police . . . took him down to the station and let him go?

SALLY: He beat me home you know. We lived about 11 miles out of town (Saleville).

N.S.: How did you feel about that?

SALLY: Awful. . . . Well, in Saleville it's very poor, I can tell you that right now. It's bad today. My daughter has been abused, she's been slapped and her husband got a gun out right in the city limits and shot it. City police came. Didn't do a thing. . . . You might as well not call 'em. It's like the sheriff told me. He said I can take 'em upstairs and book 'em and they can beat me back down.

Many cases revealed ways in which some police tend to take the batterer's side, share the batterer's understandings of the situation, or have similar interests in asserting a man's right to control his wife. It is possible that when police fail to take these situations seriously, we are also witnessing misogyny.

A good illustration of what I mean by common interests among men emerged in a conversation with Chuck, a Lovelace patrol officer. He felt that under certain conditions a "good man" might assault a woman.

> **CHUCK:** It's a frustrating situation. . . . There's times that . . . I have to . . . arrest a gentleman . . . and actually the woman really deserved it. . . . [S]he does stuff that would actually cause a good man to slap a woman.
>
> **N.W.:** Give me some ideas.
>
> **CHUCK:** Like a woman's cheatin' on her husband. And he catches her at it.

Police officers varied considerably in their attitudes toward domestic calls. Many felt frustrated because in most cases the victim did not file a criminal complaint against her abuser. Few officers expressed either an awareness or a concern over the social and economic difficulties faced by battered women, that among other things, worked against her filing criminal charges. According to police, if battered women remained with their batterers, it was because they had chosen to.

Officer Davis viewed many victims of domestic violence as being manipulative and rather undeserving of police support. His outlook betrayed more than a hint of misogyny.

> **DAVIS:** A lot of them were fabricated. . . . [T]hat man has taken all that he can take. . . . [T]hat's the way he lashes out . . . and boom. Call the State Police. I want his ass out of here. And I just don't really see that's right. . . . It's bullshit is what it is.
>
> **N.W.:** As a rough guess, what would you say the percentage of bullshit ones is to legit ones?
>
> **DAVIS:** Probably 70–30.

Kindra reported that one state trooper who attended a domestic call at her residence was hostile to her.

> **KINDRA:** I told them [state police] that I was leaving my husband, he was violent and that he's destroyed my trailer three times this week. But this one cop [state trooper] came in and he was real cocky and smart and he just walked into every room. He even walked in my kitchen and looked at what I had for dinner. . . . But they do this stuff. They try to make you look bad. . . . [T]hen I started to get my stuff together. . . . I came out with the one suitcase. And I had a laundry basket upstairs with clothes. And he told me: "You're gonna have to carry light." I said: "Well, I have to have her [Kindra's daughter] school clothes. I have to have my clothes." And he said: "Well, you can always come back and get the rest of your stuff."

This last comment told Kindra that the officer was not listening when she told him earlier that she would not return to the site of the abuse. She said he told her: "Well, I'm not a U-Haul service. . . . I don't have time for this."

Chief Jones of the Lovelace Police was active in a local campaign against domestic violence. He also sits on the Board of Directors of a local spouse-abuse shelter. In addition, Jones is active at the state level on the Attorney General's Task Force on Domestic Violence. As a chief, he is both strong and dictatorial. Internal discipline at the Lovelace Police Department is tight. Jones' influence over the policing of domestics may not have been possible in a larger department, where it might be easier for middle managers to subvert the directives of the chief. In a small town, it is easier for the chief to know if things are not being done the way he or she wants them done. Most battered women I interviewed found the response time of most other municipal police agencies to be problematic. The faster response times of the Lovelace Department were unusual, but nevertheless serve to remind us that if local police are, for whatever reasons, committed to confronting domestic violence, then the small town in rural areas may be capable of producing swift and consistent responses to family violence.

Theme Three: Isolation from Potentially Supportive Institutions

Rural battered women experience acute difficulties in using the supportive services of the state, however limited they may be. These acute difficulties and limited state provisions tend to reproduce, in a complex and often contradictory fashion, the power relations of rural patriarchy.

Institutional provisions in rural areas have mixed and contradictory effects. The ethnographic findings do not suggest that all institutional support neatly reproduces the structure of patriarchy. Neither does the ethnographic evidence suggest a monolithic role of the state *vis-à-vis* domestic violence. A monolithic interpretation of institutional provision denies the historical and cultural complexity of the relationship between the state and gender relations in rural regions. It also minimizes the complex intersection of classism, racism, and sexism. Put simply, state institutions do make provisions that respondents report as being beneficial in their lives. I therefore reject interpretations of the state that argue that institutional provisions are either "band aid" sources of legitimation or ameliorative measures that make little or no real difference to battered women. However, it must also be said that battered women in rural areas experience unique difficulties in accessing the potentially helpful services of the state. It is to these difficulties that I now turn.

Lack of Privacy   Many respondents pointed to a lack of privacy in rural life in general. Interviewees knew personnel who worked in schools, welfare agencies, churches, county politics, and the criminal justice system. On many occasions this lack of privacy worked against battered women pursuing various forms of assistance (see also Davenport and Davenport, 1979; Navin, Stockum, and Campbell–Ruggaard, 1993; and Bushy, 1993).

Lack of Childcare Services   In Kentucky, there are fewer regulated daycare facilities than in any other state. Consequently, even if battered women do leave their abusers and have the chance to engage in wage work, the lack of adequate daycare facilities will seriously limit their ability to take those jobs. Without the financial contribution of the male wage, women's prospects of surviving independently are bleak in any economy that underpays them and makes little provision for childcare. Rural battered women's "choices" often boil down to remaining with abusers and enduring or resisting violence, leaving the abuser and entering wage work in a hostile gendered capitalist economy. If women elect the latter "option," they must give up, often for the first time, their everyday job of parenting their children. For some respondents, this possibility pushed them more toward the welfare "option."

Inadequate Health Services   Health services are particularly scarce in rural Kentucky. People often must travel long distances to see a physician. This is especially the case with women's reproductive health. The most recent figures on abortion rates in Kentucky show that 10.4 abortions were performed per 1,000 women in 1987, compared to 26.7 per 1,000 nationally. Part of this disparity reflects the acute difficulties Kentucky women face in gaining access to abortion services. Battered women's limited access to health services may seriously affect their post-battering experiences. Many shelter workers in Kentucky complained of the unwillingness of doctors to intervene or to report cases of spousal abuse (as they are required to do by law). Likewise, doctors appear to be unfamiliar with the dynamics of domestic violence. Part of this may be related to the rural milieu, where physicians feel that domestic violence belongs within families, rather than out in the open. However, the problem of doctors failing to report family violence is not limited to rural areas (see Council on Scientific Affairs, 1992; and Council on Ethical and Judicial Affairs, American Medical Association, 1992).

Inadequate Schooling We must also note that rural women receive less schooling than their urban counterparts. Rural patriarchal values posit women as being less in need of schooling and more in need of a husband and children. This lack of schooling has important implications for battered women, who, without academic qualifications, have a much harder time surviving independently of the financial support of violent partners.

The Church and Patriarchal Ideology Several authors have noted the role of the church and fundamentalist religion as disseminators of patriarchal ideology (see Kuczynski, 1981; Whipple, 1987; Navin et al., 1993). Religious influences seem to be stronger in rural communities and are more likely to militate against battered women leaving violent men. These influences may include the power of religious ideology and local preachers who advise battered women to "weather the storm" with their abusers. The religious rationale behind discouraging women from leaving is often pitched in terms of maintaining the sanctity of the marital bond and also in terms of wives (not husbands) fulfilling their duty to stay in the marriage.

Interviewees reported the strong influence of religion in social and cultural life in Kentucky. Lovelace Police Chief Jones, who won a federal grant of $10,000 to work on rural domestic violence issues, used some of the money to print informative pamphlets. A key point he made in the pamphlet concerned the erroneousness of religious beliefs that argued that battered married women should remain with abusive men. These beliefs, as Jones noted, were prevalent especially in the more remote rural areas.

Likewise, some battered women reported the influence of religion on family values. Kindra described her mother-in-law as being strongly influenced by religion and the family as a whole as believing that marriages should last forever, whatever the problems. According to Kindra, "it has a lot to do with the religious beliefs of their mom."

Institutional Politics and the Absence of Women One possible reason for the death of social services for women in Kentucky may be the under-representation of women in the state legislature. Some leaders of the KDVA commented that the interests of battered women would be better served if more women were legislators. In 1992, Kentucky ranked last among the states, with only six women out of 138 legislators (five in the House and only one in the State Senate). Across the United States, nearly one-fifth of all legislators are women. In the U.S. Congress in 1992, the number of women Senators rose from three to six, while women Representatives in the House rose from 28 to 47. In Kentucky, the proportion of female legislators actually decreased in 1992, from nine to six.

It is not my suggestion that more female representatives will solve the problem of rural domestic violence. Neither do I wish to imply that the polity can undo the structure of patriarchy. Nevertheless, shelter directors and KDVA leaders argue strongly that more women representatives would at least sensitize the polity to women's issues.

Patronage Politics and Compromised Policing In those rural areas where sheriffs, county attorneys, and judges are elected, the enforcement of domestic violence laws may depend, in part, upon the political connections of the batterer and the battered woman. Unlike in urban areas, county law enforcement officials in rural regions often have personal relationships with the electorate who voted them into office.

My ethnographic data suggest that these local allegiances influence the way in which officials respond to domestic altercations. As elected officials, sheriffs perform a variety of administrative duties besides law enforcement. The role of the sheriff in policing varies considerably. In Dolphin County, for example, the sheriff seemed to be minimally involved in law enforcement. This was especially true with domestics. A number of victims and spouse-abuse shelter employees reported that the Dolphin County sheriff's response to domestics amounted to no response at all. In neighboring Rhino County, the sheriff appeared to be much more involved in all aspects of law enforcement work. Both he and his deputies attended domestics.

Sheriff's deputies reported that they had secured their jobs because they knew the sheriff. Most deputies did other work to supplement their pay. Neither sheriffs nor their deputies need have had any law enforcement experience. Rather, there is a network of men in the counties with the political connections necessary to qualify as deputies. This appointment system is reminiscent of the old patronage style of policing, whereby ward bosses gave out jobs to police officers in return for future favors, or as a reward for past favors.

Attorney Carr commented that the nature of the sheriff's response sometimes depended on the numbers of potential voters the victim or the batterer could influence.

> **CARR:** I think . . . it goes back to the political systems in these small counties. . . . They look at who has the biggest family and they kind of judge it on that. If the man is from out of town, I think she might get more help if she's got a big family in that county.

In rural areas the police reported a very informal system of serving Emergency Protective Orders. Some sheriffs serve Emergency Protective Orders by telephoning abusers and asking them to come in to collect the summons. The procedure depends upon sheriffs and their deputies knowing a large number of the men that they police. According to most officers interviewed, the telephone method of serving papers works well and offenders appreciate the informality and implied trust. Apparently, in only a few cases did abusers abscond after being called. However, the possibility of suspected abusers disappearing after being called by the sheriff seems to be real. This possibility could expose victims to more violence. Undoubtedly, the telephone approach saves the sheriff time. If the abuser refuses to come to the sheriff's office, the sheriff can develop a plan of action. However, if the abuser agrees to come in, then the sheriff can be fairly certain that the abuser will be cooperative. The attendance of the abuser after a phone request for attendance may hail a certain solidarity between sheriff and abuser as to the rules of the game. A batterer might think that his offense is less serious because the sheriff telephoned him rather than sought him out to serve the summons. With "serious" crimes like burglary, theft, robbery, and drug dealing, the police usually do not telephone suspects and ask them to drop by the office. The failure to serve papers may also signal the sheriff's reluctance to serve papers on friends and acquaintances.

Rural Policing and Subterranean Economies
Research by Davis and Potter (1991) in the rural counties of Kentucky's Appalachian region reveals that bootlegging is conducted by small groups of people with intimate ties to local politicians and criminal justice personnel. This form of organized crime is not seen as deviant behavior by rural citizens. On the contrary, bootleggers provide a much needed commodity and Davis and Potter argue that bootlegging is viewed as "respectable business" (*Ibid.*: 155). This lucrative illegal operation is also linked to other illegalities, including gambling, prostitution, and the sale of drugs, illegal weapons, and stolen goods (*Ibid.*: 146). These researchers also point to a symbiotic relationship between bootleggers and local police. They note that in a recent trial of six eastern Kentucky law

enforcement officers (four sheriffs, a police chief, and a deputy sheriff), it was suggested that the officers, all from dry counties, had "protected marijuana and cocaine shipments . . . and facilitated the bootlegging business in their capacity as law enforcement officers" (*Ibid.*: 156). They also note that if a sheriff were to move against bootleggers, he would have a "very difficult time" getting reelected (*Ibid.* 156).

My ethnographic data suggest that if law enforcement personnel are involved in activities like bootlegging, they will be compromised around the enforcement of domestic violence laws. First, to enforce the domestic violence laws against a batterer who is either a consumer or supplier of illegal goods or services (liquor, gambling, prostitution, drugs, illegal weapons, and stolen property) might expose the corrupt officer, or the officer who turns a blind eye, to the wrath of the batterer, who might then be inclined to blow the whistle on the officer. Second, enforcing the law against someone involved in the popular activity of supplying illegal goods and services might greatly diminish a sheriff's chances of reelection.

State trooper Goople noted that sheriff's departments may not pursue batterers because of the close and potentially corrupt ties between batterers, their extended families, and sheriff's department personnel.

N.W.: I've heard from . . . battered women that sheriff's departments haven't responded because . . . they've been involved in other activities with the husbands.

GOOPLE: Well, I think there's probably some accuracy to it.

Ariel lived in a secluded part of Mule County. She was the only battered woman with a bachelor's degree that I interviewed. Ariel made numerous references to the corrupt activities of local criminal justice officials. She appeared to be well informed and her allegations of impropriety were consistent with the comments of other respondents.

N.W.: Any suspicion . . . that the Bleakville sheriff's department knew about illegal gambling and drinking?

ARIEL: They know about everything over there.

N.W.: Do you have any sense that the sheriff's department is connected with illegal activity?

ARIEL: Yeah. I've been there. You know, when they're there.

Janis said she felt that all the things she reported to state police would get back to her abuser. She alluded to the existence of a "mini-Mafia," but declined to elaborate.

JANIS: He (state trooper) was good buddies with the brother of my abuser. And that's the same way with the sheriff's department. That's the main reason why they didn't respond. They asked these people (abuser, his brother, and their friends) before they ever ran for sheriff, if they should. In other words, they was gettin' their okay to do this. The people that I was with are almost mini-Mafia. That's as far as I want to go on that. I don't want to dig myself a hole here.

CONCLUSION: RURAL VOICES, THEORETICAL THEMES, AND SOCIAL POLICY

. . . I can only enumerate a few of the policy implications that emerge from the theoretical themes and empirical information presented in this article. While acknowledging the need for deep-seated structural change, the following recommendations will also focus on the kinds of ameliorative policies suggested by the ethnographic data.

1. The structural conditions experienced by women in Kentucky must change before any change in violence against women will occur. Ultimately, the nature of gender relations must change.

2. Following from the above, to live independently of violent men, Kentucky women require more and better jobs. The Homeless Job Training Initiative (HJTI program, funded by the U.S. Department of Labor) seeks to train and place homeless battered women in jobs and help them move toward economic independence. At a minimum, this program should be greatly expanded to provide support for larger numbers of battered women in spouse-abuse shelters. This expansion should recognize the need not to merely feed women into the gendered capitalist labor market, but rather to change that market and make it more sensitive to the long-term needs of women.

3. If issues central to the lives of Kentucky women (childcare services, educational opportunities, housing, health care, and transportation services) are to come to the fore in the arena of institutional politics, more women representatives will be needed at national, state, and local levels.

4. Perhaps even more important is the paradoxical suggestion that some (organized) attempt be made to create networks of women in rural areas. These groups may come together to discuss any number of issues. Their "women only" make-up would be emblematic of their politicality. The purpose of such groups would be to break down the isolation that women experience in the rural setting. One way of doing this might be to increase the number of spouse-abuse shelters and to expand outreach programs from these shelters. Historically, such group networking has taken place to a limited degree through Homemaker Clubs, which organized meetings among farm women.

5. We might envisage a program of government assistance for increasing telephone subscription rates in rural regions. More telephone contact would reduce isolation, although this would not stop violent men from terminating phone services when it suited their needs.

6. More must be done to confront the problem of local police officers being compromised around the enforcement of arrest laws. This involves much more than sensitizing and training police officers and other criminal justice personnel as to how to handle domestics. Reducing unemployment and poverty may lessen the need to make money by illegal means and thereby reduce the need for an underground economy that local police connive in or turn a blind eye to. If these changes were combined with the legalization of alcohol, this connivance would be further reduced to the point that elected officers may be much less compromised in domestic altercations.

7. Following from point six, it is essential for much more networking to take place between shelters and other agencies, including police and social services. The shelter should be the focal point of this liaison network. The aim should be to educate area agencies and to better coordinate the provision of essential services such as the issuance of protective orders and the uncompromised execution of arrest laws.

In one rural shelter in Kentucky, staff have been authorized to fill out Emergency Protective Orders (EPOs) for battered women. This saves women from the need to get these orders from the local court. The orders, once served on the abuser by the local sheriff, provide women with (legal, not de facto) protection from their abuser, until the case is heard in court and a more permanent order is put in place by the district judge.

8. We need much more information on domestic violence and policing in rural areas. We must be sensitive to regional cultural differences and guard against essentializing the concept of rural patriarchy. Rural culture differs in Oregon, Kentucky, and upstate New York, and the idiosyncrasies of these cultural differences must be factored into the formulation of policy. This involves a thorough investigation of the regional intersection of class, race, and gender relations as historically enduring indices of social conflict.

Finally, domestic violence clearly cannot be explained in terms of economic class factors. While it may or may not be accurate to argue that domestic violence occurs more frequently in poorer families (the majority of police officers in the study made this point), it is difficult to use a class analysis to explain why men commit much more violence than the women they cohabit with in poverty. Consequently, economic changes that bring jobs to rural areas and reduce poverty may not directly reduce levels of domestic violence. My ethnographic findings suggest that economic change be implemented in tandem with changes in the field of gender relations.

REFERENCES

BACHMAN, RONET. 1992. "Crime in Nonmetropolitan America: A National Accounting of Trends, Incidence Rates, and Idiosyncratic Vulnerabilities." Rural Sociology 57,4: 546–560.

BUSHY, ANGELINE. 1993. "Rural Women: Lifestyle and Health Status." Rural Nursing 28,1: 187–197.

Council on Scientific Affairs, American Medical Association. 1992. "Violence Against Women: Relevance for Medical Practitioners." Journal of the American Medical Association 267,23 (June 17): 3184–3189.

Council on Ethical and Judicial Affairs, American Medical Association. 1992. "Physicians and Domestic Violence: Ethical Considerations." Journal of the American Medical Association 267,23 (June 17): 3190–3193.

DAVENPORT, J. AND J. DAVENPORT, III. 1979. "The Rural Rape Crisis Center: A Model." Human Services in the Rural Environment 6,3.

DAVIS, R.S. AND GARY W. POTTER. 1991. "Bootlegging and Rural Entrepreneurship." Journal of Crime and Justice 14,1: 145–159.

DOBASH, R. EMERSON AND RUSSELL DOBASH. 1992. Women, Violence, and Social Change. London and New York: Routledge. 1979. Violence Against Wives. New York: Free Press.

EDWARDS, SUSAN. 1989. Policing Domestic Violence: Women, the Law, and the State. Newbury Park, New Jersey: Sage.

FASSINGER, P.A. AND H.K. SCHWARZWELLER. 1984. "The Work of Farm Women: A Midwestern Study." H.K. Schwarzweller (ed.), Research in Rural Sociology and Development. Greenwich, Conn.: JAI: 37–60.

GAGNE, PATRICIA L. 1992. "Appalachian Women: Violence and Social Control." Journal of Contemporary Ethnography 20,4 (January): 387–415.

HANMER, JALNA AND SHEILA SAUNDERS. 1984. Well Founded Fear. London. Hutchinson.

HANMER, JALNA, JILL RADFORD, AND ELIZABETH STANKO. 1989. Women, Policing, and Male Violence: International Perspectives. New York: Routledge.

KALMUSS, D. AND M. STRAUSS. 1982. "Wife's Marital Dependency nd Wife Abuse." Journal of Marriage and Family 44: 277–286.

KUCZYNSKI, K. 1981. "New Tensions in Rural Families." Human Services in the Rural Environment 6,3: 54–56.

MACIONIS, JOHN J. 1993. Sociology. Englewood Cliffs, New Jersey: Prentice Hall.

NAVIN, SALLY, ROBERT STOCKUM, AND JULIE CAMPBELL–RUGGAARD. 1993. "Battered Women in Rural America." Journal of Humanistic Education and Development 32 (September): 9–16.

PAGELOW, MILLIE. 1981. Woman Battering. Newbury Park, Cal.: Sage.

PAHL, JAN (ed.). 1985. Private Violence and Public Policy. London: Routledge, Kegan, and Paul.

PIZZEY, ERIN. 1974. Scream Quietly or the Neighbors Will Hear. Harmondsworth: Penguin.

RADFORD, JILL AND DIANA RUSSELL (eds.). 1992. Femicide. New York: Twayne Publishers.

REINHARZ, SHULAMIT. 1992. Feminist Methods in Social Research. New York: Oxford University Press.

RUSSELL, DIANA. 1990. Rape in Marriage. Bloomington and Indianapolis: Indiana University Press.

SALTIEL, JOHN, JACK GILCHRIST, AND ROBERT HARVIE. 1992. "Concern About Crime Among Montana Farmers and Ranchers." Rural Sociology 57,4: 535–545.

SHERMAN, LAWRENCE. 1992a. Policing Domestic Violence: Experiments and Dilemmas. New York: Free Press.
1992b. "Reply to Binder and Meeker: Implications of a Failure to Read the Literature." American Sociological Review (October): 888–889.

SHERMAN, LAWRENCE W. AND R.A. BERK. 1984. "The Minneapolis Domestic Violence Experiment." Washington, D.C.: Police Foundation Reports.

STANKO, ELIZABETH. 1991. Everyday Violence. London: Pandora.
1989. "Missing the Mark? Police Battering." Hanmer et al. (eds.), Women, Policing, and Male Violence: International Perspectives. New York: Routledge: 46–69.

STEWART, HESTER R. AND JUDITH S. PAYNE. 1991. Women in Kentucky: A Documented Profile. Kentucky: Cabinet for Workforce Development.

TONG, ROSE MARIE. 1984. Women, Sex, and the Law. Totowa, New Jersey: Rowman and Allenheld.

WALBY, SYLVIA. 1990. Theorizing Patriarchy. Cambridge, Mass.: Basil Blackwell.

WHIPPLE, V. 1987. "Counseling Battered Women from Fundamentalist Churches." Journal of Marital and Family Therapy 13: 251–258.

WRIGHT, J.D., PETER ROSSI, AND KATHLEEN DALY. 1983. Under the Gun: Weapons, Crime, and Violence. New York. Aldine.

CRITICAL THINKING QUESTIONS

1. Why are rural law enforcement officers reluctant to intervene to help battered women who ask for their help?

2. How does discrimination that is institutionalized in the economy and education contribute to the abuse of women in rural areas?

3. Websdale says that the abuse of rural women is perpetuated by a "rural patriarchy." Explain what he means by that term.

4. What social policies would help reduce the abuse of women in rural areas? What keeps such policies from being implemented?

Reading 27

Out in This World: The Social and Legal Context of Gay and Lesbian Families

Katherine Arnup

In this article, Arnup looks at the legal difficulties gay and lesbian parents encounter when they seek custody or visitation rights with their children at the time of divorce or when they try to adopt.

On a recent car trip through Virginia, a small roadside sign caught my attention: "*You are leaving Henrico County*." Henrico County: the jurisdiction where Sharon Bottoms lost custody of her child; the jurisdiction where lesbian mothers still risk the automatic loss of their children. I looked over at my 13-year-old daughter, fast asleep in the passenger's seat, and thought once again about the fragility of our lives.

Lesbian and gay parents first came to public attention in the 1970s as lesbian mothers began to fight for custody of their children conceived within heterosexual relationships. Until then, few outside of the "homosexual" community knew of the existence of lesbian and gay parents. In just over two decades, that situation has changed dramatically. Widely cited figures suggest that 10% of women are lesbians and that between 20 and 30% of lesbians are mothers (Herman, 1988: 12). In addition, untold numbers of gay men have become parents in heterosexual relationships prior to "coming out," as well as through adoption and fostering and a variety of co-parenting arrangements (Miller, 1979). A recent study estimated that there are "between three and eight million gay and lesbian parents in the United States, raising between six

Source: © 1999, Binghamton, NY: The Haworth Press, Inc. *Journal of Gay & Lesbian Social Services*, Vol. 10, No, 1, 1–25.

and 14 million children" (Martin, 1993). While no figures are available for Canada, we can assume that, proportionately, the number of lesbian and gay parents is equally high.

Perhaps as a result of the recent media trend of "gay marketing" and "lesbian chic," many people assume that discriminatory treatment of lesbian and gay parents is a relic of the past. In fact, lesbian and gay parents continue to face homophobia in courts, classrooms, and communities across North America. In many jurisdictions, homosexuality is still considered a "crime against nature," and a revelation of homosexual activities can lead to criminal charges and imprisonment (*Bowers v. Hardwick*, 1986). Even in jurisdictions where same-sex sexual activities are no longer criminalized, lesbians' and gay men's relationships with each other[1] and with their children remain largely outside of the law. While a limited number of jurisdictions have adopted policies and laws sanctioning lesbian and gay adoptions, many others have affirmed their opposition to *any* form of parental relationship for lesbians and gay men.

A recent custody case in Richmond, Virginia serves as a startling reminder of the fact that the issue of child custody for lesbian and gay parents is far from resolved. In September 1993, Henrico County Juvenile and Domestic Relations Court Judge Buford M. Parsons, Jr. awarded custody of Tyler Doustou to his maternal grandmother, removing the two-year-old child from the care of his biological mother and her lesbian partner. The judge's ruling was based solely on the fact that the child's mother is a lesbian. The decision is particularly significant in light of the overwhelming judicial preference for awarding custody to a natural or legally recognized parent over the claims of third parties.[2] In his judgement, Parsons relied on *Roe v. Roe,* a 1985 Virginia Supreme Court case that found homosexual parents to be unfit parents with no custodial rights to their children (*Roe v. Roe,* 1985).[3] In that case, the court found that living with a lesbian or gay parent placed "an intolerable burden" on a child. Although Bottoms, the mother in *Roe v. Roe,* was successful in her initial appeal of the decision (Wartick, 1993), that ruling was overturned by the Virginia Supreme Court, which determined that the appeals court had not given enough attention to the facts of the case (*Bottoms v. Bottoms,* 1995). A bid to appeal that ruling was unsuccessful and Tyler remains in the custody of his grandmother. Sharon Bottoms' recent efforts to expand visitation with Tyler were also thwarted, as the judge instead tightened visitation, changing weekly visits to every other weekend, and forbidding Bottoms' partner from having any contact with the child (GLPCI Network, 1996).

An equally dramatic decision was reached in a Pensacola, Florida contest between a lesbian mother and her former husband, a convicted murderer. In August, 1995, Judge Joseph Tarbuck granted custody of an 11-year-old girl to her father, John Ward, a man who murdered his first wife, apparently in the midst of a bitter custody dispute. In removing the girl from her mother's home where she had been living since her parents' separation in 1987, Judge Tarbuck declared that it was important to give the girl a chance to live in "a non-lesbian world" (*Ottawa Citizen,* February 3, 1996, A2). Apparently, in the eyes of the court, a murderer was preferable to a "sex deviant." The decision was upheld on appeal.[4]

This article explores the changing legal treatment of lesbian and gay parents in the United States and Canada during the past two decades. Through an examination of recent American and Canadian child custody, access, and adoption cases in which sexual orientation has been a factor, I will document the homophobic laws and policies which still face lesbian and gay families, as well as the important legal and political victories that we have achieved. I will argue that, despite these victories, opposition to our families remains strong, within both formal political parties and the Christian Right. As well, strategic and philosophical divisions within the lesbian and gay movements, witnessed during the 1994 debate over Bill 167 [legislation which would have conferred a range of benefits and responsibilities on same-sex couples] in Ontario, and the debates over the Defense of Marriage Act (1996) in the United States, threaten to undermine the solidarity so essential to our success. As I will argue throughout the paper, lesbians and gay men must work to resolve our differences as we continue to support our families and to mobilize for change.

Although both lesbians and gay men are affected by homophobic laws and policies, gender remains an important factor in determining the impact of family law on our lives. As Susan Boyd and I have argued, "In the realm of reproduction, women and men, regardless of their sexual orientation, are undeniably constituted differently. Indeed, for lesbians and gay men, these differences may be even more significant than for heterosexual men and women" (Arnup and Boyd, 1995). Lesbians can choose to conceive and give birth to children, sometimes with a little help from a friend or a sperm bank. In contrast, gay men cannot father a child without the intimate cooperation of a woman, in either a co-parenting or a surrogacy relationship. These fundamental biological differences mean that issues such as access to donor insemination and other reproductive technologies may be of primary concern to lesbians, while surrogacy, foster parenting, and adoption may be priorities for gay men seeking to become parents. Furthermore, because women tend to be the primary caregivers within heterosexual marriages, custody has been the paramount legal issue for lesbian mothers upon divorce, while access and visitation have been the main areas of contention for gay fathers. As I will argue in this article, these gender-based differences have, on occasion, led to political and legal conflicts between lesbians and gay men.

CUSTODY AND ACCESS

Prior to the 1970s, few lesbian mothers contested custody in court. Fearing public exposure and recognizing that they were almost assured of defeat at the hands of a decidedly homophobic legal system, many women relinquished custody, in exchange for "liberal" access to their children. On occasion, lesbian mothers were able to make private arrangements with former husbands, often concealing their sexual orientation in order to retain custody of the children. Such arrangements are still common today, although the numbers are impossible to determine, given the necessarily private nature of the agreements.

During the 1970s and 80s, with the support of the gay and lesbian movements and of feminist lawyers and friends, lesbians began to contest and, in a limited number of cases, win the custody of their children conceived within heterosexual marriages. In addition, increasing numbers of gay men attempted to secure reasonable access to and, in some instances, custody of their children. In their deliberations in these cases, judges have adopted a range of approaches. As author Robert Beargie (1988) notes: "At one end of the scale is the *per se* category in which a parent's homosexuality creates an unrebuttable presumption that the parent is unfit." Such an approach means that homosexuality in and of itself renders a parent unfit, regardless of any evidence to the contrary.

While in a number of American jurisdictions homosexuality *per se* remains a bar to custody and access, judges in Canada and in many American states have adopted the *nexus* approach; here, the court seeks to determine what effect, if any, the parent's sexual orientation will have on the well-being of the child

(Gross, 1986; Arnup, 1989). In a 1980 decision in the Ontario Court of Appeal, Mr. Justice Arnup explained:

In my view homosexuality, either as a tendency, a proclivity, or a practiced way of life is not in itself alone a ground for refusing custody to the parent with respect to whom such evidence is given. The question is and must always be what effect upon the welfare of the children that aspect of the parent's makeup and lifestyle has. (*Bezaire v. Bezaire*, 1980)

In the nexus approach, then, each case must be judged on the basis of its evidence; in order to deny custody or access to a homosexual parent, it must be demonstrated that the parent's sexual orientation will have a negative effect upon the child.

How can we resolve the apparent contradiction between the fact that, in most jurisdictions, homosexuality *per se* is no longer a barrier to custody and access (Rubenstein, 1993) and the fact that many judges continue to deny custody and access to lesbian and gay parents? The answer lies in large measure in the enormous amount of judicial discretion that is afforded to judges in family court matters. Under current family law provisions in Canada and the United States, the paramount standard applied in custody and access disputes is "the best interests of the child." No precise rule or formula exists, however, for determining *which* household or family arrangement operates in the child's best interests. Until recently in Canada, and still in many jurisdictions in the United States and elsewhere, parental fitness represented a key element of the "best interests" criteria. Judges relied on a variety of factors for determining the "fitness" of each parent, including past and present sexual conduct, the grounds for the termination of the marriage, the guilt or innocence of each party, and the "quality" of the home to assist them in determining the best custody arrangements for the children. These tests were used to brand virtually every lesbian and gay man who attempted to gain custody as an "unfit" parent.

With the passage of family law reform legislation in the 1980s, criteria for determining
custody were amended and, as a result,
parental behavior *in and of itself* could no
longer be considered a bar to custody. In Ontario, for example, the *Children's Law Reform Act*
(CLRA) specifies that the "best interests of the
child" shall be the determining factor. The legislation directs the judge to consider "all the
needs and circumstances of the child," including the relationship between the child and
those persons claiming custody, the preferences of the child, the current living situation
of the child, the plans put forward for the child,
the "permanence and stability of the family
unit with which it is proposed that the child will
live," and the blood or adoptive links between
the child and the applicant (CLRA, 1980). The
section explicitly states that "the past conduct
of a person is not relevant to a determination of
an application . . . unless the conduct is relevant to the ability of the person to act as a parent of a child" (CLRA, 1980).

While the revised legislation might appear
to improve a lesbian or gay parent's chances
for success, there are a number of ways these
provisions can be used to rule against their application for custody. First, a judge may refuse
to recognize a "homosexual" family as a permanent and stable family unit. Homosexuals
are not permitted to marry and therefore cannot meet this standard heterosexual measure
of "stability." In a 1981 North Dakota case, for
example, the judge noted that a significant
factor in denying custody to the mother was
the fact that her relationship with her partner
"never can be a legal relationship" (*Jacobson v.
Jacobson,* 1981). The "closeted" nature of many
gay and lesbian relationships (*Ewankiw v.
Ewankiw,* 1981) and the absence of any census
category to "capture" same-sex partnerships
(Arnup, 1995), also render it virtually impossible to offer statistical evidence of the longevity
of same-sex relationships. Given these obstacles, a lesbian or gay parent may well be unable
to demonstrate the "permanence and stability"
of their "family unit."

Political involvement in the lesbian and
gay movements may also be used to find that

a lesbian or gay parent is unable to provide a
"suitable" home. Coupled with a lack of "discretion" on the part of a lesbian or gay parent, political activity spells the death knell for
the custody application of a lesbian or gay
parent. *Case v. Case,* the first reported[5] Canadian case to deal specifically with the issue of
lesbian custody, exemplifies this result. In July
1974, Mr. Justice MacPherson of the Saskatchewan Queen's Bench granted custody of
the two children to their father. In considering the significance of the mother's lesbianism, the judge rejected the *per se* approach,
noting that "it seems to me that homosexuality on the part of a parent is a factor to be considered along with all the other evidence in
the case. It should not be considered a bar in
itself to a parent's right to custody" (*Case v.
Case,* 1974). That statement is contradicted by
the judge's discussion of the mother's
"lifestyle." Describing the father as a "stable
and secure and responsible person," the
judge added that, "I hesitate to put adjectives
on the personality of the mother but the evidence shows, I think, that her way of life is ir-
regular." In considering her role as Vice
President of the local gay club, he added, "I
greatly fear that if these children are raised by
the mother they will be too much in contact
with people of abnormal tastes and proclivities" (*Case v. Case,* 1974). Thus, while Mrs.
Case's lesbianism was not in itself a bar to custody, her lesbian "lifestyle" was. In similar
cases, judges have deemed activities like attending rallies and dances, exposing children
to other lesbians and gay men, and discussing
political issues openly in the home to be negative factors in considering the application of
lesbian mothers for custody of their children
(Arnup, 1989).

In marked contrast to the politically active
lesbian or gay parent stands the "good" homosexual parent, a person who is "discreet,"
and appears to the outside world to be a single
(read: heterosexual) parent. Discretion on
the part of a homosexual parent has repeatedly been cited as the rationale for awarding
custody to a lesbian or gay parent. In *K. v. K.,*
a 1975 Alberta custody dispute, the judge

drew a comparison between Mrs. K. and Mrs. Case (the mother in the preceding case):

> The situation before this court is, in my view, different. Mrs. K. is not a missionary about to convert heterosexuals to her present way of life. She does not regard herself as gay in the sense that heterosexuals are "morose" . . . Mrs. K. is a good mother and a warm, loving, concerned parent. (*K. v. K.*, 1975)

Having had the opportunity to examine both Mrs. K. and her lover, the judge concluded that "their relationship will be discreet and will not be flaunted to the children or to the community at large." On that basis, Mrs. K. was awarded custody of her child.

Discretion played an important role in a 1991 Saskatchewan case, in which custody of two children was awarded to their aunt, a woman who had been involved in a lesbian relationship for 12 years. In discussing the relationship between the two women the judge noted:

> I found these two women to be rather straightforward. Their relationship does not meet with the approval of all members of society in general. They were neither apologetic nor aggressive about their relationship. They are very discreet. They make no effort to recruit others to their way of living. They make no special effort to associate with others who pursue that lifestyle. In short, D. and H. mind their own business and go their own way in a discreet and dignified way. (*D.M. v. M.D.*, 1991)

On occasion, where it has been determined that homosexuality may negatively affect the children, judges have attempted to minimize its effects by preventing the lesbian or gay parent from engaging in an open, same-sex relationship. In a 1980 Ontario case, the trial judge ordered a lesbian mother to live alone. "I am attempting to improve the situation," he explained, "and this includes negativing any open, declared, and avowed lesbian, or homosexual relationship" (*Bezaire v. Bezaire*, 1980). When Mrs. B. failed to meet this condition, the original order, granting her custody of her two children, was quickly reversed.

Imposing such conditions is a common practice in cases involving a lesbian or gay parent. The practice is based on the assumption that a parent's homosexuality may negatively affect the child, but that those effects can be overcome if the parent meets certain conditions, such as not cohabiting or sharing a bedroom with a lover, and not showing affection of any kind in front of the child. On occasion, judges have ordered that visitation take place only in the absence of the same-sex partner. Paula Brantner explains the unfairness of these conditions: "Heterosexual parents are not routinely asked to forgo sexual relationships with other adults to obtain custody of their children—lesbian and gay parents are." The impact of these conditions on the lives of lesbian and gay parents is severe. Brantner notes: ". . . gay parents are forced to make impossible and intolerable decisions. Parents who fail to comply with the court's restrictions may lose their children. If they do comply, they may lose their partners or the ability to be openly gay and to maintain contact with other gay persons, which takes its own psychological toll" (Brantner, 1991).

The judicial effort to limit or terminate a lesbian or gay relationship is particularly disturbing in light of the research (albeit limited) which suggests that lesbian mothers' psychological health and well-being is associated with their ability to be open about their sexual orientation "with their employer, ex-husband, children, and friends, and with their degree of feminist activism" (Patterson, 1996). As well, living with a partner was, not surprisingly, correlated with both parental happiness and financial stability, factors which, presumably, would also contribute to the well-being of the children.

The contradiction between the rejection of the *per se* approach and the setting of punitive conditions is evident in dozens of cases involving lesbian and gay parents. As early as 1974, an Australian judge noted that "[t]he days are done when courts will disqualify a woman from the role of parent merely because she has engaged or is engaging in some form of extramarital sex, be it heterosexual or homosexual." Despite this statement, Judge Bright ordered the mother not to sleep in her lover's bedroom overnight or to let her lover sleep in her bedroom overnight. As well, the children were required to visit a psychiatrist at least once a year (*Campbell v. Campbell*, 1974).

A 1989 British Columbia decision provides particularly dramatic evidence of the endurance of these practices. Ian Jeffrey Saunders enjoyed regular access with his child for four years following the dissolution of his marriage until his ex-wife discovered that, in the words of Judge Wetmore, "the father had entered into a complete homosexual relationship with one E. L." Following this discovery, the mother refused to allow any overnight access. In the initial hearing on the case, the judge decided against the father, largely based on the fact that the men were living in a single room apartment. Shortly thereafter the men's relationship ended, and access resumed informally. Eventually, the two men reestablished their relationship, and moved into a two bedroom apartment. On the basis of the improved accommodation, the father applied once again for overnight and holiday access. His claim was rejected by Provincial Court Judge B. K. Davis, who chose to ignore the social worker's conclusion that "the two [men] would be as discreet as heterosexual couples when children are in the home." Saunders' appeal of that judgement was dismissed.

In his judgement dismissing the appeal, Judge Wetmore noted that "Saunders and Leblanc are unwilling to hide their relationship from the child, by LeBlanc being absent during overnight visits." "Surely it cannot be argued that the exposure of a child to unnatural relationships is in the best interests of that child of tender years," the appellate judge opined. Noting that he was charged with the responsibility of assessing "community standards as reflected by the thinking members of society," he concluded:

> I am not convinced, and neither was the Provincial Court Judge, that the exposure of a child of tender years to an unnatural relationship of a parent to any degree, is in the best interests of the development and natural attainment of maturity of that child. That is the issue, not the rights of homosexuals. (*Saunders v. Saunders*, 1989)

A 1987 Missouri decision had a strikingly similar result for a lesbian mother appealing the restricted access she had been granted. While the mother had initially been awarded custody of the four children, that order was reversed when the mother's lesbianism was presented in a new trial. The court noted that the town in which the family lived was a "small, conservative community . . . Homosexuality is not openly accepted or widespread. We wish to protect the children from peer pressure, teasing, and possible ostracizing they may encounter as a result of the 'alternative lifestyle' their mother has chosen." Regarding the mother, the judge noted:

> We are not presuming that Wife is an uncaring mother. The environment, however, that she would choose to rear her children in is unhealthy for their growth. She has chosen not to make her sexual preference private but invites acknowledgment and imposes her preference upon her children and her community. The purpose of restricting visitation is to prevent extreme exposure of the situation to the minor children. We are not forbidding Wife from being a homosexual, from having a lesbian relationship, or from attending gay activist or overt homosexual outings. We are restricting her from exposing these elements of her 'alternative lifestyle' to her minor children. (*S.E.G. v. R.A.G.*, 1987)

As the cases discussed above suggest, regardless of how "good" lesbian or gay parents may be, they cannot be "good enough" parents unless they are willing to abandon, or, at the very least, hide their same-sex relationship. As *Saunders* v. *Saunders* reveals, lesbian and gay parents must be willing to forego the possibility of a committed sexual relationship, at least while the children are present. Their children must be their first, and indeed their only priority, even if it means the demise of their committed homosexual relationship. As Judge MacKinnon noted in denying custody to a lesbian mother in a 1987 British Columbia case, in resuming cohabitation with her partner "without leave of the court," "she left no doubt as to the priority of her relationship with her companion. It was the paramount consideration. She wanted custody. It was, however, not at the sacrifice of the homosexual relationship" (*Elliott* v. *Elliott,* 1987).

The judicial approaches discussed previously present lesbian and gay parents seeking court-ordered custody with a number of difficult choices. If, for example, a woman presents herself in court as an "avowed lesbian," if she admits to coming out at work or at her children's school, she stands less chance of winning custody of her children, especially if she meets a determined challenge from her ex-husband. Within this legal context, most lesbians "choose" to act as "straight" as possible to win custody of their children. As Nancy Polikoff, mother, writer, lawyer, and long-time activist in the struggle for lesbian custody rights, notes:

> While no formula will guarantee victory in courtroom custody disputes involving lesbian mothers or gay fathers, one thing is clear: the more we appear to be part of the mainstream, with middle class values, middle-of-the-road political beliefs, repressed sexuality, and sex-role stereotyped behavior, the more likely we are to keep custody of our children. On the other hand, communal child-rearing arrangements, radical feminist activism, sexual experimentation—these choices are all predictably fatal to any custody action. The courtroom is no place in which to affirm our pride in our lesbian sexuality, or to advocate alternative child-rearing designed to produce strong, independent women. (Polikoff, 1986: 907)

Such strategies tell us far less about the belief systems of lesbian and gay parents than about the attitudes and prejudices of the courts.

It has been argued that gay men face much more judicial resistance to their parental relationships than lesbian mothers. Darryl Wishard (1989) claims that "more courts have granted lesbian mothers the right to custody of their children than have granted custody to homosexual fathers." A number of explanations have been offered, including the supposed judicial preference for maternal custody (Brophy, 1985; Boyd, 1989), assumptions about paedophilia, and fears of AIDS. Such a claim cannot be upheld, however, without much more quantitative evidence. It is arguable that the reason for this discrepancy lies in the fact that many gay men choose not to seek custody, either because they are afraid that their custodial bid will be unsuccessful, or perhaps more commonly, because they, like their heterosexual counterparts, do not wish to have primary care and custody of their children (Millbank, 1992).

Regardless of the validity of the claim that gay fathers suffer greater judicial discrimination than lesbian mothers, it is clear that, in the past ten years, the specter of AIDS (Acquired Immune Deficiency Syndrome) has been a deterrent to gay men's efforts to forge relationships with their children following separation and divorce. This would appear to be the case even when a father is not HIV positive, presumably because of the strong ideological connection between gay men and AIDS and the resulting presumption that gay fathers will inevitably expose their children to the virus. In judicial decisions, HIV-positive fathers have been ordered to refrain from kissing their children and to visit with their children only under supervision. A California court ordered a gay man to be tested for HIV before visitation was determined (Isbell, 1992). While in this respect at least gay fathers face an almost insurmountable burden of proof, I would argue that, despite the vast discrepancy in the rate of HIV infection between lesbians and gay men, the custodial claims of both gay men and lesbians are hampered by the "automatic" connection in the public (and judicial) mind between homosexuality and AIDS, as well as by the alleged (and false) connections between homosexuality and paedophilia (Weston, 1991).

THE LESBIAN "BABY BOOM"

While initially most homosexual parents who came to public attention were women who had conceived and given birth to children within heterosexual partnerships or marriages, in the past fifteen years, increasing numbers of lesbians have chosen to conceive and bear children, either on their own, or within a lesbian relationship. Since the late 1970s, an undetermined number of lesbians have requested artificial insemination services at infertility clinics and sperm banks across North America. Many of these requests were denied once the applicant's sexual orientation was revealed. In some instances women were informed that the clinic had decided not to inseminate any single woman, claiming that they feared single mothers would launch child support suits against the medical facility should the insemination be successful or that they would become embroiled in a legal contest should the lesbian couple's relationship subsequently dissolve (Arnup, 1994).

To date, no court decisions have been issued concerning infertility clinics which discriminate against single women or lesbians. In the only documented American case, a woman launched a legal action against Wayne State University when its medical centre rejected her application for artificial insemination. Fearing the repercussions of a protracted legal battle, the clinic abandoned its restrictive policy, granting her application before the case could be heard by the courts (*Smedes v. Wayne State University,* 1980). In Canada, a similar complaint was upheld by the British Colombia Council of Human Rights in August 1995. The complaint, alleging discrimination on the basis of sexual orientation and family status, was filed by Sandra Benson and Tracy Potter against Dr. Gerald Korn for his refusal to provide artificial insemination services to them solely on the grounds that they are lesbians. The women initially complained to the British Columbia College of Physicians and Surgeons who denied their claim (*Gazebo Connection,* September 1993). The B. C. Council of Human Rights awarded Benson and Potter $2500 as compensation for emotional injury and $896.44 for expenses. Although applicable only in British Columbia, the decision represents an important precedent in the struggle for the provision of donor insemination services for lesbians.

In light of access barriers to clinical services, it is not surprising that many lesbians prefer to make private insemination arrangements. Here, however, an important issue faced by lesbian mothers is the legal status of the sperm donor. While artificial insemination was initially treated by the courts as the legal equivalent to adultery against the woman's husband, gradually the courts have moved to a position that recognizes the child as the legitimate offspring of the recipient's husband, provided he has consented to the insemination procedure. The husband is thereby legally obligated to support the child. Most legislation now specifies that the parental rights and obligations of the donor are replaced by the paternal rights of the husband.

The issues are considerably more complex in the case of a lesbian or unmarried heterosexual woman and a known donor. To date, no Canadian cases have been reported, but in six of the seven reported American cases, sperm donors seeking paternity rights have had at least some of their claims upheld by the courts. The decisions have ranged from placing the sperm donor's name on the child's birth certificate to granting access rights (Arnup, 1994; Arnup and Boyd, 1995). Such decisions have been made *even* in cases where the insemination was performed by a licensed practitioner, thereby ignoring relevant legislation which extinguished the rights and obligations of donors. In a 1989 case, the Oregon Appeal Court concluded that, despite the statute, the donor had shown himself interested in performing the duties of a father and was therefore entitled to seek paternity rights similar to those of an unwed father.[6] In a similar Colorado case, the Colorado Supreme Court ruled in favor of the donor, crediting his claims of having bought toys, clothing, and books for the child, as well as establishing a trust fund in the child's name, as evidence of his desire to parent (Interest of R. C., 1989).

A lower court ruling in the sixth American case promised to reverse this trend. In an April 1993 proceeding before the Family Court of the City of New York, a sperm donor (Thomas

S.) sought a declaration of paternity over the objections of the child's biological mother (Robin Y.) and her partner, the child's co-mother. The donor, a gay man, had agreed initially that he would have no rights or obligations to the child and that he would recognize the women as the child's co-mothers. Having had no contact with the child for the first three and a half years of her life, he began seeing her only after contact was initiated by the women, in response to requests from their other daughter regarding her biological origins. Five years later the donor decided that he wished to see the child without her co-mothers and to introduce the child to his biological family, both actions that the parties had agreed (prior to the insemination) would not be taken. For reasons he did not specify, he did not feel "comfortable" introducing the child's mothers to his parents. When the women refused to comply with the request, he commenced an action for paternity and visitation.

At the lower court level, the judge denied the donor both paternity and visitation rights. Judge Kaufmann ruled that a declaration of paternity "at this late time in [the child's life] would not be in her best interests." In a stunning recognition of lesbian families, Judge Kaufmann declared that "in the family, there has been no father." Because the donor had agreed to respect that family and had made no effort to "father" the child in her early years, the judge denied his claim. That ruling was overturned on November 17, 1994 on appeal. At the Appellate Division of the Supreme Court of New York, in a 3 to 2 decision, the court ruled that Thomas S. was entitled to an order of filiation. The issue of visitation was remanded for a further hearing (*Thomas S. v. Robin Y.*, 1994). When the mothers declared their intention to appeal the decision, Steel declined to oppose the appeal, thereby leaving the result on the books. As Nancy Polikoff (1996) has noted, Steel's withdrawal from the appeal "leaves intact the appeals court decision vesting donors with full rights of parenthood."[7]

In the final American decision, the Oregon Court of Appeal upheld a lower court decision

which denied the sperm donor any paternal rights. In that case, the donor had signed an agreement waiving his paternal rights. When a dispute arose over visitation, the parties entered into mediation. After several sessions, they reaffirmed and resigned their original agreement (*Leckie v. Voorhies*, 1993). It was on that basis that the appeal court upheld the original decision.

While all of the cases to date have involved only the issues of access and a declaration of paternity, the implications extend far beyond those claims. A declaration of paternity can accord any or all of the following: sole or joint physical or legal custody, visitation, decision-making in such areas as education, religion, and health care, custody in the event of the mother's death, denial of permission to change residence or to adopt, obligation to provide child support, and inclusion of the donor's name as father on the child's birth certificate (NCLR, 1994). As the National Center for Lesbian Rights has noted: "in our system of law there are only two options. Either the donor is merely a donor, with no parental rights or relationship with the child whatsoever, or he is a father, with all of his parental rights intact. There are no gray areas in the law here, and, when in doubt, the courts tend to grant donors full parental rights in cases involving single mothers" (NCLR, 1994). Clearly, these cases have far-reaching implications for the lives of lesbian mothers and their children.

On this issue, perhaps more than on any other, the interests of lesbians and gay men may diverge. While the debate on the rights of sperm donors in Thomas S. did not take place exclusively along gender lines, gender *was* a key factor in the discussion.[8] Supporters of the lesbian mothers argued that Robin and Sandy alone, as the child's mothers and primary caregivers, ought to have the exclusive right to make decisions in their daughters' lives. On the other side, supporters of Thomas S. argued that, as the child's biological father, he should be entitled to legal protection of his parental relationship, regardless of the wishes of her mothers. In a position which has an alarming resonance with the arguments of fathers' rights advocates, Thomas S.'s attorneys maintained that biology, not daily care and control, should be the determining factor in conflicts between lesbian mothers and known donors. Indeed, Thomas' arguments on appeal amounted to a denial of Ry's lesbian family, as he referred to Robin Y. as an "unmarried woman" to whom he had "repeated 'access'" during the period of conception (*Thomas S. v. Robin Y.,* 1994). He argued further that public "policy favors the requirement that a child be provided with a father as well as a mother." Such arguments, perhaps even more than the litigation itself, raised considerable alarm within lesbian communities, causing many women to reconsider the merits of anonymous donors.

In a recent article, Fred Bernstein (1996) argues that "involved" sperm donors like Thomas S. should be entitled to legal protection of their relationship with their children. Attempting to steer a middle ground between the positions adopted by both Thomas S. and Robin Y., the author maintains that "relationships between donors and their biological children, when encouraged by the mothers, deserve legal recognition" (p. 52). Rather than extending full paternal rights to the "involved donor," such legal protection would merely preserve the donor-child visitation at the level which existed prior to the commencement of litigation. In the absence of such protection, Bernstein argues, gay men will be barred from one of the few avenues to parental relationships open to them. As well, lesbians, wary of the legal challenges made by known donors, will lose a potentially large pool of donors. While I remain somewhat skeptical of the practicality of Bernstein's solution, I believe that the lesbian and gay movements must begin to address these issues, which, in the absence of discussion, threaten to cause an enormous rift in our already embattled communities. I would argue that sperm donors must be able to "contract away" any legal rights and obligations over their prospective offspring. In the event that the re-lationships should change following the birth of the child, a new agreement, specifying the newly agreed-upon arrangements, could be drafted. Mechanisms through which these changes can be achieved—e.g., mediation, counseling, or the involvement of some other third party—should be specified in the original donor contract.

In marked contrast to sperm donors, the legal status of non-biological lesbian mothers has for the most part been denied by the courts in both the United States and Canada (Polikoff, 1990–91). Disregarding non-biological mothers' often substantial contributions to child care and financial support, courts have repeatedly *refused* to grant their claims for visitation rights upon dissolution of the lesbian relationship or custody rights upon the death of the biological mother. In a 1991 case involving two children conceived through artificial insemination, the California Court of Appeal refused to grant custodial or visitation rights to the non-biological mother, despite evidence of her substantial involvement in her children's lives. While recognizing that both women had agreed, before conception, that the non-biological mother would act as a parent of the children, the court determined that "expanding the definition of a 'parent' in the manner advocated by appellant could expose other natural parents to litigation brought by child care providers of long-standing, relatives, successive sets of step-parents or other close friends of the family" (*Nancy S. v. Michele G.,* 1991). Similar decisions have been made in a number of other American states.

In addition to denying custodial and visitation claims, courts have also resisted attempts to impose financial obligations upon non-biological mothers following dissolution of a lesbian relationship. In the only reported Canadian case dealing with this issue, the judge rejected a lesbian mother's application for support for herself and her children born during the course of her relationship with her former lesbian partner. The court sided with the non-biological mother who had vigorously maintained that she had no legal obligation to support either the biological mother or the children (*Anderson v. Luoma*, 1986). Indeed, even the judge appeared to be somewhat taken aback by the stance adopted by Luoma, the non-biological parent, noting that she downplayed "her involvement [with the children] almost to the point of being a disinterested bystander," claiming that her former partner had been on a "frolic of her own when she had the children." Despite his own view that Anderson, Luoma and the children had "worked and played as a 'family-like' unit," however, the judge was unable to stretch the opposite-sex definition of spouse to impose a financial obligation of support on Luoma. Thus, as Karen Andrews (1995) has argued: "*Anderson v. Luoma* stands for the unhappy proposition that a lesbian can behave as despicably as any man who evades his parenting and child support obligations and because she is outside the statutes, she can get away with it." In one of the few cases to contradict this trend, a New South Wales Supreme Court Judge ruled in February 1996 that a lesbian must pay her former lover a lump sum of $113,000 for support of the couple's two children. The women had cohabited between 1986 and 1994, and the children were born in 1989 and 1992. The judge ruled that "it is inconceivable for the defendant now to seek to make no contribution whatsoever to the upbringing of these children" (Parent Network, 1996). It is too early to determine whether this decision may reflect a shift in judicial decision-making in this area.

As more lesbian couples choose to become parents, courts will be faced increasingly with the issue of the rights and responsibilities of non-biological lesbian mothers. Many areas of children's (and parents') lives are affected, including medical authorization, visitation, support, and custody upon dissolution of the parental relationship, and guardianship in the event of the death of the biological mother. To date, in an effort to secure legal rights for the non-biological parent, lesbian parents have sought a variety of legal mechanisms including guardianship, joint custody, and second-parent adoption.

Second-parent adoption, the option used by step-parents in heterosexual relationships when they create a new parenting arrangement following the dissolution of the original marriage, allows the "new" parent to assume rights and responsibilities without requiring the original parent of that sex to forfeit his or her parenting status. Such an option has not been widely available to lesbian and gay parents.[9]

In May 1995, lesbian mothers in the province of Ontario won an important legal victory, when Judge Nevins granted second-parent adoptions to four lesbian couples (Re. K., 1995). In a far-reaching decision, Judge Nevins rejected all of the standard arguments used to deny parental rights to homosexuals, concluding that:

> When one reflects on the seemingly limitless parade of neglected, abandoned and abused children who appear before our courts in protection cases daily, all of whom have been in the care of heterosexual parents in a "traditional" family structure, the suggestion that it might not ever be in the best interests of these children to be raised by loving, caring and committed parents, who might happen to be lesbian or gay, is nothing short of ludicrous. (Re. K., 708)

Ontario thus joins the growing list of jurisdictions in which second-parent adoptions can be granted to lesbian and gay couples (Re. C.E.G., No. 1, 1995; Re. C.E.G., No. 2, 1995).

In all other jurisdictions, only one parent of each sex can have legal rights to a child. Thus, the birth mother must relinquish her rights to enable the non-biological mother to adopt the child. In granting a second-parent adoption, a New York State judge recently commented that requiring the biological mother to relinquish her rights "would be an absurd outcome which would nullify the advantage sought by the proposed adoption: the creation of a legal family unit identical to the actual family setup" (GLPCI Network, Summer 1994). An alternative in jurisdictions where second-parent adoption is not available is joint custody, a legal arrangement available to heterosexual parents upon dissolution of their relationship. This option is also being pursued by lesbian parents as a means to gain parental rights for non-biological mothers. Joint custody grants only a temporary status for the co-mother, however, and is still subject to challenges by biological relatives of the child.

While both second-parent adoption and joint custody hold some promise as ways of gaining legal rights for non-biological mothers, the effort to secure them may also pose a danger for lesbian families. As Nancy Polikoff (1990) has noted: "The stress of entering the legal system and potentially submitting the family to evaluation according to standards rooted in homophobia and heterosexism is as much a deterrent as the uncertainty of asserting untested legal theories" (p. 526). Lesbian families pursuing such options must weigh carefully the financial and emotional costs of state intervention against the benefits of the legal recognition of their family constellation, should their application be successful.

The final area which I wish to consider is adoption and foster parenting. For untold years, lesbians and gay men have become parents through these mechanisms. Here, legal measures designed to limit homosexuals' access to children have forced prospective adoptive or foster parents to present themselves to social service agencies as single individuals, regardless of their relationship status. The question of adoption reveals in a dramatic fashion the fact that many segments of society still harbor irrational and unfounded fears and prejudices about the dangers posed by relationships between lesbians or gay men and children. Those fears persist despite the almost complete lack of evidence of child abuse perpetrated by lesbians or gay men. Thus, lesbians and gay men wishing to adopt or foster children still face enormous barriers. For example, with the exception of British Columbia, lesbians and gay men in Canada cannot adopt a child as a couple. Instead, one of the members of a couple must apply for adoption. If that application is successful, then the partner may, in some jurisdictions, apply for a second-parent adoption.

Adoption can follow several routes including public adoption through a publicly mandated or chartered agency such as the Children's Aid Society, private adoption through an independent agency, independent adoption assisted through the court by privately hired lawyers, and international adoption, usually arranged privately and shepherded through the immigration and family court systems with fairly minimal state oversight. With the exception of public adoption, all of these forms are costly, and any type of adoption is fraught with uncertainty and long periods of waiting. For lesbians and gay men wishing to adopt, however, these problems are compounded by legal barriers. In only two states in the United States, New York and California, are lesbians and gays legally protected against discrimination in the adoption process. Even that protection does not mean, of course, that individuals will not face discrimination; it offers some limited guarantee that an individual will not be turned down solely on the basis of sexual orientation. In two other states, Florida and New Hampshire, openly lesbian and gay prospective parents are prohibited by law from adoption. In Ohio, the Supreme Court interpreted the state adoption law in such a way as to allow a gay man to adopt. In all other states, no specific legislation related to sexual orientation and adoption exists (Miller, 1993). It must be noted, however, that in 38 American states, the Department of Social Services is administered by the county, as opposed to state regulated. That means that there can be huge variations across the state on how decisions on adoption and fostering for same-sex couples are determined.

For gay men, for whom fewer avenues to parenting are available, these barriers may be especially punishing. Yet, ironically, during the 1994 debate in Ontario over Bill 167 [legislation designed to extend a range of rights and obligations to same-sex partners and their offspring], it was primarily gay men who were prepared to urge the New Democratic Party government to abandon the adoption issue, arguing that its "controversial" nature threatened to jeopardize the entire bill. That move, and its aftermath, highlighted once again the need for ongoing political discussion of the complex issues that face our families.

CONCLUSION

The legal position of lesbian and gay parents has improved considerably since the first lesbian custody cases began to appear before the courts in Canada, the United States and elsewhere, some twenty years ago. Lesbian and gay families are gaining visibility and acceptance in schools, day care centers, and communities across North America. Lesbians and gay men are contesting homophobic laws and practices in the areas of adoption, foster parenting, and child custody. The passage on May 8, 1996 of Bill C-33, legislation which amended the Canadian Human Rights Act to include sexual orientation as a prohibited ground for discrimination, is the latest in a series of important victories. Today, it is no longer a certainty in most jurisdictions that lesbian or gay parents will lose custody of their children. Despite these gains, however, lesbian and gay parents still risk losing their children and many are fighting these battles every day. As activists, as advocates, as parents and as friends, we must work together to support their struggles, and to fight for legal recognition of our families. Recognition in the courts will give legal foundation to the legitimacy of claims-making on behalf of the equality rights of our children. Further recognition of their equality rights can move us closer to the assurance of equality of access and treatment in the other arenas of social policy that have a direct effect on families.

NOTES

1. The Defense of Marriage Act (DOMA), passed by Congress and signed by President Clinton in September 1996, defines marriage as "a legal union between one man and one woman as husband and wife." Under this legislation, same-sex unions could not be marriages.

2. Grandparents fall within the category of third parties. It is worth noting that Tyler's biological father supported Sharon Bottoms' bid for custody.

3. The Virginia Supreme Court found that living conditions would "impose an intolerable burden upon her [the child] by reason of the social condemnation attached to them." The court noted as well that "the father's unfitness is manifested by his willingness to impose this burden upon [his daughter] in exchange for his own gratification." 694.

4. Mary Ward subsequently died of a heart attack on January 21, 1997 at the age of 47.

5. Not all cases which appear before the courts are reported in legal journals. It is a common practice in cases in which homosexuality or lesbianism is a factor to seal the records, ostensibly to protect the privacy of the individuals involved. This practice presents a problem for both lawyers and researchers in the field of lesbian custody. Those cases which are reported become accessible to judges and lawyers for their use in future cases, and thereby assume an importance beyond their individual significance.

6. In *Kevin N. McIntyre v. Linden Crouch*, while the insemination was not performed by a licensed practitioner, the court determined that the relevant Oregon legislation regarding donor insemination did apply. That legislation specified that, when an insemination is performed by a licensed practitioner, the donor has "no right, obligation or interest with respect to a child born as a result of artificial insemination" and the child has "no right, obligation or interest with respect" to the donor. ORS 109.239 section 5, 1 and 2. *McIntyre v. Crouch*, 780 P. 2d 239 (Or. App. 1989). Despite that finding, the court ruled that, if the donor could demonstrate that an agreement had existed between himself and the mother regarding his parental involvement with the child, then his constitutional rights would have been violated. They directed him to a lower court to make arguments on this issue.

7. Thomas Steel died of complications from AIDS on July 18, 1998.

8. Indeed, the majority in the appellate court decision defined the case explicitly in gender terms. "The notion that a lesbian mother should enjoy a parental relationship with her daughter but a gay man should not is so innately discriminatory as to be unworthy of comment." *Thomas S. v. Robin Y.*, 618 N.Y.S.2d 360 (App. Div. 1994).

9. According to a 1996 newsletter of the Gay and Lesbian Parents Coalition International (GLPCI), the following jurisdictions have granted at least one second-parent adoption: Alaska, California, Colorado, District of Columbia, Illinois, Indiana, Iowa, Massachusetts, Michigan, Minnesota, Nevada, New Jersey, New York, Ohio, Oregon, Pennsylvania, Rhode Island, Texas, Vermont, and Washington. England also recently granted a second-parent adoption. GLPCI Network, Winter/Spring 1996 Issue, 14. On November 4, 1996, full adoption rights were extended to same-sex couples in British Columbia. The Parent's Network, 2, 2 (June/July 1996).

REFERENCES

ANDREWS, K. (1995). Ancient affections: Gays, lesbians and family status. In K. Arnup (Ed.), *Lesbian parenting: Living with pride and prejudice* (pp. 367–382). Charlottetown: Gynergy.

ARNUP, K. (1994). Finding fathers: Artificial insemination, lesbians, and the law. *Canadian Journal of Women and the Law 7(1)*, 97–115.

ARNUP, K. & BOYD, S. (1995). Familial disputes? Sperm donors, lesbian mothers, and legal parenthood. In D. Herman & C. Stychin (Eds.), *Legal inversions: Lesbians, gay men, and the politics of law* (pp. 79–102). Philadelphia: Temple University Press.

ARNUP, K. (1989). Mothers just like others: Lesbians, divorce, and child custody in Canada. *Canadian Journal of Women and the Law, 3*, 18–32.

ARNUP, K. (1995). Still hidden in the household. Paper presented at the Annual Meeting of the Canadian Lesbian and Gay Studies Association, Montreal, PQ.

BATEMAN, M. (1992). Lesbians, gays and child custody: An Australian legal history. *Australian Gay and Lesbian Law Journal, 1*, 49–62.

BEARGIE, R. A. (1988). Custody determinations involving the homosexual parent. *Family Law Quarterly, 22 (1)*, 71–86.

BERNSTEIN, F. A. (1996). This child does have two mothers . . . and a sperm donor with visitation. *Review of Law and Social Change, 22 (1)*, 1–58.

BEZAIRE V. BEZAIRE, 20 R.F.L. (2d) 365 (Ont. C.A. 1980).

BOTTOMS V. BOTTOMS, 457 S.E. 2d 102 (Va. 1995).

BOWERS V. HARDWICK, 106 S.Ct. 2841 (1986).

BOYD, S. (1989). From gender specificity to gender neutrality? Ideologies in Canadian child custody law. In C. Smart & S. Sevenhuijsen (Eds.), *Child care and the politics of gender* (pp. 126–157). London: Routledge.

BRANTNER, P. A. (1991). When mommy or daddy is gay: Developing constitutional standards for custody decisions. *Hastings Women's Law Journal, 3 (1)*, 105–107.

BROPHY, J. (1985). Child care and the growth of power: The status of mothers in child custody disputes. In C. Smart & J. Brophy (Eds.), *Women in Law* (pp. 97–116). London: Routledge.

CASE V. CASE, 18 R.F.L. 138 (Sask. Queen's Bench, 1974).

Children's Law Reform Act, R.S.O., c. 68, section 24 (1980).

D.M. V. M.D. 94 Sask. R. 315; S.J. No. 672 (1991).

ELLIOTT V. ELLIOTT, B.C.J. No. 43 (BCSC), 22 (1987).

EWANKIW V. EWANKIW, M.J. No. 692 (Man. Q.B., Family Division, 1994).

GLPCI Network (1996 Fall), p. 3.

GROSS, W. (1986). Judging the best interests of the child: Child custody and the homosexual parent. *Canadian Journal of Women and the Law, 1*, 505–531.

HERMAN, E. (1988). The romance of lesbian motherhood. *Sojourner: The Women's Forum*, March.

Interest of R.C. 775 P2d 27 (Colo. 1989).

ISBELL, M. T. (1992). *HIV and family law: A survey*. Toronto: Lambda Legal Defense and Education Fund.

JACOBSON V. JACOBSON, 314 N.W. 2d 78 (N.D. 1981).

K. v. K., 23 R.F.L. 63 (Alta. Prov. Ct, 1975).

LECKIE V. VOORHIES, Case No. 60-92-06326 (Ore. Circuit Court, April 5, 1993), (unreported); and *Leckie v. Voorhies*, No. A79785, May 25, 1994, 128 Ore. App. 289.

Lesbian couple charge doctor and college with discrimination (September 1993), *Gazebo Connection, 14 (8)*, 2.

MARTIN, A. (1993). *The lesbian and gay parenting handbook*. New York: Harper Collins.

MCGUIRE, M. & ALEXANDER, N. (1985). Artificial insemination of single women. *Fertility and Sterility, 43*, 182–184.

MILLBANK, J. (1992). Lesbian mothers, gay fathers: Sameness and difference. *Australian Gay and Lesbian Law Journal, 2*, 21–40.

MILLER, B. (1979). Gay fathers and their children. *The Family Coordinator, 28*, 544–52.

National Center for Lesbian Rights (1994). Lesbians choosing motherhood: Legal implications of donor insemination and co-parenting. Reprinted in William B. Rubenstein (Ed.), *Lesbians, gay men, and the law*. New York: New Press, 543.

Ottawa Citizen, February 3, 1996, A2.

PATTERSON, C. J. (1996). Lesbian and gay parents and their children. In R. C. Savin-Williams & K. M. Cohen (Eds.), *The lives of lesbians, gays, and bisexuals: Adults to children* (pp. 281–298). Orlando, FL: Harcourt Brace.

POLIKOFF, N. (1986). Lesbian mothers, lesbian families: Legal obstacles, legal challenges. *Review of Law and Social Change, 14*, 907–916.

POLIKOFF, N. D. (1990–91). This child does have two mothers: Redefining parenthood to meet the needs of children in lesbian-mother and other nontraditional families. *Georgetown Law Journal, 78*, 459–575.

POLIKOFF, N. (1996). What's biology got to do with it? Cited in Fred A. Bernstein, This child does have two mothers . . . and a sperm donor with visitation. *Review of Law and Social Change, 22 (1)*, note 218, p. 37.

ROE V. ROE, Record No. 832044, Supreme Court of Virginia, 228 Va. 722; 324 S.E. 2d 691; 1985 Va. LEXIS164, January 18, 1985.

RUBENSTEIN, W. B. (Ed.) (1993). *Lesbians, gay men, and the law*. New York: New Press.

SAUNDERS V. SAUNDERS (1989), 20 R.F.L. (3d) 368 (B.C. Co. Ct.).

S.E.G. V. R.A.G. 735 S.W. 2d 164 (Mo. Ct. App. 1987); cited in William Rubenstein, (Ed.) (1993). *Lesbians, gay men, and the law* (pp. 496–497). New York: New Press.

SMEDES V. WAYNE STATE UNIVERSITY, No. 80-725-83 (E.D. Mich., filed July 15, 1980).

THOMAS S. V. ROBIN Y. 1994 N.Y. App. Div., Lexis 11385.

WARTIK, N. (1993, November/December). Virginia is no place for lesbian mothers. *Ms.*, 89.

WESTON, K. (1991). Parenting in the age of AIDS. In *Families we choose: Lesbians, gays, kinship*. New York: Columbia University Press.

WISHARD, D. R. (1989). Out of the closets and into the courts: Homosexual fathers and child custody. *Dickinson Law Review, 93*, 420.

CRITICAL THINKING QUESTIONS

1. What difficulties do lesbian and gay parents encounter in court when attempting to secure custody or visitation with their children?

2. What are the social and legal reasons behind arguments against allowing gay men and lesbians to be recognized as parents? Are these arguments valid? Why or why not?

3. How are the law and the judicial decisions on which it is based affected by cultural beliefs about gay men and lesbians? Should efforts at legal equity for lesbian and gay parents focus on changing public attitudes, the law, or both? Explain.

Reading 28

Legal Scholars of Gay Rights Offer Strategies to Combat the "Apartheid of the Closet"

D. W. Miller

> *In this article, Miller focuses on the many ways that discrimination against gay men and lesbians is institutionalized in U.S. law.*

FOR A FEW gay Vermonters, such as Lois Farnham and Holly Puterbaugh, Independence Day came early this year. On July 1, the pair's pursuit of happiness led them to the city clerk's office in South Burlington, where they became one of the first gay couples in the country to join in a "civil union" akin to marriage.

The women called it the end of a "27-and-a-half-year engagement." It was also the culmination of their civil-rights lawsuit, which had convinced the state's highest court that the Vermont constitution gave them the same rights as those of heterosexual citizens, including many of the legal benefits of marriage.

In New Jersey, however, James Dale wasn't celebrating. In the same week, the U.S. Supreme Court ended his long fight to resume volunteering as an assistant scoutmaster. The Boy Scouts of America won the right to

Source: Reprinted with permission from *The Chronicle of Higher Education* 46, no. 46 (July 21, 2000): A15–16.

exclude Mr. Dale and other gay people from positions of leadership, on the grounds that they cannot be proper role models for its members. The justices ruled by a vote of 5 to 4 that the Boy Scouts' freedom of association trumps New Jersey's antidiscrimination law.

A modest advance in a small, liberal state. A major disappointment in the very chamber where "separate but equal" lost all legitimacy. It's no wonder that some legal scholars who study gay rights are dissatisfied with the pace of gay liberation.

"There has been tremendous progress," says Evan Gerstmann, an assistant professor of political science at Loyola Marymount University, "but much less than people think." Even today, agrees William N. Eskridge, a law professor at Yale University, gay people suffer an "apartheid of the closet"—a separate set of laws "that are hard to defend on legal grounds, on political grounds, or even on moral grounds."

SOME IMPORTANT LEGAL VICTORIES

To be sure, the law has become more hospitable to gay rights in recent decades. Dozens of states and localities, for instance, have repealed bans on consensual sodomy or added "sexual orientation" to their anti-discrimination laws. But gay people cannot receive a marriage license, gay soldiers cannot serve openly, and—in some states—gay teachers are forbidden to discuss their orientation in the classroom lest they "promote" homosexuality.

Although the Supreme Court just four years ago protected the political prerogatives of gay people in *Romer v. Evans,* a case that relied on constitutional principles rooted in the civil rights victories of the 1950s, scholars like Mr. Gerstmann and Mr. Eskridge are not waiting for a replay of the civil rights revolution in the courts. They urge advocates to fight their battles with other tools, and in other arenas.

The Court's ruling in *Romer* seemed like a milestone. It struck down a voter-approved amendment to Colorado's constitution, Amendment 2, that would have nullified all attempts to add sexual orientation to statewide and local nondiscrimination laws. In its opinion, the Court said for the first time that a law that disadvantages gay people cannot stand if it serves no goal more reasonable than indulging the "animus" of the straight majority.

The Court thereby invoked the equal-protection clause of the 14th Amendment, which has long been crucial in protecting black people and other racial and ethnic groups from discriminatory laws and policies. Enacted shortly after the Civil War to shield newly freed slaves from oppression by a white majority, the 14th Amendment says in part that "no state shall deny to any person within its jurisdiction the equal protection of the laws."

Since 1938, the Supreme Court has construed that clause to mean that the government may not pass laws that burden protected, or "suspect," classes of people unless those laws are narrowly tailored to serve a compelling state interest. Laws subjected to such "strict scrutiny" rarely stand. By the 1970s, the list of suspect classes included the categories of race, national origin, alien status, and, as "quasi-suspect," birth legitimacy and gender.

"THE CONSTITUTIONAL UNDERCLASS"

Mr. Gerstmann argues, in *The Constitutional Underclass: Gays, Lesbians, and the Failure of Class-Based Equal Protection* (University of Chicago Press, 1999), that having created a powerful tool for protecting minority groups, the Court since the early 1970's has resisted expanding its aegis to include any new groups, including gay people. "Declaring any minority a suspect class," he writes, "is strong medicine, often resulting in the substitution of judicial judgment for democratic decision making in all areas of law affecting the protected group," a substitution the Supreme Court is reluctant to make.

Because of this reluctance, he says, *Romer* "did very little for gays and lesbians. They still get less protection than racial minorities or women. It was limited to the situation at hand and did not extend gay rights in any way."

That's because the justices neither elevated gay people to the same status as members of racial minority groups nor declared any general principles for deciding future cases. By holding the law to a standard normally reserved for suspect classes without admitting it was doing so, he writes, "the Court could strike down Amendment 2 without obligating itself to apply a heightened level of scrutiny to any other law disadvantaging gays and lesbians."

That sleight of hand is not limited to sexual orientation, he adds. The court has managed to exclude any new groups by fudging the distinction between class and classification. When vulnerable groups such as the poor, the elderly, or gay people have requested the strict scrutiny of laws that burden them as a class, the Court has required them to prove that they lack political power or share a history of discrimination. Yet it has sided with white plaintiffs—who could never meet that threshold—in striking down affirmative-action programs that impermissibly use race as a classification.

Mr. Gerstmann notes that amendment 2 supporters claimed that gay people wanted local antidiscrimination ordinances to grant them "special rights." As long as the Court interprets the 14th Amendment in terms of suspect classes of people, he argues, many Americans will continue to oppose such protections as special rights.

A MATTER OF MORAL CONSCIENCE

Dissatisfaction with the prevailing view of equal protection has led legal scholars to offer alternative weapons for advocates' constitutional arsenal. Mr. Gerstmann wants judges to junk class-based analysis of the equal-protection clause altogether. "The judiciary should invoke the Constitution's equal protection not on behalf of classes," he says, but on behalf of rights, such as the right to full political participation or an equal education. That, he says, is how the court wielded the 14th Amendment in *Brown v. Board of Education,* when it declared that segregated schools were inherently unequal.

Even if equal-protection arguments worked, says David A. J. Richards, a professor of law at New York University, he would question the common wisdom of using the Civil Rights movement as a model for the advancement of gay rights. That analogy, he argues, implies that sexual orientation could be constitutionally protected from discrimination only if it were, like race, an immutable and conspicuous fact of nature.

While scientists debate the origins of sexual preferences, he says, gay people should secure their rights as a matter of identity and moral conscience. He looks to the First Amendment to protect them, on the grounds of religious toleration.

"Americans, who are very tolerant of almost any religious group, nonetheless are deeply intolerant when it comes to gay and lesbian

advocacy," he says. Gay identity is a form of "ethically based conscientious conviction" entitled to equal respect with other forms of convictions, he writes in *Identity and the Case for Gay Rights* (Chicago, 1999). "Yet many laws target just such convictions."

For instance, he argues, the military's "don't ask, don't tell" policy claims to punish only homosexual conduct, not homosexual identity. But the military infers such conduct whenever gay soldiers express their sexual identity, such as by declaring "I am gay" or participating in a commitment ceremony with a same-sex partner.

Moreover, he argues, "some forms of legal discrimination against gay people cannot be justified or understood as anything other than sectarian expressions of moral disapproval enacted into law." That, he writes, is exactly what the First Amendment was created to prevent.

Yale's Mr. Eskridge also believes that gay-rights advocates could fashion a stronger shield against certain kinds of discrimination from the first amendment. He argues that the amendment's guarantee of free speech ought to include the expression of sexuality. In fact, he believes the Supreme Court has already made that interpretation—but only selectively.

As the court has read the First Amendment, he writes in *Gaylaw: Challenging the Apartheid of the Closet* (Harvard University Press, 1999), it has "protected gender-bending literature . . . , assured gay people rights to associate in clubs and college campuses, and protected the right to come out of the closet—but not when the person coming out is a state employee or military person, when the association involves the sale of liquor, or the gender-bending literature is explicitly homoerotic."

If it were applying the First Amendment consistently, he argues, the court would have reinstated a school guidance counselor who was fired after revealing her bisexuality. And it would have protected a gay Naval officer who came out to his superior soon after President Clinton announced his intention to ban discrimination against gay people in the armed forces.

NO MAGIC BULLET

Gay-rights litigators say they value the contributions of legal scholars, many of whom help them hone arguments for promising test cases. But they disagree that their legal briefs lack the proper ammunition.

"I don't think the equal-protection clause is useless," says Matthew Coles, a lawyer for the American Civil Liberties Union's Lesbian and Gay Rights Project. "There has been a string of district court cases post-*Romer* that have struck down laws based on 'animus.'" He expects to carry the equal-protection flag into battle against sodomy laws and discrimination in both the workplace and family court.

"We're not looking for a be-all, end-all fix from the courts, certainly not the Supreme Court, because there is no permanent fix," says Beatrice Dohrn, legal director for Lambda Legal Defense and Education Fund, the gay-rights group that took the Boy Scout case to the Supreme Court. "It's much more of a social movement."

"There is no magic bullet in legal discourse, ever," agrees William Rubinstein, a former gay-rights lawyer who teaches law at the University of California at Los Angeles. "We tend to think of *Brown v. Board of Education* as the important watershed" in the Civil Rights movement. But even that is now disputed. For one thing, the Court took its time in instructing states on how to end legal segregation. For another, he says, "We thought that a lot of racism was legally constructed. But we're still stuck with it."

Gay-rights advocates, he says, can still learn a valuable lesson from the civil rights era: Don't expect the courts to lead society where it isn't ready to go. In other words, the real battleground is the culture at large. "Court decisions have never been the leading edge for gay rights," says John D'Emilio, a historian in the gender and women's studies department at the University of Chicago at Illinois. Instead, he says, advocates must keep challenging the straight majority to reconsider its prejudices.

SHIFTING LEGAL GROUND

The opportunities for such education are everywhere, as the ground under gay rights continues to shift. Some legislatures repeal antisodomy laws, while others refuse to grant gay parents custody of children after divorce. High courts in Hawaii and Alaska rule that their state constitutions require gay marriage, and voters amend them.

That gay advocacy has become so robust, scholars say, is one thing for which judges do deserve some credit. In fact, one of the unheralded victories of the civil rights era is a string of free-speech cases that bolstered black people's participation in public debate. Since the 1970's, the free expression of gay publications, gay employees, and gay student groups has similarly won favor in the Supreme Court.

"The trick is to combine expression and equality claims," says Nan D. Hunter, a former gay-rights litigator and a professor at the Brooklyn College of Law. That strategy, she says, worked in a recent Utah case in which a high-school teacher was fired as her school's volleyball coach after revealing that she was gay. A federal judge eventually ruled that the school had both violated her free-speech rights and denied her equal protection out of prejudice.

Oddly enough, the pursuit of cultural change turns the logic of victory and defeat upside down.

The Boy Scouts may have won the right to exclude gay leaders, but only at the expense of declaring that their objection to homosexuality is a fundamental part of their message. That may cost them members and donations. "The Boy Scouts have taken on a stigma of being antigay," says Ms. Hunter. "It's the kind of case you win even if you lose."

CRITICAL THINKING QUESTIONS

1. In what ways are lesbians and gay men discriminated against in the law?

2. Compare and contrast the legal status of gay men and lesbians today with that of African-Americans in the 1950s and 1960s.

3. If, according to the U.S. Constitution, all people are entitled to equal protection under the law, how is it that gay men, lesbians, and other sexual and gender minorities continue to be treated according to legal standards different from those applied to the rest of society?

Getting Involved

1. Contact the office of the public defender in your area. Tell them you are a college student and that you would like to "shadow" one of the attorneys for a day. In that role, take notes about the types of cases the attorneys handle and the number of clients they see. Ask them about what their day or week is normally like, the number of cases they currently handle, and the amount of time and resources they put into each case, on average. Compare your findings with those of classmates who shadowed a prosecuting attorney.

2. Contact the office of the prosecuting attorney in your area. Tell them you are a college student and that you would like to "shadow" one of the attorneys for a day. In that role, take notes about the types of cases the attorneys handle and the number of clients they see. Ask them about what their day or week is normally like, the number of cases they currently handle, and the amount of time and resources they put into each case, on average. Compare your findings with those of classmates who shadowed a public defender.

3. Contact your local police or sheriff's department and ask to "ride along" with an officer for an evening. Talk to the officer about how she or he determines who might or might not be a criminal suspect, and observe who is stopped and who is arrested. Also talk to the officer about his or her opinions of domestic violence laws, battered women, and the role of the police in handling such cases. Take notes about how the officer handles any domestic cases that arise. Discuss your findings with your classmates.

Site-Seeing

1. For more information on police brutality, visit the web site of the Human Rights Watch at **http://www.hrw.org/wr2k/Us.htm.**

2. To learn more about efforts to fight discrimination in criminal justice, visit the web site of the American Civil Liberties Union at **http://www.aclu.org/issues/criminal/hjcj.html.**

3. For more information on legal issues facing gay men, lesbians, and transgenders, visit the web site of the Lamda Legal Defense and Education Fund at **http://www.lamdalegal.org.**

Chapter 5

Violent Barriers to Equality

Just as there are cultural and structural barriers to equality, violence is a means by which inequality is maintained. Violence can be used to intimidate women and racial, ethnic, sexual, and gender minorities from exercising rights they have. Violence, or even the threat of it, limits individuals' mobility, affects their health, and may cost them their lives. The articles in this section focus on just some of the ways that violence limits the life chances of minority group members and, for many people, continues to be a barrier to full participation in society.

In some instances, minority group members are targeted by members of the dominant group, who believe that white heterosexual men are now the subjects of discrimination in hiring, education, and other opportunities for advancement. In these instances, minority group members are targeted because their group is perceived as receiving unfair advantages. Each year, minority group members are victims of nearly 8,000 hate crimes—illegal acts motivated by bias against women and racial, ethnic, and sexual minorities (U.S. Department of Justice, 2000). In the first article in this chapter, hate groups, such as the Ku Klux Klan and other neo–nazi organizations, play a significant role in disseminating messages that encourage and condone violence toward minorities. Herbert focuses on the role of white power music in drawing young people to neo-Nazi organizations. He uses the powerful and offensive lyrics of some of the more popular songs of the white power movement to show how music may be used to recruit members and incite hate crimes. Still, Herbert maintains that censorship is not the answer to controlling white power groups or reducing hate crimes. Instead, he argues that people should become aware of the problem and work to end the hatred that fuels the movement. Only then will the backlash against the gains of minority groups be stemmed.

Of course, not all violence against minority groups comes from organized outsiders. In the second article in this chapter, Anderson explores what he calls the "code of the streets" in poor, urban, African-American neighborhoods. He argues that even with institutionalized barriers to racial equality—poor education, lack of job opportunities, and racial profiling—most African Americans are hardworking, law-abiding citizens. Still, Anderson shows how institutionalized barriers to middle-class status, combined with a long history of racism and discrimination in the United States, combine to lure African-American boys and men into gangs, where they can establish a sense of belonging, safety, and manhood by engaging in illegal activities. Interestingly, in an era of greater equality for women, Anderson demonstrates that men are no longer the only group to use violence to establish "manhood." Today, he argues, teenage girls are mimicking the violence and bravado of their male peers to win respect and avoid victimization. Although the odds are stacked against poor, urban African Americans, when young people use violence to gain status and respect within their peer groups, they fall into a trap that limits their long-term chances to succeed in life or even to survive.

The central point of Anderson's article—that institutionalized barriers to full participation in society result in violence—is echoed in the third article in this chapter. Focusing on personal experiences as a Native American and his observations as attorney general of Idaho, EchoHawk discusses the violence of Indian youth. The author provides an overview of the history of discrimination and genocide—the systematic extermination or destruction of a racial or cultural group—carried out by European Americans against Native Americans in the nineteenth century. He explains how continued discrimination and prejudice are related to higher rates of alcoholism and drug abuse, problems in the family, and ultimately the violent behavior of young people who have no role models to show them an honorable way of life. EchoHawk explains that the problems of today's youth are rooted in the racist practices of several generations of people. He notes that just as institutionalized discrimination caused today's problems, it will take a special, institutionalized effort to correct the mistakes of the past.

EchoHawk shows how the violent behavior of young people is rooted in structural inequality, which is translated into problems in the home. Similarly, over the past thirty years, feminists have argued that the abuse of women—sometimes referred to as domestic violence—is based on structural inequalities and cultural beliefs about the inferiority of women. For more than three decades, feminists have demanded that institutionalized programs and policies be established to end the abuse of women in their own homes. As a result, a number of changes have been made in the criminal justice system—including the arrest of suspected batterers, emergency protective orders, and court-appointed advocates to assist victims as they find their way through the system. Still, as we saw in the chapter on institutional discrimination, each year some 2 million women are assaulted by their intimate partners (Bachman & Saltzman, 1994; Straus & Gelles, 1990). And beatings can become lethal. Nearly a third of all female homicide victims are killed by husbands, former husbands, or boyfriends (U.S. Department of Justice, 2001).

As the authors of the fourth article explain, the most lethal time for a battered woman is when she is trying to leave the relationship. In this article, Erez and Belknap draw on the words of battered women who have sought help from the police and courts to show just some of the ways the system fails to protect these victims. The authors also show the vital difference that caring and dedicated authorities can make in helping women to escape violent relationships. By comparing the effects of officers, prosecutors, and judges who are dedicated to ending violence against women to that of authorities who are less concerned, the authors demonstrate how the perpetuation of violence against women continues to be built into the "criminal processing system," which more often than not fails to offer justice to battered women.

Violence in the home is a tremendous barrier to women's equality with men. Indeed, in the fifth article, which is an introduction to a special volume of a journal dedicated to the issue of wife rape, Yllö argues that this form of violence has been one that feminist researchers and activists have been reluctant to address. She contends that as long as rape within marriage is ignored, and thereby accepted, patriarchal marriage, which is at the heart of men's dominance over women, will be maintained. If we are ever to eliminate violent barriers to equality for women, it seems that the home is the first place in which intensified efforts are warranted.

The last three decades have witnessed an upsurge of programs to address violence against women. But what happens when men victimize other men, or when women assault men? In the sixth article, Donnelly and Kenyon focus on sexual assault crisis centers and examine how the services that they provide are limited by gender stereotypes. The authors argue that adult males are victims of sexual assault, but because of the stigma ascribed to men who are raped, they are less likely than women to report the assault to the police. Donnelly and Kenyon examine the role that gender stereotypes play in the provision of services to men who are victims of sexual assault. They find that male sexual assault victims are likely to encounter difficulties in receiving support from police and feminist rape crisis centers, in large part because many professionals wrongly believe that men cannot be raped. As a result of gender stereotypes such as these, men who are victims of rape or sexual assault are less likely than women to report their victimization to authorities; less likely to receive needed support, medical treatment, and therapy; and therefore more likely to suffer more severe long-term consequences of their victimization.

Just as woman abuse, wife rape, and the sexual victimization of men may be perpetuated by the individuals who staff organizations and social institutions responsible for helping victims, the conditions that give rise to violence against sexual minorities can be built into a social institution. Those conditions can be made worse when men who have been ridiculed by their fathers and socialized into stereotypical masculinity, are forced to live closely together in an institution known for "making men" out of boys. In the seventh article in this section, Hackett tells the story of the murder of U.S. Army Private Barry Winchell, who was known to date a preoperative transsexual—a male who lives as a woman and who hopes to have sex reassignment surgery. Winchell met his girlfriend at a club, where she performs as a woman. Because of his relationship, Winchell was rumored to be gay. Although he had been harassed by his peers and superior officers for being gay, the Army's "don't ask, don't tell" policy toward homosexual soldiers precluded him from reporting the abuse. In the end, Winchell was beaten to death by a fellow soldier, who was anxious to prove his masculinity by killing someone suspected of being gay.

Taken together, the articles in this chapter demonstrate just some of the ways that violence impedes equal opportunities for women and racial, ethnic, and sexual minorities. Members of these groups are targeted by white supremacist groups who wish to terrorize minority groups so that they will not assert their rights. Moreover, historical and present-day institutional and cultural barriers to equality work to entrap minority group members into poverty. Structurally and culturally barred from opportunities that would gain them upward mobility in mainstream society, many turn to violence, as much to thwart would-be attackers as to win them the respect of their peers.

Just as violence is built into the social fabric of impoverished minority groups, it is an integral part of the patriarchal family. In a society that assumes that the home is a haven in a heartless world, it is particularly cruel that so many women are victims of the physical, mental, and sexual abuse of their intimate partners. The articles in this chapter demonstrate how violence is linked to contemporary notions of masculinity, and how the stage for proving one's masculinity can be set by institutions such as the military and the family. Ironically, when men are the victims of violence, these same ideas about "real men" often preclude them from getting the help they need from authorities and professionals whose job it is to protect and serve. Clearly, then, violence is an impediment to equality of opportunity, directly affecting the lives of victims and perpetrators, limiting their life chances and keeping them from full participation in society.

REFERENCES

BACHMAN, R., AND L.E. SALTZMAN. 1995. *Violence Against Women: Estimates from the Redesigned Survey.* BJS Publication No. 154-348. Washington, DC: U.S. Department of Justice, Bureau of Justice Statistics.

STRAUS, MURRAY A. AND RICHARD J. GELLES. 1990. *Physical Violence in American Families: Risk Factors and Adaptations to Violence in 8,145 Families.* New Brunswick, NJ: Transaction.

U.S. Department of Justice. 2000. *Uniform Crime Reports: Hate Crime—1999.* Federal Bureau of Investigation: Criminal Justice Information Services (CJIS) Division.

U.S. Department of Justice. 2001. "Who Are the Victims." Violence Against Women Office.

Reading 1

High-Decibel Hate

Bob Herbert

In this article, Herbert focuses on the role of white power music in drawing young people to neo-Nazi organizations.

You kill all the niggers, and you gas all the Jews,
  Kill a gypsy and a Commie, too.
You just killed a kike, don't it feel right?
Goodness gracious, Third Reich.

The hatemongers have gone global, aided by the Internet and the unmistakable drawing power of white power music. The music

Source: Originally published in the *The New York Times,* August 20, 2001.

is mostly an amateurish mix of punk and heavy metal, with "vocalists" screaming and screeching lyrics like those above (from a song called "Third Reich," recorded by the Canadian band Rahowa, which is short for Racial Holy War).

White power music is a growing phenomenon. Hammerfest 2000 didn't get a lot of news coverage, but it was the most successful white power concert in the U.S. last year. It was held in October and drew racist skinheads galore to the town of Bremen, Ga., which has a population of 4,500 and is about 50 miles west of Atlanta.

Local officials are still embarrassed and reluctant to talk about the event.

The two-day concert was a raging success for hard-core fans of Hitler and lynching and the developing ideology of "pan-Aryanism." A group called the Bully Boys drove the Nazi-saluting crowd into a frenzy with a song called "Six Million More." And all other references there to the extermination of Jews and gays and the mass killing of blacks were warmly received.

The Intelligence Project of the Southern Poverty Law Center, which tracks the activities of hate groups, reported that "Hammerfest 2000 drew fans from Austria, Canada, France, Ireland, the Netherlands and Spain, as well as from across the United States. The concert culminated months of worldwide networking by sponsors Panzerfaust Records and Resistance Records, the premier neo-Nazi music labels in the U.S."

Call it the commodification of hate. In the new world order, everybody's an entrepreneur. It's just that some products are more egregious than others.

The music helps the hatemongers in a number of ways. Proceeds from concerts, compact discs and related items help finance the operations of major neo-Nazi and racist revolutionary groups. And in conjunction with the Internet and the cheap air fares that have eased international travel, the music has helped link racist groups throughout Europe and the Americas.

"The music has also been terribly, terribly important in bringing young kids into this movement," said Mark Potok, who edits Intelligence Report, a magazine published by the Intelligence Project.

More than anything else, he said, the music is luring the new recruits.

The crowds at the concerts sing along, dance, hurl one another into mosh pits, salute swastikas and shout "Heil Hitler."

"I've talked to many people who have come out of this movement," Potok said. "To a man and to a woman, they say it was the music, more than any other influence, that brought them to the movement in the first place."

The latest edition of Intelligence Report notes that "Internet-based 'radio' shows stream racist music around the world at all hours of the day. In the United States, racist music from 123 domestic bands and 229 foreign ones is available online from more than 40 distributors."

Impressionable youngsters in Jackson, Miss., in Oldham, England (where race riots erupted in May), or in Krakow, Poland, can listen to the same racist music—songs about barbecuing Turks or hunting blacks or torturing Jews.

The world is already ablaze with ethnic and religious hatred. So hate music, which deliberately encourages the violent tendencies of its practitioners and its fans, is fuel for an already raging fire.

In the United States this music is protected by the same Constitution that allows me to speak freely in this column. So this is not a call for censorship. What is important is that people of good will be made aware of a phenomenon so corrosive to a free society. It shouldn't be allowed to flourish in the dark. You don't want to censor this garbage. But you do want to throw a spotlight on it.

CRITICAL THINKING QUESTIONS

1. How is the fear of the spread of white power music similar to and different from fears about rock 'n' roll, heavy metal, grunge, or rap music?

2. In what ways is the music of the white power movement used to influence the thinking and behavior of group members? Will eliminating white power music reduce hate crimes? Explain.

3. Herbert argues against censoring white power music. Why? Do you agree or disagree? Explain.

Reading 2

The Code of the Streets

Elijah Anderson

In this article, Anderson argues that racism and discrimination are strong forces that can push some African-American boys and men into gangs, where they are more likely to be violent in order to prove themselves as men and to gain the respect that mainstream society denies them.

Of all the problems besetting the poor inner-city black community, none is more pressing than that of interpersonal violence and aggression. It wreaks havoc daily with the lives of community residents and increasingly spills over into downtown and residential middle-class areas. Muggings, burglaries, carjackings, and drug-related shootings, all of which may leave their victims or innocent bystanders dead, are now common enough to concern all urban and many suburban residents. The inclination to violence springs from the circumstances of life among the ghetto poor—the lack of jobs that pay a living wage, the stigma of race, the fallout from rampant drug use and drug trafficking, and the resulting alienation and lack of hope for the future.

Simply living in such an environment places young people at special risk of falling victim to aggressive behavior. Although there are often forces in the community which can counteract the negative influences, by far the most powerful being a strong, loving, "decent" (as inner-city residents put it) family committed to middle-class values, the despair is pervasive enough to have spawned an oppositional culture, that of "the streets," whose norms are often consciously opposed to those of mainstream society. These two orientations—decent and street—socially organize the community, and their coexis-

Source: Reprinted from *The Atlantic Monthly* 273, no. 5 (May 1994): 80–93 with permission from the author.

tence has important consequences for residents, particularly children growing up in the inner city. Above all, this environment means that even youngsters whose home lives reflect mainstream values—and the majority of homes in the community do—must be able to handle themselves in a street-oriented environment.

This is because the street culture has evolved what may be called a code of the streets, which amounts to a set of informal rules governing interpersonal public behavior, including violence. The rules prescribe both a proper comportment and a proper way to respond if challenged. They regulate the use of violence and so allow those who are inclined to aggression to precipitate violent encounters in an approved way. The rules have been established and are enforced mainly by the street-oriented, but on the streets the distinction between street and decent is often irrelevant; everybody knows that if the rules are violated, there are penalties. Knowledge of the code is thus largely defensive; it is literally necessary for operating in public. Therefore, even though families with a decency orientation are usually opposed to the values of the code, they often reluctantly encourage their children's familiarity with it to enable them to negotiate the inner-city environment.

At the heart of the code is the issue of respect—loosely defined as being treated "right," or granted the deference one deserves. However, in the troublesome public environment of the inner city, as people increasingly feel buffeted by forces beyond their control, what one deserves in the way of respect becomes more and more problematic and uncertain. This in turn further opens the issue of respect to sometimes intense interpersonal negotiation. In the street culture, especially among young people, respect is viewed as almost an external entity that is hard-won but easily lost, and so must constantly be guarded. The rules of the code in fact provide a framework for negotiating respect. The person whose very appearance—including his clothing, demeanor, and way of moving—deters transgressions feels that he possesses, and may be considered by others to possess, a measure of respect. With the right amount of respect, for instance, he can avoid "being bothered" in public. If he is bothered, not only may he be in physical danger but he has been disgraced or "dissed" (disrespected). Many of the forms that dissing can take might seem petty to middle-class people (maintaining eye contact for too long, for example), but to those invested in the street code, these actions become serious indications of the other person's intentions. Consequently, such people become very sensitive to advances and slights, which could well serve as warnings of imminent physical confrontation.

This hard reality can be traced to the profound sense of alienation from mainstream society and its institutions felt by many poor inner-city black people, particularly the young. The code of the streets is actually a cultural adaptation to a profound lack of faith in the police and the judicial system. The police are most often seen as representing the dominant white society and not caring to protect inner-city residents. When called, they may not respond, which is one reason many residents feel they must be prepared to take extraordinary measures to defend themselves and their loved ones against those who are inclined to aggression. Lack of police accountability has in fact been incorporated into the status system: the person who is believed capa-

ble of "taking care of himself" is accorded a certain deference, which translates into a sense of physical and psychological control. Thus the street code emerges where the influence of the police ends and personal responsibility for one's safety is felt to begin. Exacerbated by the proliferation of drugs and easy access to guns, this volatile situation results in the ability of the street-oriented minority (or those who effectively "go for bad") to dominate the public spaces.

DECENT AND STREET FAMILIES

Although almost everyone in poor inner-city neighborhoods is struggling financially and therefore feels a certain distance from the rest of America, the decent and the street family in a real sense represent two poles of value orientation, two contrasting conceptual categories. The labels "decent" and "street," which the residents themselves use, amount to evaluative judgments that confer status on local residents. The labeling is often the result of a social contest among individuals and families of the neighborhood. Individuals of the two orientations often coexist in the same extended family. Decent residents judge themselves to be so while judging others to be of the street, and street individuals often present themselves as decent, drawing distinctions between themselves and other people. In addition, there is quite a bit of circumstantial behavior—that is, one person may at different times exhibit both decent and street orientations, depending on the circumstances. Although these designations result from so much social jockeying, there do exist concrete features that define each conceptual category.

Generally, so-called decent families tend to accept mainstream values more fully and attempt to instill them in their children. Whether married couples with children or single-parent (usually female) households, they are generally "working poor" and so tend to be better off financially than their street-oriented neighbors. They value hard work and self-reliance and are willing to sacrifice for their children. Because they have a certain amount of faith in mainstream society, they harbor hopes for a better future for their children, if not for themselves. Many of them go to church and take a strong interest in their children's schooling. Rather than dwelling on the real hardships and inequities facing them, many such decent people, particularly the increasing number of grandmothers raising grandchildren, see their difficult situation as a test from God and derive great support from their faith and from the church community.

Extremely aware of the problematic and often dangerous environment in which they reside, decent parents tend to be strict in their child-rearing practices, encouraging children to respect authority and walk a straight moral line. They have an almost obsessive concern about trouble of any kind and remind their children to be on the lookout for people and situations that might lead to it. At the same time, they are themselves polite and considerate of others, and teach their children to be the same way. At home, at work, and in church, they strive hard to maintain a positive mental attitude and a spirit of cooperation.

So-called street parents, in contrast, often show a lack of consideration for other people and have a rather superficial sense of family and community. Though they may love their children, many of them are unable to cope with the physical and emotional demands of parenthood, and find it difficult to reconcile their needs with those of their children. These families, who are more fully invested in the code of the streets than the decent people are, may aggressively socialize their children into it in a normative way. They believe in the code and judge themselves and others according to its values.

In fact the overwhelming majority of families in the inner-city community try to approximate the decent-family model, but there are many others who clearly represent the worst fears of the decent family. Not only are their financial resources extremely limited, but what little they have may easily be misused. The lives of the street-oriented are often marked by disorganization. In the most desperate circumstances people frequently have a limited understanding of priorities and consequences, and so frustrations mount over bills, food, and, at times, drink, cigarettes, and drugs. Some tend toward self-destructive behavior; many street-oriented women are crack-addicted ("on the pipe"), alcoholic, or involved in complicated relationships with men who abuse them. In addition, the seeming intractability of their situation, caused in large part by the lack of well-paying jobs and the persistence of racial discrimination, has engendered deep-seated bitterness and anger in many of the most desperate and poorest blacks, especially young people. The need both to exercise a measure of control and to lash out at somebody is often reflected in the adults' relations with their children. At the least, the frustrations of persistent poverty shorten the fuse in such people—contributing to a lack of patience with anyone, child or adult, who irritates them.

In these circumstances a woman—or a man, although men are less consistently present in children's lives—can be quite aggressive with children, yelling at and striking them for the least little infraction of the rules she has set down. Often little if any serious explanation follows the verbal and physical punishment. This response teaches children a particular lesson. They learn that to solve any kind of interpersonal problem one must quickly resort to hitting or other violent behavior. Actual peace and quiet, and also the appearance of calm, respectful children conveyed to her neighbors and friends, are often what the young mother most desires, but at times she will be very aggressive in trying to get them. Thus she may be quick to beat her children, especially if they defy her law, not because she hates them but because this is the way she knows to control them. In fact, many street-oriented women love their children dearly. Many mothers in the community subscribe to the notion that there is a "devil in the boy" that must be beaten out of him or that socially "fast girls need to be whupped." Thus much of what borders on child abuse in the view of social authorities is acceptable parental punishment in the view of these mothers.

Many street-oriented women are sporadic mothers whose children learn to fend for themselves when necessary, foraging for food and money any way they can get it. The children are sometimes employed by drug dealers or become addicted themselves. These children of the street, growing up with little supervision, are said to "come up hard." They often learn to fight at an early age, sometimes using short-tempered adults around them as role models. The street-oriented home may be fraught with anger, verbal disputes, physical aggression, and even mayhem. The children observe these goings-on, learning the lesson that might makes right. They quickly learn to hit those who cross them, and the dog-eat-dog mentality prevails. In order to survive, to protect oneself, it is necessary to marshal inner resources and be ready to deal with adversity in a hands-on way. In these circumstances physical prowess takes on great significance.

In some of the most desperate cases, a street-oriented mother may simply leave her young children alone and unattended while she goes out. The most irresponsible women can be found at local bars and crack houses, getting high and socializing with other adults. Sometimes a troubled woman will leave very young children alone for days at a time. Reports of crack addicts abandoning their children have become common in drug-infested inner-city communities. Neighbors or relatives discover the abandoned children, often hungry and distraught over the absence of their mother. After repeated absences, a friend or relative, particularly a grandmother, will often step in to care for the young children, sometimes petitioning

the authorities to send her, as guardian of the children, the mother's welfare check, if the mother gets one. By this time, however, the children may well have learned the first lesson of the streets: survival itself, let alone respect, cannot be taken for granted; you have to fight for your place in the world.

CAMPAIGNING FOR RESPECT

These realities of inner-city life are largely absorbed on the streets. At an early age, often even before they start school, children from street-oriented homes gravitate to the streets, where they "hang"—socialize with their peers. Children from these generally permissive homes have a great deal of latitude and are allowed to "rip and run" up and down the street. They often come home from school, put their books down, and go right back out the door. On school nights eight- and nine-year-olds remain out until nine or ten o'clock (and teenagers typically come in whenever they want to). On the streets they play in groups that often become the source of their primary social bonds. Children from decent homes tend to be more carefully supervised and are thus likely to have curfews and to be taught how to stay out of trouble.

When decent and street kids come together, a kind of social shuffle occurs in which children have a chance to go either way. Tension builds as a child comes to realize that he must choose an orientation. The kind of home he comes from influences but does not determine the way he will ultimately turn out—although it is unlikely that a child from a thoroughly street-oriented family will easily absorb decent values on the streets. Youths who emerge from street-oriented families but develop a decency orientation almost always learn those values in another setting—in school, in a youth group, in church. Often it is the result of their involvement with a caring "old head" (adult role model).

In the street, through their play, children pour their individual life experiences into a common knowledge pool, affirming, confirming, and elaborating on what they have observed in the home and matching their skills against those of others. And they learn to fight. Even small children test one another, pushing and shoving, and are ready to hit other children over circumstances not to their liking. In turn, they are readily hit by other children, and the child who is toughest prevails. Thus the violent resolution of disputes, the hitting and cursing, gains social reinforcement. The child in effect is initiated into a system that is really a way of campaigning for respect.

In addition, younger children witness the disputes of older children, which are often resolved through cursing and abusive talk, if not aggression or outright violence. They see that one child succumbs to the greater physical and mental abilities of the other. They are also alert and attentive witnesses to the verbal and physical fights of adults, after which they compare notes and share their interpretations of the event. In almost every case the victor is the person who physically won the altercation, and this person often enjoys the esteem and respect of onlookers. These experiences reinforce the lessons the children have learned at home: might makes right, and toughness is a virtue, while humility is not. In effect they learn the social meaning of fighting. When it is left virtually unchallenged, this understanding becomes an ever more important part of the child's working conception of the world. Over time the code of the streets becomes refined.

Those street-oriented adults with whom children come in contact—including mothers, fathers, brothers, sisters, boyfriends, cousins, neighbors, and friends—help them along in forming this understanding by verbalizing the messages they are getting through experience: "Watch your back." "Protect yourself." "Don't punk out." "If somebody messes with you, you got to pay them back." "If someone disses you, you got

to straighten them out." Many parents actually impose sanctions if a child is not sufficiently aggressive. For example, if a child loses a fight and comes home upset, the parent might respond, "Don't you come in here crying that somebody beat you up; you better get back out there and whup his ass. I didn't raise no punks! Get back out there and whup his ass. If you don't whup his ass, I'll whup your ass when you come home." Thus the child obtains reinforcement for being tough and showing nerve.

While fighting, some children cry as though they are doing something they are ambivalent about. The fight may be against their wishes, yet they may feel constrained to fight or face the consequences—not just from peers but also from caretakers or parents, who may administer another beating if they back down. Some adults recall receiving such lessons from their own parents and justify repeating them to their children as a way to toughen them up. Looking capable of taking care of oneself as a form of self-defense is a dominant theme among both street-oriented and decent adults who worry about the safety of their children. There is thus at times a convergence in their child-rearing practices, although the rationales behind them may differ.

SELF-IMAGE BASED ON "JUICE"

By the time they are teenagers, most youths have either internalized the code of the streets or at least learned the need to comport themselves in accordance with its rules, which chiefly have to do with interpersonal communication. The code revolves around the presentation of self. Its basic requirement is the display of a certain predisposition to violence. Accordingly, one's bearing must send the unmistakable if sometimes subtle message to "the next person" in public that one is capable of violence and mayhem when the situation requires it, that one can take care of oneself. The nature of this communication is largely determined by the demands of the circumstances but can include facial expressions, gait, and verbal expressions—all of which are geared mainly to deterring aggression. Physical appearance, including clothes, jewelry, and grooming, also plays an important part in how a person is viewed; to be respected, it is important to have the right look.

Even so, there are no guarantees against challenges, because there are always people around looking for a fight to increase their share of respect—or "juice," as it is sometimes called on the street. Moreover, if a person is assaulted, it is important, not only in the eyes of his opponent but also in the eyes of his "running buddies," for him to avenge himself. Otherwise he risks being "tried" (challenged) or "moved on" by any number of others. To maintain his honor he must show he is not someone to be "messed with" or "dissed." In general, the person must "keep himself straight" by managing his position of respect among others; this involves in part his self-image, which is shaped by what he thinks others are thinking of him in relation to his peers.

Objects play an important and complicated role in establishing self-image. Jackets, sneakers, gold jewelry, reflect not just a person's taste, which tends to be tightly regulated among adolescents of all social classes, but also a willingness to possess things that may require defending. A boy wearing a fashionable, expensive jacket, for example, is vulnerable to attack by another who covets the jacket and either cannot afford to buy one or wants the added satisfaction of depriving someone else of his. However, if the boy forgoes the desirable jacket and wears one that isn't "hip," he runs the risk of being teased and possibly even assaulted as an unworthy person. To be allowed to hang with certain prestigious crowds, a boy must wear a different set of expensive clothes—sneakers and athletic suit—every day. Not to be able to do so might make him appear socially deficient. The youth comes to covet such items—especially when he sees easy prey wearing them.

In acquiring valued things, therefore, a person shores up his identity—but since it is an identity based on having things, it is highly precarious. This very precariousness gives a heightened sense of urgency to staying even with peers, with whom the person is actually competing. Young men and women who are able to command respect through their presentation of self—by allowing their possessions and their body language to speak for them—may not have to campaign for regard but may, rather, gain it by the force of their manner. Those who are unable to command respect in this way must actively campaign for it—and are thus particularly alive to slights.

One way of campaigning for status is by taking the possessions of others. In this context, seemingly ordinary objects can become trophies imbued with symbolic value that far exceeds their monetary worth. Possession of the trophy can symbolize the ability to violate somebody—to "get in his face," to take something of value from him, to "dis" him, and thus to enhance one's own worth by stealing someone else's. The trophy does not have to be something material. It can be another person's sense of honor, snatched away with a derogatory remark. It can be the outcome of a fight. It can be the imposition of a certain standard, such as a girl's getting herself recognized as the most beautiful. Material things, however, fit easily into the pattern. Sneakers, a pistol, even somebody else's girlfriend, can become a trophy. When a person can take something from another and then flaunt it, he gains a certain regard by being the owner, or the controller, of that thing. But this display of ownership can then provoke other people to challenge him. This game of who controls what is thus constantly being played out on inner-city streets, and the trophy—extrinsic or intrinsic, tangible or intangible—identifies the current winner.

An important aspect of this often violent give-and-take is its zero-sum quality. That is, the extent to which one person can raise himself up depends on his ability to put another person down. This underscores the alienation that permeates the inner-city ghetto community. There is a generalized sense that very little respect is to be had, and therefore everyone competes to get what affirmation he can of the little that is available. The craving for respect that results gives people thin skins. Shows of deference by others can be highly soothing, contributing to a sense of security, comfort, self-confidence, and self-respect. Transgressions by others which go unanswered diminish these feelings and are believed to encourage further transgressions. Hence one must be ever vigilant against the transgressions of others or even *appearing* as if transgressions will be tolerated. Among young people, whose sense of self-esteem is particularly vulnerable, there is an especially heightened concern with being disrespected. Many inner-city young men in particular crave respect to such a degree that they will risk their lives to attain and maintain it.

The issue of respect is thus closely tied to whether a person has an inclination to be violent, even as a victim. In the wider society people may not feel required to retaliate physically after an attack, even though they are aware that they have been degraded or taken advantage of. They may feel a great need to defend themselves *during* an attack, or to behave in such a way as to deter aggression (middle-class people certainly can and do become victims of street-oriented youths), but they are much more likely than street-oriented people to feel that they can walk away from a possible altercation with their self-esteem intact. Some people may even have the strength of character to flee, without any thought that their self-respect or esteem will be diminished.

In impoverished inner-city black communities, however, particularly among young males and perhaps increasingly among females, such flight would be extremely difficult. To run away would likely leave one's self-esteem in tatters. Hence people often

feel constrained not only to stand up and at least attempt to resist during an assault but also to "pay back"—to seek revenge—after a successful assault on their person. This may include going to get a weapon or even getting relatives involved. Their very identity and self-respect, their honor, is often intricately tied up with the way they perform on the streets during and after such encounters. This outlook reflects the circumscribed opportunities of the inner-city poor. Generally people outside the ghetto have other ways of gaining status and regard, and thus do not feel so dependent on such physical displays.

BY TRIAL OF MANHOOD

On the street, among males these concerns about things and identity have come to be expressed in the concept of "manhood." Manhood in the inner city means taking the prerogatives of men with respect to strangers, other men, and women—being distinguished as a man. It implies physicality and a certain ruthlessness. Regard and respect are associated with this concept in large part because of its practical application: if others have little or no regard for a person's manhood, his very life and those of his loved ones could be in jeopardy. But there is a chicken-and-egg aspect to this situation: one's physical safety is more likely to be jeopardized in public *because* manhood is associated with respect. In other words, an existential link has been created between the idea of manhood and one's self-esteem, so that it has become hard to say which is primary. For many inner-city youths, manhood and respect are flip sides of the same coin; physical and psychological well-being are inseparable, and both require a sense of control, of being in charge.

The operating assumption is that a man, especially a real man, knows what other men know—the code of the streets. And if one is not a real man, one is somehow diminished as a person, and there are certain valued things one simply does not deserve. There is thus believed to be a certain justice to the code, since it is considered that everyone has the opportunity to know it. Implicit in this is that everybody is held responsible for being familiar with the code. If the victim of a mugging, for example, does not know the code and so responds "wrong," the perpetrator may feel justified even in killing him and may feel no remorse. He may think, "Too bad, but it's his fault. He should have known better."

So when a person ventures outside, he must adopt the code—a kind of shield, really—to prevent others from "messing with" him. In these circumstances it is easy for people to think they are being tried or tested by others even when this is not the case. For it is sensed that something extremely valuable is at stake in every interaction, and people are encouraged to rise to the occasion, particularly with strangers. For people who are unfamiliar with the code—generally people who live outside the inner city—the concern with respect in the most ordinary interactions can be frightening and incomprehensible. But for those who are invested in the code, the clear object of their demeanor is to discourage strangers from even thinking about testing their manhood. And the sense of power that attends the ability to deter others can be alluring even to those who know the code without being heavily invested in it—the decent inner-city youths. Thus a boy who has been leading a basically decent life can, in trying circumstances, suddenly resort to deadly force.

Central to the issue of manhood is the widespread belief that one of the most effective ways of gaining respect is to manifest "nerve." Nerve is shown when one takes another person's possessions (the more valuable the better), "messes with" someone's woman, throws the first punch, "gets in someone's face," or pulls a trigger. Its proper display helps on the spot to check others who would violate one's person and also helps to build a reputation that works to prevent future challenges. But since such a show of nerve is a forceful expression of disrespect toward the person on the receiving end, the victim may be greatly offended and seek to retaliate with equal or greater force. A display of nerve, therefore, can easily provoke a life-threatening response, and the background knowledge of that possibility has often been incorporated into the concept of nerve.

True nerve exposes a lack of fear of dying. Many feel that it is acceptable to risk dying over the principle of respect. In fact, among the hard-core street-oriented, the clear risk of violent death may be preferable to being "dissed" by another. The youths who have internalized this attitude and convincingly display it in their public bearing are among the most threatening people of all, for it is commonly assumed that they fear no man. As the people of the community say, "They are the baddest dudes on the street." They often lead an existential life that may acquire meaning only when they are faced with the possibility of imminent death. Not to be afraid to die is by implication to have few compunctions about taking another's life. Not to be afraid to die is the quid pro quo of being able to take somebody else's life—for the right reasons, if the situation demands it. When others believe this is one's position, it gives one a real sense of power on the streets. Such credibility is what many inner-city youths strive to achieve, whether they are decent or street-oriented, both because of its practical defensive value and because of the positive way it makes them feel about themselves. The difference between the decent and the street-oriented youth is often that the decent youth makes a conscious decision to appear tough and manly; in another setting—with teachers, say, or at his part-time job—he can be polite and deferential. The street-oriented youth, on the other hand, has made the concept of manhood a part of his very identity; he has difficulty manipulating it—it often controls him.

GIRLS AND BOYS

Increasingly, teenage girls are mimicking the boys and trying to have their own version of "manhood." Their goal is the same—to get respect, to be recognized as capable of setting or maintaining a certain standard. They try to achieve this end in the ways that have been established by the boys, including posturing, abusive language, and the use of violence to resolve disputes, but the issues for the girls are different. Although conflicts over turf and status exist among the girls, the majority of disputes seem rooted in assessments of beauty (which girl in a group is "the cutest"), competition over boyfriends, and attempts to regulate other people's knowledge of and opinions about a girl's behavior or that of someone close to her, especially her mother.

A major cause of conflicts among girls is "he say, she say." This practice begins in the early school years and continues through high school. It occurs when "people," particularly girls, talk about others, thus putting their "business in the streets." Usually one girl will say something negative about another in the group, most often behind the person's back. The remark will then get back to the person talked about. She may retaliate or her friends may feel required to "take up for" her. In essence this is a form of group gossiping in which individuals are negatively assessed and evaluated. As with much gossip, the things said may or may not be true, but the point is that such imputations can cast aspersions on a person's good name. The accused is required to defend herself against the slander, which can result in arguments and fights, often over little of real substance. Here again is the problem of low self-esteem, which encourages youngsters to be highly sensitive to slights and to be vulnerable to feeling easily "dissed." To avenge the dissing, a fight is usually necessary.

Because boys are believed to control violence, girls tend to defer to them in situations of conflict. Often if a girl is attacked or feels slighted, she will get a brother, uncle, or cousin to do her fighting for her. Increasingly, however, girls are doing their own fighting and are even asking their male relatives to teach them how to fight. Some girls form groups that attack other girls or take things from them. A hard-core segment of inner-city girls inclined toward violence seems to be developing. As one thirteen-year-old girl in a detention center for youths who have committed violent acts told me, "To get people to leave you alone, you gotta fight. Talking don't always get you out of stuff." One major difference between girls and boys: girls rarely use guns. Their fights are therefore not life-or-death struggles. Girls are not often willing to put their lives on the line for "manhood." The ultimate form of respect on the male-dominated inner-city street is thus reserved for men.

"GOING FOR BAD"

In the most fearsome youths such a cavalier attitude toward death grows out of a very limited view of life. Many are uncertain about how long they are going to live and believe they could die violently at any time. They accept this fate; they live on the edge. Their manner conveys the message that nothing intimidates them; whatever turn the encounter takes, they maintain their attack—rather like a pit bull, whose spirit many such boys admire. The demonstration of such tenacity "shows heart" and earns their respect.

This fearlessness has implications for law enforcement. Many street-oriented boys are much more concerned about the threat of "justice" at the hands of a peer than at the hands of the police. Moreover, many feel not only that they have little to lose by going to prison but that they have something to gain. The toughening-up one experiences in prison can actually enhance one's reputation on the streets. Hence the system loses influence over the hard core who are without jobs, with little perceptible stake in the system. If mainstream society has done nothing *for* them, they counter by making sure it can do nothing *to* them.

At the same time, however, a competing view maintains that true nerve consists in backing down, walking away from a fight, and going on with one's business. One fights only in self-defense. This view emerges from the decent philosophy that life is precious, and it is an important part of the socialization process common in decent homes. It discourages violence as the primary means of resolving disputes and encourages youngsters to accept nonviolence and talk as confrontational strategies. But "if the deal goes down," self-defense is greatly encouraged. When there is enough positive support for this orientation, either in the home or among one's peers, then nonviolence has a chance to prevail. But it prevails at the cost of relinquishing a claim to being bad and tough, and therefore sets a young person up as at the very least alienated from street-oriented peers and quite possibly a target of derision or even violence.

Although the nonviolent orientation rarely overcomes the impulse to strike back in an encounter, it does introduce a certain confusion and so can prompt a measure of soul-searching, or even profound ambivalence. Did the person back down with his respect intact or did he back down only to be judged a "punk"—a person lacking manhood? Should he or she have acted? Should he or she have hit the other person in the mouth? These questions beset many young men and women during public confrontations. What is the "right" thing to do? In the quest for honor, respect, and local status—which few young people are uninterested in—common sense most often prevails, which leads many to opt for the tough approach, enacting their own particular versions of the display of nerve. The presentation of oneself as rough and tough is very often quite acceptable until one is tested.

And then that presentation may help the person pass the test, because it will cause fewer questions to be asked about what he did and why. It is hard for a person to explain why he lost the fight or why he backed down. Hence many will strive to appear to "go for bad," while hoping they will never be tested. But when they are tested, the outcome of the situation may quickly be out of their hands, as they become wrapped up in the circumstances of the moment.

AN OPPOSITIONAL CULTURE

The attitudes of the wider society are deeply implicated in the code of the streets. Most people in inner-city communities are not totally invested in the code, but the significant minority of hard-core street youths who are have to maintain the code in order to establish reputations, because they have—or feel they have—few other ways to assert themselves. For these young people the standards of the street code are the only game in town. The extent to which some children—particularly those who through upbringing have become most alienated and those lacking in strong and conventional social support—experience, feel, and internalize racist rejection and contempt from mainstream society may strongly encourage them to express contempt for the more conventional society in turn. In dealing with this contempt and rejection, some youngsters will consciously invest themselves and their considerable mental resources in what amounts to an oppositional culture to preserve themselves and their self-respect. Once they do, any respect they might be able to garner in the wider system pales in comparison with the respect available in the local system; thus they often lose interest in even attempting to negotiate the mainstream system.

At the same time, many less alienated young blacks have assumed a street-oriented demeanor as a way of expressing their blackness while really embracing a much more moderate way of life; they, too, want a nonviolent setting in which to live and raise a family. These decent people are trying hard to be part of the mainstream culture, but the racism, real and perceived, that they encounter helps to legitimate the oppositional culture. And so on occasion they adopt street behavior. In fact, depending on the demands of the situation, many people in the community slip back and forth between decent and street behavior.

A vicious cycle has thus been formed. The hopelessness and alienation many young inner-city black men and women feel, largely as a result of endemic joblessness and persistent racism, fuels the violence they engage in. This violence serves to confirm the negative feelings many whites and some middle-class blacks harbor toward the ghetto poor, further legitimating the oppositional culture and the code of the streets in the eyes of many poor young blacks. Unless this cycle is broken, attitudes on both sides will become increasingly entrenched, and the violence, which claims victims black and white, poor and affluent, will only escalate.

CRITICAL THINKING QUESTIONS

1. What does Anderson mean by "the code of the streets"? What factors contributed to the emergence of this code?

2. In your opinion, to what extent are the problems of the African-Americans described by Anderson related to poverty? To what extent are they related to racism? Discuss how poverty and racism intersect in the lives of the African-Americans in Anderson's article.

3. If you were the mayor of an urban area, what programs and social policies would you favor to help break the "code of the streets" and the violence associated with it?

Reading 3

Factors Contributing to Juvenile Violence in Indian Communities

Larry EchoHawk

> *In this article, EchoHawk discusses the impact of historical events and the resulting cultural values in the violence that Native Americans experience in their daily lives.*

I address this topic not just as a law teacher. Rather, I present a message that flows mainly from my personal and professional life experiences.

Source: Reprinted from *BYU Journal of Public Law* 13, no. 1 (1998): 69–76.

My thoughts run deeper than simply recognizing readily identifiable factors, such as alcohol and drug abuse, domestic violence, child abuse, teen pregnancy, gangs, and school dropouts, that contribute to juvenile violence across America. Instead, I will speak about the source of these problems that presently afflict

Indian reservation communities. These comments hopefully will provide some new perspective as we try to solve the growing problem of juvenile violence that is destroying the future of Indian youth.

In my childhood I experienced some measure of domestic violence, child abuse, and law breaking. These traumatic experiences were caused by my father's abuse of alcohol. There were times when I wondered if my family would stay together. Fortunately, my father stopped drinking during my teenage years and our family life got better. Today my father and mother are my greatest heroes because of the challenges they overcame and the lessons they taught to their six children.

I begin my perspective by sharing two experiences that I will tie in at the conclusion of my remarks. The first experience came about as I was finishing my undergraduate education at Brigham Young University. My oldest brother, John EchoHawk, was completing his law school education at the University of New Mexico. John took the time to have a serious conversation with me wherein he encouraged me to go to law school. I remember thinking that was the wildest idea I had ever heard of because I had played football in college and had prepared myself to be a high school teacher and coach, not a lawyer. I asked my brother why I should go to law school. I will never forget his response. He said that it would give me the "power to change." I am embarrassed to admit that what I thought he was talking about was a change for "me." I thought to myself, yes, as a lawyer I will have more money, which will mean a newer car, a bigger house, and a better living. But that is not what he was talking about. He went on to explain that a legal education would give me the "power to change" life for people in need. Specifically, he talked about the need to right the wrongs that had been done to Native American people. He spoke with sincerity and conviction. I was convinced.

For the past 28 years I have watched my brother John work tirelessly as a lawyer to achieve justice and prosperity for Indian people. As executive director for a large public interest law firm, the Native American Rights Fund, he

has had an enormous beneficial impact in preserving and protecting the rights of Native Americans. I have tried to do my best to follow his example, working for the interest of Indian people and others in need. In particular, I have seen the needs of troubled youth, both Indian and non-Indian, as I worked as a court-appointed criminal defense counsel, tribal attorney, state legislator, prosecuting attorney, state Attorney General, and criminal law professor.

The second experience I want to share has vivid visual roots in my memory. I remember walking down the center line of a rural highway in Southwest Idaho. It was a dark and foggy day in January of 1994. It is a powerful memory because of what I saw at that time. There were cars parked on both sides of this highway, stretching for nearly a mile. These were police cars, with overhead lights flashing. There were uniformed officers standing at attention next to these cars.

I had just left a memorial service held in a packed high school gymnasium located in the small town of New Plymouth, Idaho. I was walking to a cemetery located a little over a mile outside of town to attend a grave-side service for a police officer, a husband, and a father of four small children, who had been gunned down by a 14 year old boy.

It was a sad, but impressive, service held at the grave site. As the service concluded, I walked up to the widow, Sherry Feldner, who was surrounded by her little children. I reached out to shake her hand and said what I thought would be appropriate under the circumstances: "On behalf of the people of the State of Idaho, I would like to express our deepest sympathy." As soon as I said these words Sherry Feldner broke down in emotion and started to cry almost uncontrollably. I hugged her to try to comfort her. It seemed like an endless amount of time passed. I felt bad that I had said something that caused the flood of emotions. Finally, she regained her composure and looked up at me. I will never forget what she said. "Please, Mr. EchoHawk, do everything you can to make sure that this does not happen to anyone else."

To her credit, as I found out later from working with her in addressing problems of juvenile delinquency in Idaho, she was not talking only about the loss of her husband, she was also referring to the tragedy that had caused a 14 year old boy to turn to violence and become a killer. His life was destroyed as well.

The words spoken by Sherry Feldner haunted me for many days thereafter. As Attorney General of Idaho I had significant responsibility in not only enforcing law, but also crafting laws to curb unlawful conduct in society. I kept asking myself: "Am I doing enough to address the growing problem of juvenile violence?" After many tormenting days I came to a realization that the problem of juvenile crime and violence is not only the responsibility of law enforcement officers—it is a "shared responsibility." Everyone has the responsibility to see to it that "this does not happen to anyone else." We must all unite and join together to fight the growing problem of juvenile violence.

Youth in all parts of America are in jeopardy of becoming either perpetrators or victims of crime and violence. Juveniles account for about 1/3 of all arrests, [1] teen pregnancy is on the increase, [2] the school dropout rate exceeds 20%, [3] gang organizations that did not exist 25 years ago beckon to our young people to become members, and the trafficking of illegal drugs surrounds our children.

When it comes to Native American youth living in reservation communities these problems are magnified. They face greater and unique challenges not only because of factors present today, but because of the influence of past conditions.

Today, American Indians are the most impoverished minority in America. According to the 1990 Census, 31% of Native Americans live below the poverty line. [4] As of 1991 the unemployment rate among Native Americans living on reservations was 45%. [5] These factors contribute to the incidence of juvenile delinquency and violence; but what is the source of these problems? The answer to this question lies in understanding the past history of Native Americans, a history that anyone working with Native American youth must know and appreciate.

I share the history of my family and my tribe, which is similar to most other Indian families and tribes who are spread across this country.

"Echo Hawk" was the name given to my great-grandfather, a Pawnee Indian who lived in the mid-1800's in what is now the State of Nebraska. He did not speak English.

Echo Hawk got his name from the Pawnee elders. Among the Pawnee, the hawk is a symbol of a warrior. My great-grandfather, a Pawnee war scout, was known for his bravery. He was also known as a quiet young man who did not speak of his accomplishments. But other members of his tribe spoke of his deeds and bravery. As they did so it was like an "echo" from one side of he village to the other. Thus, he was named "Echo Hawk," the hawk whose deeds are echoed. I am very proud of my name and my Indian heritage. But there is also a painful history in my family and my tribe.

When the white man first came in contact with the Pawnee Indians, it was estimated that the Pawnees numbered between 15,000 and 20,000. Under the laws of the United States, the Pawnee Tribe had the right to occupy over 23 million acres of land in Nebraska. They were one of the most free, independent, and self-sustaining of people on the face of the earth.

But in the winter of 1874, when Echo Hawk was 19 years old, the Pawnee Indians were forcibly removed from the Nebraska homeland to a tiny reservation in the Oklahoma Indian Territory to make way for non-Indian settlers. No longer were the Pawnee people allowed to visit their ancestral grave sites. No longer were they permitted to seek visions on the high grassy plains of Nebraska. No longer were they able to sustain themselves by pursuing the great buffalo herds.

This is a painful history. But the most painful part for me is the realization that when the Pawnees were relocated on the reservation in Oklahoma, they did not number 20,000. They did not number 10,000. They did not even number 1,000. There were less than 750 Pawnee people remaining alive. Echo Hawk was one of the few surviving Pawnees.

The pain was not confined to Echo Hawk's generation. As a boy my father was taken from his parents and placed in a government boarding school distant from the reservation. He was dressed in a gray uniform. His hair was cut. He was beaten if he spoke his native Pawnee language.

In my generation, my older sister was sent home from public school because she was the wrong color. And I remember sitting in an elementary school classroom listening to my teacher speaking of Indian people as "savage, blood thirsty, heathen, renegades." I put my head down and cringed to think she was speaking of my family in those terms. It was very difficult for me to have positive self-esteem after listening to those descriptive words.

Thus, when I think about the factors that contribute to social problems on Indian reservations I cannot help but focus on the past history of Indian people. I blame government policy that stripped Indians of the homelands, their spiritual roots, and their way of life. I fault government policy that forced a free and self-sustaining people into a state of dependency on government rations and annuities. I lament the loss of traditional Indian family values and family bonds, a loss brought about by government policies of forced assimilation. And I recognize the detrimental impact of low self-esteem brought about by racial stereotypes, prejudice and discrimination. It is no wonder that these factors have left recent generations of Native Americans with few role models for their children to emulate. It is no wonder that many young Native Americans have been raised without much hope or dreams. It is no wonder that alcohol and drug abuse, the scourge of Indian Country, has claimed the lives of many, too many, fathers, mothers, sons, and daughters of Indian families.

But out of this pain was born some promise. Of the six children born to my parents, all six had the opportunity to go to college. We succeeded because of the values taught in our home by our parents and because finally government policies opened the doors of educational opportunity. My mother, who had an eighth grade education instilled in her six children a thirst for education. My father taught us the value of hard work. Our country invested in our education. And a black civil rights leader speaking from the steps of the Lincoln Memorial gave us hope and the power to dream.

I believe in America. I believe in the Spirit of America that says that this is a land of opportunity for all people, regardless of race, ethnic heritage, religion, gender, or economic station in life.

Along with my brothers and sisters, I have realized the best that this country has to offer, the full promise of America. But for too many the pain goes on and the promise of America is unfulfilled. I have seen faces of despair and unhappiness.

I have seen hatred on the face of Barrett Enno, a 19 year old Native American charged and convicted of first degree murder. Information gathered for his sentencing disclosed a history of physical abuse and dysfunction in his family. One particular event in this history is memorable. He was beaten and required to kneel in the corner of his bedroom with urine soaked underpants placed over his head because he had wet the bed.

I have seen a lack of hope on the face of Hoskie Lansing, an 18 year old Navajo Indian charged with rape. He was living in a state of idleness, with little parental care and supervision, causing a lack of values and respect for others.

I have seen pain on the face of Bobby Red Cap, an 18 year old Ute Indian, as he was awaiting transport to a federal correctional institution for a manslaughter conviction. He had acted in a fit of rage and had stabbed another Indian boy in the heart with a knife. He turned to violence as a means of dealing with problems that charged his emotions.

I have also seen despair on the face of Larry Sayatcitty, an 18 year old Navajo Indian, convicted of manslaughter in the death of his younger cousin. He had fallen victim to the influence of alcohol and had driven while he was drinking. He lost control and his cousin was thrown from the pickup truck and killed.

The pain goes on for Indian tribes too. For 500 years they have struggled to survive. During the past 200 years they have had their powers of self-government diminished. They have lost millions of acres of their land. Fortunately, they have not been utterly destroyed, and in the past 25 years they have won important legal victories which recognize their tribal sovereignty.

As general counsel for Idaho's largest Indian tribe, the Shoshone-Bannock Tribes, I have watched tribes devote their time, energy, and resources in the battle to restore their powers of self-government. They have fought fiercely to keep from losing their lands, natural resources, and tribal sovereignty.

Now, however, tribes are faced with losing their most important resource—their children. As social problems affecting young Indian people increase, the hope of achieving true self-determination and prosperity within tribal communities decreases. Legal rights won in the courtroom and in the Congress seem incomplete without the promise of a future generation positioned to reap the benefits of these hard fought battles.

What is the solution for stemming the tide of juvenile violence?

Let me respond to that question this way. In 1992, I was invited to be a principal speaker on the final night of the Democratic National Convention held in New York City at Madison Square Garden. You might imagine that if you were given eight minutes to address a national TV audience that you would give careful thought about what you would say. After careful thought, I chose a Native American concept of governance as the centerpiece of my message.

When the white man first came in contact with Native Americans in the northeastern region of this country, they learned of a concept of government used by the Iroquois Confederacy known as "The Seventh Generation." They said:

> In our way of life, in our government, with every decision we make, we always keep in mind the Seventh Generation to come. It's our job to see that the people coming ahead, the generations still unborn, have a world no worse than ours—and hopefully better.
>
> When we walk upon Earth, we always plant our feet carefully because we know faces of our future generations are looking up at us from beneath the ground. We never forget them." [6]

The concept of the Seventh Generation is a worthy guide for any government, but it is especially important for tribal leaders to keep in mind as they struggle to decide how to use their limited resources to combat pressing modern day problems.

We must turn our hearts to our children. Our children hold our future in their hands. If the hands of our children are strong, capable, and caring, our future is very bright. With proper care now, those hands will some day build our houses and schools. With proper care now, those hands will some day write beautiful poetry and play fine music. With proper care now, those hands will some day perform delicate surgery and soothe the sick. Most important of all, they will hold smaller hands in a gentle grasp, preparing yet another generation to reach out for the future.

But without proper care, those hands will shape a much different, much darker, world. They will clench into fists; they will brandish guns; they will grab selfishly, or strike out in anger, or curl up in despair. We cannot afford to let this happen.

Is there hope? Yes.

Today we answer that question within our hearts by our personal commitment to our work and responsibilities. We must view our job as more than just a career or profession. Our job in working with troubled Indian youth must be a personal crusade to offer hope to those children that need hope so desperately.

In closing, I challenge you to recognize that we have a "shared responsibility" for the welfare of Indian youth. I challenge you to work together and offer hope by creating one seamless system in your community that meets the special needs of troubled Native American youth. I challenge you to help troubled Indian youth to realize the promise of America.

You have the "power to change." You have the power to reduce the pain and bring forth the promise of America.

NOTES

1. See Federal Bureau of Investigations, Juvenile Crime, FBI L. ENFORCEMENT BULL., July 1, 1998, at 24.

2. See Rhonda Rowland, Teen Pregnancies on Upswing in the U.S. (last modified April 3, 1996) **http:cnn.com/HEALTH/9604/02/teenpregnancy/index. html.**

3. See generally *USA Today* Editorial Page, Schools Need to Answer to Rising Dropout Rates, *USA TODAY,* Oct. 14, 1997, at 14A.

4. DAVID H. GETCHES ET AL., FEDERAL INDIAN LAW 15 (4th ed. 1998).

5. *Id.*

6. STEVE WALL & HARVEY ARDEN, WISDOM-KEEPERS—MEETINGS WITH NATIVE AMERICAN SPIRITUAL ELDERS 68 (1990) (quoting Oren Lyons, Faithkeeper of the Turtle Clan of the Onondaga Nation and Spokesman for the Six Nations Iroquois Confederacy, concerning oral tradition of the Iroquois Great Law of Peace).

CRITICAL THINKING QUESTIONS

1. Compare and contrast the experiences of the African-Americans in Anderson's article to those of the Native Americans in Echo-Hawk's article.

2. Compare and contrast the factors that resulted in the code of the streets in Anderson's article to those that resulted in alcoholism, drug abuse, family problems, and violence among the Native Americans described by EchoHawk.

3. Each of the groups discussed by Anderson and EchoHawk are trapped in poverty. In what ways are their problems caused by poverty? In what ways are their problems caused by racism? In what ways are their problems caused by the intersection of racism and poverty?

Reading 4

In Their Own Words: Battered Women's Assessment of the Criminal Processing System's Reponses

Edna Erez and Joanne Belknap

In this article, Erez and Belknap explore some experiences of battered women as they seek services from the criminal justice system. The authors highlight women's negative and positive experiences with law enforcement and discuss ways that the criminal justice system contributes to the perpetuation of violence against women.

The questions most frequently posed about the behavior of battered women are "Why do they stay?" and "Why don't they cooper-

Source: Edna Erez and Joanne Belknap, "In Their Own Words: Battered Women's Assessment," *Violence and Victims,* Vol. 13, No. 3, 1998 © 1998. Adapted with permission of Springer Publishing Company, Inc., New York 10012.

ate with the people trying to help them?" These questions are asked not only by the public at large, but also by criminal processing agents (e.g., police officers, prosecutors, and judges), and even by battered women's advocates.

In response to these questions, it is important to acknowledge that many battered women do leave, some at the beginning and others in the later stages of abusive relationships. But a more fruitful approach for understanding the dynamics of staying, leaving and cooperating is to ask "What happens when battered women try to leave?" and "Why are violent men allowed to stay?" (see Hoff, 1990; Jones, 1994; Mahoney, 1991).

Research on woman battering has established that the most dangerous and lethal situations are when the women try to leave (e.g., Campbell, 1992; Mahoney, 1991). This phenomenon is so common that it has received a special label, "separation assault" (Mahoney, 1991). And at the time that women (and often their children) are facing increased danger, they often also encounter police, prosecutors, and judges who are "sick of" battered women returning to their abusers, or offer little assistance in avoiding further abuse. There are numerous accounts of battered women who have sought help from the authorities but have not received it (e.g., Browne, 1987; Cahn, 1992; Jones, 1994; Rosewater, 1988). In response to the notion that battered women stay because they develop "learned helplessness" (Walker, 1979), some experts have argued that it is those with the authority to control and penalize batterers (the police, prosecutors, and judges) who exhibit "learned helplessness" (Gondolf, 1988).

Given this observation, it may be useful to examine the applicability of the concept of "victim/witness cooperation" to women—the degree to which victims/witnesses assist police, prosecutors, or judges in bringing their offender to justice (see McLeod, 1983). Because attempts to leave the batterer or use the formal system to intervene are often accompanied with an increased risk of abuse by the batterer and inadequate responses by the authorities, the issue of victim/witness cooperation for battered women becomes particularly complex.

Research has established that all crime victims are reluctant to cooperate with authorities when the costs of cooperation (such as psychological stress and exposure to retaliation) are high (Davis, 1983). For many battered women, the keen role that "fear of reprisal" plays in their willingness to cooperate when the system gets involved has been clearly established (e.g., Ewing, 1987; Singer, 1988).

Many battered women who attempt to use the system face a significant threat of retaliation. They therefore need not only the information and assistance accorded to victims/witnesses regarding participation, but also increased advocacy and protection (Hart, 1993). Moreover, the greatest commonality battered women share as victims are difficulties in safe and effective participation as witnesses in the processing of their cases. These barriers often take many forms, including victim-blaming comments and attitudes by authorities (Hart, 1993). Thus, although all crime victims in similar circumstances may be reluctant to cooperate with the authorities who attempt to bring their offenders to just-ice (Davis, 1983), battered women have been uniquely singled out by system's agents as "problematic" victims/witnesses.

Assessments of battered women's cooperation with the system conducted thus far have been largely based on officials' perceptions and attitudes, or used related documentation (such as police or court reports). There has been limited research on battered women's cooperation and participation utilizing data derived from the victims themselves. The current study takes the latter approach, giving battered women "voice" concerning their experiences and perceptions of the system's response. This "voice" illuminates the dynamics of battered women's interactions with the system, and highlights the way officials' responses have both encouraged and dissuaded victims from pursuing their cases and leaving abusive relationships.

As this study reveals, battered women are not a homogenous group in their circumstances and in their needs. Different women express different wishes or requests regarding support for stopping the abuse and leaving their abusive relationships. When battered women receive "unhelpful" treatment—ranging from indifference to hostility—they are disappointed and frustrated with a system that is supposed to serve their needs. This study suggests that despite a quarter of a century of feminist scholars' and activists' campaigning to change the systemic responses to woman battering, there has not been a significant change in the sexist and victim-blaming attitudes of legal agents who serve domestic violence victims. Although few sympathetic police officers, prosecutors, judges or other public officials may make a difference in how some victims perceive the accessibility of the system's services, by and large what is delivered to battered women in terms of help in stopping the abuse remains a lottery. The research literature reviewed in the following section and the current study's findings highlight this "lottery" phenomenon: Criminal processing authorities (e.g., police, prosecutors, and judges) who offer appropriate responses are rare, and receiving meaningful assistance is generally a random event.

RESEARCH ON SYSTEMIC RESPONSES TO BATTERING

The Police

The bulk of existing research on systemic responses to woman battering focuses on the police. Studies on police response to woman battering utilized data gathered from the police themselves, via surveys or observations (e.g., Belknap, 1995; Oppenlander, 1982; Worden & Pollitz, 1984), police reports (e.g., Buzawa & Austin, 1993; Sherman & Berk, 1984) or from battered women (e.g., Bachman & Coker, 1995; Brown, 1984; Gagne, 1992; Websdale 1995a, 1995b; Websdale & Johnson, 1997). Research suggests that battered women are more likely than other victims to volunteer to name their assailants (Oppenlander, 1982) yet police are often more concerned with and spend more time with batterers than their victims (Brown, 1984; Oppenlander, 1982; Websdale, 1995a; Websdale & Johnson, 1997).

Although research reports that many battered women view the police as at least a little helpful (Brown, 1984; Kennedy & Homant, 1983), research on police indicates that the poice typically avoid arresting batterers (Bachman & Coker, 1995; Belknap, 1995; Bell, 1985; Brown, 1984; Burris & Jaffe, 1983; Dobash & Dobash, 1979; Edwards, 1989; Erez, 1986; Finesmith, 1983; Forrell, 1990–91; Gondolf & Fisher, 1988; Gondolf & McFerron, 1989; Smith & Klein, 1984; Stanko, 1985; Worden & Pollitz, 1984; Zoomer, 1989; Zorza, 1992), even in departments with pro-arrest policies (Balos & Trotzky, 1988; Bourg & Stock, 1994; Ferraro, 1989; Kennedy & Homant, 1983; Lawrenz, Lembo, & Schade 1988; Pastoor, 1984; Websdale, 1995a; Websdale & Johnson, 1997). Moreover, police inadequately and infrequently refer victims and offenders to social agencies (Belknap & McCall, 1994; Brown, 1984; Oppenlander, 1982).

The sparse research addressing battered women's assessment of how police responses affected their decisions concerning accessing the system emphasizes the significance of both positive and negative police responses. For instance, half of the battered women in one study reported that police encouragement was a major factor motivating them to request a restraining order (Fischer & Rose, 1995). In another study, battered women were more likely to take out warrants against their abusers when police explained their legal rights. On the other hand, victims who perceived police responses to them as "negative," were more likely to report feelings of self-blame (Brown, 1984).

The Courts

The plight of battered women in the court is particularly complex. As Jones (1994) noted, there is an inherent paradox in attempts to use the court's traditional approach of an adversarial legal system in domestic violence cases. Domestic "disputants" who enter the courtroom are hardly ever free-standing adversaries, in what is considered as an adversarial system of law. Battered women commonly find it difficult and complex to portray their dilemmas to judges, because their "adversary" is at once their assailant and husband or intimate. Whatever battered women may request of the court concerning their batterer—that he be locked up forever or be freed—they are likely to be reminded that the man is their husband, in the first instance, or that their complaint is disqualified, in the second. To actually help battered women in the courts, Jones (1994: 25) suggests, the myth of adversarialism must be addressed.

The sparse research on court processing of woman battering cases provides support to the problematic application of adversarial proceedings in domestic violence cases. Similar to research on police encounters with battered women, victims in the court frequently drop out of the process. Also, court officials establish unique policies for woman battering cases, and react in ways that effectively minimize the likelihood of their violent incidents becoming viable. For example, one study found that the overwhelming majority (four-fifths) of woman battering cases were dismissed, mostly because the victim requested it be dropped or did not show up in court (Quarm & Schwartz, 1985). Studies on prosecutors' handling of woman battering cases found that routine procedures are modified (Cahn, 1992) and prosecutors often establish a "cooling off" period (Ferraro & Boychuck, 1992) solely for these cases. Yet, a recent study found that battered women's decisions to pursue restraining orders were most strongly motivated by reaching a sense of "enough," following a prolonged history of violence and abuse (Fischer & Rose, 1995), indicating that this may be an important point in battered women's decision to leave and to "cooperate" with the authorities. Evaluations of the effectiveness of restraining orders, however, have shown them to be largely unenforced and ineffective (Chaudhuri & Daly, 1992; Grau, Fagan, & Wexler, 1985; McCann, 1985).

Research has found that the main reason battered women drop their cases is fear of reprisal (Quarm & Schwartz, 1985), or the frustration they feel when serious assaults against them are classified as misdemeanors (Hart, 1993; Langan & Innes, 1986). Battered women lose interest in prosecution when their victimizations are trivialized, concluding that "the costs and risks of prosecution outweigh the potential consequences for assailants" (Hart, 1993 p. 627).

With regard to the relationship between victim/witness cooperation and prosecution outcomes, some suggest that victim/witness cooperation is essential (e.g., McLeod, 1983) while others claim that such cooperation is not critical for conviction (e.g., Davis 1983; Ferraro & Boychuck, 1992). One study found that half of the battered women who requested that charges be dropped still cooperated with the prosecution (Ferraro & Boychuck, 1992). Another study, however, reported that "no drop" court policies, recently instituted in various jurisdictions, may be effective in the unintended direction: battered women who were able to drop charges were at lower risk for subsequent violence than women who were not allowed to drop charges (Ford & Regoli, 1992). The conclusion of this study was that victims were empowered by both their alliance with the authorities and their ability to drop charges.

Placing the onus of the decision to pursue a case against a batterer solely on whether the victim is not too afraid to testify against him, may be short-sighted and unwarranted for successful prosecution. For this reason, many jurisdictions have adopted "no drop" policies. Analogous to the mandatory arrest policy for police, the "no drop" court policies enable prosecutors to control decision making by precluding the victim from dropping charges (Cahn, 1992, p. 168). Yet, regardless of the existence or wisdom of "no drop" policies, it is well documented that officials taking woman battering seriously and victim advocates informing battered women of resources and services are pivotal for successful prosecution (Ferraro & Boychuck, 1992; Ferraro & Johnson, 1983; Ford & Regoli, 1992; Goolkasian, 1986; Martin, 1988; Mullarkey, 1988). Positive or encouraging responses by officials also play a considerable role in women's decisions to leave or cooperate, as do negative and inadequate responses in battered women's decisions to stay or drop. The effect of officials' responses on victims' actions, and battered women's views concerning recent system's policies designed for increasing victim cooperation, emerge in the data presented in the remainder of this article.

METHOD

Names of woman battering victims were taken from the records of the Victim Assistance Program affiliated with the prosecutor's office in two counties in Ohio. Altogether, 498 victims who were seen or assisted through these offices during 1993 were identified. Because the prosecutor's office has been occasionally in contact with the victims (e.g., follow-ups or routine inquiries about the domestic situation), and based on the professional judgment of the domestic violence special prosecutor concerning the potential risk to the victims by contacting them for the purpose of the study, this office agreed to serve as a link between the researchers and the victims. Surveys were sent by the prosecutor's office to

the respondents' addresses as they appeared in the case records. In using this mechanism to contact the victims, it was felt that any danger to the victims (many of whom tend to stay with the abuser) was minimized, giving them (and their abusers, as the case may be) a sense of remaining in the system's institutional memory. . . .

RESULTS

Sample Description

The respondents were all women and the majority (84%) were Anglo; the remainder were African American (16%). The mean age was 34.4 and both the mode and median was 36. For most of them (58%) it was the first marriage, for 29% their second marriage and 8% were not married. About one-fifth (24%) had one child with the batterer, 34% had two children, 25% had 3 or more children and 16% of the respondents had no children with the batterer.

The overwhelming majority (90%) of the victims initiated the contact with the criminal processing system concerning the battering; in the remaining 10% of the cases either a neighbor or a friend notified the police. Of those initiating contact with the criminal processing system, the majority (82%) initiated the contact by calling the police, 14% initiated a complaint through the prosecution and the remainder through other means, such as contacting legal aid, a private attorney, friends, or the batterer's parole officer. For two-thirds of the victims this was not the first time they contacted the system, and some of them reported up to ten prior contacts. For the majority of the respondents (90%), the specific incident that brought them to the prosecutor's office resulted in an injury. For over half (53%) of the victims this was not their first contact with the courts. Over a quarter of the victims had four or more contacts (the mean was 3.4).

Victims' Interactions With Police

The majority (66%) of the victims stated that the police did not collect any evidence with which to prosecute the offender. In the cases in which they collected evidence, it was most often pictures or talking to witnesses.

In response to a question about positive or encouraging behavior exhibited by the police, over two fifths (43%) of the victims stated that they encountered encouraging comments from the police concerning going forward with their complaint. Examples of encouraging comments or behaviors, in the words of the respondents, were the following:

"The different officers were very encouraging to continue to call and issue restraining orders to press charges and not then drop them."
"They had a way of talking to me that led me to trust them, and carry on further with the prosecution."
"He recommended me going to the hospital and attaching the ER report to the police report."
"One officer advised me to insist to the prosecutor that action be taken."
"They arrested him immediately."

Some of the victims noted comments that they believed were meant to be encouraging or helpful, but which the victims found to be somewhat insensitive or lacking in understanding or appreciation regarding the plight of battered women. Examples include suggesting the victim "press charges or shut up," or threats that if the victim stayed and called them again "there would be no one there" for them.

When respondents were asked to specify whether they encountered discouraging comments by the police, a higher proportion (49%) of the victims claimed that they experienced discouraging comments or attitudes by the police. Examples included comments such as the following:

"They discouraged me from filing charges."
"One policeman acted as if nothing happened and wouldn't listen to me."
"One time an officer knew Mike (my husband) and told him 'you need to leave this bitch alone'."
"The police acted as if it was my fault because I was married. One policeman said, if he was my husband, he'd beat me."

Other victims mentioned police comments which may suggest an attempt to mediate the situation, but which the victims found inappropriate or indicative of misunderstanding the problem or the injury, or victim-blaming, such as:

"It's just as much your fault as his."
"I was told I shouldn't make my abuser angry. I should try to make him happy."
"The obnoxious PLSD officer told me and my 10 yr. old daughter to mop up the blood, not just to help. Very cold and uncaring."

Some victims mentioned that police used evidentiary or procedural rules or reminders about "the real world" to discourage them from bringing the batterer to justice, such as informing them that prosecution would be difficult with "only" the victim's testimony, informing them that protection orders were "as good as a piece of toilet paper," and a detective who yelled at a victim and implied she was lying.

The overwhelming majority of the victims (98%) claimed that they cooperated with police requests for information. The most common reasons respondents provided for cooperating with the police were a need to protect themselves or fear of their abuser, having nothing to lose, and wanting to do something about the situation, including having the offender arrested or brought to justice.

The victims described various types of abuse which were quite disturbing, but for which there were not always visible signs or witnesses. The majority of the victims (96%) felt they presented to the police the abusive behavior of their batterer accurately, while 4% thought they minimized the abuse. It may be argued that this small percentage is a methodological artifact, and that in-depth interview may have disclosed the tendency of battered women to become desensitized to the enormity of their abuse. Some stated that they were more likely to minimize the injuries at the beginning than the later stages of the abusive relationship (consistent with Ferraro and Johnson's [1983] findings). Similarly, 91% thought they presented their injury accurately to the police and 9% thought they minimized it. No respondents thought they exaggerated it. However, half (50%) of the victims thought that the police minimized the extent of their injury; in the words of one victim:

> "The police minimized it. Told me I didn't need stitches—I received 6 stitches at hospital."

Sixteen percent of the victims thought the police did not believe their version of the event that led to the court case. Some felt that the officers sided with their abuser (consistent with Oppenlander (1982)), and did not properly assess the danger of the situation:

> "One officer seemed to want to cover up (at the time) for my ex-husband."
> " . . . when he held a gun to me and they were called . . . they didn't make either one of us leave. They laughed."

Over two thirds (71%) of the victims stated that some criminal processing agent tried to convince them to drop their complaint, most often this included statements such as:

> "I was going overboard."
> "Not enough physical evidence to convince the judge and no witnesses other than my children."
> "Prosecutor suggested to drop the complaint, because most women do."
> "They mentioned 'I love you' from the abuser."
> "A judge felt we should 'try to patch things up.'"

Victims' Interactions With Prosecution

Half of the victims (51%) claimed that they were encouraged to follow through with prosecution, while the other half (49%) stated they were discouraged from following through. Examples of encouraging comments were the following:

> "He would go to jail and he wasn't allowed to have any contact with me whatsoever."
> "The prosecutor told me he could get him if I went there with it."
> "This kind of stuff had been going on for quite some time, and they referred me to the battered women's hotline and the kind of help I could get."
> "Police records explained; they seem more understanding and acted like they believed."
> "She (the prosecutor) was very friendly and supportive, and said, nobody, male or female, should go through any kind of abuse."
> "He took my statement in a careful and accurate manner making sure not to exclude anything."

Some victims stated, however, that the prosecutors' doubts and reluctance to pursue the case were disturbing to them, such as telling the victims they did not believe them or that they (the victims) would not follow through with the prosecution of their batterers. Others felt that putting the responsibility on them to decide what to do, or continuously asking them what they want to do, was not helpful or desirable.

Respondents described instances of discouraging comments, attitudes or messages conveyed by the prosecution. In the words of the respondents:

"He seemed like I was wasting his time."

"He wanted to know what happened if I said or did anything to upset the batterer."

"They refused to do anything even though I had a Protection Order."

"He said the abuser would just get a fine—no jail."

"He (the prosecutor) was pretty obnoxious, real busy, just like cattle, he did not seem to care. He didn't look at anything until the day of the hearing."

"He excused the violence because of the abuser's deformed hand."

Some victims conceded, however, that what seemed at first discouraging comments turned out to be useful in the end:

"I was forced to sign a paper saying I would not change my mind about prosecuting in order to get help. Later I was very thankful I had to do this."

Over half (51%) of the victims stated that the prosecutor asked them questions about whether they provoked their abuser, such as "Why were you there?" and "How did you start the problem?" About one fifth (19%) of the victims felt the prosecutor did not believe their version of the event that led to the court case, and over two thirds (38%) thought the prosecutor minimized the extent of their injury.

The overwhelming majority of the victims (98%) stated they cooperated with the prosecutor's request to provide information. Reasons for cooperating commonly were the following:

"To make sure he was brought to justice."

"I wanted something to be done about this, because my children and I were forced to leave the home and stay at the battered women's shelter and I wanted him out of the home so we could return."

Court Experiences

About half (49%) of the victims had testified in court. Inconsistent with the popular notion of noncooperative victims, the most common reasons the battered women reported for not testifying were that they were not asked to testify (26%), intimidated by the abuser (22%), or not notified (11%). These percentages may be a result of the small sample which may include the less severe abuse and dangerous situations. It is possible that in more dangerous cases victims would be more reluctant to testify. Less frequent reasons included dropped charges in exchange for uncontested divorce or cases which were not scheduled yet. In response to the question 'why they did not testify,' victims comments included the following:

"We had a daughter together."

"My second attempt to have someone 'hear' me; the prosecutor said it would not hold up in court."

"After I found out that they weren't going to do anything, I packed up the kids and moved to Florida."

About one fifth (19%) of the victims thought the extent of the batterer's abusive behavior was minimized in the court; the remainder thought it was presented accurately. Similarly, 26% thought their injuries were minimized when presented in court. About three quarters of the victims requested a Temporary Protection Order (TPO) and practically all of them received it. Consistent with research reviewed earlier, over half

(58%) thought the TPO was not helpful in guaranteeing their safety. Reasons mentioned were that:

> "It never meant nothing to him. It never stopped him from coming over."
>
> "A TPO is not worth the paper its wrote on even the police say that if your abuser wants to abuse, they will."
>
> "When he got a letter ordering him to stay away from me, he put it in his pocket, broke into my home—when I arrived he beat me again because I had the letter sent to him."
>
> "He still has keys and police can not always sit in front of my house."

One third of the victims (33%) stated they encountered comments, questions or attitudes by the judge that they found objectionable. Examples included:

> "She had her mind made up before I could speak. She never listened to the problem, instead concentrated on another aspect of the case which had very little to do with the case."
>
> "It seemed like it was just hurried thru to get on to the next case."
>
> "He said it just seemed like a custody battle."

Some victims were disturbed by court procedures and evidentiary rules, such as not allowing children who had witnessed the abuse to testify, or having to rely on inadequate Legal Aid attorneys. The victims also experienced various types of inappropriate or irrelevant questioning. Sixteen percent of the victims stated that the judge asked them whether they had provoked the abuse, and half of them stated that the judge inquired about divorce proceedings.

Close to half of the victims (48%) stated they dropped the complaint, most commonly because of fear for their safety (36%). Over one third (38%) of the cases were dismissed and fewer than one third (31%) resulted in conviction. Over two thirds of the victims (68%) thought the disposition of the batterer was too lenient and one third thought it was appropriate. Examples of why they thought the disposition was lenient covered various aspects. Some mentioned the restrictions of overburdened prisons and jails:

> "The overcrowding of the jails has been the excuse for staying free. They took him to jail on Friday after Sunday morning he was back at the house. He is supposed to finish his jail time, 2 years later, soon but that probably will not happen."
>
> "He always gets a tough sentence then always gets out because he is a good inmate or gets out into some 'program' and don't even do half his time till he comes after me again!"

Others felt that the sentences do not take into consideration the welfare of victims and their families:

> "I think if a man or woman can't control their temper and it goes so far there is abuse (physical). They shouldn't have visitation because sooner or later the child may get abused."

Victims' Opinions of Various Procedural and Court Issues

Almost two thirds (65%) of the victims thought that victims of domestic violence should be allowed to drop charges in order to improve their domestic situation, and 15% thought they should not be allowed to drop charges (21% had no opinion). Some responses against allowing victims to drop charges included:

> "If this is a repeat offense; or even the first time, I feel these abusers need to learn they can't do this & get away with it."
>
> "No, dropping charges will not improve the situation; it will just enable it to continue."

On the other hand, those who felt the victim should be allowed to drop the charges, offered reasons such as:

"It's still my choice—why should I get arrested for not showing up or dropping charges."

"Yes, I'm more afraid than anything for the kids."

Victims were also asked whether they thought that battered women should be subpoenaed to testify in court. About half (49%) thought they should be required to testify in court, and (39%) did not know how to answer. Some reasons for requiring victims to testify were as follows:

"No one will know unless you tell what happened."

"Because I think the abuser should have to sit there and hear what I have to say."

"So the offender case can be prosecuted better."

"They know what has happened. Of course the abuser will lie about it, he knows he did wrong and don't want to go to jail."

Respondents who thought that victims should not be required to testify reasoned as follows:

"Because you been through enough."

"Too much turmoil and pain of having to face the abuser."

About two thirds of the victims (65%) thought that the use of depositions [sworn testimony given in an attorney's office] in lieu of court appearances would increase domestic violence victims' cooperation with prosecution. One victim explained her reasons for preferring depositions, and not having her as the major mobilizer of the criminal case, as follows:

"Yes, excellent idea. Can't stress how much difference I feel this would make. Plus in my case, taking the responsibility of pressing charges from me and giving it to the state really made a difference. I could have pressed charges against the drunk who held the knife to my throat, bounced me off walls, raped me and deprived me of sleep while threatening me and calling me names, but the kind, loving man who would do anything for me in the morning would have talked me out of it."

Victims' Assessment of Factors Affecting Cooperation

The victims were requested to rate the importance of various reasons for which they were unwilling to cooperate with prosecution. Fear of the batterer received the highest score, with a mean of 4.51 (on a scale of 1–5 where 5 is the highest score); followed by the ineffectiveness of the system (4.35), concern for the children (4.02), distrust of the criminal processing system (4.02), difficult experiences with the criminal processing system (3.87), emotional dependency on the batterer (3.74), economic dependency on the abuser (3.47), and the least influential factor was lack of support from the family (2.62). Other reasons for not cooperating with the prosecution given by victims included the following:

"We need lots of emotional support from family friends and court-victims are very confused and scared."

"It's really scary and it takes a lot of guts to come forward about domestic violence. You've already been threatened, beaten and traumatized by the abuser, after you come forward, you fear for your life!"

"The system doesn't work well enough."

Respondents offered a variety of factors as the most important ones to have helped them to follow through with their cases. These factors included the safety and welfare of themselves and their family. Comments about victims' own safety included the following:

"My life and where it was going and my daughter, seeing him the way he was."

"The fear of him continuing to try and hurt me and his threats to kill me."

"Fear of my life being taken."

Other comments emphasized the welfare of the children:

"I have a child. I want to protect him from any harm. Also my divorce visitation and how and when the father can see the child is determined by the outcome of domestic violence charges."

"Repeatedly forgave him and finally realized the abuse wouldn't stop due to drugs and alcohol. My daughter was also getting to an age where she was seeing more of the abuse and it was not easy to hide it from her."

"Seeing the fear in my children's faces and also my son got hurt this time. I thought to myself, I'd rather be dead than live like this any longer."

Consistent with Fischer and Rose's (1995) analysis of "enough is enough," an important factor was victims' determination not to put up with the abuse any longer. Comments included the following:

"I was tired of being abused. I wanted him to leave me alone."

"I did want something to come out of this to prove I was not going to put up with it any longer."

"I was sick of it! I was determined to get out of the situation of almost 4 years."

"I was tired of being beaten by my ex-husband. No one seems to care until you're dead. Then it's too late. We need help at the time not after we're dead."

Another factor commonly mentioned as helping in following through with the case was help and support from family. Comments included the following:

"I had so many people that know my situation, had seen the abuse, verbal as well as physical and know how scary it can be to be the focus of an abuser."

"His sisters that finally observed what was going on. They encouraged that I go ahead and put him in jail and straighten him out."

Several victims mentioned criminal processing agents helping them to follow through with the complaint. Respondents mentioned the police, prosecutor, victim assistance staff and other victims' services workers. Their responses highlight the importance of supportive criminal processing reactions:

"Officer Copeland searched me out in the courthouse and let me know that the only way to stop the cycle is to confront and make him (the abuser) know you'll not let this drop. The other sheriffs were helpful in encouraging me to not give up, it takes time to build a case."

"The first time I went to the prosecution office, I ended up filling out papers and when it was my turn to go in, I ran out because I didn't have the guts to go through with it. But during this whole episode, I had met a police officer who had dealt with my ex-husband before in arrest and stuff, and he went out of his way to talk to me and offered to go up there with me, and he did the next day. He had seen plenty of cases like this, and gave me the trust and courage that I was going to be all right."

"The policeman that let me know he was concerned and he cared enough to give me the information I needed to follow through with the proceedings. Before policemen only put the batterer more close to myself and danger."

Victims were requested to rank the behavior of various agents and players in terms of encouraging them to follow through with the case (on a scale from 1 to 5 where 5 is the highest). Family or friends scored the highest (mean = 4.17). They were followed by victim assistance staff (4.08), and prosecutor (3.70). The judge, defense attorney and police received the lowest means (3.32, 3.14 and 3.00, respectively). It is notable that the police received the lowest score among criminal processing actors, even lower than the defense attorneys [who represent the abuser].

Respondents were asked to rank the behavior of various agents and players in terms of the discouraging effect they had on them regarding following through with the complaint. The police were ranked the highest, with a mean of 2.95, on a scale from 1 to 5 (where 5 is the highest), followed by judges (2.85), defense attorneys (2.83), prosecutors (2.69), and the victim's family (2.19).

The reasons victims listed for reluctance to follow through with the court case received the following means: fear of the batterer was the highest (4.68), followed by ineffectiveness of the system (4.44), emotional ties to abuser (3.76), attitudes of criminal processing personnel (3.69), concern for the integrity of the family (3.51), economic considerations (3.46), and lastly, improvement in the relationship with the abuser (3.33).

Victims' Satisfaction With System's Agents and Penalties

The major reasons for willingness to cooperate with the criminal processing system were 1) stopping the abusive behavior (4.77), followed by 2) sending a message that the behavior is criminal (4.26), and 3) punishing the abuser (4.13). Much lower scores were given to reasons such as helping in the divorce proceedings (3.08) and negotiating some advantage in the relationship with the abuser (2.68).

Victims were asked to rank the level of satisfaction with the various system's personnel. Victim assistance staff received the highest score (3.89), followed by prosecutors (3.31), judges (3.25), and police (3.14). Victims' level of satisfaction with the process received a score of 2.77, and satisfaction with the outcome was 2.22.

Respondents ranked the importance of various considerations in determining whether an abuse was prosecuted. The highest score was given to the fact that the behavior violates the law (4.66), followed by the prior record of the batterer (4.58), the abuser's attitudes (4.53), the seriousness of the offense (4.26), and the likelihood of conviction (4.13). The wish of the victim and the victim advocate's opinion ranked somewhat lower (3.84 and 3.79, respectively).

Slightly over half of the victims (54%) thought they were adequately informed about the prosecution process or what was expected of them in the criminal processing process, almost one third (30%) did not, and the remainder had no opinion. The majority (57%) also stated they were aware of what they could expect from the justice system in terms of support. The majority of the victims (60%) also stated that they tried other avenues besides the criminal processing system, to deal with the abuse. These included marital counseling, individual counseling (for the victim), threatening to leave, trying to get his alcohol and drug abuse under control, buying a "big dog," and buying a gun. Notably, over three quarters (77%) of the respondents said they would use the criminal processing system to deal with future abuse.

The victims were asked to rank the appropriateness of various penalties imposed on batterers. On a scale from 1 to 5, where 5 is the highest, jail sentence ranked the highest (mean = 4.22), followed by fine (3.16), probation with batterers' treatment program (2.96), and pretrial diversion with counseling (2.83). The other penalties commonly imposed by the courts received less than the middle-range response: probation with individual counseling (2.61), suspended sentence (2.09), and the lowest score was given to probation (1.87).

DISCUSSION

The victim responses portrayed the inordinate difficulties and frustrations they had experienced because of their domestic violence situation. Victims reported incessant threats, abuse, confusion and pain. They and their families were exposed to danger on a daily basis. Many tried, unsuccessfully, to resolve the problem without resorting to the criminal processing system. Following contacts with the police and encounters with prosecutors or judges, many realized that the system had a limited capability or investment in helping or providing them with meaningful relief from their abusers. Their responses also reflected the contradictions inherent in the criminal processing system's attempt to approach these incidents as "just another crime," and particularly, the problematic use of adversarial proceedings when parties are simultaneously family members and assailants.

The results also show that the attitudes, comments, opinions or assumptions of criminal processing personnel who deal with battered women can be, and often are, harmful and demoralizing to victims. Inappropriate or inadequate system responses may cause battered women a deeper despair than the abuse itself. Negative comments or discouraging attitudes by criminal processing agents underline victims' powerlessness and helplessness. The data suggest that if police officers side and identify with the abuser, if they cannot appreciate the fear or vulnerability of the victim, if they do not recognize the power imbalance between the parties (all of these situations were mentioned as problems by the victims), these agents exacerbate the situation.

Similarly, if prosecutors do not try to treat the case as more than a constellation of pieces of evidence, if they give up at the outset because the evidence may look too weak or unconvincing, or if they are quick to point out the little impact the criminal processing machinery can have on the batterer or the situation, they have undermined victims' determination to follow through.

Even though victims viewed the abuse as a criminal act for which the most appropriate penalty would be a jail sentence, most of them believed that their problems with abuse could not be solved effectively by the criminal processing system. As in prior research findings, the single most important barrier for the women's cooperation was their fear of the batterer. Yet, they viewed a sympathetic criminal processing system response as critical to their determination to follow through with the process. The ranking of the police, who are the first to be called to the crime scene, was particularly notable in the victims' assessment of the system's response. Contrary to studies which consistently find that crime victims rank the overall performance of the police the highest of all agents (e.g., Erez, Roeger, & Morgan, 1997), the abused women in this study ranked police the lowest of all the authorities they encountered.

Nonetheless, the victims' responses suggest that criminal processing agents can and do make some difference. Several respondents stated that when agents show understanding and appreciation of the battered women's plight, or when criminal processing personnel treat the cases with persistence and compassion, domestic violence victims can sustain the frustration they face, or withstand the difficulties they have to overcome to reach a satisfactory solution. Respondents provided several examples in which the most important factor in their ability to follow through with the complaint was a police officer who cared and helped, a prosecutor who was determined to assist them, and of course, victim-assistance personnel who provided support and encouragement. Yet, based on the data reported here, such helpful responses are rare: to battered women, the criminal processing system remains a lottery.

The results also show that victims do not have a unified approach or identical opinions on many issues pertaining to their participation in the criminal processing system. Some want to maintain the choice of initiating or dropping a complaint or a charge, others prefer to have this choice taken from them and given to criminal processing agents. Some want to be "forced" (subpoenaed) to testify and follow through, others would rather have the decision left to them. Here, as in other situations in which criminal processing policies have been designed without input from the victims themselves (e.g., mandatory arrest, see Bowman, 1992), the "one size fits all" solution to battered women's plight is not likely to alleviate problems. The victims' responses suggest that such an approach is likely to deepen the sense of powerlessness and exacerbate the frustration characteristic of those enmeshed in battering relationships.

The conclusion that clearly emerges from this group of victims is that they want to retain choice and wish to be treated as autonomous individuals in the attempt to stop the abuse (see also Ferraro, 1995). Uniform policies of "mandatory arrest," "no drop," or "being subpoenaed to testify" cannot do justice to victims who are varied in their domestic situations, and consequently in the strategies they choose to deal with the abuse. The survey used in this study did not account for the economic resources, social supports, job and other opportunities of these women, and thus could not address how these factors might relate to the victims' assessment of the criminal processing system's responses to them. It is possible that women with more options are less likely to be dependent on the police and courts to rectify their situations and to find safety. Future research needs to address the effects of these factors on battered women's use of the system.

The results of this survey of victims also suggest that, while the criminal processing machinery has a limited ability to help, it can also make a difference. In designing and practicing an effective systemic response to women battering, the victims' voice can provide useful directions. It is important that policy makers and practitioners become acquainted with the variety of opinions battered women hold and the different preferences they have for stopping abuse.

REFERENCES

BACHMAN, R., & COKER, A. L. (1995). Police involvement in domestic violence. *Violence and Victims, 10,* 98–106.

BALOS, B., & TROTZKY, K. (1988). Enforcement of domestic abuse act in Minnesota: A preliminary study. *Law & Inequality, 6,* 83–125.

BELKNAP, J. (1995). Law enforcement officers' attitudes about the appropriate responses to woman battering. *International Review of Victimology, 4,* 47–62.

BELL, D. J. (1985). A multiyear study of Ohio: Urban, suburban, and rural police dispositions of domestic disputes. *Victimology, 10,* 301–310.

BOURG, S., & STOCK, H. V. (1994) A review of domestic violence arrest statistics in a police department using a pro-arrest policy: Are pro-arrest policies enough? *Journal of Family Violence, 9,* 177–189.

BOWMAN, C. G. (1992). The arrest experiments: A feminist critique. *Journal of Criminal Law & Criminology, 83,* 201–209.

BROWN, S. E. (1984). Police responses to wife beating: Neglect of a crime of violence. *Journal of Criminal Justice, 12,* 277–288.

BROWNE, A. (1987). *When battered women kill.* New York: Free Press.

BURRIS, C. A., & JAFFE, P. (1983). Wife abuse as a crime: The impact of police laying charges. *Canadian Journal of Criminology, 25,* 309.

BUZAWA, E. S., & AUSTIN, T. (1993). Determining police response to domestic violence victims. *American Behavioral Scientist, 36*(5), 610–623.

CAHN, N. R. (1992). Innovative approaches to the prosecution of domestic crimes. In E. S. Buzawa and C. G. Buzawa (Eds.), *The changing criminal justice response* (pp. 161–180). Westport, CT: Auburn House.

CAMPBELL, J. (1992). If I can't have you, no one can. In J. Radford & D. E. H. Russell (Eds.), *Femicide: The politics of woman killing* (pp. 99–113). New York: Twayne Publishers.

CHAUDHURI, M. & DALY, K. (1992). Do restraining orders help? Battered women's experience with male violence and legal process. In E. S. Buzazea & C. G. Buzawa (Eds.), *Domestic violence: The changing criminal justice response* (pp. 227–252). Westport, CT: Auburn House.

DAVIS, R. C. (1983). Victim/witness noncooperation: A second look at a persistent phenomenon. *Journal of Criminal Justice, 11,* 287–299.

DOBASH, R. E., & DOBASH, R. P. (1979). *Violence against wives.* New York: Free Press.

EDWARDS, S. S. M. (1989). *Policing "domestic" violence: Women, the law and the state.* London: Sage.

EREZ, E. (1986). Intimacy, violence, and the police. *Human Relations, 39,* 265–281.

EREZ, E., & BELKNAP, J. (1998). Battered women and the criminal justice system: The perspectives of the service providers. *European Journal on Criminal Policy and Research, 6,* 37–57.

EREZ, E., ROEGER, L., & MORGAN, F. (1997). Victim harm, impact statements and victim satisfaction with justice: An Austrian Experience. *International Review of Victimology, 5*(1): 37–60.

EWING, C. P. (1987). *Battered women who kill.* Lexington Books.

FERRARO, K. J. (1995). Battered women and criminal justice. Addendum to the American Society of Criminology Task Force Report on Violence Against Women, submitted to Attorney General Janet Reno, August.

FERRARO, K. J., & BOYCHUCK, T. (1992). In E. S. Buzawa & C. G. Buzawa (Eds.), *Domestic violence: The changing criminal justice response* (pp. 209–225). Westport, CT: Auburn House.

FERRARO, K. J., & JOHNSON, J. M. (1983). How women experience battering. *Social Problems, 30,* 325–339.

FINESMITH, B. K. (1983). Police responses to battered women: A critique and proposals for reform. *Seton Hall Law Review, 14,* 74–109.

FISCHER, K., & ROSE, M. (1995). When 'enough is enough': Battered women's decision making around court orders of protection. *Crime & Delinquency, 41,* 414–29.

FORD, D. A., & REGOLI, M. J. (1992). The preventive impacts of policies for prosecuting wife batterers. In E. S. Buzawa & C. G. Buzawa, *Domestic violence: The changing criminal justice response* (pp. 181–207). Westport, CT: Auburn House.

FORRELL, C. (1990–91). Stopping the violence: Mandatory arrest and police tort liability for failing to assist battered women. *Berkeley Women's Law Journal, 6,* 215–262.

GAGNE, P. L. (1992). Appalachian women: Violence and social control. *Journal of Contemporary Ethnography, 20,* 387–415.

GONDOLF, E. W., with FISHER, E. R. (1988). *Battered women as survivors: An alternative to treating learned helplessness.* New York: Lexington Books.

GONDOLF, W. W., & McFERRON, J. R. (1989). Handling battering men: Police action in wife abuse cases. *Criminal Justice & Behavior, 16,* 429.

GOOLKASIAN, G. A. (1986). Confronting domestic violence: The role of criminal court judges. *National Institute in Justice/Research in Brief* (November): 1–8.

GRAU, J., FAGAN, J., & WEXLER, S. (1985). Restraining orders for battered women: Issues of access and efficacy. In C. SchWeber & C. Feinman (Eds.), *Criminal justice politics and women: The aftermath of legally mandated change* (pp. 13–28). New York: Haworth Press.

HART, B. (1993). Battered women and the criminal justice system. *American Behavioral Scientist, 83,* 73–119

HOFF, L. A. (1990). *Battered women as survivors.* London: Routledge & Kegan Paul.

JONES, A. (1994). *Next time, she'll be dead: Battering and how to stop it.* Boston: Beacon Press.

KENNEDY, D. B., & HOMANT, R. J. (1983). Attitudes of abused women toward male and female police officers. *Criminal Justice & Behavior, 10,* 391–405.

LANGAN, P. A., & INNES, C. A. (1986). Preventing domestic violence against women. Bureau of Justice Statistics, Special Report, August, Washington, D.C.

LAWRENZ, F., LEMBO, J. F., & SCHADE, T. (1988). Time series analysis of the effect of a domestic violence directive on the number of arrests per day. *Journal of Criminal Justice, 16,* 493–498.

MAHONEY, M. (1991). Legal images of battered women: Redefining the issue of separation. *Michigan Law Review 90,* 2–94.

MARTIN, M. (1988). A social worker's response. In N. Hutchings (Ed.), *The violent family* (pp. 53–61). New York: Human Sciences Press.

McCANN, K. (1985). Battered women and the law: the limits of legislation. In J. Brophy & C. Smart (Eds.), *Women-in-law: Exploration in law, family and sexuality* (pp. 71–96). London: Routledge & Kegan Paul.

McLEOD, M. (1983). Victim noncooperation in the prosecution of domestic assault. *Criminology, 21*(3), 395–416.

MULLARKEY, E. (1988). The legal system for victims of family violence. In N. Hutchings (Ed.), *The violent family* (pp. 43–52). New York: Human Sciences Press.

OPPENLANDER, N. (19.82). Coping or copping out. *Criminology, 20,* 449–465.

PASTOOR, M. K. (1984). Police training and the effectiveness of Minnesota 'domestic abuse' laws. *Law and Inequality, 2,* 257–607.

QUARM, D., & SCHWARTZ, M. (1985). Domestic violence in criminal court: An examination of new legislation in Ohio. In C. Scheber & C. Feinman (Eds.), *Criminal justice politics and women: The aftermath of legally mandated change* (pp. 29–46). New York: Haworth Press.

RADFORD, J. (1987). Policing male violence-Policing women. In Hanmer, J. & Maynard, M. (Eds.), *Women, violence and social control* (pp. 30–45). Atlantic Heights, New Jersey: Humanities Press.

ROSEWATER, L. B. (1988). Battered or schizophrenic? Psychological tests can't tell. In K. Yllö & M. Bograd

(Eds.), *Feminist perspectives on wife abuse* (pp. 200–216). Newbury Park: Sage.

SHERMAN, L. W., & BERK, R. A. (1984). The specific deterrent effects of arrest for domestic assault. *American Sociological Review, 49,* 261–272.

SINGER, S. I. (1988). The fear of reprisal and the failure of victims to report a personal crime. *Journal of Quantitative Criminology. 4*(3), 289–302.

SMITH, D. A., & KLEIN, J. R. (1984). Police control of interpersonal disputes. *Social Problems 31,* 469–481.

STANKO, E. A. (1985). *Intimate intrusions: Women's experience of male violence.* London: Routledge & Kegan Paul.

WALKER, L. E. (1979). *The battered woman.* New York: Harper & Row.

WEBSDALE, N. (1995a). An ethnographic assessment of the policing of domestic violence in rural eastern Kentucky. *Social Justice, 22,* 102–122.

WEBSDALE, N. (1995b). Rural woman abuse: The voices of Kentucky women. *Violence Against Women, 1,* 309–338.

WEBSDALE, N., & JOHNSON, B. (1997). The policing of domestic violence in rural and urban areas: The voices of battered women in Kentucky. *Policing and Society, 6,* 297–317.

WORDEN, R. E., & POLLITZ, A. A. (1984). Police arrests in domestic disturbances. *Law & Society Review, 18,* 105.

ZOOMER, O. J. (1989). Policing woman beating in the Netherlands. In J. Hanmer & E. A. Stanko (Eds.), *Women, policing, and male violence: International perspectives* (pp. 125–154). London: Routledge.

ZORZA, J. (1992). The criminal law of misdemeanor violence, 1970–1990. *Journal of Criminal Law & Criminology, 83,* 46–72.

CRITICAL THINKING QUESTIONS

1. According to the battered women interviewed by Erez and Belknap, how effectively does the criminal justice system respond to their needs?

2. What distinguishes police, prosecutors, and judges who show an understanding and commitment to ending domestic violence from their peers who do not? What difference does this make in the lives of women who are battered?

3. Based on the findings of Erez and Belknap, design a program to improve the response of police, prosecutors, and judges to battered women's need for assistance.

Reading 5

Wife Rape: A Social Problem for the 21st Century

Kersti Yllö

In this article, Yllö contends that feminists and social scientists have all but ignored rape within marriage, thereby accepting it as a part of patriarchal marriage, which is at the heart of men's dominance over women.

It is 1999, and this special issue on sexual assault in marriage is, to my knowledge, the first issue of a scholarly journal fully devoted

Source: Reprinted from *Violence Against Women* 5, no. 9 (September 1999): 1059–1063. Reprinted by permission of Sage Publications, Inc.

to this topic. In the past 30 years, we have seen a proliferation of research on (roughly in order of their emergence as social problems) child abuse, rape, battering, child sexual abuse, elder abuse, date rape, and lesbian battering. Hundreds of journal issues and books have been devoted to these forms of violence and rightly so. However, despite the overall recognition of the epidemic of male violence, there remains a troubling silence surrounding sexual violence toward wives and cohabitors. Academics and activists (with a few notable exceptions) have said little and done less about marital rape. A recent survey of 621 rape crisis centers and battered women's shelters, for example, found that only 4% included wife rape as an issue of concern in their mission statements (Bergen, 1996). Scholars have written only three books on the topic (Bergen, 1996; Finkelhor & Yllö, 1985; Russell, 1982). With this issue, *Violence Against Women* takes an important step in furthering research and advocacy on rape in marriage.

The articles in this issue contribute to a small, but important body of knowledge about marital rape. Kathleen Basile (1999, this issue) addresses the crucial issue of consent and coercion in her article on "Rape by Acquiescence." Her analysis of how and why women "give in" to unwanted sex in marital and cohabiting relationships contributes to our understanding of the key element of rape. Although consent is always at issue in the definition of rape, it is nowhere more complex and murky than in marriage, where "I do" has historically been regarded as a permanent consent decree.

Patricia Mahoney's analysis of National Crime Victimization Survey data (1999, this issue) provides some of the best quantitative data on wife rape since Diana Russell's (1982) groundbreaking survey on sexual assault was conducted 20 years ago. Mahoney documents one of the central characteristics of rape in marriage. It is rarely a one-time assault; rather, it is an ongoing aspect of the relationship. She reports that marital rape survivors are 10 times more likely to experience multiple assaults than survivors of stranger or acquaintance rape. These data speak to a point that David Finkelhor and I (1985) have often repeated: When you are raped by a stranger, you live with a frightening memory, but when you are raped by your husband, you live with your rapist.

Mahoney also reports that in comparison to other survivors, wives are less likely to seek help from police, get medical attention, or obtain other agency help, even when they have been severely assaulted. Jackie Campbell and Karen Soeken address the consequences of the patterns Mahoney describes. In their community sample of battered women, they found that the women who had been sexually assaulted by their partners (in addition to being physically assaulted) had significantly more health problems and gynecological symptoms than women who had "only" been physically abused. Furthermore, they found that the sexually assaulted women had elevated risk factors for homicide even when seriousness of physical abuse and demographic variables were controlled.

These studies are a significant addition to our understanding of wife rape and its consequences, and I am encouraged by that. Still, I am troubled by the fact that so few articles have been published on this subject. I am concerned that this issue may represent the bulk of current research on rape in marriage. I hope that I am not alone in wondering why.

Over the years, I have been amazed at how difficult it is to raise the issue of wife rape and how easily it disappears from our discourse, despite the consistent and extraordinary efforts of Laura X and other activists. In the last decade, the only incident of marital rape to receive national attention was the Bobbitt case, and we can be quite sure that if Lorena had not taken the response to her assault into her own hands, we never would have heard about it. Why is the problem of rape in marriage so elusive?

I have come to the conclusion that there is something about the very concept of marital rape that impedes our work. It contains a cultural contradiction inherent in no other form of violence and it goes to the very heart of the institution of marriage. In our contemporary romantic image of marriage, love and sex are inextricably linked and form the very foundation of the relationship. The wedding both legitimates and celebrates this sexual bond. The very idea of this bond turning into sexual bondage falls outside of this frame of reference.

Underneath the modern image (and in many ways, the reality) of marriage, the history of the institution continues to affect us deeply. It is only within the last century in developed countries that wives are no longer regarded as their husbands' chattel. Rape laws were developed to protect men's property (virgin daughters and wives) from other men. The fact that marital rape was not criminalized in all of the United States until 1993 illustrates the tenacity of traditional notions. Moreover, we are now confronted by the activism of the political right, which is nostalgic for the old arrangements in which wives not only submit to their husbands, but according to the Southern Baptist Convention, do so graciously.

It is easy to understand why the conservatives as well as the romantics ignore the issue of marital rape; for them, for different reasons, it is simply an oxymoron. It is more difficult to explain why the feminist movement itself has had so little engagement with this epidemic form of violence against women. It is not just that sexuality is a tough subject to address. Sex (and not just gender) has been at the core feminist analysis from the beginning of the second wave. I have talked to many, many academics and activists in an effort to come to an understanding of our reluctance to confront wife rape. Interestingly, in this age of "tell-all" Jerry Springer, we talk about our discomfort with what seems like the ultimate invasion of privacy. As Campbell and Soeken indicate in their article (1999, this issue), women were initially screened for physical abuse, but because of the fear of being too intrusive at first contact, forced sex was not included in the questions. This is the current approach of choice for researchers and practitioners, and there are good reasons for it. But, this approach is not without problems.

Advocates, who have heard in horrific detail about brutal physical violence, share their concerns about exploring the specifics of sexual abuse. It just seems too intimate, and the violation of that intimacy is precisely the core of wife rape. We feel as though we violate a sacred intimacy when we ask about the violation of that intimacy. And, by not asking, we help preserve the right to violate that intimacy.

I would suggest that there is something peculiar about our thinking about marital sex and the privacy that surrounds it that is reminiscent of a previous generation's reluctance to confront wife beating. The idea that you do not interfere with what goes on behind closed doors reflected an acceptance of male entitlement in marriage. We have now opened the front door and rejected the idea that male privilege in the household can be maintained through physical violence. Because we have yet to fully open the bedroom door, I wonder if we are ambivalent about what is supposed to happen in there. What entitlement to sex does/should marriage confer? At what point and in what ways should we intervene?

I don't know the answers to these questions, but I do know that the best way to find them is through wide-ranging discussion about the issue. We knew almost nothing about battering 30 years ago. Through the combined efforts of researchers, practitioners, activists, and battered women themselves (not to suggest that these are mutually exclusive categories), we have made enormous progress. Listening to battered women has been critical to our efforts. We need to continue this collaborative work with attention specifically to sexual violence in intimate relationships. We need to reach out to survivors of wife rape so that they can be heard and so that they can help shape the nature and scope of our interventions. We also need to include the full diversity of marital rape survivors so that we can better understand and respond to the culturally specific dimensions of the problem.

The title of this commentary frames wife rape as a social problem for the 21st century. In doing so, I wanted to point out that despite our success in criminalizing marital rape (and that is no small feat), rape in marriage remains a private trouble rather than a public issue, to use C. Wright Mills's (1959) terms. This century will end without a significant public consciousness that sexual assault within marriage is a serious social problem. However, I am convinced that this is a problem we will confront in the near future.

The institution of marriage is being changed by those within it who struggle to make it a more just institution and by those who choose alternative intimate relationships. Its core heterosexual bond is being challenged by gays and lesbians who want access to the privileges that marriage grants in our society. The exclusion of gays and lesbians from marriage and the acceptance of rape within it preserve the heart of patriarchal marriage. Although we are well along the path, the transformation of marriage into an equal partner relationship is by no means inevitable. There are many conflicting parties in the contentious struggle over what marriage will be in the next century. But I am an optimist, and I am convinced that we can and will address wife rape as a serious social problem. Women's equality depends on it.

REFERENCES

BASILE, K. C. (1999). Rape by acquiescence: The ways in which women "give in" to unwanted sex with their husbands. *Violence Against Women*, 5(9), 1036–1058.

BERGEN, R. K. (1996). *Wife rape: Understanding the response of survivors and service providers.* Thousand Oaks, CA: Sage.

CAMPBELL, J. C., & SOEKEN, K. L. (1999). Forced sex and intimate partner violence: Effects on women's risk and women's health. *Violence Against Women*, 5(9), 1017–1035.

FINKELHOR, D., & YLLÖ, K. (1985). *License to rape: sexual abuse of wives.* New York: Free Press.

MAHONEY, P. (1999). High rape chronicity and low rates of help-seeking among wife rape survivors in a non-clinical sample: Implications for research and practice. *Violence Against Women*, 5(9), 993–1016.

MILLS, C. W. (1959). *The sociological imagination.* New York: Oxford University Press.

RUSSELL, D. E. H. (1982). *Rape in marriage.* New York: Macmillan.

CRITICAL THINKING QUESTIONS

1. In your opinion, is marital rape a problem that affects only individual victims, or does it serve to maintain men's domination and privilege over all women in society? Explain.

2. Yllö argues that challenging the right of men to rape their wives is similar to the demands by gay men and lesbians to be granted the right to marry. How are these two issues related?

3. How might married women work with gay men and lesbians to work toward their common goals? What has so far prevented them from working together on issues they have in common?

Reading 6

"Honey, We Don't Do Men"

Denise A. Donnelly and Stacy Kenyon

In this article, Donnelly and Kenyon document gender stereotypes behind the operations of sexual assault crisis centers. Most centers either have never considered or have refused to provide services to men who have been sexually assaulted.

. . . Even though support for victims of sexual assault has grown tremendously over the past

Source: Denise A. Donnelly and Stacy Kenyon *Journal of Interpersonal Violence*, Sep96, Vol. II. Issue 3, p. 441, 8p. © 1996 Reprinted by permission of Sage Publications.

25 years, we rarely hear about the sexual assault of adult males. Only prison assaults (Groth & Burgess, 1980; Scacco, 1982) and assaults on male children and teens (Bolton, Morris, & MacEachron, 1989; Groth & Burgess, 1980)

have generated much interest. Less than a dozen studies of noninstitutionalized adult male victims exist, and these generally focus on very small clinical populations (Collins, 1982; Kaufman, DiVasto, Jackson, Voorhees, & Christy, 1980; Mezey & King, 1992; Sarrel & Masters, 1982).

Given the sparseness of literature in this area, it is easy to assume that sexual victimization does not happen to men. There is increasing evidence, however, that men do experience sexual assaults, perpetrated on them by both men and women (Collins, 1982; Kaufman et al., 1980; Mezey & King, 1992; Sarrel & Masters, 1982; Struckman-Johnson, 1988). Records gathered by crisis centers and hospital emergency rooms indicate that males make up from 1% to 10% of all reports received (Kaufman et al., 1980; Sarrel & Masters, 1982). One study of date rape (Struckman-Johnson, 1988) revealed that 9% of men had been forced to engage in sex during their college years.

The full extent of male sexual victimization is obscured by traditional male gender role socialization. Males are socialized to be strong, sexually aggressive, and always in control. Males are seen as better able to defend themselves against attack (Groth & Burgess, 1980) and less likely to be harmed than women (Smith, Pine, & Hawley, 1988). Given these powerful social norms, it is extremely difficult for a male to admit to having been sexually assaulted (Groth & Burgess, 1980).

Only a fraction of sexual offenses against women are reported to authorities (Stuart & Greer, 1984). Because fewer cultural, social, and physical supports exist for males, they report at even lower rates. In fact, most male victims come to the attention of medical professionals when they request care for nonsexual physical injuries sustained in the assault (Kaufman et al., 1980).

There are other important male-female differences. Kaufman et al. (1980) found that male victims are generally younger than female victims, more likely to have multiple attackers, receive other (nonsexual) injuries more often, and are more likely to be socially or economically unstable. Males, like females, may be ashamed of their victimization; feel violated, helpless, and fearful; and suffer from postrape trauma (Collins, 1982; Kaufman et al., 1980). Because they are less likely to ask for assistance in dealing with their attacks, the consequences of sexual assault may be compounded and even more severe for males than for females. Thus responsive and understanding provision of services that make seeking and receiving attention less traumatic is vitally important for male victims.

STUDY OBJECTIVES

The goal of this exploratory study was to investigate the responses of law enforcement, medical professionals, rape crisis centers, and mental health professionals to male sexual assault victims. We were especially interested in how gender role stereotypes affected three areas: whether service providers saw male sexual assault as a problem, services offered to male victims, and service providers' views of the victims.

METHODOLOGY

Operationalizing Sexual Victimization

Definitions of male sexual victimization vary widely from state to state. In Georgia, where our research was conducted, the law defines rape as a crime committed solely by men against women. "A person commits the offense of rape when he has carnal knowledge of a female forcibly and against her will. Carnal knowledge in rape occurrs when there is penetration of the female sex organ by the male sex organ" (GCA 26-2001, section 16-6-1). Thus vaginal penetration has to take place for rape to occur. The victimization of males falls under the category of sodomy or aggravated sodomy. State law further defines sodomy as,

A person commits the offense of sodomy when he performs or submits to any sexual act involving the sex organs of one person and the mouth or anus of another. A person commits the offense of aggravated sodomy when he commits sodomy with force and against the will of the other person. (GCA 26-2002, section 16-6-2)

Notice that sodomy has both a consensual and nonconsensual component, but rape does not. In other states, rape is more broadly defined as attempted or actual penetration of the vagina or the anus. Both definitions are limited, because in reality sexual victimization encompasses a wide variety of offenses, including anal penetration (either by another man's penis or by a foreign object), forced oral-genital contact, fondling, forcible intercourse with a woman, and other forms of forced, unwanted sexual interaction. Thus, for the purposes of our study, we define sexual victimization as any forced and unwanted sexual contact (other than verbal harassment) perpetuated on an adult male that leads to emotional or physical injury.

Sample

For this research we used the Yellow Pages in a large metropolitan area to identify a convenience sample of rape crisis service providers. All 41 agencies advertising rape crisis or sexual assault services were contacted by telephone, and knowledgeable respondents within each organization were located. Each took part in a brief phone interview, with 30 participating in follow-up interviews.

The follow-up interviews (on which this article is based) were conducted with representatives from 4 law enforcement agencies, 10 hospitals or medical facilities, 8 mental health agencies specializing in sexual assault, and 8 community crisis or rape crisis centers. Interviews were conducted using a semistructured interview guide and lasted an average of 1 hour. Of the 30 agency representatives who took part in this phase, 11 indicated that they did not provide services to males. Nineteen were amenable to serving male victims, but only 4 had actually dealt with a male victim in the past year. Five more had dealt with at least one male victim at some time in the past. The other 10 could "theoretically" provide services to men but had never been called on to do so.

FINDINGS

Of the four agencies providing services to male sexual assault victims within the past year, one was a community-based men's center (serving a primarily gay clientele) that spoke with approximately one sexually assaulted male per week. Another was a hospital-based rape crisis center that received around two calls from male victims each month. A private counselor specializing in men's issues had seen a total of 14 sexual assault victims over the preceding 12 months. At the low end of the continuum, one law enforcement agency had seen two men within the past year.

We visited five agencies that did not see adult male victims routinely but had at some point in the past. Generally, their experience with men was limited to one or two occasions in recent memory. Male sexual assault victims were so unique that they tended to stand out in the minds of these professionals. In several cases, the assault included not only forced sex but murder or mutilation as well.

The 10 agencies that had never seen male victims, but theoretically could, said that they would deal with them in the same way as female victims. Most of these respondents felt that sexual assaults against men weren't really a problem, however, because they never saw male victims. Few acknowledged that the reason might be that they were unresponsive to these men's needs.

As expected, common stereotypes about male rape were voiced in many of the interviews that we conducted. Consistent with the findings of Smith et al. (1988), some of the more negative responses to our questions reflected these stereotypical attitudes. Many believed that men couldn't be raped or that they were raped only because they "wanted to be." One law enforcement representative bluntly stated, "Honey, we don't do men." She laughingly asked, "What would you want to study something like that for? Men can't be raped." Other respondents indicated that they did not treat men because they saw no need for it. Typical of this group was a nurse who asserted, "We don't see men, probably because so few get raped." Another law enforcement representative (who rarely saw male sexual assault victims) took her sentiments a step farther. He said,

> Most males that are fondled or sodomized are males that want to be sodomized. We don't have too many that are unwontedly sodomized. If they are, they don't come to us to report it. . . . We just don't see that many adult males, so that leads me to believe that there is just not a problem.

The similarities between this statement and those made about female victims in the past are chilling, recalling times when women were thought to have "asked for it" and to have "secretly desired being raped." Although attitudes about female rape victims have changed, attitudes toward male victims lag behind.

As a counselor in the gay community pointed out, the perception that a man cannot be forcefully sodomized or sexually aroused against his will is incorrect:

> It is frequently done more than one on one. . . . You find out there were two or three [and that no element of consent was involved]. . . . [Another] one of the things that a lot of people forget is the humiliation factor. Pressure upon the prostate can produce erection, even orgasm. . . . Imagine the humiliation if through the activity your body betrayed you and produced an erection or even ejaculated. The answer is that this is a mechanical function, but it is a terrifying adjunct to the assault.

Agencies that reported treating male victims tended to have less stereotypical attitudes than those not treating males. Although most did not

see a large number of male victims, about half of this group had seen at least one in the past. Typical of contacts within these agencies were respondents who felt that male sexual assaults occur much more frequently than are reported. Many of these respondents also made statements about the difficulties that male victims face because of societal attitudes about men and masculinity. As one respondent pointed out, "I think the problem for the male is that society teaches that women can be assaulted, but nobody will talk about a man being assaulted. You hear some men say that they'd rather be dead . . . than sexually assaulted." Another said, "My hunch is that it [male rape] is underreported because men don't want to report something that's just not macho." Because victims are easily stereotyped as gay, heterosexual men are embarrassed to disclose their victimization. One crisis center counselor noted,

> I . . . think that another of society's stigmatisms (*sic*) is that men who rape are homosexuals, and men who get raped are homosexual. . . . From statistics, and from what we know, I truly believe that most of the assaults that occur are by heterosexual males . . . and that many victims are probably also heterosexual.

This doesn't mean that reporting is any easier for gay men. In fact, gays may be especially vulnerable to sexual assault and have even more reasons not to report. As a counselor at a center that serves mostly gay men pointed out,

> There are three types of sexual assaults that trouble the gay community. One of our big secrets is date or acquaintance rape. Battering and sexual assault also occur in ongoing gay relationships [just like in heterosexual ones]. This is a Catch-22 for the gay community. Gay men [who are assaulted by other gays] are a lot less likely to report than straight men, because they are not taken as seriously, or are seen as two queens having a lover's quarrel. Stranger assault is probably the biggest problem though—homophobic violence committed by "heterosexual" men against gay men. . . .

Another respondent (a private counselor who also works primarily with the gay community) succinctly summed up the situation when he said,

Gay men don't want the intrusion of reporting—too many questions asked, and too many homophobic responses. . . . Straight men don't want to be seen as gay, so they don't report. . . . Law enforcement isn't very sympathetic to the needs of men who are assaulted. . . . Reporting is inconvenient, and most victims feel that it won't accomplish anything, anyway.

Another reason why so few males report sexual assault is that many rape crisis services are geared specifically toward the needs of women. Over one third (37%) of the agencies that we initially contacted said that they would not provide services to a male victim. Most were reluctant to elaborate on their reasons, saying only that they "were not set up to treat men." A male respondent in private practice, however, had an interesting theory about this. He felt that ownership of the problem of rape had become a feminist issue and that it was difficult for some feminist organizations to relinquish their "turf." Admitting to the existence of male victims would undermine many of their basic premises (and open up the competition for funding). As he put it, "Feminists are wise in not mainstreaming their organizations. It is unfortunate, however, that their turf defense may be at the expense of services badly needed by another population."

DISCUSSION AND CONCLUSION

As the interviews clearly indicate, gender role stereotypes influence providers' perceptions of male sexual assault victims and the actual services that are offered. Professionals with less stereotypical attitudes generally recognize that men can be victims and respond to them sympathetically. Because of traditional stereotypes of men as "always in control sexu-

ally," some providers feel, however, that males cannot be raped and thus perceive the problem as inconsequential. They often fail to recognize the victimization of men or offer responsive services. Another harmful stereotype that hinders service provision is that sexual violence against males is a gay problem having little relevance for heterosexual men. Because agencies may be blaming, unsympathetic, or simply refusing to admit that male rape can happen, many men who need help never report. Because of this underreporting, official statistics on the number of men who are raped are quite low. As our research suggests, however, unofficial numbers are probably much higher.

Interestingly, we found that the two groups least likely to acknowledge and deal with the sexual assault of men were male law enforcement personnel and feminist-based rape crisis center or hotline workers. What these groups —one typically masculine and one typically feminist—had in common were their doubts that men could be raped and their views of male rape as nonproblematic.

The "culture of masculinity" was evident in many of the statements made by law enforcement. For male law enforcement officers, admitting that men can be raped introduces the possibility of their own victimization. Their way of dealing with the reality of male vulnerability was simply to refuse to acknowledge that men could be victims or to stereotype them as "queens" or "two fairies having a lover's quarrel." The respondents making these comments typically did so in a "joking" manner accompanied by self-conscious laughter. Several tried repeatedly to change the subject. To protect their views on men and masculinity, they simply would not acknowledge the possibility of male rape.

Interestingly enough, feminist-based hotline and crisis center workers also refused to entertain the idea that men could be sexual assault victims. These women saw violence as a female problem—one perpetrated (almost) solely by males. The idea of men as victims, or women as assailants, was simply not acceptable. One respondent pointed out that if male rape were acknowledged as a problem, then men would "co-opt" the publicity and resources needed for women, just as had almost happened in the early days of the movement against woman battering. She felt that the small number of men who were victimized did not justify risking resources that could be used to assist women.

Both perspectives are commentaries on the role of men and women in our society and speak to the devaluation of that which is female. The law enforcement officials (with hypermasculine viewpoints) viewed male rape victims as "like women." They spoke of them as being gay—queens and fairies—not "real men," but pseudowomen. Victims were viewed as weak, passive, and unable to defend themselves. Similarly, the feminist respondents also saw women as "different" from men. They bought into the idea that women don't commit violence and that men are rarely victims because of their strength and power. Both views impede gender equality by failing to realize that humans are multifaceted, and by forcing men and women into narrow, stereotypical roles, we are harming both.

As our study has shown, these gender role stereotypes contribute to men's reluctance to report acts of sexual violence and also can lead to nonexistent or nonresponsive service provision. Our findings raise troubling questions about gender, sexuality, power, and assault. Until rape is redefined as a violent crime against one person by another, until women are seen as powerful agents, until the "myth of male invulnerability" is eliminated, and until homophobia is dealt with, male victims of this traditionally female crime will remain sadly underserved.

REFERENCES

BOLTON, F., MORRIS, L., & MACEACHRON, A. (1989). *Males at risk: The other side of child sexual abuse.* Newbury Park, CA: Sage.

COLLINS, G. (1982, January 18). Counseling male rape victims. *New York Times,* p. A15.

Georgia Code Annotated. 2002. Section 16-6-2. The State of Georgia.

Georgia Code Annotated. 2001. Section 16-6-1. The State of Georgia.

GROTH, A., & BURGESS, A. (1980). Male rape: Offenders and victims. *American Journal of Psychiatry,* 137(7), 806–810.

KAUFMAN, A., DIVASTO, P., JACKSON, R., VOORHEES, D., & CHRISTY, L. (1980). Male rape victims: Noninstitutionalized assault. *American Journal of Psychiatry,* 137(2), 221–223.

MEZEY, G., & KING, M. (1992). *Male victims of sexual assault.* Oxford: Oxford University Press.

SARREL, P., & MASTERS, W. (1982). Sexual molestation of men by women. *Archives of Sexual Behavior,* 11(2), 117–131.

SCACCO, A. (Ed.). (1982). *Male rape,* New York: AMS Press.

SMITH, R., PINE, C., & HAWLEY, M. (1988). Social cognitions about adult male victims of female sexual assault. *Journal of Sex Research,* 24(1), 101–112.

STRUCKMAN-JOHNSON, C. (1988). Forced sex on date: It happens to men, too. *Journal of Sex Research,* 24, 234–241.

STUART, I., & GREER, J. (1984). *Victims of sexual aggression: Treatment of children, women, and men.* New York: Van Nostrand Reinhold.

CRITICAL THINKING QUESTIONS

1. According to Donnelly and Kenyon, why do most sexual assault crisis centers ignore or avoid male victims? Why are male victims of sexual assault less likely than female victims to report the crimes that have been committed against them?

2. How are stereotypes about male victims of sexual assault associated with mainstream ideas about masculinity? How are these stereotypes associated with men's violence toward one another and toward women?

3. Can advocates for male sexual assault victims work with advocates for female victims? Would it be better, in your opinion, for them to establish separate sexual assault crisis centers for men only? What are the benefits and costs of each strategy?

Reading 7

The Execution of Pvt. Barry Winchell The Real Story Behind The 'Don't Ask, Don't Tell' Murder

Thomas Hackett

> *In this article, Hackett focuses on the violent death of a soldier who dated a transsexual. He highlights the ways that prejudice, stereotypes, and institutional policies contributed to this incident.*

Fort Campbell, a United States Army base that straddles the Tennessee-Kentucky border, is home to the famed 101st Airborne Division, which spearheaded the D-Day assault and held the line at the Battle of the Bulge. This is a huah post—one dedicated to the fighting grunt, the Army infantryman. Some 20,000 GIs live and train on these 164 square miles of Cumberland River bottomland. The sight of tanks rumbling down Screaming Eagle Boulevard and the sound of heavy artillery thumping in the distance are constants of everyday life here. Troops jog in tight formation down Air Assault Street and line up for calisthenics outside the white clapboard war-fighting center, where generals dream up mock battles. Even with these martial rituals, Fort Campbell has the familiarity of a middle-class suburb going about its day-to-day business. Young families scurry to soccer practice and swimming lessons, piling in and out of minivans at the Taco Bell and Burger King, the bingo parlor and bowling alley on post. But with no nostalgic bastions and battlements or high-tech planes and ships to marvel at, the lowly cherry private, shunted off to gray brick-and-concrete barracks at the north end of the post, has to find his own inspiration for serving in today's army.

Source: Thomas Hackett, "The Execution of Private Barry Winchell: The Real Story Behind the 'Don't Ask, Don't Tell' Murder." *Rolling Stone,* 3/2/2000 Issue 835, 80–86.

Pvt. Barry Winchell, a twenty-one-year-old from Kansas City, Missouri, was one of those earnest young men. He enlisted in 1997 and within a few months joined Delta Company, 502nd Infantry regiment, 101st Airborne, trained to fire heavy weapons like the .50-caliber machine gun and the 40 mm grenade launcher. He was by all accounts a good soldier, with ambition and skill and the beginnings of a life plan.

In the early hours of July 5th, 1999, Winchell was murdered on the third-floor landing of his barracks, bludgeoned to death with a baseball bat by a fellow soldier. The initial account of the murder was straightforward. The Army called his death the result of "an altercation between soldiers." In fact, it was that; Barry Winchell had been in a fistfight with his assailant the day before the attack, and on that Fourth of July night, with staff sergeants nowhere in sight, the soldiers had all gotten very drunk at the barracks.

But the Army did not report at first that Winchell was actually sound asleep in his cot when he was attacked. Nor did the Army reveal that he had been the target of steady harassment by other soldiers for months, that he had been ostracized and isolated, taunted even by his superiors, because he was believed to be gay. Finally, the Army did nothing to suggest the close and complicated relationship that Winchell had with his roommate, whose own sexual uncertainty contributed to the tormented atmosphere in the barracks and whose Louisville Slugger ended up in the killer's hands on the fatal night.

Not all of these complicating details emerged at two separate court-martial proceedings in December and January. Trials, especially those conducted by the military, demand a narrative without ambiguities or cloudy motivations. Yet the forces at work in this particular incident—identity and sexuality, affection and attraction, desire and disdain—cannot be easily simplified. What is clear is that three confused young men came to the Army with questions about their manhood, hoping they could figure out what to make of their troubled lives. Instead they found a place where those questions aren't tolerated.

Barry Winchell never caused trouble, though his life was not always easy. When he was four, he, his mother and his two older brothers fled his father and lived for a short time in their car. Barry struggled academically, not learning the alphabet until third grade and dropping out of high school. But in other respects he was a typical American boy, and his childhood became a happier one after his mother's remarriage, to a likable man with a career in the aerospace industry. Barry was in the Cub Scouts and Boy Scouts and Rocket Club. There were piano lessons, and then long hair and a heavy-metal band for which he played bass guitar and wrote songs. He went to the prom with the girl he said he hoped to marry. He had "his share of teenage things," says his mother, a psychiatric nurse who works with troubled kids. "His friends had drug and alcohol problems. That was the group he was accepted by, and I'm sure he did some of that himself. But he believed that you have to make a decision to become the man you want to be, and part of being a man is accepting the consequences of your actions."

That's largely what attracted Winchell to the Army: the opportunity to prove his mettle. "Before he enlisted, he told me he'd seen all the movies—that he knew all about the Army," says his stepfather, Wally Kutteles. "I told him it wasn't going to be like the movies. I told him, 'Somebody is going to chew you out, and you'll have to be able to take it. You're going to have to stand up and be a man.' He said, 'I can do that.'"

Winchell's parents began to see an amazing transformation after he enlisted. During basic training at Fort Benning, Georgia, he wrote cheerful letters home, peppered with jokes about the privations of military life. He announced that he wanted to be the best soldier there ever was. He showed a dazzling aptitude for the workings of machinery. He pored over weaponry manuals and became the best marksman in his company—his captain even encouraged him to become a helicopter pilot. Just about every week he'd call his parents, pretending at first to be down in the dumps, only to surprise them with news of more praise or another award.

The guys in his company even called him "Top Gun," he told his stepfather.

That was a small but understandable lie. Although Winchell was doing well and earning encouragement from his superiors, he was far from being a figure of envy. In fact, during the last three months of his life, he was ridiculed daily by his fellow soldiers, for Winchell had fallen in love with a man—and not just any man, but a veteran of the Gulf War who worked in a nightclub as a drag queen.

Winchell's main tormentor, who started the taunting and then turned it into a company-wide blood sport, was also his roommate. He was the one who first introduced Winchell to gay nightlife in Nashville.

That roommate, Spc. Justin Fisher, was the company character—a charismatic, mouthy rebel who was a few years older than most of the others. He was a hellion, his fellow soldiers say, whose idea of a good time usually meant flirting with trouble. He'd get drunk, fight, pass out, and afterward there'd always be a good story to tell. Like the time when he loaned clothes to a friend before they went out on the town in Nashville; in the car on the way home, he forced the friend to undress and drive home to the base in his underwear. Fisher liked to concoct schemes of going into the nearby town of Clarksville, Tennessee, equipped with walkie-talkies, and pulling off some heist. Hanging around Fisher, you might get in trouble yourself, says Pvt. Bill Marsh, who had briefly roomed with him, but it was usually worth it: You were going to have a good time.

"Basically, he had too much fun. He didn't care what anyone thought of him. He'd be making fun of NCOs [non-commissioned officers], basically telling them, 'You can't break me.' They'd make him do push-ups all the time, and he'd be laughing. He did it to everybody, always trying to find out how far he could go."

Fisher's cocksure persona was in marked contrast to the frightened child he had once been. He grew up first with an alcoholic father, who berated him for failing at sports, and later with a physically abusive stepfather whose home he left before finishing high school. Fisher talked big, but back in Lincoln, Nebraska, he'd made his living at maintenance jobs—roofing, painting houses—or working at a McDonald's. He had fathered an infant son, and in March 1997 he joined the Army, he told friends, in order to support his child.

But he also liked the idea of playing with guns, posing with guns, aiming the barrel at whoever was taking the picture, looking like a badass. Soldiers said he was obsessed with thugs, real and fictional, like Al Pacino in Scarface and the sadistic Mr. Blond in Reservoir Dogs. Home on leave in July 1998, he bought a Louisville Slugger baseball bat to use on a guy he'd heard was harassing his youngest sister. And though he didn't have the guns to go with it, he owned a double-harness holster. "He thought he was his own personal crime boss," a soldier named Nikita Sanarov testified. "He was always plotting his own crimes. He liked to plot revenge on someone who had stolen something of his—handcuffing the guy, plunging his head in a tub and burning a cigarette into his flesh. He liked the idea of interrogating someone like that. He wanted to be the Man." It was mostly talk, but not entirely. Justin Fisher never took the bat to his sister's tormentor, but he did enter the Army with an arrest on record for having the makings of a pipe bomb.

"He wasn't a shitbag," Bill Marsh says. "But if he didn't like you, he'd make sure you learned the hard way."

In May, 1998, Fisher and Winchell were randomly assigned to the same third-floor dorm unit, one of twelve apartments in their three-story building. They had a rocky friendship from the start—what one soldier called "a love-hate relationship." Some quarrel was always brewing. Winchell smoked, which Fisher hated. And Winchell was something of a mama's boy, someone who wanted to please authority figures. He was just the kind of person who would annoy Fisher, who bragged that whenever he felt stressed out, he went into his room, locked the door and beat the crap out of his roommate. He took to calling Winchell "my bitch." Again, it was mostly talk—but the bickering did sometimes turn violent. The one fight for which both were written up, a couple of months after they came to Fort Campbell, started as a boozy argument about who should clean their room. Fisher wound up sitting on Winchell's chest and punching him in the face. Finally, he struck Winchell in the head with a metal dustpan. The gash required several stitches.

The blood that spattered on the walls and ceiling during that incident would become a point of pride with Fisher. He showed it off to anyone who came by, refusing to let Winchell clean it. Yet they remained roommates. Winchell once told his older brother Scan on the phone that Fisher was a "psychopath," but he said it with a note of admiration. The next time Scan called, he heard the two of them horsing around like kids. When their company captain asked whether they wanted to be separated after the bloody dustpan incident, they declined.

"'We just had a spat,'" Cpt. Daniel Rouse recalled one of them saying. "'We like each other.'"

Justin Fisher's role as the company bad boy wasn't compromised when he returned to the post last March raving about a gay club he had visited in Nashville and the amazing "girl" he'd seen lip-syncing to Madonna in a pink negligee, sequined thong bikini and go-go boots. The next night, he got Winchell to drive him and two other soldiers back to the Connection, in the city's warehouse district. It is a huge club, a kind of gay emporium—48,000 square feet, with Saturday night crowds of 2,000 people packing its showroom, dance floor, country & western bar, restaurant and boutique.

Nashville is about an hour's drive southeast of Fort Campbell, and its resident drag queens say they're accustomed to catching the wide eyes of soldiers on the town. They say they often end up playing a transitional role for nervous young men unable to admit that they might be gay. "It's really killing when that happens," says Calpernia Addams, who served in the Navy for four years and now performs as a drag queen. His name has been legally changed, and he won't say what it used to be; he took Calpernia from Julius Caesar's wife and Addams from The Addams Family. Both as a man and in drag, as a soldier and a civilian, he's seen the pattern: A boy enlists thinking the military will make him a real man, but on some debauched and drunken night at a loud club in a strange city, where it's dark and men are dancing chest to chest, this bright, glittering thing—this man—but a man more womanly than any woman he's ever known—catches his eye.

The object of Justin Fisher's fascination that disorienting weekend last March was Calpernia Addams.

"They were all there on a Sunday night, hooting and hollering every time I came on-stage," recalls Addams, 29, who is tall and delicate, with pale skin, surgically enhanced lips and a voluptuous figure. "I met Fisher and at first didn't notice Barry, because he was so quiet. Fisher looked at me kind of like boys look at strippers. His eyes were darting all around, not looking me in the eye. I think he found me attractive and was unnerved. The next weekend, they all came again, and afterward we went to an afterhours club."

By the time the soldiers and drag queens got them, Addams and Winchell had discovered one another and started to hit it off. "So Fisher asked me to set him up with another female impersonator," Addams recalls. "He said, 'What about Kimmie—hook me up.'"

Kim Wayne Mayfield goes by the name Kimmie Satin, but unlike Addams, he hasn't legally changed his name. Even with plucked eyebrows and shaved legs, he is unmistakably a man, with a stubbly chin and a conspicuous Adam's apple.

"They come on Friday, Saturday nights, these little jarhead freaks from Fort Campbell who want a blow job with a drag queen," says Mayfield. "You see a dozen every night, and they will all say they're straight. They seem to think that being with me doesn't make them gay. They can say in their mind, 'I didn't know it was a man till we were finished,' or something fucked-up like that. So for me, it's a kind of a revenge, saying, 'Yeah, you dog homosexuals, but you'll go home with me in a heartbeat.'"

Mayfield, 31, says his relationship with Fisher never went beyond petting. In all, he saw Fisher only three or four times, usually with a group of other soldiers. Fisher was memorable, though, if only because he seemed so happy and horny and full of life. He wasn't especially handsome (friends mention his big ears and tangled teeth), but he had a presence.

"I remember fooling around, getting him all worked up, as hard as a rock," Mayfield says. "He was asking me if it still works. He was very aggressive, his hands were all over me, grabbing my butt. But there was also this nice little moment when he put his arm around my hip and I snuggled up to him."

So Fisher and Mayfield had only a passing, teasing attraction, but Winchell and Addams had found a bond surprisingly old-fashioned: a man in uniform and a country girl. "It was a really nice relationship," says Spc. Phillip Ruiz, one of the soldiers who went along to the Connection. And within a few weeks of meeting, they were spending their free time together.

"If a straight man is sort of the Holy Grail for a drag queen, a military boy is even better," Addams says, eating lunch at a Taco Bell on post, nondescript in a long denim skirt and a cardigan sweater over a halter top. "I was lonely, and when you meet someone who's attractive and has a good job and treats you nice, well, that's a very hard-to-find package, and I latched right onto it."

Addams has been taking female hormones for two years, and, as evidence of his transformation, last year took fifth place at something called the National Entertainer Awards, winning for the best evening gown. "I don't consider myself a slut," he says in a voice that's huskier than he would wish. "I know there's a very Jerry Springer-esque element to my life, but I try to present a classy image." The truth is, despite the showgirl style, Addams says he wants nothing more than to be a housewife in a suburban home, married to a 1950s version of the American man.

Winchell felt comfortable being that man, Addams says. As a preoperative transsexual, Addams has no trouble passing as a woman, and that's exactly how Barry treated him—like a girlfriend. "It's kind of a cliché to say he had a childlike quality, but that's what he had," Addams says. "He was always treating me like a lady, bringing me jewelry and things. Barry was the type of man who could undo the jelly jar if it was stuck. He was one of the only people in his circle that had his own car. It had leather seats, and it rode real smooth."

Soon, Addams was taking up all of Winchell's free time. Weekends, instead of hanging out and drinking with the guys from the barracks, he'd drive down to Nashville and keep Addams company in his dressing room. They'd go to movies together, holding hands. Then Addams would ride with Winchell back to the post, saying goodbye outside the gate so nobody would see them together.

That precaution wasn't enough to insulate Winchell, however. Beginning with the first Nashville adventure, the intimidation Fisher dished out took a darker turn. The first night they all visited the clubs together had been a drunken and disordered one. Fisher had kept everyone waiting till the wee hours as he disappeared into the back room of an after-hours club with Kimmie Satin—bragging, when he finally emerged, "I just fucking made out with that chick!" "What chick?" Ruiz asked. "You know, that guy over there." Riding back to base, Fisher suddenly started slapping at Winchell, then choking him. Fisher tore off his shirt and announced that he'd wanted to kick Winchell's ass for a long time. Ruiz and the others managed to calm him down until he passed out in the back seat.

The next day—in what might well be interpreted as a veiled confession of his own indiscretions—Fisher told his sergeant that someone in the unit, he wouldn't say who, had been intimate with another man. He

told different versions of this story to his fellow soldiers. In one, he said he'd dropped Winchell off at a gay bar, later returning to find him having oral sex with a man. Another version had him waking up in the barracks and seeing Winchell going down on a woman who, upon closer inspection, turned out to be a man. A soldier would later testify that in front of others, Fisher would ask Winchell "what it was like to suck cock." Friends noticed the vicious pleasure that Fisher—emboldened by the typical knee-jerk hostility to homosexuals one would expect to find in an all-male Army unit—now took in jeering at Winchell, "calling him a dumb fuck, a queer luck, a fucking faggot," as Spc. Edgar Rosa recalled. Through last May and June, he'd strut around the barracks saying he wished his roommate would die. "He tried to get Winchell to hit him, to ruffle his feathers and then put him in his place, screaming at him, calling him one of those names," testified Rosa.

When the taunting started, Ruiz reminded Fisher of his own misadventures in Nashville: "I said, 'Dude, you kissed a guy!' He said he didn't remember any of that, that he was too drunk."

People who knew both men have speculated that perhaps Fisher's anger came from jealousy—that he was attracted to either Addams or Winchell. Possibly, his own shame led him to punish someone else for having homosexual desires. Calpernia Addams and Kimmie Mayfield believe the murder had everything to do with Fisher's conflicted and uncontrollable feelings.

"Little psychological dramas that most people could control, Fisher had to act out," Addams says. "He would go off. Maybe it was not having me, or maybe he wanted Barry."

One particular incident gave Addams reason to wonder. Sometime in May, he recalls, Winchell told him that he woke one night to find Fisher groping him. "He told me he jumped up and said, 'What the hell are you doing?'" Addams says. "And Fisher said, 'Oh, I'm just drunk.' And Barry said, 'Well, get off.' When he mentioned it to me, he was like,

'This really weird thing happened.' It freaked him out."

Fisher's friends are flummoxed by these conjectures. In the three months that he roomed with Fisher, Pvt. Bill Marsh saw no indication that Fisher was remotely attracted to men. Neither did Pvt. Phil Frenz in the months that the two were in adjoining cells at Fort Knox. That Fisher had gone to a gay club and met up with drag queens—that didn't surprise them. He was a nervy guy who did the unpredictable.

During his court martial, however, Fisher would admit from the stand to being "afraid of my manhood." His and Winchell's escapades at the gay club, he said, were "a secret between us." In a misguided play for sympathy, Fisher addressed Winchell's parents directly. "Who do you think took him to the gay bar?" he asked. "It was me."

The statement hung in the air, raising questions: Why had Fisher been so intent on tormenting Winchell for something he himself had done? Was there more to it, some intimacy between them that he would not say?

But no one—not Army prosecutor Capt. Gregg Engler, nor Fisher's civilian attorney Michael Love, nor military judge Col. Kenneth Pangburn—would touch those questions. A forensic psychiatrist, Dr. Keith Caruso, would only testify that, whether or not Fisher was gay, he was certainly sexually confused and curious. Ever since Fisher was fourteen, Caruso noted, he had been secretly wearing women's underwear.

Whatever Fisher's personal quirks might have been, they didn't explain his increasing vindictiveness toward Winchell. "He was jealous over something," says Spc. Clayton MckInzie, a friend of Winchell's. "The last few weeks, it was real worse."

What started as a private conflict between two men quickly began to spread and infect the whole unit like a virus. Fisher's slurs reached the ears of all ninety men in the five platoons that constitute Delta Company, from private to section leader to platoon sergeant to sergeant. "Pretty much everyone called him derogatory names," said platoon Sgt. Michael Kleifgen, who was friendly with Winchell.

"They called him a faggot, I would say, on a daily basis."

One day, apparently thinking he was being big-brotherly, Kleifgen raised with Winchell the forbidden subject of sexual orientation. "I asked if he was gay," Kleifgen testified at a hearing. "He said no. I left it at that." The sergeant then silenced the courtroom by saying, straightfaced, "The military has a policy of 'Don't ask, don't tell.'"

Army spokeswoman Maj. Pamela Hart has said that if Winchell felt threatened, he could have talked to his superiors or to the post's Equal Opportunity Office. Yet Winchell did complain to Cpt. Daniel Rouse. Rouse told his men to "Knock that shit off," but nothing more was done to stop the harassment.

"Everybody was having fun," said Kleifgen, adding that it was the kind of vulgar, easygoing razzing that came with the territory, especially in all-male infantry units like Delta Company.

But even Kleifgen was alarmed by hearing his immediate superior, 1st Sgt. Roger Seacrest, say of Winchell, "The faggot has got a fucking drinking problem, and I'm going to do something about it." In fact, Kleifgen took the unusual (and professionally risky) step of reporting Seacrest to the post's inspector general. He also brought the matter to the attention of the company commander.

"It was basically blown off," he said. "I filed a formal complaint. Nothing was done about it."

A group called the service-members Legal Defense Network, initiating its own investigation of Winchell's death after receiving anonymous tips from Fort Campbell soldiers, was the first to bring the military's transgressions to light. The organization saw the killing as a case of systemic homophobia, set against the backdrop of ambivalence about gays in the military. If the activists are right, it would make Winchell's slaying the first gay-bashing death in the armed services since 1992, when Seaman Allen Schindler died of massive head injuries from an unprovoked beating at the hands and feet of fellow military men. This happened not long before the controversial "Don't ask, don't tell" policy was implemented. In a bathroom of a park in Sasebo, Japan, near a U.S. Naval installation, Schindler had his ribs broken, his skull fractured, his nose and jaw broken, his liver turned to pulp, his aorta torn, his bladder ripped open and his face so badly beaten he could only be identified by the tattoos on his arms. The Navy tried to cover up the murder and almost succeeded. Told that her son died accidentally after falling in a brawl, Schindler's mother was not informed that he was being discharged because he was gay—or that a plea agreement allowed one of his assailants to serve only a four-month sentence.

When President Clinton was elected, a week after Schindler's death, many hoped for an executive order that would delegitimize the military's hostility toward gay soldiers as authoritatively as President Truman had ended its racial segregation in 1948. Instead, Clinton stumbled into a policy that has satisfied almost nobody, perplexing gay and antigay soldiers alike while continuing to trip up presidential candidates. And intolerance has actually intensified: The number of gay and lesbian soldiers drummed out of the service has nearly doubled in the six years since they were allowed to serve if they kept their sexual preferences private, according to the SLDN, which also reports six times as many incidents of harassment.

Although the policy is now on every soldier's lips, many think that it implies another phrase: Don't ask, don't tell, but harass all you want. They complain that it's become a soft army now and that, with recruitment down, too many "weak" soldiers have been let into their ranks. They wonder why someone who is gay would join the military in the first place. If gay men are allowed to enlist, says one soldier interviewed at Fort Campbell, they "need to be harassed more than they are."

"For generations," Randy Shilts wrote in Conduct Unbecoming, his sweeping 1993 history of gays in the U.S. armed forces, "the military has been an institution that has promised to do one thing, if nothing else, and that is to take a boy and make him a man." Allowing gays and lesbians to serve seems to flout that belief system. Barry Winchell was sexually curious, yet he was clearly meeting the Army's tests of manliness. Without combat, young male soldiers

wonder whether it isn't all a myth, this glorified idea of the Army as a proving ground.

Listening to soldiers complain about the Army, one can see how the occasional display of aggression might momentarily assuage the disappointments. A soldier griped, one bored night at the post's bowling alley, "Our job basically consists of ironing our uniforms."

So into this atmosphere poisoned with prejudice and dangerous notions of manliness stumbled someone ill-equipped to keep his bearings: an eighteen-year-old private named Calvin Glover. He had been in the Army eight months, at Fort Campbell only since April, and had never been involved in the unpleasantness between Winchell and Fisher. Glover was just another lost soul who, at seventeen and with nothing else working out in his life, had given himself to the Army, one of the last organizations that would have him.

To Glover, the Army represented independence. His divorced parents thought it offered just the opposite: the supervision he'd always needed. Growing up in Oklahoma, he'd shuttled back and forth between his mother's place in Sulphur and his father's in Ada, mostly fending for himself. There were no Boy Scouts and Rocket Clubs in his youth. Making few friends, he drank, took drugs, dropped out of school in eighth grade, got expelled from a youth shelter in Tulsa and returned three times to the same home for troubled teenagers in Ada.

"He was very confused about life," his father said. "He was out of control," his mother said. "I thought the Army would be the place where he could get the role models he needed. I felt it was the place to help him grow up."

It hadn't, though. Glover found the same difficulty making friends in Delta Company that he'd had at home. He tried hard enough, says Ruiz; he just didn't know how to fit in, how to shoot the breeze until a mutual regard developed: "He was just kind of a goober—goofy, fidgety, always saying dumb things—who desperately wanted acceptance." Around the barracks, Glover became known for acting on dares, for going too far in his attempts to belong. The guys in his company thought his bragging about drugs and crimes laughably pathetic. Justin Fisher was just the kind of charismatic badass Glover was always trying too hard to be. As Fisher told tales of hits and heists, Glover tried to match him, spinning yarns about taking methamphetamines for five days straight and robbing banks. When he felt people weren't listening, he'd start throwing beer bottles and swinging baseball bats to get their attention.

"He wasn't a squared-away soldier," said one soldier in his unit. "He always seemed like he was on something," said another.

"Teenagers all have problems, but Cal wants to belong to something so bad," his father said later in court. "He lived in fear of being rejected and humiliated. He would do anything to feel important and accepted." Certainly the image of Glover as a "homophobic tormentor" (as the *New York Times* described him) didn't jibe with the frightened, emotionally needy boy he seemed to be in person, bashfully saying hello to anyone who would look his way. During his trial, as he sat trying to compose the apology he would read to Winchell's family, Glover seemed small and meek, like a chastened schoolboy in detention hall. Just about everyone who met Glover's beseeching eyes—even Winchell's parents—would admit to feeling some pity for him despite themselves. Just as Barry Winchell had found a sense of acceptance and belonging with Calpernia Addams and the gay friends he'd made at the Connection, Glover, too, had felt secure and at ease among flamboyant gay teenagers. Cynthia Brown, director of the Ada Youth Shelter, saw that side of Glover beneath all the bluster and posturing. She was called to testify on his behalf.

"Calvin," she blurted from the witness stand, facing him, "I know you're not going to want me to say this, but I don't see how anyone can call you homophobic when you were painting your nails and fixing your hair."

For the long Independence-day weekend, Barry Winchell decided to stay on base and save his money for the visit his parents were planning, for his twenty-second birthday, at the end of August. He had recently been nominated for Delta Company's soldier of the month award; he had some studying to do if he was going to win the honor and get accepted to warrant officer school. That's all he talked about the last time he called his mother on Thursday, July 1st.

He didn't mention the steady abuse he had been taking of late. But he did tell a friend that, with all the hostility in the air, he was afraid someone was going to get hurt, either Fisher or himself.

On a sweltering Saturday night, he joined a dozen other soldiers who had nowhere else to go that weekend, meeting at the concrete picnic table outside his barracks. They passed the evening drinking from a keg, telling stories, playing whiffle ball on the scruffy lawn, listening to a blaring stereo. Calvin Glover was there, "trying to impress us, to show us how tough he was," recalled Pfc. Arthur Hoffman. "He was loud in a bragging type of way. Really pushing it."

Justin Fisher was there, too, having a good time getting under Glover's skin, prodding him to tell more of his incredible exploits. From time to time, Glover would realize that Fisher was mocking him. "No, really," Fisher would say, "I'm sorry, man. . . . I was only teasing. Go on, really. . . . "

And Glover did. At some point, Winchell lost patience with Glover's lies and Fisher's cruel encouragement. "You're just a cherry private, Glover!" Winchell said in exasperation. "Why don't you take your drunk ass to bed?" Drunk and revved up, Glover pounced on Winchell. Fisher stopped him, laughing, then said, "If you think you can do it, go ahead."

Winchell stayed seated, smoking, unafraid. Over and over, Glover tried to swipe the beer out of his hand. "Suddenly, Winchell sprung up from the table and hit Glover three or four times, throwing him down on the ground," Hoffman said. "He had him down in a couple of seconds. He had no trouble subduing him."

It was beautiful, the soldiers would say, seeing the company loudmouth bested by the company faggot. Instead of feeling he'd just won a reprieve from the ridicule, however, Winchell was upset. In fact, he was crying as he tried to patch it up with Glover.

"It's cool, right?" he said, trying to shake Glover's hand, offering him another beer and some Southern Comfort. But with Fisher reminding him how he'd just had his ass kicked, the gesture only added to Glover's humiliation.

"It's not cool!" Glover said. "I could fucking kill you. A faggot cannot kick my ass."

By the next day, though, July 4th, the incident seemed all but forgotten—except by Justin Fisher. "You know how people have that voice in their head that they're going over the line? Fisher didn't have that," says Ruiz. "With him, it was relentless."

Repeatedly, Fisher tormented Glover, telling him he didn't "have a hair on his ass" if he was going to let "a fucking faggot" like Winchell take him down.

"Glover didn't react," Spc. Carlos Rodriguez said. "In fact, Glover and Winchell were playing whiffle ball together. Winchell apologized, and Glover took it. Later they were sitting, just talking. Winchell was showing Glover how to juggle."

Around 2 A.M. that second night—the keg running dry, the party breaking up—Winchell left Glover and Fisher and the others and went to bed. It was his turn to watch the company mascot, a dog named Nasty, so he set up a cot on the third-floor landing just outside his room rather than risk Fisher's wrath should the dog make a mess. He made his bed carefully, folding three blankets lengthwise as a makeshift mattress. The next morning, life would return to normal. He could go back to being an ordinary soldier, maybe even soldier of the month.

No one disputes that at around 3 A.M. that morning, Calvin Glover beat Barry Winchell to death with Justin Fisher's baseball bat. Gregg Engler said in court that the attack was prompted by Glover's shame at losing a fight to a homosexual, plain and simple. Glover's defense attorney, Maj. David Robertson—adding to Glover's own tearful admission at the beginning of his trial that he was "just really drunk"—blamed Fisher's influence, saying

that Fisher saw an opportunity to manipulate an impressionable soldier into fulfilling his own vicious wish to harm Winchell. Portrayed as a cunning malefactor, as a "manipulative gay-hater" who "despised" Winchell, Fisher had used Glover "as his weapon of choice," Robertson argued.

The prosecution and the defense agreed that the July 4th keg party ended peacefully. After Winchell had gone to sleep, Fisher brought Glover back to his room, where they kept drinking while listening to the soundtrack of the movie Psycho. At this point their stories diverge. Fisher has told investigators that Glover walked around the room for about ten minutes with a "psychotic" look on his face, making violent chopping motions in the air with the baseball bat. He says Glover left the room, while he—not knowing Glover "had that much rage in him"—lay down and listened to his stereo. Twenty minutes later Glover was back in the room, apologizing for getting blood all over Fisher's bat.

Glover said that in Fisher's room, just before the murder, Fisher continued giving him a hard time about losing the fight, saying how much he hated Winchell himself. Glover said he was goaded into settling the score—Fisher's exact instruction was to "go outside and kill that motherfucker," Glover told a prison guard, who later testified. He also claimed that as he returned the bat, Fisher, enamored of mob movies, acknowledged his complicity, saying, "We're family now—this stays in the family."

Fisher has admitted to making the solemn mafioso pact and to washing the baseball bat. Yet as Glover ran from the barracks after the attack, disposing of his bloody clothes in a Dumpster, Fisher remained, pulling the fire alarm, waking other men to get help.

Groggy-eyed soldiers rushed to the scene and found Winchell with blood streaming from his left ear, his eye sockets turning black from cerebral hemorrhaging, his brain oozing from a gaping crack in his skull, his entire head swelling to the size of a basketball.

By the time the paramedics arrived, at 3:30 A.M.—the 911 system on base wasn't working, and ambulances were slow in coming—Fisher was covered head to foot in blood, still going berserk. "Oh, God, help me," Staff Sgt. Bradley Hardin recalls Fisher screaming in a panic, "I think he's dying."

Everyone remembers those words. But they also remember Fisher saying something else as the ambulance drove Winchell away. For a while, Fisher stood silently on the scruffy lawn outside the barracks with all of the others. Glover stood there, too, covered in sweat, with bits of grass on his face and in his hair, having apparently fallen while frantically trying to hide evidence. The soldiers regarded both of them warily. Then, quite suddenly, Fisher started screaming again, this time at the ambulance driver as he pulled away.

"No balls!" he yelled. "No balls! Let him die! Let him die!" Winchell never regained consciousness; he died the next day at Vanderbilt University Medical Center from blows to the left temple, the left forehead, the jaw, the back of the head, the neck—to no other part of his body than his head.

"Calvin, tell me real slow," his father, Rue Glover, said in a cowboy's drawl minutes after his son was convicted of premeditated murder. "What changed?"

Some would say that essentially nothing had changed for Calvin Glover—that he had simply shown the world who he already was when he entered the Army, that sooner or later he was bound to make a dreadful mess of his life. But some had the opinion that joining the Army was the fateful change in Calvin Glover's life. Talking to soldiers at bars on and off post, you mostly heard that the murder of Pvt. Barry Winchell had been politicized and sensationalized by reporters and activist organizations, and by politicians anxious to overturn an unpopular policy. It wasn't prejudice that caused Winchell's death, they said; it was more a matter of the stupidity that breaks out when bored young men, already primed for violence, start drinking. Still, the more soldiers talked, the more resentful they became of the Army's handling of the murder, believing that its vigorous but narrow prosecution of the crime ignored the Army's own responsibility for the corrosive

atmosphere it permitted and for the miseducation it gave Calvin Glover.

Phil Frenz, who spent roughly equal time with both Fisher and Glover at Fort Knox's prison, doesn't believe either soldier harbored any deep hatred of homosexuals. "It's just that being in the infantry, they got this whole macho thing going on when it comes to gay people," he said by telephone. "And in my personal opinion, the Army played a big factor in this, because it kind of brainwashes you. The Army is not going to go all out and say, 'Hate him,' but the NCOs, the way they react to gay guys, it transfers over to you. People use the term faggot all the time, but, like, if you use the term nigger, if you didn't get your ass beat right then and there, you'd get brought up on an Article Thirty-two [disciplinary action] or a court martial. You'd be fucked. But call a guy a faggot— nothing. They'd laugh at it. That's just normal. So if you're openly gay, of course you're going to get a lot of shit for it. That's the Army."

In December, Calvin Glover was sentenced to life in prison for murder. In January, Justin Fisher pleaded guilty to charges of obstruction of justice, making false statements and providing alcohol to a minor, getting a twelve-and-a-half-year sentence and avoiding a trial on the more serious charge of accessory to murder. Both are incarcerated at Fort Leavenworth Military Prison, in Kansas. Fort Campbell's commanding general has announced an investigation into whether officers ignored reports of Pvt. Winchell's harassment. Defense Secretary William S. Cohen has asked the Pentagon to conduct spot checks to determine if anti-gay harassment is occurring at other military bases.

There seems to be plenty of blame to go around. Winchell's parents, Patricia and Wally Kutteles, say they are grateful for the opportunities and challenges the infantry offered their son, and they believe he met a few good men in Delta Company. (They believe, too, that he met a good man in Calpernia Addams—someone who, if nothing else, proved to be a caring friend during what was surely a difficult time in Barry's life.) But they are also now convinced that a misguided policy not only failed to protect their son but killed him. So in the final analysis, Patricia Kutteles does hold the military to blame for what happened—just as much to blame as Glover and Fisher are—and plans to pursue a wrongful-death suit in civil court against the Army.

"I think there was concern and affection for Barry in the unit," she said after her son's killers were sentenced. "But there was a mentality, a mind-set in the Army, that contributed to his death. His superior officer's silence condoned the harassment. It sent a message to these soldiers that if you label someone, it's OK."

CRITICAL THINKING QUESTIONS

1. Explain how the institutional policies of the military contribute to violence against sexual minorities.

2. Use Hong's point in the previous article about the association between masculinity and violence to explain why Justin Fisher attacked and killed Barry Winchell.

3. How is the violence of Justin Fisher related to homophobia? Explain.

Getting Involved

1. The Public Broadcasting System's web site has practical information on organizing a community- or campus-based forum to eliminate hate crimes. Visit **http://www.pbs.org/niot/** and collect information on how this can be done. Then work with student groups to organize such a forum on your campus or in your community.

2. Contact Men Against Violence at Louisiana State University, Room 275, Student Health Center Building, Infirmary Road, Baton Rouge, LA 70803 (Phone (225) 388-5718; Fax (225) 388-1278; e-mail: **MAV@lsu.edu**) for information on starting a group chapter on your campus. When you have the information, contact the student health center or women's center on your campus and tell them you are interested in working with others to start a Men Against Violence chapter on your campus.

3. Contact a representative of the rape crisis center on your campus or in your community. Volunteer to work at the center and to help them find ways to develop or improve programs to address wife rape and/or the sexual assault of men.

Site Seeing

1. To learn more about hate crimes and hate groups, visit the Anti-Defamation League's web site at **http://www.adl.org/hate-patrol/main.html.**

2. For more information on Men Against Violence visit **http://www.Geocities.com/MAVatLSU.**

3. To learn more about violence against gay men and lesbian women and some community responses to this victimization, visit the New York City Gay and Lesbian Anti-Violence Project web site at **http://www.avp.org/.**

Chapter 6

Theoretical Perspectives on Race, Class, Gender, and Sexualities

The United States professes to be a nation that takes in the tired, hungry, poor, and downtrodden from throughout the world and gives them limitless opportunities to compete for a standard of living unavailable in most other places in the world. Yet, as we have seen, inequalities of opportunity are built right into our social institutions. Those institutions then give some groups unearned advantages and deny others a fair chance to compete. We have seen just some of the ways that this system is supported by the belief that those who work hard and play by the rules are destined to get ahead in life and that those who do not succeed are lazy and untalented. Not surprisingly, many students find it depressing to learn that the "land of opportunity" is really a land of unfair chances, in which the ability to succeed in life is determined, in large part, by one's race, ethnicity, social class, gender, and sexuality.

Learning about the ways that inequality is built into our social system is only the first step in understanding the dynamics of inequality. Thus far, we have learned the "who," "what," "when," "where," and "how" of inequality; what we still do not know is the "why." That is the question the articles in this section begin to address.

In the first article, Hudson argues that the United States was founded on racist principles that have become a cornerstone of American culture. The principles underlying U.S. culture, Hudson argues, define racism and inequality as "right" or just, and affirmative action as "wrong" or unfair. To help us understand how things got this way, he provides a brief overview of the racist, sexist, and class-based assumptions on which the United States was founded. Hudson argues that the doctrine of "majority rule," which is at the heart of our democratic system, was not established to represent the interests of all people. Rather, it was put in place to protect the property rights and privileges of white male property owners. It is this system and the institutionalized racism built into it that the civil rights movement of the 1950s and 1960s challenged. To a certain extent, the civil rights movement expanded the meaning of majority rule to include the right of people of color to vote, run for office, and get a good education. Hudson argues that the successes of the civil rights movement have subsequently been labeled as problematic by right-wing, conservative groups. These groups claim that racism entails only personal prejudice and interpersonal acts of discrimination and that programs to address institutionalized discrimination, such as affirmative action or busing, constitute unfair advantages for people of color.

In the end, Hudson addresses the question: Why does racial inequality continue in the United States? His answer is that conservative groups have succeeded in labeling programs aimed at undoing institutionalized discrimination as "reverse discrimination," thus "un-American." Right-wing groups tout the idea that the only inequalities that continue today are based upon differences in intelligence, talent, and motivation. If there are differences in the achievement of racial groups, conservatives maintain that the unequal status is deserved.

Many scholars recognize that there has been a backlash against the gains of the civil rights, feminist, and gay and lesbian movements of the twentieth century. But not all resistance to the inclusion of women, people of color, and sexual minorities has been as organized as the right-wing movements discussed by Hudson. In the second article in this section, Kimmel focuses on the role men have played in perpetuating gender, racial, sexual, and class-based inequalities. Kimmel argues that all men are unaware of themselves as gendered, just as whites are often unaware of themselves as having a race, or heterosexual people are unaware of their sexual orientation. Kimmel maintains that whether or not we are aware of the privileges we enjoy because of gender, race, social class, or sexual orientation, each of us participates in a cultural system that distributes power on the basis of these statuses. As members of society, we either challenge current beliefs, structural arrangements, and customs, or we simply accept them for what they are and go along with them, thus perpetuating the status quo. In other words, by not being part of the solution, men are part of the problem of gender inequality, just as whites who take for granted the privilege race brings them are part of the problem of racial inequality.

However, a lack of awareness is only part of the reason that inequalities continue to be perpetuated today. Kimmel examines the role that men have played in constructing history as we know it and establishing the cultural values that guide our society today. He maintains, for example, that our mainstream ideas about masculinity are based upon the idea that "real men" successfully compete in a marketplace oriented toward extreme individualism. This idea about what makes a "real man" makes it difficult for society to recognize the efforts of men who have been structurally prohibited from competing in the workplace, business, or politics.

Kimmel's article focuses in an abstract way on just some of the ways that social statuses based on race, class, gender, or sexuality can and do intersect in the lives of individuals. In the third article, Espiritu provides a specific example of how the intersection of these statuses can affect a particular group of people—in this case, Asian Americans. Espiritu argues that white women tend to focus on gender as the primary source of oppression, while people of color focus on race or ethnicity. Espiritu argues that by focusing on *either* race *or* gender, women and men of color overlook the intersection of race, class, and gender and ignore the experiences of those with multiple minority group statuses. In particular, the author explains that Asian men accept dominant ideas about masculinity and endeavor to assert their power in the family, sometimes through violence toward women and children.

At the same time, Asian women, recognizing the ways that the masculinity of Asian men has been debased in U.S. society, may adhere to ideals of racial solidarity and submit to the dominance of the men in their lives. Further, because racial issues in the United States tend to be thought of in "black and white" terms, the experiences of Asian, Hispanic, Native American, and other people of color tend to be sidelined and overlooked. Espiritu argues that until we move beyond binary examinations of race, class, and gender and find ways to consider the intersections of various minority group statuses, we will continue to reinforce a social system that privileges some groups at the expense of others.

Along these lines, in the fourth article—an interview conducted by Lowe—Angela Davis discusses a number of issues regarding race, class, gender, and sexuality, including some of the reasons that women of color have resisted mainstream feminism. Like Espiritu, Davis recognizes that white feminists have a tendency to think of gender as the underlying source of women's oppression. Therefore, they miss the sources of oppression and inequality that are rooted in race, class, and sexuality, as well as the intersection of these statuses.

Davis, however, discusses the dominance of capitalism in the United States and its spread throughout the world as a source of oppression for all women, people of color, and those who are poor or working class. With the decline of industry in the United States, unskilled and semiskilled jobs that once provided good benefits and wages moved overseas where manufacturers now pay people in poor countries a fraction of what U.S. workers once earned. These jobs have been replaced, in part, by positions in the growing prison industry, where women, people of color, and members of the working class are paid lower wages to guard a growing inmate population made up primarily of poor women and people of color. Davis argues that women, people of color, the working class and poor, as well as sexual minorities, must recognize the commonality of their oppression and form coalitions with one another, on both a national and an international basis. Until these groups can overcome the desire to emphasize what is different about their identities and social experiences, all of these minority groups will continue to struggle as much with one another as against the capitalist system that benefits by oppressing all.

Although three of the first four articles in this section touch briefly on sexuality, none of them provides a theoretical explanation of the way that oppression may be rooted in gender and the patriarchal order. In the last article, Lorber addresses these issues, first by examining the theoretical debate over issues such as heterosexuality, prostitution, pornography, and transgenderism. She begins by explaining that feminists disagree over whether heterosexuality, prostitution, and pornography are forms of sexual violence used by men to oppress women. Radical feminists tend to believe that men are inherently more sexually aggressive and violent than women. Further, they believe that heterosexuality, prostitution, and pornography are all potential means by which men exercise dominance over women through violence and sexual exploitation. Radical feminists maintain that prostitution and pornography encourage men to objectify, dominate, and express violence toward women.

Lorber explains that other feminists argue that gender is one of many social statuses, including race, ethnicity, social class, and sexuality, that intersect to affect the sexual experiences that women have. Sexuality is an important aspect of life, and women must maintain the right to express themselves through heterosexual relationships and as prostitutes and in pornography, if that is what they choose to do. Rather than protecting all women from all men, these feminists argue that it would be better to address inequalities based upon race, class, and sexuality that intersect with gender to affect women's lives and experiences differently.

Finally, Lorber examines sexuality and gender and argues that bisexuals and transgenders—transsexuals and cross-dressers, for example—challenge our ideas about the social order and how to challenge it. In the end, Lorber argues, theorists and activists have worked to recognize a "hierarchy of domination," in which those who are oppressed in one instance might be the oppressor in another. If we are ever to challenge the inequalities facing us today, we must move beyond binary ideas about good and bad, oppressor and oppressed, that are rooted in the idea that subordination is based on race *or* ethnicity *or* social class *or* gender *or* sexuality. Instead, we must recognize the complex ways in which these statuses intersect with one another, as well as the ways that inequality is maintained through social interaction, our belief systems, and our structural arrangements.

Taken together, these articles show us that although it is important to recognize the way that inequalities are based on race, ethnicity, social class, gender, *or* sexuality, in order to understand why inequality continues today, we must look at the way they intersect with one another. We must consider the historical context of oppression based upon these statuses, as well as recognize the role that backlash movements play in challenging gains that have been made in equalizing opportunities. Further, people must recognize the ways in which they, personally, benefit from systems that oppress some groups by privileging others. And we must find ways, as minority group members, to work with others who are like us in some ways and different in others, to challenge the unequal system of opportunities that is so deeply entrenched in the United States.

Reading 1

Simple Justice: Affirmative Action and American Racism in Historical Perspective

J. Blaine Hudson

In this article, Hudson argues that the U.S. democratic principle of majority rule was founded upon racist ideals and goals. Social movements that oppose the gains of the civil rights movement often draw upon these ideals, which means that achieving equality will be difficult, if not impossible, for African Americans.

Affirmative action is quintessentially a question of race, rights and justice in a nation long and deeply divided by color prejudice. Because of

Source: Black Scholar, Vol. 25, Issue 3 (Summer 1995), 16–23.

this, one cannot comprehend affirmative action *within* a framework shaped by and saturated with the racial mythology of American history, which terms racism and inequality "right" and affirmative action, as an alternative vision for American society, "wrong." The current controversy over affirmative action and the possibilities of its resolution can be understood only by examining and deconstructing American racism from the perspective of its victims. Although race will be the central focus, this discussion must include gender inequality, which is targeted by affirmative action, and class inequality—which is not, but should be. This difficult and unsettling examination, as with all paradigm-shifts, requires a reassessment of first principles and underlying premises.

WORKING DEFINITIONS

How one thinks about race and racism is often limited and distorted by the "received knowledge" of American culture. Consequently, before proceeding with an analysis, a few working definitions and clarifying distinctions may be helpful.

First, all races belong to one human species, *Homo sapiens sapiens*. Within this species, *races are global human populations distinguished by genetically transmitted physical characteristics*—with skin color being the most common distinguishing characteristic. Major racial groups are recognized through "innate" physical differences, but these, as opposed to ingrained cultural differences, are only "skin deep" (Hudson 1995).

Thus, while race has an elusive biological meaning, the social and political constructions of race determines its significance in human affairs.

Second, race and ethnicity are often confused with one another. *Ethnic groups are social formations within larger racial groups distinguished by religious, cultural, linguistic or other variable traits.* In other words, constructions of race are larger in scale and more fundamental, while ethnic groups are merely parts of each racial mosaic. This rather technical point is extremely important since theories dealing with ethnicity are commonly misapplied to race, e.g., that racial integration and ethnic assimilation are identical processes (Franklin 1991).

Third, *racism is the belief or set of beliefs that one's race is superior to others*. Furthermore, there are three types/levels of racism:

- individual racism;
- institutional racism; and
- cultural racism

These forms of racism are interdependent and mutually reinforcing. Yet, while individual racism is important to individuals to varying degrees, institutional and cultural racism have more to do with economic power and relations, and affect the lives of millions of Americans—whether they are racist as individuals or not (Omi & Winant 1986). Affirmative action has polarized American society precisely because it is a means of attacking institutional and cultural racism. Furthermore, American racism involves two sets of beliefs or values: beliefs concerning the "nature" of persons of color; and beliefs concerning the "nature" of persons of presumably unmixed European descent. Only the first constellation of beliefs is usually studied.

The legions of stereotypes used to describe persons of color are familiar and some are so commonplace that few Americans question their validity, e.g., that African Americans are superior athletes. But, what of the other dimension of racism—how whites see themselves? If one wishes to understand racism and other forms of injustice, one must study the beliefs and behaviors of the perpetrators, rather than the victims, of racial injustice. An overview of this irrational cultural sub-stratum is most revealing.

AMERICAN RACISM PAST: THE ANGLO-SAXON MYTH

The roots of American racism lie deep in the European and American past (Jordan 1968). The colonists who established the first citizenry of the US derived primarily from the British Isles. They were largely Protestant in their religious leanings and identified strongly with a myth of Anglo-Saxon racial superiority

(Horsman 1981). This myth was a complex blend of history and fantasy. Historically, the Angles and Saxons (and Jutes) were Germanic tribes that invaded England and displaced the aboriginal Celts during the later stages of the Roman Empire period. Although rather barbaric by Roman standards, those Anglo-Saxons, according to myth, prided themselves on their racial purity, their physical prowess and beauty, their rare love of independence and their "gift" for creating democratic institutions. They themselves would be conquered by the Normans in 1066, but Anglo-Saxon myth would become its popularity in England and her colonies well into the 17th century (Horsman 1981).

Many of the founders of American democracy were dedicated proponents of this Anglo-Saxon myth. Thomas Jefferson, for example, held the conviction that US independence would allow for the full and unencumbered expression of the Anglo-Saxon gift for sound, democratic government (Horsman 1981). While the concept of a union of states was actually derived from the model of the Iroquois Confederacy, it is important to remember that only racially pure Anglo-Saxons were presumed to possess this gift and only they were considered fit to share in the bounty of the new nation.

As the nineteenth century unfolded, many whites advanced increasingly radical views of race and nationalism. These views fixed on the Indo-European roots of Caucasian peoples— and the superiority of the Germanic, now dubbed the Aryan, branch of the "white race." Their concept of superiority was not only racist, but ethnocentric as well in positing that Northern Europeans were superior to all other European/Caucasians (e.g., the Gallic, the Slavic and the Mediterranean types), below which were the other races of humankind.

Early in the 20th century, the Aryan/Anglo-Saxon myth became an ideological blueprint for a modern new world order. In this century, under the skillful, ruthless and maniacal leadership of a "true believer," this myth seduced a nation and unleashed madness upon the world. That leader was Adolf Hitler and that nation was Nazi Germany.

AMERICAN DEMOCRACY: "MAJORITY RULE"

A nation founded on the notion of racial superiority stands in absolute contradiction to the concept of democracy. In democratic states, all people are, in theory, citizens, and all or some combination of three types of human political rights govern their social and political interactions (Guinier 1994):

1. majority rights—embodied by the principle of majority rule;
2. group rights—embodied by the principle of protecting the rights of "minority" groups (in either homogeneous or plural societies), however comprised, against the "tyranny of the majority"; and
3. individual rights—embodied by the principle of protecting the rights of individuals against the depredations of other individuals, groups or the majority itself.

Not coincidentally, in the history of the US, only two of these sub-categories have been defined and protected by the letter of the law. In theory, the US Constitution establishes a government based on the rule of the majority. In actuality, the affluent framers of the Constitution abhorred the possibility of racial pluralism, could not imagine gender equality and distrusted the laboring masses. "Majority rule" was, in fact, the rule of affluent white males under a body of laws designed (by them) to protect their property and privilege. This was, admittedly, a tremendous improvement over arbitrary and capricious rule by the "divine right of kings." It was also far from true democracy. However, the appearance of democracy was created by a strict racial construction of US citizenship and the denial of rights to those defined as non-citizens.

THERE HAVE BEEN TWO VISIONS—and two political, social, cultural and economic agendas in American history related to race and citizenship. One has conceived of this nation as a white man's country, won by right of conquest and settled by whites of mainly Anglo-Saxon ancestry—a country whose bounty should benefit elite whites alone. This vision prevailed through most of American history and has remained a unifying principle in the twentieth century. Its message has been broadly idealistic and democratic, but its advocates have practiced racism, sexism, exclusion and elitism.

The other vision has conceived of this nation as embodying the promise and possibility of freedom and equality within (i.e., by gender, age, ethnicity) and across racial boundaries. This vision has animated progressive (and sometimes radical) political and social movements throughout American history, such as the anti-slavery movement, the women's movement, aspects of the labor and populist movements. Essentially, this vision has taken "American ideals" seriously.

These two visions have not produced "one nation" unified by a broad consensus regarding its identity, values and goals. Rather, the agendas shaped by these discordant and conflicting visions have been a veritable "point-counterpoint" of American history.

AMERICAN RACISM, PRESENT: NEOCONSERVATISM

Largely because of its embarrassing association with Nazism, the "raw" form of the Anglo-Saxon myth would become "politically incorrect" after World War II. However, its deeper meanings and political agenda would be perpetuated in the ideology of neoconservatism in contemporary America.

BY 1965, THE CIVIL RIGHTS MOVEMENT had achieved its greatest triumphs. The legal basis for racial or caste segregation had been undermined. However, the political victories of this era were, in essence, a three-way compromise between "old style" segregation, the type of token desegregation envisioned by most white Americans in the 1940s and 1950s—and the ideal of full empowerment and full participation for people of color in the mainstream of American life. In the middle, the federal government and the civil rights moderates attempted to navigate the treacherous straits between racial segregation, which was both

obsolete and an international embarrassment (in the Cold War and the age of decolonialization), and a truly democratic, pluralistic society—which most white Americans simply would not accept.

While it is easy and even fashionable to trivialize the impact of the civil rights era, the end of legal segregation changed American society profoundly. For a great many whites, the "American way of life," based on the institutionalization of the Anglo-Saxon myth, seemed in jeopardy. Consequently, the partial successes of the Civil Rights movement produced a powerful and increasingly coherent and coordinated response: the racial ideology now known as neoconservatism (Franklin 1991; Omi & Winant 1986).

Whether termed "white backlash," the "silent majority," the "new right," the "far right," the "Christian right," et al., the neoconservatives were unified by their aversion to both the form and substance of the racial reforms of the Civil Rights era. As to their own beliefs, the neoconservatives were "true Americans" dedicated to upholding the sanctity of American values—in the eighteenth and nineteenth century sense of Anglo-Saxonism/Aryanism and the belief in Manifest Destiny (Franklin 1991). They presently tried to argue that their Americanism was not racist—1965 was not 1765, or 1865, or even 1940—since this type of conservative "racial project" had become associated with images of Bull Connor in Birmingham (1963) and other race-baiters. How, then, to convey the racial meanings of the past without using the rhetoric and symbols of the past, i.e., how to be racist without appearing to be so? How, then, to preserve elite white male supremacy without advocating the restoration of legal segregation? Between 1965 and 1975, largely through trial and error, a neoconservative strategy evolved that stressed:

1. majority (i.e., white) and individual rights as the foundations of American democracy;
2. the acceptance of a narrow and restrictive definition of racism—limited primarily to varieties of individual prejudice—while systemic and cultural racism were exempted from critical analysis;

3. the acceptance of deterministic and normative explanations of racial, gender and class inequality that "blamed the victims"; and

4. an ahistorical understanding of racism, racial inequality and other forms of oppression, i.e., a type of "ditto-head" know-nothingism.

Taken together, this strategy allowed the neoconservatives to appropriate the rhetoric, in many cases, of the civil rights movement itself. For example, neoconservatives argued that, after the civil rights "revolution," special initiatives to impose or promote racial equality were no longer necessary and, furthermore, were violations of the rights of whites as individuals and as a group. Discrimination was discrimination, and objectionable as such. In other words, creating inequality was the "American way," but efforts to eliminate inequality were anathematized as "reverse discrimination," which was, of course, "un-American."

Selling this hypocrisy effectively depended on the ability of the neoconservative movement to sell two crucial supporting assumptions. The first assumption holds that persons of color are genetically and culturally different from and inferior to whites. Consequently, rather than racial inequality being caused by white racism (i.e., by the actions of whites and the operations of institutions created and controlled by whites), racial inequality simply reflects the natural inequality that exists between groups in a hierarchy of races, i.e., the natural order. This is the central argument advanced most recently in *The Bell Curve* (1994) as it relates to intellectual capacity by race and class. While this myth is patently racist, and logically and empirically flawed (Hudson 1995), we cannot overlook the other stated or implied criticism of affirmative action, i.e., that "less qualified" or "unqualified" women and persons of color are given unfair preference over "better qualified" or "the best qualified" persons—who are, presumably, white and usually male as well.

Beyond the assumption of fixed and immutable genetic inferiority, there is the corollary assumption of cultural or characterological inferiority. This myth emphasizes the behavioral dysfunctionality of persons of color, individually and collectively, i.e., the degree to which persons of color are unprepared for, or incapable of meeting, the demands of life in contemporary American society. Consequently, the preoccupation with "pathological" families, teenage mothers, "welfare queens," black criminals, drug addicts and teenage "gangbangers" allows neoconservatives to transpose or hopelessly confuse the causes of inequality with the effects of inequality. In other words, exaggerated and stereotypical caricatures of the uncivilized behavior of *some* persons of color are used to explain or justify the unequal status of all persons of color. Through this feat of intellectual *legerdemain*, neoconservatives relieve themselves of all responsibility for the unequal conditions and treatment endured by persons of color, women and the poor by blaming the victims (Hudson 1995).

Another subtle, but crucial, ingredient in the ideological witches' brew of neoconservatism is the contention that racism itself is purely a matter of individual prejudice and that the institutional and cultural manifestations of racism are no longer significant. This limited definition misrepresents racism and the causes of racial inequality, and its acceptance leads to the familiar dead-end, talk-show debates regarding "black racism" and absurdities such as "the color complex," while obscuring the most pernicious forms of white racism. Obviously, any individual can be prejudiced, but individual racial prejudice is only one, and the least dangerous, form of racism.

Admittedly, racism promotes self-hatred in its victims and divides oppressed groups against themselves from within. Furthermore, it is also quite easy to confuse justifiable feelings of anger and resentment toward whites—based on how persons of color have been treated by whites—with racism.

From the perspective of social-psychology, racism can be defined as a "cultural neurosis," a societal "mental illness." Accordingly, at any given time in American history, most white Americans have suffered from this affliction. Empirical research indicates that, depending on the historical period, 10–25 percent of white Americans were "clinically racist," another 10–25 percent were essentially non-racist, while the remaining 50–80 percent were "conforming racists" who accepted the racial status quo (Bowser & Hunt 1981; Hudson & Hines-Hudson 1994; Ostow 1991; Pettigrew 1979). This perspective supports and corresponds to the "two visions" referenced previously. Most significantly, the role of the large "conforming majority" underscores the importance of cultural and institutional racism—and how values and institutions, once established by the few, are seldom questioned and challenged by the many.

Thus, once stripped of its ideological pretensions, the buttressing of the social structure which maintains these power relations is the overarching goal of the neoconservative movement. In essence, the neoconservative argument is a straightforward racial ideology:

> Racism is purely an expression of individual prejudice. Inequalities by race (and, by extension, gender and/or class) reflect the natural order. Whites owe persons of color (and women and the poor) nothing. Therefore, demands for racial equality are unjustified, unfair to whites and "un-American."

It is important not to equivocate with respect to the meaning of neoconservatism. This ideology has dominated American politics for a generation—and has succeeded in claiming the "moral high ground" in the minds of millions of Americans who are threatened by change and receptive to a kind of respectable racism that does not appear to be racist at all. However, this new racism is little more than a Madison Avenue version of the old racism—an old poison in an attractive new bottle.

INEQUALITY, RESPONSIBILITY, AND JUSTICE

The second assumption of neoconservatism contends that affirmative action is unfair, that it penalizes guiltless white "bystanders" of this historical era for the wrongs committed by whites under slavery and segregation. This assumption seems superficially and intuitively right, but is inherently specious.

When legal segregation ended (1954–1965), African American leaders and some white supporters recognized that court decisions and protective legislation were only a first step toward achieving the goal of racial equality. The legacy of 246 years of bondage followed by another century of segregation was a vast social, cultural, economic and political gulf between racial groups. Of all the "next steps" available, as in 1864–1865, two corrective or compensatory options were most obvious.

One was reparations which, in theory, would eliminate inequality directly—by transferring wealth and power from those who had expropriated and enjoyed them illegitimately—to those who had been so victimized. Economic inequality would be "repaired" by a redistribution of wealth; political inequality would be "repaired" by a redistribution of power. It is not difficult to understand why white Americans have never been fond of this concept. However, regardless of the repeated attempts to dismiss the case for reparations, it retains a certain power, simplicity, coherence and, most importantly, appropriateness to the problem at hand that cannot be ignored. However, while the nation at least experimented briefly with land redistribution following emancipation, direct economic empowerment was never considered seriously during the civil rights era.

The other corrective measure was affirmative action or some type of selective reparations on the "installment plan." Rather than transfer wealth and power outright affirmative action programs would negate, insofar as is possible, white privilege in American institutional life and thus enable African Americans to progress, at however rapid or glacial a pace, toward equality. Toward this end, beginning with Executive Order 8802 (1941), the legal basis for racially discriminatory employment practices was systematically undermined. As singular achievements in this long process, the 1964 Civil Rights Act and Executive Order

11246 (1965) prohibited discrimination in general based on race, color, religion, and national origin, and gave the federal government the power to enforce this prohibition. Protection against sex (or gender) discrimination was included under Executive Order 11375 in 1968 (Babcock et al.1975).

Consequently, by the end of the civil rights era, the majority of US citizens had decided that legal segregation was wrong and had come to accept the principle of equality of opportunity as a process and a goal, while retreating from a commitment to equality of result. As with the end of slavery, the triumph over legal segregation was a monumental victory after a protracted struggle, but a victory that seemed increasingly hollow as the nation turned sharply toward neoconservatism and old patterns of segregation and inequality persisted or re-surfaced in the post civil rights era.

For example, the percentage of African Americans in the middle-income range (and above) more than doubled between 1960 and 1975, increasing from roughly 10–12 percent to nearly 30 percent (Landry 1987). However, this percentage subsequently declined to roughly 25 percent by 1990 (Hacker 1992), while the percentage of whites in the same income ranges remained double that of African Americans (and Latinos and Native Americans). Moreover, the 1990 mean family incomes of African Americans, Latinos and Native Americans were only roughly 60 percent of mean white family incomes and roughly 35 percent were impoverished compared to roughly 15 percent of white families (Hacker 1992). Furthermore, residential segregation by race remained commonplace throughout the nation—2 complicating the issues of school and workforce desegregation. Resegregation (through tracking), and unequal treatment and outcomes by race remained commonplace in American education. The American workforce was desegregated primarily at the bottom or in occupational categories wherein persons of color were "service providers," while the power positions were monopolized by white males (Franklin 1991).

A CHOICE OF FUTURES

Only by falsifying or ignoring the American past and the realities of the American present can the logic of affirmative action be made to seem illogical. Racism, and other forms of inequality will not simply wither away. If the people of the US wish to escape the grip of their racial past, a strategy to effect substantive and lasting change must emphasize the following, at minimum:

1. Genuine commitment to eliminating racism and racial inequality—and all other forms of inequality. No more; no less. A first expression of this commitment must be a clear and suitably broad definition of racism, based on an accurate account of American history, which stresses the centrality of institutional and cultural racism.

2. Statutory or Constitutional recognition of the principle of group rights—particularly as related to racial, class and gender groups. Recognition of such rights for all would protect "minority" groups from the "tyranny of the majority" and would facilitate the evolution of a new social contract and plural society.

3. More, rather than less—and strong, rather than weak, affirmative programs are needed. The failures of halfhearted or ill-conceived affirmative action initiatives do not invalidate the concept, i.e., because the implementation of affirmative action (by those who often oppose it) is flawed does not mean that the concept is flawed.

4. Quotas, or targets/goals, for which responsible persons will be held accountable must be a central feature of affirmative action programs. Inequality is quantifiable and its reduction/elimination can be monitored objectively. There must be some way of "keeping score," otherwise mountains of process and "good faith efforts" will bury a few molehills of results.

5. Affirmative action alone, even in its most effective form, is insufficient. Consequently, the issue of reparations for African Americans should be revisited and at least a limited reparations program should be implemented. In other words, something tangible must be done to address the massive

and long-standing inequalities that exist between blacks (and most persons of color) and white Americans. However, simplistic notions of cash payments, tax amnesties or rebates, et al., should be evaluated carefully since giving people money (much as a poor person winning the lottery) in an economy they do not control virtually guarantees that most of that money will soon flow back into the hands of those who do control the economy. The distribution of wealth and power must be equalized in the short-term and in ways that "level the playing field" and prevent the restoration of inequality. A compensatory strategy that fails to effect these ends is inadequate. Thus, there should be a simple, inverse relationship between reparations and affirmative action: The more reparations, the less affirmative action—and vice versa.

6. An effective strategy must anticipate new forms and expressions of racial, gender and class discrimination and oppression that may evolve in response to changing American and global realities. Americans once believed that ending slavery would end racism and racial inequality, but segregation, a new form of oppression, evolved after emancipation. Americans once believed that ending legal segregation would end racism. Wrong again, and institutional/structural inequality followed the end of legal segregation. Racism has proven itself to be deeply ingrained, remarkably resilient and immensely profitable. The effort to end human inequality is one in which there may be no final victory—only a long, unending struggle against human greed and fear.

Given the extent to which neoconservatism and even more radical rightists ideologies have shaped contemporary American culture, few Americans would support even a mild version of this strategy today. The proponents of the new racism, in striving to dismantle even the weak affirmative action efforts that exist at present, are working diligently to preserve a nation with a gaping abyss between "haves" and "have-nots." Their willingness and ability to mount this challenge attests to the strength and wide acceptance of neoconservative ideology, and the organization and financing of the neoconservative political project. How-

ever, the neoconservatives do not represent all Americans or even the majority of Americans—if that majority understands its larger long-term interests.

Toward the end of his life, James Baldwin (1985) wrote: "History, I contend, is the present—we, with every breath we take, every move we make, are History." There are choices before this nation that proceed from very different ethical and political premises. Persons of color, women and the poor have a right to know what their citizenship truly means—and whether they can expect simple justice from their fellow citizens.

REFERENCES

BABCOCK, B. A., A. E. FREEDMAN, E. H. NORTON, AND S. C. ROSS. 1975. *Sex discrimination and the Law: Causes and Remedies.* Boston: Little, Brown and Company.

BALDWIN, J. 1985. *The Evidence of Things Not Seen.* New York: Holt, Rinehart and Winston.

BOWSER, B. P., AND R. G. HUNT. 1981. "The Impact of Racism on White Americans." Beverly Hills, CA: Sage Publications.

FRANKLIN, R. S. 1991. *Shadows of Race and Class.* Minneapolis: University of Minnesota Press.

GUINIER, L. 1994. *The Tyranny of the Majority: Fundamental Fairness in Representative Democracy.* New York: The Free Press.

HACKER, A. 1992. *Two Nations: Black and White, Separate, Hostile and Unequal.* New York: Scribners.

HILL, H. AND J. E. JONES, JR., EDS. 1993. *Race in America: The Struggle for Equality.* Madison: University of Wisconsin Press.

HORSMAN, R. 1981. *Race and Manifest Destiny: The Origins of American Racial Anglo-Saxonism.* Cambridge: Harvard University Press.

HUDSON, J. B. 1995. Scientific Racism: "The Politics of Tests, Race and Genetics." *The Black Scholar,* 25 (1): 3–10.

HUDSON, J. B. AND B. M. HINES-HUDSON 1994. "Racial Attitudes in the Workplace: A Study of a Public Service Agency." Unpublished report (submitted for publication). University of Louisville.

JORDAN, W. D. 1968. *White over Black: American Attitudes Toward the Negro, 1550–1812.* Chapel Hill: University of North Carolina Press.

LANDRY, B. 1987. *The New Black Middle Class.* Berkeley: University of California Press.

OMI, M. AND H. WINANT. 1986. *Racial Formation in the United States: From the 1960s to the 1980s.* New York: Routledge and Kegan Paul.

OSTOW, M. 1991. "A Psychoanalytic Approach to the Problem of Prejudice, Discrimination, and Persecution." In *Opening Doors: Perspectives on Race Relations in Contemporary America,* edited by H. J. Knopke, R. J. Norrell, and R. W. Rogers. Tuscaloosa: The University of Alabama Press.

PETTIGREW, T. F. 1979. "Racial Change and Social Policy." *Annals of the American Academy of Political and Social Sciences,* 441: 114–131.

2. In what ways are the successes of the civil rights movement defined as problematic? Who sees these social changes as "bad"?

3. What are the ways in which personal and institutionalized forms of prejudice and discrimination affect people's lives?

CRITICAL THINKING QUESTIONS

1. Why is the doctrine of majority rule seen as a means of oppression instead of a solution to inequalities?

Reading 2

Invisible Masculinity

Michael S. Kimmel

In this article, Kimmel argues that men are not aware of the centrality of gender in social life and that this perpetuates gender-based inequality in society.

American men have no history. Sure, we have stacks of biographies of the heroic and famous, and historical accounts of events in which men took part, like wars, strikes, or political campaigns. And we have group portraits of athletes, soldiers, and the men who run unions and political parties. There are probably thousands of histories of institutions that were organized, staffed, and run by men.

So how is it that men have no history? Until the intervention of women's studies, it was women who had no history, who were invisible, the "other." Still today, virtually every history book is a history of men. If a book does not have the word "women" in its title, it is a

Source: Reprinted by permission of Transaction Publishers from *Society* 30, no. 6 (September/October 1993): 28–35. © 1993 by Transaction Publishers.

good bet that the book is about men. But these books feel strangely empty at their centers, where the discussion of men should be. Books about men are not about men as men. These books do not explore how the experience of being a man structured the men's lives, or the organizations and institutions they created, the events in which they participated. American men have no history as gendered selves; no work describes historical events in terms of what these events meant to the men who participated in them as men.

What does it mean, then, to write of men as men? We must examine the ways in which the experience of manhood has structured the course and the meanings of the activities of American men—great or small. We must chart the ways in which meanings of manhood have changed over the course of American history.

And we must explore the ways in which the pursuit of that elusive ideal of manhood, and our relentless efforts to prove it, have animated many of the central events in American history.

This is not to say that simply looking at the idea of manhood, or injecting gender into the standard historical approach, will suddenly, magically, illuminate the American historical pageant. We cannot understand manhood without understanding American history—that is without locating the changing definitions of manhood within the larger context of the economic, political, and social events that characterize American history. By the same token, American history cannot be fully understood without an understanding of American men's ceaseless quest for manhood in the evolution of those economic, political, social, and cultural experiences and events.

Such a perspective should shed new light on the events that dot our history and the lives of the men who made them. Composer Charles Ives insisted that Impressionistic music was "sissy" and that he wanted to use traditional tough guy sounds to build a more popular and virile music. Architect Louis Sullivan, the inventor of the skyscraper, described his ambition to create "masculine forms"—strong, solid, tall, commanding respect. Political figures, like the endless parade of presidential hopefuls, have found it necessary both to proclaim their own manhood and to raise questions about their opponents' manhood.

Think about the 1840 presidential campaign, when William Henry Harrison's supporters chastised Martin Van Buren as "Little Vanny," and a "used up man." Andrew Jackson vented his manly rage at "effete" bankers and "infantilized" Indians. Theodore Roosevelt thundered about the strenuous life while he prepared invasions of Panama and the Philippines. Then there was Lyndon Johnson's vainglorious claim during the Tet offensive of the Vietnam War that he did not just "screw" Ho Chi Minh, but "cut his pecker off!" After the vice-presidential debate with Geraldine Ferraro in 1984 George Bush boasted that he had "kicked a little ass." Then he squared off with television commentator Dan Rather in 1988 to dispel his wimp image. From the founding of the Republic, presidents have demonstrated their manhood in the political arena and have sent millions of America's young men to die to prove it.

If the pursuit of manhood has been a dominant theme in American history, at least rhetorically and metaphorically, why do American men still have no history? In part because they do not even know what questions to ask.

In the past twenty-five years, the pioneering work of feminist scholars, both in traditional disciplines and in women's studies, has made us increasingly aware of the centrality of gender in shaping social life. In the past, social scientists would have only listed class and race as the master statuses that defined and proscribed social life. But today, gender has joined race and class as one of the axes around which social life is organized, and through which we can gain an understanding of our own experiences. Feminist scholars rightfully focused their attention on women—on what Catharine Stimpson calls the "omissions, distortions, and trivializations" of women's experiences—and the spheres to which women have historically been consigned, like private life and the family.

Women's history has sought to rescue from obscurity the lives of significant women who had been ignored or whose work had been minimized by traditional androcentric scholarship. It also has examined the lives of ordinary women of the past, the struggles of laundresses, factory workers, pioneer homesteaders, or housewives in carving out lives of meaning and dignity in a world controlled by men. Whether the focus is on the exemplary or the ordinary, feminist scholarship has made clear that gender is central to women's lives.

Now, we need to go further. We need to include men. Historian Natalie Zemon Davis urges us to be "interested in the history of both women and men." She says, "We should not be working on the subjected sex any more than a historian of class can focus exclusively on peasants. Our goal is to understand the significance of the sexes, of gender groups in the historical past."

The problem with such advice is that, to men at least, gender often remains invisible.

Strange as it may sound, men are the "invisible" gender. Ubiquitous in positions of power everywhere, men are invisible to themselves. Courses on gender in the universities are populated largely by women, as if the term only applied to them. "Woman alone seems to have 'gender' since the category itself is defined as that aspect of social relations based on difference between the sexes in which the standard has always been man," writes historian Thomas Lacquer. As the Chinese proverb has it, the fish are the last to discover the ocean.

This fact was made clear to me in a seminar on feminism I attended in the late 1970s. There, in a discussion between two women, I first confronted this invisibility of gender to men. The two women, one white, the other black, were discussing whether all women were, by definition, "sisters," because they all had essentially the same experiences and because all women faced oppression by men. The white woman asserted that the fact that they were both women bonded them, in spite of racial differences. The black woman disagreed.

"When you wake up in the morning and look in the mirror, what do you see?" she asked.

"I see a woman," replied the white woman.

"That's precisely the problem," responded the black woman. "I see a black woman. To me, race is visible every day, because race is how I am not privileged in our culture. Race is invisible to you, because it's how you are privileged. It's why there will always be differences in our experience."

This startling exchange made me groan—more audibly, perhaps, than I intended. Being the only man in the room, someone asked what my response had meant.

"Well," I said, "when I look in the mirror, I see a human being. I'm universally generalizable. As a middle class white man, I have no class, no race, no gender. I'm the generic person!"

Sometimes, I like to think that it was on that day that I became a middle-class white man. Sure, I had been all this before, but it had not meant much to me. Since then, I have begun to understand that race, class, and gender do not refer only to people marginalized by race, class, or gender. Those terms also describe me. I enjoy the privilege of invisibility. The very processes that confer privilege to one group and not to another group are often invisible to those upon whom that privilege is conferred. What makes us marginal or powerless are the processes we see, partly because others keep reminding us of them.

American men have come to think of themselves as genderless, in part because they can afford the luxury of ignoring the centrality of gender. So military, political, scientific, or literary figures are treated as if their gender, their masculinity, had nothing to do with their military exploits, policy decisions, scientific experiments, or writing styles and subjects. And the disenfranchised and oppressed are those whose manhood is not considered to be equal.

By contrast, the quest for manhood—the effort to achieve, to demonstrate, to prove their masculinity—is one of the animating experiences in the lives of American men. That men remain unaware of the centrality of gender in their lives perpetuates the inequalities based on gender in our society, and keeps in place the power of men over women, and the power some men hold over other men, which are among the central mechanisms of power in society.

Invisibility reproduces inequality. And the invisibility of gender to those privileged by it reproduces the inequalities that are circumscribed by gender. The centrality of gender and the process by which it has come to be seen as central are political processes that involve both power and resistance to power. It was feminism and gay liberation, and feminism's academic sister, women's studies, that brought gender into public discourse, making femininity and masculinity problematic, and demanding a transformation of existing gender relations. It was feminist-inspired research that made social and cultural analysts aware of the ubiquitous yet subtle way in which the gender factor permeates the social fabric.

To speak and write about gender is to enter a political discourse, to become engaged with power and resistance. It is about the resources that maintain power, the symbolic props that extend power, and the ideological apparatuses that develop to sustain and legitimate power. The historical construction of gender is a process through which various forms of power are reproduced and power becomes indelibly inscribed onto everyday life. It is impossible to speak of the historical construction of gender without speaking about power. In fact, power is so central to the historical construction of masculinities that it has been invisible to most social scientists who have studied it. Thus social theory and social science have done exactly what cannot be done: analyze masculinity without discussing power.

The historical construction of masculinities, the reproduction of gendered power relations, involves two separate dimensions, each of which was rendered invisible—first by classical social theory, and more recently by the academic discourse that made "sex roles" appear as historically invariant, fixed, static, and normal. Masculinities are constructed in a field of power: 1) the power of men over women; 2) the power of some men over other men.

Men's power over women is relatively straightforward. It is the aggregate power of men as a group to determine the distribution of rewards in society. Men's power over other men concerns the distribution of those rewards among men by differential access to class, race, ethnic privileges, or privileges based on sexual orientation—that is, the power of upper and middle class men over working class men; the power of white and native-born men over non-white and/or non-native born men; and the power of straight men over gay men. The constituent elements of "hegemonic" masculinity, the stuff of the construction, are sexism, racism, and homophobia. Masculinities are constructed by racism, sexism, and homophobia, and social science has been ever complicit.

These dimensions of power were embedded within academic discourses by a sleight of hand. A version of white, middle class, heterosexual masculinity emerged as normative, the standard against which both men and women were measured, and through which success and failure were evaluated. This nominative version—enforced, coercive, laden with power—academic social science declared to be the "nominal" version.

Making the nominative into the normal has been the discursive mechanism by which hegemonic masculinity was constituted. As anthropologist Maurice Bloch writes, "It is precisely through the process of making a power situation appear as a fact in the nature of things that traditional authority works." It has been the task of academic social science to make this power situation appear as "a fact in the nature of things."

This process has not been a single, linear process, but a series of empirical specifications of the traits, attitudes, and behaviors that define vague social science concepts like "identity," "self," or "deviance." These, in turn rest on a series of theoretical inversions and appropriations whose origins lie at the center of what we commonly call classical social theory. From Thomas Hobbes and John Locke through Karl Marx, Max Weber, Emile Durkheim, and Sigmund Freud several currents run consistently. All proclaim "man" as his own maker; the phrase "homo faber" is more than a metaphor, it is about men's reproductive capacity, men's ability to give birth to themselves. This man exists originally outside society—hence the axiomatic centrality of the problematic relationship between the individual and society—and he has to be brought into society through socialization. This passage—from the state of nature into civil society—is a gendered creation myth. It is about men's power to give birth to society.

The myth goes something like this: Originally, there was chaos, but men created society to get out of this chaos. As political theorist Carole Pateman writes, "The conventional understanding of the 'political' is built upon the rejection of physical birth in favor of the masculine creation of (giving birth to) social and political order." Just as John Locke made a distinction in *Second*

Treatise on Government between "the labor of our body and the work of our hands," so too did social theorists claim a difference between labor that produces no lasting product because its possessor is dependent, and labor that transforms nature into something of value, the work, which is independent of the producer's survival needs and may outlast him. Labor, as in women's work, as in "going into labor" does not count; what counts is work.

This process of self-creation is fraught with anxiety and tension. If we are a nation, as Henry Clay coined the term in 1832, of "self-made men," then the process of self-making, of identity formation, is a public enactment, performed before the valuative eyes of other men. Nineteenth-century masculinity was a masculinity defined, tried, and tested in the marketplace. This was potentially terrifying, since the market is unstable, and it is potentially a "site of humiliation" as Henry David Thoreau called it just before he tried to escape to Walden Pond. A definition of manhood based on self-creation in the marketplace is a masculinity specific to an industrial capitalist marketplace. The generic man turns out to be a very specific construction: he is a white middle class entrepreneur.

It is this man's chronic anxiety that forms the backbone of the canon of classical sociological theory. Consider this passage from Tocqueville's *Democracy in America* (1835):

> An American will build a house in which to pass his old age and sell it before the roof is on; he will plant a garden and rent it just as the trees are coming into bearing; he will clear a field and leave others to reap the harvest; he will take up a profession and leave it, settle in one place and soon go off elsewhere with his changing desires . . . At first sight there is something astonishing in this spectacle of so many lucky men restless in the midst of abundance.

What a lucky man, indeed—chronically restless, temperamentally anxious, a man in constant motion to prove what ultimately cannot be proved: that he is a real man and that this identity is unthreatened by the actions of other men.

Now consider three more passages from the same canon. Marx and Engels writing in *The Communist Manifesto* (1848):

> The bourgeoisie cannot exist without constantly revolutionizing the instruments of production, and thereby the relations of production, and with them the whole relations of society. Conservation of the old modes of production in unaltered form, was, on the contrary, the first condition of existence for all earlier industrial classes. Constant revolutionizing of production, uninterrupted disturbance of all social conditions, everlasting uncertainty and agitation distinguish the bourgeois epoch from earlier ones.

And Max Weber in *The Protestant Ethic and the Spirit of Capitalism* (1905):

> Where the fulfillment of the calling cannot directly be related to the highest spiritual and cultural values, or when, on the other hand, it need not be felt simply as economic compulsion, the individual generally abandons the attempt to justify it at all. In the field of its highest development, in the United States, the pursuit of wealth, stripped of its religious and ethical meaning, tends to become associated with purely mundane passions, which often actually give it the character of sport.

And finally, Freud in his essay "The Dissection of the Psychical Personality" (1933):

> We are warned by a proverb against serving two masters at the same time. The poor ego has things even worse: it serves three severe masters and does what it can to bring their claims and demands into harmony with one another. These claims are always divergent and often seem incompatible. No wonder that the ego so often fails in its task. Its three tyrannical masters are the external world, the superego and the id. . . . Thus the ego, driven by the id, confined by the super ego, repulsed by reality, struggles to master its economic task of bringing about harmony among the forces and influences working in and upon it; and we can understand how it is that so often we cannot suppress a cry: "Life is not easy!"

These descriptions of the bourgeoisie under capitalism, of the fate of the Protestant work ethic under the ever rationalizing spirit of capitalism, or of the arduous task of the autonomous ego in psychological development are a common part of social science training. Does anyone ever mention that in all four cases the theorists were describing men? And not just generic mankind, but a particular type of masculinity, a definition of manhood that derives its identity from participation in the marketplace, from interaction with other men in that markeplace—a model of masculinity whose identity is based on homosocial competition?

How could men feel secure in their manhood? How could men determine that they had made the grade and were successful as real men? If the marketplace, the very arena in which they had established to demonstrate manhood was now so fraught with peril and danger, where could they go?

Enter academic social science at the turn of the twentieth century. Academic social science was, in part, an effort at historical restoration, that would rescue a model of masculinity that structural change had rendered anachronistic and reapply it to re-establish traditional power relations between women and men and between some men and other men. Academic social science provided the empirical measures for masculinity. If it could not be achieved in the marketplace, it could be demonstrated by the display of various gender-appropriate traits, attitudes, and behaviors that have become associated with masculinity. It was social science's task to enumerate those traits and attitudes, and then generalize them as the normal traits associated with adulthood, thus problematizing women and "other" men—men of color, gay men, nonnative born immigrant men.

This did not take place in a vacuum. The turn of the century was a time of dramatic change, in which the traditional foundations of gender identity—control over one's labor, ownership of the products of that labor, geographic and social mobility, domestic dominion over women and children—were eroding. Rapid industrialization, which brought changes in the scale and process of production; the closing of the frontier; challenges by women to the separation of spheres; new waves of swarthy immigrants and black migrants to the cities, and the emergence of a visible gay male subculture in the northern cities—all threatened hegemonic masculinity's sense of empowerment. Many efforts to resist proletarianization in the late nineteenth century—from the Knights of Labor to the Populist movement—used images of the heroic artisan to animate their defensive gender resistance. Everywhere, cultural critics observed masculinity to be in crisis.

This was true in private life as it was in public discourse. No sooner were the structural foundations of traditional masculinity eroding than it became clear that women had taken over the "making of men." The "feminization" of culture included women's control of the chief institutions of childhood socialization—church, school, home. Women were teaching boys to be men. Not only did classical social theory posit the primacy of production over reproduction, it set about reappropriating reproduction as well. Like the fraternal orders of the nineteenth century, in which men imitated women's reproductive powers and gave symbolic birth to one another through initiation rituals, twentieth-century American and European social theory marginalized women's sphere and then colonized it.

How did academic social science go about this process of propping up a threatened gender identity for American men? Most often, it meant pushing those potential threats to the margins, to reestablish the public arena as a safe space for men to be men with other men. This meant marginalizing women, and reasserting the dominance of middle class white men over men who were non-white, non-heterosexual, non-native born. Immigrant men, homosexual men, and black men were all tainted with the same problem: they were not properly manly. Some were unable to exercise manly self-control over primitive impulses, others were overly refined and effeminate; both effeminacy and primitivism were indications of insufficient manhood.

The more explicitly racist political agenda was left to the anthropologists. Just as sociology was taking on the central problem of measuring manhood, as a way to assure its biological possessors that they were, in fact, its social heirs, anthropology was busy measuring facial angles, brain bumps, brain weights, and other pseudo-racial characteristics, to demonstrate the natural superiority of whites over blacks, and making sure that those heirs were exclusively white. Not to be outdone, sociologists employed their newfound love of statistics to demonstrate that if present rates of fertility continued, white women would be committing "race suicide" if they failed in their patriotic duty to reproduce.

Much turn-of-the-century anthropological and sociological discourse sought to reimpose biological inevitability in the inequalities between women and men, and among men. Men and women were the way they were because they were biologically programmed to be that way. Prescriptive literature on child rearing and marriage manuals urged a return to traditional arrangements, often using the veneer of science or religion to make their point. Physical differences in size, weight, muscular strength, and brain weight were all used to shore up traditional hierarchical arrangements, and to resist women's entry into the public sphere.

"I think the great danger of our day is forcing the intellect of woman beyond what her physical organization will posssibly bear," wrote the Reverend John Todd. Let us instead, he counseled, "[g]ive woman all the advantages and all the education which her organization, so tender and delicate, will bear, but don't try to make the anemone into an oak, nor to turn the dove out to wrestle with storms and winds, under the idea that she might just as well be an eagle as a dove."

The consequences of anti-feminist diatribes in the construction of masculinities were significant. Keeping women back corresponded to maintaining some men's power over other men. Harvard professor Edward Clarke's celebrated work *Sex in Education* (1873) spelled it all out clearly. If women continue to enter schools and universities and push for entry into the professions, "it re-

quires no prophet to foretell that the wives who are to be mothers in our republic must be drawn from transatlantic homes."

Feminism implied "race suicide," which contravenes the inevitability of patriarchy. Biological models asserted that variations from the hegemonic model were themselves biological anomalies, problems inherent in the organism itself, and not subject to cultural mediation. This was extremely reassuring to parents.

The emergence of Freudian psychoanalytic theory and its popularization undermined such misplaced complacency and, together with the rise of feminism and the "invention" of homosexuality in the late nineteenth century, propelled parental anxiety about the acquisition of appropriate gender identity in their sons to new heights. Freud, after all, linked gender identity with sexual organization, both spatially and temporally. The moment of the resolution of the Oedipal complex allowed the boy to identify with father (gender identity) and become symbolically capable of possessing mother (heterosexual). The boy becomes a gendered man and a heterosexual simultaneously. More central still: gender identity and sexual organization are achieved through struggle between the individual boy and his parents.

Thus it was the parents who bore the responsibility for ensuring this passage, and the burden of blame if the child failed. And failure to acquire appropriate gender identity has serious, and suddenly observable consequences: girls could identify with father and renounce mother's passivity (feminism) and boys could fail to identify with father and thus seek sexual gratification from father-substitutes (homosexuality).

Popular magazine articles, prescriptive literature, the emerging advertising industry and, of course, academic social science combined to present a solution to increasingly anxious parents. Gender identity could be measured by the acquisition of specific attitudes, behaviors, and values. If the child acquired these traits, he or she would certainly develop appropriate gender identity and hence avoid the problems of "inversion." Parents sought signs of appropriate gender identity everywhere—in foods, play activities, fantasies, and clothing. And what was defined as "appropriate" gender identity was of course the traditional, hegemonic, white middle-class, heterosexual masculinity.

What history had begun to usher out, academic social science revived with a vengeance. This project lies at the core of social science; it was how social science began its quest for acceptance as a legitimate science. Social science operationalized sexism, racism, and homophobia and called it masculinity. We made power relations measurable, and hence, invisible as power relations. This reached its apotheosis in academic psychology in 1936 with the publication of Lewis Terman and Catherine Cox Miles' masterpiece *Sex and Personality.* Just a few years after he developed the Stanford-Binet IQ test, Terman and his assistant Miles developed the M-F scale, an inventory of gendered behaviors, attitudes, and information by which parents could plot their child's successful acquisition of gendered identity. The books a child reads, his or her dreams of the future, level and types of knowledge, and interpretation of inkblots were all used to assess appropriate gender identity. Science thus proved that "a spirit of adventure or independence in the subject are predominantly male; admissions of fear and of humanitarian tendencies, of care for personal appearance, or of liking for social gatherings are predominantly female."

The consequences were significant. Here are Terman and Miles on the ecology of homosexuality:

> [T]oo demonstrative affection from an excessively emotional mother, especially in the case of a first, last, or only child; a father who is unsympathetic, autocratic, brutal, much away from home, or deceased; treatment of the child as a girl, coupled with lack of encouragement or opportunity to associate with boys and to take part in the rougher masculine activities; overemphasis of neatness, niceness, and spirituality; lack of vigilance against the danger of seduction by older homosexual males.

It became firmly established that gender identity was a fundamental component of identity since it determined sexual organization, and that gender identity was reamed through the successful mastery of a variety of props. Freudian assumptions grounded what Joseph Pleck called the "male sex role identity" model of masculinity, that static, ahistorical container of attitudes, behaviors, and values that are appropriate to men and define masculine behavior.

The acquisition of gender appropriate behavior, the mastery of the male sex role, was a central theme in academic social science, especially with the emergence of structural-functionalism immediately after the Second World War. Parsons took Freudian assumptions about the necessity of identification with father and generated an entire theory of male aggression. In his essay "Certain Primary Sources and Patterns of Aggression in the Social Structure of the Western World" (1947), Parsons argues that the need for the boy to repudiate maternal nurture to achieve a healthy masculine identity means that "when he revolts against identification with his mother in the name of masculinity," he unconsciously associates "goodness" with femininity, so that becoming a "bad boy" becomes a positive goal. The social consequences of masculinity as a reaction formation are critical among Western men who are peculiarly susceptible to the appeal of adolescent assertiveness as masculine behavior.

Parsons conceptualized a social phenomenon—male aggression—as the aggregate of individual psychologies. His academic anxiety over its consequences informed a generation of social psychologists who explained everything from juvenile delinquency, teenage gang behavior, and playground bullies, to southern racism and political authoritarianism.

In his classic study of juvenile delinquency, *Delinquent Boys: The Culture of the Gang* (1955), Albert K. Cohen applies a Parsonian model, arguing that the sources of delinquency are to be found in "sex role anxieties and the masculine protest." Goodness represents the mother against which the young boy is rebelling and "engaging in bad behavior acquires the function of denying his femininity and therefore asserting his masculinity." This, Cohen writes, is the motivation to juvenile delinquency.

What Cohen observed for delinquents, Theodor Adomo and his collaborators observed for racists, Nazis, and others with an "authoritarian personality." Hypermasculinity was actually a compensatory mechanism to mask insecure gender identity. The authors of *The Authoritarian Personality* (1950) thus speculate:

> One might expect [authoritarian] men to think of themselves as very masculine, and that this claim would be the more insistent the greater the underlying feelings of weakness . . . There seems to be, in the high scoring men, more of what may be called pseudo-masculinity—as defined by boastfulness about such traits as determination, energy, industry, independence, decisiveness, and will power—and less admission of passivity.

"In the end," Adorno wrote later, "the tough guys are the truly effeminate ones, who need the weaklings as their victims in order not to admit that they are like them . . . the opposites of the strong man and compliant youth merge in an order which asserts unalloyed the male principle of domination."

These brief citations are moments in the social scientific construction of masculinity. Like vacation snapshots, they are pale proof that the events took place, that we were really there, but they cannot convey the visceral sensations of the traveller's immersion in another culture. Legitimating white middle class heterosexual masculinity, that is, maintaining men's power over women and some men's power over other men, was a central project of early twentieth-century social science.

Classical theorists noticed that identity had become destabilized, but without a gender perspective, they were unable to understand the dynamics of that destabilization and attributed it to capitalism, rationality, democracy, or the quest for autonomy. Empirical social science was equally blind to gender, but

social scientists knew the crisis of masculinity demanded resolution. And they believed they could help.

Many social scientists still till the same barren empirical, or theoretical earth. Social scientists often appear to enjoy humiliating themselves by declaring the biological bases for human action, thus, in effect, putting themselves out of work. Similarly, many psychological models of moral development, identity construction, or developmental stages have used hegemonic masculinity as the template against which both women and potentially competing masculinities would be judged. And forms of masculinity that vary from the hegemonic norm are declared problematic and deviant by social scientists who have studied working class men, black men, or gay men. . . .

Of course, it was the women's movement that launched the most sustained critique of academic social science and challenged it to make gender visible and thus to de-center hegemonic masculinity from its place of privilege within academic discourse, that is, to render it problematic. It has been, by definition, a political project, because it seeks to transform the hegemoic into a pluralistic set of variations, to challenge the mechanisms by which hegemony has been constituted. It is a project that seeks to deconstruct masculinity as a singular, monolithic category capable of being used against marginal groups, and to reconstruct masculinities as a set of possible gendered identities, each different, and all equal.

CRITICAL THINKING QUESTIONS

1. Why do most men fail to perceive gender as a relevant social status?

2. Is awareness of our social statuses sufficient to alleviate prejudice and discrimination? Explain.

3. How do popular definitions of masculinity and manhood work to maintain social inequalities?

Reading 3

Race, Gender, Class
in the Lives of Asian American

Yen L. Espiritu

In this article, Espiritu focuses on the way that individuals tend to think in terms of singular minority statuses, such as on the basis of race or gender. The author notes that such thinking marginalizes the experiences and needs of those with multiple minority statuses.

Societies tend to organize themselves around sets of mutually exclusive binaries: white or black, man or woman, professional or laborer, citizen or alien. In the United States, this binary construction of difference—of privileging and empowering the first term and reducing and disempowering the second—structures and maintains race, gender, and class privilege and power (Lowe, 1991; Grozs, 1994). Thus, white / male / professional / citizen constitutes the norm against which black / female / laborer / alien is defined (Okihiro, 1995). Normed on this white, male, bourgeois hierarchy, working class immigrant women of color are subordinated and suppressed (Mohanty, 1991). There is also another kind of dualism, one that treats race, gender, and class as mutually exclusive categories. White feminist scholars engage in this either/or dichotomous thinking when they assert that gender oppression transcends divisions among women created by race, social class and other forms of difference. Similarly, men of color rely on dualism when they insist that the system of racial oppression takes precedence over that of gender oppression.

By privileging either race or gender or class instead of recognizing their interconnections, this dichotomous stance marginalizes the experiences of those who are multiply disadvantaged (Crenshaw, 1990). As a multiply disadvantaged people, Asians in the United States complicate

either/or definitions and categories and carve out for themselves a "third space" as "neither/nor" and as "both/and" (Kim, 1993). Because of their racial ambiguity, Asian Americans have been constructed historically to be both "like black" and "like white," as well as *neither* black nor white.

Similarly, Asian women have been both hyperfeminized and masculinized, and Asian men have been both hypermasculinized and feminized. And in social class and cultural terms, Asian Americans have been cast both as the "inassimilable alien" and the "model minority" (Okihiro, 1995). Their ambiguous, middling positions maintain systems of privilege and power but also threaten and destabilize these constructs of hierarchies. This essay discusses how Asian Americans, as racialized "others" who occupy a "third" position, both disrupt and conform to the hegemonic dualism of race, gender, and class.

The problems of race, gender, and class are closely intertwined in the lives of Asian American men and women. It is racial and class oppression against "yellows" that restricts their material lives, (re)defines their gender roles, and provides material for degrading and exaggerated sexual representations of Asian men and women in U.S. popular culture. Asian Americans have always, but particularly since the 1960s, resisted race, class, and gender exploitation through political, economic, and cultural activism. As a result, the objectification of Asian Americans as exotic aliens who are different from,

Source: Reprinted from the journal *Race, Gender & Class: Vol 4, No 3, 1997 (12–19).*

and inferior to, white Americans has never been absolute.

On the other hand, in demanding legitimacy, some Asian Americans have adopted the either/or dichotomies of the dominant patriarchal structure, "unwittingly upholding the criteria of those whom they assail" (Cheung, 1990). Lisa Lowe (1991:31) argued that "in accepting the binary terms ("white" and "nonwhite," or "majority" and "minority") . . . , we forget that these binary schemes are not neutral descriptions." For example, men who have been historically devalued are likely to take their rage and frustration out on those closest to them (Lipsitz, 1988:204–205; Crenshaw, 1990:185–189). Having been forced into "feminine" subject positions, some Asian American men seek to reassert their masculinity by physically and emotionally abusing those who are even more powerless: the women and children in their families. In particular, men's inability to earn a family wage and subsequent reliance on their wives' income undermines severely their sense of well-being. Though it is useful to view male tyranny within the context of racial inequality and class exploitation, it is equally important to note that this aggression is informed by Eurocentric gender ideology, particularly its emphasis on oppositional dichotomous sex roles. Because these Asian American men can see only race oppression, and no gender domination, they are unable, or unwilling, to view themselves as both oppressed and oppressor. This dichotomous stance has led to the marginalization of Asian American women and their needs. Concerned with recuperating their identities as men and as Americans, some Asian American political and cultural workers have subordinated feminism to nationalist concerns. From this limited standpoint, Asian American feminists who expose Asian American sexism are cast as "antiethnic," criticized for undermining group solidarity, and charged with exaggerating the community's patriarchal structure to please the larger society. In an analysis of the display of machismo among Mexican immigrant men, Pierrette Hondagneu-Sotelo (1994:193–94) characterized these men's behaviors as "personally and collectively constructed performances of masculine gender display . . . [which] should be distinguished from structurally constituted positions of power." In other words, these displays of male prowess are indicators of "marginalized subordinated masculinities."

The racist debasement of Asian men makes it difficult for Asian American women to balance the need to expose the problems of male privilege with the desire to unite with men to contest the overarching racial ideology that confines them both. As Asian American women negotiate this difficult feat, they, like men, tend to subscribe to either/or dichotomous thinking. They do so when they adopt the fixed masculinist Asian American identity, even when it marginalizes their positions, or when they privilege women's concerns over men's or over concerns about other forms of inequality. Both of these positions advance the dichotomous stance of man and woman, gender or race or class, without recognizing the "complex *relationality* that shapes our social and political lives" (Mohanty, 1991:13). Finally, Asian American women enforce Eurocentric gender ideology when they accept the objectification and feminization of Asian men and the parallel construction of white men as the most desirable sexual and marital partners.

Traditional white feminists likewise succumb to binary definitions and categories when they insist on the primacy of gender, thereby dismissing racism and other structures of oppression. The feminist mandate for gender solidarity accounts only for hierarchies between men and women and ignores power differentials among women, among men, and between white women and men of color. This exclusive focus on gender makes it difficult for white women to see the web of multiple oppressions that constrain the lives of most women of color, thus limiting the potential bonding among all women. Furthermore, it bars them from recognizing the oppression of men of color: the fact that there are men, and not only women, who have been "feminized" and the fact that white, middle class women hold cultural power and class power over certain groups of men (Cheung, 1990:245–46; Wiegman, 1991:311).

In sum, Asian American men, Asian American women, and white women unwittingly comply with the ideologies of racialized patriarchy. Asian American men fulfill traditional definitions of manhood when they conflate might and masculinity and sweep aside the needs and well-being of Asian American women. Asian American women accept these racialized gender ideologies when they submit to white and Asian men or when they subordinate racial, class, or men's concerns to feminism. And white women advance a hierarchical agenda when they fail to see that the experiences of white women, women of color, and men of color are connected in systematic ways.

BEYOND DUALISM: CONSTRUCTING AN "IMAGINED COMMUNITY"

As a multiply marginalized group, Asian Americans pose a fundamental problem to the binary oppositions that structure and maintain privilege and power in the United States (Okihiro, 1995). The conditions of their lives challenge the naturalism of these dualisms and reveal how multiple structures of difference and disempowerment reinforce one another. In other words, they show how race, gender, and class, as categories of difference, do not parallel but instead intersect and confirm each other (Wiegman, 1991:311). The task for feminist theory, then, is to develop paradigms that articulate the complicity among these categories of oppression, that strengthens the alliance between gender and ethnic studies, and that reach out not only to women, but perhaps also to men, of color (Cheung, 1990:245).

A central task in feminist scholarship is to expose and dismantle the stereotypes that traditionally have provided ideological justifications for women's subordination. However, ideologies of manhood and womanhood have

as much to do with class and race as they have to do with sex. Class and gender intersect when the culture of patriarchy, which assigns men to the public sphere and women to the private sphere, makes it possible for capitalists to exploit and profit from the labor of both men and women. Because patriarchy mandates that men be the breadwinners, it pressures them to work in the capitalist wage market, even in jobs that are low paying, physically punishing, and without opportunities for upward mobility. In this sense, the sexual division of labor within the family produces a steady supply of male labor for the benefit of capital. The culture of patriarchy is also responsible for the capitalist exploitation of women. The assumption that women are not the main income earners in their families, and therefore can afford to work for less, provides ideological justification for employers to hire women at lower wages and in poorer working conditions than exist for men (Hossfeld, 1994:74). On the other hand, in however limited a way, wage employment does allow women to challenge the confines and dictates of traditional patriarchal social relations. It affords women some opportunities to leave the confines of the home, delay marriage and childbearing, develop new social networks, and exercise more personal independence (Lim, 1983:83). As such, wage labor both oppresses and liberates women, exploiting them as workers but also strengthening their claims against patriarchal authority (Okihiro, 1994:91). But this potential liberation is limited. As Linda Y.C. Lim (1983:88) pointed out, because capitalist employment and exploitation of female labor [are] based on patriarchal exploitation, "The elimination of these conditions may well bring about an elimination of the jobs themselves."

U.S. capital also profits from racism. In the pre-World War II era, white men were considered "free labor" and could have a variety of jobs in the industrialized economic sector, whereas Asian Men were racialized as "coolie labor" and confined to nonunionized, degrading low paying jobs in the agricultural and service sectors. Asian immigrants faced a special disability: They could not become citizens and thus were a completely disfranchised group. As noncitizens, Asian immigrants were subjected to especially onerous working conditions compared to other workers, including longer hours, lower wages, more physically demanding labor, and more dangerous tasks. The alien, and thus rights-deprived, status of Asian immigrants increased the ability of capital to control them; it also allowed employers to use the cheapness of Asian labor to undermine and discipline the white small producers and white workers (Bonacich, 1984:165–66).

The post-1965 Asian immigrant group, though much more differentiated along social class lines, is still racialized and exploited. In all occupational sectors, Asian American men and women fare worse than their white counterparts. Unskilled and semiskilled Asian immigrant labor is relegated to the lower-paying job brackets of racially segregated industries. Due to their gender, race, and noncitizen status, Asian immigrant women fare the worst because they are seen as being the most desperate for work at any wage (Hossfeld, 1994:75). The highly educated, on the other hand, encounter institutionalized economic and cultural racism that restricts their economic mobility. In sum, capitalist exploitation of Asians has been possible mainly because Asian labor had already been categorized by a racist society as being worth less than white worker's labor. This racial hierarchy then confirms the "manhood" of white men while rendering Asian men impotent.

Racist economic exploitation of Asian Americans has had gender implications. Due to the men's inability to earn a family wage, Asian American women have had to engage in paid labor to make up the income discrepancies. In other words, the racialized exploitation of Asian American men has historically been the context for the entry of Asian American women into the labor force. Access to wage work and relative economic independence, in turn, has given women solid ground for questioning their subordination. But progress has been slow and uneven. In some instances, more egalitarian divisions of labor

and control of domestic resources have emerged. In others, men's loss of status in the public and domestic spheres has placed severe pressures on the traditional family, leading at times to resentment, verbal or physical abuse, and divorce.

Moreover, Asian women's ability to transform traditional patriarchy is often constrained by their social-structural location in the dominant society. The articulation between the processes of gender discrimination, racial discrimination of (presumed or actual) immigrant workers, and capitalist exploitation makes their position particularly vulnerable. Constrained by these overlapping categories of oppression, Asian American women may accept certain components of the traditional patriarchal system to have a strong and intact family—an important source of support to sustain them in the work world (Glenn, 1986; Kibria, 1990). Indeed, in this hostile environment, the act of maintaining families is itself a form of resistance. Finally, women's economic resources have remained too meager for them to maintain their economic independence from men. Therefore, some Asian American women may choose to preserve the traditional family system, though in a tempered form, because they value the promise of male economic protection. As Evelyn Nakano Glenn (1986:218) pointed out, for Asian Americans, the family has been "simultaneously a unity, bound by interdependence in the fight for survival, and a segmented institution in which men and women struggled over power, resources, and labor."

To recognize the interconnections of race, gender, and class is also to recognize that the conditions of our lives are connected to and shaped by the conditions of others' lives. Thus men are privileged precisely because women are not, and whites are advantaged precisely because people of color are disadvantaged. In other words, both people of color and white people live racially structured lives, both women's and men's lives are shaped by their gender, and all of our lives are influenced by the dictates of the patriarchal economy of U.S. society

(Wiegman, 1991:311; Frankenbert, 1993:1). But the intersections among these categories of oppression mean that there are also hierarchies among women and men and that some women hold cultural and economic power over certain groups of men. On the other hand, the "intersecting, contradictory, and cross-category functioning of U.S. culture" (Wiegman, 1991:331) also presents opportunities for transforming the existing hierarchical structure. If Asian men have been "feminized" in the United States, then they can best attest to and fight against patriarchal oppression that has long denied all women male privilege. If white women recognize that ideologies of womanhood have as much to do with race and class as they have to do with sex, then they can better work with, and not for, women (and men) of color. And if men and women of all social classes understand how capitalism distorts and diminishes all peoples' lives, then they will be more apt to struggle together for a more equitable economic system. Thus, to name the categories of oppression and to identify their interconnections is also to explore, forge, and fortify cross-gender, cross-racial, and cross-class alliances. It is to construct what Chandra Mohanty (1991:4) called an "imagined community": a community that is bounded not only by color, race, or class but crucially by a shared struggle against all pervasive and systemic forms of domination.

REFERENCES

BONACICH, E. 1984. Asian Labor in the Development of Hawaii and California. Pp. 130–185 in *Asian Workers in the United States before World War II*, edited by L. Cheng & E. Bonacich. Berkeley: University of California Press.

CHEUNG, K. K. 1990. "The Woman Warrior Versus the Chinaman Pacific: Must a Chinese American Critic Choose Between Feminism and heroism? Pp. 234–251 in *Conflicts in Feminism*, edited by M. Hirsch and EP. Keller. New York: Routledge.

CRENSHAW, L. 1989. "Demarginalizing the Intersection of Race and Sex: A Black Feminist Critique of Antidiscrimination Doctrine, Feminist Theory and Antiracist Politics." Pp. 139–167 in University of Chicago Legal Forum: Feminism in the Law: Theory, Practice and Criticism. Chicago: University Press.

FRANKENBERG, R. 1993. *White Women, Race, Matters: The Social Construction of Whiteness*. Minneapolis: University of Minnesota Press.

GLENN, E. N. 1986. *Issei, Nisei, War Bride: Three Generations of Japanese American Women at Domestic Work*. Philadelphia: Temple University Press.

GLENN, E. 1994. *Volatiles Bodies: Toward a corporeal Feminism*. Bloomington: Indiana University Press.

HOSSFELD, K. J. 1994. "Hiring Immigrant Women: Silicon Valley's Simple Formula." Pp. 65–93 in *Women of Color in US Society*, edited by M. Baca Zinn & B. T. Dill. Philadelphia: Temple University Press.

KIM, E. 1993. Preface. Pp. vii–xiv in *Charlie Chan is Dead: An Anthology of Contemporary Asian American Fiction*, edited by J. Hagedoen. New York: Penguin.

LIM, L. Y. C. 1983. Capitalism, Imperialism, and Patriarchy: The Dilemma of Third World Women Workers in Multinational Factories. Pp. 70–91 in *Women, Men and the International Division of Labor*, edited by J. Nash and M. P. Fernandez-Kelly. Albany: State University of New York Press.

LOWE, L. 1991. Heterogeneity, Hybridity, Multiplicity: Marking Asian American Difference. *Diaspora*, 1 24–44.

MOHANTY, C. T. 1991. "Cartographies of Struggle: Third World Women and the Politics of Feminism." Pp. 1–47 in *Third World Women and the Politics of Feminism*, edited by C. T. Mohanty, A. Russo, & L. Torres. Bloomington: University of Indiana Press.

OKIHIRO, G. Y. 1995 (November). *Reading Asian Bodies, Reading Anxieties*. Paper presented at the University of California. San Diego Ethnic Studies Colloquium, La Jolla.

CRITICAL THINKING QUESTIONS

1. Why does the author argue that Asian-American women are more oppressed than white women?

2. What are the difficulties in focusing on the intersection of race *and* gender as opposed to examining only the ways in which inequality is maintained on the basis of race *or* gender?

3. If Asian-American women share commonalities with Asian-American men, as well as with other women, with whom should they work to effectively overcome their own oppression? What difficulties might they have in doing this?

Reading 4

Reflections on Race, Class, and Gender in the USA

In this article, Angela Davis discusses a number of issues regarding race, class, gender, and sexuality, including the need for minority groups, the poor, and members of the working class to form coalitions and work with one another for social change.

LISA LOWE: Please begin by considering the social, political, and economic shifts that have taken place in the United States during the period of the 1960s to the 1990s. I would like to invite you to characterize what, in your opinion, has shifted and what has not. . . .

ANGELA DAVIS: There are many ways to talk about the relationship between the '60s and the '90s. The social movements of the '60s—the civil rights movement, various movements of Native Americans, Chicanos/Latinos, Asian Americans, the women's movement, the student movement—did bring about significant, if not radical, transformations. Much of what we can call progressive change, particularly in the area of race, can be attributed to struggles waged by those movements. At the same time, a new terrain was established, which at times appears to contradict the meaning of the movements of the '60s. Did we work so hard in order to guarantee entrance of a conservative black man [Clarence Thomas], who opposes affirmative action and women's reproductive rights, into the Supreme Court? Rather than simply despair that things are taking a reactionary turn, I think it is important to acknowledge the extent to which the black movement allowed for the emergence of a much more

powerful black middle class and the breakup of an apparent political consensus. There are similar middle-class formations among other racial ethnic groups. So the question today is not so much how to reverse these developments to re-find ourselves, based on a kind of nostalgic longing for what used to be, but rather, to think about the extent to which movements for racial and gender equality can no longer be *simply* based on questions of desegregation. A different kind of "political," a different kind of politics, really, has to inform this movement. . . .

LL: When Stuart Hall talks about the convergence of the different contradictions of race, class, and gender, he suggests that the material conditions of a given historical moment make a certain contradiction rise to the surface. Could you speak about the conditions of our current moment in relation to these contradictions, addressing the ways that capitalism utilizes racism and sexism? Has the conjunction of race, class, and gender shifted in our contemporary period?

AD: Well, one of the strongest factors that has brought about the current set of transformations is deindustrialization. And the increased mobility of capital. And what I would say initially is that the collapse of an international socialist community—for good reasons, one can point out—which has led to the assumption that capitalism is the only future alternative makes it increasingly difficult to draw connections between the deteriorating conditions in

Source: Lisa Lowe, "Angela Davis: Reflections on Race, Class, and Gender in the USA" [interview with Davis conducted by Lowe], *The Politics of Culture in the Shadow of Capital,* ed. by Lisa Lowe and David Lloyd, 303–23. © 1997, Duke University Press. All rights reserved. Reprinted with permission.

communities of color and the restructuring of global capitalism, for example, the focus on crime as the most serious social problem, and the rise of the punishment industry. Another example is the related criminalization of single mothers of color through the ideological representation of the "welfare queen" as the reproducer of poverty. So the connection between the globalization of capital and these developments—which began with the Reagan–Bush administration, but have reached their peak recently—aren't generally made.

LL: Are you saying that because of global restructuring, the proletarianization of women of color in the United States is simultaneous with the exploitation of women in the so-called third world? In other words, that both exploitations are specific to the global restructuring of capitalism?

AD: Absolutely. But at the same time, what I'm trying to get at is the way in which these developments are actually represented within social movements, for example, within the black community, the increased focus on young black males, which is important, but dangerous at the same time. Important because of the fact that black youth, young black men, certainly are very much at risk since a quarter of them are under the direct jurisdiction of the criminal justice system, either in prison, on parole, or on probation. But at the same time, the demonization and criminalization of young black women is often totally neglected. What is also neglected is the fact that the rate of increase in the incarcerated population of women is about twice the rate of increase in the rate of incarceration of men.

Consider the recent movement spearheaded by Reverend Ben Chavis and Minister Farrakhan of the Nation of Islam, which calls upon black men to reassert their primacy within black families and communities. A Washington demonstration of "a million black men" in the fall of 1995 is predicated on the fact that women will stay at home in support of "their men." Cer-

tainly, in this period of increased mobility of capital, there is a gendered assault on young black men—jobs that used to be available have migrated to other parts of the world. However, to assume that saving black communities is equivalent to saving black men harks back to a dangerous, unreflected masculinist nationalism that informed black movements earlier on. There are productive ways in which a gender analysis can specifically identify ways in which men are disproportionately affected by deindustrialization. Moreover, during this period, if black men choose to organize as men, questions such as male support of women's reproductive rights and of lesbians' right to adopt and male opposition to violence against women should be emphasized. Rather than male primacy in families and communities, gender equality in private as well as public spheres needs to be foregrounded.

LL: From your vantage point now, when you think about the breakup and the transformations of black liberation struggles in the '60s, what is your understanding of the relationship between the external assault from the FBI, the police, and the state and the internal difference and conflict about priorities, about methods?

AD: In a sense, the external assaults worked hand in hand with the internal contradictions. We know that J. Edgar Hoover identified the Black Panther Party as the greatest threat to the internal security of the country, and that the FBI orchestrated assaults from one end of the country to the other, in collaboration with local police departments. This has been documented. What has not been taken as seriously is the internal struggles within radical black and Latino organizations. It was the inability to address questions of gender and sexuality that also led inevitably to the demise of many organizations. Many elder activists, as well as people who had not yet been born during the era, mourn the passing of the Black Panther Party, and nostalgically look back to that period as one in which questions of who and what constituted the enemy were crystal clear. The recent film by Melvyn Van Peebles represents the Black Panther Party in that kind of nostalgic and romantic way. If you look at Elaine Brown's book, which has been abundantly criticized—for good reasons, in part—she does reveal the extent to which the BPP and many of its fraternal organizations were very much informed by masculinist notions of what it meant to engage in struggle. These notions of struggle depended on the subordination of women, both ideologically and in practice. The women were responsible for a vastly disproportionate amount of work in a struggle constructed as one for the freedom of "the black man." This kind of critique has to continue. A number of recent Ph.D. dissertations look at women's roles in organizations like the Young Lords, the Black Panther Party, the Brown Berets, and the American Indian Movement. Tracy Matthews, who was in the history department at the University of Michigan, has written her dissertation on women in the Black Panther Party. Hopefully there will be a nice collection of books coming out in the next few years, which will begin to demystify the images of radical organizations of people of color in the late '60s and early '70s, for the sake of young people who desire to do activist work in the contemporary period.

LL: Can I ask a little more about a different kind of contradiction? In *Racial Formation in the United States,* Michael Omi and Howard Winant argue that during the period of civil rights struggles, civil rights legislation was in a way the state's attempt to appropriate and co-opt certain parts of the broader, wider variety of social movements pressuring for more change on race.[1] Would you agree with this analysis?

AD: During the civil rights era, the primary struggles were for legal transformation. It was important at the time to break down the legal barriers, to change the laws, to challenge the juridical status of people of color. Parenthetically, one of the real weaknesses of the civil rights movement was its paradigmatic black–white focus on race. But Omi and Winant point out correctly that social movements addressed issues that went beyond the legal construction of race. Beyond voting rights and desegregation, issues of education, health care, police repression, issues of jobs, etc. were raised. Organizations like SNCC [Student Nonviolent Coordinating Committee] that were rooted in voter registration and desegregation struggles initially focused on those issues, but then went on to address questions that emerged from the urban northern black communities as well.

LL: They don't argue, of course, that there was total co-optation. But rather that civil rights legislation was the response of the state to activist social movements, some of which could have called for much more radical change. . . .

In a way, it goes along with what you were pointing out earlier, that Clarence Thomas is where he is because of affirmative action and the contradictions of liberalism. Yet, despite such contradictions, we must still insist on the concept of rights, and humanity, and fight to keep in place the legislation that is now under attack.

AD: Yes, but the assumption that the state is the primary guardian of the victories that were won by the Civil Rights Movement has led to a great deal of chaos, and an inability to conceptualize where social movements can go from here. At the same time, many of the leaders of the Civil Rights Movement now occupy putative positions of power within the state structure. Look, for example, at Ron Dellums, who was initially associated with the Black Panther Party in Oakland, California. As a matter of fact, he was elected to Congress on the basis of his militant and radical positions. For the past twenty-five years, he's had to negotiate very different kinds of positions. His work within Congress has been very important. But the constituencies which were activist constituencies became electoral constituencies. With the election of Clinton, which ended the Republican Reagan–Bush era, there was the assumption that now, yes, the state will fulfill the goal that was set for it during the transformative period of the civil rights struggle. And that, as a matter of fact, the reliance on the new administration led to the absorption of oppositional organizations—and sometimes almost entire movements—into state structures.

LL: With the priority, would you say, on enfranchisement and assimilation into the state, as opposed to working for a larger transformation?

AD: That is true, and it is a rather complicated process. In many instances people truly believe that they will be able to bring about radical transformations from and within new positions of state power. The work that I am doing on prisons is a case in point. Many people whose connection with prison issues comes from their earlier involvement in oppositional struggles—who were involved in and in some instances were initiators of the prisoner rights movement— are now working within correctional bureaucracies. Here in San Francisco, the current sheriff and assistant sheriff have a long history of involvement in progressive movements. The assistant sheriff spent many years in prison during the '60s and early '70s and was associated with George Jackson and the internal prisoner movement. He was one of the founders of the California Prisoners Union. Now he inhabits the very positions which were once occupied by his adversaries. Under his leadership people have been hired to work within the jail structures who are former prisoners (such as myself and Johnny Spain, once of the San Quentin Six) and who were once visible as militant activists (such as Harry Edwards, who organized the protests at the 1968 Mexico City Olympics). The assumption, of course, is that these individuals will press for transformation. However, under such conditions transformation is conceptualized very differ-

ently. The formulation of radical prison work as leading toward the reduction of prison populations and the abolition of jails and prisons as the primary means of addressing social problems such as crime, unemployment, under-education, etc. recedes and is replaced with the goal of creating better, more progressive jails and prisons. I am not suggesting that we should not use whatever political arenas are available to us. However, once one becomes integrated into state structures, it becomes increasingly difficult to think about ways of developing radical oppositional practices.

LL: You have always been a voice for feminist concerns within black liberation struggles, yet it has been difficult for Marxist antiracist work to find a "home" in feminism as it has existed in the US women's movement. In *Women, Race, and Class,* but also in your lectures "Facing Our Common Foe" and "We Do Not Consent," you argue that racism and classism affect the construction of political agendas even and especially in the white women's movement regarding race and reproductive rights.[2] I wonder if you could discuss the struggles within US feminism in the last decade. You argue eloquently that historically rape has been defined as rape of the white woman's body, who is the property of elite white men, which obscures the possibility of thinking of black women's bodies as victims of rape, or victims of assault, and subordinates the issue of black women's health. Has the antiracist critique successfully changed white feminism?

AD: From one vantage point, those critiques have been very successful. Which isn't to say that hegemonic white feminism . . . has really substantively changed. But it is no longer possible to ignore issues of race. Even those who only pay lip service to race analysis understand this. Twenty-five years ago, dominant feminism began to evolve as if women of color did not exist. As a result, vast numbers of women of color who were interested in women's issues did not associate themselves with early feminist approaches. Toni Morrison, who is very much associated with black feminists today, wrote an article in the early 1970s in the *New York Times Magazine* in which she argued that feminism belonged to white women and had no relevance for black women. The most interesting developments in feminism, I think, over the past couple of decades have occurred within the theories and practices of women of color. US feminism would not be what it is today, US feminisms would not be what they are today, if it hadn't been for the intervention by women of color. So I think that's a very positive sign. At the same time, within communities of color, feminism has become a much more powerful force and has had an impact on all kinds of issues, on the way issues are constructed, the way campaigns are developed. The critique has to continue, though; I'm not suggesting that the work has been done. It's a lot more complicated today. Women of color who refer to themselves as feminists still find that it is not easy to identify as a feminist. For one, feminism is often considered obsolete. There are a number of new works that have been published by young feminists, both feminists of color and white feminists, that, in order to dissociate themselves from traditional feminism, tend to revert to prefeminist ideas.

LL: I would like to ask you to situate yourself in women of color discourse. . . . I understand the genealogy of your work and practice as articulating a feminist antiracist critique within the Marxist critique of capitalism. Yours is a most important synthesis that really advances women of color critique. Please share your thoughts about women of color as a political project and as a research project.

AD: Well, I don't know if we can talk about women of color politics in a monolithic way.

LL: It's perhaps even difficult to understand it as a social movement. In a way it's a critique that has various locations.

AD: There've been really interesting developments over the past fifteen years or so, since most people date the development of women of color as a new political subject from 1981, when *This Bridge Called My Back* was published.[3] Women of color conceptualized as a political project, to borrow Chandra Mohanty's notion, is extremely important. You might also use Omi and Winant's notion and argue that it is possible to think about women of color as a different kind of racial formation. And the work that you, Lisa, have done on women of color emphasizes the fact that it is a provisional identity that allows the move beyond identity politics articulated in the traditional way. The fact that race is placed at the forefront of women of color politics is important, because it also challenges the influence of nationalism on identity politics. Women of color formations are compelled to address intersectionality and the mutual and complex interactions of race, class, gender, and sexuality. That is what is so exciting about the possibilities of women of color research and organizing strategies. For the last four years or so I have been working with the Research Cluster for the Study of Women of Color in Collaboration and Conflict. Many students and faculty involved locate their work within a progressive scholarly and activist tradition that seeks to bring about structural and ideological change. The Women of Color Resource Center here in the San Francisco Bay Area attempts to forge stronger ties between researchers and grassroots organizers. Asian Immigrant Women's Advocates (AIWA) is one of the groups associated with the Women of Color Resource Center. This organization traces its genealogy back to the Third World Women's Alliance founded in 1970. This means that what we call women of color work predates 1981, the year in which *This Bridge Called My Back* was published, which is usually evoked as the originating moment of women of color consciousness. During the earlier era, the anti-imperialist character or third world women's work inflected it with a strong anticapitalist kind of critique. The influence of Marxism is still very much visible in, for example, the Combahee River Collective manifesto. While it is important to affirm the momentous cultural work initiated with the publication of *This Bridge*, the earlier, more explicitly anticapitalist traditions should not be erased.

LL: And those connections are like a history that needs still to be written.

AD: Yes. What we call women of color work or US third world women's work can be traced back to the civil rights era. During the 1964 campaign spearheaded by SNCC [the Student Non-violent Coordinating Committee] in Mississippi, Georgia, and Alabama, there was an emergent antimasculinist critique, directed against the obstinately male leadership. This critique crystallized in an internal organization of black women, which later established itself as an autonomous organization, the Black Women's Alliance. While cross-racial coalitions were not as self-conscious as they tend to be today, the political projects to which Puerto Rican women (antisterilization work, for example) and Asian American women (Vietnam solidarity work, for example) were drawn, were also embraced by the Black Women's Alliance, which later reconceptualized itself as a Third World Women's Alliance. Some of the same women associated with those efforts in the late '60s—like Elizabeth Martinez, Linda Burnham, Fran Beal—continue to be active through organizations like the Women of Color Resource Center. Around the same time, numerous lesbians of color organizations emerged. In fact, the term *lesbian of color* acquired currency before *women of color* entered into our political vocabulary. In other words, although we refer to "women of color" as a new political subject, there is a rich, unexplored history of women of color political projects. We shouldn't assume that women of color work has been going on for only a decade or so.

LL: Or that it's a reaction against . . .

AD: . . . what we used to call white middle-class feminism. NOW was founded in 1964. We can also trace the emergence of a radical women of color feminism back to the same year. . . .

LL: You mention the focus on women of color "in collaboration and conflict." . . . What are the difficulties and the opportunities for black, Chicana-Latina, and Native and Asian American women working together? What are the specific issues for each group that need to be addressed in order for coalition to take place? What sorts of things keep coming up?

AD: This work is very difficult. Coalition building has never been easy. But I think it might be more productive to move away from constructions of women of color as a coalition. The assumption behind coalition building is that disparate groups or individuals come together with their own separate—and often racially based—agendas, which have to be negotiated and compromised in order for the group to come together. Coalitions also have an ephemeral and ad hoc character. I am not suggesting that the concept *women of color* is not here to stay, but I do think that it might be a very difficult political project. First of all, not all "women of color" choose to embrace this identity. In fact, an Asian-American woman who might prefer to call herself Chinese American might be equally reluctant to identify as a woman of color. But that's all right. There is no hard and fast requirement in the sense that a woman of African descent has little choice but to identify as black. However, those who do involve themselves in women of color projects need to make strong commitments—to borrow Jacqui Alexander's formulation—"to become fluent in each other's stories."

This is not to say that significant women of color work has not taken place within coalitional formations. There is, for example, the Women of Color Coalition on Reproductive Health that has brought together representatives from four different health organizations: the Asian Women's Health Organization, the Latina Women's Health Project, the National Black Women's Health Project, and the Native American Women's Health Organization. This coalition played an important role at the UN Conference on Reproductive Rights which took place in Cairo the year before the women's conference and NGO forum in Beijing. However, it has been beset with serious problems that afflict many coalitional forms, which emanate from the difficulties of compromise and agenda negotiation. Women of color work also takes place within caucus and task-force formations that often develop within predominantly white organizations such as the National Women's Studies Association and the National Coalition Against Domestic Violence. It is interesting that women of color formations emerged within both of these organizations in 1981—a pivotal year for women of color. Early on, women of color groups also organized within a number of lesbian groups.

The groups I find most interesting, however, are those that consider "women of color" a point of departure rather than a level of organizing which rises out of and breaks down into a series of racially specific agendas: in other words, those organizations that challenge the census-category approach to "women of color." Which means that women of color work can foreground race at a time when dominant discourse attempts to erase it, yet at the same time avoid the pitfalls of essentialism. I referred earlier to the Women of Color Resource Center. This organization develops projects which bring grassroots organizers and scholars together. It also sponsors projects like AIWA—Asian Immigrant Women's Advocates—which in turn appeals to all women of color (and white women as well) to support campaigns like the Jessica McClintock

boycott. I have also referred to the Women of Color Research Cluster, which does not establish its agenda by considering so-called priority issues.

A woman of color formation might decide to work around immigration issues. This political commitment is not based on the specific histories of racialized communities or its constituent members, but rather constructs an agenda agreed upon by all who are a part of it. In my opinion, the most exciting potential of women of color formations resides in the possibility of politicizing this identity—basing the identity on politics rather than the politics on identity.

LL: You have written about visiting Egypt, and the complications of being both a black woman activist and yet also a "representative" from the United States, a dominant first world power.[4] Taking up these complications, I wonder if you could comment about the importance, the possibilities, and the difficulties of work between radical US women and women in the third world.

AD: Women's organizations have been engaged in international solidarity work at least since the previous century, since the beginning of this century. I think it's important to acknowledge this internationalism. Some of this work was supported by the former socialist countries: the former Soviet Union, the German Democratic Republic, where the NGO Women's International Democratic Federation was located. Women for Racial and Economic Equality, a US-based organization, has ties with women's organizations all over the third world. I am suggesting that there are precedents for the kind of organizing across borders that women are presently attempting to do. However, during the earlier period, women's organizations tended to be rather confined to specific agendas: peace, for example, which was certainly important. But now the possibilities are vaster, considering the globalization of capital and the circuits that have been opened up by migrating corporations. In other words, it is even more important today to do transnational organizing—around labor issues, sexual trafficking, and violence against women. While there is not enough time to make specific reference to all the current international struggles US women are and need to be connected with, I would like to mention the need to strengthen women of color work in opposition to the economic embargo of Cuba. Cuban women are hurt most by the blockade and are on the front lines of opposition. Alice Walker and I are presently helping to organize a campaign to "Boycott the Blockade." In general, considering the impact of NAFTA, the need for networking and international organizing among women trade unionists in Canada, the United States, and Mexico is especially great. Considering the global assembly line—and the extent to which immigrant women working within the United States may work for the same corporations that are exploiting women in Asia, in Canada, in Mexico—organizing possibilities are vast.

LL: Yes. Can I ask you about immigration, since we touched on that? How do you think the influx of Asians and Latin Americans into the United States, particularly since 1965, has changed communities of color and race relations in the United States? Is the current policing of immigration and immigrant communities an index of similar, yet different, contradictions than those that operated in the 1960s?

AD: Well, it's no longer possible to talk about issues of race in exclusively black and white terms. While large communities of color that are not black—Native American, Asian, Latina/o—have parallel histories of racism, oppression, and militant resistance, civil rights discourse established terms that were largely based on a certain construction of black history that excluded women, gays and lesbians, and other marginalized groups. Especially since questions of immigration are moving to the fore, it is no longer possible to confine race discourse and antiracist activism to

a simple black–white binary. New issues, new problems, new contradictions have emerged and old ones have been uncovered. Many veteran activists bemoan the fact that there are so many tensions and contradictions within and among communities of color and that it can no longer be assumed that a person who is not white will necessarily assume progressive positions on racial issues—on affirmative action, for example. They bemoan the fact that you cannot expect a person of color by virtue of his/her racial location to speak out against racism, regardless of the group targeted. This has become especially apparent in the failure of significant numbers of black organizations to actively mobilize against Proposition 187 in California and similar measures in other states. I am afraid that the impact of anti-immigrant rhetoric on black communities is inhibiting the development of a political awareness of the radical potential of Latin American and Asian immigrant workers. It used to be the case that within the more progressive sectors of the trade union movement, black workers were acknowledged as a radical and militant force. Today, if there is any hope for the labor movement, it will come, in my opinion, from the new forms of organizing that immigrant workers are developing.

LL: Asian women and Latinas in the garment industry.

AD: Yes. Absolutely. What is really exciting are the new forms of organizing that aren't contained within single trade unions, nor are they focused on narrow trade union issues. It's been virtually impossible within the labor movement over the decades to address issues that aren't traditional union issues. Like wages, benefits, workplace—these are extremely important. But there are also issues that go beyond the workplace that affect workers as well.

LL: Childcare, language.

AD: Yes. Environmental issues, as well. I'm thinking about the work that's being done in Los Angeles immigrant communities, a project that is a multi-union effort with a community base. Considering these new forms of resistance, there are ways to think about these changes in an optimistic way.

LL: Yes. I really agree. We could say that even though there's been an intensification of the exploitation of women of color and third world women, it has also generated new methods and strategies for addressing that exploitation.

Regarding different organizing strategies for the new kinds of populations of workers and the specificities of labor exploitation under new capitalist modes like "mixed production" and "flexible accumulation," perhaps we can get back to the initial discussion of the shifts over the past thirty years. We know that conditions have worsened particularly for the women in communities of color. What kinds of activist projects are possible now? In these times, how do we measure what significant change means?

The Southwest Network for Environmental and Economic Justice is really interesting to me, the group under which AIWA along with La Fuerza Unida organized the Levi Strauss boycott. It seems that the issues of the environment, health, and toxic waste dumping are places where labor concerns and racialized community concerns come together.

AD: Exactly. The environmental justice movement is a relatively new and very promising organizing strategy in communities of color. New strategies are also suggested by the workers' centers in Chinatown that link work against exploitative sweatshop conditions with campaigns against domestic violence and simultaneously make appeals for multiracial solidarity. We will have come a long way if we succeed in convincing a significant number of black women's organizations, for example, to support Asian immigrant women's labor and community struggles. This would be yet another form of women of color consciousness that is politically rather than racially grounded and at the same time anchored in a more complex antiracist consciousness.

LL: There's a project in San Diego called Beyond Borders that has a support committee for *maquiladora* workers in Baja California, Mexico, and Central America. They document working conditions and occupational health and safety violations in the *maquilas,* publicize the attacks on workers' rights to organize, and promote cross-border worker organizing by connecting US trade unionists with their counterparts in Mexico. Interestingly enough, a number of the women who work in this group are Asian American.

AD: This kind of cross-racial, cross-border organizing needs to be encouraged in many different contexts.

LL: You've done considerable work with women in prisons, political prisoners, and prisoners' rights. Could you say a bit about your different projects with prisoners?

AD: My work with prisoners—both research and organizing work—has been one of the most consistent themes of my political life. It seems that the struggle to free political prisoners is unending. The campaign to free Mumia Abu-Jamal is a case in point. With respect to women prisoners, I am presently working on a project with Kum-Kum Bhavnani, who teaches sociology at UC-Santa Barbara and has a similar political history. We have interviewed women prisoners in an attempt to add new voices to the debate around prisons and to suggest that abolitionist strategies need to be taken seriously. In general, we need more activist projects against the proliferation of prisons, against what Mike Davis calls the "prison-industrial complex."[5] Our earlier discussion of labor is relevant here, too. There is a dangerous privatization trend within the correctional industry, which involves not only the privatization of entire state correctional systems and some sectors of the federal system, but the increasing reliance on prison labor by private corporations as well. The state of California can boast of the largest prison systems in the country—and one of the largest in the world. The Department of Corrections in California has established a joint venture system, which invites corporations to establish their shops on prison grounds. The advertising scheme represents prisoners as a cheap labor force that does not require employers to respect minimum wage provisions or provide health benefits. One advertisement points out that prison workers never ask for paid vacations or have transportation or babysitting problems. This means that prisoners are considered cheap labor in the same sense that immigrants within the United States and third world workers abroad are treated as the most profitable labor pools. Rather than crossing national borders, corporations simply go behind prison walls.

LL: Perhaps that's the "Made in the USA" label.

AD: Yes, that's the "Made in the USA" label at 50 cents an hour with no benefits. Prisoners have been unsuccessfully trying to organize labor unions for decades. Perhaps we need to think about organizing that will bring together prisoners, prisoners' rights groups, immigrant worker organizations, and some of the traditional labor unions. In other words, there *is* a place for coalitions. While I find identity-based coalitions problematic, I do concur with Bernice Reagon when she says that coalition work must be central in late twentieth-century political organizing. However, I think that we should focus on the creation of unpredictable or unlikely coalitions grounded in political projects. Not only prisoners, immigrant workers, and labor unions, but also prisoners and students, for example. This might be the most effective way to contest the shifting of the funding base for education into prison construction and maintenance. One of the other coalitions that should be encouraged is between welfare rights and gay and lesbian organizations. Both welfare mothers and gays and lesbians are directly targeted by conservative emphasis on "family values."

LL: Such a coalition could include legal and undocumented immigrants, too, if it were organized around the proposed Personal Responsibilities Act, which bars not only undocumented immigrants but legal permanent residents from receiving federal benefits.

AD: That's right. We might also think about coalition work that would bring together legal and undocumented immigrant youth, on the one hand, and young African-American and Latino-American youth, on the other, who are all targeted by a devious criminalization process that replaces a legitimate need for jobs, education, and health care with a very effective demonization of these groups. And it is certainly time to revive the demand for a reconsideration of the eight-hour workday. A shorter workday could help provide jobs for undocumented immigrants as well as the vast unemployed sectors among youth in communities of color. If the new cultural arenas that have developed over the past decade are utilized, young activists might be able to create powerful campaigns.

NOTES

1. Michael Omi and Howard Winant, *Racial Formation in the United States, from the 1960s to the 1990s* (New York: Routledge, 1994).
2. Angela Y. Davis, *Women, Race, and Class* (New York: Random House, 1981), chapters 11 and 12. "Facing Our Common Foe: Women and the Struggle against Racism" and "We Do Not Consent: Violence against Women in a Racist Society," in Angela Y. Davis, *Women, Culture, and Politics* (New York: Random House, 1988).
3. Cherríe Moraga and Gloria Anzaldúa (eds), *This Bridge Called My Back: Writings by Radical Women of Color* (New York: Kitchen Table Press, 1981).

4. Angela Y. Davis, "Women in Egypt: A Personal View," in *Women, Culture, and Politics.*

5. Mike Davis, "A Prison-Industrial Complex: Hell-Factories in the Field," *The Nation*, 260, no. 7 (1995), 229–34.

CRITICAL THINKING QUESTIONS

1. According to Davis, why have so many women of color resisted mainstream femi-nism? With whom have they tended to work to gain civil rights and equal opportunities?

2. What is the role of capitalism, both in the United States and globally, in the perpetua-tion of inequalities based on race, gender, and social class?

3. How has growth in the prison system con-tributed to the maintenance of inequalities of race, gender, and social class?

Reading 5

Embattled Terrain: Gender and Sexuality

Judith Lorber

In this article, Lorber discusses the differences among different branches of feminism and high-lights debates about the issues of heterosexuality, prostitution, pornography, and transgen-derism. She argues that it is important to examine issues of gender and sexuality as they intersect with race and social class and to recognize hierarchies of domination, in which those who are oppressors in one instance may be members of an oppressed group in a different situation.

In much recent feminist scholarship, the inclu-sion of gender as an organizing principle has enlarged the arena of shared concepts, re-search questions, and policy stances. With sex-uality, however, many issues have two (or more) often embattled sides. Some of the debates in-volved are whether heterosexuality in Western societies is still dominated by men's objectifica-tion and exploitation of women's bodies or whether women are initiators and equal part-ners in consensual heterosexual encounters, whether prostitution is sex work or sexual slav-ery, and whether pornography is universally harmful or can be a legitimate part of varied sexual repertoires. These are divisive political

Source: Lorber, J. 1999. "Embattled Terrain: Gender and Sexuality." pp. 416–448 in Myra Marx Feree, Judith Lor-ber, and Beth Hess (Eds.) *Revisioning Gender.* Thousand Oaks, CA: Sage Publications, 1999.

splits, with some feminists fighting for women's freedom from sexual oppression and others for women's freedom to be sexual (Chancer 1998:1–58). The theoretical divisions center on concepts of sexuality, heterosexual relation-ships, and men's personal and structural domi-nance. Although feminists don't all line up on one side or the other, the debates have been in-tense. Chancer targets the "internal conun-drum" of contemporary feminism as the source of the intensity—the intertwining of the per-sonal and the political. In the case of sexuality, she says, "the feminist critique . . . raised the possibility that the very *fulfillments* and *pleasures* of the personal could also be the *undoing* and *bane* of the political" (p. 43).

Another set of issues concerns the origins and stability of heterosexual and homosexual sexuality and the significance of bisexuality. The area of transgendering (from cross-dressing to medicalized sex change) has raised questions of transgression and conformity. Here the debates, equally impassioned, are over the politics of identity. Transgendering and bisexuality implicitly deny the essentiality of binary, clearly distinguishable gender and sexual categories and their usefulness in theory, research, and politics (Lorber 1996; McIntosh 1993; Namaste 1994; Parlee 1996). The reaction by some lesbian and gay activists to transgressions that blur the boundaries illustrates the paradox that without clear categories, you have neither a politics of identity nor a politics of transgression (Gamson 1995). As Gamson (1996) says, "Both the category-strippers and the category-defenders are right: fixed identity categories are both the basis for oppression and the basis for political power" (p. 35).

At the heart of all of these debates are conceptualizations of gender and sexuality. Gender is not a homogeneous category, but involves status, identity, and display. *Gender status*—being taken as a man or woman—in Western society implies dominance and assertiveness. *Gender identity*—the sense of self as a man or a woman, which can have various sexual identifications—presents interaction and legal issues. *Gender display*—being a feminine versus being masculine according to late-twentieth-century postindustrial norms and expectations—involves sexualized behavior and appearance. *Sexuality* involves desired and actual sexual attraction, emotions, and fantasies, not just behavior. A *sexual identity* involves self-identification and a lifestyle; a *sexual status* involves social recognition of the identity (Klein, Sepekoff, and Wolf 1985; Person 1980). In the past decade, bisexuals and transgenders have become recognized social categories along with gays and lesbians, but the boundaries and definitions of each group, as well as their relationships to gender and sexual identity, transgression, and politics, present fascinating theoretical and conceptual issues (Bornstein 1994; Bristow and Wilson 1993; Garber 1992, 1995; Tucker 1995).

In the following analysis of the feminist discourse on gender and sexuality, I will argue that one side of these debates construes gender sta-

tuses, identities, and displays as both binary and stable, almost "essential," whereas the other sees them as derived from socialization and social context and thus potentially both multiple and fluid. Although these contrasting views are often implicit, they have political implications for feminist stances on sexuality. Liberal feminism's emphasis on sexual freedom assumes malleability and individual agency, whereas radical feminism's more pessimistic view of the pervasive sexual oppression of women by men reflects a belief in men's deep-seated proclivities for domination and control, often through violence. Psychoanalytic feminism sees men's sexual domination in heterosexual relationships as rooted in their unconscious and unlikely to change unless there are radical changes in gendered parenting. Lesbian feminists, like gay theorists and activists, recognize the political perils of claims of biology or early childhood imprinting as the origins of sexual orientation, but in organizing around identity, have tended to emphasize permanence in commitment to a gay or lesbian sexual status. Social constructionists analyze the historical and cultural context in which sexuality is "scripted," focusing politically on what sexual behaviors are approved, tolerated, and tabooed for women and men of different social groups. Sexuality, in this perspective, is a product of learning, social pressures, and cultural values. Legal penalties, job loss, and violence uphold the heterosexual social order, often defeating individual attempts at resistance and rebellion, but because everything is socially produced, as social values change, so do the strictures on sexual behavior. Postmodern feminism and queer theory take the most extreme view on the fluidity of gender and sexuality, arguing that they are performances complete with costume changes and episodic dramatic narratives; individuals can deliberately produce conformity or varying degrees of social subversion.

The following discussion of heterosexuality, prostitution, pornography, and transgendering examines the theoretical assumptions on gender and sexuality in the different perspectives and the consequent political outcomes. I end this chapter with the possibilities of a theoretical convergence, although I am pessimistic about the political conflicts ending soon.

HETEROSEXUALITY: RAPE OR CROSS-PURPOSES?

In the 1980s, radical feminists such as MacKinnon (1989) expanded the concept of patriarchy by defining it as a worldwide system of subordination of women by men through violence and sexual exploitation. At the core of the radical feminist view is the belief that all men are capable of, if not prone to, rape, and all women are potential victims (Russell 1998). Thus, the threat of sexual violence is one of the most powerful means of men's control of women (Brownmiller 1975). Even if the violence is not direct, high culture and mass media sexualize and objectify women's bodies, encouraging attitudes that women are sexually available for any man's use (Kaplan 1983; Millett 1970). Sexual harassment is one of the most common manifestations of the covert sexual violence in Western societies: Unwanted sexual invitations, sexually loaded remarks and jokes, and inappropriate comments on dress or appearance—on the job, in school, and on the street—are routine experiences for women and girls. Overt sexual violence is manifest in all-too-frequent stranger, date, and gang rape and in sexual murders (Bart and Moran 1993; Caputi 1987; Crosette 1997).

The radical feminist concept of sexual violence was extended to romantic heterosexual relationships. The contention is that if all men derive power from their dominant social status, then any sexual relationship between women and men is intrinsically unequal: "Sexuality is conceived as . . . nothing less than the dynamic of sex as social hierarchy, its pleasure the experience of power in its gendered form" (MacKinnon 1989:xiii). Consent by women to heterosexual intercourse is by this definition, not true consent, because it is often forced by emotional appeals and threats to end the relationship. If a woman fears that a date or friend or lover or husband will use physical violence

if she does not give in, and she "consents," it is tantamount to rape. In this analysis, the line between consensual sex and rape is often hard to discern. According to MacKinnon (1987), men may clearly distinguish between "normal sex" and acts of sexual violence, but women do not:

> We have a deeper critique of what has been done to women's sexuality and who controls it. What we are saying is that sexuality in exactly these normal forms often *does* violate us. So long as we say that those things are abuses of violence, not sex, we fail to criticize what has been made of *sex,* what has been done to us *through* sex, because we leave the line between rape and intercourse, sexual harassment and sex roles . . . right where it is. (pp. 86–87)

In sum, in the radical feminist view, men's sexuality is imbued with barely concealed aggression. The finding that 25 percent of women in a U.S. national survey had experienced unwanted sex supports this view (Laumann et al. 1994). Radical feminists contrast men's sexuality with women's mutuality and tenderness: "Feminine sexuality, unlike the mediation of the visible which sustains phallic desire, is of the register of touching, nearness, presence, immediacy, contact" (Gallop 1982:30). Lesbian sexuality would then be the antithesis of male sexuality, especially anonymous "bath-house" encounters. Valverde (1985) says that because lesbian relationships reflect mother-daughter love, they are more emotionally encompassing and more powerfully erotic than heterosexual relationships are for women: "Because of this 'emotionalism' that women are conditioned to have, and the inevitable associations of the lover's body with the nurturing, all-powerful body of the mother, love between women can create some of the strongest bonds in human experience" (pp. 90–91).

The social constructionist view of sexuality agrees that in Western societies, men's sexual behavior is more instrumental and aggressive than women's, but places more emphasis on socialization and context than on innate differences in female and male sexuality. Some heterosexual and lesbian women enjoy sado-masochistic sex (English, Hollibaugh, and Rubin 1981). For many men, heterosexual as well as homosexual, objectified sexuality is not "good sex" (Stoltenberg 1990:101–14). However inequality in sexual relationships is almost expected in contemporary society. A study of college-age women and men in dating relationships found that both felt the man appropriately had more power in the relationship; male-dominant relationships were also more long-lasting than female-dominant relationships, which were seen as nonnormative (Felmlee 1994).

In another study, women's and men's attitudes toward sexuality were not that different. Narratives on their sex lives written by White, middle-class, mostly heterosexual college students in the 1980s showed that women as well as men felt that they had a right to experiment sexually, that men as well as women were romantic, and that everyone believed that sex with affection was the best kind (Moffatt 1989:181–270). To be sexually eclectic, a man had to be able to respect his sex partner, whether their relationship was casual or long-term. Similarly, "to be an authentic sexual liberal, a woman, correspondingly, had to stop believing that if she fooled around she was a slut. Also, like a male romantic, she had to modify the neotraditional woman's stance so that she herself could enjoy casual sex without commitment" (p. 223).

Although there are both gender differences and significant overlap in current attitudes toward sexual behavior, women and men seem to be at cross-purposes in heterosexual relationships. For heterosexual men, norms of masculinity forbid open displays of affection for their men friends, to whom they are intensely loyal, even though they rely on women for emotional sustenance (Herek 1986). Women who become heterosexual relegate their emotional bonds with other women to "backup," while they search for one man to invest in emotionally for a long-term relationship (Cancian 1987). In their peer groups, the closeness of men's bonding is masked by sex talk, especially boasts of sexual conquests. The heterosexual

boy's goal is supposed to be conquest: "To the young man, the woman becomes, in the most profound sense, a sexual object. Her body and mind are the object of a sexual game, to be won for his personal aggrandizement. Status goes to the winner, and sex is prized not as testament of love but as testimony to control of another human being" (Anderson 1990:114).

These sexual attitudes are deeply embedded in Western culture. The contradictions of men's continuing attachment to their friends and sexual objectification of women, and women's needing their friends for emotional solace while they pursue unrewarding romances, have been depicted in the songs, folklore, and fortune-telling rituals of the precommunist Russian working class (Bobroff 1983), the bawdy songs and stories of today's working-class Mexican men (Peña 1991), the street lore of late-twentieth-century African Americans (Anderson 1990:112–19), the sexual fantasies of White middle-class college students of the 1980s (Moffatt 1989:181–270), and the sexualization of adolescent girls in Germany in the 1970s (Haug et al. 1987).

According to psychoanalytic feminism, this asymmetry in heterosexual relationships is the outcome of the Oedipus complex—the psychological separation from the mother as a child develops a sense of individual identity but at the same time continues to want emotional closeness with her (Chodorow 1976). In Freudian theory, boys have to separate from their mothers and identify with their fathers in order to establish their masculinity. They develop strong ego boundaries and a capacity for the independent action, objectivity, and rational thinking so valued in Western culture, but also learn to repress their emotional attachment to their mothers.

Women are a threat to men's independence and masculine sexuality because they remind men of their dependence on their mothers. However, men need women for the emotional sustenance and intimacy they rarely give each other. Their ambivalence toward women is reflected in their proclivities to control women emotionally and objectify them sexually. In contrast, girls continue to identify with their mothers, and so they grow up with fluid ego boundaries that make them sensitive, empathic, and emotional. It is these qualities that make them potentially good mothers and responsive to men's emotional needs. But because the men in their lives have developed personalities that make them emotionally guarded, women turn to other women for intimacy. Thus, Rich (1980) contends that heterosexuality arises through the repression of a continuum of lesbian emotionality and desire by an intense process of socialization.

Whether the source is patriarchal oppression, social scripting, or the Oedipus complex, feminists have shown that men's sexuality holds many dangers for women, especially young women. Must they then constantly be protected from men's sexual predatoriness? The prevalence of rape, especially gang rape in supposedly friendly territory like fraternity houses, would so indicate (Sanday 1981). But some young women argue that such protection puts them back into the days of the taboo against premarital sex and the glorification of virginity (Roiphe 1993). Sexual protection laws for women have a long history of racial and ethnic contamination in the United States. Black women's and White women's legal standing as accusers of Black men and White men in rape cases are hardly equal. As Crenshaw (1991) notes:

> Rape statutes generally do not reflect *male* control over *female* sexuality, but *white* male regulation of *white* female sexuality. . . . When Black women were raped by white males, they were being raped not as women generally, but as Black women specifically. Their femaleness made them sexually vulnerable to racist domination, while their Blackness effectively denied them any protection. This white male power was reinforced by a judicial system in which the successful conviction of a white man for raping a Black woman was virtually unthinkable. (pp. 68–69)

A social construction analysis of rape shows that it is embedded in cultures and social attitudes, not in men's intrinsically violent sexuality. Reeves Sanday's (1981) cross-cultural analysis of 95 nonindustrial societies found that in 18 percent there was a high incidence of rape and concomitant cultural approval, whereas rape was rare or absent and culturally condemned in 47 percent). In the rape-free societies, women were respected for their procreative and productive roles, power was balanced between women and men, and interpersonal violence in general was condemned. In the rape-prone societies, men were dominant and regarded women as property, hostility was fostered between women and men, and sexual assault was part of the generalized use of violence in social conflict.

Even in a rape-prone society, not all men rape. To find out under what circumstances men in the United States commit rape, Scully and Marolla interviewed convicted rapists and compared them to other felons in the same prisons (Scully 1990). The rapists they interviewed were poorly educated and had held low-status jobs; many were serving sentences for more than one crime. The majority were under 35 years old; 54 percent were Black and 66 percent of their victims were White; 46 percent were White, and two of their victims were Black. [These statistics reflect the prison population. In the majority of rapes in the United States, the victim and the perpetrator are of the same race (Scully 1990:145–49).] More than half had not lived with their biological parents when growing up, and about half had grown up in violent families. Their adolescent and adult sex lives had been active and unremarkable; almost half were either married or cohabiting at the time of the rape. The felons who were committed for crimes other than rape had similar social backgrounds, so there was nothing in upbringing or social characteristics that distinguished the rapists. What did distinguish the men convicted of violent sexual behavior was their hostility toward women and rigid beliefs that women should be sexually faithful and men should be tough, fearless, and able to conquer women sexually and defy authority. They also believed, more strongly than other felons, that women's own behavior causes men to rape, that women could avoid rape if they tried, that women secretly want to be raped and enjoy it, and that women use the charge of rape vindictively against innocent men. Some took pleasure in sexual violence, others in subduing a proud women; for still others, it was a bonus in a burglary or mugging. Given the culture's approval of sexual violence, Scully calls rape a low-risk, high-reward crime (pp. 137–69).

The social context of gang rapes shows that they are also rooted in gender norms of masculinity and a sexual double standard that blames the woman for complicity (Chancer 1987; Martin and Hummer 1989; Sanday 1990). In addition, gang rapes, or date rapes that turn into gang rapes, are part of men's bonding rituals in Western cultures. In an analysis of gang rapes in the United States, Reeves Sanday (1990) found a common pattern: "A vulnerable young woman, one who is seeking acceptance or who is high on drugs or alcohol, is taken to a room. She may or may not agree to have sex with one man. She then passes out, or is too weak or scared to protest, and a train of men have sex with her" (p. 1). This pattern "appears to be widespread not only among fraternities but in many other exclusively male contexts at colleges and universities in the United States, such as organized sports. It or its equivalent is also found outside universities where men band together in clubs, work groups, athletic teams, military units, and business conventions—in all the settings associated with the term 'stag party'" (p. 4). She argues that this behavior is a manifestation of both homosociality and homophobia: "In group sex, homoerotic desires is simultaneously indulged, degraded, and extruded from the group. The fact that the woman involved is often unconscious highlights her status as a surrogate victim in a drama where the main agents are males interacting with one another" (pp. 12–13). The sexual show of masculinity is for each other, to show they are "real men." Men close ranks around one another when accused of gang rapes, and their families and communities also support their behavior by decrying the promiscuity or irresponsibility of the victims, even when they are from the same community

(Chancer 1987; Lefkowitz 1997; Martin and Hummer 1989).

From a social constructionist view, women need protection from the discourse of heterosexuality and its continued double standard, not men's sexuality. However, the double standard that condones and often glorifies men's sexual aggressiveness and condemns the same behavior in women reflects the dominance and subordination in the gendered social order. In the radical feminist view, that is the heart of sexual politics. By controlling women's bodies, men control a great part of women's lives. Sexual violence is one end of a continuum, not a pathology separate from what is normal. The viewpoints in the debate over heterosexuality and the politics of rape are not so far apart, but the continued virulence of the argument over whether women are constant victims of men's tacit and open sexual violence or are, for the most part, equal agents, speaks to a resonance with experiences that women cannot deny, even when they do not want to blame men in general. There is an ambivalence here that muddies feminist responses to men's egregious public sexual acting out and makes it difficult to maintain clear guidelines in cases of sexual harassment. As Chancer (1998) says, "Even today, the pleasures of sexuality and the pain inflicted by sexism remain stubbornly enmeshed in male-dominated societies like our own; it is difficult to extricate erotic joy from oppressive vulnerability" (p. 1).

So is the choice, as Segal (1994:318) puts it, feminism or fucking? Hardly, in her view: "Sexual pleasure is far too significant in our lives and culture for women not to be seeking to express our agency through it" (pp. 313–14). Sexual oppression is our lives, too, but for many of us lucky enough to have escaped physical violence, not our whole lives. A view of sexual behavior as socially constructed and contextualized, with a variety of behaviors and relationships, offers a perspective for an analysis of heterosexuality that does not preclude political activism against rape and violence, but also allows for heterosexual women's desires and sexual initiatives (Richardson 1996; Wilkinson and Kitzinger 1993).

PROSTITUTION: SEX WORK OR SEXUAL SLAVERY?

A similar ambivalence imbues feminist positions on prostitution and other forms of sex work, some taking the point of view that it is women's right to use their bodies to make money (Chapkis 1997; Jenness 1990) and others claiming that prostitutes are virtual slaves in a worldwide sex industry (Barry [1979] 1983, 1995).

In the eighteenth and nineteenth centuries in Europe and the United States, women's selling or bartering sex for gifts, money, or favors was brought into public discourse and became subject to control and regulation by medicine and law, which had supplanted religion as the prime agencies of social control (Foucault 1978). Prostitution (known as "vice") became immoral work. Working-class women who had been able to augment their poor salaries or survive in hard times by selling sex were publicly stigmatized by vice campaigns (Corbin 1990; Hobson 1987; Rosen 1982; Walkowitz 1980). Condemned as sources of disease and moral pollution, they were subjected to medical examinations and treatment under contagious disease statutes or sent to prison as law-breakers. Their customers, of course, were rarely included in these cleanup campaigns, although the ostensible intent was to protect customers' wives and unborn children from the scourge of syphilis. It was as difficult for middle-class feminists as for men reformers to see the working-class woman who sold sex as someone making a rational decision: "Middle class reformers could not grasp the motivations, moral codes, and survival strategies of poor women—that prostitution could appear as a viable alternative to low wages and lack of employment options. . . . Consequently, they advocated protection rather than punishment, which translated into poli-cies that imposed strong controls over young women's lives, work, leisure, and relationships" (Hobson 1987:5). The result, as with so many other attempts to regulate sexual behavior, was to transform formerly private acts into a public problem and to stigmatize the women involved.

Today, prostitution is likely to be part of other illegal activities, especially selling drugs and organized crime, but even where it is not, it is usually an illegal way of making money (Miller 1986). Barry (1995) considers the global sex industry a form of sexual slavery because vulnerable young women from poor countries are lured by false promises into emigrating to rich countries, where they are frequently confined to brothels, deprived of their passports, and financially exploited. In many newly developing economies, especially in Southeast Asia and Eastern Europe, prostitution has become an export and tourist industry.

Just as the nineteenth-century campaign against prostitution implicated women in the spread of syphilis and gonorrhea, so, in the fight to halt the spread of AIDS, women sex workers were accused of being one of the main sources of HIV infections in heterosexual men (Campbell 991; King 1990). In actuality, a woman is much more vulnerable to HIV infection from intercourse with an HIV-positive man than a man is from an HIV-positive woman—an ejaculation is an excellent conveyor of the virus, and semen stays in the vagina for days (Padian, Shiboski, and Jewell 1991). Ironically, it is harder for women to insist on condom use or safer sex practices in love relationships than in casual encounters or when partners are paying for sex (Osmond et al. 1993). . . .

Attempting to reconcile the feminist positions about prostitution, Overall (1992) comes to the conclusion that it "makes sense to defend prostitutes' entitlement to do their work but not to defend prostitution itself as a practice under patriarchy" (p. 723). In this view, because women have fewer resources than men, and poor women, especially those from disadvantaged racial groups, have both limited economic choices and a degraded status, prostitution as work is intrinsically exploitative. However, sympathy and protection for the prostitute and condemnation of the worldwide sex industry does not point to clear policies. If feminists call for state intervention in the sex trade, some women will inevitably be criminalized for work that may be their only source of income or a considerably better source of income than a sweatshop factory job or round-the-clock domestic service. If adult sex work were decriminalized and workers better paid, unionized, entitled to benefits like health care and vacation pay, and there were no racial ethnic preference or children working in prostitution or pornography, would sex work still be an anathema? Or would there still be a revulsion against the sale of what should be an act of desire, if not affection?

A feminist analysis of prostitution has to look at the economic, gender, sexual, and psychological aspects (Chancer 1998:188–97; Hoigard and Finstad 1992). As work, the way it is organized and the extent of the workers' bargaining power are crucial elements. Child laborers of any kind are likely to be exploited. It does make a difference in sex work, as in any other kind of employment, whether the worker is a casual, off-the-books seller of services for money, food, clothes, jewelry, or drugs, or a "professional." Any permanent worker benefits from unionization or some sort of collective representation, as well as a clean, safe place to work, health services, sick leave, and vacations with pay (Alexander 1998). . . .

Both economic exploitation and sexual stigmatization victimize prostitutes—men and boys, women and girls. Patriarchy can certainly be blamed—it interpenetrates with capitalism, militarism, and imperialism in the sex industry in wartime and peacetime, encouraging and feeding on the belief that men must have constant and varied sexual services (Bailey and Farber 1992; Kazuko 1994). But women are implicated here, too, as upholders and beneficiaries of the economic, social, sexual, and gender arrangements that use other women and men as prostitutes and kept lovers, and at the same time excommunicate them from "polite society." A feminist analysis that sweeps everything together under one rubric, patriarchal sexual exploitation or free-agent sex work, loses the knowledge of sex

workers' lives and customers' motivations, which are differentially shaped by gender statuses within social structures, as well as by cultural values and economic opportunities and constraints.

PORNOGRAPHY: VIOLENCE AGAINST WOMEN OR EROTIC ENHANCEMENT?

Pornography is an even more embattled area in feminism than prostitution, with some feminists calling for its complete suppression and others arguing against censorship. Still others tout its erotic worth.

The radical feminist view on pornography is that the symbolic sexual plunder of women in high culture and the mass media is often no different from the explicit sexual violence in hard-core productions (Dworkin 1987; Griffin 1982; MacKinnon 1987:125–213; Nead 1990). Both demean and exploit women. In many nineteenth-century paintings by men of artists' models, ballerinas, and barmaids, Nochlin (1988:34, 37–56) points out, the women selling services are also selling themselves sexually.

However, the radical feminist view goes much further, arguing that pornography is harmful to all women because of its conflation of sexuality and violence. MacKinnon (1987) says: "In pornography the violence *is* the sex. The inequality is the sex. Pornography does not work sexually without hierarchy. If there is no inequality, no violation, no dominance, no force, there is no sexual arousal" (p. 160). Russell (1998) argues that pornography feeds into western culture's misogyny and is an explicit encouragement to rape.

The pornographer's view of sexuality is no less essentialist than the radical feminist view, but there is much more overlap in the depiction of women's and men's sexual behavior. Pornography portrays women as sexual objects of men's lust and at the same time as sexually demanding and virtually insatiable; it portrays men as objectified by their enlarged penises, always sexually arousable and performance-perfect. The sex act is genitally specific and ends in explosive orgasms for the man and the woman—the "money shot" (Brod 1995; Faludi 1995; Williams 1989).

But there are sexual and symbolic gender differences between men and women actors. In her discussion of the pornographic portrayal of orgasm, Williams (1989) notes that it is male-focused not only for ideological reasons, but because there is a problem with the representation of female orgasms: "The irony . . . is that, while it is possible, in a certain limited and reductive way, to 'represent' the physical pleasure of the male by showing erection and ejaculation, this maximum visibility proves elusive in the parallel confession of female sexual pleasure. Anatomically, female orgasm takes place . . . in an 'invisible place' that cannot be easily seen" (p. 49). Women depict sexual desire in visual pornography (and in prostitution) without necessarily being aroused; as sexual actors in pornography (and in prostitution), men have to be aroused: "The male actor cannot merely depict arousal, because the audience looks for his erection as the sign of arousal. The only men who could depict arousal without enacting it are those who could sustain an erection in the absence of arousal" (Soble 1986:129; see also Faludi 1995).

Men's evident sexual prowess in visual pornography glorifies them as superstuds, so acting in pornographic films or live sex acts, posing for pornographic photographs, or selling sexual services does not debase them as much as it does women (Soble 1986:129–30). As audience, men spectators can identify with the studs and feel powerful; in gay pornography, a homosexual viewer can identify with the aggressive partner (Kimmel 1990:247–87). However, some men using pornography identify with the women as well, and women viewing pornography with men partners often find it sexually arousing (Putnam forthcoming).

Taking a Marxist perspective, Soble (1986) contends that under capitalism, "the use of pornography is an attempt to recoup in the domain of sexual fantasy what is denied to men in production and politics" (p. 81). Soble sees men who use pornography as powerless, although there is no evidence that it is used more by working-class men. In contrast, radical feminists see men who use pornography as potentially if not actually dangerous to women by virtue of their participation in a culture that encourages men's violence as a means of subordinating women. As for women's consensual participation in pornography, as actors or spectators, they would argue that it is a co-optation of women's sexual freedom to ends that are ultimately harmful to them.

The contrasting position—that pornography is erotica—puts it into the realm of fantasy and sexual enhancement. What pornography offers men, says Segal (1998) in an article critical of antipornography feminism, is fantasies of "infantile grandiosity" that they are sexually inexhaustible and irresistible and that there is always a ready and willing woman available: "Whether we respond with derision, sympathy, horror or indifference to what this suggests about men's ruling sexual trepidations will influence the stand we take on pornography" (p. 46). She argues that there is little proof that these fantasies inevitably translate into violence against real women. In her view, pornography is the least effective of the "phallocentric and misogynistic discourses fashioning our images of gender and sexuality" (p. 51), so its suppression would not do much to change the ways of our world (see also Chancer 1998:61–81). However, studies of the effects of pornography on men's attitudes toward women do demonstrate an increasing callousness and trivialization of the effects of rape (Donnerstein and Linz 1990; Zillmann and Bryant 1990).

In the psychoanalytic feminist view, women are objectified because they represent the female sexual identification and emotionality men had to repress in order to become like their fathers. If not only pornography but all of the mass media (and much of high culture as well) produce images of women that legitimate men's sexual objectification of them— what Kaplan (1983) calls "the male gaze"— why target pornography? Women as performers cannot escape men's voyeuristic gaze: In film, men directors look at them, men actors look at them, and men spectators look at them. Thus, no matter what role women play, they are sexualized because men look at them as desired or despised objects, and "men do not simply look; their gaze carries with it the power of action and of possession that is lacking in the female gaze" (p. 311).

As a result of this cultural phallocentricity, most of the sexual imagery in Western culture does not depict women's sexuality as experienced by women. . . .

Suppose we lived in a scrupulously equal world where women and men had equal power, and all forms of sexuality were recognized as equally valid. Would there be equal numbers of pornographic magazines, movies, strip shows, erotic dancers, and any other sexual productions for heterosexual, homosexual, bisexual, transvestite, and sadomasochistic women as for the same groups of men? Would movies, television, books, and popular songs show women as sexual pursuers equally with men? Would pornography still be violence?

LESBIGAYS, TRANSGENDERS, AND QUEERS: WHO'S WHO?

The feminist sex wars of the 1980s (Ferguson et al. 1984; Vance 1984) have not disappeared, but they have been superseded somewhat by the current arguments over bisexuality and transgendering. Framed by similar theories of gender and sexuality as essential or socially constructed, the issues here are the stability of sexual choice, the boundaries of sexual identities, and the politics of transgression (Gamson 1995, 1998; McIntosh 1993; Wilson 1993).

Fifty years ago, Kinsey used a seven-point scale to place people on a heterosexual-homosexual continuum of sexuality, from all male-female sexual acts to all male-male or all female-female (Kinsey, Pomeroy, and Martin 1948; Kinsey et al. 1953). What was revolutionary at the time were Kinsey's statistics showing that a significant proportion of Americans fell into the middle ranges of the scale: They had engaged in both heterosexual and homosex-

ual sex. Yet no one seemed to pay much attention to what we now call bisexuality. All the rhetoric was in terms of binary sexual identities—heterosexual or homosexual.

With the advent of the women's and the homosexual rights movements of the 1970s, it became clear that sexuality is gendered and that there are at least four sexual identities: heterosexual women and men, and lesbians and gays. The new nomenclature for homosexuals reflected the political and lifestyle split between lesbians and gays (McIntosh 1993; Taylor and Whittier 1992). Lesbian idealization of emotionally intimate sexuality and coupling was congruent with the feminist valorization of women's nurturant and expressive qualities. In contrast, the gay movement's pre-AIDS political stance called for liberation through anonymous and promiscuous sexual acts, almost a caricature of conventional masculine sexuality. Each type of sexual behavior could be attributed to female-male differences (sexuality as biology) or to choice and commitment (sexuality as socially constructed). Given that there are many gay men in long-term coupled relationships, often raising children (Weston 1991), and that there are lesbians who enjoy sadomasochistic sex and multiple partners (Hollibaugh and Moraga 1983), the evidence would seem to be on the side of a socially constructed sexual orientation rather than intrinsic male-female characteristics.

However, the debate over the origins and stability of homosexuality continues among sexologists and psychiatrists (Docter 1988; Green and Money 1969; Stoller 1985; Walters and Ross 1986) and among gays and lesbians writing about themselves (Abelove, Barale, and Halperin 1993; Bristow and Wilson 1993; Greenberg 1988; Kitzinger 1987; Stein 1992; Whisman 1996). Studies of *bisexuality* (serial or simultaneous same- and cross-sex sexual relationships) have shown how difficult it is to document the conventional sexual categories empirically (Klein and Wolf 1985; Rust 1995; Tucker 1995). Are we talking about desire, preference, identity, or social status? Sexual identities—heterosexual, homosexual, bisexual—are responses not just to psychic input but also to social and cultural strictures and pressures from family and friends. Because Western culture now constructs sexuality dichotomously (Laqueur 1990), many people whose sexual inclinations and experiences are bisexual are forced to choose between a heterosexual and homosexual identity as their "real" self.

Rust's (1992, 1993) research on bisexual and lesbian sexual identity found that 90 percent of the self-identified lesbians who answered her questionnaire had heterosexual relationships, 43 percent after coming out as lesbians, but these were discounted; what counted for these lesbians were their current relationships. The women who identified themselves as bisexual, in contrast, put more emphasis on their sexual attraction to both women and men. Assuming that all self-identified gay men and lesbians have exclusively same-sex partners not only renders invisible the complexities of sexuality but can also have disastrous health outcomes, as has been found in the spread of HIV infection and AIDS among lesbians (Goldstein 1995).

Gender shapes bisexual relationships as much as it does those that are heterosexual and homosexual. One early study found great variations in feelings and behavior within a small sample of bisexuals, but although gender was irrelevant to their choice of partner, sexual scripting was not only gendered, but quite conventional, with both women and men saying that women partners were more emotionally attuned and men partners more physically sexual (Weinberg, Williams, and Pryor 1994). The authors say that this gender-typing is paradoxical:

> In a group that often sets itself against societal norms, we were surprised to discover that bisexual respondents organized their sexual preferences along the lines of traditional gender stereotypes. As with heterosexuals and homosexuals, gender is the building material from which they put together their sexuality. Unlike these groups, however, the edifice built is not restricted to one gender. (p. 57)

Rust (1995) found that her bisexual respondents spoke of being attracted to another person because of particular personality characteristics, ways of behaving, interests, intellect, looks, style. The physical sex, sexual orientation, masculinity, femininity, and gender markers are just the beginning set of parameters, and they might differ for a quick sexual encounter, a romantic liaison, a long-term relationship. Rather than comparing categories of gender or sexuality, researchers might want to compare types of relationships.

As for group identification, gender and sexuality can play out in many ways (Connell 1992). Sedgwick (1990) notes that some homosexuals (e.g., gay drag queens and butch lesbians) want to cross into the other gender's social space, whereas for others (e.g., macho gay men and lesbian separatists), "it is instead the most natural thing in the world that people of the same gender, people grouped under the single most determinative diacritical mark of social organization, people whose economic, institutional, emotional, physical needs and knowledges may have so much in common, should bond together also on the axis of sexual desire" (p. 87).

The issues of gender identification and display that Sedgwick raises are even more problematized by transgenders—transsexuals, transvestites, and hermaphrodites. Transsexuals are individuals with cross-gender identification; some pass as members of the desired gender more or less permanently through cross-dressing and renaming, while others undergo medicalized sex change (hormones and surgery) and change their legal and marital status as well (Bolin 1988; Morris 1975). Although the initial medical research on transsexuals (Green and Money 1969) accepted their insistence that they had believed they belonged in the opposite gender from early childhood (indeed, that was a condition for the surgery), stories began to emerge of the deliberate use of their mothers' hormones by boys and other manipulations of the medical teams (Garfinkel 1967:285–88). And it was also startling to those believing in clear-cut sex and sexual categorization to find that there are transsexuals who are homosexual in desire and behavior, both before and after surgery (Bolin 1988; Feinbloom et al. 1976).

Hermaphrodites and pseudohermaphrodites are people born with ambiguous genitalia or hormonal input (Fausto-Sterling 1993). In the Dominican Republic, there has been a genetic phenomenon in which children who looked female at birth and were brought up as girls produced male hormones at puberty. Their genitalia masculinized, their voices deepened, and they developed a male physical appearance (Imperato-McGinley et al. 1979). Most gradually changed to men's social roles—working outside the home, marrying, and becoming heads of households. Not all those who lived as men had fully functioning genitalia, and all were sterile. Some researchers who studied these pseudohermaphrodites claim that those who decided they would adopt men's identities and social roles despite having been raised as girls "appear to challenge both the theory of the immutability of gender identity after three or four years of age and the sex of rearing as the major factor in determining male-gender identity" (Imperato-McGinley et al. 1979:1236). They stress the effects of the hormonal input and secondary male sex characteristics at puberty. Others question whether the pseudohermaphrodites were reared unambiguously as girls, given their somewhat abnormal genitalia at birth, arguing that the community recognized and had names for a third sex category (Herdt 1990). At puberty, although virilization was not total, it provided the opportunity for the choice of the more attractive social role. In Papua New Guinea, many of these children were identified by experienced midwives at birth and reared anticipatorily as boys (Herdt 1990; Herdt and Davidson 1988). They went through boys' rituals as they grew up, but their identity as adult men was stigmatized; because of their small penises, they did not allow themselves to be fellated by adolescent boys, which made them fully men in that culture.

In Westernized countries, "clarifying" surgery has usually been done right after birth on children born with ambiguous genitalia to support an unambiguous gender categorization (Kessler 1990, 1998). In the past few years, there has been an intersex movement in protest against what is felt to be genital mutilation and the ruin of future sexual pleasure (Angier 1997; Cowley 1997). The sexual potentialities of true hermaphrodites with male and female genitalia who are not surgically altered can be gleaned from Fausto-Sterling's (1993) account of Emma, who was born in 1937 with a penis-like clitoris as well as a vagina. Raised as a girl, Emma used her penis in sexual relationships with women, and her vagina in sexual relations with her husband. She refused to have vaginal closure and to live as a man because it would have meant a divorce and her having to get a job. Emma's gender identity was that of a woman; she was physiologically bisexed, and thus able to be heterosexual in her sexual relations with her husband as well as with her women lovers.

Transvestism, or cross-dressing, is a familiar phenomenon in many societies throughout history, with many combinations and permutations of gender and sexual display, identity, and social status (Epstein and Straus 1991; Kates 1995; Nanda 1990; Williams 1986). In Western societies, women have dressed as men to work in nontraditional jobs, join the military, or enter other places where women are not allowed (Wheelwright 1989; Woodhouse 1989). Others cross-dress for performances (drag queens and kings), for parties and parades, for sexual pleasure, and just for kicks (Ekins 1997; Garber 1992). The two types of gender display—passing and transgressive—have totally different implications for gender identity and gender politics.

Passing both normalizes and disrupts conventional gender categories. Those who construct their gender against their sex assignment, whether through cross-dressing or surgical alteration of genitalia, reaffirm the conventional categories of man and woman, typically dressing conservatively and making their genitalia congruent with their outward gender display. Against this almost essentialist perspective, their own behavior sabotages the essentiality of the categories; in Garber's (1992) words, anyone who passes successfully (by crossing any boundaries) possesses "extraordinary power . . . to disrupt, expose, and challenge, putting in question the very notion of the 'original' and of stable identity" (p. 16). But only if they "unmask." Transgenders who pass as normal women or men achieve a successful transformation, but their achievement (and the gender resistance it entails) must remain a secret. As Gagné and Tewksbury (1998) say of their transgendered respondents:

> The need to come to terms with and publicly proclaim an alternative gender identity outweighed the fear of rejection and desire for self-preservation. But the need to avoid social erasure compelled a complete (even if temporary) transformation. For most, identity achievement entailed the public expression of gender in ways that reflected an internalized sense of self, not one externally imposed upon them. Often this required enacting the gender of the "opposite" sex/gender category, the only known possibility available. (p. 86; see also Gagné, Tewksbury, and McGaughey 1997; Shapiro 1991)

Queers openly subvert binary gender and sexual categories through their deliberate mixtures of clothing, makeup, jewelry, hairstyles, and behavior. Transgression—queering—is their goal. By not constructing gender and sexuality in expected ways, they make visible, in Butler's (1990) term, the performativity on which the whole gender order depends. In their self-presentation, mixtures of partners in relationships, nonconventional combinations of housemates, and in-your-face political acts and cultural performances, they are saying to heterosexuals, "Get over it" and "Get used to it" (Warner 1993). Yet the more outrageous the behavior, the more boundaries get drawn between "them" and "us" (Gamson 1998).

Despite the attempts of queer theorists to include lesbians, gays, bisexuals, transgenders, and hermaphrodites under one transgressive category, they themselves have broken up into multiple groups with different political goals. Lesbians, gays, and bisexuals are grouping under the rubric "lesbigay" in academic centers, and there is a *Journal of Gay, Lesbian, and Bisexual Identity*, which was started in 1996. Their agenda is the decentering of heterosexuality and the expansion of sexual possibilities. Nonetheless, there is still uneasiness between lesbians and bisexuals over the politics of identity, because the political stance of those lesbians and gays who argue that homosexuality is not a matter of choice is undermined by bisexual behavior and politics (McIntosh 1993; Rust 1995).

Transsexuals and transvestites now often call themselves transgenders. Although cross-dressing is a standard phase on the road to sex-change surgery, many transvestites do not even want to change their gender, let alone their genitalia. Ekins (1997) distinguishes three patterns among men—those related to sex ("body femaling"), sexuality ("erotic femaling"), and role behavior ("gender femaling"). Hermaphrodites are in an even more anomalous position. They can choose to live as men or women, but if they do not have "clarifying" surgery, their genitalia will not match their gender status. Even if they do have surgery, they are usually infertile. Although there has been some shared activism with groups opposing female genital mutilation (but not around infertility), for the most part hermaphrodites feel they don't fit in with any other gender, sex, or sexual group. It is not surprising that they have developed their own identity politics with a separate organization, Intersex Society of North America, which publishes a journal on the Internet, *Hermaphrodites with Attitude* (see also Angier 1996).

The double identity of belonging and not belonging to a category of stigmatized people has created hostility toward transsexuals and transgenders among some feminists and toward bisexual women among some lesbians. As Raymond (1979) says in arguing that male-to-female transsexuals are not women:

We know that we are women who are born with female chromosomes and anatomy, and that whether or not we were socialized to be so-called normal women, patriarchy has treated and will treat us like women. Transsexuals have not had this same history. No man can have the history of being born and located in this culture as a woman. He can have the history of *wishing* to be a woman and of *acting* like a woman, but this gender experience is that of a transsexual, not of a woman. Surgery may confer the artifacts of outward and inward female organs but it cannot confer the history of being born a woman in this society. (p. 114; for a response, see Stone 1991)

On lesbian politics and bisexuality, Rust (1995) says: "Lesbians have become invested in a gender-based definition of lesbianism. Bisexuals, by challenging both dichotomous gender and dichotomous sexuality, challenge the very existence of lesbianism" (p. 59).

In sum, the content of the transgressions (gender status, sexual behavior, sexual identity, appearance, genitalia) and the divisions between those who want to pass as normal women and men and those who are open gender rebels make it theoretically and politically impossible to speak of "transgenders" as a unified category. This fragmentation of identity groups and their conflicting agendas undermine the possibilities for unified political action. As Gamson (1995) says, "In the contemporary American political environment, clear identity categories are both necessary and dangerous distortions, and moves to both fix and unfix them are reasonable" (p. 401). Without a political agenda for change, transgressiveness soon loses its sting:

We transgress in order to insist that we are there, that we exist, and to place a distance between ourselves and the dominant culture. But we have to go further—we have to have an idea of how things could be different, otherwise transgression ends in mere posturing. In other words, transgression on its own leads eventually to entropy, unless we carry within us some idea of transformation. It is therefore not transgression that should be our watchword, but transformation. (Wilson 1993, 116)

(IN)CONCLUSION

In this chapter, I have shown that the feminist differences over heterosexuality, prostitution, pornography, and multiple sexualities are to a great extent based on contrasting theories of gender. One gender perspective relies on clear and dichotomous categories of women and men with different sexual needs and behavior. In the contrasting perspective, gender is one of the social statuses that intersect with all the socially significant statuses, especially race and ethnicity, social class, sexual orientation, and age.

At the beginning of the second wave, radical feminists conceptualized women as an oppressed class whose bodies were under siege by dominant men. Today, there is much more emphasis on how the multiplicities and intersections of race, ethnicity, social class, and gender construct a hierarchy of domination in which the same people can be both oppressed and oppressors. There is also a recognition that a group identity is forged by socialization, education, economic and political opportunities, cultural values, history, place of residence, and sexual orientation, and that being a woman or a man intertwines with and shapes these experiences. To the extent that gender continues to structure social orders and power imbalances, it will be a prime organizing force in individual and group identity and in the social patterning of sexual behavior. But as postmodern theorists have shown, gender itself is a problematic category (Butler 1990; Flax 1987). Does a dual viewpoint that recognizes gender as structure and gender as performance offer policies for social change? If we want to redress the inequalities evident in the power of men over women's sexuality and in heterosexuality as the default sexuality, there has to be both behavioral change and a restructuring of laws and family relationships. Getting people to understand the constrictions of gender and sexual norms and expectations and encouraging resistance to them in daily life will not necessarily change social structures. Individuals and groups of people may resist or rebel, but the social order is very slow to change.

Queer theory emphasizes the impact of presentation of the self in the guise and costume most likely to produce or parody conformity. Postmodern feminism is mainly concerned with deconstructing cultural productions, but its techniques have also been used on the more iron-bound and controlling discourses embedded in legal, religious, and political texts. Social construction feminism's analyses of the institutional and organizational practices that maintain the sexual/gender order could be combined with postmodern feminism and queer theory's deconstruction of how individuals do and undo gender and sexuality. Social construction feminism argues that the social order is constantly restabilized by individual action, but postmodern feminism and queer theory have shown how individuals can consciously and purposefully create disorder and instability, opening the way to social change. Postmodern feminism and queer theory's playfulness has the intent of making us think about what we take for granted—that men and women, homosexuals and heterosexuals, males and females, are totally different creatures, and that we cannot make and remake ourselves. Social construction feminism can show where the structural fault lines are, which would offer places for individuals, organizations, and social movements to pressure for long-lasting restructuring and a more equal social order for all kinds of people. Of course, rebels and transgressors will always find new contradictions, because, as queer theory teaches us, social orders can always use a little disorder.

REFERENCES

ABELOVE, HENRY, MICHÈLE AINA BARALE, AND DAVID M. HALPERIN, eds. 1993. *The Lesbian and Gay Studies Reader.* New York: Routledge.

ANDERSON, ELIJAH. 1990. *Streetwise: Race, Class, and Change in an Urban Community.* Chicago: University of Chicago Press.

ANGIER, NATALIE. 1996. "Intersexual Healing: An Anomaly Finds a Group." *New York Times,* February 4, Week in Review, p. 14.

———. 1997. "New Debate over Surgery on Genitals." *New York Times,* May 13, pp. C1, C6.

BAILEY, BETH AND DAVID FARBER. 1992. *The First Strange Place: Race and Sex in World War II Hawaii.* Baltimore: Johns Hopkins University Press.

BARRY, KATHLEEN. [1979] 1983. *Female Sexual Slavery.* New York: New York University Press.

———. 1995. *Prostitution of Sexuality: Global Exploitation of Women.* New York: New York University Press.

BART, PAULINE B. AND EILEEN G. MORAN, eds. 1993. *Violence against Women: The Bloody Footprints.* Newbury Park, CA: Sage.

BOBROFF, ANNE. 1983. "Russian Working Women: Sexuality and Bonding Patterns in the Politics of Daily Life." Pp. 206–27 in *Powers of Desire: The Politics of Sexuality,* edited by Ann Snitow, Christine Stansell, and Sharon Thompson. New York: Monthly Review Press.

BOLIN, ANNE. 1988. *In Search of Eve: Transsexual Rites of Passage.* South Hadley, MA: Bergin & Garvey.

BORNSTEIN, KATE. 1994. *Gender Outlaw: On Men, Women, and the Rest of Us.* New York: Vintage.

BRISTOW, JOSEPH AND ANGELIA R. WILSON, eds. 1993. *Activating Theory: Lesbian, Gay, and Bisexual Politics.* London: Lawrence & Wishart.

BROD, HARRY. 1995. "Pornography and the Alienation of Male Sexuality." Pp. 393–404 in *Men's Lives,* 3d ed., edited by Michael S. Kimmel and Michael A. Messner. Boston: Allyn & Bacon.

BROWNMILLER, SUSAN. 1975. *Against Our Will: Men, Women and Rape.* New York: Simon & Schuster.

BUTLER, JUDITH. 1990. *Gender Trouble: Feminism and the Subversion of Identity.* New York: Routledge.

CAMPBELL, CAROLE A. 1991. "Prostitution, AIDS and Preventive Health Behavior." *Social Science and Medicine* 32:1367–78.

CANCIAN, FRANCESCA M. 1987. *Love in America: Gender and Self-Development.* New York: Cambridge University Press.

CAPUTI, JANE. 1987. *The Age of Sex Crime.* Bowling Green, OH: Bowling Green University Popular Press.

CHANCER, LYNN. 1987. "New Bedford, Massachusetts, March 6, 1983–March 22, 1984: The 'Before and After' of a Group Rape." *Gender & Society* 1:239–60.

———. 1998. *Reconcilable Differences: Confronting Beauty, Pornography, and the Future of Feminism.* Berkeley: University of California Press.

CHAPKIS, WENDY. 1997. *Live Sex Acts: Women Performing Exotic Labor.* New York: Routledge.

CHODOROW, NANCY. 1976. "Oedipal Asymmetries and Heterosexual Knots." *Social Problems* 23:454–68.

CONNELL, R. W. 1992. "A Very Straight Gay: Masculinity, Homosexual Experience, and Gender." *American Sociological Review* 57:735–51.

CORBIN, ALAIN. 1990. *Women for Hire: Prostitution and Sexuality in France after 1850.* Translated by Alan Sheridan. Cambridge, MA: Harvard University Press.

COWLEY, GEOFFREY. 1997. "Gender Limbo." *Newsweek,* May 19, pp. 64–66.

CRENSHAW, KIMBERLÉ. 1991. "Demarginalizing the Intersection of Race and Sex: A Black Feminist Critique of Antidiscrimination Doctrine, Feminist Theory, and

Antiracist Politics." Pp. 57–80 in *Feminist Legal Theory: Readings in Law and Gender,* edited by Katharine T. Bartlett and Rosanne Kennedy. Boulder, CO: Westview.

CROSETTE, BARBARA. 1997. "Violation: An Old Scourge of War Becomes Its Latest Crime." *New York Times,* June 14, Week in Review, pp. 1, 6.

DOCTER, RICHARD F. 1988. *Transvestites and Transsexuals: Toward a Theory of Cross-Gender Behavior.* New York: Plenum.

DONNERSTEIN, EDWARD AND DANIEL LINZ. 1990. "Mass Media, Sexual Violence, and Male Viewers: Current Theory and Research." Pp. 219–32 in *Men Confront Pornography,* edited by Michael S. Kimmel. New York: Meridian.

DWORKIN, ANDREA. 1981. *Pornography: Men Possessing Women.* New York: Perigee.

———. 1987. *Intercourse.* New York: Free Press.

DWORKIN, ANDREA AND CATHARINE A. MACKINNON. 1988. *Pornography and Civil Rights.* Minneapolis: Organizing Against Pornography.

EKINS, RICHARD. 1997. *Male Femaling: A Grounded Theory Approach to Cross-Dressing and Sex-Changing.* New York: Routledge.

ENGLISH, DEIRDRE, AMBER HOLLIBAUGH, AND GAYLE RUBIN. 1981. "Talking Sex: A Conversation on Sexuality and Feminism." *Socialist Review* 11, no. 4:43–62.

EPSTEIN, JULIA AND KRISTINA STRAUS, eds. 1991. *Body Guards: The Cultural Politics of Gender Ambiguity.* New York: Routledge.

FALUDI, SUSAN. 1995. "The Money Shot." *New Yorker,* October 30, pp. 64–87.

FAUSTO-STERLING, ANNE. 1993. "The Five Sexes: Why Male and Female Are Not Enough." *Sciences* (March-April):20–25.

FEINBLOOM, DEBORAH HELLER, MICHAEL FLEMING, VALERIE KIJEWSKI, AND MARGO P. SCHULTER. 1976. "Lesbian/Feminist Orientation among Male-to-Female Transsexuals." *Journal of Homosexuality* 2, no. 1:59–71.

FELMLEE, DIANE H. 1994. "Who's on Top? Power in Romantic Relationships." *Sex Roles* 31:275–95.

FERGUSON, ANN, ILENE PHILIPSON, IRENE DIAMOND, AND LEE QUINBY, AND CAROLE S. VANCE AND ANN BARR SNITOW. 1984. "Forum: The Feminist Sexuality Debates." *Signs* 10:106–35.

FLAX, JANE. 1987. "Postmodernism and Gender Relations in Feminist Theory." *Signs* 12:621–43.

FOUCAULT, MICHEL. 1978. *The History of Sexuality.* Vol. 1, *An Introduction.* Translated by Robert Hurley. New York: Random House.

GAGNÉ, PATRICIA AND RICHARD TEWKSBURY. 1998. "Conformity Pressures and Gender Resistance among Transgendered Individuals." *Social Problems* 45:81–101.

GAGNÉ, PATRICIA, RICHARD TEWKSBURY, AND DEANNA MCGAUGHEY. 1997. "Coming Out and Crossing Over: Identity Formation and Proclamation in a Transgender Community." *Gender & Society* 11:478–508.

GALLOP, JANE. 1982. *The Daughter's Seduction: Feminism and Psychoanalysis.* Ithaca, NY: Cornell University Press.

GAMSON, JOSHUA G. 1995. "Must Identity Movements Self-Destruct? A Queer Dilemma." *Social Problems* 42:390–407.

———. 1998. "Publicity Traps: Television Talk Shows and Lesbian, Gay, Bisexual, and Transgender Visibility." *Sexualities* 1:11–41.

GARBER, MARJORIE. 1992. *Vested Interests: Cross-Dressing and Cultural Anxiety.* New York: Routledge.

———. 1995. *Vice Versa: Bisexuality and the Eroticism of Everyday Life.* New York: Simon & Schuster.

GARFINKEL, HAROLD. 1967. *Studies in Ethnomethodology.* Englewood Cliffs, NJ: Prentice Hall.

GOLDSTEIN, NANCY. 1995. "Lesbians and the Medical Profession: HIV/AIDS and the Pursuit of Visibility." *Women's Studies* 24:531–52.

GREEN, RICHARD AND JOHN MONEY, eds. 1969. *Transsexualism and Sex Reassignment.* Baltimore: Johns Hopkins University Press.

GREENBERG, DAVID F. 1988. *The Construction of Homosexuality.* Chicago: University of Chicago Press.

GRIFFIN, SUSAN. 1982. *Pornography and Silence: Culture's Revenge against Nature.* San Francisco: Harper & Row.

HAUG, FRIGGA ET AL. 1987. *Female Sexualization: A Collective Work of Memory.* London: Verso.

HERDT, GILBERT. 1990. "Mistaken Gender: 5α-Reductase Hermaphroditism and Biological Reductionism in Sexual Identity Reconsidered." *American Anthropologist* 92:433–46.

HERDT, GILBERT AND JULIAN DAVIDSON. 1988. "The Sambia 'Turnim-man': Sociocultural and Clinical Aspects of Gender Formation in Male Pseudohermaphrodites with 5α-Reductase Deficiency in Papua, New Guinea." *Archives of Sexual Behavior* 17:33–56.

HEREK, GREGORY M. 1986. "On Heterosexual Masculinity: Some Psychical Consequences of the Social Construction of Gender and Sexuality." *American Behavioral Scientist* 29:563–77.

HOBSON, BARBARA MEIL. 1987. *Uneasy Virtue: The Politics of Prostitution and the American Reform Tradition.* New York: Basic Books.

HOIGARD, CECILIE AND LIV FINSTAD. 1992. *Backstreets: Prostitution, Money, and Love.* Translated by Katherine Hanson, Nancy Sipe, and Barbara Wilson. University Park: Pennsylvania University Press.

HOLLIBAUGH, AMBER AND CHERRIÉ MORAGA. 1983. "What We're Rollin' Around in Bed With: Sexual Silences in Feminism." Pp. 394–405 in *Powers of Desire: The Politics of Sexuality,* edited by Ann Snitow, Christine Stansell, and Sharon Thompson. New York: Monthly Review Press.

IMPERATO-MCGINLEY, JULIANNE, RALPH E. PETERSON, TEOFILO GAUTIER, AND ERASMO STURLA. 1979. "Androgens and the Evolution of Male-Gender Identity among Male Pseudohermaphrodites with 5α-Reductase Deficiency." *New England Journal of Medicine* 300:1233–37.

JENNESS, VALERIE. 1990. "From Sex as Sin to Sex as Work: COYOTE and the Reorganization of Prostitution as a Social Problem." *Social Problems* 37:403–20.

KAPLAN, E. ANNE. 1983. "Is the Gaze Male?" Pp. 309–27 in *Powers of Desire: The Politics of Sexuality,* edited by Ann Snitow, Christine Stansell, and Sharon Thompson. New York: Monthly Review Press.

KATES, GARY. 1995. *Monsieur d'Eon Is a Woman: A Tale of Political Intrigue and Sexual Masquerade.* New York: Basic Books.

KESSLER, SUZANNE J. 1990. "The Medical Construction of Gender: Case Management of Intersexed Infants." *Signs* 16:3–26.

———. 1998. *Lessons from the Intersexed.* New Brunswick, NJ: Rutgers University Press.

KIMMEL, MICHAEL S., ed. 1990. *Men Confront Pornography.* New York: Meridian.

KING, DONNA. 1990. "Prostitutes as Pariah in the Age of AIDS: A Content Analysis of Coverage of Women Prostitutes in the *New York Times* and the *Washington Post* September 1985–April 1988." *Women and Health* 16:135–76.

KINSEY, A. C., W. B. POMEROY, AND C. E. MARTIN. 1948. *Sexual Behavior in the Human Male.* Philadelphia: W. B. Saunders.

KINSEY, A. C., W. B. POMEROY, C. E. MARTIN, AND P. H. GEBHARD. 1953. *Sexual Behavior in the Human Female.* Philadelphia: W. B. Saunders.

KITZINGER, CELIA. 1987. *The Social Construction of Lesbianism.* Newbury Park, CA: Sage.

KLEIN, FRITZ, BARRY SEPEKOFF, AND TIMOTHY J. WOLF. 1985. "Sexual Orientation: A Multi-variable Dynamic Process." *Journal of Homosexuality* 11, nos. 1–2:35–49.

KLEIN, FRITZ, AND TIMOTHY J. WOLF, eds. 1985. *Two Lives to Lead: Bisexuality in Men and Women.* New York: Harrington Park.

LAQUEUR, THOMAS. 1990. *Making Sex: Body and Gender from the Greeks to Freud.* Cambridge, MA: Harvard University Press.

LAUMANN, EDWARD O., JOHN H. GAGNON, ROBERT T. MICHAEL AND STUART MICHAELS. 1994. *The Social Organization of Sexuality: Sexual Practices in the United States.* Chicago: University of Chicago Press.

LEFKOWITZ, BERNARD. 1997. *Our Guys.* Berkeley: University of California Press.

LORBER, JUDITH. 1996. "Beyond the Binaries: Depolarizing the Categories of Sex, Sexuality, and Gender." *Sociological Inquiry* 66:143–59.

MACKINNON, CATHARINE A. 1987. *Feminism Unmodified: Discourses on Life and Law.* Cambridge, MA: Harvard University Press.

———. 1989. *Toward a Feminist Theory of the State.* Cambridge, MA: Harvard University Press.

MARTIN, PATRICIA YANCEY AND ROBERT A. HUMMER. 1989. "Fraternities and Rape on Campus." *Gender & Society* 3:457–73.

MCINTOSH, MARY. 1993. "Queer Theory and the War of the Sexes." Pp. 30–52 in *Activating Theory: Lesbian, Gay, and Bisexual Politics,* edited by Joseph Bristow and Angelia R. Wilson. London: Lawrence & Wishart.

MILLER, ELEANOR M. 1986. *Street Women.* Philadelphia: Temple University Press.

MILLETT, KATE. 1970. *Sexual Politics.* Garden City, NY: Doubleday.

MOFFATT, MICHAEL. 1989. *Coming of Age in New Jersey: College and American Culture.* New Brunswick, NJ: Rutgers University Press.

MORRIS, JAN. 1975. *Conundrum.* New York: Signet.

NAMASTE, KI. 1994. "The Politics of Inside/Out: Queer Theory, Poststructuralism, and a Sociological Approach to Sexuality." *Sociological Theory* 12:220–31.

NANDA, SERENA. 1990. *Neither Man or Woman: The Hijiras of India.* Belmont, CA: Wadsworth.

NEAD, LYNDA. 1990. "The Female Nude: Pornography, Art, and Sexuality." *Signs* 15:323–35.

NOCHLIN, LINDA. 1988. *Women, Art, and Power and Other Essays.* New York: Harper & Row.

OSMOND, MARIE WITHERS, K. G. WAMBACH, DIANE HARRISON, ET AL. 1993. "The Multiple Jeopardy of Race, Class, and Gender for AIDS Risk among Women." *Gender & Society* 7:99–120.

OVERALL, CHRISTINE. 1992. "What's Wrong with Prostitution? Evaluating Sex Work." *Signs* 17:705–24.

PADIAN, NANCY S., S. C. SHIBOSKI, AND N. P. JEWELL. 1991. "Female-to-Male Transmission of Human Immunodeficiency Virus." *Journal of the American Medical Association* 266:1664–67.

PARLEE, MARY BROWN. 1996. "Situated Knowledges of Personal Embodiment: Transgender Activists' and Psychological Theorists' Perspectives on 'Sex' and 'Gender.'" *Theory and Psychology* 6:625–45.

PEÑA, MANUEL. 1991. "Class, Gender, and Machismo: The 'Treacherous-Woman' Folklore of Mexican Male Workers." *Gender & Society* 5:30–46.

PERSON, ETHEL SPECTOR. 1980. "Sexuality as the Mainstay of Identity: Psychoanalytic Perspectives." *Signs* 5:605–30.

PUTNAM, MICHAEL. Forthcoming. "Private 'I's: Investigating Men's Experiences of Pornographies." Ph.D. dissertation, City University of New York.

RAYMOND, JANICE G. 1979. *The Transsexual Empire: The Making of the She-male.* Boston: Beacon.

RICH, ADRIENNE. 1980. "Compulsory Heterosexuality and Lesbian Existence." *Signs* 5:631–60.

RICHARDSON, DIANE, ed. 1996. *Theorizing Heterosexuality: Telling It Straight.* Buckingham: Open University Press.

ROIPHE, KATIE. 1993. *The Morning After: Sex, Fear and Feminism on Campus.* Boston: Little, Brown.

ROSEN, RUTH. 1982. *The Lost Sisterhood: Prostitution in America, 1900–1918.* Baltimore: Johns Hopkins University Press.

RUSSELL, DIANA E. H. 1998. *Dangerous Relationships: Pornography, Misogyny, and Rape.* Thousand Oaks, CA: Sage.

RUST, PAULA. 1992. "The Politics of Sexual Identity: Attraction and Behavior among Lesbian and Bisexual Women." *Social Problems* 39:366–86.

————. 1993. "'Coming Out' in the Age of Social Constructionism: Sexual Identity Formation among Lesbian and Bisexual Women." *Gender & Society* 7:50–77.

————. 1995. *Bisexuality and the Challenge to Lesbian Politics: Sex, Loyalty, and Revolution.* New York: New York University Press.

SANDAY, PEGGY REEVES. 1981. "The Socio-cultural Context of Rape: A Cross-cultural Study." *Journal of Social Issues* 37:5–27.

————. 1990. *Fraternity Gang Rape: Sex, Brotherhood and Privilege on Campus.* New York: New York University Press.

SCULLY, DIANA. 1990. *Understanding Sexual Violence: A Study of Convicted Rapists.* Boston: Unwin Hyman.

SEDGWICK, EVE KOSOFSKY. 1990. *Epistemology of the Closet.* Berkeley: University of California Press.

SEGAL, LYNNE. 1994. *Straight Sex: Rethinking the Politics of Pleasure.* Berkeley: University of California Press.

————. 1998. "Only the Literal: The Contradictions of Anti-pornography Feminism." *Sexualities* 1:43–62.

SHAPIRO, JUDITH. 1991. "Transsexualism: Reflections on the Persistence of Gender and the Mutability of Sex." Pp. 148–79 in *Body Guards: The Cultural Politics of Gender Ambiguity,* edited by Julia Epstein and Kristina Straus. New York: Routledge.

SOBLE, ALAN. 1986. *Pornography: Marxism, Feminism and the Future of Sexuality.* New Haven, CT: Yale University Press.

STEIN, EDWARD, ed. 1992. *Forms of Desire: Sexual Orientation and the Social Constructionist Debate.* New York: Routledge.

STEINEM, GLORIA. 1978. "Erotica and Pornography: A Clear and Present Difference." *Ms.,* November, pp. 53–54, 75, 78.

STOLLER, ROBERT J. 1985. *Presentations of Gender.* New Haven, CT: Yale University Press.

STOLTENBERG, JOHN. 1990. *Refusing to Be a Man: Essays on Sex and Justice.* New York: Meridian.

STONE, SANDY. 1991. "The *Empire* Strikes Back: A Post-transsexual Manifesto." Pp. 280–304 in *Body Guards: The Cultural Politics of Gender Ambiguity,* edited by Julia Epstein and Kristina Straus. New York: Routledge.

TAYLOR, VERTA AND NANCY E. WHITTIER. 1992. "Collective Identity in Social Movement Communities: Lesbian Feminist Mobilization." Pp. 104–29 in *Frontiers in Social Movement Theory,* edited by Aldon Morris and Carol McClurg Muellen. New Haven, CT: Yale University Press.

TUCKER, NAOMI, ed. 1995. *Bisexual Politics: Theories, Queries, and Visions.* New York: Harrington Park.

VALVERDE, MARIANA. 1985. *Sex, Power and Pleasure.* Toronto: Women's Press.

VANCE, CAROLE S., ed. 1984. *Pleasure and Danger: Exploring Female Sexuality.* Boston: Routledge & Kegan Paul.

WALKOWITZ, JUDITH R. 1980. *Prostitution and Victorian Society: Women, Class, and the State.* Cambridge: Cambridge University Press.

WALTERS, WILLIAM W. A. AND MICHAEL W. ROSS. 1986. *Transsexualism and Sex Reassignment.* Oxford: Oxford University Press.

WARNER, MICHAEL, ed. 1993. *Fear of a Queer Planet: Queer Politics and Social Theory.* Minneapolis: University of Minneapolis Press.

WEINBERG, MARTIN S., COLIN J. WILLIAMS, AND DOUGLAS W. PRYOR. 1994. *Dual Attraction: Understanding Bisexuality.* New York: Oxford University Press.

WESTON, KATHLEEN M. 1991. *Families We Choose: Lesbians, Gays, Kinship.* New York: Columbia University Press.

WHEELWRIGHT, JULIE. 1989. *Amazons and Military Maids: Women Who Cross-Dressed in Pursuit of Life, Liberty and Happiness.* London: Pandora.

WHISMAN, VERA. 1996. *Queer by Choice: Lesbians, Gay Men and the Politics of Difference.* New York: Routledge.

WILKINSON, SUE AND CELIA KITZINGER, eds. 1993. *Heterosexuality: A Feminism and Psychology Reader.* London: Sage.

WILLIAMS, LINDA. 1989. *Hard Core: Power, Pleasure, and the "Frenzy of the Visible."* Berkeley: University of California Press.

WILLIAMS, WALTER L. 1986. *The Spirit and the Flesh: Sexual Diversity in American Indian Culture.* Boston: Beacon.

WILSON, ELIZABETH. 1993. "Is Transgression Transgressive?" Pp. 107–17 in *Activating Theory: Lesbian, Gay, and Bisexual Politics,* edited by Joseph Bristow and Angelia R. Wilson. London: Lawrence & Wishart.

WOODHOUSE, ANNIE. 1989. *Fantastic Women: Sex, Gender, and Transvestism.* New Brunswick, NJ: Rutgers University Press.

ZILLMANN, DOLF AND JENNINGS BRYANT. 1990. "Pornography, Sexual Callousness, and the Trivialization of Rape." Pp. 207–18 in *Men Confront Pornography,* edited by Michael S. Kimmel. New York: Meridian.

CRITICAL THINKING QUESTIONS

1. What is the radical feminist argument regarding heterosexuality, prostitution, and pornography? What is the position of feminists who disagree with them?

2. Why do feminists disagree about the issues of prostitution and pornography?

3. According to the arguments presented by Lorber, where does gender rank among the social statuses in defining inequalities? What does she mean by a hierarchy of domination? Is this concept useful? Why or why not?

Getting Involved

1. Take an informal survey of students on your campus. Stand in a busy, public location (such as outside the cafeteria at lunch time) and ask students if they have a moment to answer three quick questions:

- Do you think inequality is a problem in the United States?
- Of the following, which is the most important reason that inequality exists today?

    racism

    sexism

    capitalism

- What is your race or ethnicity? What is your gender?

Work with a partner to record students' responses. Examine the data you collected to determine which source of oppression is the most important by the gender and racial or ethnic group of your respondents.

2. Visit the web sites of several state departments of corrections. Find the statistics about demographics of inmates in these correctional systems. Also look for the salaries offered for new correctional officers. Compare this information with data from your state as a whole regarding demographics and average household income. What does this data suggest to you about who is in prison, both as inmates and as staff?

3. Interview students on your campus. Ask male students to define for you what it means to be a man and what the term masculinity means to them. What characteristics are common in their answers. Also, ask students (both male and female) what it means to be successful. Analyze the responses you get to these two questions, looking for similarities and differences.

Site-Seeing

1. To learn more about the issue of reparations to the descendants of African-American slaves, visit the web site sponsored by the African American Reparation Action Network at **http://www.angelfire.com/super/freedom.**

2. For more information on men's studies and a discussion of academic issues involved in the study of masculinities, visit the American Men's Studies Association web site at **http://www.mensstudies.org/.**

3. To learn more about the life, work, and theoretical perspective of Angela Davis, visit the web page about her set up by the Public Broadcasting System at **http://www.pbs.org/wgbh/pages/frontline/shows/race/interviews/davis.html.**

4. To find out more about Asian-American women and their views on feminism, visit the Asian American Women Speak web site at **http://www.geocities.com/Tokyo/Bay/9897/women/.**

Chapter 7

Social Movements And Resistance

Over the past fifty years, people of color, women, and sexual minorities have achieved many civil rights that were once denied them. This progress is the result, in large part, of the work of activists in the civil rights, feminist, gay and lesbian, and transgender social movements. Despite these gains, however, all of these groups have a long way to go before they achieve full equality of opportunity in U.S. society. Moreover, social class has remained a primary source of inequality. Over the last several decades, the poor and working classes have lost ground. With the decline in labor union membership, deindustrialization, outsourcing, and the globalization of our economy, workers have lost a great deal of the power they once wielded in the workplace. Their children are likely to be the first generation in U.S. society to be worse off than their parents. Furthermore, with the welfare reform of the Clinton Administration, the poor have less of a safety net today than in the last forty years.

When considering issues of race, class, gender, and sexuality, the picture is not clearly one of progress or setbacks. Nor is it one of a race won or lost. To provide a better understanding of where we stand today, the articles in the last section examine the challenges that continue to face people of color, the poor, members of the working class, women, sexual minorities, and transgenders, as well as some of the ways that they continue to resist oppression.

In the first article, Ladner briefly summarizes some of the major accomplishments of the civil rights movement. She argues that the success of that movement led other minority groups, such as women, gay men and lesbians, and many other groups to believe they had the right to pressure the government to correct institutional barriers to equality. With the entry of these groups into the political domain, Ladner argues that it has been difficult for the civil rights movement to maintain the coalition of sympathetic whites and labor and church leaders that resulted in its success. Today, she maintains, U.S. citizens cannot agree on whether the problems that continue to plague African Americans, which are largely rooted in poverty, are class-based or race-based issues. Indeed, they cannot even agree on whether the government is responsible for addressing these inequalities.

Ladner argues that the civil rights movement faces two major challenges if it is to succeed in the twenty-first century. The first is that it must find ways to address the persistence of racial inequalities in income, education, health, housing, and criminal justice. The second is that the movement must develop a more fluid understanding of racial and class-based inequality. This model must address the issues of all people of color, as well as the problems facing poor whites. Any future success of the civil rights movement rests on its ability to build coalitions with the poor and all people of color and to address the inequalities that continue to plague these groups.

One of the problems that continues to face poor people, particularly those of color, is an issue known as environmental racism—an institutionalized practice of unfair enforcement of environmental policies that results in exposure to unsafe and unhealthy physical environments for poor people and for racial and ethnic minorities. In the second article, Bullard documents just some of the ways that environmental racism results in greater health risks for people of color than for whites, even among people of the same social class. He examines social movements that have mobilized against environmental racism and some of the ways activists have worked to help people protect themselves from exposure to toxic elements. These efforts have succeeded in changing some environmental policies, stopping the placement of certain nuclear power plants and garbage incinerators, for example, and reduced exposure to other health hazards. In the end, Bullard argues that environmental protection is a right that the government has systematically failed to provide to the poor and people of color. He says that these groups must remain vigilant or they will be overrun by the interests of wealthy whites, who advocate placing environmental hazards in neighborhoods other than their own.

Although many inequalities, including environmental racism, disproportionately hurt the poor, discrimination is not limited to the economically disadvantaged. In the third article, Gregory and Jacobs look at the efforts of black models to resist racism in the fashion industry. According to those models, people of color are grossly under-represented in all aspects of the fashion industry. Moreover, the authors maintain that the exclusion of people of color from advertising has a negative effect on the self-esteem of minority youth. The movement advocates that African Americans boycott clothing designers and manufacturers who fail to use black models in their advertisements and instead to "buy black."

African Americans have long understood the importance of standing together and using their economic clout to force social change. In the fourth article, Fletcher questions whether the union movement will have a similar resolve as it tries to represent the interests of working people in the United States and throughout the world. The author explains that at one time, unions refused to represent women or people of color and that whenever there have been divisions among workers, capitalists have moved in to take advantage of them. Fletcher argues that there is no question that members of the working class share a number of issues, in both the U.S. and global economies, but that race and gender have once again become issues that threaten to divide the union movement. The author asserts that unions must be willing to address issues at the intersection of race, gender, and social class if they are to achieve unity and fully represent the interests of all members of the working class.

Just as women and men of color have had difficulties getting unions to recognize and address issues of sexism and racism, women of color have often found that the feminist movement has failed to represent their interests adequately. In the fifth article, Zia explains that many people believe the myth that the feminist movement is a "white thing," a misconception that prevents many women of color from becoming involved in the women's movement. Drawing on historical examples of the involvement of strong women of color in the feminist movement, as well as providing statistics on the number of women of color in leadership positions of mainstream feminist organizations, Zia argues that women of color have long played an important role in the feminist movement. Nonetheless, she asserts that women of color continue to face significant barriers in their efforts to exercise power in leadership roles of mainstream feminist organizations. They also encounter difficulties in getting these organizations to recognize fully the issues that women of color face. Still, Zia maintains that social change for women of color will be achieved as they work in coalition with white women to end sexism, and with men of color to end racism.

Although women and people of color have achieved some level of success in getting the feminist movement and labor unions to address issues of importance to them, gay men, lesbians, and bisexuals have often had to organize among themselves, with little or no outside support, to advocate for their rights. In the sixth article, Raeburn examines the workplace activism of lesbians, gay men, and bisexuals to win nondiscrimination policies that include extending health insurance and other benefits to the partners of sexual minorities. She says that those corporations that made "gay-friendly" changes in their employment policies did so only under organized pressure from groups representing gay men, bisexuals, and lesbians. Raeburn argues that although this minority group has a long way to go before it achieves workplace equity, bisexuals, gay men, and lesbians achieved enough success in the late twentieth century to have their agenda named "the workplace issue of the '90s."

The workplace unity of gay men, lesbians, and bisexuals is just one domain where the organized efforts of minority groups have achieved success. In the seventh article, Cusac discusses the unity that was evident among gays, lesbians, bisexuals, and transgenders in 1969, during the Stonewall riot—an event widely recognized as touching off the gay and lesbian rights movement. Since that time, however, the author laments that in its search for respectable representatives of the community, the movement has marginalized or excluded some members, including transgenders and bisexuals. Cusac argues that the Stonewall riot was about achieving radical sexual equality for all, but that the promise of Stonewall is one the movement seems to have left behind.

In the last article, Dahir examines the controversy within the gay, lesbian, and bisexual movement about whether transgenders should be included. The author draws on interviews with several activists to point out just some of the ways that transsexuals and cross-dressers have been either marginalized within the movement or excluded altogether. Many transgenders argue that they are marginalized within the movement by activists who think of them as "freaks" who are an embarrassment to the movement. Moreover, Dahir looks at the efforts of the gay, lesbian, and bisexual movement to pass federal legislation that would outlaw discrimination against them in employment. Many transsexual and cross-dressing leaders argue that the movement has worked to exclude transgenders in that legislation, in large part because passing it would be easier if they were left out.

Taken together, these articles show us several important trends and challenges within groups seeking to end institutionalized and cultural barriers to equality. First, all of the groups we have examined in this book—racial and ethnic minorities, the poor and the working class, women, sexual minorities, and transgenders—have organized to demand social change. And they have succeeded in winning some of their demands. Second, each group has issues in common with others. Racial and ethnic minorities often share poverty and its associated social problems with poor white women and men. But they also have issues specific to themselves as people of color, including lack of representation in the media and lack of forceful representation by labor unions. Similarly, labor unions—which have traditionally represented working-class men—must now represent people of diverse backgrounds who share social class but have a number of differing workplace issues. For women, these include issues related to fertility and sexuality. For people of color, they include race-based discrimination. For gay men, lesbians, and bisexuals, these issues often include homophobia. And transgenders encounter transphobia because as they publicly change genders, they challenge deep-seated assumptions about the natural correlation between biological sex and cultural gender presentations.

Some of the greatest successes of the social movements of the twentieth century came about when people organized on the basis of a singular identity—African Americans in the civil rights movement, women in the feminist movement, and sexual minorities in the gay and lesbian movement. But the greatest challenges of the movements of the twenty-first century center on how these groups will maintain their individual group identities, which are the basis of solidarity, while at the same time creating coalitions and working with those who share common problems. Furthermore, these movements must work to address the issues confronting people with multiple minority statuses and to find ways to confront the intersections of race, class, gender, and sexuality. When it comes to inequality, this is, perhaps, the greatest challenge of the twenty-first century.

Reading 1

A New Civil Rights Agenda

Joyce A. Ladner

> *In this article, Ladner provides a brief summary of some of the major accomplishments of the civil rights movement and argues that as new groups have entered the fight for civil rights, it has been difficult to maintain a unified front.*

Few issues in American life have been as intransigent as race. In every century, race has presented the nation its greatest paradoxes,

Source: Reprinted from *Brookings Review* 18, no. 2 (Spring 2000): 26–28. Used by permission of the Brookings Institute Press, Washington, D.C.

challenges, and opportunities, calling into question time and again the principle of equality on which it was founded.

During the 1950s and 1960s, the golden era of civil rights activism, the civil rights movement mobilized the nation's collective consciousness around issues of racial equity. The

U.S. Supreme Court officially ended legal school segregation in *Brown v. Board of Education of Topeka, Kansas* in 1954. Congress passed the landmark Civil Rights Act of 1964 and the Voting Rights Act of 1965. Black political participation increased dramatically. In 1964, only 5 blacks served in the U.S. Congress. By 1998, the number had grown to 39.

But the victories of the movement, however decisive they seemed at the time, did not bring the long-term parity that activists and policymakers hoped for. Bread-and-butter issues such as unemployment, substandard housing, inferior education, unsafe streets, escalating child poverty, and homelessness supplanted the right to vote, eat at a lunch counter, and attend desegregated schools. As new issues arose, appearing and intensifying in ways that fell beyond the scope of the legislation and social reforms, the old civil rights model—one that relied mostly on judicial and protest remedies—seemed less and less effective in dealing with them.

CONTRIBUTIONS OF THE MOVEMENT

The civil rights movement made lasting contributions to the nation. Above all, it helped eliminate the legal apartheid that had dogged the United States since its earliest days. It also created a national expectation that individuals and groups had the right to petition their government to right legal wrongs affecting them. In its wake there developed a broad base of constituent interest groups—women, the elderly, children's rights advocates, the handicapped, homosexuals, environmentalists—that emphasize the rights of affected parties to be a critical part of the decisions affecting their interests.

Ironically, the emergence of those constituent groups, each with its own divergent interests, made it much more difficult to sustain the old civil rights coalition of members of labor, the faith communities, and sympathetic whites and blacks to advance the new issues of post–civil rights America. Indeed, the dominant ethos of the sixties, racial integration and equality, has given way to an implicit but insidious assumption by many whites and blacks today that voluntary racial isolation and segregation are acceptable even among those whose fundamental interests are similar.

The American citizenry is also divided over whether the unfinished civil rights agenda has its origins in race or social class, and even whether government reforms such as affirmative action should address the lingering problems. The compelling evidence of African-American progress found in the burgeoning middle class helps explain why opponents of a race-based agenda feel the way they do. Meanwhile poverty in a large and intractable black underclass reaches deep into inner cities and rural communities nationwide and decisively constricts the life chances for affected parties, particularly children.

THE UNFINISHED CIVIL RIGHTS AGENDA

Two issues remain on the civil rights agenda. The first is addressing the persistence of racial disparities. The second is redefining the agenda to fit a vastly changing American demographic profile.

Black-white inequality persists in income, education, health, housing, technology access, and safe communities. The national media increasingly report on racial profiling in what has come to be euphemistically referred to as "driving while black," in the denial of equal access to rent or purchase housing, and in disparities in arrests and sentencing in the criminal justice system.

Many still view government intervention as the most effective means to provide the leadership to eliminate the disparities. But others argue that the responsibility for solving these problems rests neither entirely with government, nor with the voluntary, private, sector, but with a coalition of government, civil society, business, and individual initiatives. They see an invigorated role for faith-based groups, particularly those serving African Americans, and also a stronger role for industry in hiring and training the most indigent and least prepared.

The second issue on the civil rights agenda involves the rapid growth in the immigrant population since 1965. Individuals of Hispanic origin now outnumber African Americans. By 2050, the majority-minority population paradigm on which race and ethnic relations have traditionally rested in this society may be a thing of the past. As a nation, we have already moved away from the traditional white-black model of race relations to one that reflects the nation's broad diversity—in race, ethnicity, gender, and lifestyle.

The increase in interracial and interethnic marriages is already changing the historical perceptions of what it is to be a member of the "white" or "black" race. High-profile individuals like golf professional Tiger Woods represent a generation of Americans who are redefining race by embracing their ethnic and racial diversity and its broader societal implications.

It is conceivable that at mid-century, Americans will view race in fluid rather than fixed and precise terms, not unlike the way Brazilians see their multiracial population.

THE NEED FOR NEW MODELS

One of the shortcomings of the civil rights movement of the 1950s and 1960s was its failure to envision the need for a fluid model of action to address new civil rights issues in the years ahead. And still the search goes on. Indeed, the issue today is how to develop flexible remedies to black-white disparity, the nation's changing racial and ethnic diversity, and white poverty. One way is to rebuild the black voluntary sector that was for a time supplanted by the black electorate. Jesse Jackson's Rainbow Coalition was a step in the direction of pitching a huge tent under whose shelter new and old minorities and the poor could find common issues and agendas. Martin Luther King's proposed Poor People's campaign in 1967 also recognized that a civil rights coalition based entirely on race would not be sufficient to address the problem of white poverty.

A new generation of civil rights leaders now focuses its work on eliminating social and economic disparities, particularly for the indigent. Using some of the sixties strategies for community organizing around advocacy and service delivery, these leaders are bringing technical proficiency to such complex problems as economic development, improvement of schools, and the organization of community development corporations whose missions range from building housing to creating mini-industries.

The most effective of these leaders are people like Bob Moses, a key voting rights activist in the South in the sixties, who now teaches math literacy to prepare poor children for the technology-driven job market; Eugene Rivers, a founder of Boston's 10-Point Coalition to disarm gangs and rehabilitate young lives; Hattie Dorsey, whose Atlanta Neighborhood Development Partnership helps rebuild decaying neighborhoods; and Robert Woodson, head of the National Neighborhood Enterprise Center, who brokered a truce among the District of Columbia's most violent gangs and placed its members in paying jobs.

Most of the successful leaders in the post–civil rights movement operate in the nonprofit sector, primarily in community-based groups. They know how to reinvent themselves and their strategies by developing cross-cultural alliances and partnerships based on technical competence as much as on common goals; build public and private resource bases; and navigate the bureaucratic governmental maze for funding. And they are actively training a new generation of young leaders to succeed them. The skills they bring to the job include expertise in planning, finance, technology, and government. They know how to design programs that are appropriate for the complex, multi-layered issues inherent in their work and how to garner the resources to rebuild decaying infrastructures and overhaul human services to make them more efficient and less costly, even while pushing constituents to practice self-sufficiency.

In conclusion, two questions stand out. First, can diverse cultural communities (such as Puerto Ricans in New York City, Central Americans or Ethiopians in Washington, D.C., Asians and Latinos in Los Angeles) and nonprofit groups in civil society coalesce with elected officials and with one another to address the post–civil rights agenda? Second, as they face increased costs along with demands for both enhanced services and fiscal accountability, how can cities (including economically and institutionally recovering venues of reinvention like Washington, D.C., and Philadelphia) support all their citizens?

CRITICAL THINKING QUESTIONS

1. How did the civil rights movement's focus on racial issues result in the successes it enjoyed? What issues did the movement overlook by not focusing on social class issues?

2. How has the activism of women, gay men, lesbians, and other minority groups affected the strategies and actions of the civil rights movement?

3. Why does the author argue that it is important for the civil rights movement to expand its focus and scope? What can the movement do to incorporate issues affecting the poor and working classes, women, sexual minorities, and transgenders? How might such inclusion affect the goals and strategies of the movement?

Reading 2

Dismantling Environmental Racism in the USA

Robert D. Bullard

In this article, Bullard explores the structure and dynamics of environmental racism, focusing on the ways that institutionalized forms of discrimination contribute to differential health outcomes for minorities. He also discusses grassroots social movement efforts to change the way environmental policies are administered.

INTRODUCTION

Despite significant improvements in environmental protection over the past several

Source: Robert. D. Bullard, "Dismantling Enviromental Racism in the USA". *Local Environment,* Vol. 4, Issue 1, 5–19, published by Taylor & Francis Ltd. www.tandf.co.uk/journals. Used by permission.

decades, millions of Americans continue to live in unsafe and unhealthy physical environments. Many economically impoverished communities and their inhabitants are exposed to greater health hazards in their homes, in their jobs and in their neighbourhoods when compared to their more affluent counterparts (Alston, 1992; Alston & Brown,

1993; Bryant & Mohai, 1992; US Environmental Protection Agency (EPA), 1992). This paper examines the root causes and consequences of differential exposure of some US populations to elevated environmental health risks.

DEFINING ENVIRONMENTAL RACISM

In the real world, all communities are not created equal. All communities do not receive equal protection. Economics, political clout and race play an important part in sorting out residential amenities and disamenities. Environmental racism is as real as the racism found in housing, employment, education and voting (Bullard, 1993a). Environmental racism refers to any environmental policy, practice or directive that differentially affects or disadvantages (whether intended or unintended) individuals, groups or communities based on race or colour. Environmental racism is just one form of environmental injustice and is reinforced by government, legal, economic, political and military institutions. Environmental racism combines with public policies and industry practices to provide benefits for whites while shifting costs to people of colour (Godsil, 1990; Colquette & Robertson, 1991; Collin, 1992; Bullard, 1993a).

From New York to Los Angeles, grassroots community resistance has emerged in response to practices, policies and conditions that residents have judged to be unjust, unfair and illegal. . . . Some of these conditions include: (1) unequal enforcement of environmental, civil rights and public health laws; (2) differential exposure of some populations to harmful chemicals, pesticides and other toxins in the home, school, neighbourhood and workplace; (3) faulty assumptions in calculating, assessing and managing risks; (4) discriminatory zoning and land-use practices; and (5) exclusionary practices that limit some individuals and groups from participation in decision making (C. Lee, 1992; Bullard, 1993b, 1994).

THE ENVIRONMENTAL JUSTICE PARADIGM

During its 28-year history, the US EPA has not always recognized that many government and industry practices (whether intended or unintended) have adverse impacts on poor people and people of colour. Growing grassroots community resistance has emerged in response to practices, policies and conditions that residents have judged to be unjust, unfair and illegal. The EPA is mandated to enforce the nation's environmental laws and regulations equally across the board. It is required to protect all Americans—not just individuals or groups who can afford lawyers, lobbyists and experts. Environmental protection is a right, not a privilege reserved for a few who can 'vote with their feet' and escape or fend off environmental stressors.

The current environmental protection apparatus is broken and needs to be fixed. The current apparatus manages, regulates and distributes risks (Bullard, 1996). The dominant environmental protection paradigm institutionalises unequal enforcement, trades human health for profit, places the burden of proof on the 'victims' and not the polluting industry, legitimates human exposure to harmful chemicals, pesticides and hazardous substances, promotes 'risky' technologies, exploits the vulnerability of economically and politically disenfranchised communities, subsidises ecological destruction, creates an industry around risk assessment and risk management, delays clean-up actions and fails to develop pollution prevention as the overarching and dominant strategy (Beasley, 1990a, b; Austin & Schill, 1991; Bullard, 1993c).

Environmental justice is defined as the fair treatment and meaningful involvement of all people regardless of race, colour, national origin or income with respect to the development, implementation and enforcement of environmental laws, regulations and policies. Fair treatment means that no group of people, including racial, ethnic or socio-economic groups, should bear a disproportionate share of the negative environmental consequences resulting from industrial, municipal and commercial operations or the execution of federal, state, local and tribal programmes and policies.

ENDANGERED COMMUNITIES

Numerous studies reveal that low-income persons and people of colour have borne greater health and environmental risk burdens than the society at large (Mann, 1991; Goldman, 1991; Goldman & Fitten, 1994). Elevated public health risks have been found in some populations even when social class is held constant. For example, race has been found to be independent of class in the distribution of air pollution, contaminated fish consumption, municipal landfills and incinerators, abandoned toxic waste dumps, the clean-up of superfund sites and lead poisoning in children (Commission for Racial Justice, 1987; Agency for Toxic Substances and Disease Registry, 1988; West et al., 1992; Bryant & Mohai, 1992; Lavelle & Coyle, 1992; Goldman & Fitten, 1994; Pirkle et al., 1994).

Childhood lead poisoning is another preventable disease that has not been eradicated. Figures reported in the July 1994 Journal of the American Medical Association from the Third National Health and Nutrition Examination Survey (NHANES III) revealed that 1.7 million children (8.9% of children aged 1–5) are lead poisoned, defined as having blood levels equal to or above 10 microg/dl. The NHANES III data found African-American children to be lead poisoned at more than twice the rate of white children at every income level (Pirkle et al., 1994). Over 28.4% of all low-income African-American children were lead poisoned compared to 9.8% of all low-income white children. During the time-period between 1976 and 1991, the decrease in blood lead levels for African-American and Mexican-American children lagged far behind that of white children.

In California, a coalition of environmental, social justice and civil libertarian groups joined forces to challenge the way the state carried out its lead screening of poor children. The Natural Resources Defense Council, the National Association for the Advancement of Colored People Legal Defense and Education Fund (NAACP LDF), the American Civil Liberties Union and the Legal Aid Society of Alameda County, California won an out-of-court settlement worth $15 million to $20 million for a blood lead testing programme. The lawsuit, *Matthews v. Coye*, involved the failure of the state of California to conduct the federally mandated testing for lead of some 557,000 poor children who received Medicaid (B. L. Lee, 1992). This historic agreement triggered similar lawsuits and actions in several other states that failed to live up to the mandates.

IMPETUS FOR POLICY SHIFT

The impetus behind the environmental justice movement did not come from within government or academia, or from within largely white middle-class nationally based environmental and conservation groups. The impetus for change came from people of colour, grassroots activists and their 'bottom-up' leadership approach. Grassroots groups organised themselves, educated themselves and empowered themselves to make fundamental change in the way environmental protection is performed in their communities.

The environmental justice movement has come a long way since its humble beginning in rural, predominantly African-American, Warren County, North Carolina, where a polychlorinated biphenyl landfill ignited protests and where over 500 arrests were made. The Warren County protests provided the impetus for a US General Accounting Office (1983) study, *Siting of Hazardous Waste Landfills and Their Correlation with Racial and Economic Status of Surrounding Communities*. That study revealed that three out of four of the off-site, commercial hazardous waste landfills in Region 4 (which comprises eight states in the South) happened to be located in predominantly African-American communities, although African-Americans made up only 20% of the region's population.

The protests also led the Commission for Racial Justice (1987) to produce *Toxic Wastes and Race in the United States,* the first national study to correlate waste facility sites and demographic characteristics. Race was found to be the most potent variable in predicting where these facilities were located—more powerful than poverty, land values and home ownership. In 1990, *Dumping in Dixie: Race, Class, and Environmental Quality* (Bullard, 1994) . . . highlighted African-Americans' environmental activism in the South, the same region that gave birth to the modem civil rights movement. What started out as local and often isolated community-based struggles against toxics and facility siting blossomed into a multi-issue, multi-ethnic and multi-regional movement.

The First National People of Color Environmental Leadership Summit (1991) was probably the most important single event in the movement's history. The Summit broadened the environmental justice movement beyond its anti-toxics focus to include issues of public health, worker safety, land use, transportation, housing, resource allocation and community empowerment (C. Lee, 1992). The meeting, organised by and for people of colour, demonstrated that it is possible to build a multi-racial grassroots movement around environmental and economic justice (Alston, 1992).

Held in Washington, DC, the day Summit was attended by over 650 grassroots and national leaders from around the world. Delegates came from all 50 states, including Alaska and Hawaii, Puerto Rico, Chile, Mexico and as far away as the Marshall Islands. People attended the Summit to share their action strategies, redefine the environmental movement and develop common plans for addressing environmental problems affecting people of colour in the USA and around the world.

On 27 October 1991, Summit delegates adopted 17 'principles of environmental justice'. . . . These principles were developed as a guide for organising and networking, and relating to non-governmental organisations (NGOs). By June 1992, Spanish and Portuguese translations of the principles were being used and circulated by NGOs and community groups at the Earth Summit in Rio de Janeiro.

Federal, state and local policies and practices have contributed to residential segmentation and unhealthy living conditions in poor, working-class and people of colour communities (Bullard & Johnson, 1997). Several recent cases in California bring this point to life (Lee, 1995). Disparate highway siting and mitigation plans were challenged by community residents, churches and the NAACP LDF, in *Clear Air Alternative Coalition v. United States Department of Transportation* (ND Cal. C-93-0721-VRW), involving the reconstruction of the earthquake-damaged Cypress Freeway in West Oakland. The plaintiffs wanted the downed Cypress Freeway (which split their community in half) rebuilt further away. Although the plaintiffs were not able to get their plan implemented, they did change the course of the freeway in their out-of-court settlement.

The NAACP LDF has filed an administrative complaint, *Mothers of East Los Angeles, El Sereno Neighborhood Action Committee, El Sereno Organizing Committee et al. v. California Transportation Commission et al.* (before the US Department of Transportation and US Housing and Urban Development), challenging the construction of the 4.5 mile extension of the Long Beach Freeway in East Los Angeles through El Sereno, Pasadena and South Pasadena. The plaintiffs argue that the mitigation measures proposed by the state agencies to address noise, air and visual pollution discriminate against the mostly Latino El Sereno community. For example, all of the freeway in Pasadena and 80% of that in South Pasadena will be below ground level. On the other hand, most of the freeway in El Sereno will be above-grade. White areas were favoured over the mostly Latino El Sereno in the allocation of covered freeway, historic preservation measures and accommodation to local schools (Lee, 1995; Bullard & Johnson, 1997).

Los Angeles residents and the NAACP LDF have also challenged the inequitable funding and operation of bus transportation used primarily by low-income persons and people of colour residents. A class action lawsuit was filed on behalf of 350,000 low-income, people of colour, bus travellers represented by the Labor/Community Strategy Center, the Bus Riders Union, the Southern Christian Leadership Conference, Korean Immigrant Workers Advocates, and individual bus travellers. In *Labor/Community Strategy Center v. Los Angeles Metropolitan Transportation Authority* (Cal. CV 94-5936 TJH Mcx), the plaintiffs argued that the Los Angeles Metropolitan Transit Authority (MTA) uses federal funds to pursue a policy of raising the costs of bus travellers (who are mostly poor and people of colour) and reducing the quality of the service in order to fund rail and other projects in predominantly white, suburban areas.

In the end, the Labor/Community Strategy Center and its allies successfully challenged transit racism in Los Angeles. The group was able to win major fare and bus pass concessions from the Los Angeles MTA. They also forced the Los Angeles MTA to spend $89 million on 278 new, clean, compressed natural gas buses.

MAKING GOVERNMENT MORE RESPONSIVE

Many of the nation's environmental policies distribute costs in a regressive pattern while providing disproportionate benefits for whites and individuals who fall at the upper end of the education and income scales. Lavelle & Coyle (1992) uncovered glaring inequities in the way the federal EPA enforces its laws:

> There is a racial divide in the way the US government cleans up toxic waste sites and punishes polluters. White communities see faster action, better results and stiffer penalties than communities where blacks, Hispanics and other minorities live. This unequal protection often occurs whether the community is wealthy or poor.

This study reinforced what many grass-roots activists have known for decades: all communities are not treated the same. Communities that are located on the 'wrong side of the tracks' are at greater risk from exposure to lead, pesticides (in the home and the workplace), air pollution, toxic releases, water pollution, solid and hazardous waste, raw sewage and pollution from industries (Goldman, 1992).

Government has been slow to ask the questions of who gets help and who does not, who can afford help and who can not, why some contaminated communities get studied while others get left off the research agenda, why industry poisons some communities and not others, why some contaminated communities get cleaned up while others are not, why some populations are protected and others are not protected, and why unjust, unfair and illegal policies and practices are allowed to go unpunished.

Struggles for equal environmental protection and environmental justice did not magically appear in the 1990s. Many communities of colour have been engaged in life and death struggles for more than a decade. In 1990, the Agency for Toxic Substances and Disease Registry (ATSDR) held a historic conference in Atlanta. The ATSDR National Minority Health Conference focused on contamination (Johnson et al., 1992). In 1992, after meeting with community leaders, academicians and civil rights leaders, the US EPA (under the leadership of William Reilly) admitted there was a problem, and established the Office of Environmental Equity. The name was changed to the Office of Environmental Justice under the Clinton Administration.

In 1992, the US EPA produced one of the first comprehensive documents to examine the whole question of risk and environmental hazards in their equity report, *Environmental Equity: reducing risk for all communities* (US EPA, 1992). The report, and its Office of Environmental Equity, were initiated only after prodding from people of colour, environmental justice leaders, activists and a few academicians.

The EPA also established a 25-member National Environmental Justice Advisory Council (NEJAC) under the Federal Advisory Committee Act. The NEJAC divided its environmental justice work into six sub-committees: Health and Research, Waste and Facility Siting, Enforcement, Public Participation and Accountability, Native American and Indigenous Issues, and International Issues. The NEJAC is comprised of stakeholders representing grassroots community groups, environmental groups, NGOs, state, local and tribal governments, academia and industry.

In February 1994, seven federal agencies, including the ATSDR, the National Institute for Environmental Health Sciences, the EPA, the National Institute of Occupational Safety and Health, the National Institutes of Health, the Department of Energy and Centers for Disease Control and Prevention sponsored a National Health Symposium entitled 'Health and research needs to ensure environmental justice'. The conference planning committee was unique in that it included grassroots organisation leaders, affected community residents and federal agency representatives. The goal of the February conference was to bring diverse stakeholders and those most affected to the decision-making table (National Institute for Environmental Health Sciences, 1995). Some of the recommendations from that symposium included the following:

- Conduct meaningful health research in support of people of colour and low-income communities.
- Promote disease prevention and pollution prevention strategies.
- Promote inter-agency co-ordination to ensure environmental justice.
- Provide effective outreach, education and communications.
- Design legislative and legal remedies.

In response to growing public concern and mounting scientific evidence, President Clinton on 11 February 1994 (the second day of the National Health Symposium) issued Executive Order 12898, 'Federal actions to address environmental justice in minority populations and low-income populations'. This Order attempts to address environmental injustice within existing federal laws and regulations.

Executive Order 12898 reinforces the 30-year-old Civil Rights Act of 1964, Title VI, which prohibits discriminatory practices in programmes receiving federal funds. The Order also focuses the spotlight back on the National Environmental Policy Act (NEPA), a 25-year-old law that sets policy goals for the protection, maintenance and enhancement of the environment. The NEPA's goal is to ensure for all Americans a safe, healthful, productive and aesthetically and culturally pleasing environment. The NEPA requires federal agencies to prepare a detailed statement on the environmental effects of proposed federal actions that significantly affect the quality of human health.

The Executive Order calls for improved methodologies for assessing and mitigating impacts and health effects from multiple and cumulative exposures, the collection of data on low-income and minority populations who may be disproportionately at risk, and impacts on subsistence fishers and wildlife consumers. It also encourages the participation of the affected populations in the various phases of impact assessment, including scoping, data gathering, alternatives, analysis, mitigation and monitoring.

The Executive Order focuses on 'subsistence' fishers and wildlife consumers. Not everybody buys their fish at the supermarket. There are many people who are subsistence fishers, fishing for protein, who basically subsidise their budgets and their diets by fishing from rivers, streams and lakes that happen to be polluted. These subpopulations may be underprotected when basic assumptions are made using the dominant risk paradigm.

THE CASE OF CITIZENS AGAINST NUCLEAR TRASH VERSUS LOUISIANA ENERGY SERVICES

Executive Order 12898 was put to the test in rural north-west Louisiana. Since 1989, the Nuclear Regulatory Commission had under review a proposal from Louisiana Energy Services (LES) to build the nation's first privately owned uranium enrichment plant. A national search was undertaken by LES to find the 'best' site for a plant that would produce 17% of the nation's enriched uranium. LES supposedly used an objective scientific method in designing its site selection process.

The southern USA, Louisiana and Claiborne Parish ended up being the dubious 'winners' of the site selection process. Residents from Homer and the nearby communities of Forest Grove and Center Springs—two communities closest to the proposed site—disagreed with the site selection process and outcome. They organised themselves into a group called Citizens Against Nuclear Trash (CANT). CANT charged LES and the federal Nuclear Regulatory Commission (NRC) staff with practising environmental racism. CANT hired the Sierra Club Legal Defense Fund and sued LES.

The lawsuit dragged on for more than 8 years. On 1 May 1997, a three-judge panel of the NRC Atomic Safety and Licensing Board issued a final decision on the case. The judges concluded that 'racial bias played a role in the selection process' (NRC, 1997). The precedent-setting federal court ruling came some 2 years after President Clinton signed Executive Order 12898. The judges, in a 38-page written decision, also chastised the NRC staff for not addressing the provision called for under Executive Order 12898. The court decision was upheld on appeal on 4 April 1998.

A clear racial pattern emerged during the so-called national search and multi-stage screening and selection process (Bullard, 1995). For example, African-Americans comprise about 13% of the US population, 20% of the Southern states' population, 31% of Louisiana's population, 35% of the population of Louisiana's northern parishes and 46% of the population of Claiborne Parish. This progressive trend, involving the narrowing of the site selection process to areas of increasingly high poverty and African-American representation, is also evident from an evaluation of the actual sites that were considered in the 'intermediate' and 'fine' screening stages of the site selection process. The aggregate average percentage of black population for a 1-mile radius around all of the 78 sites examined (in 16 parishes) was 28.35%. When LES completed its initial site cuts, and reduced the list to 37 sites within nine parishes (i.e. the same as counties in other states), the aggregate percentage of black population rose to 36.78%. When LES then further limited its focus to six sites in Claiborne Parish, the aggregate average percentage of black population rose again, to 64.74%. The final site selected, the 'LeSage' site, has a 97.1% black population within a 1-mile radius.

The plant was proposed on Parish Road 39 between two African-American communities, just 0.25 miles from Center Springs (founded in 1910) and 1.25 miles from Forest Grove (founded in the 1860s just after slavery). The proposed site was in a Louisiana parish that has a per capita earnings average of only $5800 per year (just 45% of the national average, $12,800), and where over 58% of the African-American population is below the poverty line. The two African-American communities were rendered 'invisible' since they were not even mentioned in the NRC's draft environmental impact statement (NRC, 1993).

Only after intense public comments did the NRC staff attempt to address environmental justice and disproportionate impact implications, as required under the NEPA and called for under Environmental Justice Executive Order 12898. For example, the NEPA requires that the government consider the environmental impacts and weigh the costs and benefits of the proposed action. These include health and environmental effects, the risk of accidental but foreseeable adverse health and environmental effects and socio-economic impacts.

The NRC staff devoted less than a page to addressing the environmental justice concerns of the proposed uranium enrichment plant in its final environmental impact statement (FEIS). Overall, the FEIS and the environmental report are inadequate in the following respects: (1) they assess inaccurately the costs and benefits of the proposed plant; (2) they fail to consider the inequitable distribution of costs and benefits of the proposed plant between the white and African-American populations; (3) they fail to consider the fact that the siting of the plant in a community of colour follows a national pattern in which institutionally biased decision-making leads to the siting of hazardous facilities in communities of colour, which results in the inequitable distribution of costs and benefits to those communities.

Among the distributive costs not analysed in relationship to Forest Grove and Center Springs are the disproportionate burden of health and safety, effects on property values, fire and accidents, noise, traffic, radioactive dust in the air and water, and the dislocation from a road closure that connects the two communities. Overall, the CANT legal victory points to the utility of combining environmental and civil rights laws and the requirement of governmental agencies to consider Executive Order 12898 in their assessments.

In addition to the remarkable victory over LES, . . . a company that had the backing of powerful US and European nuclear energy companies, CANT members and their allies won much more. They empowered themselves and embarked on a path of political empowerment and self-determination. During the long battle, CANT member Roy Madris was elected to the Claiborne Parish Jury (i.e., county commission), and CANT member Almeter Willis was elected to the Claiborne Parish School Board. The town of Homer, the nearest incorporated town to Forest Grove and Center Springs, elected its first African-American mayor, and the Homer town council now has two African-American members. In autumn 1998, LES sold the land on which the proposed uranium enrichment plant would have been located. The land is going back into timber production—as it was before LES bought it.

CONVENT RESIDENTS VERSUS SHINTECH PLANT

Battle lines are now drawn in Louisiana on another national environmental justice test case. The community is Convent and the company is Shintech. The Japanese-owned Shintech, Inc. has applied for a Title V air permit to build an $800 million polyvinyl chloride (PVC) plant in Convent, Louisiana—a community that is over 70% African-American and where over 40% of the residents fall below the poverty line. The community already has a dozen polluting plants and a 60% unemployment rate. The plants are very close to residents' homes. Industries are lured into the black community with the promise of jobs. But, in reality, the jobs are not there for local residents.

The Shintech case raises environmental racism concerns similar to those found in the failed LES siting scheme. The US EPA is bound by Executive Order 12898 to ensure that "no segment of the population, regardless of race, color, national origin, or income, as a result of EPA's policies, programs, and activities, suffer disproportionately from adverse health or environmental effects, and all people live in clean and sustainable communities". The Louisiana Department of Environmental Quality is also bound by federal laws to administer and implement its programmes, mandates and policies in a non-discriminatory way.

Any environmental justice analysis of the Shintech proposal will need to examine the issues of disproportionate and adverse impact on low-income and minority populations near the proposed PVC plant. Clearly, it is African-Americans and low-income residents in Convent who live closest to existing and proposed industrial plants and who will be disproportionately affected by industrial pollution (Wright, 1998). African-Americans comprise 34% of the state's total population. The Shintech plant would be located in a parish, St James Parish, that ranks third in the state for toxic releases and transfers. Over 83% of St James Parish's 4526 residents are African-

American. Over 17.7 million pounds of releases were reported in the 1996 toxic release inventory. The Shintech plant would add over 600,000 pounds of air pollutants annually. Permitting the Shintech plant in Convent would add significantly to the toxic burden borne by residents, who are mostly low-income and African-American.

After more than 18 months of intense organising and legal manoeuvering, residents of tiny Convent, Louisiana, and their allies forced Shintech to scrap plans to build the PVC plant. The decision came in September 1998, and was hailed around the country as a major victory against environmental racism. The driving force behind this victory was the relentless pressure and laser-like focus of the local Convent community.

CONCLUSION

The environmental protection apparatus in the USA does not provide equal protection for all communities. The current paradigm institutionalises unequal enforcement, trades human health for profit, places the burden of proof on the 'victims' and not on the polluting industry, legitimates human exposure to harmful chemicals, pesticides and hazardous wastes, promotes 'risky' technologies, exploits the vulnerability of economically and politically disenfranchised communities and nations, subsidises ecological destruction, creates an industry around risk assessment and delays clean-up actions, and fails to develop pollution prevention, waste minimisation and cleaner production strategies as the overarching and dominant goal.

The environmental justice movement emerged in response to environmental inequities, threats to public health, unequal protection, differential enforcement and disparate treatment received by the poor and people of colour. This movement has redefined environmental protection as a basic right. It has also emphasised pollution prevention, waste minimisation and cleaner production techniques as strategies to achieve environmental justice for all Americans without regard to race, colour, national origin or income.

Both race and class factors place low-income and people of colour communities at special risk. Unequal political power arrangements have also allowed poisons of the rich to be offered as short-term economic remedies for poverty of the poor. However, there is little or no correlation between the proximity of industrial plants in communities of colour and the employment of nearby residents. Having industrial facilities in one's community does not automatically translate into jobs for nearby residents. More often than not, communities of colour are stuck with the polluting industries and poverty, while other people commute in for the jobs.

Governments must live up to their mandate of protecting all peoples and the environment. The call for environmental and economic justice does not stop at US borders but extends to all communities and nations that are threatened by hazardous wastes, toxic products and environmentally unsound technology. The environmental justice movement has set out the clear goal of eliminating the unequal enforcement of environmental, civil rights and public health laws, the differential exposure of some populations to harmful chemicals, pesticides and other toxins in the home, school, neighbourhood and workplace, faulty assumptions in calculating, assessing and managing risks, discriminatory zoning and land-use practices, and exclusionary policies and practices that limit some individuals and groups from participation in decision-making.

The solution to environmental injustice lies in the realm of equal protection for all individuals, groups and communities. Many of these problems could be eliminated if existing environmental, health, housing and civil rights laws were vigorously enforced in a non-discriminatory way. No community, rich or poor, urban or suburban, black or white, should be allowed to become a 'sacrifice zone' or dumping ground.

REFERENCES

Agency for Toxic Substances and Disease Registry (1988) *The Nature and Extent of Lead Poisoning in Children in the United States: a report to Congress* (Atlanta, GA, US Department of Health and Human Services).

ALSTON, D. (1992) Transforming a movement: people of color unite at summit against environmental racism, *Sojourner,* 21(1), pp. 30–31.

ALSTON, D. & BROWN, N. (1993) Global threats to people of color, in: R. D. Bullard (Ed.) *Confronting Environmental Racism: voices from the grassroots* (Boston, MA, South End Press).

AUSTIN, R. & SCHILL, M. (1991) Black, brown, poor, and poisoned: minority grassroots environmentalism and the quest for eco-justice, *The Kansas Journal of Law and Public Policy,* 1(1), pp. 69–82.

BEASLEY, C. (1990a) Of pollution and poverty: keeping watch in cancer alley, *Buzzworm,* 2(4), pp. 39–45.

BEASLEY, C. (1990b) Of poverty and pollution: deadly threat on native lands, *Buzzworm,* 2(5), pp. 39–45.

BRYANT, B. & MOHAI, P. (1992) *Race and the Incidence of Environmental Hazards* (Boulder, CO, Westview Press).

BULLARD, R. D. (1993a) *Confronting Environmental Racism: voices from the grassroots* (Boston, MA, South End Press).

BULLARD, R. D. (1993b) Race and environmental justice in the United States, *Yale Journal of International Law,* 18(1), pp. 319–335.

BULLARD, R. D. (1993c) Environmental racism and land use, *Land Use Forum: a journal of law, policy & practice,* 2(1), pp. 6–11.

BULLARD, R. D. (1994) *Dumping in Dixie: race, class and environmental quality* (Boulder, CO, Westview Press).

BULLARD, R. D. (1995) Prefiled written testimony at the CANT vs. LES hearing, Shreveport, Louisiana.

BULLARD, R. D. (1996) *Unequal Protection: environmental justice and communities of color* (San Francisco, CA, Sierra Club Books).

BULLARD, R. D. & JOHNSON, G. S. (1997) *Just Transportation: dismantling race and class barriers* (Gabriola Island, BC, New Society Publishers).

COLLIN, R. W. (1992) Environmental equity: a law and planning approach to environmental racism, *Virginia Environmental Law Journal,* 13(4), pp. 495–546.

COLQUETTE, K. C. & ROBERTSON, E. A. H. (1991) Environmental racism: the causes, consequences, and commendations, *Tulane Environmental Law Journal,* 5(1), pp. 153–207.

Commission for Racial Justice (1987) *Toxic Wastes and Race in the United States* (New York, United Church of Christ).

GODSIL, R. D. (1990) Remedying environmental racism, *Michigan Law Review,* 90(394), pp. 394–427.

GOLDMAN, B. (1991) *The Truth about Where You Live: an atlas for action on toxins and mortality* (New York, Random House).

GOLDMAN, B. & FITTEN, L. J. (1994) *Toxic Wastes and Race Revisited* (Washington, DC, Center for Policy Alternatives, NAACP, United Church of Christ).

JOHNSON, B. L., WILLIAMS, R. C. & HARRIS, C. M. (1992) *Proceedings of the 1990 National Minority Health Conference: focus on environmental contamination* (Princeton, NJ, Scientific Publishing).

LAVELLE, M. & COYLE, M. (1992) Unequal protection, *The National Law Journal,* 21 September, pp. 1–2.

LEE, B. L. (1992) Environmental litigation on behalf of poor, minority children: *Matthews v. Coye:* a case study, paper presented at the Annual Meeting of the American Association for the Advancement of Science, Chicago, IL (9 February).

LEE, B. L. (1995) Civil rights remedies for environmental injustice, paper presented at the Transportation and Environmental Justice: building model partnerships Conference, Atlanta, GA (11 May).

LEE, C. (1992) *Proceedings: the First National People of Color Environmental Leadership Summit* (New York, United Church of Christ Commission for Racial Justice).

MANN, E. (1991) *LA's Lethal Air: new strategies for policy, organizing, and action* (Los Angeles, CA, Labor/Community Center).

National Institute for Environmental Health Sciences (1995) *Proceedings of the Health and Research Needs to Ensure Environmental Justice Symposium* (Research Triangle Park, NC, NIEHS).

NRC (1993) Draft Environmental Impact Statement for the Construction and Operation of Claiborne Enrichment Center, Homer, Louisiana, Docket No. 70-3070, Louisiana Energy Services, L.P. (November).

NRC (1997) Final initial decision—Louisiana Energy Services, US NRC, Atomic Safety and Licensing Board, Docket No. 70-3070-ML (1 May).

PIRKLE, J. L., BRODY, D. J., GUNTER, E. W., KRAMER, R. A., PASCHAL, D. C., GLEGAL, K. M. & MATTE, T. D. (1994) The decline in blood lead levels in the United States: the National Health and Nutrition Examination Survey (NHANES III), *Journal of the American Medical Association,* 272, pp. 284–291.

US EPA (1992) *Environmental Equity: reducing risk for all communities* (Washington, DC, US EPA).

US General Accounting Office (1983) *Siting of Hazardous Waste Landfills and Their Correlation with Racial and Economic Status of Surrounding Communities* (Washington, DC, Government Printing Office).

WEST, P., FLY, J. M., LARKIN, F. & MARANS, P. (1992) Minority anglers and toxic fish consumption: evidence of the state-wide survey of Michigan, in: B. Bryant & P. Mohai (Eds) *Race and the Incidence of Environmental Hazards* (Boulder, CO, Westview Press).

WRIGHT, B. H. (1998) *St. James Parish Field Observations* (New Orleans, LA, Deep South Center for Environmental Justice, Xavier University).

CRITICAL THINKING QUESTIONS

1. What is environmental racism? Explain why it is likely to affect poor people more than members of the middle class.

2. Why does environmental racism affect people of color more negatively than whites?

How does social class affect how people are negatively affected?

3. What environmental issues might draw people of different backgrounds together to fight against environmental racism?

Reading 3

The Ugly Side of the Modeling Business

Deborah Gregory and Patricia Jacobs

In this article, Gregory and Jacobs report on the activism of African-American models who fight prejudice and discrimination in the fashion industry.

On a chilly afternoon last winter, the atmosphere inside Club USA—one of New York City's hottest nightspots—matched the outdoor temperature, but for a different reason: America's Black supermodels were in revolt. The Black Girls Coalition (BGC), a consortium of fashion models formed in 1988 by supermodel Iman and former model Bethann Hardison (now owner of the modeling agency Bethann Management Co., Inc.) to aid the homeless, had chosen this site for a press conference to speak out on an issue that's been hidden beneath the glamour and glitter of the profession: namely, racism within the fashion and modeling business.

About 20 strong, almost all of BGC's members were in attendance—among them Karen Alexander, Cynthia Bailey, Tyra Banks, Kersti Bowser, Naomi Campbell, Peggy Dillard, Iman, Coco Mitchell, Gail O'Neill, Beverly Peele, Phina, Karla Otis, Akure Wall, Veronica

Source: Reprinted from *Essence* magazine 24, no. 5 (September 1993): 89–92.

Webb, Roshumba Williams and the designated leader, Bethann Hardison.

Also present were more than 100 members of the press representing Black and White American and European publications, who got an earful from the Black beauties gathered to expose the industry's ugly side. Accustomed to being seen and not heard, the models—who for the most part were stripped of their ready-to-work glamour-girl makeup—nonetheless took their turn at the podium and spoke candidly about the everyday injustices that exist within their "workplace."

Among the specific grievances addressed: the gross underrepresentation of African-Americans in fashion advertising (television commercials, billboards, magazines, catalogs, in-store promotions), designer shows and even the editorial pages of consumer magazines. "People don't realize there are hundreds of jobs related to the fashion industry, from being a makeup artist to scouting locations for a photo shoot," said a Black fashion editor at a women's magazine. "But you can practically count on both hands the number of Blacks who have any of these jobs in what's become a very closed arena." This is despite the fact that collectively African-Americans spend over $16 billion on clothing annually, according to the Consumer Expenditure Survey, and will represent approximately 13 percent of the total population by the year 2000, according to the U. S. Census Bureau.

WHAT PRICE BEAUTY?

As "soldiers" at the forefront of the style wars, the models also expressed outrage at other more subtle but unmistakable signs of racism that exist in their field: everything from the lack of Black behind-the-scenes fashion personnel—art directors, editors, designers, photographers—to being controlled around the clock right down to how they wear their locks, or indeed, told whether or not they can even wear "locks." Many, instead, are forced to wear wigs, falls and weaves.

"In more than ten years as a model," explained Coco Mitchell, "I've always had to look like what other people wanted me to look like, never how I wanted to." Most of the models admitted to being under pressure to have flowing hair that emulates that of the White models. Two have refused to give in to such pressure, however: Roshumba Williams and British-born Phina both wear their hair natural and closely cropped. Phina, in fact, stepped on these shores wearing her hair in spiky twists. "I wear my hair like this because I want to—not because I am militant, as I am so often told," she explains. "I think it's really sad that time and time again I'm asked to adhere to a certain look or value that is justifiable only to certain people." Adds Roshumba, "I'm constantly arriving at a photographer's studio and being told that I have to wear a wig." Roshumba, though, is one of the few Black models who still gets a lot of work while sporting her short natural.

The grievances of the Black models were dramatically supported in a groundbreaking study conducted by the City of New York's Depart-

ment of Consumer Affairs in 1991. The report, titled "Invisible People," looked at how often Blacks and other ethnic groups were used in magazine and catalog advertising—and the findings were shocking. A paltry 3.4 percent of all consumer-magazine advertisements depicted African-Americans—despite the fact that we comprise approximately 11.3 percent of the readership of all consumer magazines and 12.5 percent of the U. S. population.

In addition to its study, New York City's Department of Consumer Affairs conducted a special survey of repeat advertisers in 634 issues of general-circulation magazines and found that some of the most prolific fashion advertisers rarely, if ever, depict Blacks (or Asian-Americans) in their ads. And when they do, it is usually as stereotypes, not consumers. The companies included Calvin Klein (out of 148 ad insertions reviewed, none depicted "identifiable minorities"), Perry Ellis, Giorgio Armani, Gucci and Guess? by Georges Marciano. In the case of Calvin Klein, one of his ad campaigns in particular—which features White rapper Marky Mark and White model Kate Moss profiling in low-slung, oversize jeans—doesn't exactly have the rap-music community singing "Hip-hop hooray." After all, it was the Black rappers who created—and still perpetuate—the urbanized, flavorized look, yet no major advertising campaigns have come their way.

When asked about the Marky Mark advertising campaign, Calvin Klein asserted that "it wasn't about Marky Mark being a White or Black rapper, but more about his body than his music. He had been wearing the underwear in his concerts and the ads were capitalizing on something he started." Marky Mark's latest contract with Klein is triple the amount of the first—and Klein's sales are up about 30 percent.

One of the reasons that the gross inequity in fashion advertisements persists, says Consumer Affairs Commissioner Mark Green, is that the Department of Consumer Affairs has no legal jurisdiction to require that ads reflect the racial makeup of magazine readership in America. There are also no laws on the books that require advertisers to "fill quotas," although according to a survey of 470 marketing and media executives conducted by *Advertising Age,* the trade publication for the advertising industry, 54.8 percent agreed that there were too few Blacks in print ads, period.

THE EFFECT ON SELF-ESTEEM

There can be no doubt that the exclusion of Blacks from ads has had a negative impact, especially on our youths, who often feel little connection to the larger society. According to Marilyn Kern-Foxworth, a journalism professor at Texas A & M University and the author of an upcoming book on Blacks in advertising, "There's been a drastic erosion of self-esteem with young African-Americans—and it's partially because the images they see of themselves are either negative, offensive, or not there." Adds Michele Wallace, author of the book *Invisibility Blues: From Pop to Theory* (Routledge, 1990), "Not seeing our images reproduced—in particular in ads that constitute such a visible medium in our society—suggests to our children that we have no power, that having power is inconceivable."

Other areas of inequity, the models say, are fashion shows and even fashion layouts in magazines—and most notably fashion-magazine covers, on which Black models are rarely seen. For example, supermodel Tyra Banks, who has appeared on 17 magazine covers in Europe, has graced only two in the United States (including the June 1993 issue of this magazine). During the press conference for *Sports Illustrated*'s venerable swimsuit issue last winter, Banks, who was the only Black model featured in the issue, noted that *Sports Illustrated* has never had a Black or Asian model on the cover of the swimsuit issue in its nearly 30 years of publishing the special issue.

As for designer shows, at the fall-winter 1993 collections that took place in March in New York City, fewer Black models were seen on the runways than in any recent season gone by. (Coincidentally, many Black supermodels were seen for the first time in years either without weaves or with drastically shorter weaves—including Naomi Campbell and Beverly Peele.) Calvin Klein's collection, for example, featured only one model of color, Aya Thorgren, who is also one of the three models to appear in Revlon's ColorStyle ads. White designer Jennifer George, however, bucked the current grunge trend and tomboy, waiflike wave of innocent White models by using all Black models to show her collection.

One Black model who can afford to take a more militant position and turn down jobs from designers she considers racist is supermodel Naomi Campbell. "What I've started to do with certain designers who simply say they don't want Black girls—not individual models—is not do their shows and not wear their clothes, even in editorials [magazine fashion layouts that feature the clothes of a particular designer]," Campbell said at the BGC press conference. "I don't see why we [Black models] should make their clothes look good and then not be represented by them in any way." Campbell, however, one of the most popular and highest-paid models of any color in the industry, is still in demand, even when she turns down work. This is a claim few other Black models can make, and it limits their ability to take controversial stands.

ON THE GOOD SIDE

It would be unfair and inaccurate to suggest that there has been no progress for Blacks in the fashion industry during the last few years. Witness, for instance, the spanking-new Armani Exchange (AX) billboards and fashion ads profiling the cool beauty of Marvin Gaye's daughter, Nona Gaye. Or the new Ralph Lauren Safari fragrance campaign with Tyra Banks (one of the first high-profile designer-fragrance campaigns depicting a Black model in recent history) resplendent in florals amid colonial African chic. Or Liz Claiborne Jewelry ads (also with Tyra). Fernando Sanchez's lingerie ads feature sultry Kara Young, and Roshumba Williams is on the pages of the Tweeds catalogs and in the

Robert Lee Morris jewelry ads for Saks Fifth Avenue. On the downside, however, none of these manufacturers advertises in any of the Black publications.

The beauty industry, which has been somewhat better than the fashion industry in recognizing the financial clout of Black women, made history when some of the biggest cosmetics firms all launched major advertising campaigns featuring products for Black women: Maybelline (Shades of You), Cover Girl and Revlon (ColorStyle). Even better: Both Revlon and Cover Girl awarded Black supermodels Veronica Webb and Lana Ogilvie, respectively, exclusive contracts to advertise their products—a lucrative domain previously reserved for such White supermodels as Christy Turlington and Linda Evangelista.

In the final analysis, what it all comes down to is power—the power to change the things we can, and the power to choose what we will change. We can choose the clothes, accessories and beauty products we buy, for instance. And we can write letters to fashion and beauty manufacturers if those products or publications don't reflect our image.

Unfortunately, when approached by New York City's Department of Consumer Affairs following its study on the lack of people of color in print advertising, not one magazine or non-Black ad agency or advertiser would agree to sign a general pledge to depict people of color more accurately on their pages and in their advertisements. "We can only hope that our new appeal to advertisers will encourage them to act in their own economic interest as well as in the public interest by including more people of color in their product promotions," stated Commissioner Mark Green. "Ad agencies can exert considerable influence on the selection of models used in ads, but advertisers pay the bills and ultimately call the shots." And as Bethann Hardison points out "It's a rare White person who helps people of color forge ahead. We have to raise their consciousness and appeal to their humanity."

The Black male model Alvin Clayton-Fernandes does not order from those mail-order catalogs that never or seldom use Black male models. Civil-rights attorney Flo Kennedy believes in the power of the boycott: "If Blacks aren't represented in a particular clothing company's advertisements, don't buy from them," she says simply.

Ultimately, as consumers we can decide where to spend our fashion dollars. Now, more than ever, there are African-American designers manufacturing style that's available at retail or in catalogs or can be custom-made. From hip-hop gear to glamour gowns, African-American designers, such as Cross Colours, Byron Lars, Tracy Reese for Magaschoni, Shaka King and Ahneva Ahneva in California, are at the forefront of our style.

Only when "buying Black" becomes a regular part of our economic lifestyle will mainstream style setters get the message and recognize that racism is not only out of fashion in the beauty business but also will not be tolerated by all those people of color who help keep the bottom line black in a multi-billion-dollar clothing industry.

CRITICAL THINKING QUESTIONS

1. In what ways is discrimination practiced in the fashion industry? What are the effects of the under-representation of African-Americans in the fashion industry on minority youth, the African-American community, and society in general?

2. Many feminists argue that the fashion industry depicts women in unrealistic ways, which is harmful to the self-esteem of adolescent girls. Defend or refute the statement that African-American women are better off than white women when they are under-represented in the fashion industry.

3. Suggest some goals that African-American and white women might have in working together to change the fashion industry so that both groups benefit. Suggest goals that these two groups might have in common with white men in changing the industry so that all groups benefit.

Reading 4

Race, Gender, and Class: The Challenges Facing Labor Educators

Bill Fletcher, Jr.

In this article, Fletcher explores the history and successes of the labor union movement, with an emphasis on whether or not labor unions are willing to address issues at the intersection of race, gender, and social class.

... The U.S. trade union movement faces an immense challenge as it enters the twenty-first century. The working class is becoming browner and more female, yet this is rarely reflected in the upper echelons of the union movement. Additionally, with organized labor representing 14 percent of the non-agricultural workforce, a serious question remains as to whether the trade union movement will rise to the occasion and represent the interests of the vast majority of the working class, or in the alternative, will it only represent those who are fortunate enough to be organized. In this situation, labor educators are called upon to dispense with their former roles. The traditional and, unfortunately, marginal role of labor educators—at least since the 1950s—within the trade union movement must be challenged in its fundamentals. In a rapidly changing world, where most of the basic assumptions of the post-World War II era (the so-called "golden age of capitalism") have been thrown out or, at the very least, called into question, immense confusion exists within the ranks of organized labor. The confusion is on many levels, concerning issues such as the nature of the economy; who are the friends and enemies of the working class; and, at a very basic level (and paradoxically, with what is generally described in the media as a thriving economy), why will the conditions for our children be worse than they were for us.

In this globalized world, differences around race and gender have risen in importance and must be front and center on the agenda of the trade union movement. There is no question but that the material basis for unity both within the U.S. working class and with working classes in other countries has increased with globalization as neo-liberal capitalism increases the disparity of wealth, throws millions of people out of work, and forces us to work harder and faster just to stand still, driving us all in a race to the bottom. It is also the case that racial, national, ethnic, and gender tensions have grown as there has been an increase in the competition for scarce resources, and a search for enemies, in this brave new world order. Unless our members, not to mention non-union workers, come to understand the dynamics of the world economy, workers will be incapable of overcoming the differences among themselves. We will find ourselves victims of the machinations of the descendants of the robber barons of the nineteenth century, who warned—in the immortal words of Jay Gould—that they could buy one section of the working class to kill off the other.

Labor educators are faced with the challenge of fighting marginalization within the trade union movement and integrating the development of a pro-worker world view into every feature of trade union activity. Our roles can no longer be limited to offering technical trainings in the various aspects of contract administration, or being called in to orchestrate conferences or facilitate meetings, but must be expanded such that in every steward training,

Source: Reprinted from *Labor Studies Journal* 25, no. 1 (Spring 2000): 104–106.

we are talking about the dynamics of the world economy. In every training of union representatives/business agents, we are discussing how sections of the working class are "played off" against one another to the detriment of our common objectives. In every training for local union officers, we are discussing bargaining strategy, not simply with one company or agency, but with the global industry, and, as such, why international worker solidarity is more than rhetoric, but is of immediate and material importance. In every membership gathering, we are discussing with the members (rather than preaching at them), the reasons why the trade union movement cannot be agnostic on issues of racism or sexism, but that these issues, and the struggles against them, must be part of the lifeblood of trade unionism; otherwise we have no unity at all.

That labor educators were willing to have a serious discussion about the intersection of race, gender and class meant that the U.S. trade union movement is beginning to turn its head toward the sun rather than hide in the shadows of ignorance. The next steps, however, are the most critical ones. We must take our growing understanding of the significance of these issues for the future of the U.S. trade union movement and integrate them into the work we conduct and the practice which we hope to improve. We cannot retain this knowledge, as if we were some elite priesthood; our job is to engage the rest of the trade union movement in a debate as to its future; a future which acknowledges the intersection of race, gender, and class, and ties all this to the question of building real working class power in the U.S.A.

CRITICAL THINKING QUESTIONS

1. What concerns do members of the working class, women, and people of color share that can or should be addressed by labor unions? In your opinion, what, if anything, should unions do to address the concerns of sexual minorities and transgenders?

2. What barriers do labor unions face in actively engaging the concerns of women and people of color? What can they do to overcome these barriers?

3. How are all poor people and members of the working class harmed by divisions in the labor union movement?

Reading 5

Women of Color in Leadership

Helen Zia

> *In this article, Zia explores the common myth that the women's movement is a "white" movement and how this belief has discouraged many women of color from joining feminist organizations. She argues that even when women of color have become active in feminist organizations, they have encountered barriers that have prevented them from rising to positions of leadership. Zia contends that feminist groups must adopt policies that promote real representation of women of color.*

Not long ago I met a friend for a dinner. She, like me, is a woman of color, active in feminist causes. She had just been offered a high-ranking staff position at a leading feminist organization, but felt ambivalent about the job. At the time, she shook her head, saying, "I can't believe I'm going to work in the

Source: Reprinted from *Social Policy* 23, no. 4 (Summer 1993): 51–55.

women's movement. If you had told me a year ago I might do this, I'd say you were crazy."

My friend is not alone in that view. It is a false but widely held belief that the women's movement is a "white thing," and that "feminist of color" is oxymoronic. This misconception is largely the result of dual phenomena. On the one hand is the tendency of the news media to simplify and reduce social movements to a single image, with one organization and one woman as representative of all women so that—guess what?—all the "representative images" are white. On the other hand, European-American feminists for many reasons have not done such a good job of dispelling the "white only" myth, whether internally or externally to the women's movement. Any feminist of color can recite all too many tales of tokenism, insensitivity to racial issues and an apparent unwillingness to share power by white feminists.

Yet the truth is, women of color have been integral to the leadership of the women's movement. In the 19th century, Sojourner Truth, Harriet Tubman and Ida Wells Barnett were powerful voices for women's rights and spoke of the linkage between racism and sexism. In more recent times, there seems to be a collective amnesia about women of color like Pauli Murray, Flo Kennedy, Shirley Chisholm, Fannie Lou Hamer, Graciela Olivarez, Patsy Mink and many others who were instrumental to the founding of the National Organization for Women and the National Women's Political Caucus. Aileen Hernandez, an African American, was president of NOW from 1970 to 1971; Irene Natividad, an Asian American, headed NWPC from 1985 to 1989; Faye Wattleton, an African American, led Planned Parenthood from 1978 to 1992.

Within women-of-color communities, groups like the National Council of Negro Women have long stood for women's concerns, while organizations like the National Black Feminist Organization, the National Black Women's Health Project, Asian Pacific Islanders for Reproductive Health, the National Latinas Caucus, and the Native American Women's Health Education Project emerged during this feminist wave.

In the absence of a deliberate effort to reclaim this history, many women of all colors have accepted the notion that the women's movement is white. This adds to the sense of entitlement and ownership of the movement that European American women may already possess, further disempowering women of color in the process. Even worse, it places a feminist of color in a dilemma—she will not only have to contend with institutional and individual racism within the women's movement, she will also incur the judgment of her community that she is selling out to a "white" cause. It is this quandary that prevents many women of color from even imagining participation in the women's movement, not to mention taking a leadership role.

MYTH AND REALITY

It's not that women of color aren't present in mainstream women's groups in meaningful numbers and positions of responsibility. A sampling of some leading feminist organizations reveals the following numbers:

- American Association of University Women: 40 women of color in a staff of 95;
- Fund for the Feminist Majority: 7 women of color out of 22 employees;
- League of Women Voters: 11 women of color—including the executive director—and 2 men of color of 45 employees;
- National Abortion Rights Action League: 6 women of color and 2 men of color out of 34 paid positions, the chair of the board is African American, and 50 percent of the board are people of color;
- National Center for Lesbian Rights: 3 lesbians of color out of 8 staffers;
- National League for Nursing: 30 women of color out of nearly 200 employees, with an Asian American chief executive officer;
- National Organization for Women: 13 women of color out of 34 employees, 14 women of color on its 37–member board, 3 women of color of 50 state coordinators;

- National Women's Political Caucus: 3 women of color on a 15-member staff, all are clerical/support personnel;
- Women's Legal Defense Fund: 7 women of color out of 20 employees.

Staff representation is not necessarily proportionate to membership, but these numbers are nonetheless a significant contrast to the mythology that women of color are not present in the mainstream women's movement.

Unfortunately, without role models and their cumulative experiences in dealing with racism and sexism, the women of color in the mainstream movement usually end up having to reinvent the same strategies to deal with the same kinds of situations. For example, when Irene Natividad was elected president of NWPC, she used her political savvy to navigate "not being minority enough for women of color, while white women rolled their eyes whenever [she] mentioned racial issues." During Aileen Hernandez's tenure at NOW, she constantly struggled to broaden the scope of "women's issues"—a necessity for activists who are involved in multiple communities. We need to learn from their solutions, not to reinvent them.

BUILDING YOUR OWN BASE

Today when feminists of color are not able to find workable solutions to issues within mainstream women's organizations, some may conclude that the women's movement is hopelessly white and hopelessly racist. But survivors of such alienating trench warfare nevertheless warn against such sweeping generalizations. "As each group of women of color discovers feminism, they believe that they discover the women's movement is racist," says Loretta Ross, who was NOW's first director of its women-of-color program. "It damages our cause to adopt an ahistorical view that the women's movement is white, which it is not. We sometimes confuse our critique of white women with a critique of feminism, as though white women and feminism are the same."

When Ross was at NOW, she built her own grassroots support network to serve as her power base—a strategy she recommends for other women of color. "Women of color who work in mainstream women's groups have to be ready for a long haul," she says. "They have to do their homework on the inner politics of the organization, to learn how to get power and how to use it. Women of color have to give up the notion that white women can do something for us. The task is to build a constituency."

A case in point is Karen Johnson, an African American who heads NOW's national racial diversity committee. She joined NOW in 1975, and was active in the San Antonio chapter. She served on the Texas NOW state council, was elected to the national board of directors, became vice president of action of another state council, and currently works on a national committee.

In other words, the politics of working in women's organizations is just like politics anywhere else, though of course feminist groups claim to uphold equal rights for all. The inattention to this principle has led some women of color to quit mainstream women's groups to organize very successful autonomous groups. When Billye Avery left the National Women's Health Network to form the National Black Women's Health Project, she created a powerful base from which to advocate for African American women's health concerns. By creating our own organizations, women of color can work as equals in coalition with counterparts from mainstream women's groups, while maintaining control of our own issues. In doing so, an additional benefit is the enhancement of the position of women of color working inside mainstream women's groups.

However, recognition by women of color that politics within the women's movement can be as down and dirty as other organizations does not take the heat off mainstream groups when it comes to dealing with issues of racism, in all its subtleties; women of color should expect feminist groups to deal with internal racism just as feminists expect other institutions to deal with internal sexism.

ADDRESSING THE ISSUES

On an institutional level, feminist groups must adopt policies that promote real representation of women of color; some groups, for example, have written such policies into their by-laws. They must pursue aggressive programs—not fringe activities—that reach women of color; they must make a conscious effort to address such issues of concern to women of color as racism, equal justice, immigration, economics. And they must work in coalition with other groups that address these issues, and devote money and other resources to promote such programs.

At the attitudinal level, women of color demand environments free from harassing or intimidating behavior—the same commitment we demand from male-dominated institutions. But that doesn't mean women of color won't have to deal one-on-one with close encounters of the racial kind. When Irene Natividad ran for the presidency of the NWPC, she didn't get the support of one of the more liberal caucuses because she presented the "wrong image" for the group; yet when one of her white opponents pulled out of the race after falling behind Natividad, she claimed she "didn't want to stand in the way of a woman of color."

Presenting the "right image" is a common euphemism for the assumption that "feminism" equals "white." When *Ms.* magazine featured on its cover a woman of color and her daughter as an example of a feminist mother and daughter, the question was raised whether "most" readers could "identify" with the image. Fortunately, the cover stayed.

Breaking through some of the informal friendship and support networks is another critical leadership issue, much as breaking down the old boys' networks at men-only clubs has been for all women. In Washington, DC, the prestigious Presidents Council—made up of the presidents of the major feminist organizations—is mostly monochromatic. Various other old girls' clubs exist throughout the women's movement, and more often than not, they are white-only. As an alternative, women of color in Washington have formed their own network, the Women of Color Leadership Council, which is open to all women of color involved in feminism.

BEYOND THE "OLD GIRLS" NETWORK

It is on this personal level that some of the most difficult choices must be made by European-American feminists. In 1990, when a young Korean American feminist reporter confronted Jimmy Breslin about some sexist columns he had written, he exploded in the newsroom in a white rage, screaming a string of racist and sexist epithets at the woman. While Asian-American, African-American and Latino groups rallied to her support, not a single feminist organization spoke up in what had begun, after all, over Breslin's gender-biased comments. One reason for the silence: Breslin's wife, a local politician who jumped to his defense, was an active player in the feminist old girls' network. The club disappointingly, though not surprisingly, failed to respond.

The women's movement as a whole still has a long way to go when it comes to women of color in leadership. As Loretta Ross points out, many women of color can't stomach the racism any more than they can stand the sexism of the civil rights movement. In 1979, Aileen Hernandez recommended that Black women not join NOW until it clearly demonstrated more concern to issues of women of color, and until its leadership included more women of color. Hernandez herself has not rejoined NOW, though, she cautions, this means little since no single organization represents the women's movement.

Still, as the numbers show, there has been some progress. At NOW, Ginny Montez, an Afro-Honduran American, is within striking distance of the presidency. And my friend, who accepted the influential position at a mainstream women's organization, has not only found the job to be a positive experience overall, but has been able to assist other women of color, both programmatically and by her example, in addition to her work on behalf of all women. That's what the leadership of women of color can mean.

CRITICAL THINKING QUESTIONS

1. What contributions have African-American women made to the feminist movement? Why have they and other women of color had difficulties in getting the feminist movement to represent their concerns?

2. What are the barriers that confront African-American women seeking leadership positions in the feminist movement?

3. How might women of color work with the civil rights movement, lesbians in the gay and lesbian movement, and transgenders in that movement to get their concerns addressed? What keeps these groups from forming stronger alliances?

Reading 6

The Rise of the Workplace Movement: Fighting for Lesbian, Gay, and Bisexual Rights in Corporate America*

Nicole C. Raeburn

> *In this article, Raeburn explores the development, strategies, and achievements of gay and lesbian employee organizations among Fortune 1000 companies.*

Despite the backlash against gay and lesbian rights occurring across the United States, a rapidly expanding number of corporations are including sexual orientation in nondiscrimination policies, adding sexual orientation to diversity training, and extending health insurance and other benefits to domestic partners of lesbian and gay employees. Equitable bene-

*This work draws from Chapters 1 and 2 of the author's book, *Inside Out: The Struggle for Lesbian, Gay, and Bisexual Rights in the Workplace* (forthcoming from University of Minnesota Press). The author gratefully acknowledges the following sources of financial support for this project: a National Science Foundation Doctoral Dissertation Research Grant; an American Sociological Association/National Science Foundation Fund for the Advancement of the Discipline Award; a Martin P. Levine Memorial Dissertation Fellowship Honorable Mention from the Sex and Gender Section of the American Sociological Association; and various scholarly and financial awards from the Ohio State University.

fits, often referred to as domestic partner benefits, represent the latest expansion in the definition of workers' rights. My study of "Fortune 1000" companies reveals that the majority of equitable benefits adopters instituted this policy change only after facing internal pressure from mobilized groups of lesbian, gay, and bisexual employees (see also Baker, Strub, and Henning 1995).

With a fledgling start in the late 1970s and early '80s, when only two major corporations witnessed the birth of gay employee networks, by the late 1980s, small numbers of lesbians and gay men began to mobilize for inclusive policies and practices in their places of work. Still, by the end of that decade, only ten gay employee groups had sprung up among the Fortune 1000. By the late 1990s, however, the numbers had swelled to over 80 documented networks, which together constitute a pioneering force for social change. Serving as powerful reminders that the state is not the sole contested terrain, these "institutional activists" (Santoro and McGuire 1997) demonstrate that committed individuals "do" politics not simply on the streets or in voting booths but in the cubicles, offices, and board rooms of companies across the country.

Amidst the longstanding backlash against gay rights in the U.S. (Adam 1995; Vaid 1995; Epstein 1999), how did the workplace movement take off and gain enough visibility and partial success such that the *New York Times* referred to gay-inclusive corporate policies as "the workplace issue of the '90s" (Baker et al. 1995)? To answer this question, I first discuss the patterned emergence and diffusion of lesbian and gay employee networks among the Fortune 1000 in relation to four main areas: the wider sociopolitical context, the larger gay and lesbian movement, the media, and institutional openings in the workplace. I then briefly address the development of interorganizational linkages among gay employee networks beginning in the early '90s. I close with a summary of the remarkable successes that the workplace movement has achieved thus far, particularly the adoption of equitable benefits in a rapidly growing number of companies. My multimethod approach utilizes surveys of 94 Fortune 1000 corporations with and without gay networks, intensive interviews with vice presidents of human resources and gay employee activists, a small number of case studies, print and virtual media on gay-related workplace topics, and extensive field data gathered from attendance at multiple workplace conferences and employee network meetings.

THE RISE AND GROWTH OF THE CORPORATE WORKPLACE MOVEMENT

Examining the number of lesbian, gay, and bisexual employee groups that have emerged each year among Fortune 1000 companies re-veals a distinctive patterning of network formations across time. Organizational births are clustered within three main periods such that the trajectory of corporate organizing can be described as follows: (1) a slow rise between 1978 and 1989; (2) rapid growth from 1990 to 1994; and (3) a decline in new organizing from 1995 to mid 1998 (when data collection ended).

During the first wave of the workplace movement, between 1978 and 1989, only 10 gay networks appeared among the Fortune 1000. The slow rate of mobilization over that 12-year stretch contrasts sharply with the next 5 years, which witnessed the birth of 50 new groups from 1990 through 1994. Put differently, while during the first wave of mobilization the organizational founding rate was less than one new group per year, that figure climbed to 10 per year between 1990 and 1994. Examining the distribution trends from the perspective of the entire organizational sample (n = 69), only 14 percent of corporate networks were born during the first wave compared to 72 percent in the second.

The third period of the workplace movement is marked by a significant decline in the pace of new organizing. Only 9 employee groups emerged between 1995 and mid 1998, which represents only 13 percent of the total sample. At first glance the decrease may appear to be an artifact of unequal time comparisons (5 years in period 2 versus 3.5 years in period 3). But this does not explain the fact that the organizational birth rate dropped from 10 new networks per year in the second wave to less than 3 per year in the third.

All of these contrasting patterns will begin to make sense when viewed through the trifocal lens of the shifting political climate, the actions of the broader gay and lesbian movement, and the variable conditions present in other institutional spheres. For now, it bears mentioning that by the end of the third period, after over 20 years of workplace mobilization, gay and lesbian employee groups had emerged in 85 documented Fortune 1000 companies, 69 of which are included in this study.

The Sociopolitical Context of Corporate Organizing

As political opportunity theorists suggest, shifts in the wider political environment help to explain the emergence and trajectory of social movements (Jenkins and Perrow 1977; Tilly 1978; McAdam 1982; Katzenstein and Mueller 1987; Tarrow 1989, 1998; McAdam, McCarthy, and Zald 1996). The rise of the gay and lesbian workplace movement and the distinctive patterns of network formation over the past 20 years likewise reflect changes in the broader sociopolitical context.

The New Right and the first wave of employee activism.   The tentative pace of early corporate organizing is hardly surprising given the rise of the New Right in the late 1970s and its consolidation of power in the 1980s. Mobilized around fiscally and socially conservative goals, including the defense of traditional gender and sexual norms, and drawing from a broad network of well organized single-issue groups, evangelical Christians, and various members of the corporate elite, the New Right took aim at the gains that had been made by the gay liberation movement in the 1970s (Adam 1995; Epstein 1999). Beginning with Anita Bryant's highly publicized "Save Our Children" campaign in 1977, which resulted in the repeal of a gay rights ordinance in Dade County, Florida, a wave of similar repeals spread across the United States (Adam 1995). The day after the Dade County repeal, California state senator John Briggs introduced the infamous Briggs Initiative, which aimed to purge the school system of gay men and lesbians as well as anyone who presented homosexuality in a positive light (D'Emilio 1992).

In response to the growing anti-gay backlash, 300,000 people turned out for San Francisco's Gay Pride Day in 1978 (D'Emilio 1992:89), and over 30 organizations sprang up across the state to fight the initiative (Epstein 1999:47), a groundswell of mobilization that historian John D'Emilio (1992:89) described

as "the most far-reaching and sustained gay organizing campaign" the movement had ever seen. Later that same year, Dan White, a disgruntled former member of the San Francisco Board of Supervisors and former police officer, assassinated Mayor George Moscone and City Supervisor Harvey Milk, one of the first openly gay office-holders in the country. When White received a manslaughter rather than murder conviction, five to ten thousand people marched on City Hall (D'Emilio 1992:92), where some smashed windows and others torched police cars to express their rage at the injustice (Adam 1995).

It was during that turbulent year of 1978 that the earliest known gay employee group formed in corporate America. Not surprisingly, its location was California, as was the case for four of the ten employee networks that emerged during the first wave of the workplace movement. During the same year, the organization then known as the National Gay Task Force released the first movement study of anti-gay workplace discrimination in the private sector. Nonetheless, aside from the second corporate network that formed in 1980, the next five years of that decade produced no other gay employee groups.

The stunted growth of the workplace movement may have stemmed from the recession of the early '80s as well since economic downturns make it more difficult for progressive social movements to advance their cause (Ryan 1992:68; Taylor and Rupp 1993; Adam 1995; Whittier 1995). Lesbians and gay men were already concerned for their economic livelihoods given their vulnerability to job loss and other forms of anti-gay employment discrimination (Weinberg and Williams 1974; Levine 1979, 1992; Lewis 1979; Blumstein and Schwartz 1983; Levine and Leonard 1984; Schneider 1984, 1986, 1988; Woods 1993; Badgett 1995; Taylor and Raeburn 1995). How much stronger the fear of coming out must have been when compounded by the rising rate of unemployment generally.

But an even more direct explanation for the five-year hiatus in corporate organizing can be found in the New Right's consolidation of power in the early '80s. The presidential election of Ronald Reagan in 1980 and the announcement of a renewed anti-gay campaign by Jerry Falwell's Moral Majority served to entrench the New Right (D'Emilio 1992), thereby forcing the gay and lesbian movement to focus on defensive rather than proactive measures (Adam 1995). Struggling against the powerful conservative momentum of the Reagan era and the rise of the AIDS epidemic, gay and lesbian activists concentrated not on gaining recognition in the workplace but rather on preventing further assaults on gay rights, battling the deadening silence of the media and political establishment over AIDS from 1981 to 1983, and then defending against the widespread panic and virulently anti-gay attacks that followed once word of the epidemic hit the news (Adam 1995; Epstein 1999).

Thus the first two gay employee networks, both in the high-tech industry, remained the solitary representatives of the corporate workplace movement from 1980 until well into the second term of Ronald Reagan, when they were finally joined by a slow trickle of other gay networks beginning in 1986. By 1989, lesbian, gay, and bisexual employees had mobilized in 10 Fortune 1000 companies. The workplace movement was thus re-awakening from the doldrum years of the early to mid '80s, a period of "abeyance," to borrow Verta Taylor's (1989) term, during which activists had been forced into a holding pattern amidst an unreceptive political climate (see also Rupp and Taylor [1987] 1990).

The revival of corporate activism by the end of the 1980s came on the heels of what Barry Adam (1995:130) called the "faltered" momentum of the New Right in the middle of the decade. These changes, compounded by sex scandals among the Christian fundamentalist leadership of the Right beginning in 1987 and Pat Robertson's failure to obtain the Republican presidential nomination in 1988, portended a shifting political environment. Lesbians and gay men then increasingly mobilized "in all spheres of civil society . . . at work, in communities, in churches, in health and social services, in sport, and in the media, education, and the arts" (Adam 1995:130).

Clinton's rise to office and the second wave of employee activism. The second wave of the workplace movement is marked by a significant jump in corporate organizing beginning in 1990, which ushered in a five-year period of rapid growth and diversification. While during the first wave of the movement it took 12 years to produce 10 gay networks, the year 1990 alone brought 10 more groups, starting a growth trend that would continue throughout the second wave of mobilization such that by 1994, 60 networks had formed among the Fortune 1000. The relative explosion of corporate organizing during the second wave corresponds to the changing political climate that eventually brought William Clinton to the presidency.

Beginning in the early '90s, the larger gay and lesbian movement encountered a more favorable set of environmental conditions, including the aggressive courting of the gay vote by Clinton (Vaid 1995). Openly gay people were prominent on Clinton's campaign team and his list of presidential appointments (Epstein 1999). Discussing other significant openings in the structure of political opportunity for the gay rights movement, Sidney Tarrow (1994) notes the split among the political elite over the definition of "family values," the electoral realignment of 1992 that brought a Democrat into the White House after 12 years of Republican occupancy, Clinton's attempt to end the longstanding military ban on gay and lesbian service members (see also Korb 1996), and the increasing presence of gay-friendly allies among civil rights groups, the women's movement, and various members of Congress.

Just days after the election, President Clinton sent a letter to the National Gay and Lesbian Task Force (NGLTF) in which he thanked members for their advocacy work and campaign support, asked for help in implementing positive change, and extended a warm welcome to those who were attending the organization's annual Creating Change conference. Describing both the immediate impact and wider significance of Clinton's gesture, one audience member later reflected, "When Urvashi Vaid [then NGLTF director] read Bill Clinton's letter . . . the crowd went wild. The President Elect's letter to *us,* lesbian, bisexual, and gay activists from all over the U.S., was at once a recognition of the role of our community in his victory and a positive sign for the future" (Bain 1992a:7; emphasis in the original).

New strategies of the Right. In 1992 the workplace movement experienced a different kind of jolt following passage of Colorado's Amendment Two. A statewide ballot initiative that legally banned civil rights protection for lesbians, gay men, and bisexuals, the measure overturned gay rights laws that had been passed in Aspen, Boulder, and Denver (Adam 1995:133; Dugan 1999). While the lesbian and gay movement was accustomed to battling the repeal of gay rights ordinances, this measure and others like it in Oregon and later in Idaho and Cincinnati, Ohio, represented a new form of legislation "that sought to make it legally impossible for gay rights laws ever to be established" (Epstein 1999:68; see also Blain 1997 and Dugan 1999). Although in 1996 the United States Supreme Court ruled the Colorado amendment unconstitutional, its passage in 1992 by 53 percent of voters led outraged lesbian and gay activists to issue a national boycott against travel to the state (Epstein 1999:68).

Nine new employee groups (13 percent of the current sample) emerged in the Fortune 1000 that year, making it the third most "fertile" year of the workplace movement's 20-year history. Commenting on the mobilizing impact of the legislation, one Colorado-based activist explained, "after voters in my district supported Amendment Two, I decided it was time for a gay employee resource group at my company." While none of the other employee networks that formed that year were located in Colorado, the New Right's success in passing a more insidious form of anti-gay legislation created a wave of gay and lesbian mobilization that reverberated across state lines and into corporations around the country.

The Impact of the Larger Gay, Lesbian, and Bisexual Movement

Taking it to the streets . . . and into the workplace. Situated within nested political environments, the workplace movement faces windows of opportunities and walls of constraint that stem not simply from actions of the state and of countermovements but also from the efforts of the wider lesbian, gay, and bisexual movement. Just as suddenly imposed grievances can incite activism, so too can movement protest itself lead to increased and more widespread mobilization (Sawyers and Meyer 1999). For example, the cluster of first-wave employee groups that sprang up during the late '80s followed the record-breaking turnout for the second National Gay and Lesbian March on Washington in 1987. In response to the New Right's vitriolic attacks and the ever expanding AIDS crisis, and in the aftermath of the *Bowers v. Hardwick* Supreme Court decision in 1986 that upheld sodomy statutes and denied lesbians and gays the right to privacy, anywhere from half a million to over 650,000 people descended on the Capitol to demand justice, equality, and a cure (D'Emilio 1992:267; Vaid 1995:99; Epstein 1999).

The radical presence at the march of newly formed ACT UP (AIDS Coalition to Unleash Power), a direct action, grassroots coalition, and the participation of 5000 activists at the national Civil Disobedience Action the following day at the Supreme Court (Vaid 1995:99), attracted considerable media attention. ACT UP expanded the strategic repertoire of the movement by reincorporating tactics that had been abandoned after the heyday of gay liberation (D'Emilio 1992; Berzon 1994; Epstein 1999). As ACT UP's "SILENCE = DEATH" slogan diffused rapidly to the public spaces of mainstream America, its message struck a responsive chord among many.

Once connected through AIDS organizing, and once empowered to be visible, many gay men and lesbians decided to mobilize in their own places of work (Stewart 1991; Meyerson and Scully 1995; Swan 1997; Scully and Creed 1998). The first gay network to emerge in a utility company, for example, grew out of the efforts of six employees who had persuaded their west coast employer to sponsor an internal AIDS hotline. Although one of the founders was a gay rights activist who had previously worked for a civil rights organization, the gay employee network started out as a purely social group. Shortly thereafter, however, members took on explicitly political aims both within and outside of the company. Many other gay networks in the Fortune 1000 likewise began as informal "support groups," but members soon expanded their goals, renamed themselves "diversity networks" or "employee resource groups" (the terms commonly used by preexisting networks for women and people of color), and sought meetings with corporate elites about the need for gay-inclusive policies (see also Swan 1997).

As alluded to above, however, the birth of several gay employee networks in the late '80s after a five-year hiatus came not simply from the mobilizing carry-overs of the AIDS epidemic. The 1987 March on Washington fanned the flames of that organizing impulse. As activist-writer Urvashi Vaid (1995:99) explained, the march and day-long demonstrations of civil disobedience "ignited gay and lesbian activism" in local communities across the country and in multiple institutional spheres, sparking a trend of movement growth and organizational diversification that continued well into the next decade. Movement scholar John D'Emilio (1992:267) commented eloquently on the impact of the 1987 march:

[T]he weekend in Washington proved uncontainable. The display of the Names Project quilt, the massive wedding ceremony at the National Cathedral, and the impressive parade of contingents from every state in the nation, struck a chord of self-respect so deep that it could not be ignored. People returned to their home communities transformed, ready to do what seemed unimaginable a few days before.

D'Emilio's words ring true in the founding account of the largest lesbian and gay employee group in the country, which I refer to as "GLUE" (Gay and Lesbian United Employees). Located in a telecommunications company and formed in 1987 by a small circle of friends who had attended the march that year, by 1996 the network had over 2000 members in 30 chapters across the U.S. Even though the organization's membership was reduced after the corporation split into separate companies, GLUE is still the largest network in the movement with 1300 members and 28 chapters nationwide. The 1987 March on Washington made such an impression on the founders that even their informational brochure mentions its significance. As explained in the pages of the flyer, GLUE's first chapter formed after some friends in the company who had been meeting informally "returned home from the March on Washington inspired, energized, and convinced that they could change their part of the world . . . that they could make [their company] a place that welcomed ALL of its employees!" (emphasis in the original).

We're here, we're queer, we're fabulous, get used to us. . . . Although GLUE witnessed the emergence of gay employee groups in six other companies between 1987 and 1989, it was not until the 1990s that gay networks began to appear in far greater numbers, due in part to an attention-grabbing development in the wider lesbian and gay movement. In 1990, word spread like wildfire about a new social movement organization called Queer Nation. Formed in New York City, where it mobilized large and visible demonstrations against gay bashings, the group distributed 15,000 flyers at the New York Lesbian and Gay Pride Parade (Epstein 1999:60). News of Queer Nation's loud and raucous entry at the pride march traveled fast, and "within days it seemed that groups calling themselves Queer Nation were springing up around the country" (Gross 1993:82, as cited in Epstein 1999:60).

Adopting a grassroots, direct action, "in-your-face" style of organizing and a binary-smashing position that rejected the notion of fixed sexual identities, Queer Nation was a purposeful reaction against the mainstream tactics and essentialist stance of the larger gay and lesbian rights movement (J. Gamson 1995). As a means of challenging what queer theorists have called heteronormativity (Ingra-ham 1994), Queer Nation claimed public—and implicitly heterosexualized—space by holding "kiss-ins" or "queer-ins" while leaflet-ing at shopping malls and bars (Epstein 1999). Posting neon-colored stickers and wearing t-shirts with confrontational slogans such as "queers bash back," members popularized the "we're here, we're queer" chant that now echoes through the crowds of marchers at pride parades across the country (Faderman 1991; Podolsky 1994; Vaid 1995).

The corporate activism that took off in the early '90s and gathered momentum through-out the second wave was, to be sure, a far cry from the transgressive style of queer politics. Nevertheless, the rise of Queer Nation and its offshoots in 1990 and the heightened militancy of ACT UP injected a new energy into the lifeblood of the larger movement, garnering an increased visibility that facilitated multiple forms of organizing. Ten gay employee groups (15 percent of the current total) formed among the Fortune 1000 in 1990, making it the second most prolific year of the workplace movement. Of course, this eruption of corporate organiz-ing was generated not simply by a spillover of ac-tivist energy from the streets to the workplace. The second wave was fueled as well by the mo-mentous turning of the media spotlight to gay and lesbian employment issues. Although queer activists were not solely responsible for this pivotal shift in media attention, their suc-cess in generating mainstream visibility clearly benefitted the campaign for equal rights in the workplace.

Mainstream media's "Year of the Queer." In a published chronicle of the lesbian and gay movement, 1990 earned the title "Year of the Queer" given the unprecedented media cov-erage of gay activism (Rouilard 1994). While media attention to movement concerns is often a crucial component of successful mobi-lization, such visibility can be exceedingly dif-ficult to come by (McCarthy and Zald 1977; McAdam 1996). Why then, in 1990, did the mainstream news establishment suddenly de-vote so much air time to queer politics?

In fact, that year queer activists targeted the media establishment directly, issuing charges of bias against the *New York Times,* the *Wash-ington Post,* and other major news carriers (Rouilard 1994:358; Vaid 1995:201). Well aware that media discourse can be harmful if coverage presents a "biased and ridiculed picture of the movement" (Klandermans and Goslinga 1996:319; see also Gitlin 1980), gay and lesbian activists mobilized within and against the main-stream media. Queer Nation, ACT UP, the Na-tional Gay and Lesbian Task Force, *OutWeek* magazine, and organized groups of lesbian and gay journalists challenged the media giants on inaccurate reporting, urged more extensive coverage of the gay community and movement, and pushed for nondiscrimination in unem-ployment (Rouilard 1994:358; Vaid 1995:201).

News executives had also been facing pres-sure from the Gay and Lesbian Alliance Against Defamation (GLAAD), which formed in 1985 to push for fairness and accuracy in the media. By 1992, the *Los Angeles Times* described GLAAD as "possibly the most successful orga-nization lobbying the media for inclusion" (GLAAD 1999). It seems likely, therefore, that the increased and more accurate coverage of gay issues beginning in 1990 stemmed in part from the self-interest of major corporate play-ers in the news industry, who were defending against public attacks that threatened their reputation as upholders of the highest jour-nalistic standards.

But expanded media access also came in response to another important force, namely, innovations in the strategic repertoire of the lesbian, gay, bisexual, and transgender move-ment. Due to the increasingly creative sym-bolic politics of "self-proclaimed queers" who were "seasoned media-savvy activists" (Rouilard 1994:357), the movement finally met what Doug McAdam (1996:346) has called "the first requirement of media coverage": it had achieved the title "newsworthy" in the eyes of media gatekeepers. Faced with tight resources and restricted access to advertising as well as media indifference to the ideologies or collective action frames that justify mobilization (Snow, Rochford, Worden, and Benford 1986; Gamson 1992a,b), not to mention the ratings-driven emphasis of news producers (McCarthy, Smith, and Zald 1996), movements must often resort to "extraordinary techniques to gain coverage" (Molotch 1979:91; see also W. Gamson 1995; J. Gamson 1998). In other words, and rather ironically, outsiders have to disrupt the public order in order to gain mainstream visibility.

As the flashy new tactics of queer activists grew ever more spectacular—figuratively and literally in the sense of a "media spectacle" (see McCarthy, Smith, and Zald 1996:309)— they brought much needed visibility not only to the street fighters themselves but to gay and lesbian issues in general. Given the dramatically disruptive nature of myriad queer actions in 1990, major television networks and newspapers suddenly began to focus on the concerns of lesbian and gay people, including their experiences with employment discrimination (Rouilard 1994). In the words of activist and writer Richard Rouilard (1994:357), "Week after week, we were six o'clock news." From AIDS activists interrupting the Rose Parade in Pasadena, California; challenging President Bush during his first speech on AIDS; halting traffic on the Golden Gate Bridge during rush hour and deadlocking 14,000 cars; to street protestors issuing a national boycott of Miller beer and Marlboro cigarettes for manufacturer Philip Morris' corporate donations to anti-gay senator Jesse Helms, the movement in 1990 at last grabbed the serious attention of the media (Rouilard 1994:357-358; Thompson 1994:359-360).

Understanding all too well that an action without media publicity amounts to a "non-event" (W. Gamson ([1995] 1997:235), Queer Nation and ACT UP planned numerous and dazzling demonstrations that made for good copy, thereby winning extraordinary coverage in mainstream news outlets (Rouilard 1994). Certainly the media framing was not always favorable, but as William Gamson ([1995] 1997:235) has so aptly put it, "No news is bad news." Whether positive or negative, media attention validates challengers as "important players" (p. 235). When in 1990 queer activism hit the news as never before, employee mobilization spiked as well. Indeed, the splash of queer actions that generated widespread press coverage in 1990 created a ripple effect as major business publications then turned their attention to sexual orientation issues in the workplace.

We're here, we're gay, and professional we'll stay. . . . Aside from winning expanded media access, queer activists provided additional aid to corporate challengers in the form of a radical flank effect (Haines 1988). Many employee activists reasoned that their "professional" requests for equality at work seemed far less threatening to corporate elites than did the militant stance of queer activists. Explicitly contrasting their tactics with those of ACT UP or Queer Nation, employee respondents repeatedly emphasized that network members always behaved "professionally" and never made "demands." While respecting the boldness of these radical groups—at times even expressing a frustrated desire to adopt similar strategies—most employee activists nonetheless defined their own collective identity through a distancing from queer politics. Queer radicals thus simultaneously inspire workplace activism and temper its apparent threat to corporate elites who, when faced with both kinds of challengers, see moderation and professionalism in one and extremism and bad press in the other.

And the movement marches on. . . . Much like the shot in the arm that the birth of Queer Nation delivered in 1990, the third national

Lesbian, Gay, and Bisexual March on Washington in 1993 stimulated the largest growth spurt that the workplace movement has ever experienced. Depending on the estimates used, the march drew to the Capitol anywhere from 300,000 to 1,000,000 participants (Epstein 1999:68). The enthusiasm generated by the march obviously carried over into the workplace wing of the movement. While in 1990 10 new gay networks had formed among the Fortune 1000, followed by 6 more in 1991 and 9 others in 1992, the number of organizational births in 1993 shot up to 17. Looked at from the perspective of the current organizational sample (n = 69), one-quarter of all corporate networks were born in 1993. With the help of the March on Washington, then, the workplace movement had grown to include 52 Fortune 1000 companies by the end of 1993.

As their numbers reached a critical mass, employee activists' grievances, goals, and successes became the subject of media attention, which in turn furthered the growth of the movement. In the next section, I examine expanded media access as both a process and an element of what I call "institutional opportunity." I touch briefly on the role of queer activism in triggering this new "issue attention cycle" (Downs 1972, as cited in McCarthy and Zald 1977:1229; McCarthy, Smith, and Zald 1996). Drawing from gay publications, mainstream news outlets, and the business press, I then analyze media representations of employment discrimination and workplace activism in order to assess the mobilizing impact of visibility.

Expanded Media Access as an Element of Institutional Opportunity: The Benefits of Mainstream Visibility for Workplace Activists

Openings in institutional arenas such as the media and the corporate sector can facilitate collective action in much the same way as shifts in the traditional political domain. Activists, however, do not simply wait for institutional opportunities such as expanded media attention. As discussed above, challengers can create

openings for themselves and others by drawing on the power of disruptive tactics or by planning other media-focused events (Gamson and Meyer 1996; McAdam 1996; Tarrow 1996, 1998; Koopmans [1993] 1997).

As queer activists in 1990 engaged in purposefully outrageous and imaginatively obtrusive acts of symbolic resistance, interrupting the flow of everyday life, the mass media finally took notice, sparking a novel period of mainstream visibility. While the news media began to cover gay issues and made much ado about the newly coined "outing" phenomenon, wherein some queer activists dragged various gay politicians and corporate powerbrokers like Malcolm Forbes out of the closet (Thompson 1994:365), the movie industry released three films in 1990 that gave additional voice and visibility to the diversity of the gay community. All three soon became queer classics: Marlon Riggs' *Tongues Untied* on the lives of black gay men, Jennie Livingston's *Paris is Burning* on drag balls in New York's black and Puerto Rican gay communities, and the even more widely seen *Longtime Companion* on the devastating impact of AIDS on a circle of affluent gay friends in New York, a film that won critical acclaim in the mainstream press (Thompson 1994:372).

Energized by the numerous queer images reflected on the big screen and in mainstream news venues, and cognizant of the opportunity afforded by this new visibility, lesbian and gay employees mobilized within their companies at a more rapid pace than ever before. With the increased media attention to queer lives in 1990, 10 new networks emerged among the Fortune 1000, thus creating in only 12 months what had taken the earlier workplace movement 12 years to achieve. The doubling of the organizational population from 10 to 20 networks meant that lesbian and gay employee groups would become far more visible not just within but also outside of the corporate arena where they arose.

"Corporate bullies" and the gay press. The jump in workplace organizing in the early '90s, however, was not simply a response to the new mainstream visibility of gay issues. The lesbian and gay movement's own media also contributed to the upswing in corporate activism. In 1990 the gay and lesbian movement's national news magazine, *The Advocate,* "changed dramatically" and adopted an "aggressive investigative reporting" style (Rouilard 1994:358), including a cover story entitled "Corporate Gay Bashing" (Hollingsworth 1990). The article attacked several major "corporate bullies" for anti-gay employment discrimination, especially their refusal to adopt domestic partner benefits. The sudden focus of *The Advocate* on the lack of equitable benefits came on the heels of the decision by Ben and Jerry's, the popular ice cream makers that pride themselves on their socially responsible reputation, to adopt the benefits in late 1989. Besides the *Village Voice* newspaper, Ben and Jerry's, with 600 employees, was the only company to have opened its healthcare plan to domestic partners (Baker et al. 1995).

Expanding on the equal rights angle, the author pointed out that "although employee benefits are, under law, considered to be part of wages," even companies with gay-inclusive nondiscrimination statements do not view the policies as applicable to benefit plans (Hollingsworth 1990:30). Some lesbian and gay employee activists now frame their arguments for equitable benefits by highlighting this inconsistency, mainly by describing the lack of benefits as compensation discrimination. At the time this article was published, however, the push for domestic partner benefits by gay employee networks had barely begun. Noting the emergence of "gay and lesbian support groups" in the corporate workplace, the author lamented their reluctance to fight for equitable benefits: "Gays and lesbians who are currently fighting employment and compensation discrimination publicly . . . can be counted on fewer than two hands" (p. 30). This cover story by the movement's national news source thus sounded a call to arms.

While bemoaning the scarcity of gay-inclusive nondiscrimination policies, let alone equitable benefits, *The Advocate* writer nevertheless made clear that as of 1990 the struggle

for gay rights in the workplace was being waged on multiple fronts: lawsuits in the court system by individuals and gay advocacy organizations, lobbying by activists for federal protection in the legislative arena, nascent attempts at shareholder activism, and mobilization efforts within corporations by "a younger generation without fear" (p. 33). The list of workplace endeavors also included a survey designed to document the hiring policies of over 300 companies, an undertaking of the Gay and Lesbian Employment Rights Project at the Interfaith Center on Corporate Responsibility in New York (p. 32). Discussing the preliminary results of the study, the author cited various corporations and whether they included sexual orientation in their nondiscrimination statements. He emphasized, however, that without municipal or state legislation to back them up, such policies are not typically treated as legally binding.

While lesbian and gay employees are painfully aware of their lack of legal rights, the wider public remains largely ignorant of the situation, perpetuated no doubt by the New Right's extensive campaigns against gay rights as "special rights" (Blain 1997; L. Duggan [1994] 1998; Dugan 1999). Nevertheless, press coverage of particularly blatant cases of discrimination can chip away at misinformation and jar people from a state of passivity. The audacity of some employers to publicly announce their anti-gay policies—and of some localities to preemptively ban any legal protections against such discrimination (Epstein 1999)—can actually be a boon to advocates of equal rights in the workplace.

Cracker Barrel's crusade and the impact of "suddenly publicized grievances." In January 1991, Cracker Barrel corporation, a chain of restaurants located in 16 southern and midwestern states, issued a press release announcing an official policy against employment of "homosexuals." Signed by the vice president of human resources, the policy mandated the termination of individuals "whose sexual preferences fail to demonstrate normal heterosexual values, which have been the foundation of families in our society" (as cited in Bain

1992b:1). The company then fired 11 gay and lesbian employees, all from jurisdictions that lacked gay rights ordinances. When word hit the national news networks, protestors quickly staged demonstrations and sit-ins at various restaurant locations, and activists from across the country issued calls for a boycott (Vaid 1995). The National Gay and Lesbian Task Force (NGLTF) launched a nationwide campaign against the company, and for the first time in the history of shareholder activism, a U.S. corporation was faced with a shareholder resolution that sought to institute explicit protections against anti-gay discrimination (Bain 1992b:1).

Much like the lunch counter sit-ins of the civil rights movement (McAdam 1983; Morris 1984), the Cracker Barrel sit-ins helped to elicit additional and "highly sympathetic" press coverage of gay employees' grievances (Bain 1992b:2). Stories appeared on programs such as *Oprah Winfrey, Larry King Live,* and ABC's *20/20* (Equality Project 1999). Even months later the company's policy was receiving national media attention. During a November 1991 segment of *20/20,* which was said to have been rescheduled so that it would air prior to Cracker Barrel's annual shareholder meeting, Barbara Walters announced that she would not patronize the chain (Bain 1992b). Dan Quayle, on the other hand, showed support for the corporation's intransigence by visiting one of the restaurants during his campaign for the presidency (Vaid 1995).

Nonetheless, the Cracker Barrel protestors had won support form several public officials and a broad range of organizations, including the NAACP, labor unions, pension funds that held stock in the company, and liberal religious institutions (Bain 1992b). The company's actions were later featured in a first-ever documentary on anti-gay workplace discrimination entitled *Out at Work.* Premiering at the Sundance Film Festival, it subsequently aired on HBO in January 1999 as part of the cable channels "America Undercover" documentary series (*Gay People's Chronicle* 1999). Long before then, however, in the words of corporate ac-

tivist and writer C. Arthur Bain (1992b:8), Cracker Barrel's decision to trumpet its policy far and wide had "brought the issue of homophobic discrimination into sharp focus in boardrooms and living rooms across the country." Thus mainstream media's Year of the Queer in 1990, followed by extensive coverage of the Cracker Barrel protests in 1991, sounded like beacons for the movement, calling "Come out, come out, wherever you are. . . ."

In addition to "suddenly imposed grievance" (McAdam 1994), which can spur people to action, the aftermath of the Cracker Barrel disclosure suggests that suddenly *publicized* grievances can have the same mobilizing impact. While the firings were certainly nothing new to the gay community, the company's brazen announcement brought into the open what other equally discriminatory employers practice but rarely codify: i.e., a ban on the hiring or promotion of "known or suspected" gay, lesbian, bisexual, and transgendered people. Thus, as the media publicized a particularly striking example of long-held grievances in the gay and lesbian community, 6 more employee networks formed among the Fortune 1000 in 1991, followed by 9 others the next year.

In 1990, the second wave of corporate activism had begun with the birth of 10 gay networks. Comparatively speaking, then, the workplace movement experienced a drop in new organizing after the Cracker Barrel story hit the news in 1991. Nonetheless, media coverage of the incident set in motion a new set of developments in corporate organizing that helped to mitigate the potentially chilling effect of the firings. Cracker Barrel's crusade against gays and lesbians persuaded many employee networks, which had been mobilizing separately, to join forces in order to share resources and hone strategies for making the workplace a safer space.

In the wake of the Cracker Barrel fury in 1991, activists from several different companies organized the first two conferences in the country to focus on lesbian, gay, and bisexual issues in the workplace. As will be discussed in a later section, both of these 1991 events constituted a critical turning point for the workplace movement. The east coast conference, which focused on educating corporate elites, generated considerable press coverage (Swan 1997). The west coast effort, called "Out and Equal in the Workplace," was organized primarily for gay and lesbian employees and was so successful that it became an annual event.

The business press takes note. Even staid, button-down business publications began to devote some of their pages to gay issues generally and the workplace movement in particular. A first in the world of business publishing, on December 16, 1991, *Fortune* magazine ran a cover story called "Gay in Corporate America," with the subheading, "What it's like, and how business attitudes are changing." Above the by-line on the first page of the featured article was the following statement, set off in bold print: "In the company closet is a big, talented, and scared group of men and women. They want out—and are making the workplace the next frontier for gay rights" (Stewart 1991:42).

Reporting that lesbians and gay men in major corporations were "rapidly forming employee groups," journalist Thomas Stewart described the agenda of this "new activism": gay-inclusive nondiscrimination policies, diversity training, and equitable benefits (p. 43). The article also mentioned one of the two conferences on gay and lesbian workplace issues that had taken place earlier that year, to which CEOs and human resource directors from companies across the country had been invited. Emphasizing the need for such events, Stewart cited one of the replies that organizers received in response to their invitation: "To all the fags, gays, homos, and lezzies. Do not mail me any of your fag shit lezzie homo paperwork to my business" (p. 56).

Citing a few of the companies that had begun to require attendance at homophobia workshops, the *Fortune* article indicated how far some segments of corporate America had come in their treatment of lesbian and gay employees. But the author was careful not to overstate the extent of progress. Stewart relayed the painful experiences of several gay professionals who were struggling with what one respondent described as "rampant homophobia" (p. 43). Commenting on the results of a 1987 *Wall Street Journal* survey, in which 66 percent of the CEOs from major corporations stated that "they would be reluctant to put a homosexual on management committees," the *Fortune* author concluded, "[W]hile attitudes may have changed since, there's no evidence of a revolution" (p. 45).

Nonetheless, without realizing it, the writer was reporting on the very beginnings of a different kind of revolution in the workplace: the rise of domestic partner benefits. In an in-laid side feature entitled "A Cutting-Edge Issue: Benefits," Stewart discussed the "historic" move by high-tech Lotus corporation in September 1991 to extend to gay domestic partners all of the benefits already offered to the spouses of heterosexual employees (p. 50). Adopted in response to the organizing work of an informal group of lesbian and gay employees who had requested the benefits over two years earlier (Laabs 1991), the policy change made Lotus, with its workforce of 3100, the first major corporate adopter of equitable benefits (Stewart 1991:50). "Will Lotus set a trend? Probably not," concluded the author. Little did he know. As I will discuss in the next section, Lotus' move reflected a significant institutional opening for the corporate workplace movement.

In sum, this cover story appearing in the widely read pages of *Fortune* magazine brought much needed visibility to the workplace movement and to the "cutting-edge" issue of equitable benefits. The author's focus on gay employment topics and his mentioning of several specific employee networks served to further expand the ranks of the movement. That same year, articles on gay issues in the workplace, including domestic partner benefits, began to appear in personnel and human resources journals as well. To this day, employee activists celebrate such articles, especially those published in outlets like *Fortune* magazine that reach far wider audiences than specialty journals. At one of the many network meetings I attended, members excitedly pored over the pages of a magazine article on gay workplace issues and then distributed copies to everyone on their mailing list, including those who worked for other companies. Thus, as greater numbers of gay employees heard about the struggles and successes of some of the early networks, many decided to mobilize in their own places of work, creating a new wave of activism that would eventually usher in a sea change in corporate America.

Institutional Openings in the Workplace: Early Adopters of Equitable Benefits and "Walking the Talk" of Diversity

The rise of domestic partner benefits.   The dawning of equitable benefits on the corporate horizon spurred many gay and lesbian employees into action. Several founders of second-wave networks said that hearing the good news about early adopters prompted them to form employee organizations in their own companies. Other gay networks decided to add domestic partner benefits to their list of goals or, if already present, to give them higher priority. While the *Village Voice* in New York City was actually the first employer in the country to adopt equitable benefits back in 1982 (Baker et al. 1995), word of the policy change did not spread far. The successful efforts of the union's gay and lesbian caucus thus went unnoticed in the wider business world. In contrast, after Lotus' decision in 1991, national newspapers started to cover stories about domestic partner benefits, which had already begun to arise in a small number of cities.

Municipal employees had first won equitable benefits in Berkeley in 1984, West Hollywood in 1985, Santa Cruz in 1986, and then Los Angeles and Takoma Park, Maryland, in 1988. (All dates are from a list provided by the Human Rights Campaign.) After Ben and Jerry's and Santa Cruz County adopted the benefits in 1989, Seattle and Laguna Beach

followed suit in 1990. When Lotus announced their decision in 1991, the momentum spread from the arena of municipal government to the business sector. The scales then began to tip away from city politics such that for every year since 1993 the majority of adopters have been companies, both large and small, followed in number by universities.

From 1982 through 1990, there were just 20 employers that had adopted domestic partner benefits, and only 4 of these were companies. The bulk of adopters during this period were either cities or counties (9), national gay rights organizations (2), or other non-profit organizations (5) such as the American Civil Liberties Union, the American Psychological Association, and Planned Parenthood. In 1991, however, with national media coverage of benefits adoption by Lotus, and the similar move by Montefiore Medical Center in the Bronx after threat of a lawsuit, other companies started to come on board. Of the 7 adopters that year, 4 were either small or large companies.

In 1992, there was an acceleration of benefits adoption: 21 employers extended their plans to cover domestic partners, including major corporations such as west coast-based Levi Strauss & Co., Silicon Valley's Borland International, MCA/Universal Studios, a few hospitals and legal firms, and five universities (Oberlin College in Ohio, University of Rochester, American University in Washington, D.C., Golden Gate University in San Francisco, and University of Iowa). Of the 21 adopters that year, only 3 were cities. The following year in 1993, 36 employers, 20 of which were companies, adopted equitable benefits. Corporate America had begun to outpace employers in other sectors and has been in the forefront of change ever since.

The vast majority of early corporate adopters extended their policies only after being persuaded to do so by groups of lesbian and gay employees (on the institutional and movement processes that brought about these groundbreaking changes, see Raeburn 2000, 2002). For the purposes of the present discussion, however, the relevance of early benefits adoption by major corporations lies in the energizing impact that it had on the workplace movement. As Lotus' policy change in the fall of 1991 jump-started the corporate campaign for equitable benefits, leading to a dramatic increase in adopters between 1992 and 1993, the pace of new organizing likewise quickened in response. While 6 networks formed among the Fortune 1000 in 1991, the next year brought 9 new groups, followed by 17 more in 1993.

"Walking the talk" of diversity. Given the buzz in the gay community about the rise of equitable benefits and the new queer visibility in mainstream media, as well as *The Advocate*'s more aggressive coverage of employment issues and employee organizing, the workplace movement picked up considerable steam in the early years of the decade. But the second wave momentum that generated new gay employee networks across the country also drew fuel from another institutional opening in the corporate world. According to many network founders, the surge of corporate organizing in the early '90s stemmed in part from the glaring omission of gay men and lesbians from their companies' newfound interest in diversity issues.

While some executives began to see diversity training and the formation of diversity task forces, councils, and/or offices as examples of corporate "best practices," lesbian and gay employees largely found themselves excluded altogether from these initiatives. Nevertheless, some corporate elites began to view diversity as a business imperative, reflecting the diffusion of what institutional scholars Frank Dobbin and John Sutton (1998) describe as a new human resources paradigm. Lesbian and gay employees saw in this expanded corporate mindset an institutional opening that offered new hope for a place at the table.

In diversity-embracing companies, gay employees watched the doors begin to open wider for people of color and women in general. Responding to this "open moment" (Gourevitch 1986) that indicated "Big Opportunity" (Gamson and Meyer 1996:280),

and taking a collective deep breath, lesbians and gay men attempted to walk through those doors as well. Although sometimes met by corporate bouncers on the other side, gay employee activists remained steadfast in their determination to join the party. The swell of workplace organizing in the first half of the '90s hence grew not simply out of a more favorable political climate or out of the expanded opportunities afforded by media visibility and early benefits adoption. The rush of corporate activism during this period was also a response to a new institutional opening available to those whose employers had begun "talking the talk" of diversity. Responding to their changing corporate culture, gay and lesbian employees stepped in—or rather "out"—to be sure that their companies would, in the words of a popular catch phrase among workplace activists, "walk the walk" when it came to addressing gay concerns.

The emergence of the largest gay employee network in the country clearly demonstrates the importance of expanded institutional opportunities at the organizational or corporate level. As already discussed, GLUE was formed in a telecommunications company by a small group of friends who were inspired by the 1987 March on Washington. But even before the march, when meeting for lunch in restaurants or after work in their homes, the friends had talked about the need for an officially recognized lesbian and gay employee organization "like the other diversity groups" in their company for women and people of color.

The majority of gay networks that eventually emerged in the Fortune 1000 likewise cited the existence of preexisting diversity groups in their companies as indirect but important motivators behind their decision to organize. These preexisting networks, which Sidney Tarrow (1998) would call "early risers," had already successfully mobilized for official recognition and resources, alerting gays and lesbians to the potential effectiveness of claims-making on the corporate elite. Thus, the changing corporate culture in some companies signaled a possible opening of opportunities for gay and lesbian employees. Tuned in to the transformations that were taking place in more and more companies whose executives saw dollar signs in the face(s) of diversity, lesbian and gay workers quickly mobilized in response.

Summary.   The markedly greater fertility of the workplace movement during the second wave was thus the fruitful result of multiple factors. The more receptive political climate and unprecedented media coverage of queer activism and employment discrimination, in combination with early institutional shifts toward corporate diversity and domestic partner benefits, made for relatively inviting waters during the early '90s. Lesbian, gay, and bisexual employees hence took the plunge in greater numbers than ever before, creating visible workplace organizations aimed at effecting widespread institutional change. While most of the first-wave networks had labored in relative isolation, gay employee groups that mobilized later could draw courage—and vastly improved networking opportunities—from the knowledge that they were not alone.

THE RISE OF INTERORGANIZATIONAL LINKAGES AMONG LESBIAN, GAY, AND BISEXUAL EMPLOYEE NETWORKS

During the second wave of the movement, between 1990 and 1994, institutional activists worked hard to create and foster interorganizational linkages among gay employee networks. These connections ranged from informal social gatherings and e-mail exchanges to more fully institutionalized networking mechanisms such as annual workplace conferences, hyper-linked web sites, and formal umbrella groups consisting of gay employee networks from a wide variety of institutional settings. In response to the burgeoning grass-roots movement for workplace equality, the two most prominent gay rights organizations in the country, the National Gay and Lesbian Task Force (NGLTF) and the Human Rights Campaign (HRC), instituted Workplace Projects in order to provide resources and additional networking opportunities for employee activists from across the country.

As the linkages among employee activists grew increasingly dense and formalized during the second wave, the workplace movement experienced a certain coming of age. Much like other rites of passage, this period of development came with its own set of tensions and a heightened reflexivity as leaders struggled over the type and degree of formalization that would best suit networking at the regional and national levels. Some local umbrella groups folded while other regional organizations attempted to broaden their geographic reach. Efforts to form umbrella networks at the national level underwent a series of bumps and starts. In all, however, these growing pains resulted in a bigger, stronger, more densely connected movement.

By the mid 1990s, after a slow and tentative start back in 1978, the workplace wing of the gay and lesbian movement had finally come into its own. Numerous umbrella groups, two national workplace projects, and an abundance of conferences and web sites that focused on gay employment issues were all well established by the middle of the decade (see Raeburn 2000, 2002). Their continued presence signifies the successful institutionalization of the workplace movement. This impressive movement infrastructure facilitated favorable mobilization and policy outcomes. In addition to sustaining the commitment of employee networks and increasing the visibility of the workplace campaign, these interorganizational structures have improved the movement's "bargaining" position in the institutional policy domain by educating corporate decision-makers as well as individual activists (Burstein, Einwohner, and Hollander 1995). Indeed, the infrastructural efforts of activists during the second wave helped the workplace movement achieve relatively remarkable policy success.

INSIDE OUT: WINNING EQUALITY IN CORPORATE AMERICA

Research shows that in 1990 just three corporations provided family and bereavement leave for lesbian and gay employees (Mickens 1994), and none provided health insurance coverage for domestic partners (Baker et al. 1995). But by the middle of the '90s, domestic partner benefits had practically become a household word given their adoption by numerous big-name companies. In 1999, the rate of adoption among major employers reached almost two per week (Herrschaft 1999).

According to the most recent figures provided by HRC's WorkNet project, as of mid-March 2002, 158 Fortune 500 companies (32 percent) had instituted equitable benefits (HRC 2002). In just the first quarter of 2001, over 20 Fortune 500 companies adopted domestic partner benefits or announced that they would do so by mid year (DataLounge 2001). This number exceeded the entire yearly total of Fortune 500 adopters in 2000. In addition to these corporations, almost 4000 other private companies, nonprofit organizations, and unions offer domestic partner benefits. The numbers of adopters in the university and government sectors are 164 and 137, respectively. In all then, nearly 4440 employers have instituted equitable benefits (HRC 2001).

My study reveals the crucial role of the workplace movement in bringing about this sea change. While institutional processes in the wider sociopolitical and corporate arenas also influence policy decisions (see Raeburn 2000, 2002), employee activists clearly spearheaded this major transformation in the business world. Of the 20 private employers who first adopted equitable benefits, at least 16 did so in response to internal mobilization (Baker et al. 1995). As of 1999, corporations with gay employee groups still constituted two-thirds of Fortune 1000 adopters (56 out of 83, or 67 percent).

Although more recent adopters do not necessarily have organized groups of gay workers, data show that lesbian and gay employees should not assume that their employers will jump on board the benefits bandwagon in the absence of internal pressure. Gays and lesbians who are standing idly by, waiting for their own employers to adopt equitable policies, should be careful of resting on others' laurels. Silence rarely brings change. In corporations without domestic partner benefits, many executives cite apparent lack of employee demand.

While many if not most social movement scholars focus on the formal political arena, the workplace movement is a potent reminder that challengers do not always target the state. The struggle for equality is waged in a wide variety of institutional arenas, including not only the workplace but also education, medicine, religion, and the military (Katzenstein 1990, 1998; D'Emilio 1992; McNaught 1993; Hodson 1995, 1996, 2001; Taylor and Raeburn 1995; Epstein 1996; Taylor 1996; Taylor and Van Willigen 1996; McNaron 1997; Meyer and Tarrow 1998; Knoke 2001). Though mobilization inside institutions often remains invisible to the wider public, "unobtrusive activists" can effect significant transformations in the institutional landscape (Katzenstein 1990, 1998). Indeed, by coming out and mobilizing at work, lesbian, gay, and bisexual employees, along with their heterosexual allies, are winning equitable policies and practices in organizations across the country. As testament to the power of activism inside institutions, their fight for equal rights reveals how committed groups of people can bring about wide-scale social change.

REFERENCES

ADAM, BARRY D. 1995. *The Rise of a Gay and Lesbian Movement.* 2d ed. New York: Twayne Publishers.
BADGETT, M. V. LEE. 1995. "The Wage Effects of Sexual Orientation Discrimination." *Industrial and Labor Relations Review* 48:726–739.
BAIN, C. ARTHUR. 1992a. "A Letter from President Elect Bill Clinton." *The Gay/Lesbian/Bisexual Corporate Letter,* November/December, p. 7.

————. 1992b. "Cracker Barrel Seeks SEC Dismissal of First Gay Rights Shareholder Action." *The Gay/Lesbian/Bisexual Corporate Letter,* September/October, pp. 1–2, 8.

BAKER, DANIEL B., SEAN O'BRIEN STRUB, AND BILL HENNING. 1995. *Cracking the Corporate Closet: The 200 Best (and Worst) Companies to Work For, Buy From, and Invest in if You're Gay or Lesbian—and Even if You Aren't.* New York: Harper Business.

BERZON, BETTY. 1994. "Acting Up." Pp. 307–308 in *Long Road to Freedom: The Advocate History of the Gay and Lesbian Movement,* edited by Mark Thompson. New York: St. Martin's Press.

BLAIN, MICHAEL. 1997. "The Politics of Victimage: Power and Subjectivity in Anti-Gay Campaigns." Paper presented at the annual meeting of the Pacific Sociological Association, San Diego, CA.

BLUMSTEIN, PHILIP AND PEPPER SCHWARTZ. 1983. *American Couples.* NY: William Morrow.

BURSTEIN, PAUL, RACHEL L. EINWOHNER, AND JOCELYN A. HOLLANDER. 1995. "The Success of Political Movements: A Bargaining Perspective." Pp. 275–295 in *The Politics of Social Protest: Comparative Perspectives on States and Social Movements,* edited by J. Craig Jenkins and Bert Klandermans. Minneapolis: University of Minnesota Press.

DataLounge. 2001. "Domestic Partner Benefits Sweeping U.S. Firms" (DataLounge news report, April 16). Retrieved July 24, 2001 (http://www.datalounge.com/datalounge/news/record.html?record=14266).

D'EMILIO, JOHN. 1992. *Making Trouble: Essays on Gay History, Politics, and the University.* New York: Routledge.

DOBBIN, FRANK, AND JOHN R. SUTTON. 1998. "The Strength of a Weak State: The Rights Revolution and the Rise of Human Resources Management Divisions." *American Journal of Sociology* 104:441–476.

DOWNS, A. 1972. "Up and Down with Ecology—the Issue Attention Cycle." *Public Interest* 28:139–171.

DUGAN, KIMBERLY B. 1999. "Culture and Movement-Countermovement Dynamics: The Struggle over Gay, Lesbian, and Bisexual Rights." Ph.D. dissertation, Department of Sociology, Ohio State University, Columbus, OH.

DUGGAN, LISA. [1994] 1998. "Queering the State." Pp. 564–572 in *Social Perspectives in Lesbian and Gay Studies: A Reader,* edited by Peter Nardi and Beth E. Schneider. New York: Routledge.

EPSTEIN, STEVEN. 1996. *Impure Science: AIDS, Activism, and the Politics of Knowledge.* Berkeley: University of California Press.

————. 1999. "Gay and Lesbian Movements in the United States: Dilemmas of Identity, Diversity, and Political Strategy." Pp. 30–90 in *The Global Emergence of Gay and Lesbian Politics: National Imprints of a Worldwide Movement,* edited by Barry D. Adam, Jan Willem Duyvendak, and André Krouwel. Philadelphia: Temple University Press.

Equality Project. 1999. "The Equality Project: Gay and Lesbian Consumers, Employees, and Investors Working Together" (Home Page). New York, NY: The Equality Project. Retrieved June 14, 1999 (http://www.equalityproject.org/).

FADERMAN, LILLIAN. 1991. *Odd Girls and Twilight Lovers: A History of Lesbian Life in Twentieth-Century America.* New York: Penguin Books.

GAMSON, JOSHUA. 1995. "Must Identify Movements Self-destruct? A Queer Dilemma." *Social Problems* 42:390–407.

————. 1998. *Freaks Talk Back: Tabloid Talk Shows and Sexual Nonconformity.* Chicago: University of Chicago Press.

GAMSON, WILLIAM A. 1992a. *Talking Politics.* New York: Cambridge University Press.

————. 1992b. "The Social Psychology of Collective Action." Pp. 53–76 in *Frontiers in Social Movement Theory,* edited by Aldon D. Morris and Carol McClurg Mueller. New Haven, CT: Yale University Press.

————. 1995. "Hiroshima, the Holocaust, and the Politics of Exclusion: 1994 Presidential Address." *American Sociological Review* 60:1–20.

————. [1995] 1997. "Constructing Social Protest." Pp. 228–244 in *Social Movements: Perspectives and Issues,* edited by Steven M. Buechler and F. Kurt Cylke, Jr. Mountain View, CA: Mayfield Publishing.

GAMSON, WILLIAM A., AND DAVID S. MEYER. 1996. "Framing Political Opportunity." Pp. 275–290 in *Comparative Perspectives on Social Movements: Political Opportunities, Mobilizing Structures, and Cultural Framings,* edited by Doug McAdam, John D. McCarthy, and Mayer N. Zald. New York: Cambridge University Press.

Gay and Lesbian Alliance Against Defamation. 1999. "A Brief Introduction to GLAAD" (GLAAD History Web site). New York, NY: Gay and Lesbian Alliance Against Defamation. Retrieved July 28, 1999 (http://www.glaad.org/glaad/history.html).

Gay People's Chronicle. 1999. "HBO Film Looks at Lesbian and Gay Workplace Bias." January 1, p. 13.

GITLIN, TODD. 1980. *The Whole World is Watching.* Berkeley: University of California Press.

GOUREVITCH, PETER. 1986. *Politics in Hard Times: Comparative Responses to International Economic Crises.* Ithaca, NY: Cornell University Press.

GROSS, LARRY. 1993. *Contested Closets: The Politics and Ethics of Outing.* Minneapolis: University of Minnesota Press.

HAINES, HERBERT H. 1988. *Black Radicals and the Civil Rights Movement, 1954–1970.* Knoxville: University of Tennessee Press.

HERRSCHAFT, DARYL. 1999. "Equality Works: Revamped WorkNet Website Empowers GLBT Workers." *HRC Quarterly,* Fall 1999, pp. 14–15.

HODSON, RANDY. 1995. "Worker Resistance: An Underdeveloped Concept in the Sociology of Work." *Economic and Industrial Democracy* 16:79–110.

————. 1996. "Dignity in the Workplace Under Participative Management: Alienation and Freedom Revisited." *American Sociological Review* 61:719–738.

————. 2001. *Dignity at Work.* New York: Cambridge University Press.

HOLLINGSWORTH, GAINES. 1990. "Corporate Gay Bashing." *The Advocate,* September 11, pp. 28–33.

Human Rights Campaign (HRC). 2002. "WorkNet Employer Database" (HRC Web site). Washington, D.C.: Human Rights Campaign. Retrieved March 15, 2002 (http://www.hrc.org/worknet/asp_search/detail_search.asp).

INGRAHAM, CHRYS. 1994. "The Heterosexual Imaginary: Feminist Sociology and Theories of Gender." *Sociological Theory* 12:203–219.

JENKINS, J. CRAIG, AND CHARLES PERROW. 1977. "Insurgency of the Powerless: Farm Worker Movements (1946–1972)." *American Sociological Review* 42:249–268.

KATZENSTEIN, MARY FAINSOD. 1990. "Feminism Within American Institutions: Unobtrusive Mobilization in the 1980s." *Signs: Journal of Women in Culture and Society* 16:27–54.

———. 1998. *Faithful and Fearless: Moving Feminist Protest Inside the Church and Military.* Princeton, NJ: Princeton University Press.

KATZENSTEIN, MARY F., AND CAROL MCCLURG MUELLER, eds. 1987. *The Women's Movements of the United States and Western Europe: Consciousness, Political Opportunity, and Public Policy.* Philadelphia: Temple University Press.

KLANDERMANS, BERT, AND SJOERD GOSLINGA. 1996. "Media Discourse, Movement Publicity, and the Generation of Collective Action Frames: Theoretical and Empirical Exercises in Meaning Construction." Pp. 312–337 in *Comparative Perspectives on Social Movements: Political Opportunities, Mobilizing Structures, and Cultural Framings,* edited by Doug McAdam, John D. McCarthy, and Mayer N. Zald. New York: Cambridge University Press.

KNOKE, DAVID. 2001. *Changing Organizations: Business Networks in the New Political Economy.* Boulder, CO: Westview Press.

KOOPMANS, RUUD. [1993] 1997. "The Dynamics of Protest Waves: West Germany, 1965 to 1989." Pp. 367–383 in *Social Movements: Readings on Their Emergence, Mobilization, and Dynamics,* edited by Doug McAdam and David A. Snow. Los Angeles: Roxbury Publishing.

KORB, LAWRENCE J. 1996. "The President, the Congress, and the Pentagon: Obstacles to Implementing the 'Don't Ask, Don't Tell' Policy." Pp. 290–301 in *Out in Force: Sexual Orientation and the Military,* edited by Gregory M. Herek, Jared B. Jobe, and Ralph M. Carney. Chicago: University of Chicago Press.

LAABS, JENNIFER J. 1991. "Unmarried . . . With Benefits." *Personnel Journal* 70:62–70.

LEVINE, MARTIN P. 1979. "Employment Discrimination against Gay Men." *International Review of Modern Sociology* 9:151–63.

———. 1992. "The Status of Gay Men in the Workplace." Pp. 251–66 in *Men's Lives,* edited by Michael S. Kimmel and Michael A. Messner. New York: Macmillan Publishing.

LEVINE, MARTIN P. AND ROBIN LEONARD. 1984. "Discrimination Against Lesbians in the Work Force." *Signs: Journal of Women in Culture and Society* 9:700–10.

LEWIS, SASHA GREGORY. 1979. *Sunday's Women: A Report on Lesbian Life Today.* Boston: Beacon Press.

MCADAM, DOUG. 1982. *Political Process and the Development of Black Insurgency, 1930–1970.* Chicago: University of Chicago Press.

———. 1983. "Tactical Innovation and the Pace of Insurgency." *American Sociological Review* 48:735–754.

———. 1994. "Culture and Social Movements." Pp. 36–57 in *New Social Movements: From Ideology to Identity,* edited by Enrique Laraña, Hank Johnston, and Joseph R. Gusfield. Philadelphia: Temple University Press.

———. 1996. "Conceptual Origins, Current Problems, Future Directions." Pp. 23–40 in *Comparative Perspectives on Social Movements: Political Opportunities, Mobilizing Structures, and Cultural Framings,* edited by Doug McAdam, John D. McCarthy, and Mayer N. Zald. New York: Cambridge University Press.

MCADAM, DOUG, JOHN D. MCCARTHY, AND MAYER N. ZALD, eds. 1996. *Comparative Perspectives on Social Movements: Political Opportunities, Mobilizing Structures, and Cultural Framings.* New York: Cambridge University Press.

MCCARTHY, JOHN D., JACKIE SMITH, AND MAYER N. ZALD. 1996. "Accessing Public, Media, Electoral, and Governmental Agendas." Pp. 291–311 in *Comparative Perspectives on Social Movements: Political Opportunities, Mobilizing Structures, and Cultural Framings,* edited by Doug McAdam, John D. McCarthy, and Mayer N. Zald. New York: Cambridge University Press.

MCCARTHY, JOHN D., AND MAYER N. ZALD. 1977. "Resource Mobilization and Social Movements: A Partial Theory." *American Journal of Sociology* 82:1212–1241.

MCNARON, TONI A. 1997. *Poisoned Ivy: Lesbian and Gay Academics Confronting Homophobia.* Philadelphia: Temple University Press.

MCNAUGHT, BRIAN. 1993. *Gay Issues in the Workplace.* New York: St. Martin's Press.

MEYER, DAVID, AND SIDNEY TARROW. 1998. *The Social Movement Society: Contentious Politics for a New Century.* Lanham, MD: Rowman and Littlefield Publishers.

MEYERSON, DEBRA E., AND MAUREEN A. SCULLY. 1995. "Tempered Radicalism and the Politics of Ambivalence and Change." *Organization Science* 6:585–600.

MICKENS, Ed. 1994. *The 100 Best Companies for Gay Men and Lesbians—Plus Options and Opportunities No Matter Where You Work.* New York: Pocket Books.

MOLOTCH, HARVEY. 1979. "Media and Movements." Pp. 71–93 in *The Dynamics of Social Movements: Resource Mobilization, Social Control, and Tactics,* edited by Mayer Zald and John McCarthy. Cambridge, MA: Winthrop Publishers.

MORRIS, ALDON D. 1984. *The Origins of the Civil Rights Movement: Black Communities Organizing for Change.* New York: Free Press.

PODOLSKY, ROBIN. 1994. "Birth of a Queer Nation." Pp. 367–369 in *Long Road to Freedom: The Advocate History of the Gay and Lesbian Movement,* edited by Mark Thompson. New York: St. Martin's Press.

RAEBURN, NICOLE C. 2000. *The Rise of Lesbian, Gay, and Bisexual Rights in the Workplace.* Ph.D. dissertation,

Department of Sociology, Ohio State University, Columbus, OH.

————. Forthcoming. *Inside Out: The Struggle for Lesbian, Gay, and Bisexual Rights in the Workplace.* Minneapolis: University of Minnesota Press.

ROUILARD, RICHARD. 1994. "Year of the Queer: 1990." Pp. 357–358 in *Long Road to Freedom: The Advocate History of the Gay and Lesbian Movement,* edited by Mark Thompson. New York: St. Martin's Press.

RUPP, LEILA J., AND VERTA TAYLOR. [1987] 1990. *Survival in the Doldrums: The American Women's Rights Movement, 1945 to the 1960s.* Columbus: Ohio State University Press.

RYAN, BARBARA. 1992. *Feminism and the Women's Movement: Dynamics of Change in Social Movement Ideology and Activism.* New York: Routledge.

SANTORO, WAYNE A., AND GAIL M. McGUIRE. 1997. "Social Movement Insiders: The Impact of Institutional Activists on Affirmative Action and Comparable Worth Policies." *Social Problems* 44:503–519.

SCHNEIDER, BETH E. 1984. "Peril and Promise: Lesbians' Workplace Participation." Pp. 211–30 in *Women-Identified Women,* edited by Trudy Darty and Sandee Potter. Palo Alto, Calif.: Mayfield Publishing Company.

SAWYERS, TRACI M., AND DAVID S. MEYER. 1999. "Missed Opportunities: Social Movement Abeyance and Public Policy." *Social Problems* 46:187–206.

————. 1986. "Coming Out at Work: Bridging the Private/Public Gap." *Work and Occupations* 13:463–87.

————. 1988. "Invisible and Independent: Lesbians' Experiences in the Workplace." Pp. 273–286 in *Women Working,* edited by Ann Stromberg and Shirley Harkess. Palo, Alto, Calif.: Mayfield Publishing Company.

SCULLY, MAUREEN, AND W. E. DOUGLAS CREED. 1998. "Switchpersons on the Tracks of History: Situated Agency and Contested Legitimacy in the Diffusion of Domestic Partner Benefits." Paper presented at the annual meeting of the Academy of Management, San Diego, CA.

SNOW, DAVID A., E. BURKE ROCHFORD, JR., STEVEN K. WORDEN, AND ROBERT D. BENFORD. 1986. "Frame Alignment Processes, Micromobilization, and Movement Participation." *American Sociological Review* 51:464–481.

STEWART, THOMAS A. 1991. "Gay in Corporate America." *Fortune,* December 16, pp. 42–56.

SWAN, WALLACE. 1997. "The Workplace Movement." Pp. 25–33 in *Gay/Lesbian/Bisexual/Transgender Public Policy Issues: A Citizen's and Administrator's Guide to the New Cultural Struggle,* edited by Wallace K. Swan. New York: Harrington Park Press.

TARROW, SIDNEY. 1989. *Struggle, Politics, and Reform: Collective Action, Social Movements, and Cycles of Protest.* Ithaca, NY: Cornell University Press.

————. 1994. *Power in Movement: Social Movements, Collective Action, and Politics.* New York: Cambridge University Press.

————. 1996. "States and Opportunities: The Political Structuring of Social Movements." Pp. 41–61 in *Comparative Perspectives on Social Movements: Political Opportunities, Mobilizing Structures, and Cultural Framings,* edited by Doug McAdam, John D. McCarthy, and Mayer N. Zald. New York: Cambridge University Press.

————. 1998. *Power in Movement: Social Movements and Contentious Politics.* 2d ed. New York: Cambridge University Press.

TAYLOR, VERTA. 1989. "Sources of Continuity in Social Movements: The Women's Movement in Abeyance." *American Sociological Review* 54:761–775.

————. 1996. *Rock-a-by Baby: Feminism, Self-Help, and Postpartum Depression.* New York: Routledge.

TAYLOR, VERTA, AND NICOLE C. RAEBURN. 1995. "Identity Politics as High-Risk Activism: Career Consequences for Lesbian, Gay, and Bisexual Sociologists." *Social Problems* 42:252–273.

TAYLOR, VERTA, AND LEILA J. RUPP. 1993. "Women's Culture and Lesbian Feminist Activism: A Reconsideration of Cultural Feminism." *Signs: Journal of Women in Culture and Society* 19:32–61.

TAYLOR, VERTA, AND MARIEKE VAN WILLIGEN. 1996. "Women's Self-Help and the Reconstruction of Gender: The Postpartum Support and Breast Cancer Movements." *Mobilization: An International Journal* 2:123–142.

THOMPSON, MARK, ed. 1994. *Long Road to Freedom: The Advocate History of the Gay and Lesbian Movement.* New York: St. Martin's Press.

TILLY, CHARLES. 1978. *From Mobilization to Revolution.* Reading, MA: Addison-Wesley.

VAID, URVASHI. 1995. *Virtual Equality: The Mainstreaming of Gay and Lesbian Liberation.* New York: Anchor Books.

WEINBERG, MARTIN S., AND COLIN J. WILLIAMS. 1974. *Male Homosexuals: Their Problems and Adaptations.* New York: Penguin.

WHITTIER, NANCY. 1995. *Feminist Generations: The Persistence of the Radical Women's Movement.* Philadelphia: Temple University Press.

WOODS, JAMES D., with JAY H. LUCAS. 1993. *The Corporate Closet: The Professional Lives of Gay Men in America.* New York: Free Press.

CRITICAL THINKING QUESTIONS

1. What strategies have sexual minorities used to achieve workplace benefits? Could these have worked better if gay men and lesbians had worked more closely with labor unions? Explain.

2. What specific social and political conditions facilitated and inhibited the success of gay and lesbian workplace activists?

3. Discuss the importance and validity of the claim that gay, lesbian, and bisexual rights are the "workplace issues of the 1990s."

Reading 7

The Promise of Stonewall

Anne-Marie Cusac

> *In this article, Cusac discusses the lack of unity among gay men, lesbians, bisexuals, and transgenders since the birth of the gay rights movement at the Stonewall Rebellion in 1969. She argues that the efforts of many activists to achieve respectability in mainstream society has caused them to marginalize and exclude more radical members of the community, thus fragmenting and weakening the movement.*

On a visit to New York City two years ago, I was intent on seeing Stonewall, a bar where three days of rioting in June 1969 touched off the grassroots gay and lesbian movement. So I asked a friend to go with me.

It was a Thursday afternoon about 4:00 P.M. The place was quiet, with three patrons besides us and a bartender. This was where it started—"the hairpin drop heard 'round the world," as it was called by the New York Mattachine Society, a gay civil rights group.

There should be something here, I told my friend, some recognition of what this place has meant to so many people. But it looked like any other dive. I drank a soda, bought a T-shirt, and we left.

This past June was the thirtieth anniversary of the Stonewall riots. And Stonewall, the building, did receive recognition in the National Register of Historic Places. There are 70,000 or so national landmarks, and this is the first one associated with gays and lesbians, says the bar's present owner, Bob Gurecki.

On June 28, 1969, the police raided the Stonewall Inn, one of many police busts in an era when it was illegal to cross-dress or dance with a partner of the same sex. But this time, the people fought back, and their defiance was contagious. Theirs was the desperate resistance of those who had learned to love the only corner that would shelter them—a seedy, mafia-run bar.

Source: Reprinted with from *The Progressive* 63, no. 8 (August 1999): 10. www.progressive.org

"Why the Stonewall and not the Sewer or the Snake Pit?" asked the *New York Mattachine Newsletter* shortly after the riots. "The answer lies, we believe, in the unique nature of the Stonewall.... It catered to a large group of people who are not welcome in, or cannot afford, other places of homosexual social gathering.... When it was raided, they fought for it.... They had nothing to lose other than the most tolerant and open-minded gay place in town."

The riots ended, amazingly, with no one dead. But the impact was immediate. "For those of us in Public Morals, after the Stonewall incident things were completely changed," said Seymour Pine, who was deputy inspector in charge of the New York City Police Department's vice squad. "They suddenly were not submissive anymore." The news spread, and four months later, *Time* and *Newsweek* featured stories entitled "The Homosexual: Newly Visible, Newly Understood" and "Policing the Third Sex."

In the early days of the popular gay and lesbian movement, there were gay be-ins in Central Park, with thousands together for the first time—many of them crying with exhilaration and grief that I can only begin to understand. There were rallies, there were organizations. And yet, as Gurecki said to me over the phone shortly after the building was recognized as a historic property, "They will always remember Stonewall, just like they remember Rosa Parks."

Stonewall matters to me—as it does to the thousands who visit the bar every weekend and the thousands more who can't get there but think of it with gratitude and affection as "our place."

I was three-and-a-half years old during the Stonewall riots. I had no idea that it happened until after I came out as a lesbian in my mid-twenties. Even so, it made the life I live possible. Stonewall, and the burgeoning movement that followed it, inspired many gay and lesbian people to live openly. Their visibility, in turn, helped me to understand that it was possible to live a different sort of life—which became for me a lesbian life. When I walk hand-in-hand with my girlfriend through the streets of Madison, Wisconsin, I credit Stonewall.

Sometimes, I think of how I might have lived had it not been for Stonewall. I imagine a civil, but quietly unhappy, married life. Who knows if that's accurate? I do know, however, that I might have suppressed any desires or ideas that didn't feel right. Others—the more visibly queer, the people who couldn't have denied their feelings even if they tried, and the outrageously brave—wouldn't have. They would have chosen lives of greater risk.

The mainstream has recently declared gays and lesbians to be a significant, meaningful, and, in some cases, ordinary segment of the population. We're on TV. We have access to the President. We're a marketing niche.

But while some lesbians and gay people celebrate our current popularity and search for "good representatives of our community," the newly legitimate gay movement seems to want to leave some members behind. I'm talking about the drag queens, who helped start the Stonewall riots (like Marsha P. Johnson and Sylvia Rivera), the bull dykes, bisexuals, and many others. Transgendered people, in particular, are the siblings many would rather forget about. They are the flamboyant people who show up in the newspaper photos and "don't really represent the lesbian and gay movement," some of us tell ourselves. They don't blend in well. They don't take the trouble to camouflage themselves, or they can't. Cross-dressers and transsexuals are also murdered frequently, though these killings get little media attention.

Why this embarrassment while we march on toward freedom? What does this mean?

I think it means that sexual desire—that mysterious, seemingly uncontrollable, and beautiful thing—still frightens most of us. And I think it means that some lesbian and gay people still dislike and fear themselves. By taking out their nervousness on the more visibly sissy, butchy, campy, bisexual, or transgendered, they give the rest of the world license to hate.

"What do you think would happen if a bunch of queens started a riot to protect a bar tonight?" I recently asked my coworker who is a queer activist.

"I don't know," she said. "What do you think?"

"I think it would seriously divide the gay movement," I said.

She paused and looked at me. "I think so, too," she said finally.

The Stonewall we celebrate represents our hidden past, when the safest places for people who were sexually different were the places heterosexuals abhorred. But Stonewall, the bar, accepted all kinds—at least in legend. According to Gurecki, it still does.

"Anybody can come in and not feel uncomfortable," he says. "That's what we were fighting about to begin with."

The promise of Stonewall is a promise of radical sexual equality. It excludes no one. It's a promise we have yet to fulfill.

CRITICAL THINKING QUESTIONS

1. The place of transgenders and bisexuals in the gay and lesbian rights movement has changed over the last three decades. How?

2. What are the positive effects of using "respectable" persons on the front lines of the gay and lesbian rights movement? What are the negative consequences of this strategy?

3. Looking at the gay and lesbian movement and other movements for equal rights, how does the exclusion of some affect the equal rights of all?

Reading 8

Whose Movement Is It?

Mubarak Dahir

In this article, Dahir discusses the controversy over transgenders in the gay, lesbian, and bisexual movement. The author explains that debate about why gay men and lesbians have excluded transgenders from the movement centers on whether or not success would be easier to achieve if certain sexual or gender minorities were not included.

Transgender activists seek allies among often-reluctant lesbians and gay men.

It happened every time Jamison "James" Green tried to enter a lesbian bar in the '70s and '80s. The bouncer would try to stop him from entering because of the way he looked. "This is a women-only bar," the bouncer would protest.

"Do you want me to show you my tits?" Green would respond.

Only after the bouncer engaged in a brief and hushed huddle with a manager would Green eventually be admitted to the bar.

For 22 years Green had sex with women and identified as a lesbian. "But [the discrimination] wasn't about whom I was sleeping with, it was about my exterior gender traits. Being challenged like that was painful," he recalls.

But once inside the bar, Green was still uncomfortable. "I felt left out in women-only spaces," he says. "The fact is, I was more male than female."

Although born with a female anatomy, Green felt like a man. In 1988 he began medical treatment to transition from female to male. Today the 50-year-old writer is president of the San Francisco-based organization Female-to-Male International. "My orientation is still toward women, so today I'm heterosexual," he says. "But I still consider myself part of the queer community."

However, many gay men and lesbians don't consider Green and others like him, referred to as transgendered, or transsexual, to be part of their political and social movement. Those skeptics look on transgendered people as part of the fringe, oddities who are a potential embarrassment to the push for mainstream acceptance. Only in the past few years have transgendered people begun winning acceptance as part of a larger alliance of gays, lesbians, and bisexuals. And while many gay and lesbian political organizations on both the local and national levels now officially recognize transgendered people in their mission statements, an often-divisive debate continues around the question of how closely connected the gay and lesbian movement and the transgender movement are and should be.

Resistance comes from both sides. "There are a lot of people in my situation—heterosexual men—who are vehemently opposed to being associated with queers," Green says.

"There are some transgendered people with homophobia," agrees Sharon Stuart, executive director of the Transgender Law Conference, an organization that helps transsexuals locate legal resources. For example, Stuart says, many cross-dressers—men who wear women's clothes but are heterosexual—resent being confused with drag queens, who are gay men who dress in women's clothes.

Still, most transgender leaders insist the opposition to a united gay, lesbian, bisexual, and transgender movement comes from gay men and lesbians.

"A significant number of gays and lesbians haven't resolved their own phobias around gender and appearance, and they're the ones most likely to object" to including transsexuals, says Nancy Nangeroni, a transgender activists who hosts *GenderTalk,* a radio show on WMBR in Cambridge, Mass.

Even the gay leaders who make distinctions between the gay rights movement and the transgender rights movement concede that the hesitancy to link the groups comes most strongly from gay men and lesbians.

"I'd say if a transgendered person doesn't have a gay orientation, he or she is not part of the gay movement," says Rich Tafel, executive director of the Log Cabin Republicans, a national gay political group. "Adding transgendered people to a mission means arguing for a group of heterosexual people too, and that is a broader coalition of people."

But, Tafel admits, much of the discrimination against transgendered people exhibited by gays and lesbians is based on fear, not philosophy. "Frankly, to a lot of gay men, transgendered people are an embarrassment. The unspoken attitude is, Let's keep them in the closet. They're freaks and they hurt us."

Tafel condemns that attitude, calling it "little more than internalized homophobia." He believes that transgendered people are more likely to be victims of discrimination and violence than lesbians or gay men because they are less likely to meld into mainstream society. He says the key to cooperation between gays and lesbians and transsexuals is "being honest and clear about who everyone is. The transgender issue confuses a lot of people, gay and straight. A lot of the opposition in the gay community is based on the fear that others will think the transgendered are just gay people with sex-change operations."

But some transgender activists say that making distinctions about experiences and political goals is what separates transgendered people from gays and lesbians in the first place. Simply asking whether transsexuals should be part of the gay rights movement shows the arrogance of a movement that is too politically narrow, says Riki Wilchins's, executive director of the gender education and advocacy group GenderPAC.

"Gayness used to be about both orientation and gender," Wilchins says. But then, she charges, some gays and lesbians staked out what has proved to be a successful, if divisive, public relations strategy in winning support from heterosexuals: "We look like you. We act like you. We're just like you. Give us our rights."

When this happened, Wilchins says, "the movement was hijacked. Now, we're just trying to reintegrate the movement again. It has left out gender queers because, let's face it, we're not like everybody else. We were the flamboyant, visible ones, so we got sacrificed for political expediency. You can sell Ellen DeGeneres on Capitol Hill. You can't sell RuPaul."

Nothing epitomizes the rift between the gay and lesbian movement and the transgendered more than the attempt to draft and pass the federal Employment Non-Discrimination Act. As currently written, ENDA, if passed, would offer federal protection against employment discrimination for gays, lesbians, and bisexuals. Transsexuals are not included in the bill.

Transgender activists uniformly condemn the exclusion from ENDA. They charge that gay and lesbian leaders and organizations, particularly Democratic congressman Barney Frank of Massachusetts and the Human Rights Campaign, a Washington, D.C.-based gay lobbying group, fought hard to keep transgendered people out of ENDA because they believed it would ease the political struggle to pass it.

Frank and HRC deny it was a matter of political self-interest. "I am not for including transgender in ENDA because [the transgendered population's] issues couldn't be addressed in this" bill, Frank says. He dismisses the notion of political embarrassment and points to his support of including transgendered people in federal hate-crimes legislation. "It's not about who is being covered, it's about what activity is being covered. Transgendered people want a law that mandates a person with a penis be allowed to shower with women. They can't get that in ENDA. They may need separate laws." Frank says there are real issues for businesses where employees must share dorms, showers, and bathrooms. He believes some transgendered people will get protection from ENDA but acknowledges it does not offer blanket coverage.

"Every civil rights legislation ever passed was partial," he says. "The notion [that] you shouldn't do anything until you can do everything is a notion for doing nothing. It's not immoral to take the gains where you can get them."

And Donna Red Wing, national field director at HRC—a group whose fundraisers have been protested by transgender activists in the past—denies her organization would ever adopt an "us versus them" approach to transsexuals. "It's dangerous to separate ourselves from transgendered people in order to be more palatable to the mainstream," she says. "And it's crazy to pretend that those who would discriminate against the transgendered wouldn't discriminate against us."

But she also says ENDA will move forward as written, without including the transgendered. The claim that transsexuals have been politically sacrificed "is an easy out," she says. "The gay and lesbian community has worked Congress for 25 years. The transgendered community has just started to lobby Congress in the past five years. Congress doesn't have any real understanding of the transgendered community. The real work is ahead of them."

Not all gay activists hold this view. "It is not just up to transgendered people to do the legwork" on educating Congress and the public, says Kerry Lobel, executive director of the National Gay and Lesbian Task Force, a political group. In 1996 the task force became the first national gay and lesbian organization to incorporate transgendered people into its mission statement. "NGLTF believes there is one movement, the GLBT movement," Lobel says. Therefore, she says, the organization cannot support ENDA without transsexual inclusion. "You can't leave some members behind now and hope they catch up later."

Transgender activists scoff at the arguments against including them in ENDA and say it is typical of the political segregation they experience from gays and lesbians.

"When the bathroom argument was raised in the fight over gays in the military, Barney [Frank] courageously denounced it as a red herring," Wilchins says. "Now he's using the same argument against the most vulnerable people in the movement." (Wilchins's group, GenderPAC, is planning to hold its fourth annual lobby effort in Washington, D.C., May 23–25, to urge representatives to include transgendered people in ENDA and the Hate Crimes Prevention Act.)

Activists say that on the local level the issue of bathrooms and showers can be easily negotiated by including language that calls on businesses to offer "reasonable accommodation." "There are so many ways to work around this," says Phyllis Randolph Frye, an attorney and transgender activist in Texas. Prejudice, not practicality, is the real obstacle, she insists. "It is a choice between political opportunism and inclusion, and ENDA is the litmus test."

But beyond political strategizing, transgendered people argue there is a deeper philosophical basis for inclusion: Gay men, lesbians, bisexuals, and transgendered people are essentially fighting the same battles against prejudice. This bond should be stronger than any difference that might separate members of the various groups.

"No one is saying that transgendered equals gay equals lesbian equals bisexual," Stuart says. "We all have our distinct identities, our distinct concerns. But what we share is more important than our differences, and that's what the larger political movement should be built upon."

As a former lesbian, Green says his years of battling discrimination with different identities has taught him that "we are all vilified in similar ways by the non-queer world. Those who hate us don't draw distinctions. Their venom is directed against all of us. I don't think we have any choice but to stick together."

CRITICAL THINKING QUESTIONS

1. What has the gay and lesbian rights movement done to exclude or marginalize transgenders?

2. What is the motivation of the leaders of the gay and lesbian rights movement for excluding or marginalizing transgenders?

3. Discuss other social movements that are guilty of excluding or marginalizing members seeking representation.

Getting Involved

1. Contact the local office of the National Association for the Advancement of Colored People (NAACP) in your area or a group representing the interests of people of color on your campus. Find out when the next meeting is scheduled, and go to it. Take note of the race or ethnicity and gender of the people in attendance. What are the issues they discuss? After the meeting, ask someone in a leadership position what other issues the group is working on. Are the issues of women of color represented? Identify an issue you are interested in working on with the NAACP, and ask what you can do to get involved with the organization.

2. Contact the local office of the National Organization for Women (NOW) or the Business and Professional Women (BPW) in your area or a women's group on your campus.

3. Contact a gay and lesbian organization in your area or on your campus. Find out when the next meeting is scheduled, and go to it. Take note of the race or ethnicity and gender of the people in attendance. What are the issues they discuss? After the meeting, ask someone in a leadership position what other issues the group is working on. Are the issues of bisexuals and transgenders represented? Are the issues specific to sexual or gender minorities of color represented? Identify an issue you are interested in working on with the group, and ask what you can do to get involved with the organization.

Site-Seeing

1. For information about the place of transgenders in the gay and lesbian movement's activism about workplace rights, visit Human Rights Campaign's web site at **http://www.gendernet.org/hrcwatch/subvert.htm.**

2. To learn more about what one union is or is not doing to address issues of race, class, gender, and sexuality in the workplace, visit the web site of the United Auto Worker's Union at **http://www.uaw.org.** Be sure to click on the site's links to current papers on the issues facing workers today.

3. For information on African-American women and feminism, visit the African-American Feminism web site at **http://www.cddc.vt.edu/feminism/AfAm.htm.**